Prentice Hall

AMERICA
HISTORY OF OUR NATION
Beginnings Through 1877

Author
James West Davidson

Boston, Massachusetts • Chandler, Arizona • Glenview, Illinois • Upper Saddle River, New Jersey

THE LANDING OF THE PILGRIMS = 1620 MABELLE L HOLMES

Acknowledgments appear on page 712, which constitutes an extension of this copyright page.

ISBN-13: 978-0-13-323005-5

ISBN-10:   0-13-323005-8

4 5 6 7 8 9 10 V057 17 16 15 14

PEARSON

Author
James West Davidson

Dr. James Davidson is coauthor of *After the Fact: The Art of Historical Detection* and *Nation of Nations: A Narrative History of the American Republic.* Dr. Davidson has taught at both the college and high school levels. He has also consulted on curriculum design for American history courses. Dr. Davidson is an avid canoeist and hiker. His published works on these subjects include *Great Heart,* the true story of a 1903 canoe trip in the Canadian wilderness.

Senior Program Consultants
Albert M. Camarillo

Dr. Albert Camarillo received his Ph.D. in U.S. history from the University of California at Los Angeles. He has been teaching history at Stanford University since 1975. Dr. Camarillo has published six books, including *Chicanos in a Changing Society: From Mexican Pueblos to American Barrios* and *California: A History of Mexican Americans.* His awards for research and writing include a National Endowment for the Humanities Fellowship and a Rockefeller Foundation Fellowship. Dr. Camarillo is the Miriam and Peter Haas Centennial Professor in Public Service.

Diane Hart

Diane Hart is a writer and consultant in history and social studies. She earned bachelor's and master's degrees in history from Stanford University and was a Woodrow Wilson Fellow. As a former teacher at the elementary, secondary, and college levels, Ms. Hart remains deeply involved in social studies education through her active participation in both the National and California Councils for the Social Studies. She has written a number of textbooks for middle school students.

Understanding by Design Consultant
Grant Wiggins

Grant Wiggins, Ed.D., is the President of Authentic Education in Hopewell, New Jersey. He earned his Ed.D. from Harvard University and his B.A. from St. John's College in Annapolis. Dr. Wiggins consults with schools, districts, and state education departments on a variety of reform matters; organizes conferences and workshops; and develops print materials and Web resources on curricular change. He is perhaps best known for being the co-author, with Jay McTighe, of *Understanding by Design* and *The Understanding by Design Handbook*, award-winning materials on curriculum.

Over the past twenty years, Dr. Wiggins has worked on some of the most influential reform initiatives in the country, including Vermont's portfolio system and Ted Sizer's Coalition of Essential Schools. He has established statewide Consortia devoted to assessment reform for the states of North Carolina and New Jersey. Dr. Wiggins is the author of *Educative Assessment* and *Assessing Student Performance*, both published by Jossey-Bass. His many articles have appeared in such journals as *Educational Leadership* and *Phi Delta Kappan*. His work is grounded in 14 years of secondary school teaching and coaching. Dr. Wiggins taught English and electives in philosophy.

Academic Reviewers

Teacher Reviewers

Partnership School Consultants

Content Consultants

Differentiated Instruction Consultants

Donald Deshler, Ph.D
Professor of Special Education (Learning Disabilities)
Director, Center for Research on Learning
University of Kansas
Lawrence, Kansas

Dr. Deshler is the Chair of Prentice Hall's Differentiated Instruction Board. He assembled a distinguished panel of national experts to serve on the board, offering extensive experience in special needs, English language learners, less proficient readers, and gifted and talented students. This team informs Prentice Hall's approach to differentiated instruction and offers guidance on the development of new materials based on this approach.

Anthony S. Bashir, Ph.D.
Coordinator for Academic and Disability Services
Emerson College
Boston, Massachusetts

Cathy Collins Block, Ph.D.
Professor of Curriculum and Instruction
Texas Christian University
Fort Worth, Texas

Anna Uhl Chamot, Ph.D.
Professor of Secondary Education
    ESL and Foreign Language Education
Graduate School of Education and
    Human Development
The George Washington University
Washington, D.C.

Susan Miller, Ph.D.
Professor of Special Education
University of Nevada, Las Vegas
Las Vegas, Nevada

Jennifer Platt, Ed.D.
Associate Dean, College of Education
University of Central Florida
Orlando, Florida

Eric Pyle, Ph.D.
Associate Professor, Geoscience Education
Department of Geology & Environmental Science
James Madison University
Harrisonburg, Virginia

Accuracy Panel

Esther Ratner, Greyherne Information Services

Colleen F. Berg, Greyherne Information Services

Mike Jankowski, M.S. Information Finders

Jane Malcolm, M.L.S. Professional Research
    Services, Tulsa, Oklahoma

Barbara Whitney Petruzzelli, M.L.S.

Amy Booth Raff, M.L.S.

Bernard Rosen, Ph.D.

PBS Videos for America: History of Our Nation ©2014

Visit your online course at www.PearsonSuccessNet.com to view the remarkable PBS videos for Pearson's *America: History of Our Nation* ©2014.

PBS educational films deliver rigorous and relevant context through rich media experiences that engage students in exploring curricular concepts and are aligned to the needs of today's teachers and learners. Students and teachers will have access to the videos through the online digital course—both in streaming and downloadable formats.

Ken Burns's *The Civil War*

PBS®

Unit 1 Beginnings of American History. . 1

Essential Question: How did the colonists, with strong roots in the past, develop their own way of life?

Unit 1 Historian's Apprentice Workshop

Surrender at Yorktown

Table of Contents

The signing of the Constitution

The Lewis and
Clark expedition

Table of Contents

San Francisco, 1850s

Unit 5 Civil War and Reunion 476

? Essential Question: How was the Civil War a political, economic, and social turning point?

The Civil War: African American soldiers

Special Features

Historian's Apprentice Workshop

Answer the Unit Essential Question by analyzing historical documents.

GEOGRAPHY AND HISTORY

Discover the role geography has played in American history.

HISTORIAN'S APPRENTICE ACTIVITY PACK

Complete the activity packs to answer essential questions about American history.

Historian's Apprentice Skills for Life

21st Century Learning

Build skills that will help you analyze American history content.

LIFE AT THE TIME

Learn more about how people lived at different places and times in history.

Links Across Time

Expand your understanding of American history by connecting the past and the present.

Literature

Experience American history through works of literature.

● INFOGRAPHIC

Understand the significance of important historical events and developments.

Explore the past through the power of technology.

MAP MASTER®
Skills Activity

PRENTICE HALL StudentEXPRESS™
Learn · Study · Succeed

History Interactive

Develop geographic literacy through dynamic map skills instruction. Learn map skills, and interact with every map online and on CD-ROM.

Activate your learning with a suite of tools online and on CD-ROM:
- Interactive Textbook
- Reading and Notetaking Study Guide
- Social Studies Skills Tutor
- Web Resources

Launch into an interactive adventure online—using special graphics in this textbook as jumping-off points—to extend your understanding of American history.

Special Features *(continued)*

History *Interactive*

Launch into an interactive adventure to extend your understanding of American history.

Biography Quest

Search for answers to mysteries about key people in American history.

Thinking Critically With Images

Illustrated Atlas of American History

Charts, Graphs, and Diagrams

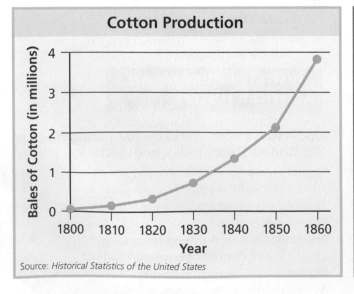

Cotton Production

Source: *Historical Statistics of the United States*

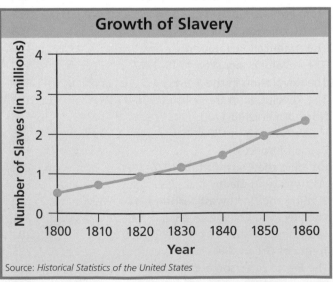

Growth of Slavery

Source: *Historical Statistics of the United States*

Timelines

Cause-and-Effect Charts

Political Cartoons

King Andrew the First

A king's crown

Trampling on rights

Reading Political Cartoons

Skills Activity

The national press ridiculed Jackson for his quick temper and steely will.

(a) Detect Points of View Name two negative images in the cartoon. Why do you think Jackson is shown stepping on the bank document?

(b) Distinguish Relevant Information Would this cartoon have the same impact in Britain if, instead of Jackson, it showed a British leader? Explain your answer.

Special Features (continued)

In-Text Sources

Gain insights by examining documents, eyewitness accounts, and other sources.

Special Features (continued)

Primary Sources

Tools to help you along the way...

Taking Notes

In history, there's a lot to read about and a lot to understand. Taking good notes is one way to help you remember key ideas and to see the big picture. This program has two ways to help you.

You can keep your notes in the *Interactive Reading and Notetaking Study Guide*. Or you can go online to take your notes. Either way, you will be able to record what you are learning. And, by the end of the year, you'll have created a perfect study tool.

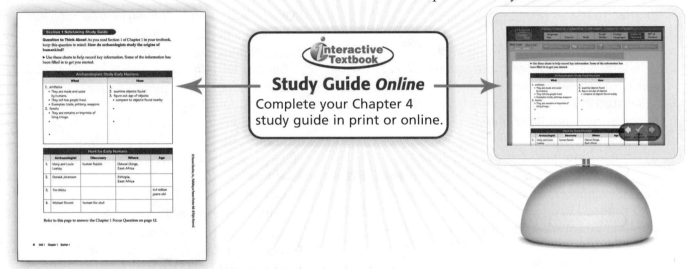

Study Guide *Online*
Complete your Chapter 4 study guide in print or online.

Monitor Your Progress

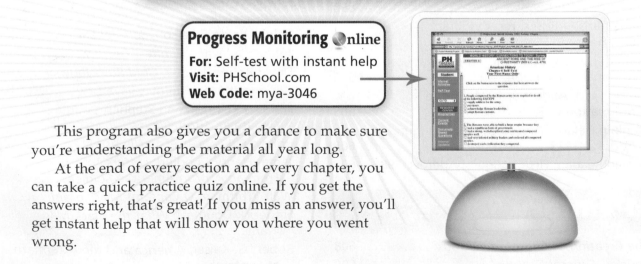

Progress Monitoring ◯nline
For: Self-test with instant help
Visit: PHSchool.com
Web Code: mya-3046

This program also gives you a chance to make sure you're understanding the material all year long.

At the end of every section and every chapter, you can take a quick practice quiz online. If you get the answers right, that's great! If you miss an answer, you'll get instant help that will show you where you went wrong.

Historian's Apprentice Toolkit

Introduction: Studying Our Past

The nation was at war with itself, the North fighting against the South. In July 1863, more than 50,000 soldiers had died at a horrible battle in Gettysburg, Pennsylvania. A few months later, President Abraham Lincoln visited Gettysburg to dedicate the battlefield as a cemetery. Lincoln spoke of the soldiers who had given their lives to keep the nation together:

> **The world will little note, nor long remember what we say here, but it can never forget what they did here.**
>
> —Abraham Lincoln, Gettysburg Address

Lincoln was partly right. The world still remembers the soldiers who died during the Civil War. But we also remember what Lincoln said and what he did for the cause of freedom. As you study American history this year, you will be asked to remember all those who came before us—soldiers and Presidents, explorers and inventors, religious leaders and business leaders, the people who wrote our Constitution, and the people who fought to end slavery.

Helping us remember the past is the job of the historian. Historians explore important questions in order to find out how people lived and why they made the decisions they did. Historians also try to understand how history affects our lives today.

On the next few pages, you will learn to think like a historian. You will also get to try out some of the tools historians use. Your Historian's Apprentice Toolkit can make your study of American history easier and more rewarding.

Union soldier

Think Like a Historian

Historical Evidence

Historians use many types of evidence to learn about the past. This evidence can be divided into primary sources and secondary sources.

Primary Sources A primary source is firsthand information about people or events. Primary sources include official documents, such as laws and public speeches, as well as eyewitness accounts, such as diaries, letters, and auto-biographies. Primary sources may also include visual evidence, such as news photographs or videotapes.

Another type of primary source is an artifact. This is an item left behind by people in the past. This might take the form of a statue, a tool, or an everyday object.

Primary sources are valuable because they are created at the time when an event occurs. But this does not necessarily make them "true." Primary sources are created by people, and they may reflect the points of view of the people who created them. The person might not have been aware of certain facts, might have been trying to impress someone, or may even have been lying. So primary sources must be evaluated carefully and considered in relation to other sources on the subject.

Secondary Sources Historians also use secondary sources. These are sources created by someone who did not actually witness events. This textbook, for example, is a secondary source. The authors gathered information from many sources to reach an understanding of what happened and why it happened. Then, they wrote their interpretation of the events. Other secondary sources include news articles and biographies.

Types of Historical Sources

Type of Source	Description	Examples

Primary Sources 	• Provide direct evidence about an event
	• Have a limited viewpoint
	• May be reliable or unreliable
	• Include objects left behind by people
		• Official documents
		• Letters and diaries
		• Speeches and interviews
		• Autobiographies
		• Photographs
		• Artifacts
		  • Tools and weapons
		  • Statues and other art

Secondary Sources 	• Consist of secondhand information about an event • Use primary sources to create a broader picture • May be reliable or unreliable	• History books • Biographies • Encyclopedias and other reference works • Internet Web sites

Using Historical Sources

Everyone who wants to know about history starts by asking questions. You might be familiar with the types of questions found in your textbook or asked by your teacher. But historians ask questions the way a detective would. Each answer is a clue that leads to another question. The questions and answers bring the historian to an understanding of events in the past.

Consider this situation. Patricia was going through some very old books she found in her great-grandmother's trunk in the attic. Between the pages of one book, she found an old letter on thin, yellowing paper. A copy of the letter is shown here at right.

While reading the letter, Patricia asked herself many questions. Some of her questions are shown at right. Trying to find the answers to the questions is the same sort of thinking that historians use to find out about the past.

June 12, 1849

Dear Sean,

Everyone was happy to get your last letter. After surviving such a long, difficult journey, it must have been wonderful to arrive at last in New York.

Where did Sean come from? Why was the trip so hard?

Things in our village are not as bad as when you left. But many children and old people are still starving, and too many people have no place to live. You were wise to go to America.

What has happened to cause these problems?

Please tell me more about your plans. After traveling for so long, why would you want to begin a new journey? Where is this place called California? And why are you so sure you can get rich there?

How does Sean plan to get rich?

I miss you. I only hope I live long enough to join you someday.

Your loving brother,
Michael

Patricia may follow several steps to find the answers to her questions.

- **Start with what is known.** Patricia knows that her ancestors came to the United States from Ireland many years ago. She thinks this letter might explain why.

- **Read and observe.** Patricia can look for further information in primary and secondary sources. She might look at a map to see where Ireland is and how far it is from New York to California.

- **Speculate.** To help get started, Patricia might make some guesses, called hypotheses, about the answers to her questions.

- **Evaluate evidence.** As Patricia finds more information, she will test her hypotheses against the information that turns up. She can always change her hypotheses as she learns more.

- **Draw conclusions.** Patricia states what she believes are the final answers to her questions.

To start her search, though, Patricia will need to practice her skills of reading like a historian and using maps. The information on the following pages will help you review some of these skills.

Read Informational Texts

Reading a magazine, an Internet page, or a textbook is not the same as reading a novel. The purpose of reading nonfiction texts is to acquire new information. On page HT 7, you'll read about some ⊙ **Reading Skills** that you'll practice as you read this textbook. Here, we'll focus on a few skills that will help you read nonfiction with a more critical eye.

Analyze the Author's Purpose

Different types of materials are written with different purposes in mind. For example, a textbook is written to teach students information about a subject. The purpose of a technical manual is to teach someone how to use something, such as a computer. A newspaper editorial might be written to persuade the reader to accept a particular point of view. An author's purpose influences how the material is presented. Sometimes, an author states his or her purpose directly. More often, the purpose is only suggested, and you must use clues to identify the author's purpose.

Distinguish Between Facts and Opinions

Active reading enables you to distinguish between facts and opinions when reading informational texts. Facts can be proved or disproved, but opinions reflect someone's own point of view.

Because newspaper editorials usually offer opinions on current events and issues, you should watch for bias and faulty logic when reading them. For example, the newspaper editorial at right shows factual statements in blue and opinions in red. Highly charged words are underlined. They reveal the writer's bias.

More than 5,000 people voted last week in favor of building a new shopping center, but the opposition won out. The margin of victory is irrelevant. Those <u>radical</u> voters who opposed the center are obviously <u>self-serving elitists</u> who do not care about anyone but themselves.

This month's unemployment figure for our area is 10 percent, which represents an increase of about 5 percent over the figure for this time last year. These figures mean that unemployment is worsening. But the people who voted against the mall probably do not care about creating new jobs.

Identify Evidence

Before you accept a writer's conclusion, you need to make sure that the writer has based the conclusion on enough evidence and on the right kind of evidence. A writer may present a series of facts to support a claim, but the facts may not tell the whole story. For example, the writer of the newspaper editorial on the previous page claims that the new shopping center would create more jobs. But what evidence is offered? Is it possible that the shopping center might have put many small local stores out of business? This would decrease employment rather than increase it.

Evaluate Credibility

Whenever you read informational texts, you need to assess the credibility of the writer. In other words, you have to decide whether the writer is believable. This is especially true of sites you may visit on the Internet. All Internet sources are not equally reliable. Here are some questions to ask yourself when evaluating the credibility of a Web site:

☐ Is the Web site created by a respected organization, a discussion group, or an individual?

☐ Does the Web site creator include his or her name as well as credentials and the sources he or she used to write the material?

☐ Is the information on the site balanced or biased?

☐ Can you verify the information using two other sources?

☐ Is there a date telling when the Web site was created or last updated?

Build Vocabulary

One of the most important tools in reading informational texts is to make sure you understand the key vocabulary used by the writer. This textbook helps you with two types of vocabulary—key terms and high-use academic words. Key Terms are words that you need to understand to read about a particular historical event or development. High-use academic words are words that will help you read any textbook.

Key Terms and High-Use Academic Words

Reading Skill

Identify Propositions The study of history often takes you inside important debates over ideas and actions. People propose their ideas and then give reasons to support those ideas. Identifying those propositions will help you to understand the beliefs and experiences of people in an earlier time. One way to identify propositions is to ask yourself what problems people had and how they proposed solving those problems.

Key Terms and People

constitution
executive
economic depression
Daniel Shays

Government by the States

As the Continental Congress began moving toward independence in 1776, leaders in the individual states began creating governments. Eleven of the 13 states wrote new constitutions to support their governments. A constitution is a document stating the rules under which a government will operate. The other two states—Rhode Island and Connecticut—kept using their colonial charters. However, they removed all references to the British king.

Writing State Constitutions In writing state constitutions, Americans were well aware of the problems that had led to the Revolution. Colonists had been unhappy with governors appointed by the British Crown. Thus, the new constitutions minimized the powers of state governors. Instead, they gave most of the power to state legislatures elected by the people.

204 Chapter 7 Creating the Constitution

❶ **Key social studies terms for each section are introduced in the section opener.**

Reading Skill

Identify Propositions The study of history often takes you inside important debates over ideas and actions. People propose their ideas and then give reasons to support those ideas. Identifying those propositions will help you to understand the beliefs and experiences of people in an earlier time. One way to identify propositions is to ask yourself what problems people had and how they proposed solving those problems.

Key Terms and People

constitution
executive
economic depression
Daniel Shays

Government by the States

As the Continental Congress began moving toward independence in 1776, leaders in the individual states began creating governments. Eleven of the 13 states wrote new constitutions to support their governments. A constitution is a document stating the rules under which a government will operate. The other two states—Rhode Island and Connecticut—kept using their colonial charters. However, they removed all references to the British king.

Writing State Constitutions In writing state constitutions, Americans were well aware of the problems that had led to the Revolution. Colonists had been unhappy with governors appointed by the British Crown. Thus, the new constitutions minimized the powers of state governors. Instead, they gave most of the power to state legislatures elected by the people.

204 Chapter 7 Creating the Constitution

❷ **Notice that they are always shown in blue type within the text narrative. Their definitions are also in blue.**

Protecting Rights The Declaration of Independence listed ways that Britain had violated the rights of colonists. To prevent such abuses, states sought to protect individual rights. Virginia was the first state to include a bill of rights in its constitution. Virginia's list included freedom of the press and the right to trial by jury, and it also barred "cruel and unusual punishments." The final clause guaranteed freedom of religion:

> "That religion, or the duty which we owe to our Creator, and the manner of discharging it, can be directed only by reason and conviction, not by force or violence; and therefore all men are equally entitled to the free exercise of religion, according to the dictates of conscience."
>
> —Virginia Bill of Rights, 1776

Vocabulary Builder
individual (in duh VIJ oo uhl)
adj. of, for, or by a single person or thing

Protecting Rights
Virginia included a bill of rights in its constitution. The Virginia bill of rights became a model for other states and, later, for the national Constitution. **Critical Thinking:** ***Link Past and Present*** *Which protections in the Virginia bill of*

❸ **High-use words are underlined in the text and defined in the margin. You can practice these words at Vocabulary Builder Online.**

🎯 Reading Skills

The History Reading Skills described on this page are important in helping you read and understand the information in this book. Each section teaches a reading skill and gives you a chance to practice the skill as you read. As you learn to use these skills, you will find that you can apply them to other books you read.

🎯 **Clarify Meaning** You can better understand what you read by using summaries and outlines and by taking notes to help identify main ideas and supporting details. **Chapters 1, 2.**

🎯 **Compare and Contrast** When you compare, you examine the similarities between things. When you contrast, you look at the differences. **Chapter 3.**

🎯 **Use Context** Learn to use context clues to help you understand the meaning of unfamiliar words and words with more than one meaning. **Chapter 4.**

🎯 **Word Analysis** Discover how to analyze words to determine their meanings. **Chapters 6, 8.**

🎯 **Understand Sequence** A sequence is the order in which a series of events occurs. Noting the sequence of important events can help you understand and remember the events. **Chapters 9, 15.**

🎯 **Analyze Cause and Effect** Every event in history has causes and creates effects. You will learn how to identify causes, which are what make events happen, and effects, which are what happen as a result of an event. **Chapters 10, 14.**

🎯 **Draw Conclusions** You will learn how to use details from primary and secondary sources to draw conclusions. **Chapters 5, 12.**

🎯 **Evaluate Information** As you read history, it is important to evaluate how writers' support their propositions, or the ideas they put forth. To do so, it is important to know how to identify and explain central issues and frame good research questions. **Chapters 7, 11, 13, 16, Epilogue.**

MAP✦MASTER®

CONTENTS

Go Online PHSchool.com The maps in this textbook can be found online at **PHSchool.com**, along with map-skills practice.

Geography and History

Historical information is not presented only in written sources. Maps are often a key to understanding what happened and why.

Do you remember when Patricia was asking questions about the letter she found? (See page HT 3.) In addition to using primary and secondary sources, Patricia could have used maps to locate Ireland and to trace Sean's route from New York to California.

In order to get the most out of maps as sources, you need to make sure that your geography map skills are strong. On the next few pages, you can review some of the basic tools historians use to understand maps and geography.

The pictures above show two different geographical regions of the United States. The Midwest (above, left) has fertile plains suitable for farming. The rocky coasts of New England (right) are home to a large fishing industry.

Five Themes of Geography

Studying the history and geography of the United States is a huge task. You can make that task easier by thinking of geography in terms of five themes. The five themes below are tools you can use to organize geographic information and to answer questions about the influence of geography and human history.

Location

1 The exact location of a country or city is expressed in terms of longitude and latitude. Relative location defines where a place is in relation to other places. For example, the exact location of the city of Chicago, Illinois, is 42° north (latitude) and 88° west (longitude). Its relative location could be described as "on the shore of Lake Michigan" or "821 miles north of New Orleans."

Place

2 Location answers the question, "Where is it?" Place answers the question, "What is it like there?" You can identify a place by such features as its landforms, its climate, its plants and animals, or the people who live there. Much of the history of the southeastern United States was shaped by the fact that it had a mild climate and fertile land suitable for large-scale farming of crops such as cotton.

Regions

3 Regions are areas that share common features. Regions may be defined by geography or culture. For example, New York is one of the Middle Atlantic states because it is located on the Atlantic Ocean. In colonial days, it was one of the Middle Colonies. And in the early 1800s, New York was one of the "free states" because slavery was banned there.

Movement

4 Much of history has to do with the movement of people, goods, and ideas from place to place. In Patricia's letter, we saw two examples of movement: the movement of immigrants to the United States from other countries and the movement of Americans from the East to the West. Both played a key role in the history and growth of the United States.

Interaction

5 Human-environment interaction has two parts. The first part has to do with the way an environment affects people. For example, people in the desert of the American Southwest developed very different ways of life from those living in the rich farmlands of California. The second part of interaction concerns the way people affect their environment. People mined silver in Nevada and harnessed the power of falling water in North Carolina. In each case, they changed their environment.

Practice Geography Skills

Look at the photographs on page HT 8 and read the caption. How do these pictures illustrate the themes of place, region, and interaction?

Globes

A globe is a model of Earth. It shows the actual shape, size, and location of each landmass and body of water.

Globes divide Earth into lines of latitude and longitude. Latitude measures distance north or south of the Equator, which is an imaginary line around the widest part of Earth. Longitude measures distance east or west of the Prime Meridian, which is an imaginary line running from the North Pole to the South Pole. The diagram below shows how lines of longitude and latitude form a grid pattern on a globe.

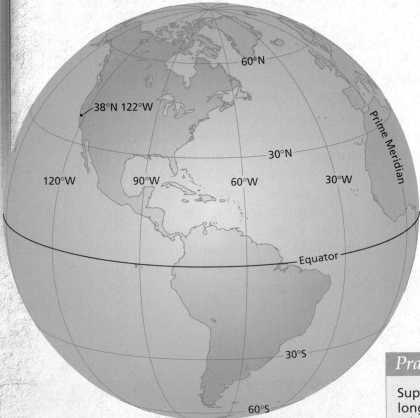

Using lines of latitude and longitude, you can locate any place on Earth. The location of 38° north latitude and 122° west longitude is written as 38° N/122° W. Only one place on Earth has this location: the city of San Francisco, California.

Practice Geography Skills

Suppose that you wanted to plan a long trip. What would be some advantages and disadvantages of using a globe?

Map Projections

Globes are accurate, but they are not easy to carry around, and they are not useful for showing smaller areas of Earth in detail. So mapmakers had to develop methods to show the curved Earth on a flat surface. These methods are known as map projections. All map projections distort Earth in some way. Below are two common types of map projections.

Mercator Projection

In the 1500s, ocean travelers relied on the Mercator projection, named after mapmaker Gerardus Mercator. The Mercator projection accurately shows direction and the shape of Earth's landmasses. However, it distorts distance and size.

Robinson Projection

The Robinson projection shows the correct shape and size of landmasses for most parts of the world. However, it does not show directions as well as a Mercator projection does. It also distorts the size of the North Pole and South Pole.

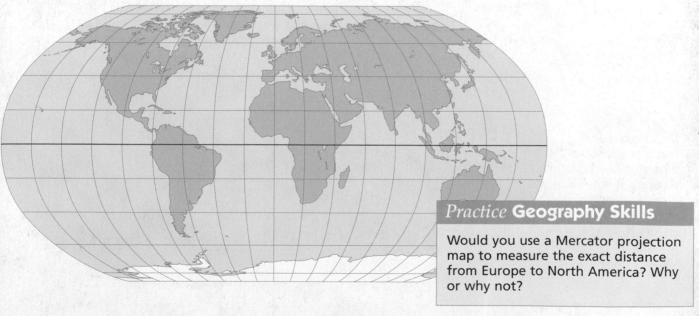

Practice Geography Skills

Would you use a Mercator projection map to measure the exact distance from Europe to North America? Why or why not?

How to Use a Map

Mapmakers provide several clues to help in understanding the information on a map. Maps provide different clues, depending on their purpose or scale. However, most maps have several clues in common.

Locator
Many maps are shown with locator maps or globes. They show where on Earth the area of the map is located.

Title
Maps have titles. The title tells you the subject of the map.

Key
Often a map has a key, or legend. The key shows the meaning of the symbols and colors used on the map.

Compass rose
Many maps show direction by displaying a compass rose with the directions north, east, south, and west. The letters N, E, S, and W are placed to indicate these directions.

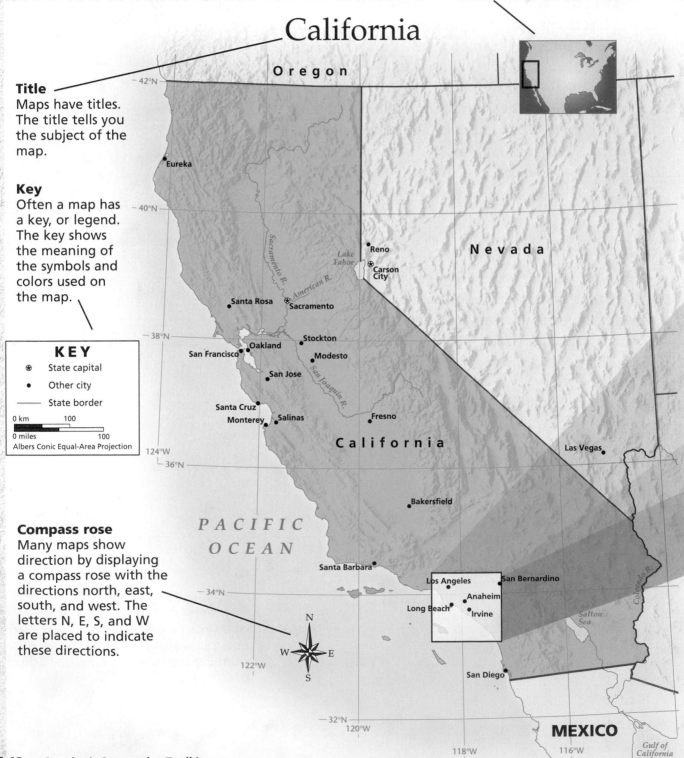

California

KEY
⊛ State capital
• Other city
— State border

0 km 100
0 miles 100
Albers Conic Equal-Area Projection

Maps of Different Scales

Maps are drawn to different scales, depending on their purpose. Here are three maps drawn to very different scales. Keep in mind that maps showing large areas have smaller scales. Maps showing small areas have larger scales.

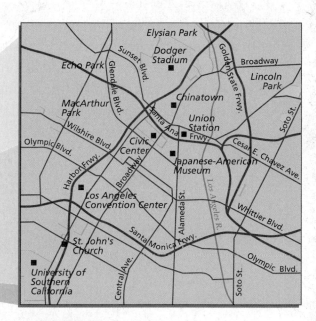

▲ Greater Los Angeles
Find the light gray square on the main map of California (left). This square represents the area shown on the map above. It shows Los Angeles in relation to nearby cities, towns, and the Pacific Ocean. It also shows some features near the city, such as the airport and major roadways.

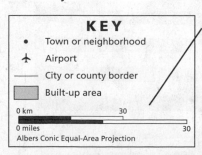

KEY
- • Town or neighborhood
- ✈ Airport
- ── City or county border
- ▨ Built-up area

0 km   30
0 miles   30
Albers Conic Equal-Area Projection

Scale bar
A scale bar helps you find the actual distances between points shown on the map. Most scale bars show distances in both miles and kilometers.

▲ Downtown Los Angeles
Find the gray square on the map of Greater Los Angeles. This square represents the area shown on the map above. This map moves you closer into the center of Los Angeles. Like a zoom on a computer or a camera, this map shows a smaller area, but in greater detail. It has the largest scale. You can use this map to explore downtown Los Angeles.

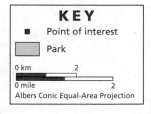

KEY
- ▪ Point of interest
- ▨ Park

0 km   2
0 mile   2
Albers Conic Equal-Area Projection

Practice Geography Skills
- What part of a map explains the colors used on the map?
- How does the scale bar change depending on the scale of the map?

Political Maps

Historians use many different types of maps. On the next four pages, you will see four maps that relate to American history. Each map shows a different area in a different way and for a different purpose.

One of the most familiar types of map is the political map. Political maps show political divisions, such as borders between countries or states. Colors on a political map help make the differences clear. Political maps also show the location of cities. This map shows the United States in 1790, at the time George Washington was President.

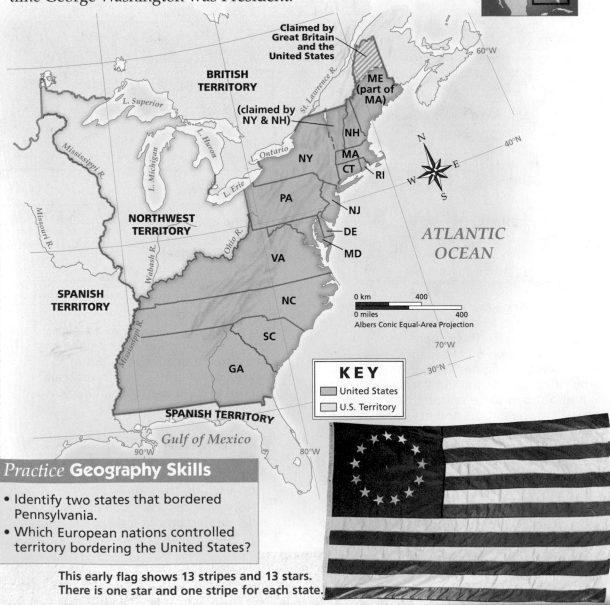

Practice **Geography Skills**

- Identify two states that bordered Pennsylvania.
- Which European nations controlled territory bordering the United States?

This early flag shows 13 stripes and 13 stars. There is one star and one stripe for each state.

Physical Maps

Physical maps show the major physical features of a region, such as seas, rivers, and mountains. The larger the scale of a physical map, the more detail it can show. For example, the map below shows the rivers that run through the American Southwest. If you compare this map to the physical map in the Atlas at the front of this textbook, you will notice that there are several rivers shown on this map that are not shown on the Atlas map.

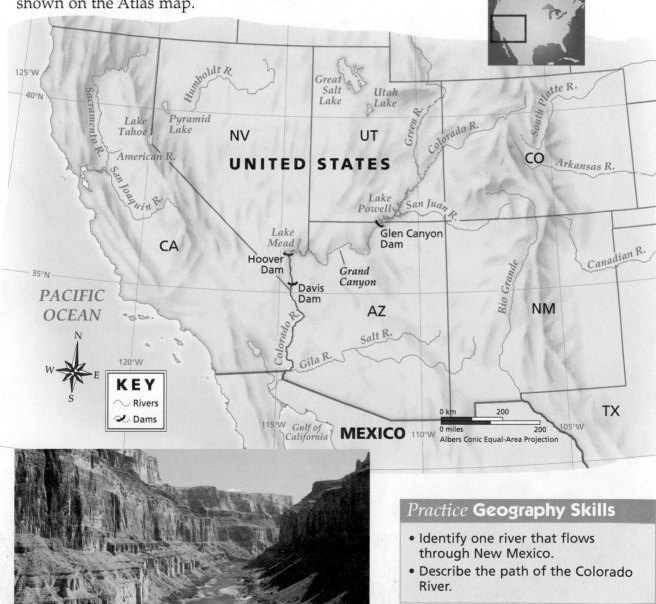

Practice Geography Skills

- Identify one river that flows through New Mexico.
- Describe the path of the Colorado River.

The Colorado River formed the Grand Canyon in Arizona.

Special-Purpose Maps
Battle Maps

In addition to political maps and physical maps, there are different types of special-purpose maps. These range from road maps to weather maps to election maps. Some special-purpose maps use arrows to show the movement of people and goods from place to place. The map below shows the battles and troop movements that led up to the Battle of Gettysburg in July 1863.

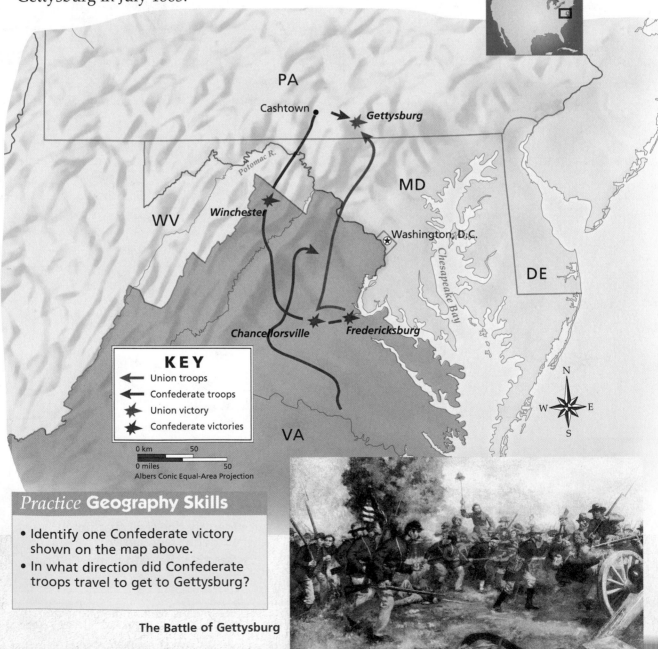

KEY

⬅ Union troops
⬅ Confederate troops
★ Union victory
★ Confederate victories

0 km   50
0 miles   50
Albers Conic Equal-Area Projection

Practice **Geography Skills**

- Identify one Confederate victory shown on the map above.
- In what direction did Confederate troops travel to get to Gettysburg?

The Battle of Gettysburg

Election Maps

Have you ever seen a newspaper or watched television during a presidential election? If you have, then you have probably seen an election map. Election maps show all of the states voting in the election. Different colors are used to show which candidates won the vote in which states. The map below shows the election of 1912, when three major candidates were running for President.

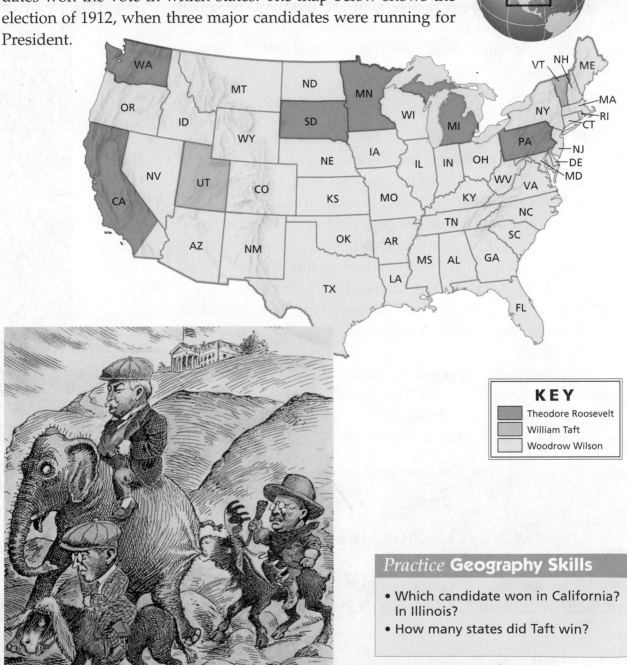

KEY
- Theodore Roosevelt
- William Taft
- Woodrow Wilson

Practice **Geography Skills**

- Which candidate won in California? In Illinois?
- How many states did Taft win?

Cartoon showing Wilson, Taft, and Roosevelt running for President in 1912

Read Visual Information

In this textbook, the information you need to know is presented in written form. Often, however, key information is also summarized in chart form. Charts organize facts and ideas in a visual way that makes them easier to understand.

The next four pages review some of the basic types of visuals you will find in this textbook. Building your ability to analyze visuals will help you get the most out of the information provided.

Timelines

Every chapter in this textbook begins with a timeline. You have used timelines before, but the ones in this book have a few special features. Most of them are made up of two parts:

- **U.S. Events** This is the main part of the timeline. It shows the events that are described in that chapter that took place within the United States.
- **World Events** This part of the timeline shows events that took place in other parts of the world during the same time period. These events are often included because they related to what was going on in the United States.

Timelines make it easier to understand the sequence of events over time. The timelines in this textbook will help you explain how major events are related to one another in time.

Practice **Chart Skills**

- How many years after gold was discovered in California was gold discovered in Australia?
- Which world event was probably related to one of the U.S. events?

U.S. Events					
Irish immigration to United States increases.	1846	1849	Gold is discovered in California.	1854	Slavery leads to violence in Kansas.

1840   **1850**   **1860**

World Events					
	1845	Famine strikes Ireland.	1851	Gold is discovered in Australia.	1854	Japan opens ports to foreign ships.

Build Chart Skills

Tables

Tables provide a simple way to organize a large amount of information graphically. A table is arranged in a grid pattern. Columns run vertically, from top to bottom. Rows run horizontally, from left to right.

This sample table summarizes some basic facts about four major wars you will learn about this year. The four wars are listed in the column at the far left, at the beginning of each row. The categories of information given about each war are listed at the top of each column.

Tables can be very large. You may have seen computer spreadsheets that include dozens of columns and rows. Yet, all tables follow the same basic grid pattern shown below.

Four American Wars

War	Dates	Opponents	Results
American Revolution	1775–1781	American colonists vs. Britain	• Colonists win. • United States wins independence.
War of 1812	1812–1814	United States vs. Britain	• No clear winner emerges. • Increased sense of national pride felt.
Mexican-American War	1846–1848	United States vs. Mexico	• United States wins. • United States gains new territory in the West.
Civil War	1861–1865	North vs. South	• North wins. • Union is preserved. • Slavery ends.

Practice Chart Skills

- What were the results of the Mexican-American War?
- In which two wars did Americans fight the same opponent?

Pie Charts

Some charts and graphs in this book show statistical information, that is, information based on exact numbers. Pie charts show statistical information in terms of percentages. The circle, or pie, represents 100 percent of a group. Each wedge of the pie represents one subgroup of the whole. The bigger the wedge is, the larger the group. This pie chart shows how the population of southern states was divided in the year 1850, when slavery was still legal in the South.

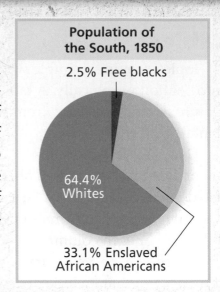

Population of the South, 1850

2.5% Free blacks

64.4% Whites

33.1% Enslaved African Americans

Line Graphs and Bar Graphs

Line graphs and bar graphs show statistical information as it changes over time. The horizontal, or side to side, axis usually tells you the time period covered by the graph. The vertical, or up and down, axis tells you what is being measured. By lining up the points on the graph with the horizontal and vertical axes, you can see how many or how much of something there was at a given time.

On a line graph, the points are connected. On a bar graph, each year is represented by a bar. The line graph (below left) and the bar graph (below right) show the same information: the number of patents, or licenses for new inventions, issued by the U.S. government.

Practice Chart Skills

- What percentage of southern society in 1850 was made up of enslaved African Americans?
- About how many patents were issued in 1860? In 1880?

U.S. Patents, 1860–1900

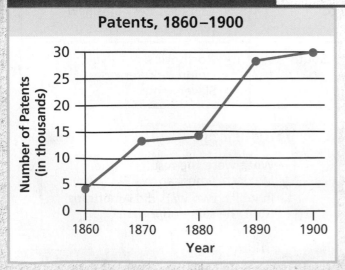

Patents, 1860–1900

Number of Patents (in thousands)

Year

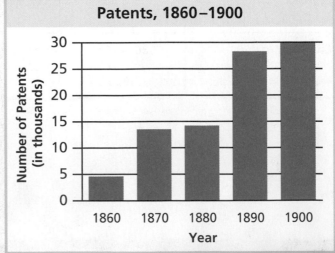

Patents, 1860–1900

Number of Patents (in thousands)

Year

When you are doing research on the Internet, it is important to evaluate the Web sites to determine if the information is valid and objective. The page below is from a Web site about Samuel F.B. Morse.

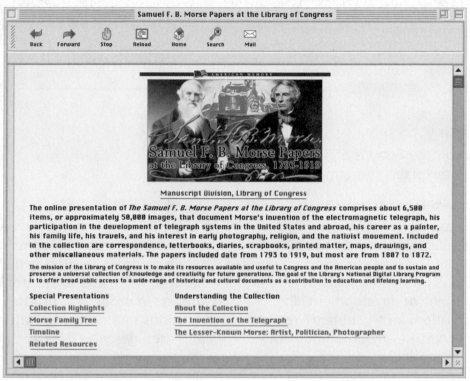

Source: The Library of Congress

Use these steps to learn how to evaluate Internet sources.

- Determine the Web site's purpose. Does the Web site provide information? Is it trying to sell something or to promote a particular point of view?
- Examine the information. Does the site include visuals? Does it include first-person accounts and other primary source materials?
- Compare the information to what you already know. Does the information agree with what you have read in a textbook or in another reliable print source? What other information is provided?
- Evaluate the source. Is the source an established organization? Can you tell who provided the information?

Practice Internet Skills

- What is the purpose of this Web site?
- (a) Who is the provider for this site? (b) If you were writing a paper about Samuel F.B. Morse, do you think you could use the information on this Web site? Why or why not?

You have learned how to use historians' tools to learn about the past. The next step is to write about what you have discovered. Historians share their findings in a variety of ways, including expository essays, narratives, research papers, and persuasive essays or speeches. You will have a chance to practice each type through end-of-section and end-of-chapter writing activities.

Expository Essays

An expository essay is a piece of writing that explains something in detail.

❶ Select and Narrow Your Topic

Define exactly what you want your essay to do. Do you want to describe a process? Compare and contrast two ideas? Explain the causes and effects of a historical event or development? Explore possible solutions to a problem? You cannot plan your essay until you know what you are trying to do in it.

❷ Gather Evidence

Create a graphic organizer that identifies details to include in your essay, such as the one shown below.

❸ Write a First Draft

Write a topic sentence, and then organize the essay based on what you are trying to do. If your essay describes a process, write about the steps of the process in order. If your essay explores solutions to a problem, state the problem, and then describe different possible solutions.

❹ Revise and Proofread

Make sure that all the details support your topic sentence.

Problem	Suggested Solutions	Evaluation of Solution
The Articles of Confederation left the nation weak because they did not provide for a central authority.	Leave the Articles alone, and persuade other countries and Americans to respect the new nation.	Not practical—what would make more established governments and local rebels accept a weak authority?
	Get rid of the Articles, and create an entirely new plan.	Possible, but it would be a huge task to start all over again.

If you were writing a problem-solution essay, you might create a chart like this to help you organize your ideas.

Research Papers

Research papers present information that you have found about a topic.

① Select and Narrow Your Topic

Choose a topic that interests you. Make sure that your topic is not too broad. For example, instead of writing a report on Native Americans, you might write a report about the Cherokees who were forced to move west in 1837 on a journey known as the Trail of Tears.

② Acquire Information

Locate several sources of information about the topic from the library or on the Internet. Be sure to evaluate the source. Is it reliable? How does the information compare to what you have found in other sources?

For each resource, create a source index card. Then, take notes using an index card for each detail or subtopic. On the card, note which source the information was taken from. Use quotation marks when you copy exact words from a source.

③ Make an Outline

Use an outline to decide how to organize your research paper. Sort your index cards in the same order.

④ Write a First Draft

Write an introduction, a body, and a conclusion. If you are preparing your first draft by hand, leave plenty of space between lines so you can go back and add details that you may have left out.

⑤ Revise and Proofread

Be sure to include transition words between sentences and paragraphs. Here are some examples:

- To describe a process: *first, next, then*
- To show a contrast: *however, although, despite*
- To point out a reason: *since, because, if*
- To signal a conclusion: *therefore, as a result, so*

Introduction

The Trail of Tears

How would you feel if soldiers came to your home and forced you to move thousands of miles away? This may sound like an impossible nightmare. But that is what happened to the Cherokee people in 1838.

Conclusion

Therefore, the Trail of Tears was a tragedy for the Cherokees and other Native Americans. Sadly, there would be more clashes with settlers in the years to come.

Narrative Essays

History is like a story. It has characters, both leaders and everyday people. It has a setting where events take place. It even has a plot, in which events unfold, conflicts arise, and resolutions occur.

1 Select and Narrow Your Topic

In this textbook, you will be asked to write narratives about the past. You might be asked to imagine a setting and describe how it affects what is happening. You might be asked to take the point of view of one of history's characters. Or you might be asked to explain the conflict or resolution of a historical situation. First, you must understand what you are being asked to do or who you are asked to be.

2 Gather Details

Brainstorm a list of details you would like to include in your narrative.

3 Write a First Draft

Start by writing a simple opening sentence that conveys the main idea of your essay. Continue by writing a colorful story that has interesting details. Write a conclusion that sums up the main points.

4 Revise and Proofread

Check to make sure you have not begun too many sentences with the word *I*. Replace general words with more colorful ones.

Persuasive Essays

A persuasive essay is a piece of writing that supports a position or opinion.

1 Select and Narrow Your Topic

Choose a historical topic that has at least two sides or two interpretations. Choose a side. Decide which argument will best persuade your audience to agree with your point of view.

2 Gather Evidence

Create a chart that states your position at the top, and then lists the pros and cons for your position in two columns below. Predict and address the strongest arguments against your viewpoint.

3 Write a First Draft

Write a strong thesis statement that clearly states your position. Continue by presenting the strongest arguments in favor of your position and acknowledging and refuting opposing arguments.

4 Revise and Proofread

Check to make sure you have made a logical argument and that you have not oversimplified the argument.

There are many types of questions in your textbook. Checkpoint Questions help you check your understanding of a small section of your reading. Check Your Progress questions at the end of each section help you practice understandings gained while reading the whole section. Likewise questions at the end of the chapter help you understand content in the chapter.

There is another type of question in this textbook that may be even more important. They are called Essential Questions. You will find them at the beginning of each unit and each chapter. They are also the basis of the Historian's Apprentice Learning System, which appears throughout this book.

Essential questions can really make you think. They don't have a right answer. They often make you think of other questions. But they are important because they get to the heart of the matter. As you think about them, you will come to deep understanding.

▲ The Essential Question for the unit is introduced on the unit opener.

▲ The Historian's Apprentice Activity Pack provides more activities to explore history.

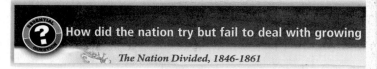

▲ The Essential Question at the beginning of each chapter helps frame your understanding of the whole chapter.

ACTIVITY

Divide into three groups to build an answer to the unit question: How was the Civil War a political, economic, and social turning point?

One group should use the Think Like a Historian documents to describe the Civil War's political effects. Another group should use the documents to describe the economic effects of the war. The last group should cover the war's social effects. After each group has had time to prepare a presentation, it should report its findings to the rest of the class in the format of a documentary news program.

▲ At the end of every unit you complete an activity that will help you show your understanding.

Unit 1

How did the colonists, with strong roots in the past, develop their own way of life?

History Interactive
Explore Historian's Apprentice Online
Visit: PHSchool.com
Web Code: mvp-1000

Across the Atlantic Sailing three small ships across the Atlantic in uncharted waters, Christopher Columbus opened the Americas to regular contact with the people of Europe.

1492

Slave Trade By the late 1600s, a steady stream of ships carried enslaved Africans to the Americas. Most enslaved Africans were forced to work on plantations in the West Indies and in South America. Slavery grew in North America after the plantations system took hold in the South.

LATE 1600s

Beginnings of American History

The Five Nations
The Iroquois of the Eastern Woodlands formed the League of the Iroquois to keep the peace among their peoples. Items like this moose-antler comb were widely used and traded among the people who belonged to the League.

1500s

THE LANDING OF THE PILGRIMS 1620

The Pilgrim Community Seeking freedom to practice their religion, Pilgrims founded the colony of Plymouth. In time, the idea of religious freedom for all would become a cornerstone of American democracy.

1620

English Colonies Flourish The English founded 13 colonies along the Atlantic coast of North America. People in the New England, Middle, and Southern colonies developed distinct ways of life. Some children attended school, where they learned reading, writing, and arithmetic.

1750

Roots of the American People

Prehistory -1500

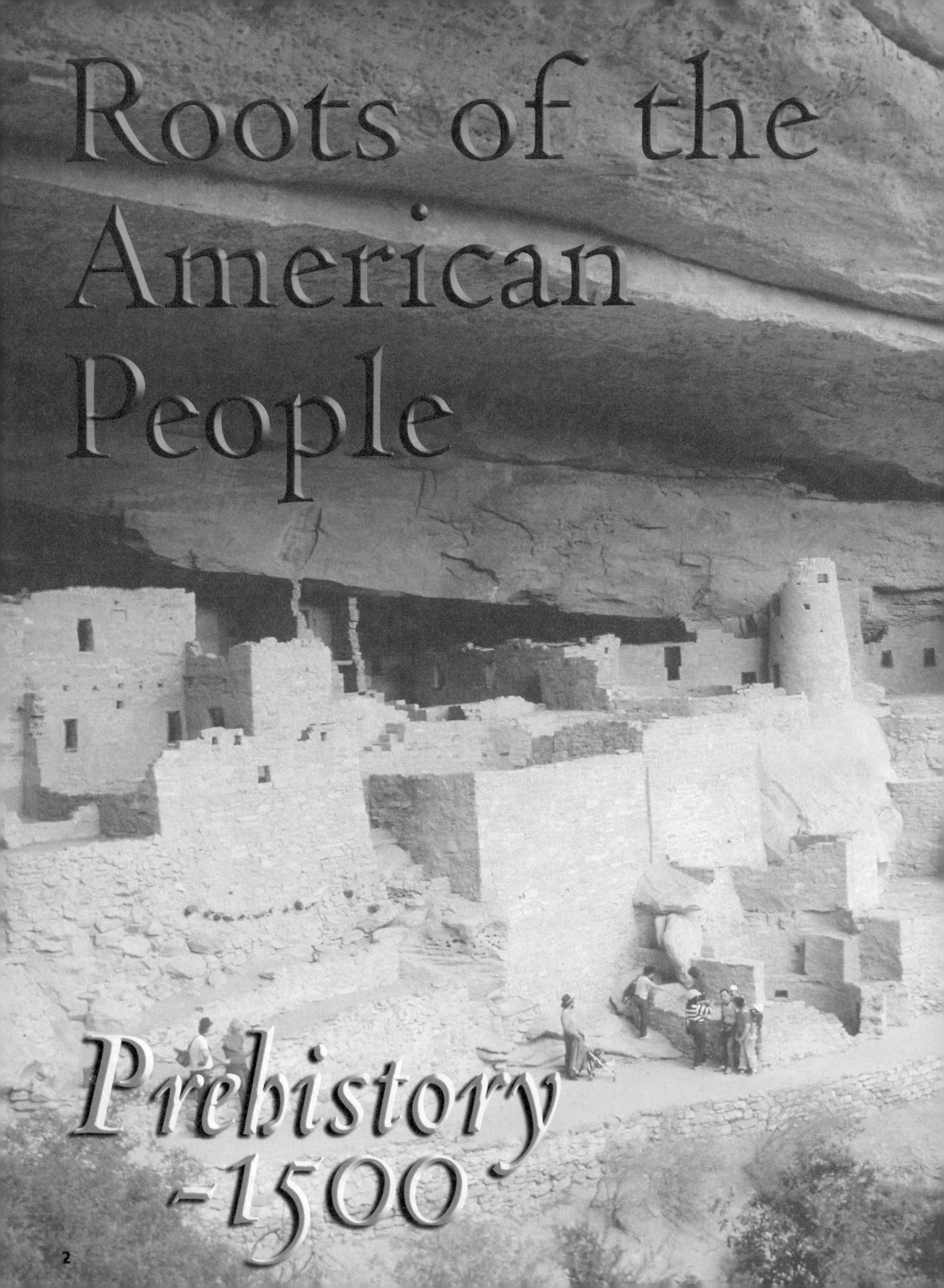

"African, European, and Indian ...in their adaptations to, and borrowings from, one another, they created truly exceptional societies."

Alan Taylor,
American Colonies:
The Settling of
North America

What You Will Learn

Section 1
THE EARLIEST AMERICANS
Early people spread across the Americas and eventually built great civilizations.

Section 2
CULTURES OF NORTH AMERICA
Peoples of North America developed a wide variety of cultures.

Section 3
TRADE NETWORKS OF ASIA AND AFRICA
A complex trade network linked Africa, Asia, and Europe.

Section 4
THE EUROPEAN HERITAGE
Traditions that came to the Americas from Europe included Judaism, Christianity, and Greek and Roman ideas about government.

Hundreds of years ago, Native Americans built these cliff dwellings at Mesa Verde in present-day Colorado.

Reading Skill
Read Actively In this chapter, you will practice active reading by taking notes and using review questions to identify main ideas and supporting details.

The World, ca. 1500

◄ Inuit igloo

NORTH AMERICA

Cheyenne tepee ▼

▲ Iroquois longhouse

Aztec temple ▶

AZTEC EMPIRE ○ Tenochtitlán

Atlantic Ocean

West Indies

N
W — E
S

Incan figurine ▶

0   1000 miles
0   1000 km
Miller Cylindrical Projection

Pacific Ocean

INCAN EMPIRE ○ Cuzco

SOUTH AMERICA

KEY
— Major trade routes
— Silk Road
◄ Voyages of Zheng He, 1405–1422
◄ Voyages of Vasco da Gama, 1497–1499

U.S. Events

Prehistory	1000	1200

World Events | 20,000–30,000 years ago | First people come to the Americas. | | 1095 | Pope calls for crusades to begin.

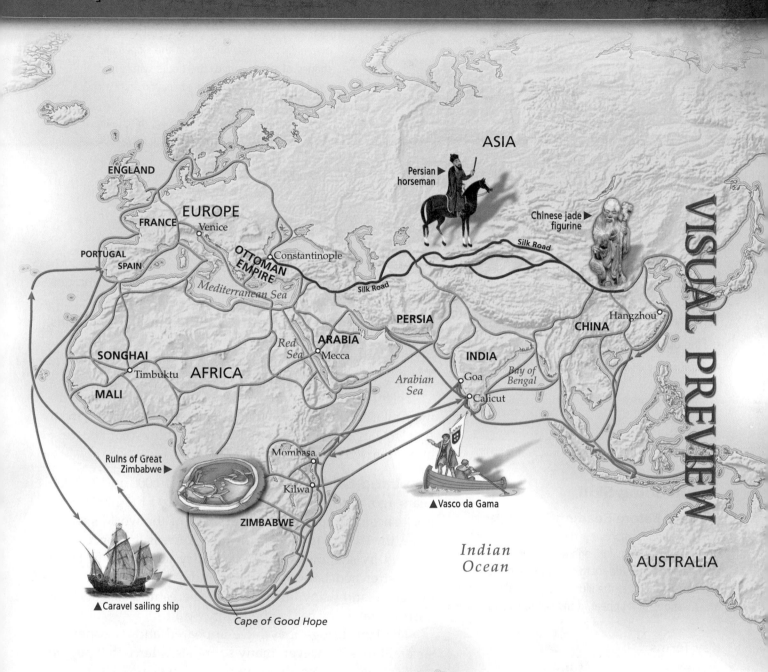

VISUAL PREVIEW

ENGLAND

EUROPE

FRANCE
Venice

PORTUGAL
SPAIN

OTTOMAN
EMPIRE
Constantinople

Mediterranean Sea

Silk Road

ASIA

Persian ▶
horseman

Chinese jade ▶
figurine

Silk Road

PERSIA

ARABIA

Red
Sea
Mecca

CHINA
Hangzhou

SONGHAI
Timbuktu

AFRICA

INDIA

Arabian
Sea

Goa
Calicut

Bay of
Bengal

MALI

Ruins of Great
Zimbabwe ▶

Mombasa

Kilwa

ZIMBABWE

▲Vasco da Gama

Indian
Ocean

AUSTRALIA

▲Caravel sailing ship

Cape of Good Hope

1200	1400	1600

1200s African empire of Mali rises.

1400s Aztecs conquer most of Mexico.

1500s Iroquois League is formed.

Ancient Pyramid Found

❝When they first saw us digging there, the local people just couldn't believe there was a pyramid. . . . It was only when the slopes and shapes of the pyramid, the floors with altars were found, that they finally believed us.❞

—Archaeologist Jesus Sanchez, describing discovery near Mexico City, 2006

◄ Mayan pyramid in Mexico

The Earliest Americans

Objectives

- Understand how people may have first reached the Americas.
- Find out how people learned to farm.
- Explore the civilizations of the Mayas, Aztecs, and Incas.

Reading Skill

Preview Before Reading The first step in active reading is to preview the text. Read the Objectives, Reading Skill, and Key Terms. Scan all the headings and side-margin notes. Read the captions and look at the illustrations. Finally, read the questions that appear at the section's end.

Key Terms

glacier
irrigation

surplus
civilization

Why It Matters Tens of thousands of years ago, no humans lived in North America or South America.

❓ Section Focus Question: How did early civilizations develop in the Americas?

The First Americans

Scientists have various ideas about how people came to the Americas. Some think that people may have come from Asia in large canoes. However, most think that the first humans arrived by land.

The Land-Bridge Theory Between 10,000 and 100,000 years ago, much of the world was covered by glaciers, or thick sheets of ice. As more and more of the world's water froze, the level of the oceans dropped. Areas that once were covered by shallow water became dry land. One of these areas stretched between Siberia and Alaska. It became a bridge of land many miles wide. The area now lies under a narrow waterway called the Bering Strait.

The land bridge may have appeared and disappeared several times. However, many scientists believe that people first came to North America between 20,000 and 30,000 years ago. They were hunters, possibly following the coast of Siberia as they hunted prehistoric mammals such as the woolly mammoth. Over thousands of years, hunting bands moved over the land. They eventually spread across North America and South America.

Other Theories Not everyone agrees with the land-bridge theory. Some scientists think that people may first have crossed the arctic waters by boat and traveled southward along the Pacific coast. This idea is known as the coastal-route theory.

Many Native Americans also dispute both the land-bridge theory and the coastal-route theory. Each group has its own tradition explaining how they settled in the lands they did. These traditions appear in their creation stories.

Learning to Farm For centuries, early humans could fill most of their needs by hunting. Game animals provided food, furs for clothing, and bones for tools.

In time, many of the larger animals began to disappear. <u>Deprived</u> of their main source of food, hunters had to change their ways of life. In many places, hunters became gatherers. They traveled from place to place, searching for wild plants and small game.

Some 8,000 years ago, gatherers in Mexico began growing food plants, including squash and lima beans. The discovery of farming transformed life. No longer did families have to wander in search of food. In dry regions, farmers developed methods of irrigation. **Irrigation** is a method to water crops by channeling water from rivers or streams. Farmers also learned how to raise animals such as cattle, pigs, and llamas.

With a more dependable food supply, the population grew more rapidly. Once Native Americans produced **surplus,** or extra, food, they traded with others. Some farming communities grew into cities. The cities became centers of government and religious life.

☑**Checkpoint** **How do scientists think people first reached the Americas?**

Vocabulary Builder
<u>deprive</u> (dee PRĪV) **v.** to take away

Preview Before Reading
Preview the matter on the following pages under the heading "Three Civilizations." What do the subheadings, images, and captions tell you?

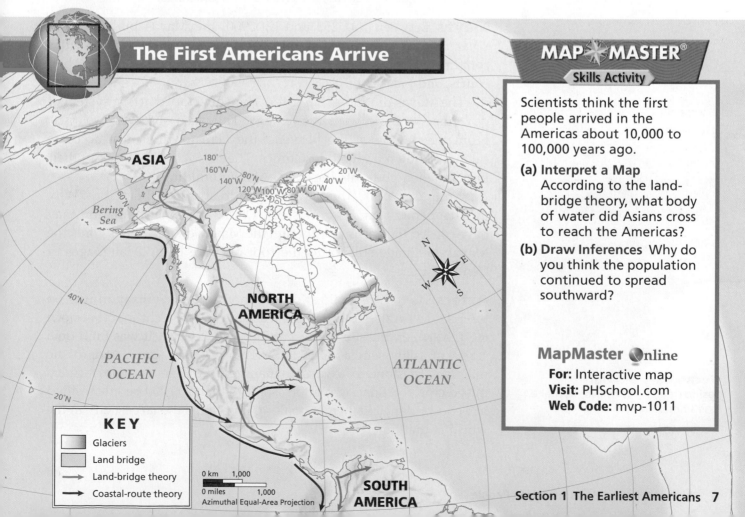

The First Americans Arrive

ASIA

Bering Sea

PACIFIC OCEAN

NORTH AMERICA

ATLANTIC OCEAN

SOUTH AMERICA

180°
160°W
140°W
120°W 100°W 80°W 60°W
0°
20°W
40°W

60°N
40°N
20°N

KEY
- Glaciers
- Land bridge
- → Land-bridge theory
- → Coastal-route theory

0 km 1,000
0 miles 1,000
Azimuthal Equal-Area Projection

MAP MASTER®

Skills Activity

Scientists think the first people arrived in the Americas about 10,000 to 100,000 years ago.

(a) Interpret a Map According to the land-bridge theory, what body of water did Asians cross to reach the Americas?

(b) Draw Inferences Why do you think the population continued to spread southward?

MapMaster Online
For: Interactive map
Visit: PHSchool.com
Web Code: mvp-1011

Tenochtitlán The Aztecs built their capital city of Tenochtitlán on a group of islands in the middle of a lake. The center of the city was dominated by a huge temple (inset). *Critical Thinking: Draw Conclusions* How does this picture support the idea that the Aztec society was highly organized?

Three Civilizations

With the development of cities came the beginnings of civilization. A **civilization** is an advanced culture in which people have developed cities, science, and industries. Over the centuries, several civilizations rose and declined in the Americas. The largest were the civilizations of the Mayas, the Aztecs, and the Incas.

Mayas Between A.D. 250 and A.D. 900, the Mayas built cities in what is now Mexico and Central America. These splendid cities contained large public plazas lined with pyramids, temples, ball courts, and palaces.

The Mayas did more, however. They developed arts, a system of government, and a written language. They also observed the stars. From their study of the heavens, they created the most accurate calendar known until modern times. They also carved stories of their past and their gods into the stones of their buildings.

Around A.D. 900, the Mayas began to abandon their cities. Why this happened remains a mystery. Disease or overpopulation may have caused the decline. Although the Mayan civilization is gone, the Mayan language still forms the root of more than 20 languages of Central America.

Aztecs As Mayan civilization declined, a new civilization was on the rise. The Aztecs built a great capital city, Tenochtitlán (tay noch tee TLAHN), on the site of present-day Mexico City. It was built on a series of islands in a large lake. The city was connected to the mainland by stone roadways. In many parts of Tenochtitlán, farmers raised crops on floating platforms. More than 200,000 people <u>resided</u> in Tenochtitlán at its height, making it perhaps the largest city in the world at that time.

Vocabulary Builder
<u>reside</u> (ree ZĪD) **v.** to live; to make one's home in

The center of the city was a sacred place with dozens of temples that honored the Aztec gods. This was appropriate because religion dominated Aztec life. To the Aztecs, prosperity depended on the good will of the gods. Like a number of other ancient peoples, the Aztecs practiced human sacrifice as an offering to their gods.

During the 1400s, Aztec armies brought half of modern-day Mexico under their control. The Aztecs proved to be effective but harsh rulers. Conquered tribes were forced to send treasure, food, and prisoners to the Aztec capital. The Aztecs forced the people they conquered to pay high taxes. Resentful subjects would eventually turn on the Aztecs when the empire most needed allies.

Incas In the 1400s, the largest empire was not in Europe or Asia. It was in South America. The vast empire of the Incas stretched down the coast of South America along the Andes, across the Atacama desert, and reached the fringes of the Amazon rain forest.

At the center of the empire was the Inca capital, Cuzco (KOOS koh). Cuzco was linked to other cities and towns by a great network of roads. A Spaniard who traveled the main Inca highway called it "the finest road to be seen in the world."

The Incas constructed buildings of huge stones carefully shaped to fit together. Their engineers built walls to hold soil in their fields, canals to carry water, and bridges over deep canyons. The Incas produced fine weavings and metalwork. Inca rulers wore gold and silver jewelry, and their palaces contained plates of gold.

☑ **Checkpoint** **Where were the Aztec and Inca civilizations located?**

☆ **Looking Back and Ahead** Most Native Americans did not live in large cities like Tenochtitlán or Cuzco. In the next section, you will learn about the ways of life of people north of Mexico.

Figure of an Inca ruler or priest

Section 1 | **Check Your Progress**

Progress Monitoring ⬤nline
For: Self-test with instant help
Visit: PHSchool.com
Web Code: mva-1011

Comprehension and Critical Thinking

1. (a) List Name one skill that people had to learn in order to grow crops.
(b) Identify Benefits What benefits could farmers get from learning to raise animals?

2. (a) Define What is a civilization?
(b) Apply Information How did the Mayas and Aztecs fit that definition?

⟳ Reading Skill

3. Preview Before Reading Preview Section 2. Read its headings, study its images and captions, and review its questions. Tell what you think Section 2 will be about. Use the headings to identify the text organization. How can you use this information to plan your reading?

Key Terms

Answer the following questions in complete sentences that show your understanding of the key terms.

4. How did the growth of glaciers affect water levels in the ocean?
5. Why was learning about irrigation important for farmers?
6. What are the advantages of having a surplus of crops?

Writing

7. Outline a paragraph in response to the following question: How did early civilizations use industry and science to improve their way of life? Then, list four or five supporting details. Next, write a concluding sentence.

Preserving Native American Culture

❝ By encouraging a greater focus on native language programs, we are not only striving to preserve the identity of the nation's tribes, but we're encouraging greater academic performance among Native American students as well. ❞

—Congresswoman Heather Wilson, on the Esther Martinez Native American Languages Preservation Act of 2006

◄ Recreation of a Native American village

Cultures of North America

Objectives
- Learn about the earliest peoples of North America.
- Discover what different groups of Native Americans had in common.
- Explore the impact of geography on Native American cultures.

🎯 Reading Skill

Apply Prior Knowledge You can prepare for reading by building on and connecting to what you already know. This can be information from an earlier section, chapter, or other reading. It can also be prior knowledge from your own life experience. Applying this knowledge while you are reading helps you interact with and engage in the text. This, in turn, will help you understand and remember what you have read.

Key Terms

culture	adobe
culture area	clan
kayak	sachem
potlatch	

Why It Matters As the Mayas, Aztecs, and Incas built civilizations in Central America and South America, diverse cultures developed to the north.

❓ Section Focus Question: How did geography influence the development of cultures in North America?

First Cultures of North America

In North America, as elsewhere, groups of people developed unique **cultures,** or ways of life. Around 3,000 years ago, various groups began to emerge in an area stretching from the Appalachian Mountains to the Mississippi Valley. We call these people Mound Builders because they constructed large piles of earth. Many mounds were burial places, but some served as foundations for public buildings. One group of Mound Builders, the Mississippians, built the first cities in North America. As many as 40,000 people may have lived in the largest Mississippian city, Cahokia, in present-day Illinois.

A far different culture, which we call the Anasazi, emerged in southern Utah, Colorado, northern Arizona, and New Mexico. They built large cliff dwellings, probably to defend against attacks by outsiders such as the Navajos or even the Aztecs. Their largest community housed about 1,000 people. The Anasazis were skilled in making baskets, pottery, and jewelry. They also engaged in trade. Mysteriously, by 1300, the Anasazis had abandoned their cliff dwellings.

From about 300 B.C. to A.D. 1450, highly skilled farmers called the Hohokam dug irrigation canals in the deserts of present-day Arizona. Trade brought them in contact with people who lived on the Gulf of California. The Hohokam traded for seashells, which they used to create jewelry and religious objects.

☑Checkpoint **For what purposes were mounds built?**

Ways of Life

Scholars classify Native Americans into several culture areas, regions in which groups of people have a similar way of life. Though these cultures were very different from one another, many shared some basic traits.

Meeting Basic Needs Early Native American societies developed a variety of ways to meet their needs. In many areas, women collected roots, wild seeds, nuts, acorns, and berries. Men hunted for game and fished. Wild game was plentiful in regions like the Pacific Coast and the Eastern Woodlands.

In many culture areas, agriculture allowed people to grow and store food. Native Americans learned to grow crops suited to the climate in which they lived. They used pointed sticks for digging. Bones or shells served as hoes. Some used fertilizer, such as dead fish, to make the soil more productive. Where Native Americans lived by farming, their population was much larger than in nonfarming areas.

Trade was a common activity in all the North American cultures. In some areas, items such as seashells or beads were used as currency. Shells, flint for making fires, copper, and salt were all important trade items.

Shared Beliefs Many Native Americans felt a close relationship to the natural world. They believed that spirits dwelled in nature and that these spirits were part of their daily lives.

Traditions reflected these beliefs. For example, the Indians of the Southeast held the Green Corn Ceremony in late summer. The ritual, which could last for more than a week, was a form of natural and spiritual renewal at the end of the growing season. The Pueblo Indians revered spirits known as kachinas. To teach their children about these benevolent spirits, the Pueblos carved kachina dolls.

Native Americans also had a strong oral tradition. Storytellers memorized history and beliefs and then recited them. In this way, their tradition was passed on from generation to generation.

☑Checkpoint **How did North American cultures meet their needs?**

Vocabulary Builder
currency (KUH rehn see) *n.* items used as money

Native American Farmers
Early farmers made and used stone tools such as the digging stick and axe shown to the left. **Critical Thinking:** *Clarify Problems Based on this picture, what difficulties might these farmers face?*

Native Americans of North America

Well before 10,000 B.C., Native Americans had spread across the North American continent. They had adapted to the various climates and living conditions of the lands in which they settled. By A.D. 1500, when the first Europeans reached the Americas, the Native Americans living in North America were a richly diverse group of people with <u>distinct</u> ways of life.

Vocabulary Builder
<u>distinct</u> (dihs TIHNKT) **adj.** clearly different in quality

Far North The people of the Arctic lived in a vast and harsh land, some of it covered with ice all year long. The people survived on fish, shellfish, and birds. They also hunted marine mammals, such as whales, seals, and walruses, from **kayaks**, small boats made from skins. In the summer, they fished on the rivers and hunted caribou.

South of the Arctic lay the dense forests of the subarctic region. With a climate too cold for farming, subarctic peoples relied on animals and plants of the forest for food. Most hunted caribou, moose, bear, and smaller animals.

Northwest Many Native Americans lived in the region of the Pacific Northwest, the land that stretches from southern Alaska to northern California. Deer and bears roamed forests rich with roots and berries. Rivers swarmed with salmon. With so much food available, people here were able to live in large, permanent settlements even though they were not farmers.

In many societies of the Northwest, high-ranking people practiced a custom called the potlatch. A **potlatch** was a ceremony at which the hosts showered their guests with gifts such as woven cloth, baskets, canoes, and furs. A family's status was judged by how much wealth it could give away.

Far West The people of the Far West lived in different geographic regions. Winters could be very cold in the forests and grasslands of the north. On the other hand, southern parts could be desertlike. In California, with its warm summers and mild winters, food was abundant. People there ate small game, fish, and berries.

Housing differed, depending on the area. Some Native Americans lived in pit houses, which were dug into the ground. Others lived in cone-shaped houses covered with bark. In the north, houses were made of wooden planks.

Southwest The area that is now Arizona, New Mexico, and the southern parts of Utah and Colorado was dry most of the year. But in late July and August, thunderstorms drenched the desert. All the groups in this area did some farming, although certain groups also followed and hunted animals. Farming peoples had to learn to collect and store the rain for the dry times.

The Pueblo people such as the Hopis and Zunis had stable towns that lasted for hundreds of years. To protect themselves from attack, they built large apartment houses made of **adobe**, or sun-dried brick.

Apply Prior Knowledge What do you know about apartment life? Use this knowledge to imagine and describe Pueblo homes.

Homes of Native Americans

Native Americans lived in several distinct culture areas. In each region, geography and climate helped shape the people's way of life.
Critical Thinking: *Apply Information* Look at the map and the pictures. Identify the group that lived in tepees.

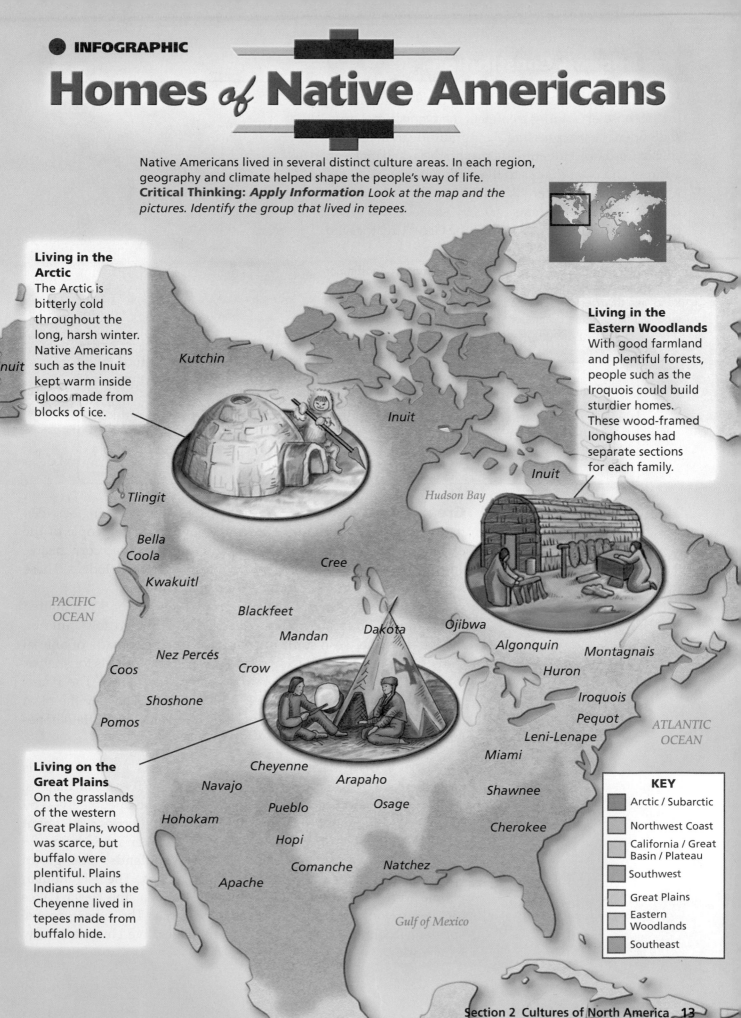

Living in the Arctic
The Arctic is bitterly cold throughout the long, harsh winter. Native Americans such as the Inuit kept warm inside igloos made from blocks of ice.

Living in the Eastern Woodlands
With good farmland and plentiful forests, people such as the Iroquois could build sturdier homes. These wood-framed longhouses had separate sections for each family.

Living on the Great Plains
On the grasslands of the western Great Plains, wood was scarce, but buffalo were plentiful. Plains Indians such as the Cheyenne lived in tepees made from buffalo hide.

Inuit

Kutchin

Inuit

Hudson Bay

Inuit

Tlingit

Bella Coola

Kwakuitl

Cree

PACIFIC OCEAN

Blackfeet

Mandan

Dakota

Ojibwa

Algonquin

Montagnais

Nez Percés

Crow

Huron

Coos

Shoshone

Iroquois

Pomos

Pequot

Leni-Lenape

ATLANTIC OCEAN

Miami

Cheyenne

Navajo

Arapaho

Shawnee

Pueblo

Osage

Hohokam

Cherokee

Hopi

Comanche

Natchez

Apache

Gulf of Mexico

KEY

■ Arctic / Subarctic
□ Northwest Coast
■ California / Great Basin / Plateau
■ Southwest
□ Great Plains
□ Eastern Woodlands
■ Southeast

The Iroquois Constitution

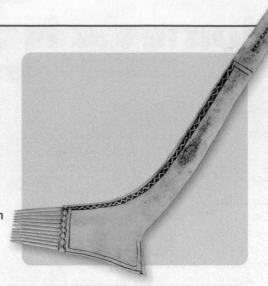

❝Whenever the Confederate Lords shall assemble for the purpose of holding a council, the Onondaga Lords shall open it by expressing their gratitude to their cousin Lords and greeting them, and they shall make an address and offer thanks to the earth where men dwell, to the streams of water . . . to the forest trees for their usefulness, to the animals that serve as food and give their pelts for clothing . . . and to the Great Creator who dwells in the heavens above.❞

—Iroquois Constitution

Items like this were widely used and traded among the people who belonged to the League of Iroquois.

Reading Primary Sources
Skills Activity

The constitution of the Iroquois League was at first a spoken rather than a written document. The excerpt above describes how members of the Iroquois League were to begin a meeting.

(a) **Apply Information** What attitude toward nature does this selection reflect?

(b) **Draw Conclusions** Why do you think members of the Iroquois League wanted to begin each meeting with a set ritual?

Great Plains The Great Plains is a vast region stretching between the Mississippi River and the Rocky Mountains. The people of the eastern Plains lived mainly by farming. Women planted corn, beans, and squash in river valleys. Many people lived in earth lodges. These buildings had log frames and were covered with soil.

Much of the western Great Plains was too dry and too matted with grass to be farmed. The treeless land provided few building materials. In the west, some people lived in tepees made of animal skins. Other Plains people dug round pits near their fields for shelter.

Hunting parties followed buffalo across the plains. The Plains people depended on the buffalo for many things. They ate the meat and used the hides to make tepees, robes, and shields. Buffalo bones were made into tools.

Eastern Woodlands Hundreds of years ago, most of what is now the eastern United States was covered by forests of maples, birches, pines, and beeches. The earliest woodlands people lived by hunting, fishing, and foraging for nuts and berries. By about A.D. 1000, a number of woodlands people had taken up farming.

Two groups dominated the Eastern Woodlands. One group spoke Algonquian (al GOHN kee un) languages. The Algonquian people were scattered through southern Canada, the Great Lakes area, and along the Atlantic coast to Virginia. The other groups, speaking Iroquoian (IHR uh kwoy an) languages, lived in what is now New York.

The Iroquois were made up of five distinct nations. Each nation was made up of **clans**, or groups of families that were related to one another. Because membership in a clan was passed from a mother to her children, women had great influence in Iroquois society. They owned all the property that belonged to a clan. Women also chose the clan's **sachem**, or tribal chief.

During the 1500s, the five Iroquois nations went through a period of constant warfare. Finally, Iroquois leaders convinced their people to make peace. They formed a union called the League of the Iroquois. It established a council to make laws to keep the peace. Each tribe was still free to deal with its own affairs.

Southeast The climate in the Southeast was mild, but the summers were steamy and hot. The land and climate supported farming. People such as the Cherokees and Creeks built houses on wooden frames, covered with straw mats. They then plastered the houses with mud clay to keep the interiors cool and dry.

The Natchez people of the Gulf Coast created a complex society. At the top stood the ruler, called the Great Sun, and the nobles. At the bottom were commoners, known as Stinkards. By law, all nobles—including the Great Sun himself—had to marry Stinkards. In this way, membership in each class kept changing.

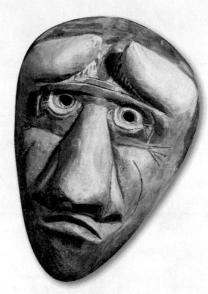

Cherokee mask

✓Checkpoint **In what culture areas was hunting the main way of life?**

⭐ **Looking Back and Ahead** In this section, you learned about Native American cultures. In the next sections, you will explore cultures that developed on the other side of the world.

Section 2 | **Check Your Progress**

Progress Monitoring Online
For: Self-test with instant help
Visit: PHSchool.com
Web Code: mva-1012

Comprehension and Critical Thinking

1. (a) Recall What role did nature play in many Native American religious beliefs?
(b) Draw Inferences How does that emphasis on nature reflect the everyday life of the people?

2. (a) Identify Identify two culture areas where farming was the main way of life.
(b) Analyze Cause and Effect Why do you think farming did not develop extensively in the Arctic and the subarctic regions?

🔄 Reading Skill

3. Apply Prior Knowledge Reread the first paragraph under the heading "Native Americans of North America." How is your culture group different from others? How is it the same? Use this knowledge to describe how Native American cultures were the same and different.

Key Terms

Fill in the blank in each question with a key term from this section.

4. The _____ of a people includes its customs, beliefs, and ways of making a living.
5. The _____ provided leadership in Iroquois communities.
6. Members of the same _____ shared a common ancestor.

Writing

7. Create a chart that shows how three different groups of Native Americans adapted to the regions in which they lived. Use the following column headings: Region, Way of Life, Diet, Shelter.

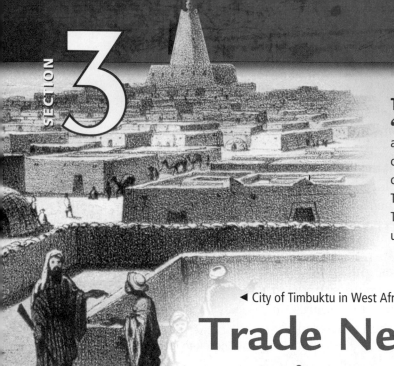

The Wealth of Timbuktu

❝ The inhabitants are very rich. . . . Grain and animals are abundant, so that the consumption of milk and butter is considerable. But salt is in very short supply because it is carried here from Tegaza, some 500 miles from Timbuktu. . . . The royal court is magnificent and very well organized. . . . This king makes war only upon neighboring enemies and upon those who do not want to pay him tribute. ❞

—Hassan ibn Muhammad, *The Description of Africa*, 1526

◀ City of Timbuktu in West Africa

Trade Networks of Asia and Africa

Objectives

- Learn about the role played by Muslims in world trade.
- Discover how great trading states rose in East Africa and West Africa.
- Find out how China dominated an important trade route across Asia.

🎯 Reading Skill

Ask Questions Asking questions when you read will help you organize your reading plan and get involved with the text. You can use your questions, for example, to set a reading purpose—answering the questions. Two ways to generate questions are to restate headings and to study the review questions at the end of the section.

Key Terms and People

Muhammad
Mansa Musa

navigation
Zheng He

Why It Matters While Native Americans were developing diverse cultures and civilizations, other civilizations thrived in Europe, Africa, and Asia.

❷ **Section Focus Question: How did trade link Europe, Africa, and Asia?**

The Muslim Link in Trade

From earliest times, trade linked groups who lived at great distances from one another. As trade developed, merchants established regular trade routes. These merchants carried their culture with them as they traveled.

By the 1500s, a complex trade network linked Europe, Africa, and Asia. Much of this trade passed through the Arabian Peninsula in the Middle East. Ships from China and India brought their cargoes of spices, silks, and gems to ports on the Red Sea. The precious cargoes were then taken overland to markets throughout the Middle East.

Rise of Islam The growth in trade was also linked to the rise of Islam. This religion emerged on the Arabian Peninsula in the 600s. Its founder was Muhammad. His followers believed him to be a prophet. He taught that there is one true God. Followers of Islam, called Muslims, believed that the Quran (ku RAHN), the sacred book of Islam, contained the exact word of God as revealed to Muhammad.

Islam was transmitted rapidly through conquest and trade. Arab armies swept across North Africa and into Spain. Muslim merchants also spread their religion far into Africa, and from Persia to India. Millions of people across three continents became Muslims.

Advances in Learning Arab scholars made remarkable contributions to mathematics, medicine, and astronomy. They helped develop algebra and later passed it along to Europe. Arab astronomers measured the size of Earth, supporting the Greek belief that Earth was a sphere. Arabs also made important advances in technology. They built ships with large, triangular sails that allowed captains to use the wind even if it changed direction.

☑**Checkpoint** **How did Islam spread?**

The African Link in Trade

Africa has a long history of trade, going back as far as 3100 B.C., when the great civilization of Egypt arose. Egyptian traders sailed throughout the eastern Mediterranean Sea and the Red Sea to bring home cedar logs, silver, and horses. Following routes south from Egypt, they traded for ivory, spices, copper, and cattle.

East African Trade Centers About A.D. 1000, trade centers began to appear in eastern Africa. The most powerful was Zimbabwe (zim BAH bway), which became the center of a flourishing empire in the 1400s. Zimbabwe lay on the trade route between the east coast and the interior of Africa. Traders passing through Zimbabwe had to pay taxes on their goods.

Trade brought prosperity to a number of cities along the east coast of Africa. Kilwa, the chief trading center, attracted merchant ships from as far away as China. Kilwa traders did a brisk trade with the African interior, exchanging cloth, pottery, and manufactured goods for gold, ivory, and furs. An active slave trade also developed between East Africa and Asia across the Indian Ocean.

Vocabulary Builder
sphere (sfeer) **n.** rounded shape

Ask Questions
Preview the headings on the next two pages. Turn them into questions that you would expect to find the answers to as you read.

Cardamom

Curry

Cumin

Merchants in the Middle East

At outdoor bazaars, Muslim merchants bought and sold goods from around the world. Probably the most valuable goods sold at this Persian bazaar were spices from Southeast Asia, such as the ones shown here. **Critical Thinking: Link Past and Present** How is this bazaar similar to a modern shopping area? How is it different?

Mansa Musa
1280?–1337

Every Muslim must make a *hajj*, or pilgrimage, to the holy city of Mecca. Mansa Musa's hajj became famous. His escort included 80 camels, each carrying 300 pounds of gold. Thousands of servants and officials accompanied the emperor across the Sahara.

Word of the emperor's hajj reached Europe. A Portuguese mapmaker described Mansa Musa as "the richest and most noble king in all the land."

West African Trade Centers Trade networks also linked the Middle East and West Africa. Desert nomads guided caravans, or groups of camels and their cargo, across the vast Sahara, the largest desert in the world.

Ghana was the first major center of trade in West Africa. The kingdom was located between the sources of salt in the desert and the gold fields farther south. By the ninth century, the demand for gold had grown in the Middle East. On the other hand, people in West Africa needed salt in their diet to prevent dehydration in the hot tropical climate. As the trade in gold and salt increased, the rulers of Ghana became rich.

Shifting trade routes and disruptions caused by war gradually led Ghana to weaken. In the 1200s, the kingdom was absorbed into the empire of Mali. Mali reached its height under the Muslim ruler Mansa Musa. As Mali prospered, its great city of Timbuktu became a center of learning. Merchants from Mali traded throughout the region for kola nuts, food, and, of course, gold.

In the 1400s, Mali had a number of weak rulers. When nomads captured Timbuktu in 1433, the empire had been in decline for some time. It would soon be replaced by Songhai.

The rulers of Songhai captured Timbuktu in 1468. Songhai rulers restored the city as a center of Islamic learning. Trade across the Sahara expanded, which brought wealth to the Songhai Empire. Salt, gold, and captives for sale as slaves passed through Songhai on the way to Muslim markets in the north.

✓**Checkpoint** What trading kingdoms arose in West Africa?

The East Asian Link in Trade

As early as 221 B.C., a strong ruler had unified China into a single empire. Later rulers added to the empire until it covered a large part of the continent of Asia. Highways, canals, and a postal system linked China together.

As China's empire expanded, so did its trade. China established trade links with India, Korea, Japan, the Middle East, and Africa. China's trade centers grew into cities. By the 1200s, Hangzhou (HAN JOW) was one of the world's largest cities.

World Traders China had a higher level of technology than any other civilization of the time. Around 1050, the Chinese invented printing with movable type. This was about 400 years before this technology was developed in Europe.

The Chinese made great advances in navigation. Navigation is the science of locating the position and plotting the course of ships. The Chinese invented the magnetic compass, which made it possible for ships to sail out of sight of land and still find their way home.

By the 1300s Chinese ships were sailing trade routes that stretched from Japan to East Africa. The Chinese explorer Zheng He made several voyages with a fleet of more than 300 giant ships. The fleet visited 30 nations throughout Asia and Africa, trading silks and pottery for spices, gems, medicinal herbs, and ivory.

Spice Trade and the Silk Road Chinese silks, bronze goods, pottery, and spices flowed west from China along a route known as the Silk Road. The Silk Road was one of the great trade routes of ancient times. It was not really a single road but a series of routes that stretched about 5,000 miles from Xi'an (SHE AHN) in China to Persia.

Merchants on the Silk Road brought silk and other goods from China across Asia for sale in Middle Eastern and European markets. Along the way they traded in the Middle East for products like cloves, nutmeg, and peppercorns from the Spice Islands in Southeast Asia. The Silk Road declined in importance when <u>alternative</u> sea routes were discovered.

☑ **Checkpoint** What was the Silk Road?

⭐ **Looking Back and Ahead** The trade links between Asia and Africa developed at a time when much of Europe was isolated. In the next section, you will learn about the development of Europe. You will also see how Europe began to look toward the riches of Asia.

This Chinese figurine is made of jade, a precious trade item.

Vocabulary Builder
<u>alternative</u> (awl TUR nuh tiv) **adj.** providing a choice between two or among more than two things

---

Progress Monitoring ⦿nline
For: Self-test with instant help
Visit: PHSchool.com
Web Code: mva-1013

Section 3 | **Check Your Progress**

Comprehension and Critical Thinking

1. **(a) Recall** What role did the Muslim world play in trade?
(b) Interpret Maps Locate the Arabian Peninsula on a world map. Why was its location ideal for a trading center?

2. **(a) Recall** Why were gold and salt important in West African trade?
(b) Contrast How did trade in East Africa differ from trade in West Africa?

🔄 **Reading Skill**

3. **Ask Questions** Look at the questions you asked, and look at the section review questions. Did the reading answer those questions? How did previewing help you set purposes and increase your understanding?

Key Terms

4. Write two definitions for the key term navigation—one a formal definition for a teacher, the other an informal definition for a younger child.

Writing

5. Consider the following thesis statement: The trading network between Asia, Africa, and Europe began a useful exchange of ideas and products. Write one or two paragraphs to develop that thesis.

Global Trade in the Fifteenth Century

For centuries, merchants and traders used land and sea routes to travel between Europe, Africa, and Asia. Before the first European voyages to the Americas, a global trading network linked the major civilizations of three continents. Gold and salt moved east from Africa while silk and spices moved west from China and India. Use the map below to trace the patterns of global trade.

Ivory

Gold

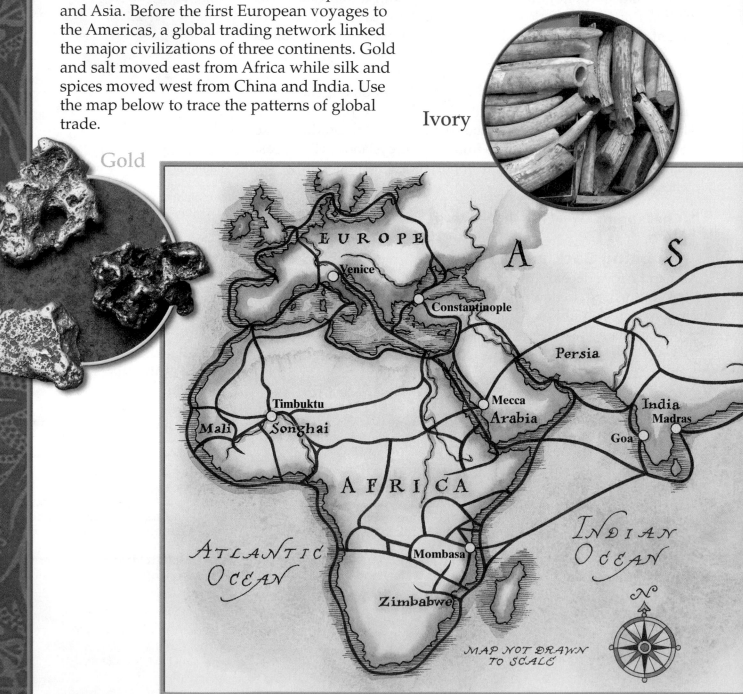

EUROPE

Venice

Constantinople

Persia

Mecca
Arabia

India
Madras

Goa

Timbuktu
Mali   Songhai

AFRICA

ATLANTIC OCEAN

Mombasa

Zimbabwe

INDIAN OCEAN

N

MAP NOT DRAWN TO SCALE

History *Interactive*
**Explore Global
Trade**

Visit: PHSchool.com
Web Code: mvl-1013

Gold, Salt, and Ivory

Trade centers in East and West Africa saw heavy traffic in gold, salt, and ivory. African gold was highly valued in the Middle East.

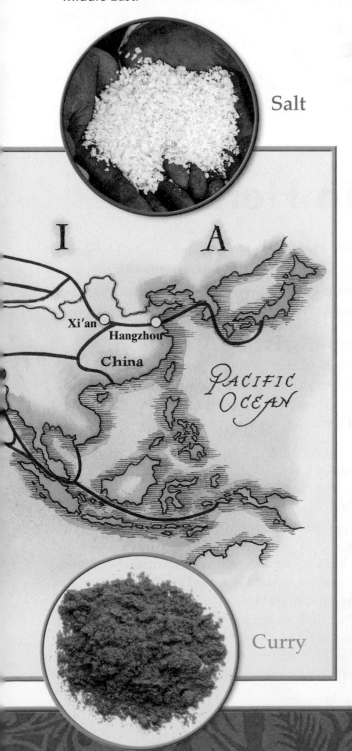

Salt

I   A

Xi'an
Hangzhou
China

PACIFIC
OCEAN

Curry

Understand Effects:

The Network Expands

When Christopher Columbus sailed west from Spain in 1492, he opened up a new era in global trade. Prior to Columbus's voyage, the Americas were isolated from the flow of goods and ideas that connected Europe, Africa, and Asia. After 1492, the old trade networks expanded across an ocean to a new world of resources.

▲ Trade flourished throughout Asia. Ships from China and India unloaded their cargoes in Arabian ports for overland transport to African or European markets.

Analyze **GEOGRAPHY AND HISTORY**

Worldwide trade allowed for the exchange of goods and ideas across continents. Write a paragraph describing how West African gold might travel to China.

Cinnamon, Pearls, and Gold

❝[I] landed and showed them a variety of merchandise, with the view of finding out whether such things were to be found in their country. This merchandise included cinnamon, cloves, seepearls, gold, and many other things, but it was evident that they had no knowledge whatever of such articles. ❞

—Vasco de Gama, *Round Africa to India*, 1497–1498

▲ European merchants sold goods from Africa and Asia.

The European Heritage

Objectives

- Understand the importance of the Judeo-Christian tradition.
- Learn how Greece and Rome shaped ideas about government and law.
- Discover the impact of the Crusades and the Renaissance on Europe.
- Find out why Europeans began to look beyond their borders.

Reading Skill

Use Graphics to Construct Meaning

Textbooks include information beyond the main text that can be useful to your understanding. Nontext material includes maps, charts, and photos. These materials often have accompanying text such as captions or titles. Use this material to gain understanding as you read.

Key Terms and People

monotheism
Jesus
salvation
direct democracy
republic

feudalism
Martin Luther
Henry the
  Navigator
Vasco da Gama

Why It Matters Through migration and trade, Europeans, Africans, and Asians exchanged goods, inventions, and ideas.

❓ **Section Focus Question: What major influences shaped European civilization?**

The Judeo-Christian Tradition

European beliefs and values were shaped by two religions of the ancient Middle East: Judaism and Christianity. The influence of these two religions is known as the Judeo-Christian tradition.

Judaism Around 1700 B.C. a religion called Judaism arose among the Israelites, a nomadic people of the Middle East. Judaism was the first major world religion to teach **monotheism**, the idea that there is only one God.

According to the Hebrew Bible, Moses taught the Israelites the values God wanted them to fulfill—love your neighbor, be kind to strangers, give charity, and pursue justice. Those teachings included the Ten Commandments, a set of religious and moral rules.

Other early religions regarded rulers as gods. Judaism held that even the most powerful ruler had to obey God's laws. This belief formed the basis for the later view that no person, no matter how powerful or wealthy, is above the law.

Christianity About 2,000 years ago, a Jewish teacher named Jesus of Nazareth began to preach in the region around the Sea of Galilee. Jesus attracted a following. Many believed that he was the Messiah, the Savior chosen by God.

The Gospels, which recount the life of Jesus, tell how crowds flocked to hear Jesus teach and perform miracles. According to the Gospels, the Roman rulers of Judea, wanting to maintain order, arrested, tried, and crucified Jesus. Followers of Jesus said that he rose from the dead three days later.

The life and teachings of Jesus inspired a new religion, Christianity. Christianity is based on the belief that Jesus was indeed the Messiah, sent by God to save the world. Christians teach that Jesus was, in fact, God in human form.

The teachings of Jesus emphasized love, mercy, and forgiveness. Jesus also taught that all people have an equal chance for salvation, or everlasting life. These beliefs appealed to many people, especially the poor and oppressed. This helped Christianity spread from the Middle East across Europe.

As Christianity spread, the Romans at first viewed it as a threat. Christians were subject to arrest and death. Later, emperors accepted Christianity and made it the official religion of the Roman Empire. As a result, it eventually became the dominant religion of all of Europe.

✓**Checkpoint** **What does Christianity teach about Jesus?**

Use Graphics to Construct Meaning
Preview the pictures in this section. What do they suggest to you about the content of the text?

The Ten Commandments

❝[I.] I the Lord am your God, who brought you out of the land of Egypt, the house of bondage. You shall have no other gods besides Me. . . .
[IV.] Remember the sabbath day and keep it holy. . . .
[V.] Honor your father and your mother, that you may long endure on the land that the Lord your God is assigning to you.
[VI.] You shall not murder. . . .
[VIII.] You shall not steal.❞

—Book of Exodus, *Tanakh*, The New Jewish Publication Society Translation of the Hebrew Bible

Painting showing Moses with the Ten Commandments

Reading Primary Sources
Skills Activity

According to the Book of Exodus, God gave the Ten Commandments to the Israelite leader Moses. Five of the Commandments are given above.

(a) **Apply Information** How does this selection reflect the Judeo-Christian idea of monotheism?

(b) **Draw Conclusions** How do the Ten Commandments say we should treat other people?

Greek and Roman Traditions

Judaism and Christianity shaped European religious and moral thinking. At the same time, the ancient civilizations of Greece and Rome shaped European political traditions. Greek and Roman ideas would later deeply influence the Founders of the United States.

Athenian Democracy In the fifth century B.C., the Greek city-state of Athens experienced a sudden explosion of learning and creativity. Perhaps its most remarkable achievement was the birth of democracy.

Athens was a direct democracy. **Direct democracy** is a form of government in which an assembly of ordinary citizens makes decisions. This differs from the modern American form of government, in which citizens elect representatives to make laws. Any adult male citizen could <u>participate</u> in the Athenian Assembly. The Athenian leader Pericles described the Athenian idea of democracy:

> "Our constitution is named a democracy, because it is in the hands not of the few but of the many. . . . We decide or debate, carefully and in person, all matters of policy."
> —Pericles, from *The History of the Peloponnesian War* (Thucydides)

Still, Athenian democracy had limitations. Women, slaves, and foreign-born people could not participate in government.

Athenians believed that a democracy depended on well-rounded, educated citizens. In Athenian schools, boys studied many areas of knowledge, from history and grammar to poetry and music. Because Athenian citizens were expected to voice their opinions in the Assembly, schools also trained students in public speaking.

Roman Government and Law While democracy was developing in ancient Greece, a few small villages in central Italy were growing into the city of Rome. Over time, the Romans developed new traditions in law and government.

Vocabulary Builder
<u>participate</u> (pahr TIHS uh payt)
v. to take part

Education in Athens
This Greek vase painting shows an Athenian school. At the center, a teacher checks a student's writing tablet. **Critical Thinking: Interpret Art** *Identify one other subject that the students at this school are learning.*

Links Across Time

2009 Congress counts electoral ballots for the 2008 presidential election.

Republican Government

509 B.C. The Roman Republic was established. The elected Senate became the chief governing and law-making body of Rome.

1787 The Founders of the United States admired the Roman Republic. When they wrote the Constitution, they gave lawmaking power to an elected Congress similar to the Roman Senate. But they divided Congress into two separate houses, the Senate and the House of Representatives.

Link to Today   Online

Congress Today Today, as in the past, the men and women of Congress make laws that affect the lives of all Americans.

For: Congress in the news
Visit: PHSchool.com
Web Code: mvc-1014

In 509 B.C., the Romans overthrew their king and set up a republic. A **republic** is a form of government in which people choose representatives to govern them. In the Roman Republic, an elected senate and assembly made the laws.

Rome's code of laws defined the rights of citizens. According to the code, everybody was equal under the law. People accused of crimes were considered innocent until proven guilty. These principles form the framework of the American system of justice.

Long years of civil war led to the collapse of the Roman republic. In 27 B.C., a noble named Octavian declared himself emperor. The Roman Empire would last for almost 500 years. During this time, Roman ideas about law and government spread over a wide area.

☑**Checkpoint** How did citizens participate in Greek and Roman government?

New Horizons

After a period of decline, the Roman Empire fell to invaders in A.D. 476. Europe fragmented into many small states. The 1,000-year period after the fall of Rome is known as the Middle Ages.

The Middle Ages By the ninth century, feudalism had arisen in Europe. **Feudalism** is a system in which a ruler grants parts of his land to lords. In exchange, lords owed the king military service and financial assistance. In turn, lords granted land to lesser lords.

Copying a Manuscript
In Europe during the Middle Ages, learning was in the hands of the Church. Monks like this one spent hours and hours each day carefully copying books by hand. **Critical Thinking: *Make Predictions*** *How might the invention of mechanical printing affect learning in Europe?*

The Roman Catholic Church had great power in the Middle Ages. Daily life revolved around the rituals of the Catholic Church. The Catholic Church was also the center of learning. Outside of members of the clergy, few people, even among the nobility, were able to read and write.

The Crusades In 1095, the leader of the Roman Catholic Church, Pope Urban II, declared a crusade, or holy war. Its object was to win back control of the region known as the Holy Land, the land where Jesus had lived and taught. There were nine crusades over the next 200 years. In the end, they failed to win permanent control of the Holy Land.

Still, the Crusades had important long-term effects. They put Europeans in closer contact with the more advanced Muslim civilization. Europeans were attracted by the rich goods they saw in the Holy Land. They tasted strange foods and spices, such as oranges, pepper, and ginger. They also learned about advanced technology used for navigation. In time, the Crusades would help inspire Europeans to look overseas for trade.

The Renaissance Beginning in the 1300s, there was a rebirth of learning that is known as the Renaissance. European scholars rediscovered the classical texts of ancient Greece and Rome. Artists reflected a new interest in subjects that had influenced ancient thinkers.

Science and invention flourished. One invention, in particular, had a great impact on society. In the mid-fifteenth century, Johann Gutenberg invented a printing press. Using movable type, the printing press enabled a printer to produce a large number of identical books in a short time. As books became more available, the ability to read became more widespread.

During the late Middle Ages, powerful nation-states emerged in Europe. Italian cities had long controlled trade on the Mediterranean. The new nations—Spain, Portugal, France, and England—would shift the important trade routes to the Atlantic Ocean.

The Reformation Since the late Roman Empire, most Europeans had belonged to the Roman Catholic Church. Not all were happy with Catholicism, however. In 1517, a German monk named Martin Luther demanded that the Roman Catholic Church reform.

When his demands were rejected, Luther rebelled against the Catholic Church authority. Followers of Luther were called Protestants, because they were protesting certain Catholic Church practices. The movement Luther led is called the Protestant Reformation. Over time, Luther's movement split, and many Protestant churches emerged. The Reformation also plunged Europe into a long series of wars between Catholic and Protestant forces.

✓Checkpoint **What was the Renaissance?**

An Age of Exploration Begins

The Renaissance, the rise of nations, and the expansion of trade set the stage for an era of exploration. The person who provided the leadership for this new era was a brother of the king of Portugal, known to history as Prince Henry the Navigator. A deeply religious man, Henry hoped not only to expand Portuguese power but also to spread Christianity to new lands.

In the 1400s, Henry set up a center for exploration at Sagres (SAH greesh) in southern Portugal. He brought mathematicians, geographers, and sea captains to this center to teach his crews everything they needed to know about navigation and mapmaking.

At Sagres, sailors learned how to use the magnetic compass to find their direction at sea. They also learned how to use an instrument called the astrolabe to determine their <u>precise</u> latitude, or distance from the equator.

Vocabulary Builder
precise (pree sīs) *adj.* exact; accurate

Using their new skills, Portuguese sailors began sailing southward along the western coast of Africa. By 1498, the Portuguese sailor Vasco da Gama passed the southern tip of Africa and continued north and east to India. Da Gama's course became an important trade route and helped boost Portuguese wealth and power. Later, Portuguese sailors pressed on to the East Indies, the source of trade in spices.

☑**Checkpoint** What was Prince Henry's goal?

⭐ **Looking Back and Ahead** By the time Vasco da Gama reached India, Prince Henry was long dead. However, his work opened the way for European sailors to reach far-flung corners of the globe. In the next chapter, you will see how these sailors linked the long-separated worlds of the east and west.

Section 4 | Check Your Progress

Progress Monitoring Online
For: Self-test with instant help
Visit: PHSchool.com
Web Code: mva-1014

Comprehension and Critical Thinking

1. (a) Recall What role did citizens play in Athens?
(b) Contrast How did Athenian democracy differ from the Roman Republic?

2. (a) Recall How did Europeans make greater contact with the outside world?
(b) Identify Benefits How might Europeans of that time benefit from increased trade?

Reading Skill

3. Use Graphics to Construct Meaning How did previewing visual material in this section help you read more actively? How did this material add detail to your understanding of European civilization?

Key Terms

Answer the following questions in complete sentences that show your understanding of the key terms.
4. How did monotheism differ from other early beliefs?

5. Why were nobles important in feudalism?
6. How are leaders chosen in a republic?

Writing

7. Some of the events covered in this section include the Crusades, feudalism, and the Renaissance. What do you think life was like in Europe before these events happened? How did life in Europe change after these events? Answer the questions in one or two paragraphs.

21st Century Learning History books are full of information. Although you cannot remember every fact, you can learn to identify the main ideas and note the details that explain and support them. The following passage is a description such as you might find in a textbook.

Native Americans developed a variety of ways to meet their basic needs for food, clothing, and shelter. In some culture areas, tribes hunted animals and gathered the nuts and fruits that grew in the wild. Other tribes depended on the sea for food. They made boats out of animal skins or carved canoes out of trees. From their boats and canoes, they speared fish or hunted marine animals such as seals, walruses, and whales.

Whether hunting, fishing, farming, or gathering wild plants, Native Americans had a great respect for the natural world. Their prayers and ceremonies were designed to maintain a balance between people and the forces of nature. They believed that they must adapt their ways to the natural world in order to survive and prosper.

Learn the Skill

Use these steps to learn how to identify main ideas and supporting details.

1 Find the main idea. The main idea is what the passage is about. Often, the main idea is stated in the first sentence of a paragraph. However, it can occur in other parts of a paragraph as well.

2 Restate the main idea. To be sure you understand the ideas expressed in the paragraph, restate the main idea in your own words.

3 Look for details. Details might include facts, reasons, explanations, examples, and descriptions that tell more about the main idea.

4 Make connections. Note how the details support and expand the main idea.

Practice the Skill

Answer the following questions based on the paragraph above.

1 Find the main idea. (a) What is the main-idea sentence in the first paragraph? (b) What is the main-idea sentence in the second paragraph?

2 Restate the main idea. Restate the main idea of each paragraph in your own words.

3 Look for details. Identify a detail that supports the main idea in each paragraph.

4 Make connections. (a) How do the details in the first paragraph help explain its main idea? (b) How do the details in the second paragraph help explain its main idea?

Apply the Skill

See the Review and Assessment at the end of this chapter.

Quick Study Guide

How did different cultures and traditions develop around the world?

Section 1
The Earliest Americans

- Most scientists believe that early people came to the Americas from Asia by way of a land bridge.
- As people learned to farm, they formed permanent settlements.
- The Mayas, Aztecs, and Incas built civilizations in Central America and South America.

Section 2
Cultures of North America

- The Mound Builders were among the earliest cultures of North America.
- People of North America developed varied ways of life, depending upon the environments in which they lived.
- The League of the Iroquois created a pact between warring nations in the Eastern Woodlands.

Section 3
Trade Networks of Asia and Africa

- The Muslim world linked Asia to Africa and Europe through trade.
- Various trading states emerged in both East Africa and West Africa.
- China dominated East Asian trade along the Silk Road.

Section 4
The European Heritage

- Judaism and Christianity formed the foundation for European religious beliefs.
- Greece and Rome shaped ideas about democratic government.
- After the Middle Ages, Europeans began to look beyond their boundaries.

(?) Exploring the Essential Question

Use the online study guide to explore the essential question.

Section 1
How did early civilizations develop in the Americas?

Section 2
How did geography influence the development of cultures in North America?

Chapter 1 Essential Question
How did different cultures and traditions develop around the world?

Section 4
What major influences shaped European civilization?

Section 3
How did trade link Europe, Africa, and Asia?

Key Terms

1. Draw a table with eight rows and three columns. In the first column, list the following key terms: glacier, irrigate, culture, clan, navigation, monotheism, direct democracy, republic. In the next column, write the definition of each word. In the last column, make a small illustration that shows the meaning of the word.

Comprehension and Critical Thinking

2. **(a) Recall** Describe the land-bridge theory that scientists have developed to explain how people first came to the Americas.
   (b) Clarify Problems Some scholars have different ideas about how people first came to the Americas. Why do you think we are not sure about this event?

3. **(a) Describe** How did the Aztecs build a large empire?
   (b) Compare What features did the Aztec civilization have in common with the civilization of the Incas?
   (c) Contrast How did the civilization of the Aztecs differ from other societies of North America?

4. **(a) Recall** What was the purpose of the League of the Iroquois?
   (b) Identify Costs and Benefits What did each Iroquois Nation give up by joining the League? What did they gain?
   (c) Draw Conclusions Why do you think the Iroquois League succeeded?

5. **(a) Describe** How did trade goods move between West Africa and the Middle East?
   (b) Apply Information Describe two ways that goods from China might have reached the trading states of East Africa.
   (c) Make Generalizations Based on your reading, write a one-sentence generalization about the importance of trade routes in Asia and Africa.

6. **(a) Summarize** Which Greco-Roman traditions influenced the shaping of government in the United States?

(b) Link Past and Present How do these Greco-Roman ideas directly impact political life in the United States today?
(c) Recall Name three major influences of the Judeo-Christian tradition on Europe.

7. **(a) Define** What were the Crusades?
   (b) Analyze Cause and Effect What were the long-range effects of the Crusades?
   (c) Draw Conclusions Do you think the Crusades were a failure or a success? Explain.

History Reading Skill

8. **Read Actively** Apply what you learned about active reading to the next chapter. Preview the headings and prereading material. Scan the graphic material. Generate two questions to help you guide your reading.

Writing

9. **Write a paragraph on the following topic:** Historical events led to increasing contacts between people in different parts of the world. **Your paragraph should:**
   - begin with a thesis statement that explains the critical events and ideas that started the move toward increasing contacts;
   - support these events or ideas with facts and examples.

10. **Write a Narrative:**
    You are a sailor who studied with the navigator Prince Henry. Write a paragraph explaining why you attended Prince Henry's school, what you learned, and your goals after leaving the school.

Skills for Life

Identify the Main Idea
Reread the text following the subheading "Far West" in Section 2, then answer the following questions.

11. What is the main-idea sentence of each paragraph?

12. Summarize the main idea of the two paragraphs in your own words.

13. What details support the main-idea sentence of the first paragraph?

Test Yourself

1. **Native American religious beliefs were based on**

   A the Ten Commandments.

   B the Quran.

   C reverence for nature.

   D the teachings of the Mound Builders.

2. **The Roman Senate was most similar to**

   A the Athenian assembly.

   B the U.S. Congress.

   C the feudal system.

   D the Aztec government.

Refer to the map at right to answer Question 3.

3. **What do the three civilizations shown on the map have in common?**

   A They were all located in South America.

   B They all traded with the Iroquois.

   C They all disappeared for unknown reasons.

   D They were all very organized societies.

Document-Based Questions

Task: Look at Documents 1 and 2, and answer their accompanying questions. Then, use the documents and your knowledge of history to complete the following writing assignment:

> Write a paragraph describing the influence of geography on the Tlingit society.

Document 1: This photograph shows the land where the people of the Pacific Northwest, such as the Tlingit and Nootka, lived. *Based on this picture, what resources did the Pacific Northwest people have for building homes and finding food?*

Document 2: In this excerpt from an oral history, a Tlingit boy describes the traditional life of his people. *Why did the Tlingit expect young people to work?*

> "Land ownership is one of the biggest laws in the Tlingit culture. You did not fish or hunt on somebody else's land without their permission. If you did and you were caught, your equipment would be broken and you would have to leave. . . .
>
> The Tlingit people subsisted in seasonal rounds. . . . They hunted black and brown bear with spear and deadfall. For wolf, coyote, and fox they used snares. They used traps to get mink, weasel, and land otter. With bow and arrow, they hunted the mountain goat. They fished Halibut, King salmon, Silver salmon, and Humpy salmon. . . .
>
> The jobs of young children long ago depended on the mental and physical capabilities. They had to do whatever they could. They had to pick berries, gather roots and plants, and clean fish. The older they got the harder the tasks became. This is how they learned."

Europe Looks Outward

With its long coastline facing the Atlantic Ocean, Portugal funded many journeys of exploration during the 1500s. This monument in Lisbon, Portugal, pays tribute to brave Portuguese explorers.

1000–1720

"This is so beautiful a place... there are trees and herbs here which would be great value in Spain... Should I meet with gold or spices in great quantity, I shall remain till I collect as much as possible."

—Journal of Christopher Columbus, October 19, 1492

What You Will Learn

Section 1
THE AGE OF EXPLORATION

The search for a water route to Asia led to the European discovery of two continents and the exchange of resources between the Eastern and the Western hemispheres.

Section 2
SPAIN'S EMPIRE IN THE AMERICAS

The Spanish established an extensive empire in the Americas and created a colonial society with a rigid class structure.

Section 3
EUROPEANS COMPETE IN NORTH AMERICA

European economic and religious conflicts quickly spilled over into North America, leading France, Holland, and England to finance explorations there.

Section 4
FRANCE AND THE NETHERLANDS IN NORTH AMERICA

Prosperous French and Dutch colonies in North America often interacted with Native Americans.

Reading Skill

Identify Main Ideas and Details In this chapter, you will learn to locate the most important ideas in a text, and the details that support them.

33

What were the causes and effects of

ESSENTIAL QUESTION

Exploration of the Americas

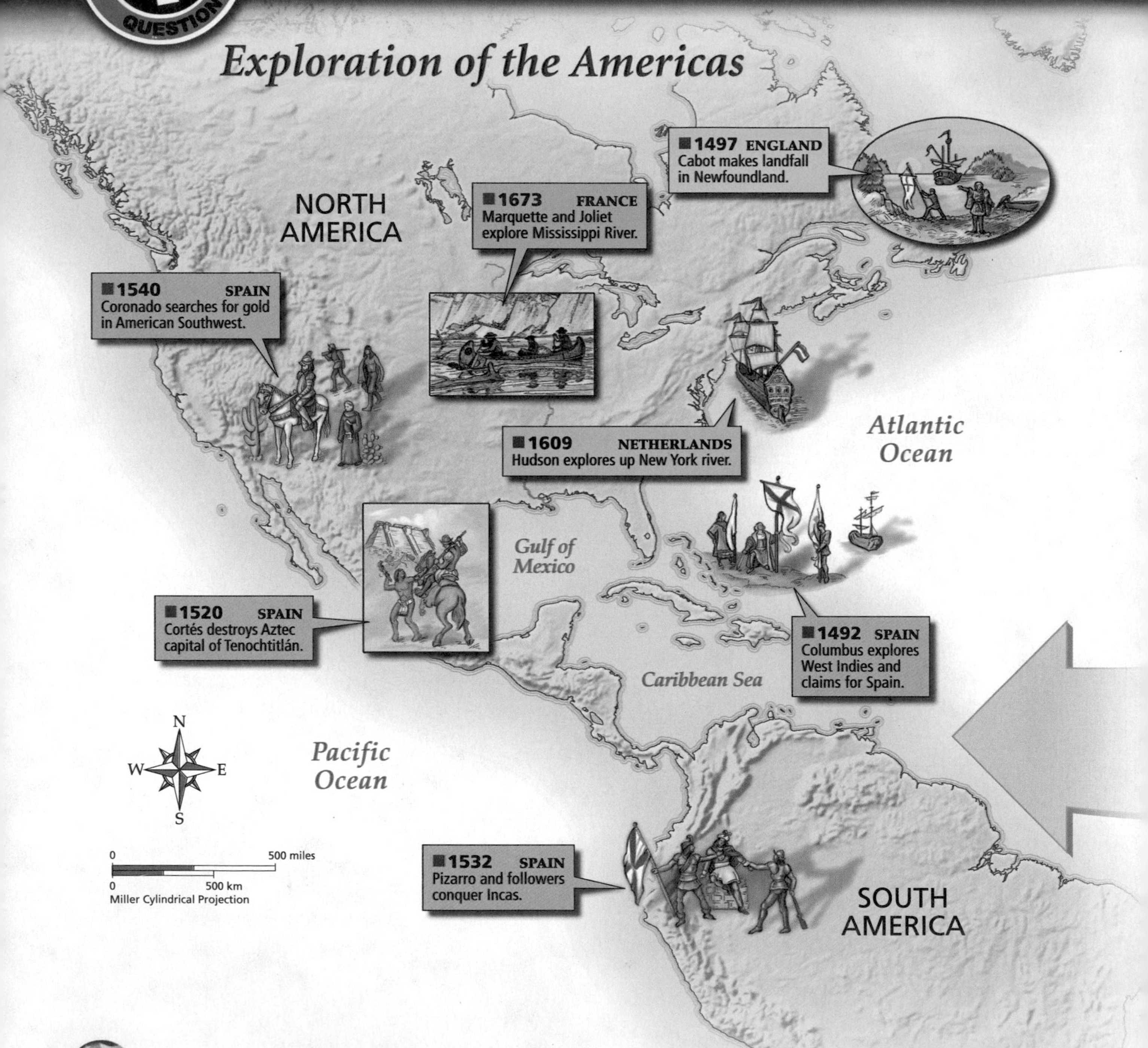

NORTH AMERICA
1497 ENGLAND
Cabot makes landfall in Newfoundland.
1673 FRANCE
Marquette and Joliet explore Mississippi River.
1540 SPAIN
Coronado searches for gold in American Southwest.
1609 NETHERLANDS
Hudson explores up New York river.
Atlantic Ocean
Gulf of Mexico
1520 SPAIN
Cortés destroys Aztec capital of Tenochtitlán.
1492 SPAIN
Columbus explores West Indies and claims for Spain.
Caribbean Sea
N
W
E
S
Pacific Ocean
0
500 miles
0
500 km
Miller Cylindrical Projection
1532 SPAIN
Pizarro and followers conquer Incas.
SOUTH AMERICA

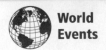

U.S. Events

1001 Vikings reach North America.

Columbus lands in the West Indies. **1492**

1000 **1400** **1500**

World Events

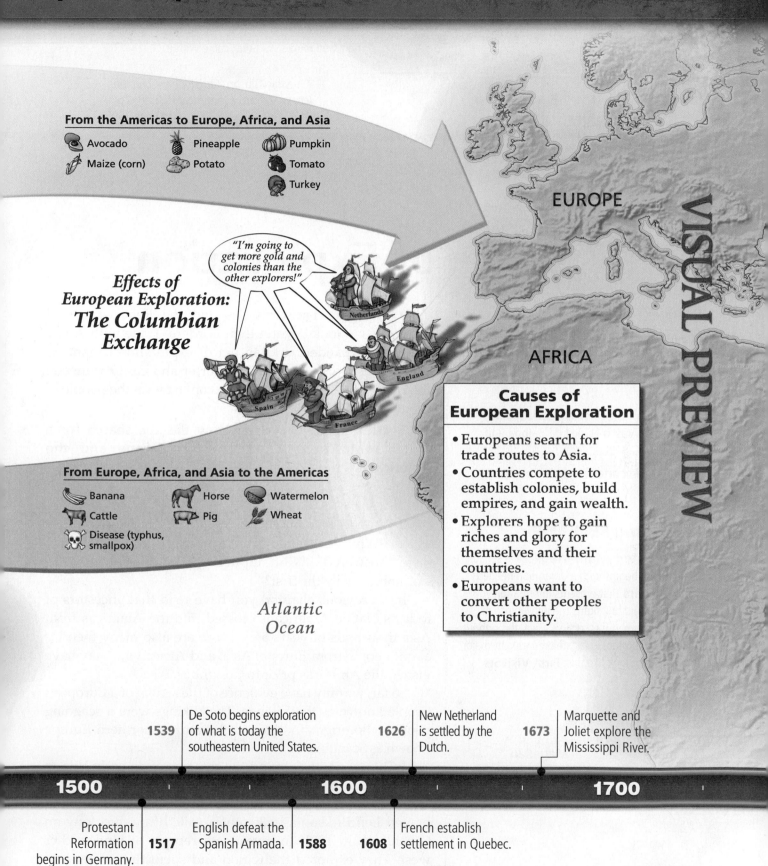

From the Americas to Europe, Africa, and Asia

Avocado   Pineapple   Pumpkin

Maize (corn)   Potato   Tomato

Turkey

Effects of European Exploration: **The Columbian Exchange**

"I'm going to get more gold and colonies than the other explorers!"

Netherlands

England

Spain

France

EUROPE

AFRICA

From Europe, Africa, and Asia to the Americas

Banana   Horse   Watermelon

Cattle   Pig   Wheat

Disease (typhus, smallpox)

Atlantic Ocean

Causes of European Exploration

- Europeans search for trade routes to Asia.
- Countries compete to establish colonies, build empires, and gain wealth.
- Explorers hope to gain riches and glory for themselves and their countries.
- Europeans want to convert other peoples to Christianity.

VISUAL PREVIEW

1539 De Soto begins exploration of what is today the southeastern United States.

1626 New Netherland is settled by the Dutch.

1673 Marquette and Joliet explore the Mississippi River.

1500   **1600**   **1700**

Protestant Reformation begins in Germany. **1517**

English defeat the Spanish Armada. **1588**

1608 French establish settlement in Quebec.

Columbus Opened the Door

❝He opened the door to European settlement of the Americas—and all the devastation, innovation, and reinvention that came with it.❞

—Christine Gibson, *Christopher Columbus, Hero or Villian*, in AmericanHeritage.com, October, 2005

◄ Columbus claims West Indies island for Spain.

The Age of Exploration

Objectives

- Explain what happened to the Vikings who explored Newfoundland.
- Describe the voyages of Christopher Columbus.
- Describe the expeditions of such Spanish explorers as Vasco Núñez de Balboa and Ferdinand Magellan.
- Explain the importance of the Columbian Exchange.

🔄 Reading Skill

Identify Stated Main Ideas Each section in this textbook begins with a paragraph headed **Why It Matters** that presents information you learned earlier and highlights the importance of what you will learn in this section. Then, throughout each section, important ideas are organized by major red headings that look like this: **First Visitors From Europe.**

Key Terms and People

Christopher Columbus
Vasco Núñez de Balboa

Ferdinand Magellan
strait
circumnavigate

Why It Matters The Crusades and the Renaissance led Europeans to look beyond their borders. Trade with Africa and Asia expanded, and an era of exploration began. As European sailors searched for shorter and easier routes to the riches of Asia, they came into contact with the people of the Americas.

❓ **Section Focus Question: How did the search for a water route to Asia affect both Europe and the Americas?**

First Visitors From Europe

If you had been in school 50 years ago and your teacher asked "Who discovered America?" you would probably have answered, "Christopher Columbus." But was Columbus really the first?

In a previous chapter, you have read that ancestors of today's Native Americans crossed into the Americas from Asia thousands of years ago. There are also many theories about people from Europe, Asia, and Africa who may have visited the Americas prior to Columbus.

So far, we only have evidence of the arrival of a European people known as the Vikings. The Vikings were a seagoing people who originally lived in the part of northern Europe known as Scandinavia.

In 1963, scientists found the remains of an early Viking settlement in Newfoundland. The findings supported the truth of old Viking stories. According to one story, a Viking named Leif Erikson and 35 others sailed from a colony on Greenland, in 1001, to investigate reports of land farther west. They explored the region and spent the winter in a place they named Vinland.

The Voyages of Columbus Vinland existed only in <u>myths</u> for the next 500 years. Whether Christopher Columbus ever heard the stories is not known. However, Columbus believed he could reach Asia and the East by sailing west across the Atlantic Ocean. He never suspected that a huge landmass was blocking the way.

Christopher Columbus grew up near Genoa, an important port on the west coast of Italy. In the 1470s, he settled in Portugal, which was Europe's leading seafaring nation. Columbus sailed on Portuguese ships, studied maps and charts, and learned about the world beyond Europe. From all this he developed his idea for a voyage to Asia.

Portugal's king showed little interest in Columbus's plan. The king hoped to reach Asia by following the route Bartholomeu Dias and other Portuguese explorers were pioneering around southern Africa. He also believed the world was larger than Columbus had calculated. Thus, in his view, the voyage would be much longer than Columbus expected. For these reasons, Portugal refused to finance such a trip.

Columbus did not give up. He moved to Spain and set his plan before King Ferdinand and Queen Isabella. They liked Columbus's plan. But it took six years before they finally agreed to provide ships for the voyage.

Setting Sail In August 1492, about 90 men—most of them Spaniards—prepared to make the voyage. Columbus's ships—the *Niña*, the *Pinta*, and the *Santa Maria*—were tiny, between 55 and 90 feet long. Sailing with the wind, they covered up to 170 miles per day.

Columbus predicted that they would reach Asia in 21 days. After a month at sea, there was no sight of land. The crew became restless and spoke of mutiny, or soldiers and sailors rebelling against their officers. Columbus held firm against the threat.

Finally, on October 12, a sailor spotted land. Coming ashore in a small boat, Columbus claimed the island for Spain. Curious islanders soon gathered on the beach. Believing he was in the Asian islands known as the Indies, Columbus called these people Indians. The next day he wrote in his journal, "I intend to go see if I can find the island of Japan."

Columbus then sailed southwest to a large island. At first he thought it was Japan. Actually, Columbus was on the island of Cuba. His guides next pointed Columbus west to the island of Hispaniola. Columbus set sail to return to Spain in January 1493.

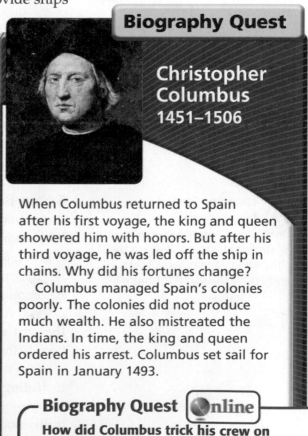

Biography Quest

Christopher Columbus
1451–1506

When Columbus returned to Spain after his first voyage, the king and queen showered him with honors. But after his third voyage, he was led off the ship in chains. Why did his fortunes change?

Columbus managed Spain's colonies poorly. The colonies did not produce much wealth. He also mistreated the Indians. In time, the king and queen ordered his arrest. Columbus set sail for Spain in January 1493.

Biography Quest **Online**

How did Columbus trick his crew on his first voyage?

For: The answer to the question about Columbus
Visit: PHSchool.com
Web Code: myd-1012

EARLY VOYAGES *of* EXPLORATION 1492-1609

During the 1400s and 1500s, a number of daring explorers started the exploration to find a sea route to Asia. **Critical Thinking:** *Draw Conclusions How did technology contribute to the age of exploration?*

The Mariner's Astrolabe
Sailors used mariner's astrolabes to determine latitude, longitude, and time of day. ▼

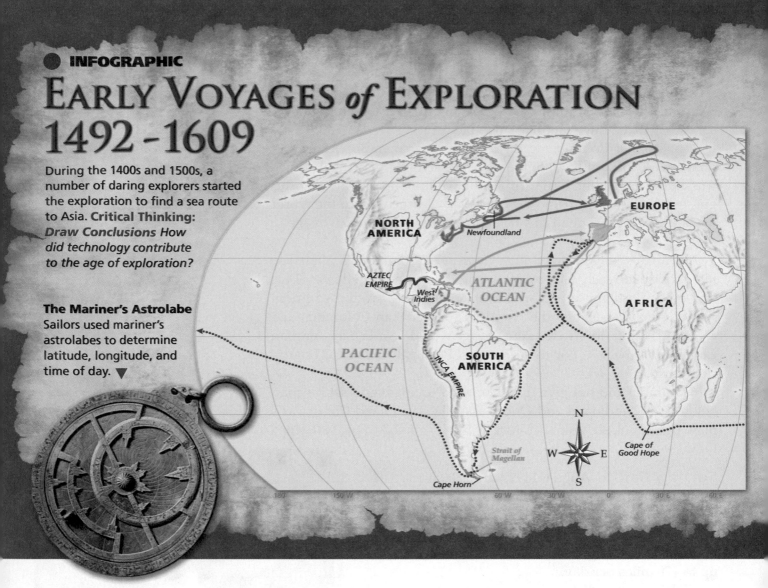

EUROPE

NORTH AMERICA

Newfoundland

AZTEC EMPIRE

West Indies

ATLANTIC OCEAN

AFRICA

PACIFIC OCEAN

SOUTH AMERICA

INCA EMPIRE

N
W — E
S

Cape of Good Hope

Strait of Magellan

Cape Horn

180 150 W 60 W 30 W 0 30 E 60 E

Identify Stated Main Ideas

What important idea from the first paragraph following the subheading "Spain Backs More Voyages" is discussed throughout the passage?

Spain Backs More Voyages In Spain, Columbus reported that there were huge amounts of gold in the land he referred to as the West Indies. The grateful monarchs made him governor of all he had claimed for Spain.

In September 1493, he sailed again for the West Indies. This time he commanded 17 ships filled with 1,500 soldiers, settlers, and priests. The Spanish planned to colonize and rule the land they thought was the West Indies. They also intended to convert the people there to Christianity.

On this second voyage, Columbus discovered other islands, including Puerto Rico. He found that the men he had left behind on Hispaniola had been killed by Indians. Not discouraged, Columbus built another settlement nearby and enslaved the local Indians to dig for gold. Within a few months, 12 of his ships returned to Spain, with gold, trinkets, and a number of captives.

On his third expedition in 1498, Columbus reached the northern coast of South America and decided it was the Asian mainland. Spain permitted him to try to prove his claims in a fourth voyage, in 1502.

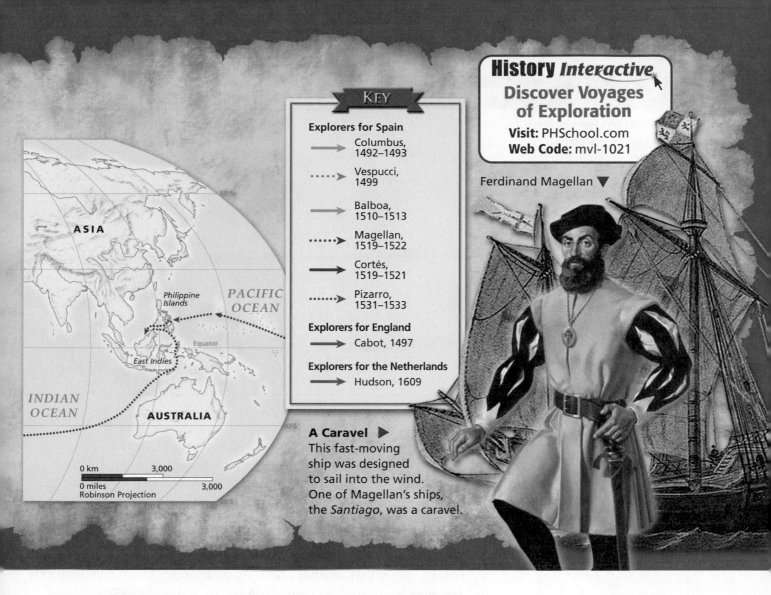

History *Interactive*
Discover Voyages of Exploration
Visit: PHSchool.com
Web Code: mvl-1021

Ferdinand Magellan ▼

KEY

Explorers for Spain

Columbus, 1492–1493

Vespucci, 1499

Balboa, 1510–1513

Magellan, 1519–1522

Cortés, 1519–1521

Pizarro, 1531–1533

Explorers for England

Cabot, 1497

Explorers for the Netherlands

Hudson, 1609

ASIA

PACIFIC OCEAN

Philippine Islands

Equator

East Indies

INDIAN OCEAN

AUSTRALIA

0 km 3,000
0 miles 3,000
Robinson Projection

A Caravel ▶
This fast-moving ship was designed to sail into the wind. One of Magellan's ships, the *Santiago*, was a caravel.

He returned to Spain two years later with his beliefs unchanged. Columbus died in 1506, still convinced that he had reached Asia.

☑ **Checkpoint** **Why were Spain's monarchs interested in the proposal Columbus made to them?**

The Continuing Search for Asia

Many explorers followed the route charted by Columbus. Another Italian explorer, Amerigo Vespucci, made two trips to the new lands. His trips convinced Vespucci that the lands he saw were not part of Asia. Upon his return to Europe, he wrote a letter describing a "new world . . . more densely peopled and full of animals than our Europe or Asia or Africa." A German mapmaker labeled the region "the land of Amerigo" on his maps. The name was soon shortened to "America."

Meanwhile, the Spanish continued to explore and colonize. In 1510, Vasco Núñez de Balboa, a Spanish colonist, explored the Caribbean coast of what is now Panama. Hacking his way across the jungle, he became the first European to set eyes on the Pacific Ocean.

The Columbian Exchange

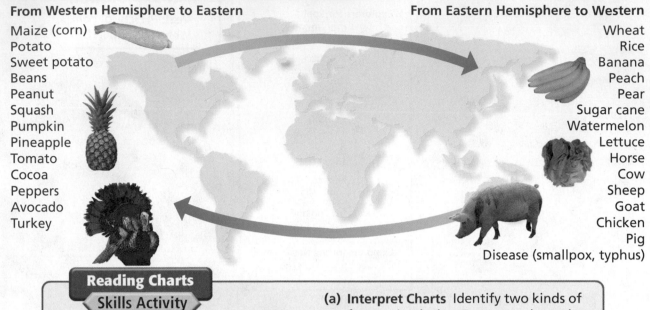

From Western Hemisphere to Eastern
- Maize (corn)
- Potato
- Sweet potato
- Beans
- Peanut
- Squash
- Pumpkin
- Pineapple
- Tomato
- Cocoa
- Peppers
- Avocado
- Turkey

From Eastern Hemisphere to Western
- Wheat
- Rice
- Banana
- Peach
- Pear
- Sugar cane
- Watermelon
- Lettuce
- Horse
- Cow
- Sheep
- Goat
- Chicken
- Pig
- Disease (smallpox, typhus)

Reading Charts
Skills Activity

The Columbian Exchange brought many European, Asian, and African goods to the Americas. At the same time, American crops and livestock were distributed to the rest of the world.

(a) Interpret Charts Identify two kinds of farm animals that Europeans brought to the Americas.

(b) Identify Benefits Who do you think benefited most from the Columbian Exchange? Explain.

The discovery that another ocean lay west of the Americas did not end the search for a water route to Asia. In September 1519, Portuguese explorer **Ferdinand Magellan** set out to find an Atlantic-Pacific passage.

For more than a year, the small fleet slowly moved down the South American coast looking for a **strait,** a narrow passage that connects two large bodies of water. As it pushed farther south than earlier expeditions, it encountered penguins and other animals that no European had ever seen before. Finally, near the southern tip of present-day Argentina, Magellan found a narrow passage. After 38 days of battling winds, tides, and currents, his ships exited what today is called the Strait of Magellan. They now entered the large ocean Balboa had seen nine or ten years earlier. Although Magellan did not realize it, Asia was still thousands of miles away.

Magellan finally reached the Philippine Islands. There, he and several others were killed in a battle with Filipinos. The survivors fled in two of the ships. One ship finally reached Spain, in September 1522. Three years after they had begun, the 18 men aboard became first to **circumnavigate,** or travel around, the entire Earth.

☑**Checkpoint** **What were the contributions of Balboa and Magellan as explorers?**

The Columbian Exchange

These early Spanish voyages set the stage for a great exchange between the Western and the Eastern hemispheres. The next century began what is now known as the Columbian Exchange, a transfer of people, products, and ideas between the hemispheres.

Many of the changes brought about by the Columbian Exchange were positive. Europeans introduced cows, hogs, and other domestic animals to the Western Hemisphere. Many food plants, such as wheat and oats, also arrived on the ships that brought the Europeans.

The exchange also had <u>negative</u> effects on the Americas. Europeans brought germs to which Native Americans had no immunity, or natural resistance. Smallpox, chickenpox, measles, and other contagious diseases killed Native Americans by the thousands.

The impact of the Americas on Europe was no less important. Europeans in the Americas found plants and animals they had never seen before either. For example, the Americas introduced llamas, turkeys, squirrels, and muskrats to the rest of the world. More important, however, were the crops that Native Americans taught the Europeans to cultivate. Today, plants that once were found only in the Americas account for nearly one third of the world's food supply.

✔Checkpoint What impact did the Columbian Exchange have on Europe?

☆ **Looking Back and Ahead** The voyages of Columbus marked the beginning of a new historical era. The foothold he established in the Caribbean would expand into a vast empire. By 1600, Spain would control much of North and South America and would be one of the world's richest nations.

Vocabulary Builder
<u>negative</u> (NEHG ah tihv) **adj.**
opposite to something regarded as positive

Progress Monitoring ⬤nline
For: Self-test with instant help
Visit: PHSchool.com
Web Code: mva-1021

Section 1 | Check Your Progress

Comprehension and Critical Thinking

1. (a) Recall Who were the Vikings?
(b) Apply Information What problems might there be with using Viking myths as historical sources?

2. (a) Recall What is the Columbian Exchange?
(b) Support a Point of View Did the Columbian Exchange bring more changes to the Americas or to Europe? Explain your view.

⟳ Reading Skill

3. Identify Stated Main Ideas Read the text under the heading "The Columbian Exchange." Identify the stated main idea and explain how the paragraphs support that idea.

Key Terms

Fill in the blanks with the correct key terms.
4. Magellan's ships sailed through a _____ in order to reach the Pacific Ocean.
5. The few survivors of Magellan's crew were the first to _____ Earth.

Writing

6. Create a timeline showing early explorations in the Americas. Choose three entries that you think are most significant. For each choice, write one or two sentences explaining why you made that choice.

Danger at Sea

When Europeans began to make voyages of discovery, they had no idea what they would find. Some of the dangers that they feared did not really exist. Other dangers were all too real. But the more they traveled, the more their views of the world changed.

◄ **Fearsome Sea Monsters**

Popular tales warned that the oceans were filled with dragons, sea serpents, and other monsters. Happily, these dangers turned out to be imaginary.

▲ **Storms at Sea**

One real danger was bad weather. A violent storm could send a ship and its whole crew to the bottom of the ocean.

▼ Getting Lost

Another real fear was that a ship might get lost in the vast, endless ocean. Fortunately, improved navigational tools, like the sextant and more accurate maps, made this danger less likely.

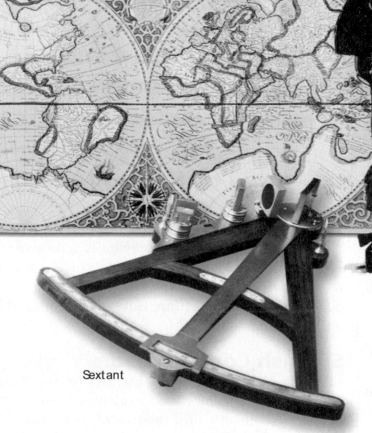

Sextant

▼ Starvation

Running low on supplies at sea meant disaster. One Spanish sailor described what happened when his ship ran out of food.

"We . . . ate only old biscuit reduced to powder, full of grubs and stinking from the dirt which rats had made on it. We drank water that was yellow and stinking."

—Antonio Pigafetta, *Journal*

Piracy ▲

When ships began to carry treasure to Europe, a new danger emerged: piracy. Pirates would attack merchant ships, steal the cargo, and often, murder the crew. Some pirates, such as Captain Kidd (shown above), became legendary for their boldness.

Analyze LIFE AT THE TIME

Imagine you are a European sailor about to go on an ocean voyage. Write a letter explaining your view of the world and why you are going on the voyage in spite of the dangers.

The Indians Fear Us

❝ The Indians of the coast, because of some fears of us, have abandoned all the country, so that for thirty leagues not a man of them has halted. ❞

—Hernando de Soto, Spanish explorer and conqueror, report on expedition to Florida, 1539

◀ Hernando de Soto

Spain's Empire in the Americas

Objectives
- Describe how the Spanish were able to defeat the empires of the Aztecs and Incas.
- Identify Spanish explorations in areas that later became part of the United States.
- Explain how society was organized in Spain's empire in the Americas.

🔄 Reading Skill

Identify Supporting Details Text includes details to support a main idea. These details might be examples, reasons, facts, or descriptions. They enable readers to understand a main idea by helping them to picture it, to make sense of its argument or to believe its accuracy. As you read Section 2, look for details that support the main ideas.

Key Terms and People

conquistador
Hernando Cortés
Moctezuma
plantation
encomienda

Bartolomé de Las
 Casas
mission
peninsular

Why It Matters Even though Columbus never realized that he had reached a region previously unknown to Europeans, his voyages gave Spain a head start on its European rivals in colonizing the Americas.

❓ Section Focus Question: How did Spain establish an empire in the Americas?

Spanish Conquistadors

By the early 1500s, the Spanish had a firm foothold in the Americas. From Spain's island colonies in the Caribbean, soldier-adventurers called **conquistadors** set out to explore and conquer a world unknown to them. They hoped for riches and glory for themselves and for Spain.

Cortés and Pizarro In 1519, conquistador Hernando Cortés sailed from Cuba to Mexico with more than 500 soldiers. The first Native Americans he met presented him with gifts of gold.

On November 8, 1519, Cortés marched into the Aztec capital city of Tenochtitlán. As the Spaniards moved closer to Tenochtitlán, many Native Americans joined them. Conquered by the Aztecs, they hated the Aztec's brutal rule.

The Aztec leader Moctezuma (mokt uh ZOO muh) (also spelled *Montezuma*) met with Cortés and tried to get him to leave by offering him gold. The gold had the opposite effect. Cortés took Moctezuma hostage and claimed all of Mexico for Spain. However, the Aztecs soon rebelled and forced the Spaniards to flee.

About a year later, Cortés returned with a larger force, recaptured Tenochtitlán, and then destroyed it. In its place he built Mexico City, the capital of the Spanish colony of New Spain.

Cortés used the same methods to subdue the Aztecs in Mexico that another conquistador, Francisco Pizarro, used in South America. Pizarro landed on the coast of Peru in 1531 to search for the Incas, who were said to have much gold. In September 1532, he led about 170 soldiers through the jungle into the heart of the Inca Empire. Pizarro then took the Inca ruler Atahualpa (ah tuh WAHL puh) prisoner. Although the Inca people paid a huge ransom to free their ruler, Pizarro executed him anyway. By November 1533, the Spanish had defeated the leaderless Incas and captured their capital city of Cuzco.

Why the Spanish Were Victorious How could a few hundred Spanish soldiers defeat Native American armies many times their size? Several <u>factors</u> explain the Spaniards' success. First among these was technology. The Indians' weapons simply were no match for the armor, muskets, and cannons of the Europeans. In addition, many of the Spaniards rode horses, which the Native Americans had never before seen. Finally, the Native Americans were divided among themselves. In Peru, a civil war had just ended. In Mexico, many Native Americans hated the Aztecs.

Vocabulary Builder
<u>factor</u> (FAK tor) **n.** important element of something

☑Checkpoint   **Why were a few Spanish conquistadors able to defeat the larger armies of the Aztecs and Incas?**

Spanish Conquistadors
The Spanish soldiers were outnumbered by the Aztecs and the Incas, yet they were able to easily defeat these empires. *Critical Thinking: Explain Problems Some Native Americans sided with the Spanish against the Aztecs and the Incas. What problems might this have caused between the groups after the battle?*

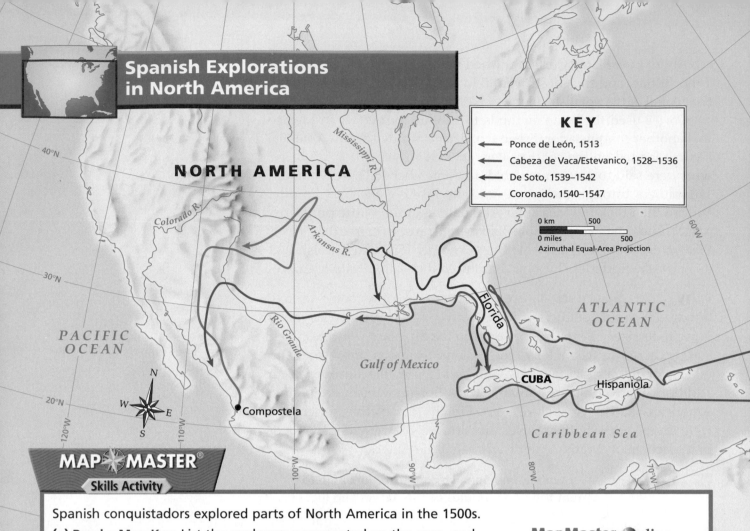

Spanish Explorations in North America

KEY

← Ponce de León, 1513
← Cabeza de Vaca/Estevanico, 1528–1536
← De Soto, 1539–1542
← Coronado, 1540–1547

NORTH AMERICA

Mississippi R.

Colorado R.

Arkansas R.

Río Grande

PACIFIC OCEAN

Gulf of Mexico

Florida

ATLANTIC OCEAN

CUBA

Hispaniola

Caribbean Sea

Compostela

0 km 500
0 miles 500
Azimuthal Equal-Area Projection

MAP MASTER
Skills Activity

Spanish conquistadors explored parts of North America in the 1500s.

(a) Read a Map Key List the explorers represented on the map, and briefly describe the area each one explored.

(b) Link Past and Present Based on this map, in what areas of the present-day United States would you expect to find Latino influence strongest?

MapMaster Online

For: Interactive map
Visit: PHSchool.com
Web Code: mvp-1022

Spanish Explorers in North America

The Spanish did not limit themselves to the exploration of what we now call Latin America. In 1513, Juan Ponce de León sailed north from Puerto Rico to investigate reports of a large island. He found beautiful flowers there, so he named the place *La Florida*. Ponce de León became the first Spaniard to set foot in what is now the United States.

Exploration along Florida's west coast began in 1528, when about 400 Spaniards landed near the present-day city of St. Petersburg. Finding none of the gold they had hoped for, they marched into northern Florida. There, under attack by Native Americans, they built five crude boats and set out to sea. About 80 survivors led by Álvar Núñez Cabeza de Vaca eventually landed at present-day Galveston Island on the Texas coast.

Starvation and disease reduced their number to 15 before Indians enslaved them. Finally, only four—including Cabeza de Vaca and Estevanico, an African slave—remained alive. After six years in captivity, they escaped and spent two more years finding their way to Mexico City. In 1536, eight years after landing in Florida, the four survivors of the 400-man expedition returned to Spanish lands.

In Mexico City, the men related stories they had heard from Native Americans about seven great cities filled with gold far to the north. Officials asked the survivors to head an expedition to find these cities. However, only Estevanico was willing to go. In 1539, he led a group into what is now western New Mexico. When Estevanico was killed by Indians, the others returned to Mexico City.

The conquistador Francisco Coronado (koh roh NAH doh) set out with about 1,100 Spaniards and Native Americans to find the golden city. Although he never found the city, he did explore much of what is now New Mexico, Arizona, Texas, and Kansas.

While Coronado was trekking through the southwest, Hernando de Soto was searching for riches in today's southeastern United States. De Soto traveled as far north as the Carolinas and as far west as Oklahoma. He died in what is now Louisiana, in 1542, having found the Mississippi River but no cities of gold.

Native Americans received harsh treatment from Spaniards.

☑Checkpoint **What regions in the present-day United States did Spaniards explore?**

Colonizing Spanish America

At first, Spain let the conquistadors govern the lands they had conquered. However, this was not successful. In order to control its new empire, Spain created a formal system of government to rule its colonies.

Harsh Life for Native Americans Within Spain's vast empire, there was little place for Native Americans except as a source of labor. Government officials granted settlers huge tracts of land to start mines, ranches, and plantations—large farms worked by laborers who live on the property. To help Spanish colonists find needed workers, the Spanish government granted *encomiendas* (ehn KOH mee ehn dahz). These were land grants that included the right to demand labor or taxes from Native Americans. The Spanish forced Native Americans to work in the gold and silver mines. Many died when the tunnels caved in. Some Spaniards protested this cruel treatment. The priest Bartolomé de Las Casas traveled through New Spain working for reform. Largely due to Las Casas's efforts, the government of Spain ordered reform of the *encomienda* system in the mid-1500s.

Like other Europeans in the Americas, the Spanish believed they had a duty to convert Native Americans to Christianity. They set up missions, religious settlements, run by Catholic priests and friars. San Francisco, San Diego, San Antonio, and a number of other U.S. cities got their start as Spanish missions in the 1700s.

The Trade in Humans As the death toll for Native Americans continued to rise, Spanish colonists looked across the Atlantic Ocean for a new source of labor.

In 1517, Spain brought about 4,000 Africans to the Caribbean islands and forced them to work there. By the middle of the 1500s, the Spaniards were shipping about 2,000 enslaved Africans each year to Hispaniola alone. You will read about the growing slave trade in another chapter.

Society in the Spanish Colonies A rigid social system based on birthplace and ethnic group developed in the Spanish colonies. At the top of the social structure were the *peninsulares,* Spanish colonists who had been born in Spain. Almost all government officials came from this class. Colonists born in America of two Spanish parents were called *Creoles.* Generally, Creoles also held important positions. Many of the wealthiest merchants and plantation owners were Creoles.

People of mixed parentage were lower on the social ladder. *Mestizos,* people of Spanish and Indian heritage, could achieve economic success as ranchers, farmers, or merchants. But entrance into the upper levels of society was impossible for them. Below mestizos were *mulattos*—people of Spanish and African heritage. Native Americans and African Americans were held at the bottom of society. This rigid class system helped Spain keep control of its empire in the Americas for more than 300 years.

☑**Checkpoint** **How were Native Americans treated under the** *encomienda* **system?**

☆ **Looking Back and Ahead** The resentment and tensions caused by the rigid class system eventually provided the seeds for revolutions in the early 1800s that ended Spain's American empire.

Vocabulary Builder
rigid (RIH jihd) *adj.* not bending; not flexible

Identifying Supporting Details
Identify two details in these two paragraphs that support the following main idea: *Spain created a formal system of government in America to rule the vast regions it claimed.* Explain how the details support the main idea.

Section 2 | **Check Your Progress**

Progress Monitoring 🌐**nline**
For: Self-test with instant help
Visit: PHSchool.com
Web Code: mva-1022

Comprehension and Critical Thinking

1. **(a) Identify** What parts of the North American continent did Spanish conquistadors explore?
(b) Apply Information How did the conquistadors help establish the Spanish Empire in the Americas?

2. **(a) Identify** What was the lasting accomplishment of Bartolomé de Las Casas?
(b) Summarize How would you describe the lives of Native Americans in New Spain?

Reading Skill

3. **Identify Supporting Details** Read the text following the subheading "Society in the Spanish Colonies." Identify three details that support its main idea: A rigid social system, based on birthplace and ethnic group, developed in Spain's colonies over time. Explain how the details support the main idea.

Key Terms

4. Write two definitions for each of the following key terms: conquistador, plantation, mission, peninsular. First, write a formal definition for your teacher. Second, write a casual definition in everyday English for a classmate.

Writing

5. **(a)** Prepare an outline you would use to write an essay describing the effects of Spanish colonization in the Americas.
(b) Then, write several sentences describing the views of Bartolomé de Las Casas and a conquistador about Spanish rule in the Americas.

◄ English warships engage the invading Spanish Armada.

Europeans Compete in North America

Objectives

- Describe the religious and economic conflicts in Europe during the Reformation.
- Explain why European powers continued to search for a new route to Asia.
- Describe the outcome of the search by explorers John Cabot and Henry Hudson for a northwest passage around the Americas.

🔄 Reading Skill

Identify Implied Main Ideas Sometimes a portion of text does not state the main idea directly. However, the text still has a main idea. This idea is implied, or suggested, by the many details contained in the text. You can identify this idea by reading all the details and developing an idea that fits all of them. State the idea to yourself in a sentence, then reread the text and confirm that the details do support it.

Key Terms and People

mercantilism   northwest passage
John Cabot   Henry Hudson

Why It Matters Spain's empire in the Americas increased Spain's wealth and power. As a result, the rulers of other European countries grew jealous. The Protestant Reformation was another source of tension. After the Roman Catholic Church rejected Martin Luther's demands for reform, Luther and other protesters formed new Protestant churches. The Protestant Reformation plunged Europe into a long series of wars between Catholic and Protestant forces.

❓ **Section Focus Question: How did conflicts in Europe spur exploration in North America?**

Conflicts in Europe

As the appeal of the Reformation increased, the split between the Catholics and the Protestants increased religious and economic tensions between countries in Europe.

Religious Conflicts By 1530, the rulers of Sweden, Denmark, and several European states had split with the Roman Catholic Church and set up Protestant churches in their countries. Elsewhere in Europe, the teachings and writings of Swiss thinker John Calvin had a great influence on the development of Protestant churches in France, Switzerland, Scotland, and the Netherlands.

English Protestants found a supporter in King Henry VIII. Henry was married to Catherine of Aragon, the daughter of King Ferdinand and Queen Isabella of Spain. When Catherine did not produce a male heir to the English throne, Henry sought to divorce her and remarry.

Mercantilism

European leaders of the time believed that the purpose of colonies was to benefit the home country. This belief was part of an economic theory known as mercantilism. According to this theory, a nation became strong by building up its gold and silver supply. One way to do this was to take gold and silver from colonies and send it to the royal treasury. **Critical Thinking: *Identify Economic Benefits and Costs* What risks did the home country take in relying on colonies to support its economy?**

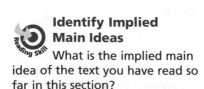

Raw Materials

Colonies
Can trade only with the home country

Such as:
• Gold
• Cotton
• Timber

Home Country
Trades to acquire wealth

Manufactured Goods

Such as:
• Clothing
• Furniture

Because Catholic law does not permit divorce, Henry asked the pope to annul, or cancel, his marriage. This had occurred before. Popes had annulled royal marriages. The pope's refusal to grant the annulment caused Henry to break with the Roman Catholic Church in 1533. He set up a Protestant church and named it the Church of England.

Economic Conflicts Religious tensions created by the Reformation inflamed rivalries that already existed among the nations of Europe. Wars were common and alliances often shifted. This uncertainty made European rulers believe they could not depend on one another to protect their country's security.

For example, Spain was unwilling to depend on Italian or Portuguese traders. As a result, the Spanish monarchs eagerly supported Columbus's search for a new route to Asia. The Spanish thought that if they could start colonies there, goods from those colonies would make Spain wealthy and powerful. Most importantly, the Spanish hoped Asian colonies would provide gold. Nearly every European nation sought gold to pay for its wars and help strengthen its armies. In fact, Spain required one fifth of all gold that Spaniards found to be sent to the king. This requirement was part of a system widely followed at the time, called mercantilism (MER kuhn tihl ihz uhm). The system of mercantilism held that colonies existed to make the home country wealthy and powerful.

The Spanish Armada England's King Henry VIII died in 1547. He was succeeded by his son Edward, who ruled only a short time before he died, too. The throne then passed to Mary I, who made plans to <u>restore</u> the Roman Catholic Church in England. However, Mary died in 1558 and Elizabeth I, a Protestant, took the throne.

Identify Implied Main Ideas

Reading Skill

What is the implied main idea of the text you have read so far in this section?

Vocabulary Builder

<u>restore</u> (ree STOR) *v.* to give back something taken away

---

The rule of the Protestant Queen Elizabeth I renewed the rivalry with Roman Catholic Spain. Spain's King Phillip II hoped to make England a Catholic nation again. Relations were also strained by English raids on Spanish ships at sea. Many of these ships carried gold from the Americas. The Spanish also resented English assistance to rebels trying to win independence in the Spanish <u>province</u> of Holland.

Vocabulary Builder
<u>province</u> (PRAHV ahns)
n. territorial district of a country

In 1588, Phillip assembled a fleet of 130 warships known as the Spanish Armada. Phillip hoped to force Elizabeth from the throne. A fleet of English ships met the Spanish off the coast of France. The smaller and faster English ships sank many of the Spanish ships. Barely half of the Spanish Armada returned to Spain.

The defeat of the Spanish Armada changed the balance of power in Europe. Spain was weakened and so was its control of the seas. This enabled countries like England and France to found colonies in the Americas. Europe's religious and economic conflicts were not settled by the defeat of the Armada, however. As England and France founded colonies, these conflicts spread to the Americas.

✓**Checkpoint** **How did economic concerns among European nations lead to conflicts?**

Asia Continues to Beckon

Columbus's return from his first voyage interested another Italian explorer, John Cabot. Cabot decided that a more northern route to Asia would be shorter and easier.

The Northern Voyages Neither Spain nor Portugal had any interest in Cabot's ideas. However, the English were interested enough to finance a voyage of exploration. Cabot left England with one ship, in May 1497. He crossed the North Atlantic and explored the region around Newfoundland. On a second voyage in 1498, Cabot may have explored the North American coast as far south as Chesapeake Bay. However, we cannot be sure. His ships disappeared without a trace.

Europeans soon realized that the lands Cabot had reached were not Asia, but a land they had never seen. England, France, and Holland all financed voyages of exploration to North America. These voyages focused on finding a **northwest passage,** a sea route from the Atlantic to the Pacific that passed through or around North America.

In 1524, another Italian explorer, Giovanni da Verrazano (vehr rah TSAH noh), searched for such a passage for King Francis I of France. Verrazano explored the Atlantic coastal region from North Carolina to Newfoundland. In doing so, he discovered the mouth of the Hudson River and New York Bay. French explorer Jacques Cartier (kar tee YAY) made three trips to North America for France. In searching for a northwest passage, he discovered the St. Lawrence River and explored it as far as present-day Montreal.

Queen Elizabeth I

With his son and a few loyal crew members, Henry Hudson was set adrift, by mutineers, in Hudson Bay. They died a lonely death somewhere on the bay.

English explorer Henry Hudson made four voyages in search of a northwest passage. Two voyages in the Arctic Ocean, during 1607 and 1608, were unsuccessful, and Hudson's English backers gave up on him. However, the Dutch grew interested in his activities and financed a third expedition in 1609. Crossing the Atlantic, Hudson reached what is now New York and explored up the river that today bears his name.

Hudson's discoveries on his third voyage convinced the English to sponsor a fourth voyage in 1610. Hudson again sailed into the Arctic, looking for a passage to the Pacific. He reached as far as Hudson Bay, which also is named for him, before the icy waters forced a halt to the voyage. In the spring of 1611, Hudson's crew, unhappy about spending the winter in this harsh land, grew desperate. They mutinied and set the explorer, his teenage son, and seven loyal crew members adrift in a small boat. The mutineers returned to England. Like John Cabot, Hudson was never heard from again.

✔**Checkpoint** **Why did explorers continue to look for routes to Asia?**

⭐ **Looking Back and Ahead** Hudson's last voyage marked the end of serious efforts to find a northwest passage. Europe's attention shifted to the lands that the voyagers had explored. In these lands, explorers reported, were vast amounts of timber, fish, and other resources. Europeans began to think of North America not as an obstacle blocking their way to Asia but as a land to be exploited for profit.

Section 3 | **Check Your Progress**

Progress Monitoring ⬤nline
For: Self-test with instant help
Visit: PHSchool.com
Web Code: mva-1023

Comprehension and Critical Thinking

1. **(a) Recall** How did the Reformation lead to religious conflict in Europe?
   (b) Apply Information Why do you think the religious tensions that developed during the Reformation among European nations spread to the Americas?

2. **(a) Summarize** How did the defeat of the Spanish Armada change the political balance of power among European countries?

(b) Analyze Cause and Effect How did the shift in the political balance of power affect the exploration of North America?

↻ **Reading Skill**

3. **Identify Implied Main Ideas** Find the implied main idea of the text under the heading "Asia Continues to Beckon." Then, combine this main idea with the main idea you identified under the heading "Conflicts in Europe" to state a single main idea for both of these portions of text.

Key Terms

Complete each of the following sentences so that the second part further explains the first part and clearly shows your understanding of the key term.

4. Spain's economy was based on the system of mercantilism, under which _____.

5. European explorers searched for a northwest passage, _____.

Writing

6. Why do you think Spain and Portugal refused to support John Cabot's proposed voyage? Write a paragraph explaining your views.

Settlement of New France

"Acting upon the information which has been given us by those who have returned from New France, respecting the good quality and fertility of the lands of that country, and the disposition of the people to accept the knowledge of God, We have resolved to continue the settlement previously undertaken there. . . .**"**

—Proclamation by the King of France to continue settling New France, 1608

◀ Settlement of Quebec in New France, 1608

France and the Netherlands in North America

Objectives

- Describe how the French colony of New France spread into the interior of North America.
- Explain how the Dutch established a thriving colony along the Hudson River.
- Explain the influence of these settlements on the Native Americans of the region.

Reading Skill

Combine Main Ideas to Construct Meaning Several main ideas are developed in each section in this textbook. Use the red heads to identify the bigger main ideas. The blue heads introduce text that further develops the main ideas. As you read Section 4, identify the main ideas and the ways in which the information helps you to understand these ideas.

Key Terms and People

Samuel de Champlain
coureur de bois

Jacques Marquette
alliance

Why It Matters European countries competed for the best trade routes and for control of lands in North America. In the early 1600s, England, France, and the Netherlands sent explorers to North America and staked claims to land there.

❓ Section Focus Question: What impact did the establishment of French and Dutch colonies in North America have on Native Americans?

New France

The French began to settle colonies in the early 1600s. In 1603, **Samuel de Champlain** made the first of 11 voyages to explore and map the lands along the St. Lawrence River. In 1608, Champlain established a settlement on the banks of the St. Lawrence, which he named Quebec. From this base he ventured east, in 1609, and explored the large lake on the border of present-day Vermont and New York that bears his name. His activities gave the French an influence in the region that lasted 150 years.

Life in New France New France, as the French colony was called, developed in quite different ways than New Spain. As you know, the Spanish sought gold, silver, and other precious minerals. The French, on the other hand, profited from fish and furs. The Spanish forced Native Americans into harsh labor. The French traded with Native Americans for the animal skins so highly valued in Europe. Beaver skins sent to Europe and made into hats were a profitable item.

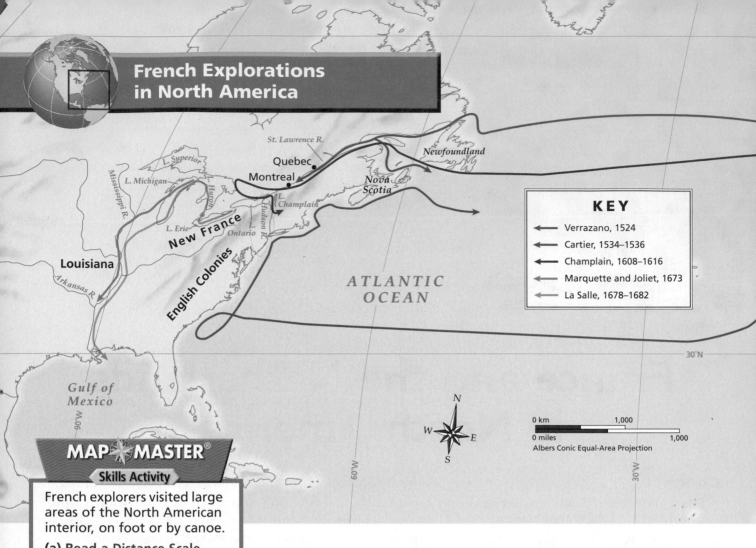

French Explorations in North America

KEY

← Verrazano, 1524
← Cartier, 1534–1536
← Champlain, 1608–1616
← Marquette and Joliet, 1673
← La Salle, 1678–1682

St. Lawrence R.
Newfoundland
Quebec
Montreal
Nova Scotia
L. Superior
L. Michigan
L. Huron
Mississippi R.
L. Erie
L. Ontario
L. Champlain
Hudson R.
New France
Louisiana
Arkansas R.
English Colonies

ATLANTIC OCEAN

Gulf of Mexico

90°W
60°W
30°W
30°N

N
W   E
S

0 km   1,000
0 miles   1,000
Albers Conic Equal-Area Projection

MAP★MASTER®

Skills Activity

French explorers visited large areas of the North American interior, on foot or by canoe.

(a) Read a Distance Scale Find the route taken by La Salle. About how many miles did he travel from Montreal to the mouth of the Mississippi River?

(b) Make Predictions What kinds of rivalries do you think the French explorations started?

MapMaster Online

For: Interactive map
Visit: PHSchool.com
Web Code: mvp-1024

Vocabulary Builder
decline (dee KLĪN) **v.** to lessen in force, health, strength, or value

This pattern was set during Champlain's first days in the Americas. He established the colony's first settlement—a trading post—in what is today Nova Scotia, in 1604. As he continued to explore the region, he convinced local Indians to bring pelts to the trading posts established by the French. Trading posts such as Quebec City and Montreal became busy centers of commerce.

Brave employees of the fur companies paddled large canoes into the wilderness to find and acquire pelts from Native Americans. *Coureurs de bois*, the French term for "runners of the woods," were independent traders who lived among the Indians. Many of them married Indian women and started families.

Not until the late 1600s did French colonists begin to farm in large numbers. One reason for this change was that the market for furs in Europe was in decline. Another reason was the disruption that Indian wars brought to the fur trade. Still another was the 3,000 French settlers—including many single young women—that King Louis XIV sent to New France in the 1660s. After the new settlers arrived, the population began to expand. New France had about 5,000 colonists by 1672.

Exploring the Mississippi The same economic and religious motives that established New France also inspired its expansion. By 1670, French missionary Jacques Marquette had founded two missions along the Great Lakes, in present-day Michigan. Meanwhile, French traders explored the Great Lakes area looking for new sources of furs.

In 1673, Father Marquette and Louis Joliet, a French Canadian trader, paddled their canoes along the shores of Lake Michigan to what is now Green Bay, Wisconsin. They made their way west until they reached the Mississippi River. For the next month they followed the river downstream, thinking that it might be the long-sought northwest passage. In July, the group reached the Mississippi's junction with the Arkansas River. Convinced that the Mississippi flowed into the Gulf of Mexico and not into the Pacific Ocean, they returned home.

Although Marquette and Joliet did not find a northwest passage, they provided the French with a water route into the heart of North America. The river's exploration was completed in 1682 by René Robert Cavelier, also known as La Salle. Reaching the river's mouth at the Gulf of Mexico, La Salle claimed the entire Mississippi Valley for France. He named the region Louisiana, in honor of King Louis XIV.

✓**Checkpoint** **What was the goal of the voyage of Marquette and Joliet on the Mississippi?**

Vocabulary Builder
motive (MOH tihv) *n.* inner drive that causes a person to do something

Combine Main Ideas to Construct Meaning
Identify three main ideas from the paragraphs following the subheading "Life in New France." Then, state the big idea of these paragraphs.

Exploring the Mississippi
This drawing shows Father Marquette and Louis Joliet traveling the unknown waters of the Mississippi River. **Critical Thinking:** *Draw Conclusions* *How would settling the Mississippi Valley benefit New France?*

Links Across Time

Wall Street

Late 1600s Built in 1653, a wall at the lower end of Manhattan protected Dutch settlers from outside attacks. Gradually, the path by the wall became an important place for merchants and traders.

1792 The New York Stock Exchange began in lower Manhattan where a group of New York businessmen met daily to buy and sell stocks. Today, Wall Street is part of the thriving commerce of New York City.

Link to Today Online

Wall Street Today How has the role of Wall Street changed in today's financial market? Go online to find out more about Wall Street today.

For: Wall Street in the news
Visit: PHSchool.com
Web Code: mvc-1024

New Netherland

Dutch land claims in North America were based on Henry Hudson's exploration of the Hudson River. In 1610, Dutch traders arrived in the Hudson River valley and began a busy trade with Native Americans. The trade was so profitable that the Dutch West India Company decided to establish a permanent colony in what the Dutch called New Netherland.

In 1624, about 300 settlers arrived from the Netherlands. Most of them settled at Fort Orange, a fur-trading post that was later renamed Albany. In 1626, another group settled at the mouth of the Hudson River. The colony's governor, Peter Minuit, purchased the island from nearby Indians. The colonists named their new home New Amsterdam. The town grew steadily as new colonists arrived. By 1653, it had a population of about 800.

New Netherland was a barrier to the English. It kept English settlers from moving westward. In 1664, English forces seized New Netherland. The new territory was renamed New York, after the king's brother, the Duke of York.

✓**Checkpoint** Why did the Dutch establish settlements along the Hudson River?

The Impact on Native Americans

As you have read, Native Americans provided fur pelts to French and Dutch traders. The Europeans gave Native Americans manufactured goods, such as cloth, iron pots and tools, and guns. Ultimately, however, the fur trade had a grave effect on Native Americans.

The French and the Dutch each made alliances with Native American peoples. An **alliance** is an agreement between parties that benefits them both. Long before the Hurons became trading partners with the French, the Iroquois and the Hurons were enemies. The Hurons became partners with the French, and the Dutch had an agreement with the Iroquois. The Iroquois, using guns from the Dutch, began to attack the Hurons. The attacks were devastating to the Hurons.

Even worse were the diseases caused by contact with Europeans. Furthermore, the overtrapping of animals weakened the food chain on which Native Americans depended. As the fur-bearing animals disappeared, the Native Americans' value to the colonists decreased. Instead, Native American land became more valuable to the colonists.

✓**Checkpoint** How did the French and Dutch settlements affect Native Americans?

☆ **Looking Back and Ahead** England did not stand by as France and Holland carved out colonies in North America. As English colonies spread over the Atlantic shores of North America, their competition with New France and New Netherland grew.

Dutch traders with Iroquois

Section 4 | **Check Your Progress**

Progress Monitoring ⓞnline
For: Self-test with instant help
Visit: PHSchool.com
Web Code: mva-1024

Comprehension and Critical Thinking

1. (a) Describe How did the colonists in New France support themselves?
(b) Compare and Contrast How did the economic activities of New France compare with those of New Spain?

2. (a) Identify Name two Dutch settlements in the Americas.
(b) Apply Information How did the geographic location of these settlements contribute to their success?

Reading Skill

3. Combine Main Ideas to Construct Meaning What is the big idea of Section 4? What smaller main ideas work together to support this big idea?

Key Terms

Answer the following questions in complete sentences that show your understanding of the key terms.
4. Who were the *coureurs de bois,* and how did they contribute to the economic success of New France?

5. What were the consequences of the Dutch alliance with the Iroquois for the Hurons?

Writing

6. In Section 2, you read about Bartolomé de Las Casas's observations concerning relations between the Spaniards and the Native Americans. Write similar eyewitness accounts of relations between Native Americans and **(a)** the French and **(b)** the Dutch in the Americas.

21st Century Learning   When you study history, you generally read about events in the sequence, or order, in which they happened. One way to understand the sequence of historical events is by creating a timeline. A timeline identifies major events and the dates that each took place. You should read a horizontal timeline from left to right. Reading a timeline helps you judge how events could be related in time.

Exploring the Americas

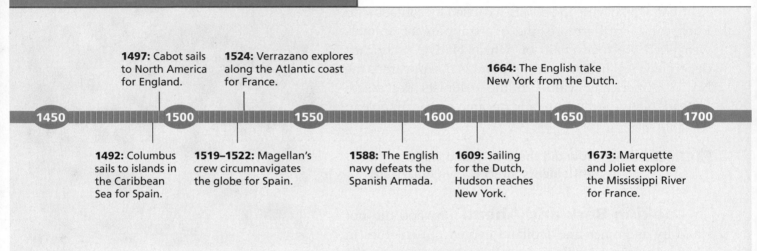

1497: Cabot sails to North America for England.

1524: Verrazano explores along the Atlantic coast for France.

1664: The English take New York from the Dutch.

1450 — 1500 — 1550 — 1600 — 1650 — 1700

1492: Columbus sails to islands in the Caribbean Sea for Spain.

1519–1522: Magellan's crew circumnavigates the globe for Spain.

1588: The English navy defeats the Spanish Armada.

1609: Sailing for the Dutch, Hudson reaches New York.

1673: Marquette and Joliet explore the Mississippi River for France.

Learn the Skill

Use these steps to understand sequence.

1 **Identify the time period covered in the timeline.** Look for the beginning date and the ending date.

2 **Figure out the intervals between each date on the timeline.** Timelines are always divided into time periods of equal length, such as 10, 50, or 100 years.

3 **Add additional events.** Include other important historical events on the timeline, based on your reading of the text.

4 **Draw conclusions.** Use the timeline to draw conclusions about the events that took place during a particular period in history. Framing questions based on the timeline can help you draw sound conclusions.

Practice the Skill

Answer the following questions about the timeline on this page.

1 **Identify the time period covered in the timeline.** (a) What is the date of the first event? (b) What is the date of the last event?

2 **Figure out the intervals between each date on the timeline.** How many years are there between each major date on the timeline?

3 **Add additional events.** What other events might you add to this timeline? Why?

4 **Draw conclusions.** How does the timeline show conflict among European nations during this period?

Apply the Skill

See the Review and Assessment at the end of this chapter.

Quick Study Guide

What were the causes and effects of European exploration of the Americas?

Section 1
The Age of Exploration

- The Vikings set up a colony in Newfoundland.
- Christopher Columbus, seeking a sea route to Asia, reached the West Indies in 1492 instead.
- European explorers continued to explore and colonize the Americas.
- The Columbian Exchange resulted in the transfer of products, people, and ideas between Europe and the Americas.

Section 2
Spain's Empire in the Americas

- Spanish conquistadors conquered Native American civilizations in the Americas.
- As the Spanish Empire grew, Native American workers were harshly treated.
- A strict class system developed in Spain's American colonies.

Section 3
Europeans Compete in North America

- During the Reformation, the authority of the Roman Catholic Church was challenged.
- The defeat of the Spanish Armada undermined Spanish control of the seas.
- European explorers continued to seek a northwest passage to Asia.

Section 4
France and the Netherlands in North America

- Colonists in New France established a fur trade with Native Americans.
- The Dutch established permanent settlements in what is now the northeastern United States.
- The French and Dutch settlements had a negative impact on Native American life.

? Exploring the Essential Question

Use the online study guide to explore the essential question.

Section 1
How did the search for a water route to Asia affect both Europe and the Americas?

Section 2
How did Spain establish an empire in the Americas?

Chapter 2 Essential Question
What were the causes and effects of European exploration of the Americas?

Section 4
What impact did the establishment of French and Dutch colonies in North America have on Native Americans?

Section 3
How did conflicts in Europe spur exploration in North America?

Key Terms

Complete each of the following sentences so that the second part further explains the first part and clearly shows your understanding of the key term.

1. Hernando Cortés and Francisco Pizarro were Spanish conquistadors_____.

2. Because Spain's empire in the Americas needed workers, the government issued *encomiendas*_____.

3. In the 1500s and 1600s, many European nations practiced mercantilism_____.

4. During a time of war, it may help to form an alliance_____.

Comprehension and Critical Thinking

5. **(a) Recall** What discoveries did Balboa and Magellan make on their voyages?
   (b) Apply Information How did the achievements of those explorers change the way in which people viewed their world?

6. **(a) Identify** What were some of the products exchanged between Europe and the Americas as a result of the Columbian Exchange?
   (b) Link Past and Present What kinds of cultural and economic exchanges occur between nations today?

7. **(a) Recall** How did the Spanish government bring order to new Spanish settlements being developed in Spanish colonies?
   (b) Apply Information How does the image below show how religion was used to bring order to the settlements?

8. **(a) List** List three ways that French and Dutch colonists affected the lives of Native Americans.
   (b) Explain Problems Why do you think England felt it was a problem when they learned of the presence of French settlements in the valleys of the Ohio and the Mississippi rivers?

9. **(a) Recall** What role did gold play in the economy of Europe during the 1500s?
   (b) Identify Costs How did mercantilism affect the growth of colonies in the Americas?

History Reading Skill

10. **Identify Main Ideas and Details** Identify the main idea of Section 2. Find details to support the main idea.

Writing

11. **Write two paragraphs:**
    Discuss the causes and effects of European exploration in the Americas.
    Your paragraphs should:
    • begin with a thesis statement that expresses a main idea about the beginning of European exploration in the Americas;
    • support the main idea with facts, examples, and other information about the era;
    • use chronological order as much as possible.

12. **Write a Persuasive Speech:**
    The year is 1510. You are an adventurer eager to continue the attempt to find a route to Asia. Prepare a speech you will give to persuade a monarch that spending money on this voyage is a wise decision.

Skills for Life

Understand Sequence
Use the chapter timeline on pages 34–35 to answer the following questions.

13. What time period is covered in the timeline?

14. Into what time intervals is the timeline divided?

15. **(a)** When did the French establish Quebec?
    (b) How many years later did Marquette and Joliet explore the Mississippi?

16. What additional events might you add to the timeline? Why?

17. What trend does this timeline show? Explain.

Test Yourself

1. **Which of the following people was the first Spaniard to set foot in what is now the United States?**

   A Christopher Columbus

   B Juan Ponce de León

   C Francisco Pizarro

   D Francisco Coronado

2. **How did Europe's attitude toward North America change after Henry Hudson's last voyage?**

   A Efforts to find a northwest passage continued.

   B French and Dutch fur traders set up more trading posts.

   C Efforts began to profit from the lands explored.

   D Most countries no longer gained from the system of mercantilism.

3. **In return for the fur pelts, what goods did the Europeans trade with Native Americans?**

   A tobacco

   B food crops

   C cloth and tools

   D pots and silk

4. **Unlike the Spaniards, French claims in North America were largely for**

   A settling farm communities.

   B economic gains.

   C establishing fur trade posts.

   D establishing lumber trade posts.

Document-Based Questions

Task: Look at Documents 1 and 2, and answer their accompanying questions. Then, use the documents and your knowledge of history to complete the following writing assignment:

> Write a two-paragraph essay describing positive and negative effects of the Columbian Exchange.

Document 1: The Columbian Exchange involved hundreds of items that enriched people's lives. But one item was deadly—European disease. Bernal Díaz del Castillo, who traveled with Hernando Cortés, describes the scene in the Aztec capital of Tenochtitlán in 1521. *What conditions did the Spanish encounter in Tenochtitlán?*

"All the houses and stockades in the lake were full of corpses. . . . It was the same in the streets and courts. . . . We could not walk without treading on the bodies and heads of dead Indians. . . . . Indeed, the stench was so bad that no one could endure it . . . and even Cortés was ill from the odors which assailed his nostrils."

Document 2: The arrival of Columbus set off a tragic chain of events for the people of the Americas. Study the graph to see how the population of central Mexico declined after the European arrival. *What happened to the population between 1500 and 1560?*

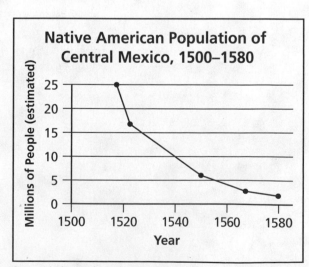

Native American Population of Central Mexico, 1500–1580

Source: Nicolás Sánchez-Albornoz, *The Population of Latin America*

Colonies Take Root

1587–1752

"*Being thus arrived in a good harbor and brought safe to land, they fell upon their knees and blessed the God of Heaven who had brought them over the vast and furious ocean....*"

—*Journal of William Bradford, 1620*

This painting shows thankful Pilgrims arriving in Plymouth, Massachusetts, in 1621.

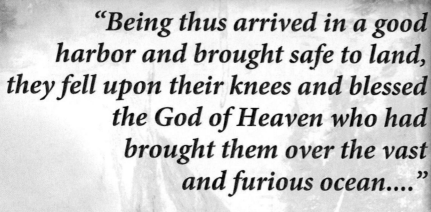

CHAPTER 3

What You Will Learn

Section 1
THE FIRST ENGLISH SETTLEMENTS

After two failed efforts in the 1580s, the English started colonies in North America in the 1600s.

Section 2
THE NEW ENGLAND COLONIES

The religious beliefs of Puritans influenced the New England Colonies.

Section 3
THE MIDDLE COLONIES

The Middle Colonies attracted a wide range of settlers and offered a haven of religious tolerance.

Section 4
THE SOUTHERN COLONIES

The Southern Colonies developed rich coastal plantations based on slavery, whereas backcountry farmers struggled to survive.

Section 5
SPANISH COLONIES ON THE BORDERLANDS

Lands from Florida to California formed the vast Spanish Empire in the Americas.

Reading Skill

Compare and Contrast In this chapter, you will learn to look for similarities and differences between events, people, and issues.

63

Colonies Take Root

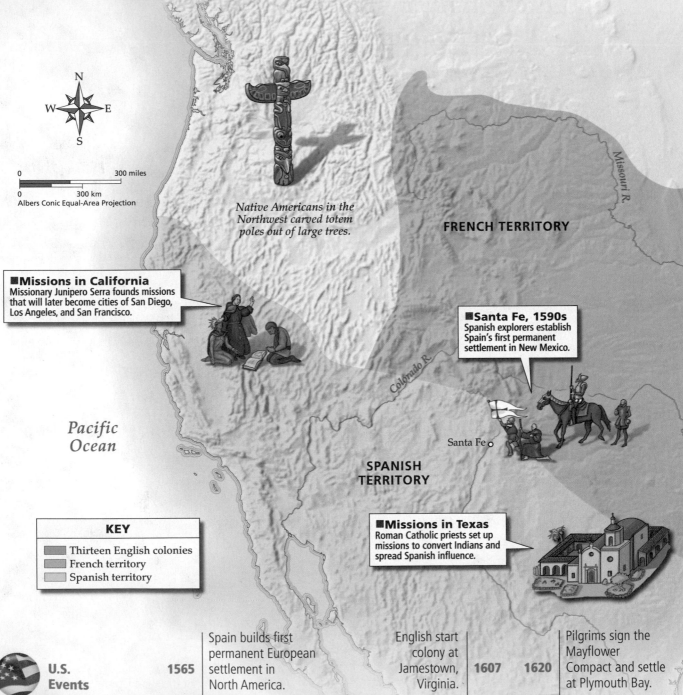

Native Americans in the Northwest carved totem poles out of large trees.

FRENCH TERRITORY

■Missions in California
Missionary Junipero Serra founds missions that will later become cities of San Diego, Los Angeles, and San Francisco.

■Santa Fe, 1590s
Spanish explorers establish Spain's first permanent settlement in New Mexico.

Pacific Ocean

Santa Fe ○

SPANISH TERRITORY

KEY
- Thirteen English colonies
- French territory
- Spanish territory

■Missions in Texas
Roman Catholic priests set up missions to convert Indians and spread Spanish influence.

0 ———— 300 miles
0 ———— 300 km
Albers Conic Equal-Area Projection

Colorado R.

Missouri R.

U.S. Events

1565 Spain builds first permanent European settlement in North America.	English start colony at Jamestown, Virginia.	**1607**	**1620** Pilgrims sign the Mayflower Compact and settle at Plymouth Bay.

1550   **1600**   **1650**

World Events

1558 Elizabeth I becomes queen of England.	**1602** Dutch start East India Company.	**1640s** The English fight a civil war.

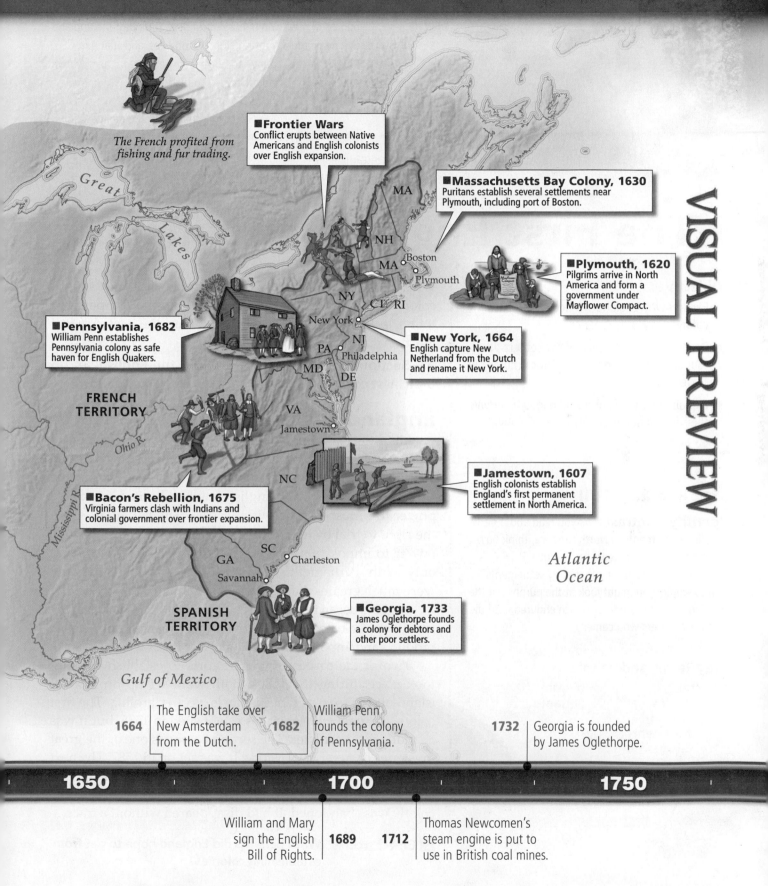

The French profited from fishing and fur trading.

■**Frontier Wars**
Conflict erupts between Native Americans and English colonists over English expansion.

■**Massachusetts Bay Colony, 1630**
Puritans establish several settlements near Plymouth, including port of Boston.

■**Plymouth, 1620**
Pilgrims arrive in North America and form a government under Mayflower Compact.

■**Pennsylvania, 1682**
William Penn establishes Pennsylvania colony as safe haven for English Quakers.

■**New York, 1664**
English capture New Netherland from the Dutch and rename it New York.

FRENCH TERRITORY

■**Bacon's Rebellion, 1675**
Virginia farmers clash with Indians and colonial government over frontier expansion.

■**Jamestown, 1607**
English colonists establish England's first permanent settlement in North America.

■**Georgia, 1733**
James Oglethorpe founds a colony for debtors and other poor settlers.

SPANISH TERRITORY

Gulf of Mexico

Atlantic Ocean

Great Lakes

MA
NH
MA
Boston
Plymouth
NY
CT RI
New York
PA
NJ
Philadelphia
MD
DE
VA
Jamestown
NC
SC
GA
Charleston
Savannah
Ohio R.
Mississippi R.

VISUAL PREVIEW

1650   **1700**   **1750**

1664 | The English take over New Amsterdam from the Dutch.

1682 | William Penn founds the colony of Pennsylvania.

1732 | Georgia is founded by James Oglethorpe.

William and Mary sign the English Bill of Rights. | **1689**

1712 | Thomas Newcomen's steam engine is put to use in British coal mines.

Moldy Rotten Peas

" The allowance in those times for a man was only eight ounces of meal and half a pint of peas for a day, the one and the other moldy, rotten, full of cobwebs and maggots . . ., which forced many to flee for relief to the [Native Americans] . . . and others . . . to filch. **"**

—General Assembly of Virginia, describing colonists' hardships, 1624

◄ Recreation of English settlement at Jamestown, Virginia

The First English Settlements

Objectives

- Explain why England wanted to establish colonies in North America.

- Describe the experience of the settlers who founded the first permanent English colony in Jamestown.

- Explain how the Pilgrims managed to survive their first years in the Plymouth Colony.

Reading Skill

Identify Contrasts As you read about early English settlements in North America, think how each of these settlements was unique. How was each different from the other early settlements? For example, you might look at the purpose of the settlements, the conditions each endured, and the types of settlers who came.

Key Terms and People

charter
John Smith
representative
   government
pilgrim
Squanto

Why It Matters As Spain, France, and Holland sought colonies in the Americas, England entered the competition, too. The English established colonies on the east coast of North America.

⑦ Section Focus Question: How did the English set up their first colonies?

England Seeks Colonies

Like most of Europe in the age of exploration, England was a monarchy. However, in England, the power of the king or queen was limited by law and by a lawmaking body called Parliament.

Ever since the 1200s, English law had limited the king's power to punish people without trial. The law guaranteed the right to trial by jury. Other provisions limited the king's power to impose new taxes. The king could set new taxes only with Parliament's consent. Still, the king's powers were much greater than those of Parliament.

England began to establish colonies in North America in the late 1500s. Colonies would provide new markets for English products and important raw materials for English industries.

Two of the earliest English efforts to establish colonies took place during the 1580s. Both were set up on a small island off the coast of what today is North Carolina. The first colony at Roanoke Island was established in 1585, but it was abandoned a year later. The second colony is one of the great mysteries of American history. It was set up in 1587. The next year, England found itself at war with Spain. No ship was able to visit the Roanoke colony until 1590. By then, the colony was abandoned. It had disappeared without a trace.

☑ **Checkpoint** What benefits did England hope to get from establishing colonies?

Founding Jamestown

In 1607, a group of wealthy people pooled their resources and made a new attempt to <u>establish</u> an English colony in North America. Eager to gain a share of the wealth of the Americas, they formed the Virginia Company of London. Some of the founders hoped to discover gold or silver. Others expected the colonists to trade with the Indians for furs, which could then be sold in Europe at a profit. Lumber also could be cut from North America's vast forests. Farmers could plant vineyards to grow grapes or mulberry trees to produce silk. England needed all of these products.

England's King James I backed the project. The king granted the merchants a charter to establish a colony called Virginia. A **charter** is a document issued by a government that grants specific rights to a person or company. It gave the Virginia Company authority over a large portion of North America's Atlantic coastline.

The first colonists arrived in Virginia in the spring of 1607. About 100 men sailed into Chesapeake Bay and built a fort they called Jamestown. It would prove to be England's first permanent settlement in North America.

Jamestown barely survived its first year. It was located on a swampy peninsula where insects thrived in warm weather. During the first summer, many colonists caught diseases, such as malaria, and died.

The colony had another serious problem. Many of the colonists had no intention of doing the hard farmwork needed to grow crops. Those men who came to the colony were not farmers. They were skilled in other trades. They spent their time looking for gold, expecting to get the food they needed from the Native Americans. The colonists found no gold. The local people, led by a chief named Powhatan, supplied some food to the colony. But it was not enough. By the spring of 1608, only 38 of the original colonists were still alive.

John Smith Takes Charge Conditions in Jamestown were extremely bad, in part because the colony was poorly led. Then, in the fall of 1608, John Smith was sent out from London to lead the colony. Smith lost no time taking command. He drew up tough, new rules. The most important rule was "He who works not, eats not."

Under Smith's firm leadership, the Jamestown colonists cut timber, put up new

Vocabulary Builder
establish (uh STAB lish) **v.** to set up, found

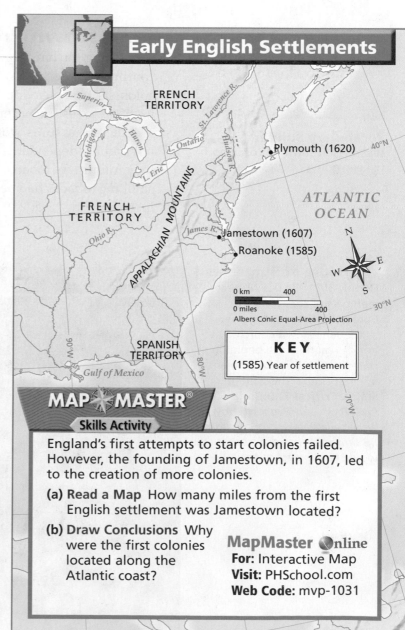

Early English Settlements

FRENCH TERRITORY

FRENCH TERRITORY

SPANISH TERRITORY

ATLANTIC OCEAN

Plymouth (1620) 40°N

Jamestown (1607)

Roanoke (1585)

L. Superior

L. Michigan

L. Huron

L. Ontario

L. Erie

St. Lawrence R.

Hudson R.

Ohio R.

James R.

APPALACHIAN MOUNTAINS

Gulf of Mexico

90°W

80°W

70°W

30°N

0 km 400
0 miles 400
Albers Conic Equal-Area Projection

KEY
(1585) Year of settlement

MAP MASTER
Skills Activity

England's first attempts to start colonies failed. However, the founding of Jamestown, in 1607, led to the creation of more colonies.

(a) Read a Map How many miles from the first English settlement was Jamestown located?

(b) Draw Conclusions Why were the first colonies located along the Atlantic coast?

MapMaster Online
For: Interactive Map
Visit: PHSchool.com
Web Code: mvp-1031

buildings, and planted crops. Meanwhile, hundreds of new colonists arrived. They included the first English women to settle in Jamestown. To get more food, Smith raided Native American villages. This angered Powhatan, who feared the English intended "to invade my people and possess my country."

The "Starving Time" In the fall of 1609, John Smith returned to England after being injured in an explosion. With Smith gone, conditions in Jamestown quickly worsened. So did relations with the Native Americans. Powhatan decided the time had come to drive the English away. First, he refused to supply them with food. The English settlers quickly ran out of food. The terrible winter of 1609–1610 is called the "starving time." By the spring of 1610, only 60 colonists were still alive.

☑ **Checkpoint** **Why did settlers in Jamestown have difficulties at first?**

Jamestown Prospers

During the hard times, the Virginia Company did not give up. It continued to send new colonists and offered free land to keep old colonists from leaving. Most important, it sent new leaders from England to restore order in the colony.

These measures would not have succeeded if the colonists had not found a dependable source of income to <u>sustain</u> the colony. What they found was tobacco, a crop native to the Americas. By the 1580s, smoking tobacco had become popular in several European countries, including England.

Vocabulary Builder
<u>sustain</u> (suh STAYN) **v.** to support; to keep going

The House of Burgesses
On July 30, 1619, the 22 elected members of the House of Burgesses first met together at the Jamestown church. That hot day marked the beginning of representative government in what is now the United States. *Critical Thinking: Link Past and Present How would a lawmaking body today be similar? What differences would you expect to see?*

Soldiers stand guard.

The governor calls the meeting to order.

The secretary records what is said at the meeting.

Farmers in Jamestown and nearby settlements in Virginia began planting tobacco in 1612. By the early 1620s, Virginia farmers were selling all the tobacco they could grow. Their success drew new colonists from England.

The House of Burgesses During these years, Virginia developed a tradition of representative government—the form of government in which voters elect people to make laws for them. In 1619, Virginia's lawmaking body, the House of Burgesses, was elected and met for the first time. The House of Burgesses could pass laws and set taxes. However, it shared power with Virginia's appointed governor, who could veto its acts. The House of Burgesses marked the start of representative government in North America.

Africans Come to Virginia In the summer of 1619, a Dutch ship arrived in Virginia from the West Indies. On board were 20 Africans, who had been captured and taken from their homeland. The Africans were sold to the Virginia colonists as slaves. However, that did not necessarily mean they would be enslaved for the rest of their lives. In the early days of the colony, enslaved people had a chance to earn their freedom after working a certain number of years. Some enslaved Africans were able to do this. Permanent slavery for Africans was not established in Virginia until the last part of the 1600s.

African American artist Romare Bearden presents the forced journey enslaved Africans made to the Americas in his painting *Roots Odyssey.*

☑**Checkpoint** **What were the responsibilities of the House of Burgesses?**

The Plymouth Colony

In England during the 1500s, people could be punished for their religious beliefs. In the 1530s, when King Henry VIII declared himself head of the Church of England, everyone was expected to follow the ways of the Church of England.

About the time Jamestown was founded, a group of people in eastern England left their homes and settled in the Netherlands. They wanted to separate from the Church of England and practice Christianity in their own way. These people, called Separatists, were often persecuted or treated badly because of their religion.

Between 1607 and 1609, several groups of Separatists settled in the Netherlands. Although they were allowed to worship as they pleased, they still were not happy. In 1620, one group of Separatists decided to leave the Netherlands and settle in Virginia. They are the people we know today as the Pilgrims. A pilgrim is a person who takes a religious journey.

The Mayflower Compact *agreement* In September 1620, about 100 Pilgrims sailed for Virginia aboard a ship called the *Mayflower*. After a long voyage, they arrived safely in North America. However, storms had blown them off course, and they landed far to the north in what today is Massachusetts. They called their new home Plymouth, after a port city in England.

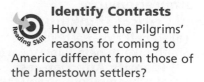

Identify Contrasts
How were the Pilgrims' reasons for coming to America different from those of the Jamestown settlers?

Squanto

Because they had landed outside Virginia, the Pilgrims believed they were not bound by the rules of the Virginia Company. But they needed rules of some sort. Before going ashore, 41 adult men signed the Mayflower Compact. It called for a government that would make and follow "just and equal laws." Officeholders would be elected by the colony's adult males.

Thus, a year after the creation of Virginia's House of Burgesses, the Pilgrims had taken a second step toward self-government in the Americas. The Mayflower Compact was the first document in which American colonists claimed a right to govern themselves.

The First Thanksgiving The Pilgrims had a very difficult first winter in Plymouth. They had arrived too late to plant crops and did not have enough food. During the winter of 1620–1621, half the colonists died from hunger or disease.

Conditions improved in the spring of 1621. As had happened at Jamestown, help from local Native Americans sustained the Pilgrims. A local chief gave the Pilgrims some food. Another Native American, named Squanto, brought the Pilgrims seeds of native plants—corn, beans, and pumpkins—and showed them how to plant them. He also taught the settlers how to catch eels from nearby rivers.

In the fall of 1621, the Pilgrims set aside a day to give thanks for their good fortune. Today's Thanksgiving holiday celebrates that occasion.

✓**Checkpoint** Why was the Mayflower Compact important?

⭐ **Looking Back and Ahead** The early settlers faced many challenges before they were able to claim success. In the next section, you will read how English settlers established additional colonies in New England.

Section 1 | **Check Your Progress**

Progress Monitoring ⊕nline
For: Self-test with instant help
Visit: PHSchool.com
Web Code: mva-1031

Comprehension and Critical Thinking

1. **(a) Recall** What actions did John Smith take to help Jamestown?
(b) Identify Alternatives What other methods do you think Smith could have used to save the colony?

2. **(a) Identify** Who were the Pilgrims?
(b) Analyze Cause and Effect How did the Pilgrims' experiences in England affect the government they established in the Plymouth Colony?

📡 **Reading Skill**

3. **Identify Contrasts** How did the government of the Jamestown settlers differ from that of the Plymouth settlers?

Key Terms
Fill in the blanks with the correct key terms.

4. The English king gave the merchants of the Virginia Company a _____ to establish a colony called Virginia.

5. English colonies in North America established a form of _____ based on elections.

Writing

6. Imagine that you are preparing a news report about the founding of Jamestown Colony. Make notes providing background information about this development. Your notes should include the economic benefits of colonialism and the particular details about how Jamestown Colony was founded.

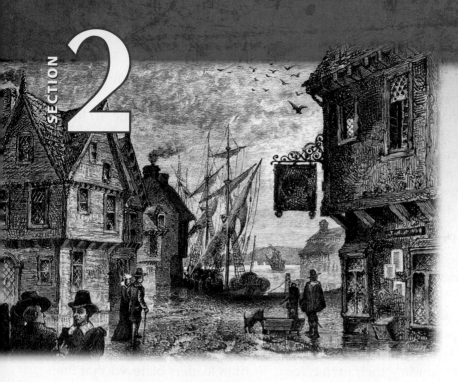

God Has Preserved Me

❝In [sixteen] sixty-one, my house was burnt, . . . and it was a most violent fire. . . . It pleased God to stir up the hearts of my loving friends to help me to the carrying on of another. . . . Thus God has all along preserved and kept me all my days.❞

—John Dane, recalling his life in New England, 1670

◀ Boston, Massachusetts, in the 1660s

The New England Colonies

Objectives

- Describe the geography and climate of the New England Colonies.

- Describe the Puritan settlement in Massachusetts.

- Identify the new settlements that developed in New England as a result of Puritan religious practices.

- Explain the changes that took place in the New England Colonies in the 1600s.

🎯 Reading Skill

Make Comparisons Despite differences, the New England colonies were alike in many ways. Look for these similarities in this section. For example, how was the climate similar in various colonies? You might also look at the shared reasons colonists had for coming to North America and at the ways that similar government structures evolved throughout New England.

Key Terms and People

John Winthrop
toleration
Roger Williams
Anne Hutchinson

Thomas Hooker
John Wheelright
town meeting
Metacom

Why It Matters Religious beliefs led the Pilgrims to move to North America and establish Plymouth Colony. Religion played a key role in other colonies that were established in New England.

❓ Section Focus Question: How did religious beliefs and dissent influence the New England Colonies?

Geography of New England

New England is in the northeastern corner of the United States. Massachusetts, Connecticut, and Rhode Island make up southern New England. New Hampshire, Vermont, and Maine make up the northern part.

Much of New England is made up of hills and low mountains. Large areas are covered by forests. The soil is thin and rocky, which makes farming difficult. There are narrow plains located along the Atlantic coast. The Connecticut River, the region's longest river, flows from New Hampshire and Vermont through Massachusetts and Connecticut before reaching the sea. Just off New England's long, jagged coastline are some of the richest fishing grounds in the world.

Winters in New England tend to be long and snowy. Summers are shorter and warm. This helped the early colonists in the region, who caught fewer diseases and lived longer than the colonists in Virginia.

✓**Checkpoint** **Why would colonists in New England have turned to fishing rather than to farming?**

Puritans in Massachusetts Bay

Similar to the Pilgrims, a group known as the Puritans had disagreements with the Church of England. Rather than split off from the established church, they wanted to reform, or change, it. In the early 1600s, the Puritans were influential in England. Many were important professionals such as merchants, landowners, or lawyers.

The 1620s brought hard times for England's Puritans. King Charles I opposed their movement and persecuted them. Hundreds of Puritan ministers were forced to give up their positions.

The Puritans Leave England A number of Puritans eventually decided to leave England and make the hazardous voyage to North America. In 1630, about 900 Puritans set off in 11 ships. They had formed the Massachusetts Bay Company, which received a charter to establish settlements in what are now Massachusetts and New Hampshire. The Puritans were led by John Winthrop, a respected landowner and lawyer.

In founding their own colony, Puritan leaders believed that their way of life would provide an example to others. As Winthrop said in a sermon during their voyage:

> **❝**Now the only way . . . is . . . to walk humbly with our God. . . . We must consider that we shall be as a City upon a Hill. The eyes of all people are upon us.**❞**
>
> —John Winthrop, "A Model of Christian Charity," 1630

Make Comparisons
Compare the reasons that England's Puritans went to North America with the reasons that the Pilgrims left England. How are they similar?

INFOGRAPHIC

SALEM WITCH Trials

Today, the Salem witch trials show how quickly false accusations can be accepted as true. **Critical Thinking: Draw Conclusions** Do you think this kind of judgment is possible today? Explain.

The Accusers
Clergymen such as Cotton Mather of Boston helped to feed the hysteria by asserting that the Devil was luring Salem's people into witchcraft.

On Trial
In 1692, hysteria about witches swept through Salem, Massachusetts. A special court tried dozens of women and men accused of witchcraft.

The Massachusetts Bay Colony The Puritans established several settlements in their colony. The main town was Boston, which was located on an excellent harbor. By 1643, about 20,000 people lived in the Massachusetts Bay Colony.

By the mid-1630s, Massachusetts Bay had an elected assembly, the General Court. Each town sent representatives to the assembly. But voting was limited to adult male members of the Puritan church. Both the General Court and the colony's governor were elected each year.

The Puritans had founded their colony so they could worship as they chose. However, they did not give non-Puritans the same right. The Puritans did not believe in religious toleration—recognition that other people have the right to different opinions.

☑Checkpoint **Why did the Puritans go to North America?**

New Colonies

Disagreements about religion led to the founding of other colonies in New England. A key dispute involved Roger Williams, minister of a church in the town of Salem. Williams believed the Puritans should split entirely from the Church of England. He also criticized colonists who had seized Native American lands. Williams specified that colonists should pay Native Americans for their land.

Williams was forced to leave Massachusetts Bay in 1635. He moved south, to what today is Rhode Island, where he bought land from Native Americans. In 1636, he founded the town of Providence.

Vocabulary Builder
specify (SPEHS ah fī) **v.** to point out in detail

The Accused
An accused woman is strapped to a dunking stool, a common form of punishment.

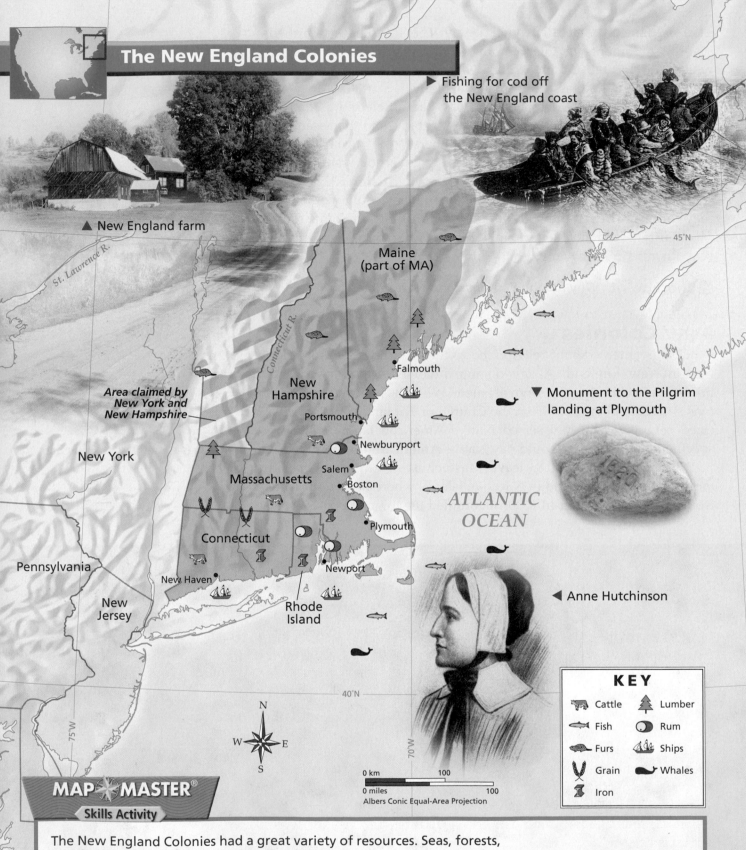

The New England Colonies

► Fishing for cod off the New England coast

▲ New England farm

Maine (part of MA)

Falmouth

New Hampshire

Portsmouth

Area claimed by New York and New Hampshire

New York

Newburyport

Salem

Boston

Massachusetts

▼ Monument to the Pilgrim landing at Plymouth

Plymouth

ATLANTIC OCEAN

Connecticut

New Haven

Rhode Island

Newport

◄ Anne Hutchinson

Pennsylvania

New Jersey

St. Lawrence R.

Connecticut R.

75°W

70°W

45°N

40°N

N
W   E
S

0 km   100
0 miles   100
Albers Conic Equal-Area Projection

KEY

🐄	Cattle	🌲	Lumber
🐟	Fish	⬭	Rum
🐟	Furs	⛵	Ships
Y	Grain	🐋	Whales
⚒	Iron		

MAP★MASTER®
Skills Activity

The New England Colonies had a great variety of resources. Seas, forests, and farms provided a good living to colonists.

(a) Read a Map In which area was fur trade important?

(b) Evaluate Information What resources were available to settlers along the Atlantic coast?

MapMaster ●nline

For: Interactive map
Visit: PHSchool.com
Web Code: mvp-1032

In 1644, the colonists in Rhode Island received a charter from the king to govern themselves. In doing so, they made an important contribution to religious toleration. They decided that Rhode Island would have no established, or official, church. People of all faiths could worship as they saw fit. Among the people who found religious freedom in Rhode Island were followers of the Jewish faith.

Anne Hutchinson's Dissent A Boston woman, Anne Hutchinson, questioned some of the Puritan teachings. She was put on trial in 1638 and was expelled from Massachusetts. Hutchinson established a settlement on an island that is now a part of Rhode Island. In 1642, she traveled farther south, into what is today New York State.

Settling Connecticut Thomas Hooker, a minister, disagreed with the Puritan leaders. He left Massachusetts with about 100 followers in 1636 and settled in what today is Connecticut. There, he founded the town of Hartford. Hundreds of Puritans followed, and soon Connecticut had several new settlements.

In 1639, the colonists drew up the Fundamental Orders of Connecticut, which established a new government with an elected legislature and governor. In 1662, Connecticut received an official charter from the king granting it self-government.

John Wheelright also was forced to leave Massachusetts. He got into trouble because he agreed with some of Anne Hutchinson's views. In 1638, Wheelright and some followers moved to New Hampshire, where they founded the town of Exeter. For a time, Massachusetts tried to control New Hampshire. Finally, in 1680, a charter from the king made New Hampshire a separate colony.

☑ **Checkpoint** **Why did Roger Williams and Anne Hutchinson leave the Massachusetts Bay Colony?**

Growth and Change

The Puritans believed that towns and churches should manage their own affairs. They also believed that people should work hard and live in strong and stable families.

Each Puritan town governed itself by setting up a town meeting—an assembly of townspeople that decides local issues. Membership in town meetings was <u>restricted</u> to male heads of households. Town meetings set local taxes and elected people to run the towns. Town meetings also gave New Englanders an opportunity to speak their minds. This early experience encouraged the growth of democratic ideas. New England became a region of towns and villages where neighbors knew one another and participated together in government.

New England families earned their livelihoods in many different ways. Farmers grew crops, but they also made leather goods and other products. Fishers caught cod and other fish that were shipped to customers in Europe. A shipbuilding industry provided many jobs. By the 1660s, more than 300 ships from New England were fishing off the coast or moving products across the Atlantic Ocean.

Vocabulary Builder
<u>restrict</u> (ree STRIHKT) **v.** to place limitations on something or somebody

Metacom, known to the English as "King Philip"

King Philip's War By the 1670s, the Native American population was decreasing, mainly because large numbers of Native Americans had died from diseases that they caught from Europeans. By 1670, there were only 12,000 Native Americans in New England, one tenth of their population 100 years earlier.

In 1675, a major conflict erupted. Opponents of the English were led by Metacom, the chief of the Wampanoag, who was also known by his English name, King Philip. His goal was to stop Puritan expansion. Other Native American groups, from Maine to Rhode Island, joined the war, some siding with the settlers. The fighting lasted a year and cost thousands of lives. Metacom and his allies destroyed 12 English towns. The uprising ended in 1676 when Metacom was captured and killed. The war's end left the English colonies free to expand.

Puritan Influence Declines By the 1670s, the outlook of New Englanders was changing. There was a new generation of people born in North America. The new generation had lost some of their parents' religious fervor, as people concentrated on running farms and businesses. In growing towns like Boston, successful merchants were becoming the new community leaders. The English colonies of New England were doing well. But the stern religious rules of the original founders now had less influence over the people who lived there.

☑Checkpoint **Why did Metacom declare war on the English colonists?**

⭐ **Looking Back and Ahead** As English colonies spread through New England, other colonies were being established to the west and south.

Progress Monitoring ⏾nline
For: Self-test with instant help
Visit: PHSchool.com
Web Code: mva-1032

Section 2 | **Check Your Progress**

Comprehension and Critical Thinking

1. **(a) Summarize** What was the geography and climate of New England?
(b) Identify Economic Costs How did geography affect the New England economy?

2. **(a) Recall** Why did Puritans establish the Massachusetts Bay Colony?

(b) Analyze Cause and Effect How did the lack of religious toleration affect politics in the Massachusetts Bay Colony?

⏺ **Reading Skill**

3. **Make Comparisons** Compare the way the English government treated the Puritans with the way the Puritans treated Anne Hutchinson. How are they similar?

Key Terms

4. Write two definitions for each key term: toleration, town meeting. First, write a formal definition for your teacher. Second, write a casual definition in everyday English for a classmate.

Writing

5. Create a concept web. Label the main oval "Religion." Then, add entries that show how religion played a major role in the settling of the New England Colonies. Add as many secondary ovals as necessary.

A Diverse Colony

❝On the island of Manhattan, . . . there may well be four or five hundred men of different sects and nations: the Director General told me that there were men of eighteen different languages. ❞

—Father Isaac Jogues, describing the Dutch settlement of New Amsterdam, 1646

◄ Dutch settlement of New Amsterdam, 1670s

The Middle Colonies

Objectives
- Describe the geography and climate of the Middle Colonies.
- Describe the early history of New York and New Jersey.
- Explain how Pennsylvania and Delaware were founded.
- Explain how the Middle Colonies changed in the 1600s and early 1700s.

🔄 Reading Skill

Identify Signal Words Signal words help readers spot comparisons and contrasts. For example, when we say, "Kentucky is warm. New York is *also* warm," the word *also* suggests that the two states and climates are similar. If the text reads, "Kentucky is warm. *Instead*, New York is cool," the word *instead* suggests that the two states and climates are different. Look for comparison and contrast signal words as you read this section.

Key Terms and People
proprietary colony   William Penn
royal colony   backcountry

Why It Matters While the New England colonies were growing, important developments were taking place in the region south of New England, known as the Middle Colonies.

❓ Section Focus Question: How did the diverse Middle Colonies develop and thrive?

Geography of the Middle Colonies

Four states made up the Middle Colonies: New York, Pennsylvania, New Jersey, and Delaware. New York, now the largest of these states, also is the farthest north. The scenic Hudson River flows south through eastern New York before reaching the sea at New York City. Long Island, the easternmost piece of New York, extends into the Atlantic Ocean for more than 100 miles. Today, New York City is the most populous city in the country.

Pennsylvania is the region's second-largest state. The southeastern section is a lowland. Philadelphia, Pennsylvania's largest city, is located there, on the Delaware River.

Most of New Jersey is a lowland along the Atlantic coast. Delaware, the region's smallest state, is on the coast directly south of New Jersey.

Middle Colony farmers had an easier time than farmers in New England. The climate was warmer, with a longer growing season. The fertile soil was well suited for crops like wheat, fruits, and vegetables.

✓**Checkpoint** What conditions in the Middle Colonies favored farming?

New York and New Jersey

New York began as the Dutch colony of New Netherland. By 1660, it was an economic success. Farmers in the Hudson River valley were prosperous. The colony was the base for a profitable fur trade between the Dutch and Native Americans. The Dutch also made money trading with merchants in the British colonies. This trade violated Britain's mercantile laws and angered the government.

One of New Netherland's major problems was its small Dutch population. Many of the colonists came from Sweden, France, and Portugal. There also were some English Puritans who had settled on Long Island. These people often were hostile to Dutch rule.

Tension also existed between England and the Netherlands. New Netherland separated England's northern colonies from its colonies farther south. Furthermore, England and Holland were rivals at trade.

New Netherland Becomes New York In 1664, England's King Charles II granted the right to all the Dutch lands in North America to his brother James. All that James had to do was conquer the territory. James sent a few warships to do the job, and the Dutch surrendered immediately. The colony was renamed New York, after James, the Duke of York. New Amsterdam, its capital, became New York City. The colony grew slowly. At the end of the 1600s, New York City was still a village on the southern end of Manhattan.

New Jersey New Jersey was established in 1665, when part of southern New York was split off to form a new colony. Like New York and several other English colonies, New Jersey at first was a **proprietary colony**—a colony created by a grant of land from a monarch to an individual or family. In 1702, New Jersey received a new charter as a **royal colony**—a colony controlled directly by the English king. New York had become a royal colony in 1685.

✓**Checkpoint** **How did New Jersey become a separate colony?**

Pennsylvania and Delaware

In the 1640s and 1650s, the Quakers were one of a number of new religious groups in England. Their ideas set them apart from most groups, including the Puritans.

The Quakers believed that all people had a direct link, or "inner light," with God. Groups of Quakers, therefore, did not need ministers. Another <u>fundamental</u> Quaker belief was that all people were equal in God's eyes. Thus, they were among the first in England to speak out against slavery. Women were considered equal to men in spiritual matters and often were leaders in Quaker meetings.

By the 1660s, there were thousands of Quakers in England. Many of them refused to pay taxes to support the Church of England. Because of their views, they often suffered from persecution. One Quaker leader was William Penn, a wealthy man who personally knew King Charles II. Penn wanted to find a place for Quakers to live

James, Duke of York

Vocabulary Builder
<u>fundamental</u> (fuhn duh MEHN tahl)
adj. most important part

where they would be safe from persecution. He used his connections to get a charter from the king for a new colony in North America. In 1681, he received an area almost as large as England itself, mainly in what is now Pennsylvania.

Penn's "Holy Experiment" Penn arrived in his colony in 1682. For his capital, Penn established a city named Philadelphia, which means "City of Brotherly Love." To attract settlers, he printed pamphlets in several languages and distributed them in England and on the European continent. Soon, new settlers began arriving from many places—England, Scotland, Wales, and Ireland. Still others came from Germany, Holland, and Switzerland.

Penn considered his colony to be a "holy experiment." His goal was to create a colony in which people from different religious backgrounds could live peacefully. In 1682, Penn wrote his Frame of Government for Pennsylvania. It granted the colony an elected assembly. It also provided for freedom of religion.

Penn tried to deal fairly with Native Americans. He did not allow colonists to settle on land until the Native Americans sold it to them. Relations between settlers and Native Americans in Pennsylvania were far from perfect. However, during Penn's lifetime they were much better in Pennsylvania than in other colonies.

Delaware: A Separate Colony People from Sweden were the first European settlers in Delaware. The Dutch took control of the territory in the 1650s, but they lost it to the English when they lost New York.

Penn's charter for Pennsylvania included Delaware. Because Delaware settlers did not want to send delegates to a distant assembly in Philadelphia, Penn gave the area its own representative assembly. In 1704, Delaware became a separate colony.

✓**Checkpoint** Why did Penn call Pennsylvania "a holy experiment"?

Identify Signal Words
What signal words suggest a contrast between Pennsylvania and the other colonies? What contrast is suggested?

William Penn and other leading Quakers make a peace treaty with Native Americans.

Growth and Change

By the early 1700s, more than 20,000 colonists lived in Pennsylvania. Fertile soil and hard work made its farms productive. Farmers grew more than they could use and sold the balance. The top cash crop, wheat, was sold to customers in New England and abroad. Because of all its wheat, Pennsylvania was called America's breadbasket. New Jersey also produced large amounts of wheat.

Manufacturing was just beginning in the Middle Colonies during the 1700s. The largest manufacturers produced iron, flour, and paper. Meanwhile, artisans in towns worked as shoemakers, carpenters, masons, weavers, and in many other trades. Among the most important artisans were coopers, who made the barrels used to ship and store flour and other foods.

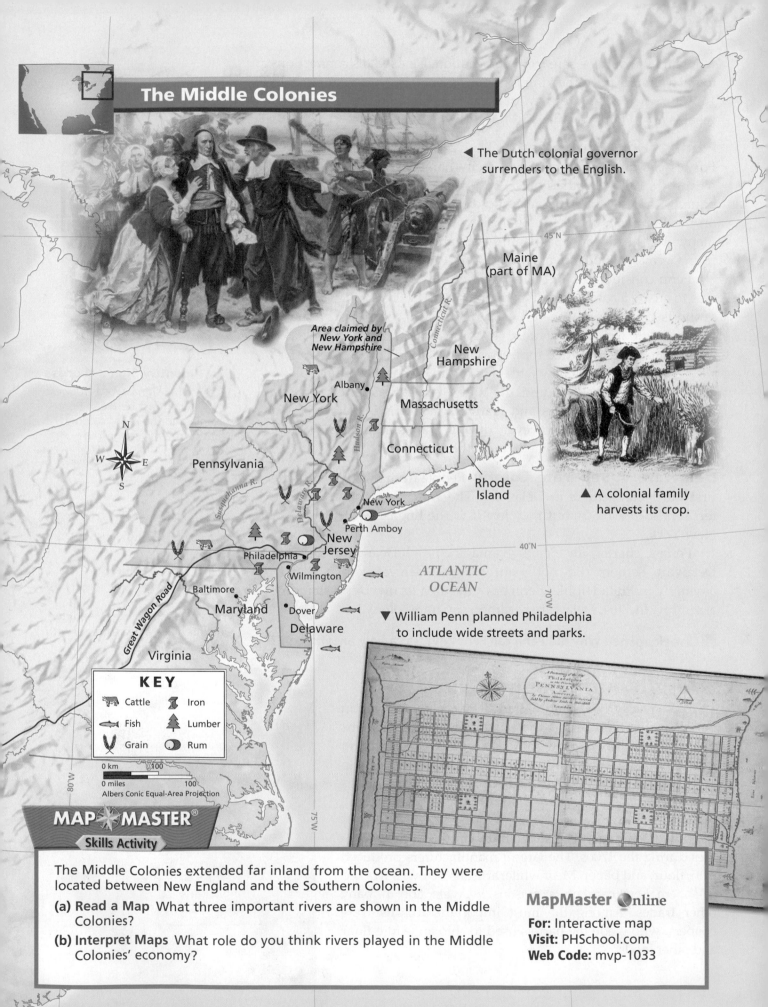

The Middle Colonies

◄ The Dutch colonial governor surrenders to the English.

45°N

Maine
(part of MA)

Area claimed by
New York and
New Hampshire

New
Hampshire

Albany

New York

Massachusetts

Connecticut

Pennsylvania

Rhode
Island

▲ A colonial family harvests its crop.

Susquehanna R.

Delaware R.

Hudson R.

Connecticut R.

New York

Perth Amboy

New
Jersey

Philadelphia

40°N

ATLANTIC
OCEAN

Wilmington

▼ William Penn planned Philadelphia
to include wide streets and parks.

Great Wagon Road

Baltimore

Maryland

Dover

Delaware

Virginia

KEY

Cattle		Iron	
Fish		Lumber	
Grain		Rum	

0 km 100
0 miles 100
Albers Conic Equal-Area Projection

75°W

70°W

80°W

MAP MASTER®
Skills Activity

The Middle Colonies extended far inland from the ocean. They were located between New England and the Southern Colonies.

(a) Read a Map What three important rivers are shown in the Middle Colonies?

(b) Interpret Maps What role do you think rivers played in the Middle Colonies' economy?

MapMaster Online

For: Interactive map
Visit: PHSchool.com
Web Code: mvp-1033

The Backcountry The western section of Pennsylvania was part of a region called the backcountry. The backcountry was a frontier region extending through several colonies, from Pennsylvania to Georgia.

Many of the people who settled in the backcountry were not English. Thousands were Scotch-Irish. Originally from Scotland, they had settled in Ireland before coming to North America. Large numbers of German immigrants began arriving early in the 1700s. The word these German newcomers used to describe themselves was *Deutsch*, for "German." Americans thought they were saying "Dutch." As a result, German immigrants in Pennsylvania were called the Pennsylvania Dutch.

By the middle of the 1700s, many settlers were pushing south and west along a route that led from Pennsylvania to Georgia. Because they often traveled in covered wagons, the route was called the Great Wagon Road. These backcountry settlers often fought with Native Americans.

Diverse and Thriving Colonies By 1750, the non-English immigrants had made the Middle Colonies the most diverse part of English North America. Philadelphia and New York were accumulating people at such a rate that they had become the largest cities and busiest ports in the colonies. All of the colonies had thriving economies.

Vocabulary Builder
accumulate (uh KYOOM yoo layt)
v. to increase in amount over time

☑ **Checkpoint** How was Pennsylvania a breadbasket?

⭐ **Looking Back and Ahead** Both the New England and Middle Colonies had many small family farms. In the next section, you will read that parts of the Southern Colonies developed a plantation economy that was far different.

Section 3 | Check Your Progress

Progress Monitoring ⬤nline
For: Self-test with instant help
Visit: PHSchool.com
Web Code: mva-1033

Comprehension and Critical Thinking

1. (a) **Recall** What was the geography and climate of the Middle Colonies?
   (b) **Identify Economic Benefits** What advantages did the geography and climate give to people living in the Middle Colonies?

2. (a) **Summarize** What were William Penn's goals for his colony?
   (b) **Compare** How did Penn's "holy experiment" differ from the Puritans' "city on a hill"?

🕐 Reading Skill

3. **Identify Signal Words** What word in the sentence that follows suggests a comparison? What similarity is being identified?
   Sentence: Both Pennsylvania and New Jersey produced a lot of wheat.

Key Terms

Answer the following questions in complete sentences that show your understanding of the key terms.

4. How was New Jersey different after it became a royal colony in 1702?

5. Why did settlers and Native Americans clash in the backcountry?

Writing

6. Imagine that you are a Pennsylvania farmer. Write a letter to a fellow farmer in New England telling him about your life in your new home. Then, write a letter that the New England farmer might send back describing his life in New England.

GEOGRAPHY AND HISTORY

Landscapes of the 13 Colonies

The physical geography of the 13 British colonies differed widely from region to region. While farmers in New England had difficulty planting crops in thin and rocky soil, farmers in the Middle and Southern colonies had better luck with more fertile soil and warmer climates.

Three Regions

Although farming was an important economic activity throughout the colonies, poor soil forced people in New England to concentrate on the sea for economic survival. For the colonists to the south, better geography yielded more favorable soils and longer growing seasons.

Because the climate of the Southern Colonies supported long growing seasons, plantation owners purchased enslaved people and used their labor to harvest rice and sugar crops. As the plantation system grew to dominate the economy of the Southern Colonies, slavery spread throughout the region.

▲ **New England** farmers had to break up rocks in the soil to clear land for crops. Because this was difficult work with only a small chance for financial success, many New Englanders relied upon fishing off the New England coast to provide for their families.

◄ Farmers in the **Middle Colonies** of Pennsylvania and New Jersey had an easier time growing crops. Better soil and a warmer climate in this region rendered huge wheat fields that gave Pennsylvania the nickname America's breadbasket.

◄ The **Southern Colonies** shared a lowland area called the Tidewater. Farmers there grew crops such as sugar, tobacco, and rice (pictured left). These crops thrived in the region's hot, humid environment. Because the Tidewater crops were grown on great stretches of land and required a great deal of labor, large farms, called plantations, developed in the South.

Analyze GEOGRAPHY AND HISTORY

Colonists in each of the three major regions of the 13 colonies learned to adapt to their environments. Write a paragraph describing how physical geography affected the output of food in the colonies.

▲ Virginia planters feast as their slaves harvest tobacco.

Persons of the Worst Character

❝ These overseers are indeed for the most part persons of the worst character. . . . They pay no regard to . . . the lodging of the field negroes. Their huts, which ought to be well covered, and the place dry where they take their little repose, are often open sheds, built in damp places; so that, when the poor creatures return tired from the toils of the field, they contract many disorders. ❞

—Olaudah Equiano, *The Interesting Narrative of the Life of Olaudah Equiano*

The Southern Colonies

Objectives

- Describe the geography and climate of the Southern Colonies.
- Describe the early history of Virginia.
- Explain how Maryland, the Carolinas, and Georgia were founded.
- Identify the factors that produced the Tidewater and backcountry ways of life.

Reading Skill

Compare and Contrast As you read about the Southern Colonies in this section, think about how they are the same and different from one another. What physical features do they share? What human features? In what ways are the communities and places different? Comparing and contrasting will help you better understand the colonies.

Key Terms and People

Nathaniel Bacon   debtor
Lord Baltimore   plantation
James Oglethorpe

Why It Matters The New England and Middle Colonies had much in common. But the two regions also differed because of local geographic conditions and other factors.

❓ **Section Focus Question: What factors influenced the development of the Southern Colonies?**

Geography of the Southern Colonies

During the 1760s, Charles Mason and Jeremiah Dixon were hired to settle a boundary dispute between Maryland and Pennsylvania. They conducted a survey—a careful measuring of an area with scientific instruments using the techniques of mathematics—that took four years to complete. The boundary they drew is known as the Mason-Dixon line. This line on a map marked much more than the boundary between two colonies. After the American Revolution, it was the dividing line between the northern states where slavery was abolished and the southern states where slavery persisted.

Five colonies were located south of the Mason-Dixon line: Maryland, Virginia, North Carolina, South Carolina, and Georgia. They shared a coastal area called the Tidewater, a flat lowland that includes many swampy areas. On its west, the Tidewater blends into a region of rolling hills called the Piedmont.

The climate of these states is warm and humid. Hot summers provide a long growing season that colonial farmers used to raise crops such as tobacco and rice. Both crops required many workers in the fields and thus were partly responsible for helping to spur the early development of slavery.

✓ **Checkpoint** What conditions favored the development of a plantation economy?

Virginia Grows

Virginia's population grew gradually during the 1600s. New settlers arriving from Europe made up for the fact that disease and difficult living conditions kept the death rate high. After 1650, the death rate fell, and the population increased more quickly. In 1640, about 10,000 settlers lived in Virginia. By 1670, the number had reached 40,000.

The makeup of Virginia's population also changed. By the 1670s, there were more children because fewer were dying at a young age. The percentage of women in the population rose as well.

Conflicts With Native Americans As Virginia's white population grew, the Native American population shrank. Disease and violence took their toll. In 1607, there had been about 8,000 Native Americans in Virginia. By 1675, only about 2,000 Native Americans were left.

Farmers took over more land to plant tobacco. This led to trouble with the Native Americans. There were two violent confrontations—one in 1622 and the other in 1644. Although the Native Americans killed hundreds of colonists, they were defeated both times. After 1644, the Native Americans living near the coast had to accept English rule.

Bacon's Rebellion There was more trouble to come. Beginning in the 1660s, wealthy Virginia tobacco planters bought most of the good farmland near the coast. That left no land for poorer colonists who wanted to start their own farms. Most of these colonists were young men who were forced to work the land for wealthier farmers. The young men also were angry because without property, they could not vote.

Many poor colonists moved inland to find good farmland. Fighting broke out with Native Americans, and people were killed on both sides. Farmers on the frontier demanded that the governor take strong measures against the Native Americans. However, the governor hesitated. He hoped to avoid an all-out war with the Native Americans, partly because he benefited from his fur trade with them.

Nathaniel Bacon became the leader of the frontier settlers. In 1675, he organized a force of 1,000 westerners and began attacking and killing Native Americans. The governor declared that Bacon and his men were rebels. Bacon reacted by attacking Jamestown, burning it to the ground, and forcing the governor to run away.

The revolt, known as Bacon's Rebellion, collapsed when Bacon became sick and died. The governor hanged 23 of Bacon's followers. Still, he could not stop English settlers from moving onto Native American lands.

✓**Checkpoint** What was the main cause of Bacon's Rebellion?

Bacon's Rebellion
Nathaniel Bacon (center) is shown here taking part in the burning of Jamestown during his 1675 rebellion. **Critical Thinking: *Explain Problems*** *How did the interests of frontier settlers differ from those of colonists in towns and on plantations?*

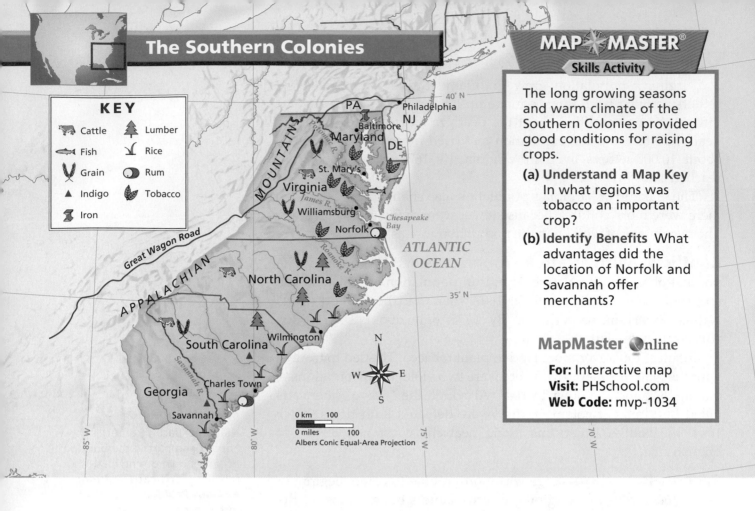

The Southern Colonies

KEY

- 🐄 Cattle
- 🐟 Fish
- 🌾 Grain
- ▲ Indigo
- ⚒ Iron
- 🌲 Lumber
- 🌾 Rice
- 🛢 Rum
- 🍃 Tobacco

MAP MASTER®
Skills Activity

The long growing seasons and warm climate of the Southern Colonies provided good conditions for raising crops.

(a) Understand a Map Key In what regions was tobacco an important crop?

(b) Identify Benefits What advantages did the location of Norfolk and Savannah offer merchants?

MapMaster Online

For: Interactive map
Visit: PHSchool.com
Web Code: mvp-1034

Vocabulary Builder
proprietor (proh PRĪ ah tor) **n.** owner of a business or a colony

Compare and Contrast
Compare and contrast the population growth, agriculture, and political tensions of Maryland with those of Virginia.

Religious Toleration in Maryland

In 1632, King Charles I granted a charter for a new colony to George Calvert, an English Catholic. Catholics suffered great discrimination in England. Calvert aimed to set up a colony where Catholics could live safely. His colony, Maryland, lay across Chesapeake Bay from Virginia.

The first settlers included both Catholics and Protestants. They grew tobacco and harvested the sea life of Chesapeake Bay. When George Calvert died, his son, Cecil Calvert, Lord Baltimore, became proprietor. As the charter required, there was a representative assembly similar to the House of Burgesses in Virginia.

Soon there was tension between Protestants and Catholics. Fearing that Catholics might lose their rights, Lord Baltimore got the assembly to pass the Act of Toleration in 1649. It welcomed all Christians and gave adult male Christians the right to vote and hold office. Although the Toleration Act did not protect people who were not Christian, it was still an important step toward religious toleration in North America.

✓ **Checkpoint** Who benefited from Maryland's toleration?

Colonies in the Carolinas and Georgia

By the 1660s, a few settlers from Virginia had moved south beyond the colony's borders. In 1663, King Charles II granted a charter for a new colony to be established there, in the area called Carolina.

The northern part of Carolina developed slowly. It lacked harbors and rivers on which ships could travel easily. Settlers lived on small farms, raising and exporting tobacco. Some produced lumber for shipbuilding.

The southern part of Carolina grew more quickly. Sugar grew well in the swampy lowlands. Many planters came from Barbados in the West Indies. They brought enslaved people to grow sugar. Soon the colonists were using slave labor to grow another crop, rice. It became the area's most important crop.

As rice production spread, Carolina's main city, Charles Town (today's Charleston), eventually became the biggest city in the Southern Colonies. By then, Carolina had become two colonies: North Carolina and South Carolina.

Georgia The last of England's 13 colonies, Georgia was founded for two reasons. First, the English feared that Spain was about to expand its Florida colony northward. An English colony south of Carolina would keep the Spanish bottled up in Florida. Second, a group of wealthy Englishmen led by James Oglethorpe wanted a colony where there would be protection for English debtors— people who owe money. Under English laws, the government could imprison debtors until they paid what they owed.

Georgia's founders wanted Georgia to be a colony of small farms, not large plantations. Therefore, slavery was banned. However, this restriction was unpopular with settlers and did not last. By the 1750s, slavery was legal in Georgia.

✓Checkpoint **Why did Oglethorpe and the other founders establish the colony of Georgia?**

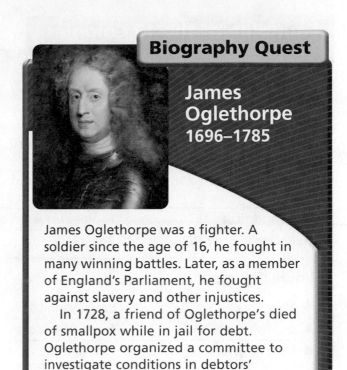

Change in the Southern Colonies

During the 1700s, the Southern Colonies developed two distinct ways of life. People along the coast lived very differently from people who settled inland on the frontier.

The Tidewater Region The most important feature of life along the coast in the Southern Colonies was the plantation, a large farm especially in a hot country where crops such as cotton, sugar, and rice are grown. This led to an economy dominated by plantations in the Tidewater region. The plantation system began in Virginia and Maryland when settlers started growing tobacco. It spread southward when planters found other crops they could export profitably to Europe.

Founding of the 13 Colonies

Colony / Date Founded	Leader(s)	Reason(s) Founded
New England Colonies		
■ Massachusetts Plymouth / 1620 Massachusetts Bay / 1630	William Bradford John Winthrop	Religious freedom Religious freedom
■ New Hampshire / 1622	Ferdinando Gorges John Mason	Profit from trade and fishing
■ Connecticut / 1636	Thomas Hooker	Expand trade; religious and political freedom
■ Rhode Island / 1636	Roger Williams	Religious freedom
Middle Colonies		
■ New York / 1624	Peter Minuit	Expand trade
■ Delaware / 1638	Swedish settlers	Expand trade
■ New Jersey / 1664	John Berkeley George Carteret	Expand trade; religious and political freedom
■ Pennsylvania / 1682	William Penn	Profit from land sales; religious and political freedom
Southern Colonies		
■ Virginia / 1607	John Smith	Trade and farming
Maryland / 1634	Lord Baltimore	Profit from land sales; religious and political freedom
■ The Carolinas / 1663 North Carolina / 1712 South Carolina / 1719	Group of eight proprietors	Trade and farming
■ Georgia / 1733	James Oglethorpe	Profit; home for debtors; buffer against Spanish Florida

Reading Charts
Skills Activity

By 1733, England had established 13 colonies on the Atlantic coast of North America. These colonies were founded for a variety of reasons.

(a) **Interpret a Chart** Identify one Middle Colony and one Southern Colony founded for religious reasons.

(b) **Understand Sequence** How many English colonies were there by 1700?

The Tidewater region in South Carolina and Georgia was well suited for rice. However, rice-growing required large numbers of workers laboring in hot, humid, unhealthy conditions. This was one reason rice-farming helped promote the spread of slavery. In time, the enslaved population outnumbered the free population of South Carolina.

The plantation system did not just create a society of slaveholders and enslaved people in the Tidewater. It also divided the white community into a small group of wealthy people and a much larger group with little or no property, most of whom were poor and lived in the backcountry South.

The Backcountry The backcountry was cut off from the coast by poor roads and long distances. Families usually lived on isolated farms. They often did not legally own the land they farmed. Many families lived in simple one-room shacks. Few families had servants or enslaved people to help them with their work. Women and girls worked in the fields with the men and boys.

In the backcountry, people cared less about rank. Life in the backcountry provided a sharp <u>contrast</u> to life near the coast. As a result, backcountry people believed that the colonial governments on the coast did not care about them. They thought that colonial government cared only about protecting the wealth of the Tidewater plantation owners.

Vocabulary Builder
<u>contrast</u> (KAHN trast) *n.* difference shown between things when compared

☑Checkpoint **How did people live in the backcountry?**

⭐ **Looking Back and Ahead** As you have seen, the English colonies developed along distinct regional lines. But Spain, too, was competing for influence in North America. It had started its own colonies long before the English arrived.

Section 4 | **Check Your Progress**

Progress Monitoring ⬤nline
For: Self-test with instant help
Visit: PHSchool.com
Web Code: mva-1034

Comprehension and Critical Thinking

1. (a) **Summarize** How did the geography of the Southern Colonies affect the kinds of crops that were grown there?
   (b) **Draw Conclusions** Why did the struggle for rich farmland affect the colonists in Virginia?

2. (a) **Recall** Why did Lord Baltimore want Maryland's Act of Toleration?
   (b) **Compare** How would you compare the motives of Lord Baltimore in founding the colony of Maryland with those of James Oglethorpe in founding Georgia?

🔵 **Reading Skill**

3. **Compare and Contrast** Compare and contrast the Tidewater and the backcountry regions of the Southern Colonies.

Key Terms
Read each sentence. If the sentence is true, write YES. If the sentence is not true, write NO and explain why.

4. **Debtors** could not be imprisoned under English law.

5. There were many **plantations** where crops such as wheat, fruits, and vegetables were grown.

Writing

6. List the different groups of people living in the Southern Colonies between 1620 and the 1700s. Write two or three sentences about each group.

Baptisms and Conquests

❝I have baptized here in these new conquests . . . about four thousand five hundreds souls, and could have baptized twelve or fifteen thousand if we had not suspended further baptisms until our Lord should bring us missionary fathers to aid us.❞

—Father Eusebio Kino, describing missionary activity in present-day Arizona, late 1600s

◄ Spain's empire extended from Florida (left) to the present-day Southwest.

Spanish Colonies on the Borderlands

Objectives
- Describe Spain's colony in Florida.
- Explain how Spain established settlements throughout much of North America.
- Describe the significance of the Spanish missions.

🔁 Reading Skill

Compare and Contrast Across Sections The colonies discussed in Sections 1 through 4 were settled primarily by people from the British Isles. Section 5 discusses Spain's colonies in North America. Recall information from Sections 1 through 4 in order to compare and contrast the English colonies with those of Spain. Examine the text in Section 5 to ask: How are these similar to or different from the colonies discussed in Sections 1 through 4?

Key Terms and People
borderland   presidio
Junípero Serra   pueblo

Why It Matters While France and England were building colonies in North America, Spain's colonies in the Americas were already hundreds of years old. Some of Spain's colonies bordered lands where French and English settlers were moving. The people of these colonies would influence each other for many years to come.

❓ Section Focus Question: How did the Spanish establish colonies on the borderlands?

Spanish Florida

Spanish explorers reached Florida early in the 1500s. In 1565, fearing that France might take over the area, Spain built a fort called St. Augustine in northern Florida. It was the first permanent European settlement in what is now the United States.

As English colonies spread southward, Spanish control was threatened. To weaken the English colonies, in 1693, the Spanish announced that enslaved Africans who escaped to Florida would be protected. They would be given land if they helped to defend the colony. During the 1700s, hundreds of enslaved African Americans fled to Florida.

Spain's Florida colony grew slowly. By 1763, there were only three major Spanish settlements there. All were centered around forts, and all were in the north. The Spanish had little control over the rest of Florida.

✓Checkpoint Why did the Spanish colonize Florida?

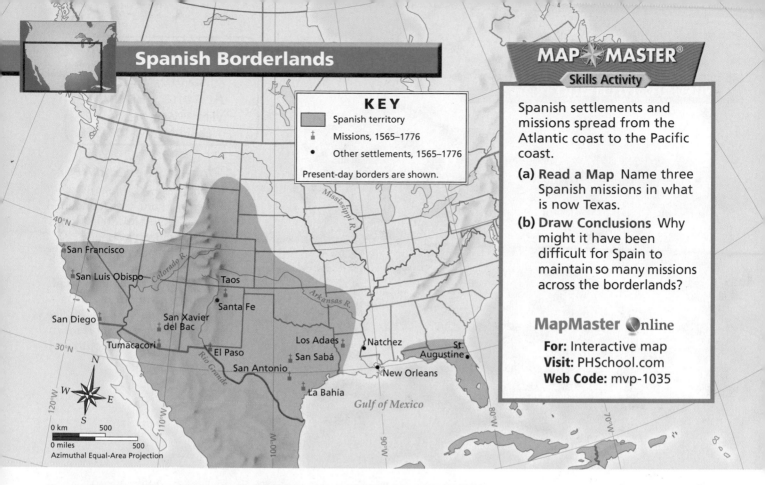

Spanish Borderlands

KEY

Spanish territory

Missions, 1565–1776

Other settlements, 1565–1776

Present-day borders are shown.

MAP MASTER®
Skills Activity

Spanish settlements and missions spread from the Atlantic coast to the Pacific coast.

(a) Read a Map Name three Spanish missions in what is now Texas.

(b) Draw Conclusions Why might it have been difficult for Spain to maintain so many missions across the borderlands?

MapMaster Online

For: Interactive map
Visit: PHSchool.com
Web Code: mvp-1035

Map labels: San Francisco, San Luis Obispo, San Diego, Tumácacori, Taos, Santa Fe, San Xavier del Bac, El Paso, San Antonio, La Bahía, Los Adaes, San Sabá, Natchez, New Orleans, St. Augustine, Colorado R., Mississippi R., Arkansas R., Rio Grande, Gulf of Mexico

0 km 500
0 miles 500
Azimuthal Equal-Area Projection

Settling the Spanish Borderlands

Spain's most important colonies were in Mexico and South America. Its territories north of Mexico were called the borderlands, meaning lands along a frontier. The main function of the Spanish borderlands was to protect Mexico from other European powers.

The borderlands began in the east with Florida. Farther west, they included most of Texas, New Mexico, Arizona, Colorado, Utah, Nevada, and California. This vast area differs greatly from place to place with humid lowlands in Texas and deserts and mountains in New Mexico, Arizona, and Utah. Colorado has highlands and mountains, while California has deserts in its southeast corner.

Juan de Oñate in New Mexico The first Spanish explorers did not start permanent settlements. Then, in 1598, Juan de Oñate (WAN day ohn YAH tay) led an expedition into New Mexico. He aimed to find gold, convert Native Americans to Christianity, and establish a permanent colony. Oñate never found gold, but in 1598 he established Spain's first permanent settlement in the region at Santa Fe.

Oñate brought more than 300 horses. At their settlements, the Spanish used Native Americans to look after the horses. When some Native Americans ran away from the Spanish, they spread the skill of horseback riding from one Native American group to another. This skill forever changed the lives of the Native Americans of the region.

The Native Americans suffered under Spanish rule. In 1680, several groups in New Mexico rebelled and drove the Spanish from the region. After that defeat, the Spanish did not return for more than 10 years.

Vocabulary Builder
function (FUHNK shuhn)
n. purpose; proper use; official duty

Vocabulary Builder
convert (kuhn VERT) **v.** to change from one religion to another

History *Interactive*

Explore an Arizona Mission
Visit: PHSchool.com
Web Code: mvl-1031

A Mission: Then and Now
The Tumacácori Mission in southern Arizona was founded in 1691 and rebuilt in 1800. It looks much as it did when Henry Cheever Pratt portrayed it in 1855 (at left). The mission is now a National Historical Park. **Critical Thinking:** *Draw Conclusions Why are abandoned missions like this one considered important to the history of the U.S. Southwest?*

Missions in Texas and Arizona Roman Catholic missionaries played a key role in colonizing the borderlands. To win Native Americans to Christianity, they established missions—religious settlements that aim to spread a religion into a new area. At the missions, priests taught about Catholicism and made Native Americans work by set rules. The missionary who led the way in spreading Spanish influence in what today is Arizona and Texas was Father Eusebio Francisco Kino.

At first, the Spanish had little success. The only early mission that took root in Texas was about 150 miles north of the Rio Grande. Although the mission failed to convert many Native Americans, it did attract Spanish colonists. This mission became the city of San Antonio.

Missions Along the California Coast Spain's California missions were especially important. Spain began colonizing California in 1769. A missionary named Junípero Serra (hoo NEE peh roh SEHR rah) played an important role in that effort. His first mission, just north of today's Mexican-American border, eventually became the city of San Diego. Serra later established other missions, including those located in what is now San Francisco and Los Angeles. Altogether, the Spanish founded almost 20 missions in California between 1769 and 1800.

Presidios and Pueblos Along with missionaries, Spain sent soldiers. They set up presidios—military posts—to defend the missions.

Compare and Contrast Across Sections

Reading Skill

Compare and contrast the role of religion in the Spanish settlements with that in the Southern Colonies and New England.

The Spanish also established what they called pueblos—civilian towns. The pueblos were centers of farming and trade. In the middle of the town was a plaza, or public square. Here, townspeople and farmers came to do business or to worship at the church. Church, shops, and homes lined the four sides of the plaza.

☑Checkpoint **What role did missionaries play in Spain's expanding North American empire?**

Life in Spanish Missions

Thousands of Native Americans labored at Spanish missions. They farmed, built churches, and learned a wide range of crafts. The Native Americans were not overworked by Spanish standards of the time. They worked from five to eight hours per day and five or six days per week. They did not work on Sundays or religious holidays.

However, the Native Americans did not have control over their lives. The missionaries punished them harshly if the Native Americans violated mission rules. Native Americans were imprisoned and often kept in shackles or whipped while tied to whipping posts.

Native Americans often rebelled against such treatment. Meanwhile, their population fell as thousands died because of poor living conditions and European diseases.

☑Checkpoint **Why did some Native Americans rebel against rules set by missionaries?**

⭐ **Looking Back and Ahead** Spain had now built a vast empire in the Americas. But the 13 English colonies were destined to grow, too. New frictions would develop within the English Empire as it grew.

HISTORIAN'S APPRENTICE ACTIVITY PACK

To further explore the topics in this chapter, complete the activity in the Historian's Apprentice Activity Pack to answer this essential question:

What was Spain's lasting influence on the United States?

Section 5 | **Check Your Progress**

Progress Monitoring ❂nline
For: Self-test with instant help
Visit: PHSchool.com
Web Code: mva-1035

Comprehension and Critical Thinking

1. **(a) Identify** Where is Saint Augustine located?
(b) Draw Conclusions Why do you think the colony failed to attract settlers?

2. **(a) Summarize** Why were the borderlands important to Spain?
(b) Apply Information How did the importance of the borderlands influence the way Spain ruled this region?

3. **(a) Recall** How did Junípero Serra help establish Spain's presence in the Americas?
(b) Link Past and Present In what way have the early Spanish missions influenced today's Americans?

🔊 **Reading Skill**

4. **Compare and Contrast Across Sections** Compare and contrast the experiences of Native Americans in Spanish settlements and in English colonies.

Key Terms

5. Draw a table with two rows and three columns. In the first column, list the following key terms from this section: presidio, pueblo. In the next column, write a definition of each word. In the last column, make a small illustration that shows the meaning of each word.

Writing

6. Review the table you created in Key Terms. Add a column to the table. Write two or three sentences for each key term. Explain how it relates to the settlement of Spanish colonies in the Americas.

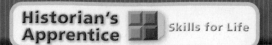

21st Century Learning   Historians use primary sources to find out information about the past from people who lived during that period. A primary source is firsthand information about people or historical events. The following primary source describes events that took place near the Jamestown Colony in 1608.

This selection is from John Smith's book *A Generall Historie of Virginia, New-England, and the Summer Isles*, published in 1624. It describes his capture by Native Americans and his rescue by Pocahontas, the daughter of the Indian chief Powhatan. Using the writing style of this period of history, Smith refers to himself in the third person, using "he" or "him" instead of "I" or "me."

Primary Source

". . . Finding he was beset with 200 savages, two of them he slew still defending himself with the aid of a savage, his guide, . . . yet he was shot in his thigh a little, and had many arrows that stuck in his clothese; but no great hurt, til at last they took him prisoner.

Six or seven weeks those barbarians kept him prisoner, . . . yet he . . . diverted them from surprising the fort . . . [gained] his own liberty, and got himself and his company such estimation among them that those savages admired him more than their own *quiyouckosuchs* [gods]. . . .

1608   At last they brought him to . . . Powhatan, their emperor. . . . Having feasted him after their best barbarous manner they could, a long consultation was held, but the conclusion was: two great stones were brought before Powhatan; then as many as could laid hands on him, dragged him to them, and thereon laid his head, and being ready with their clubs to beat out his brains, Pocahontas, the king's dearest daughter, . . . got his head in her arms, and laid her own upon his to save him from death."

Learn the Skill
Use these steps to read a primary source.

1. **Identify the source.** Ask questions that help you identify the writer or speaker.

2. **Identify the author's purpose for writing.** Often, eyewitnesses might want to inform or persuade the reader to share their views.

3. **Recognize the author's point of view.** Distinguish between facts and the author's opinion.

4. **Evaluate whether the source is reliable.** Consider who wrote the primary source and the information presented. Compare this information with what you know about the subject.

Practice the Skill
Answer the following questions about the primary source on this page.

1. **Identify the source.** (a) Who wrote this excerpt? (b) When did the events occur?

2. **Identify the author's purpose for writing.** Why did the author write this source?

3. **Recognize the author's point of view.** What is the author's opinion of Native Americans?

4. **Evaluate whether the source is reliable.** Is this a reliable source for learning about the history of the Jamestown Colony? Explain.

Apply the Skill
See the Review and Assessment at the end of this chapter.

How did the English start colonies with distinct qualities in North America?

Section 1
The First English Settlements

- The English colony at Jamestown is founded in 1607.
- English Pilgrims seeking religious freedom settled the Plymouth Colony.

Section 2
The New England Colonies

- Puritans seeking religious freedom settled the Massachusetts Bay Colony in 1630.
- People unhappy with the Puritans' religious intolerance founded Rhode Island, Connecticut, and New Hampshire.

Section 3
The Middle Colonies

- After the English takeover, New Netherlands was renamed New York.
- Pennsylvania was founded in 1681 by a Quaker, William Penn.

Section 4
The Southern Colonies

- Maryland was founded as a colony where Catholics could worship freely.
- Large plantations marked the Tidewater region, and small farms dominated the backcountry.

Section 5
Spanish Colonies on the Borderlands

- Spain had large colonies in the Caribbean, Mexico, and South America.
- Spanish missions sought to convert Native Americans to Christianity.
- Spain established presidios and pueblos throughout the borderlands.

? Exploring the Essential Question

Use the online study guide to explore the essential question.

Section 1
How did the English set up their first colonies?

Chapter 3 Essential Question
How did the English start colonies with distinct qualities in North America?

Section 2
How did religious beliefs and dissent influence the New England Colonies?

Section 5
How did the Spanish establish colonies on the borderlands?

Section 3
How did the diverse Middle Colonies develop and thrive?

Section 4
What factors influenced the development of the Southern Colonies?

Key Terms

Answer the following questions in complete sentences that show your understanding of the key terms.

1. How did the charter of the Virginia Company help the colonization of the Americas?

2. What problems resulted because Puritans did not believe in religious toleration?

3. What groups settled in the backcountry?

4. How did town meetings affect the governing of New England colonies?

5. Why was New Jersey a royal colony?

Comprehension and Critical Thinking

6. **(a) Recall** What was the Mayflower Compact?
   (b) Apply Information Why do you think the Mayflower Compact is an important part of our country's history?

7. **(a) Identify** Who were the Puritans and the Pilgrims?
   (b) Compare and Contrast How would you compare and contrast the Pilgrims and Puritans?
   (c) Synthesize Do you think Puritans and Pilgrims would worship together in America? Explain.

8. **(a) Summarize** How does the Edward Hicks painting below show the nature of William Penn's dealings with Native Americans?
   (b) Contrast How would you contrast the way colonists in Pennsylvania and in Massachusetts got along with Native Americans?

9. **(a) Identify** How was land farmed in the Tidewater region and in the Virginia backcountry?
   (b) Draw Conclusions Would a farmer living in the Tidewater or in the backcountry be more likely to support the Virginia government? Explain.

History Reading Skill

10. **Compare and Contrast** Choose any two colonies from among those discussed in Chapter 3. Make a list of three important features of the colonies. Then, compare and contrast these features in the two colonies you have chosen.

Writing

11. **Write two paragraphs on the following topic:** Describe the factors that led to the establishment of English and Spanish colonies in the Americas.

12. **Write a Dialogue:** Write a conversation that Roger Williams might have had with William Penn. Include issues about how their colonies were settled.

Skills for Life

Read a Primary Source

Use the primary source below by William Bradford, governor of the Plymouth Colony, to answer the questions that follow.

> [1621] "[What] was most sad and lamentable was that in two or three months' time, half of their company died, . . . being infected with the scurvy and other diseases. . . . [I]n the time of most distress, there were but six or seven sound persons who . . . spared no pains night or day, but with abundance of toil and hazard to their own health fetched them wood, made them fires . . . made their beds . . . and all this willingly . . . without any grudging in the least."
>
> —from the book *Of Plymouth Plantation, 1620–1647*, by William Bradford

13. Who wrote these observations?

14. Why did the author write this source?

15. How does the author show his feeling about the people who cared for the sick colonists?

16. Do you think the author gives an accurate view of the events? Why?

Test Yourself

1. **Which of the following established the right of American colonists to govern themselves?**

   A mercantilism

   B pueblo

   C proprietary colony

   D Mayflower Compact

2. **The followers of Nathaniel Bacon**

   A supported the governor of Virginia.

   B had a profitable fur trade with the Native Americans.

   C were poor farmers seeking good farmland.

   D were fully represented in the House of Burgesses.

3. **What geographical feature helped New England colonists?**

   A long growing seasons

   B mountains

   C natural harbors

   D fertile soil

Refer to the passage below to answer Question 4.

> Roger Williams said that **"**God Land will be as great a God with us English as God Gold was with the Spanish.**"**

4. **Which event can be judged as a result of English colonists' push for land in the Americas?**

   A Spanish expeditions to find gold

   B King Philip's War

   C the election of the House of Burgesses

   D John Smith's return to England

Document-Based Questions

Task: Look at Documents 1 and 2, and answer their accompanying questions. Then, use the documents and your knowledge of history to complete this writing assignment:

> Write a short essay explaining why these two documents were important in the development of democratic government in America.

Document 1: The Ordinance for Virginia, dated July 24, 1619, called for the creation of an assembly chosen by and made up of colonists. The House of Burgesses, as the assembly is known, marked the beginning of representative government in America. *What powers did the Burgesses have?*

> **"**And this General Assembly shall have free Power . . . to make, ordain, and enact such general Laws and Orders, for the Behoof [good] of the said Colony, and the good government thereof. . . .**"**

Document 2: In 1620, the Pilgrims arrived in America. While still aboard the *Mayflower,* they drew up and signed the Mayflower Compact. *What powers did the Mayflower Compact give the Plymouth settlers?*

> **"**We . . . combine ourselves together into a civil Body Politick, . . . [to] enact, constitute, and frame, such just and equal Laws, Ordinances, Acts, Constitutions and Offices, from time to time, as shall be thought most meet and convenient for the general Good of the Colony; unto which we promise all due Submission and Obedience.**"**

Life in the Colonies

1650-1750

"*...Here every man may be master of his own labour and land...and if he have nothing but his hands he may set up his trade, and by industry grow rich.*"

—New England colonial farmer

This needlework depicts the fine clothing and refined manners of wealthy colonists. Most members of colonial society did not enjoy such an elegant lifestyle.

CHAPTER 4

What You Will Learn

Section 1
GOVERNING THE COLONIES
English ideas about government, individual rights, and trade deeply affected colonial life.

Section 2
COLONIAL SOCIETY
Although colonial society was divided into different social and economic classes, it was far less rigid than European society of the time.

Section 3
SLAVERY IN THE COLONIES
By the 1700s, slavery had become a part of American life, serving the economic interests of both northern traders and southern planters.

Section 4
THE SPREAD OF NEW IDEAS
Religion played a key role in colonial life, while the European Enlightenment influenced scientific and political thought.

Reading Skill
Determine Meaning From Context In this chapter, you will practice using context and word clues to understand unfamiliar passages in a text.

How did colonial life take shape?

Life in the English Colonies

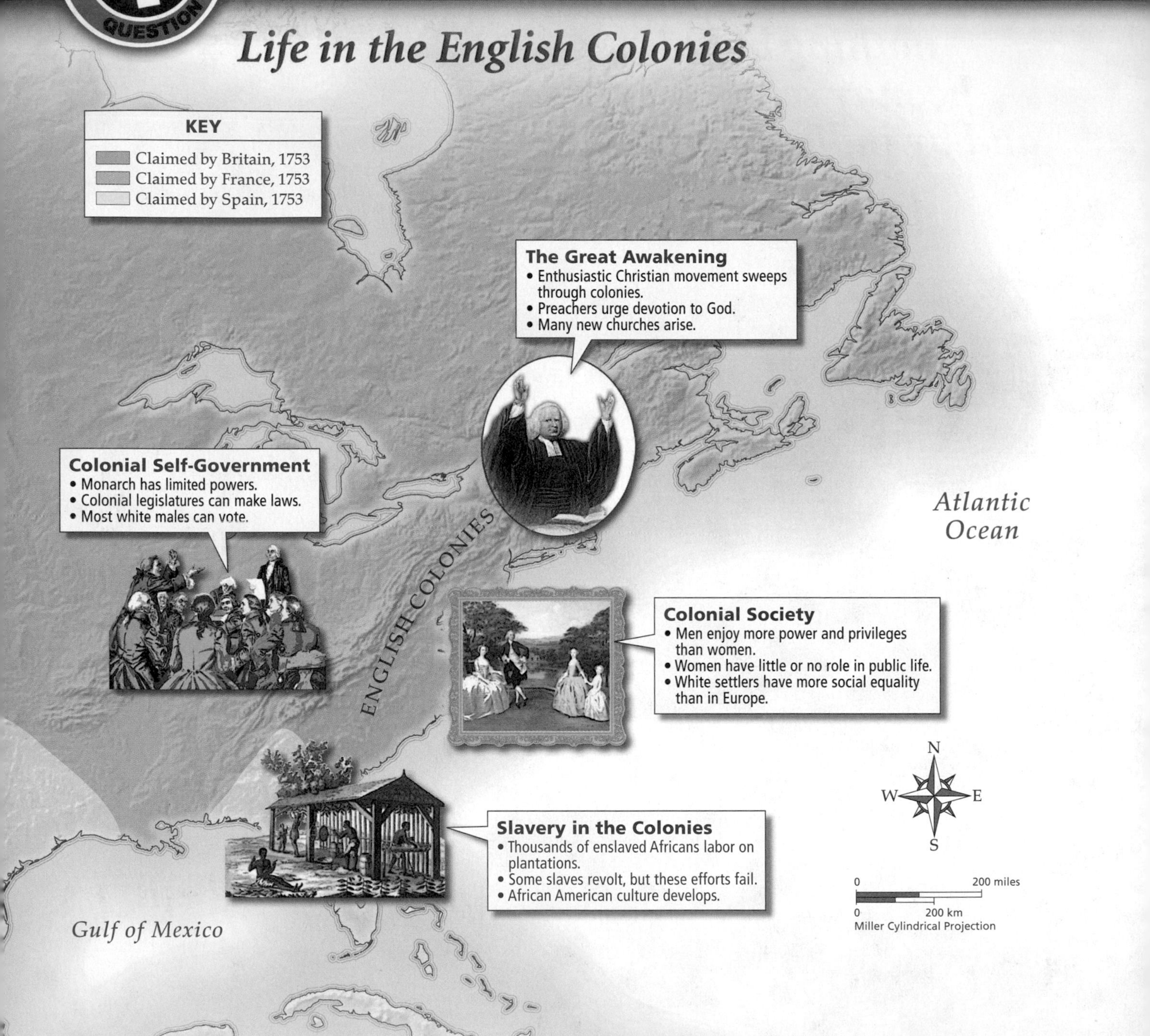

KEY

- Claimed by Britain, 1753
- Claimed by France, 1753
- Claimed by Spain, 1753

The Great Awakening
- Enthusiastic Christian movement sweeps through colonies.
- Preachers urge devotion to God.
- Many new churches arise.

Colonial Self-Government
- Monarch has limited powers.
- Colonial legislatures can make laws.
- Most white males can vote.

Colonial Society
- Men enjoy more power and privileges than women.
- Women have little or no role in public life.
- White settlers have more social equality than in Europe.

Slavery in the Colonies
- Thousands of enslaved Africans labor on plantations.
- Some slaves revolt, but these efforts fail.
- African American culture develops.

Atlantic Ocean

ENGLISH COLONIES

Gulf of Mexico

N
W   E
S

0   200 miles
0   200 km
Miller Cylindrical Projection

U.S. Events **1647** Massachusetts requires large towns to have public schools.

1663 First major slave revolt occurs in Gloucester, Virginia.

1700s Triangular slave trade brings increasing numbers of enslaved Africans to the colonies.

1650   **1675**   **1700**

World Events **1650s** Parliament passes Navigation Acts.

1689 English Bill of Rights is issued.

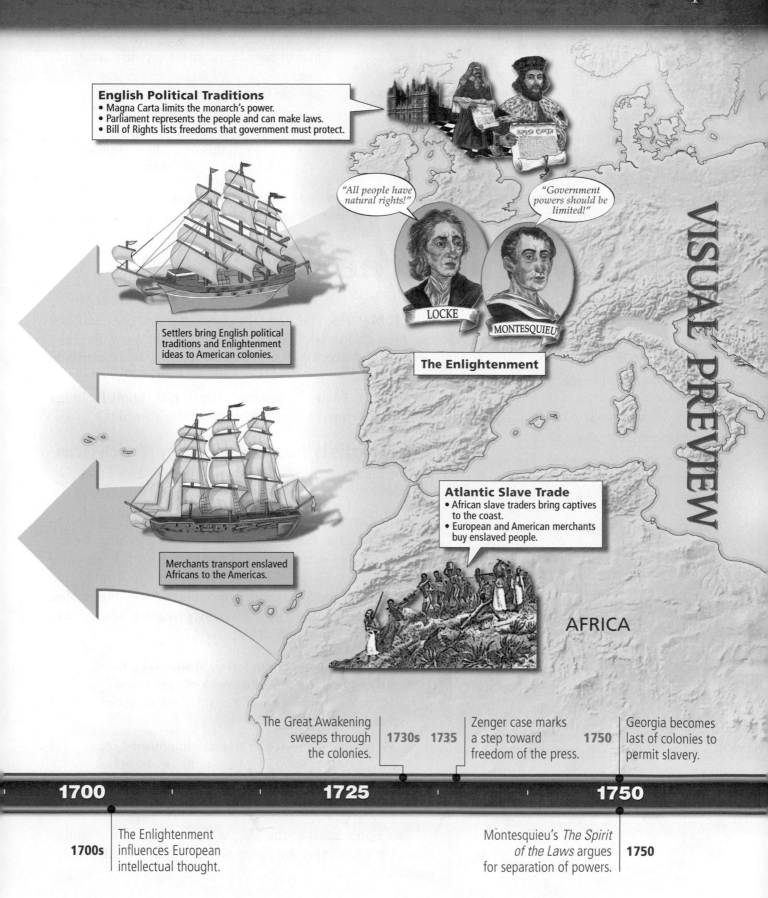

English Political Traditions
• Magna Carta limits the monarch's power.
• Parliament represents the people and can make laws.
• Bill of Rights lists freedoms that government must protect.

"All people have natural rights!"

"Government powers should be limited!"

LOCKE

MONTESQUIEU

The Enlightenment

Settlers bring English political traditions and Enlightenment ideas to American colonies.

Merchants transport enslaved Africans to the Americas.

Atlantic Slave Trade
• African slave traders bring captives to the coast.
• European and American merchants buy enslaved people.

AFRICA

VISUAL PREVIEW

The Great Awakening sweeps through the colonies.

1730s **1735**

Zenger case marks a step toward freedom of the press.

1750

Georgia becomes last of colonies to permit slavery.

1700   **1725**   **1750**

1700s The Enlightenment influences European intellectual thought.

Montesquieu's *The Spirit of the Laws* argues for separation of powers. **1750**

An Assembly Yearly Chosen

"For the well governing of this province . . ., there shall be an assembly yearly chosen, by the freemen thereof, to consist of four persons out of each country . . . [to] prepare bills in order to pass into laws; impeach criminals, and redress grievances. "

—William Penn, on the governing of Pennsylvania, 1710

◀ William Penn (right) receives the charter for Pennsylvania from King Charles II.

Governing the Colonies

Objectives

- Explain how English political traditions influenced the 13 colonies.
- Describe the responsibilities of early colonial governments.
- Identify John Peter Zenger's role in establishing freedom of the press.
- Understand how the Navigation Acts affected the colonies' economy.

Reading Skill

Use Word Clues to Analyze Meaning
When you encounter an unfamiliar word, look for clues within the word itself. For example, to understand the term *notable*, the familiar word *note* is helpful. If *note* means "to notice or remember," then *notable* may mean "worth remembering or noticing." Also, consider whether the word seems to be a verb, an adjective, or a noun.

Key Terms

legislature
bill of rights
habeas corpus

freedom of the press
libel

Why It Matters The New England, the Middle, and the Southern colonies developed in some unique ways. But they were all English colonies, and they therefore shared a common English heritage.

? Section Focus Question: How did English ideas about government and trade affect the colonies?

The English Parliamentary Tradition

The English colonists brought with them the idea that they had political rights. This idea was rooted in English history.

Magna Carta In 1215, English nobles forced King John to sign the Magna Carta, the Latin name meaning "great charter." The Magna Carta was the first document to place restrictions on an English ruler's power. It limited the monarch's right to levy taxes without consulting the nobles. It also protected the right to own private property and guaranteed the right to trial by jury:

"31. Neither we nor our [officials] shall take, for our castles or for any other work of ours, wood which is not ours, against the will of the owner of that wood. . . .

39. No free man shall be taken or imprisoned . . . except by the lawful judgment of his peers, or by the law of the land. "

—Magna Carta

The rights listed in the Magna Carta were at first limited to nobles. Over time, the rights were extended to all English citizens.

Parliament Under the Magna Carta, nobles formed a Great Council to advise the king. This body developed into the English Parliament (PAHR luh mehnt). Parliament was a two-house legislature. A **legislature** is a group of people who have the power to make laws. The House of Lords was made up of nobles, most of whom inherited their titles. Members of the House of Commons were elected. Only a few rich men and landowners had the right to vote for the House of Commons.

Parliament's greatest power was the right to approve new taxes. No monarch could raise taxes without the consent of Parliament. This "power of the purse" gave Parliament a degree of control over the monarch.

In the 1640s, power struggles between King Charles I and Parliament led to the English Civil War. Parliamentary forces eventually won the war, executed the king, and briefly ruled England. In 1660, the monarchy was restored. Still, Parliament <u>retained</u> its traditional rights.

English Bill of Rights An event in 1688 further boosted parliamentary power. Parliament removed King James II from the throne and invited his daughter Mary and her husband William to rule England. This event was called the Glorious Revolution. In 1689, King William and Queen Mary signed the English Bill of Rights. A **bill of rights** is a written list of freedoms that a government promises to protect.

Vocabulary Builder
<u>retain</u> (ree TAYN) **v.** to keep

English Bill of Rights

These selections from the English Bill of Rights deal with the powers of Parliament:

4. **❝**That levying money for or to the use of the crown . . . without grant of Parliament . . . is illegal; . . .
6. That the raising or keeping a standing army within the kingdom in time of peace, unless it be with the consent of Parliament, is against the law; . . .
8. That election of members of Parliament ought to be free;
9. That the freedom of speech and debates or proceedings in Parliament ought not to be impeached [challenged] or questioned in any court or place out of Parliament.**❞**

—English Bill of Rights

William and Mary

Reading Primary Sources
Skills Activity

The English Bill of Rights was issued under William and Mary in 1689. It guaranteed the powers of Parliament and the basic rights of English citizens.

(a) Interpret a Primary Source Summarize item 4 in your own words.
(b) Draw Conclusions Why do you think Parliament included item 9 in the Bill of Rights?

The English Bill of Rights restated many of the rights granted by the Magna Carta, such as trial by jury. It upheld **habeas corpus,** the principle that a person cannot be held in prison without being charged with a specific crime. Finally, the Bill of Rights required that Parliament meet regularly and declared that no monarch could <u>levy</u> taxes or raise an army without the consent of Parliament.

☑**Checkpoint**   **How was the power of English monarchs limited?**

Colonial Self-Government

The legal rights that Englishmen had won over the centuries led the colonists to expect a voice in their government. The ideas of limited monarchy and representative government were dear to them. In their new land, colonists wanted to take part in governing themselves.

Colonial Legislatures As you have read, from 1619 the Virginia Company allowed the House of Burgesses to make laws for the Jamestown Colony. The House of Burgesses became the first legislature in English North America. Massachusetts colonists also set up a legislature called the General Court in 1629. Five years later, Massachusetts colonists gained the right to elect delegates to the General Court.

On the other hand, the English government gave William Penn outright ownership of Pennsylvania. The governor and a large council made laws that an assembly could only approve or reject. But the Pennsylvania colonists wanted to draw up laws themselves. In 1701, they forced Penn to agree that only the General Assembly could `make laws. The king could overturn laws passed by the General Assembly, but neither Penn nor his council had any part in lawmaking.

By 1760, every British colony in North America had a legislature of some kind. However, the legislatures still clashed at times with the colonial governors appointed by the king.

The Right to Vote In many ways, the colonies offered settlers greater political rights than they would have had in England. From 50 to 75 percent of white males in the American colonies could vote. This was a far greater percentage than in England.

Still, the right to vote did not extend to everyone in the colonies. English women—even those who owned property—could not vote in any colony. Neither could the Native Americans who still lived on land claimed by the colonists. Finally, no Africans, whether free or enslaved, could vote.

☑**Checkpoint**   **Which groups of people were permitted to vote in colonial elections? Which were not permitted to vote?**

Links Across Time

Making State Laws

1619 The House of Burgesses became the first colonial legislature. For the next 155 years, the Burgesses helped govern the affairs of the Virginia Colony.

1776 After the United States declared independence from Britain, Virginia replaced the House of Burgesses with the General Assembly. The other states also set up state legislatures to make laws.

Link to Today

State Legislatures Today There are 50 separate state legislatures operating in the United States. What issues do these lawmakers face?

For: State legislatures in the news
Visit: PHSchool.com
Web Code: mvc-1041

THE
New-York Weekly JOURNAL

Containing the freshest Advices, Foreign, and Domestick.

MUNDAY November 12, 1733.

There are two Sorts of Monarchies; an absolute and a limited one. In the first, the Liberty of the Press can never be maintained . . .

Penalty for Criticism
British authorities burned John Peter Zenger's *Journal* newspaper publications as a punishment for criticizing the governor. **Critical Thinking: Link Past and Present** *How did the jury's verdict in Zenger's trial help to pave the way for freedom of the press in the United States?*

Freedom of the Press

The colonists expected to enjoy the traditional rights of English subjects. A notable court case in 1735 helped establish another important right. This was **freedom of the press,** the right of journalists to publish the truth without restriction or penalty.

John Peter Zenger, publisher of the *New York Weekly Journal,* was arrested for printing a series of articles that criticized the governor. Zenger was charged with **libel,** or the publishing of statements that damage a person's reputation. Under modern American law, statements must be untrue in order to be considered libel. However, English law at the time punished writings that criticized the government—even if the statements were true.

At Zenger's trial, Zenger's lawyer, Andrew Hamilton, admitted that Zenger had printed the statements against the governor. However, Hamilton argued that the articles Zenger published were based on fact and, therefore, should not be considered libel. Hamilton told the jury:

> ❝By your verdict, you will have laid a noble foundation for securing to ourselves, our descendants, and our neighbors, the liberty both of exposing and opposing tyrannical power by speaking and writing truth.❞
>
> —Andrew Hamilton, in A Brief Narrative of the Case and Trial of John Peter Zenger

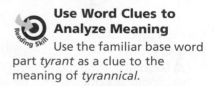

Use Word Clues to Analyze Meaning
Use the familiar base word part *tyrant* as a clue to the meaning of *tyrannical.*

The jurors agreed. They found that Zenger was not guilty of libel.

The Zenger case later helped establish a fundamental principle. A democracy depends on well-informed citizens. Therefore, the press has a right and responsibility to keep the public informed of the truth. Today, freedom of the press is recognized as a basic American liberty.

✔**Checkpoint** **Why was the Zenger case important?**

Regulating Trade

As you have read, under the theory of mercantilism, colonies existed in order to serve the economic needs of their parent country. They were a source of raw materials and a place to sell the home country's goods.

In 1651, the English Parliament passed the first of several Navigation Acts to support mercantilism. By these laws: (1) Shipments from Europe to English colonies had to go through England first. (2) Any imports to England from the colonies had to come in ships built and owned by British subjects. (3) The colonies could sell key products, such as tobacco and sugar, only to England. This helped create jobs for English workers.

In many ways, the Navigation Acts benefited the colonies. Colonial traders had a sure market for their goods in England. Also, the law contributed to a booming shipbuilding industry in New England.

Still, as colonial trade expanded, many colonists came to resent the Navigation Acts. In their view, the laws favored English merchants. Colonists felt that they could make more money if they were free to sell to foreign markets themselves. Some colonists got around the Navigation Acts by smuggling—that is, by importing and exporting goods illegally.

A Boston merchant counts up the profits from shipping.

✔**Checkpoint** **Why did many colonists resent the Navigation Acts?**

☆ **Looking Back and Ahead** As the 13 colonies grew, colonists established lawmaking bodies and developed the economy. In the early days, England's monarchy and Parliament influenced the decisions the colonies made. Yet, the colonies were far from England, and colonists were developing their own ideas. In the next section, you will look at the structure of colonial society.

Section 1 | **Check Your Progress**

Progress Monitoring Online
For: Self-test with instant help
Visit: PHSchool.com
Web Code: mva-1041

Comprehension and Critical Thinking

1. **(a) Identify** What political rights had England's citizens won by 1688?
   (b) Apply Information Why do you think those living in the 13 colonies believed they were entitled to those rights?

2. **(a) Recall** What were the Navigation Acts?
   (b) Identify Economic Costs and Benefits How did the Navigation Acts affect the colonial economy?

Reading Skill

3. **Use Word Clues to Analyze Meaning** Use its part of speech to help you analyze the meaning of *boomed* in this sentence: As a result of a law that allowed colonists to build their own ships, the shipbuilding industry in New England *boomed*.

Key Terms

Complete each of the following sentences so that the second part further explains the first part and clearly shows your understanding of the key term.

4. Based on English traditions, colonial legislatures _____.
5. The English Bill of Rights protected the rights of individuals, including habeas corpus, _____.
6. John Peter Zenger was accused of libel, _____.

Writing

7. List at least two examples from colonial society to support this main idea: English colonists believed they should have the same freedoms as English citizens.

▲ A colonial farm

A Cold North Wind

❝Wednesday. A fine clear morning with a cold north wind. My heart is burnt with anger and discontent, want of every necessary thing in life and in constant fear of gaping creditors consumes my strength and wastes my days. The horror of these things, . . . like to so many horse leeches, preys upon my vitals.❞

—Diary of Mary Cooper, Long Island, New York, 1769

Colonial Society

Objectives
- Learn about life on a colonial farm.
- Describe the roles of men, women, and children in colonial America.
- List the class differences that existed in colonial society.

🎯 Reading Skill

Use Sentence Clues to Analyze Meaning To find a word's meaning, you may examine other words within the same sentence for clues. For example, you may find familiar descriptive words near the unfamiliar word or find details that suggest a possible meaning. Ask: How is the unfamiliar word connected to a familiar word in the sentence? How is the word described?

Key Terms
extended family
apprentice
gentry
middle class
indentured servant

Why It Matters People in England's colonies enjoyed the traditional political rights of English citizens. This heritage, along with other shared characteristics, helped to create a unifying culture among the colonists.

❓ **Section Focus Question: What were the characteristics of colonial society?**

The Family in Colonial Times

The family played an important role in colonial America. Many people lived with their extended families. An **extended family** is a family that includes, in addition to the parents and their children, other members such as grandparents, aunts, uncles, and cousins.

On a Farm Most colonists lived on farms, where a large family was considered an advantage. Many hands were needed to operate a farm. Usually, farms were widely separated, often by dense forests. This made it necessary for families to be closely knit and self-sufficient. On a farm, each member of the family had many responsibilities. Family members helped plant, cultivate, and harvest crops. There were always fences to mend, animals to tend, and wood to chop.

By today's standards, farmhouses were not very comfortable. Most were made of wood and had few rooms. People sat on stools or benches and slept on planks. Some houses had mattresses of corncobs. There were few utensils, and they were crudely made. In the New England and the Middle colonies winters were cold, and the only source of heat in each house might be a fireplace in the kitchen room. On cold winter nights, the family might huddle around the fire telling stories and shelling nuts.

In a Town In the colonies' few cities and towns, it was easier for single people to sustain themselves. However, family ties were still held in the highest regard. In Puritan New England, single men and women were expected to live with a family as a servant or a boarder.

☑**Checkpoint** Why was a large family useful on a farm?

Men, Women, and Children

The lives of men and women differed. Even on the frontier, where families had to labor together to survive, men and women generally took on different roles. A North Carolina settler wrote:

> **❝**Men are generally of all trades, and women the like within their spheres. . . . Men are generally carpenters, joiners, wheelwrights, coopers, butchers, tanners, shoemakers, tallow-chandlers, watermen, and what not; women soap-makers, starch-makers, dyers, etc. He or she that cannot do all these things, or has not slaves that can, over and above all the common occupations of both sexes, will have but a bad time of it.**❞**
>
> —John Urmstone, letter, July 7, 1711

A husband and father controlled a family's income and property. Other family members were expected to accept his authority. In addition to fulfilling their home duties, men represented their families in public life as voters and, sometimes, as officeholders.

Roles of Women In colonial America, most women were expected to marry men chosen by their parents. In choosing, parents considered a man's property, his religion, and their own family interests. Romantic love was not considered the most important reason for marriage. Furthermore, when a woman married, her property and any money she might earn became her husband's. A woman often bore her husband many children. She was expected to be his faithful helper in every way.

Besides childcare, a woman had many <u>domestic</u> responsibilities. She cooked, did the laundry, and spun yarn into cloth that she made into family clothing. Outside, she took care of the garden, milked the cows, tended the chickens, churned butter, and preserved food. If the family had money, she might have help from servants.

Sometimes, however, the line blurred between women's work and men's work. On the western frontier, a woman might help plow or pitch hay. If she lived in a town, she might keep a shop or an inn, or work as a baker, a printer, or even an undertaker. Her husband or sons might help make cloth, if needed.

Women had little or no role in public life. They could not hold office or vote. On the western and southern frontiers, however, the rules were sometimes bent. For example, Mary Musgrove Matthews, a woman of English and Creek ancestry, advised Georgia governor James Oglethorpe on Indian affairs.

Vocabulary Builder
<u>domestic</u> (doh MEHS tihk)
adj. having to do with the home or household; pertaining to a country's internal affairs

COLONIAL WOMEN

Most women in colonial homes were required to handle a wide variety of tasks. In addition to domestic chores, women often worked in the fields along with the men. **Critical Thinking: Compare and Contrast** *How might a woman's responsibilities differ if she lived in a town? How might they be similar?*

History Interactive
Explore the Lives of Colonial Women
Visit: PHSchool.com
Web Code: mvl-1042

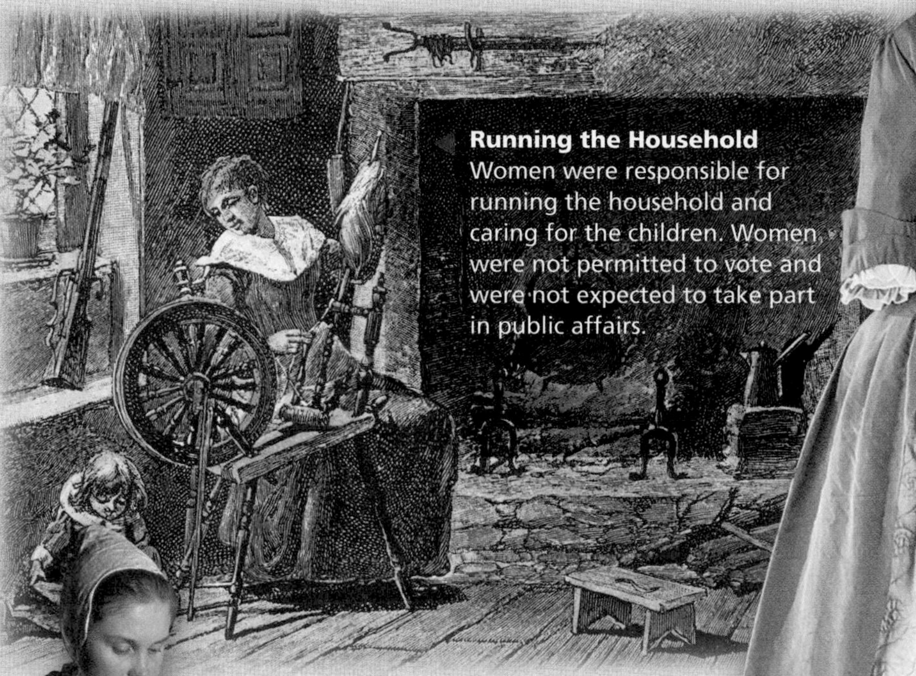

Running the Household
Women were responsible for running the household and caring for the children. Women were not permitted to vote and were not expected to take part in public affairs.

◀ **Preparing a Meal**
In colonial times, preparing meals from scratch took a great deal of time and effort.

Making Clothes
Women's duties included making most of the clothes worn by their families. Among the gentry, women might wear fancier dresses sewed by professional seamstresses.

Milking the Cows ▶
Families that owned cows had fresh milk to use and sell.

Colonial butter churn ▶

Children's dolls were made from elaborate materials or cornhusks.

Young People If they survived infancy, colonial children had about seven years before they were required to work. In these years, they could pass the time playing. Children played many games that are still familiar. Marbles, hopscotch, leapfrog, and jump rope were all popular.

The toys colonial children played with were usually homemade. Girls enjoyed dolls made of cornhusks and scraps of cloth, while boys built houses of corncobs. Sometimes, a spinning top would be fashioned out of a bit of leftover wood and string. Children whose families were well-to-do had fine dolls and toy soldiers that were made in Europe.

By the age of seven, most children had work to do. They might do household or farm chores, or, if they were poor, they might become servants in other families. On farms, children were expected to fetch water and wood and to help in the kitchen and in the fields. Older children had greater responsibilities. Boys were expected to work the fields with their fathers, while girls labored beside their mothers learning how to run a house. Parents believed that tasks like these prepared children for adult life.

Boys who were learning trades, such as making shoes or building furniture, began as apprentices. An **apprentice** is someone who learns a trade by working for someone in that trade for a certain period of time. The apprentice would live in the home of a master artisan. At the end of his apprenticeship, the young man was prepared to work independently.

☑**Checkpoint**   **How did the jobs of boys and girls differ?**

Social Classes

Many European colonists came to America hoping to build a better life than they could have in Europe. In England and other European countries, land was the main measure of wealth. Land in Europe, however, was in the hands of a relative few. America appeared to have land in abundance, offering immigrants the chance to own land. The possibility of owning land played a large part in the appeal of life in America.

In Europe, a person's <u>prospects</u> were determined by birth. Those who were born wealthy generally stayed wealthy. Those who were born poor had little opportunity to improve their station in life. By contrast, in colonial America there was more social equality among settlers—at least among white settlers. Still, there were many class distinctions.

The Gentry A group known as the gentry were the upper class of colonial society. The gentry included wealthy planters, merchants, ministers, royal officials, and successful lawyers. Prosperous artisans, like goldsmiths, were often considered gentry as well. The gentry were few in number, but they were the most powerful people. For example, in Virginia, some 50 plantation-owning families held most of the land and power.

Vocabulary Builder
<u>prospect</u> (PRAHS pehkt)
n. expectation; something to look forward to happening

In New York, wealthy Dutch estate owners lived in luxury. Their homes featured gold mirrors, clocks, richly carved furniture, and jewels. These things were far beyond the means of ordinary colonists.

Because many official jobs paid no salary, few but the gentry could afford to hold office. They felt that serving the community in public office was both their duty and their right, and most people agreed.

The Middle Class The great majority of colonists from Europe were what colonists called "the middling sort." Neither rich nor extremely poor, this **middle class** was made up of small planters, independent farmers, and artisans. Middle-class men could vote, and a few held office. This middle class was mostly white, but some of its members were of African descent. About 1 percent of African Americans were free during the colonial period.

The growth of the middle class gave the poor something to hope for and work for. The poor who were free might never be rich, but they could always maintain the hope that some day they would be middle class. In this way, the colonies were different from England and the rest of Europe. Not only could people move around the land, they could acquire property and move up the social scale.

Indentured Servants Lower on colonial America's social scale, and just above enslaved Africans, were farmhands and indentured servants. An **indentured servant** signed a contract to work from 4 to 10 years in the colonies for anyone who would pay for his or her ocean passage to the Americas. In the 1600s, most indentured servants came from England. In the 1700s, a growing number came from Ireland and Germany.

Reading Skill

Use Sentence Clues to Analyze Meaning Who belonged to the middle class in colonial times? What does *middle class* mean?

Life Among the Gentry

The gentry lived a more comfortable life than most colonists. Servants attended to many of their needs. **Critical Thinking: *Compare and Contrast*** *How do the comforts of the family in this picture compare to those of a middle-class family today?*

An indentured servant assists a colonial bricklayer.

During the time of service, indentured servants had few, if any, rights. They were bound to obey their masters, who could work them almost to death. Those who disobeyed or tried to run away risked being whipped or having time added to the service.

At the end of a term, an indentured servant received a set of clothes, tools, and 50 acres of land. About 1 indentured servant in 10 became a prosperous landowner. Another 1 in 10 became an artisan. The others either returned home to Europe or joined a class of landless, poor whites. The hardships they endured drove many poor whites to resent wealthy landowners.

Free African Americans Free people of African ancestry were never a large portion of the colonial population. By the time the first census was taken in 1790, there were nearly 60,000 free people of African ancestry, compared with more than 757,000 enslaved.

Free African Americans were allowed to own property, even in the South. This permitted them to become slaveholders. Some free blacks purchased relatives who were enslaved and set them free. Still, the lives of free African Americans were restricted. Most African American property owners were not allowed to vote or sit on juries.

✔**Checkpoint** How might one become a member of the middle class?

☆ **Looking Back and Ahead** Life in America offered more opportunities than did life in England. This was especially true for the poor and middle class. However, if indentured servants occupied the lowest level of white society in the English colonies, one group was even more disadvantaged. In the next section, you will look in detail at the enslaved Africans who were brought to America against their will.

Section 2 | Check Your Progress

Progress Monitoring ⊘nline
For: Self-test with instant help
Visit: PHSchool.com
Web Code: mva-1042

Comprehension and Critical Thinking

1. (a) **Summarize** Describe the responsibilities that children in colonial times were expected to meet.
(b) **Link Past and Present** How do these responsibilities differ from those of children today?
(c) **Draw Conclusions** How might you explain this difference?

2. (a) **Recall** Identify the social classes in colonial society.

(b) **Apply Information** Which two groups had the most privileges and opportunities? Which two groups had the least?

🎯 **Reading Skill**

3. **Use Sentence Clues to Analyze Meaning** Use sentence clues to analyze the meaning of *prospects* in the following sentence: In many countries, a person's *prospects* for success in life are determined by birth.

Key Terms

4. Write two definitions for each key term: extended family, apprentice, gentry, middle class, indentured servant. First, write a formal definition for your teacher. Second, write a casual definition for a classmate.

Writing

5. Write a paragraph describing the importance of work in colonial society.

Those Who Shall Be Whipped

❝ Be it enacted . . . that every . . . Negro or slave that shall be taken hereafter out of his master's plantation, without a ticket, or leave in writing, from his master or mistress . . . shall be whipped. ❞

—South Carolina slave law, 1712

◄ Enslaved people were brought to the West African coast for shipment to the Americas.

Slavery in the Colonies

Objectives

- Describe the conditions under which enslaved Africans came to the Americas.
- Explain why slavery became part of the colonial economy.
- Identify the restrictions placed on enslaved Africans in the colonies.
- Describe how African culture influenced American culture.

Reading Skill

Use Paragraph Clues to Analyze Meaning When you encounter an unfamiliar word, read the nearby sentences for clues. You may find clues in examples or descriptions. Sometimes a nearby sentence includes a contrast clue to what the word *does not* mean.

Key Terms

triangular trade   slave code
racism

Why It Matters Spanish and Portuguese settlers were the first to bring Africans to the Americas as a source of slave labor. Slavery spread to the colonies of other European countries. Millions of Africans were transported to the colonies against their will.

❓ **Section Focus Question: How did slavery develop in the colonies and affect colonial life?**

The Atlantic Slave Trade

Some scholars estimate that more than 10 million enslaved Africans were transported to the Americas between the 1500s and the 1800s. The Spanish and Portuguese brought the first Africans to the Americas. The British, Dutch, and French also entered the slave trade. In time, English colonists—especially from New England—were actively shipping enslaved Africans across the Atlantic.

Slave traders set up posts along the West African coast. Africans who lived along the coast made raids into the interior, seeking captives to sell to the Europeans. Bound at the leg and neck, captives were forced to march as far as 300 miles to the coast. Half of these captives died along the way.

Middle Passage Once they arrived at the coasts, captives were traded for guns and other goods. They were then loaded onto slave ships and transported across the Atlantic on a brutal voyage that became known as the Middle Passage.

To increase their profits, some slave-ship captains crammed the maximum number of captives on board. As many as 350 people might be bound together in a tiny space below deck, without light or air. Other captains provided better conditions, in the hope that more captives would survive in good health and fetch a higher price.

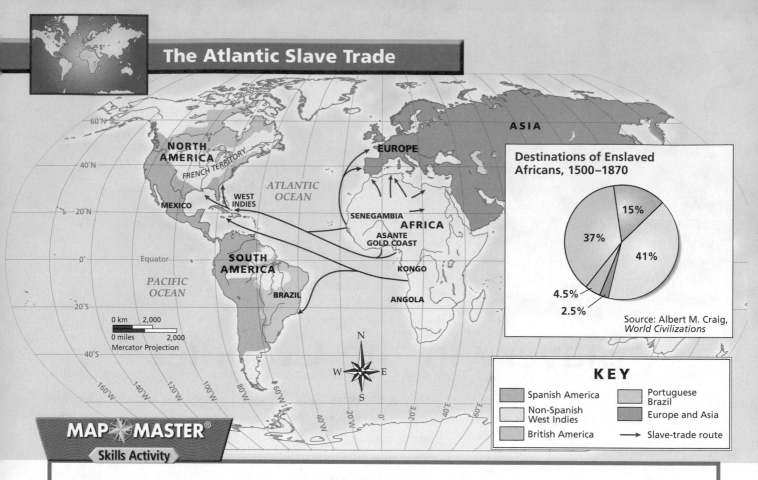

The Atlantic Slave Trade

Destinations of Enslaved Africans, 1500–1870

15%
37%
41%
4.5%
2.5%

Source: Albert M. Craig, *World Civilizations*

KEY

- Spanish America
- Non-Spanish West Indies
- British America
- Portuguese Brazil
- Europe and Asia
- → Slave-trade route

MAP MASTER
Skills Activity

The slave trade linked the Americas with Europe and western Africa.

(a) Evaluate Information How did British trade in slaves compare to that of the Spanish and Portuguese?

(b) Identify Costs Did the slave trade help or hurt western Africa? Explain your reasoning.

MapMaster Online

For: Interactive map
Visit: PHSchool.com
Web Code: mvp-1043

Olaudah Equiano told of being captured in western Africa when he was a boy. He later described the conditions aboard a slave ship:

> **Use Paragraph Clues to Analyze Meaning** Use the quoted paragraph's description and examples of *inconceivable* to analyze the word's meaning.

> "The closeness of the place, and the heat of the climate, added to the number in the ship, which was so crowded that each had scarcely room to turn himself, almost suffocated us. . . . The shrieks of the women, and the groans of the dying, rendered the whole a scene of horror almost inconceivable."
> —The Interesting Narrative of the Life of Olaudah Equiano

As a result of such conditions, from 15 to 20 percent of enslaved Africans died or committed suicide during the Middle Passage.

Once slave ships reached the Americas, healthy men, women, and children were put on the auction block. They might be sold one by one or in groups. Family members were often separated at this stage. The vast majority of those sold ended up on plantations in the Spanish colonies, Brazil, or the Caribbean. (See the pie chart above.) But for some 500,000 enslaved Africans, their final destination was British North America.

Triangular Trade By about 1700, slave traders in the British colonies had developed a regular routine, known as the triangular trade. The **triangular trade** was a three-way trade between the colonies, the islands of the Caribbean, and Africa.

On the first leg of the three-leg voyage, ships from New England carried fish, lumber, and other goods to the Caribbean islands, or West Indies. There, Yankee traders bought sugar and molasses, a dark syrup made from sugar cane. The ships then sailed back to New England, where colonists used the molasses and sugar to make rum.

On the second leg, ships carried rum, guns, and other goods from New England to West Africa. There, merchants traded the goods for enslaved Africans. On the final leg, ships carried their human cargo to the West Indies for sale. With the profits from selling enslaved Africans, traders bought more molasses.

Many New England merchants grew wealthy from the triangular trade. In doing so, they often disobeyed the Navigation Acts, which required them to buy only from English colonies. Because demand for molasses was so high, traders also made purchases from other European colonies in the West Indies. They then smuggled their cargoes into New England.

An advertisement for a colonial slave auction

☑ **Checkpoint** **What was the Middle Passage?**

Slavery in the Colonies

Slavery had existed since ancient times. However, in many cultures, slavery was not for life. In some early Christian societies, for example, slaves were freed if they became Christians. In many African societies, people captured in war were often enslaved for only a few years. Then, they were freed and became full members of the community. In the Americas, however, a harsher system of slavery developed over time.

Slavery Takes Root The first Africans who reached Jamestown may have been treated as servants. But by the late 1600s, ships were bringing growing numbers of enslaved Africans.

Why did slavery take root? One reason was the plantation system. The profits that could be made from tobacco and rice led planters to import thousands of enslaved Africans to work the fields. The southern economy came to depend on slavery.

Planters preferred slaves over servants. Indentured servants were <u>temporary</u>. Once their terms were over, they could go. Also, as conditions improved in England, fewer servants came to America.

Vocabulary Builder
<u>temporary</u> (TEM poh rehr ee)
adj. not permanent

Enslaved for Life As the need for cheap labor grew, colonies made slavery permanent. In 1639, Maryland passed a law stating that baptism did not lead to liberty. This meant people could be enslaved for life. In 1663, a Virginia court held that any child born to a slave was a slave too.

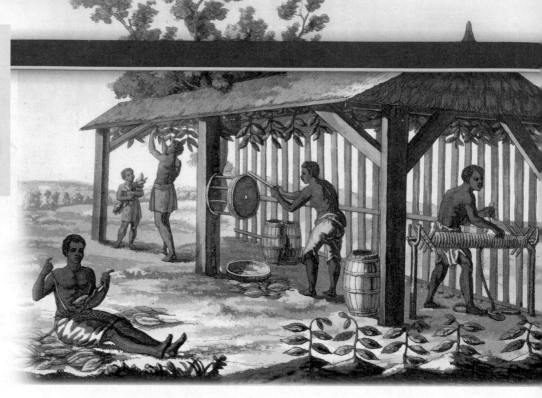

Slave Labor Preparing tobacco was one of the tasks performed by enslaved workers at a Virginia plantation in the 1700s. *Critical Thinking: Draw Conclusions How did the cultivation of crops such as tobacco and rice encourage the growth of slavery in North America?*

Vocabulary Builder
revolt (ree VOHLT) *v.* to rebel; to participate in an uprising

Early on, there were attempts to stop slavery. In 1652, Rhode Island passed the first antislavery law. However, it did not survive long, because Rhode Island shippers made high profits from the slave trade. Georgia had a ban on slavery until the 1750s and then lifted it. Slavery became legal in all the colonies.

Not every African in America was a slave, but slavery came to be restricted to people of African descent. Thus, slavery was linked to racism. **Racism** is the belief that one race is superior or inferior to another. Most English colonists believed themselves superior to Africans. Also, some colonists believed that they were helping Africans by introducing them to Christianity and European ways.

Resistance to Slavery As the number of enslaved people grew, whites began to worry that they would revolt. The first serious slave revolt took place in 1663, in Gloucester, Virginia. The rebels were betrayed, probably by an indentured servant, and the uprising failed. Soon, other revolts occurred in Connecticut and Virginia.

Fearing more trouble, colonial authorities wrote **slave codes**, or strict laws that restricted the rights and activities of slaves. Under the codes, enslaved people could not meet in large numbers, own weapons, or leave a plantation without permission. It also became illegal to teach enslaved people to read and write. Masters who killed enslaved people could not be tried for murder. Slave codes gave masters more control over enslaved Africans. It also made it harder for escaped slaves to survive.

The new laws did not stop resistance. In 1739, an enslaved Angolan named Jemmy led a revolt in South Carolina. He and his followers killed more than 20 whites before they were defeated. Revolts continued to flare up until slavery itself ended in 1865.

✓**Checkpoint** What was the purpose of slave codes?

African Cultural Influences

The lives of enslaved Africans differed greatly from colony to colony. Only 10 percent of the enslaved population lived north of Maryland. In cities of the North, they were often hired out to work as blacksmiths or house servants. On small farms, they might work alongside the owner. Over time, they might buy their freedom.

Even in the South, the lives of enslaved Africans varied. On rice plantations in South Carolina, Africans saw few white colonists. As a result, more than any other enslaved Africans, these workers kept the customs of West Africa. They reproduced the African grass baskets used to sift rice. They spoke Gullah, a special dialect that was created on the west coast of Africa during slave times. This dialect blended English and several African languages. Even today, some residents of the coastal South speak Gullah.

Enslaved Africans in colonies, such as Virginia and Maryland, were less isolated from white society. Still, many African customs survived. Craftsworkers in cities used African styles to create fine quilts, furniture, carved walking sticks, and other objects. The rhythm of drums used for communication by Africans found its way into American music. The banjo came from Africa as well. African folk tales became a part of American culture.

☑ **Checkpoint** **What cultural influences did Africans bring to America?**

⭐ **Looking Back and Ahead** In this section, we have seen how millions of Africans were transported to the colonies against their will. In the next section, we shall see how education and religion developed in colonial America.

Section 3 | **Check Your Progress**

Progress Monitoring Online
For: Self-test with instant help
Visit: PHSchool.com
Web Code: mva-1043

Comprehension and Critical Thinking

1. (a) Recall Why did fewer indentured servants come to America in the 1700s?
(b) Analyze Cause and Effect How did the plantation system and the lack of indentured servants affect the status of Africans in America?

2. (a) Identify Why did the Gullah dialect appear in South Carolina?
(b) Compare and Contrast In general, how did the experience of enslaved Africans in the North differ from that of enslaved Africans in the South?

Reading Skill

3. Use Paragraph Clues to Analyze Meaning Some paragraphs give you examples and descriptions of unfamiliar words. Reread the second paragraph under the heading "African Cultural Influences." Use paragraph clues to explain the meaning of *dialect* in that context. Explain the clues you used.

Key Terms

Answer the following questions in complete sentences that show your understanding of the key terms.
4. What was triangular trade?

5. How did racism affect the status of Africans in America?
6. Why did white colonists create slave codes?

Writing

7. Create an outline for an essay that discusses the geographic and economic factors that resulted in some colonies using slave labor more than other colonies.

Study Diligently

"Apply yourself, without delay, to the study of the law of nature. I would recommend to your perusal, Grotius, Puffendorf, Locke, Montesquieu, and Burlemaqui. . . . If you attend, diligently, to these [writers], you will not require any other."

—Alexander Hamilton, praising Enlightenment thinkers, 1775

◄ Harvard College, in Massachusetts, was the first college in the colonies.

The Spread of New Ideas

Objectives

- Describe the education colonial children received.
- Summarize the development of poetry and literature in colonial America.
- Explain how the Great Awakening affected the colonies.
- Explain how the colonies were affected by the spread of new ideas.

Reading Skill

Use Context to Determine Meanings When the clues you have tried do not work, broaden the context. Where else might you have encountered this word? Do you remember it from films or books? Was it defined in previous sections? Can you find examples of it elsewhere? Finally, imagine yourself in a situation like the one in which the word appears.

Key Terms and People

public school
dame school
Anne Bradstreet
Phillis Wheatley
Benjamin Franklin

Jonathan Edwards
natural rights
divine right
separation of powers

Why It Matters You have learned how English colonists shared certain cultural characteristics. In the 1700s, new ideas had a lasting impact on the colonists' thinking.

❓ **Section Focus Question: How did ideas about religion and government influence colonial life?**

The Importance of Education

To Puritans, education went hand in hand with religion. In early New England, everyone was expected to read the Bible.

Puritan Beginnings The Puritans passed laws to promote education. They required parents to teach their children and servants to read. Another law required every town with at least 50 families to start an elementary school. Every town with 100 families had to have a grammar school for older students.

These Massachusetts laws were the beginning of public schools in America. A **public school** is a school supported by taxes. Puritan schools were very different from the public schools of today, however. Puritan schools were run with both private and public money. In addition, Puritan education laws were not completely compulsory. Some towns paid a fine rather than set up a school. Laws that required all children to attend school did not begin until the late 1800s.

Colonial Schools Another difference between colonial schools and modern public schools is that colonial schools included instruction in religion. Most schools in the 1600s were under religious sponsorship. Schools in New Netherland (later New York) were run by the Dutch Reformed Church. Pennsylvania schools were run by the Quakers.

In addition to religion, colonial elementary schools taught basic skills such as reading, writing, and arithmetic. Many students learned lessons from a hornbook, a paddle-shaped board with a printed lesson on top, protected by a transparent piece of animal horn. The hornbook might have the ABCs, the Roman numerals, and the Lord's Prayer so that children could copy and memorize them. A reading book called the *New England Primer*, first published in the 1680s, became widely used.

In the South, people were separated by great distances, so there were few schools. Members of the gentry often hired private tutors to instruct their children. Children from poorer families often received no formal education at all.

Some colonial elementary schools admitted girls. Others taught them only in summers or when boys were not in school. Girls might also attend **dame schools**, schools that women opened in their homes to teach girls and boys to read and write.

Education for African Americans
Most colonial schools were restricted to white children. However, in New York, an Anglican church group ran a school for free African Americans, as well as for Native Americans and poor whites.

Some Quaker and Anglican missionaries taught enslaved people to read. After slave codes in the South outlawed this, some enslaved people passed along their learning in secret. Still others taught themselves from stolen or borrowed books.

Colonial Education
Young children were often educated in dame schools, such as the one shown. **Critical Thinking: Evaluate Information** *Look at the page from the* New England Primer, *below. What kinds of lessons does it include?*

Now the Child being entred in his Letters and Spelling, let him learn these and such like Sentences by Heart, whereby he will be both instructed in his Duty, and encouraged in his Learning.

The Dutiful Child's Promises,

I Will fear GOD, and honour the KING.
    I will honour my Father & Mother.
I will Obey my Superiours.
I will Submit to my Elders.
I will Love my Friends.
I will hate no Man.
I will forgive my Enemies, and pray to God for them.
I will as much as in me lies keep all God's Holy Commandments.

▲ Page from the the *New England Primer*

Hornbook ▶

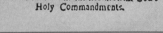

Upper Levels After elementary school, some boys went on to grammar school. Grammar schools were similar to modern high schools. They prepared boys for college. Students learned Greek and Latin, as well as geography, mathematics, and English composition.

The first American colleges were founded largely to educate men for the ministry. The Puritan general council <u>financed</u> what became Harvard College. Opening in 1638, Harvard was the first college in the English colonies. In 1693, colonists in Virginia founded the College of William and Mary, the first college in the South.

✓**Checkpoint** **How did education differ for girls and boys?**

Roots of American Literature

The earliest forms of colonial literature were sermons and histories. Books such as John Smith's *General History of Virginia* and William Bradford's *Of Plymouth Plantation* provided lively accounts of life in the first colonies.

Poetry The first colonial poet was Anne Bradstreet. Her book *The Tenth Muse, Lately Sprung Up in America* was first published in 1650, in England. It was not published in Boston until after her death. Bradstreet's poems, such as "Upon the Burning of Our House" and "To My Dear and Loving Husband," expressed the joys and hardships of life in Puritan New England.

A later poet, Phillis Wheatley, was an enslaved African in Boston. Her first poem was published in the 1760s, when she was about 14. Her works were in a scholarly style that was then popular in Europe.

Ben Franklin Perhaps the best-loved colonial writer was Benjamin Franklin. At age 17, Ben moved from Boston to Philadelphia and started a newspaper, the *Pennsylvania Gazette*. It became the most widely read newspaper in the colonies.

Franklin's most popular work was *Poor Richard's Almanack*, published every year from 1733 to 1753. The *Almanack* was full of pithy sayings that usually had a moral. These included "Eat to live, not live to eat" and "God helps them who help themselves." Franklin also published a vivid autobiography.

Franklin was far more than a writer. He was a businessman, community leader, scientist, inventor, and diplomat. He founded a library and a fire department, made discoveries about electricity, and invented such useful items as bifocal eyeglasses and a stove. As you will see, he also became one of the founders of the United States.

✓**Checkpoint** **How did Ben Franklin contribute to American literature?**

Vocabulary Builder
<u>finance</u> (Fī nans) **v.** to supply with money; to manage monetary situations

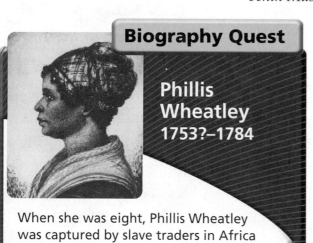

Biography Quest

Phillis Wheatley
1753?–1784

When she was eight, Phillis Wheatley was captured by slave traders in Africa and sent to Boston. But she was luckier than most enslaved Africans. The family she worked for educated her and gave her time to write.

Wheatley won fame as a poet and later gained her freedom. Sadly, her last years were full of hardship. She is recognized today as America's first poet of African descent.

Biography Quest **Online**

How did Wheatley meet George Washington?

For: The answer to the question about Wheatley

Visit: PHSchool.com

Web Code: mvd-1044

The Great Awakening

From the start, religion played a critical role in the 13 English colonies. In Plymouth and Massachusetts Bay, religious leaders set extensive rules on moral and religious matters. Even in colonies that were founded primarily for economic reasons, such as Jamestown, early laws required colonists to attend church regularly.

By the 1700s, rules on religion had become less strict in many of the colonies. The Puritan tradition gradually declined in New England. Still, churches remained centers of faith and community life in all of the colonies.

Religious Revival An emotion-packed Christian movement swept through the colonies in the 1730s and 1740s. This period of religious revival is called the Great Awakening. The Great Awakening began as a reaction against what some Christians saw as a decline of religious zeal in the colonies. Leaders such as Massachusetts preacher Jonathan Edwards called on people to examine their lives and commit themselves to God. In a famous sermon, Edwards warned sinners what would happen to them after they died unless they changed their ways and sought forgiveness:

> **❝**The God that holds you over the pit of hell, much as one holds a spider, or some loathesome insect, over a fire, abhors you, and is dreadfully provoked; his wrath towards you burns like fire; he looks upon you as worthy of nothing else, but to be cast into the fire.**❞**
>
> —Jonathan Edwards, Sinners in the Hands of an Angry God

Forceful preachers quickly spread the Great Awakening throughout the colonies. George Whitefield, an English minister, made several tours of the colonies. His listeners often wept with emotion. After a Whitefield visit to Philadelphia, Benjamin Franklin observed that "one could not walk thro' the Town in an Evening without Hearing Psalms sung in different Families of every Street."

Impact of the Great Awakening The Great Awakening led to the rise of many new churches. Methodists and Baptists, which had been small sects or groups, grew quickly. The Presbyterian, Dutch Reformed, and Congregationalist churches split between those who followed the new movement and those who did not. In time, the growth of new churches led to more tolerance of religious differences in the colonies.

Use Context to Determine Meaning Use the clues in the surrounding sentences and your own knowledge about colonial life to determine the meaning of the word *extensive*.

Religious Awakening
Traveling preachers, such as English evangelist George Whitefield (below), provoked a broad religious revival in the 1730s and 1740s. **Critical Thinking: *Draw Conclusions*** *Why might the Great Awakening have unsettled many prominent church leaders of the time?*

Divine Right Versus Natural Rights

	Divine Right	Natural Rights
Where does the right to govern come from?	From God to the ruler	From the people
Where do people's rights come from?	From the ruler	From God to the people
What happens if a government violates people's rights?	People must obey ruler	People can change their government

Reading Charts
Skills Activity

Did the right to rule come from the will of God or from the people? The answer to this question would alter the course of history in nations around the world.

(a) **Read a Chart** Which column represents the views of John Locke?

(b) **Draw Conclusions** Which of those views would be most attractive to the American colonists? Explain.

Vocabulary Builder
reinforce (ree ihn FORS) **v.** to make stronger; to strengthen; to make more effective

The Great Awakening was one of the first national movements in the colonies. It <u>reinforced</u> democratic ideas. People thought that if they could decide on their own how to worship God, they could decide how to govern themselves.

✔**Checkpoint** How did the Great Awakening affect American society?

The Enlightenment

Starting in the late 1600s, a group of European thinkers came to believe that all problems could be solved by human reason. They ushered in a new intellectual movement that became known as the Enlightenment. Enlightenment thinkers looked for "natural laws" that governed politics, society, and economics. The Enlightenment reached its height in France in the mid-1700s. However, some of its key ideas came from an Englishman, John Locke.

Locke In 1690, Locke published *Two Treatises on Government*. In this influential work, Locke argued that people have certain **natural rights,** that is, rights that belong to every human being from birth. These rights include life, liberty, and property. According to Locke, these rights are inalienable, meaning that they cannot be taken away.

Locke challenged the idea of divine right. **Divine right** is the belief that monarchs get their authority to rule directly from God. According to this belief, any rights that people have come to them from the monarch. By contrast, Locke stated that natural rights came from God. He argued that people formed governments in order to protect their rights. They give up some individual freedoms but only to safeguard the rights of the community.

Locke's reasoning led to a startling conclusion. Because government exists to protect the rights of the people, if a monarch violates those rights, the people have a right to overthrow the monarch. This idea would later shape the founding of the United States.

Montesquieu A French thinker, the Baron de Montesquieu (MON tehs kyoo), also influenced American ideas. In his 1748 book *The Spirit of the Laws*, Montesquieu argued that the powers of government should be clearly defined and limited. Furthermore, he favored separation of powers, or division of the power of government into separate branches. Separation of powers, he said, protects the rights of the people because it keeps any individual or group from gaining too much power.

Montesquieu suggested that government should be divided into three branches: a legislative branch to make laws, an executive branch to enforce the laws, and a judicial branch to make judgments based on the law. He wrote:

Montesquieu

> **"**There would be an end to everything, were the same man or the same body . . . to exercise those three powers, that of enacting laws, that of executing the public resolutions, and of trying the causes of individuals.**"**
>
> —Baron de Montesquieu, *The Spirit of the Laws*

As you will see, this division of power would become the basis of government in the United States.

☑ **Checkpoint** **What was the goal of Enlightenment thinkers?**

⭐ **Looking Back and Ahead** By the 1770s, educated colonists had come to accept the idea that they were born with certain natural rights. As you will see in the next chapter, this belief would set the stage for conflict with the English king and Parliament.

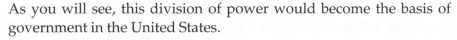

Section 4 | **Check Your Progress**

Progress Monitoring Online
For: Self-test with instant help
Visit: PHSchool.com
Web Code: mva-1044

Comprehension and Critical Thinking

1. **(a) Recall** What role did religion play in colonial schools?
   (b) Support Generalizations Find at least two facts to support the following generalization: Education was important to the colonists.

2. **(a) Describe** What was the Great Awakening?

(b) Analyze Cause and Effect What was one effect of the Great Awakening?

🎯 **Reading Skill**

3. **Use Context to Determine Meaning** Reread the quotation by Jonathan Edwards in this section. Use context to determine the meaning of *abhors*. Explain the clues you used.

Key Terms

4. Write two definitions for each key term: public school, dame school, natural rights, separation of powers. First, write a formal definition for your teacher. Second, write a definition in everyday English for a classmate.

Writing

5. Write two to three closing sentences for an essay on the Enlightenment. Focus particularly on the impact of this movement.

How I Became a Printer
by Benjamin Franklin

Prepare to Read

Introduction

It took Benjamin Franklin 17 years to finish his *Autobiography,* and it was not published until after his death. Today, it is recognized as a classic of early American literature. The book covers only the first 51 years of Franklin's long life, so it does not tell of his later role in the founding of the United States.

Reading Skill

Analyze Autobiographical Approach Writers of autobiographies often convey their attitudes and beliefs as they are conveying a story. As you read, look for clues about Franklin's attitude toward the government. Do you think Franklin approves of the Assembly's actions against James?

Vocabulary *Builder*

As you read this literature selection, look for the following underlined words:

chandler (CHAND ler) *n.* person who makes or sells candles, soap, and other items made from the fat of animals

tedious (TEE dee uhs) *adj.* boring

censure (SEHN sher) *v.* to condemn or criticize

admonish (ad MAHN ihsh) *v.* warn

Background

Tithing (TĪTH ing) is the practice of giving one tenth of one's earnings to the church annually. Here, Franklin jokingly implies that his father wished to follow this same tradition by giving the tenth of his children, Benjamin, rather than a tenth of his earnings.

I was put to the grammar-school at eight years of age, my father intending to devote me, as the tithe of his sons, to the service of the Church. My early readiness in learning to read (which must have been very early, as I do not remember when I could not read), and the opinion of all his friends, that I should certainly make a good scholar, encouraged him in this purpose of his. . . . But my father, in the mean time, from the view of the expense of a college education, which having so large a family he could not well afford . . . took me from the grammar-school, and sent me to a school for writing and arithmetic. . . . At ten years old I was taken home to assist my father in his business, which was that of tallow-<u>chandler</u> and soapboiler. . . . Accordingly, I was employed in cutting wick for the candles, filling the dipping mold and the molds for cast candles, attending the shop, going of errands etc.

I disliked the trade, and had a strong inclination for the sea, but my father declared against it. However, living near the water, I was much in and about it, learned early to swim well, and to manage boats; and when in a boat or a canoe with other boys, I was commonly allowed to govern, especially in any case of difficulty; and upon other occasions I was generally a leader among the boys. . . .

From a child I was fond of reading, and all the little money that came into my hands was ever laid out in books. . . .

This bookish inclination at length determined my father to make me a printer, though he had already one son (James) of that profession. In 1717 my brother James returned from England with a press and letters to set up his business in Boston. I . . . signed the indenture when I was yet by twelve years old. I was to serve as an apprentice till I was twenty-one years of age, only I was to be allowed journey-man's wages during the last year. In a little time I made great proficiency in the business, and became a useful hand to my brother.

Though a brother, he considered himself as my master, and me as his apprentice, and accordingly, expected the same services from me as he would from another, while I thought he demeaned me too much in some he required of me, who from a brother expected more indulgence. Our disputes were often brought before our father, and I fancy I was either generally in the right, or else a better pleader, because the judgment was generally in my favor. But my brother was passionate, and had often beaten me, which I took extremely amiss; and thinking my apprenticeship very <u>tedious</u>, I was continually wishing for some opportunity of shortening it, which at length offered in a manner unexpected.

One of the pieces in our newspaper on some political point, which I have now forgotten, gave offense to the Assembly. He [James] was taken up, <u>censured</u>, and imprisoned for one month, by the speaker's warrant, I suppose, because he would not discover [reveal] his author. I too was taken up and examined before the council; but, though I did not give them any satisfaction, they contented themselves with <u>admonishing</u> me, and dismissed me. . . .

During my brother's confinement, which I resented a good deal, notwithstanding our private differences, I had the management of the paper; and I made bold to give our rulers some rubs in it, which my brother took very kindly. . . . My brother's discharge was accompanied with an order of the House (a very odd one), that "James Franklin should no longer print the paper called the New England Courant."

There was a consultation held in our printing-house among his friends, . . . it was finally concluded on as a better way, to let it be printed for the future under the name of BENJAMIN FRANKLIN; . . . the contrivance was that my old indenture should be returned to me, with full discharge on the back of it, to be shown on occasion, but to secure to him the benefit of my service, I was to sign new indentures for the remainder of the term, which were to be kept private. A very flimsy scheme it was; however, it was immediately executed, and the paper went on accordingly, under my name for several months.

From *The Autobiography of Benjamin Franklin,*
by Benjamin Franklin. © 2003. Yale University Press.

☑ **Checkpoint** **What plan did Franklin's brother approve to keep publishing the newspaper after his confinement?**

Ben Franklin (center)

Analyze Autobiographical Approach

Throughout the story, Franklin conveys his feelings about his brother. When his brother is imprisoned, Franklin takes action by giving the Assembly "some rubs in." Do you think he does this more out of family loyalty or because he supports a free press?

Analyze **LITERATURE**

Benjamin Franklin disliked being his brother's apprentice. Imagine that you are Franklin. Write a letter to the *New England Courant* expressing your opinion about the fairness or unfairness of being made an apprentice at the age of 12.

If you liked this passage, you might want to read *The Printer's Apprentice* by Stephen Krensky, illustrated by Madeline Sorel. Yearling. 1996.

Compare and Contrast

21st Century Learning

A Venn diagram is a graphic organizer that shows similarities and differences. You can use a Venn diagram to compare and contrast information about any two items, including time periods, historical events, people, and ideas. Aspects of the two items that are different appear outside the shared area where the circles intersect. Aspects that are similar are listed within the shared area.

Copy and complete the Venn diagram below to compare and contrast information about colonial women and women today. Use information that follows the subheading "Roles of Women" in Chapter 4, Section 2, and your own knowledge about contemporary American women.

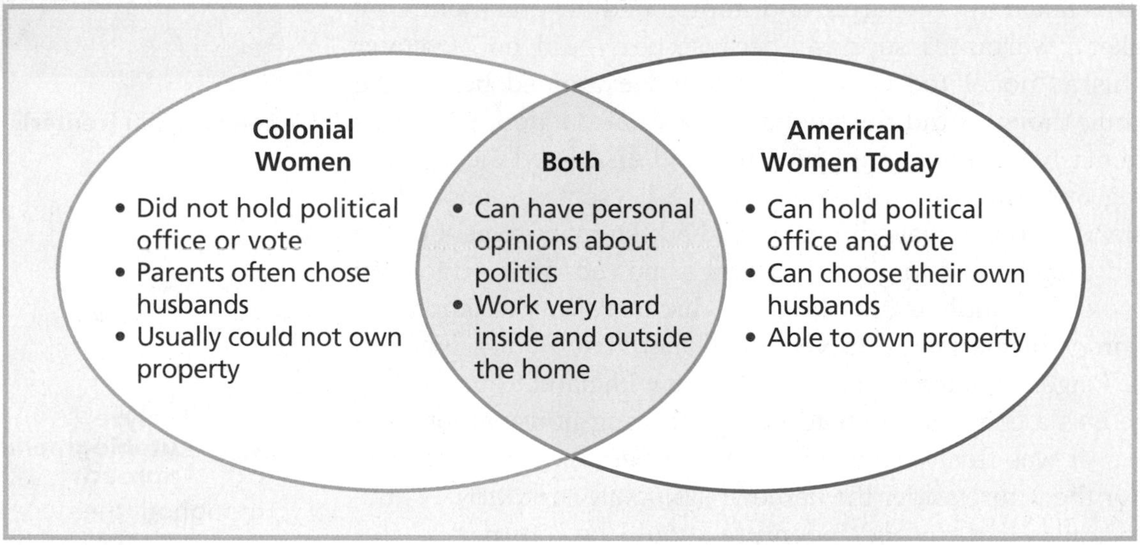

Colonial Women
- Did not hold political office or vote
- Parents often chose husbands
- Usually could not own property

Both
- Can have personal opinions about politics
- Work very hard inside and outside the home

American Women Today
- Can hold political office and vote
- Can choose their own husbands
- Able to own property

Learn the Skill

Use these steps to create a Venn diagram.

1 **Identify the subject.** Decide what items you will compare and contrast on the Venn diagram. Write a title summarizing the subject of the organizer.

2 **Identify the differences.** Write the differences between the items being compared in each circle under the appropriate heading.

3 **Identify the similarities.** Write the similarities between the items being compared in the intersecting circle under the heading "Both."

4 **Draw a conclusion about the subject.** Use the information on the Venn diagram to write a sentence summarizing the conclusions.

Practice the Skill

Answer the following questions about the Venn diagram on this page.

1 **Identify the subject.** What is a good title for the Venn diagram on this page?

2 **Identify the differences.** What is a difference between colonial women and American women today?

3 **Identify the similarities.** What is a similarity between colonial women and American women today?

4 **Draw a conclusion about the subject.** Based on the information in the Venn diagram, what is one conclusion you can draw about colonial women and American women today?

Apply the Skill

See the Review and Assessment at the end of this chapter.

How did colonial life take shape?

Section 1
Governing the Colonies

- The Magna Carta and English Bill of Rights guaranteed the rights of English citizens.
- By 1760, each of the 13 colonies had a legislature to make laws.
- The trial of John Peter Zenger helped establish the idea of freedom of the press.
- England passed the Navigation Acts to regulate colonial trade.

Section 2
Colonial Society

- In colonial society, men, women, and children had clearly defined roles.
- Colonial America offered poor and middle-class whites the opportunity to own land and improve their social status.

Section 3
Slavery in the Colonies

- More than 10 million Africans were transported to the Americas in the Atlantic slave trade.
- The plantation economy of the South became dependent on the labor of enslaved African Americans.
- Slave codes did not stop occasional slave revolts.

Section 4
The Spread of New Ideas

- Education during colonial times was influenced by religion.
- Colonial era literature included poetry, sermons, and popular writing.
- The Great Awakening of the 1730s and 1740s led to the rise of new churches.
- Enlightenment thinkers influenced ideas about government and natural rights.

? Exploring the Essential Question

Use the online study guide to explore the essential question.

Section 1
How did English ideas about government and trade affect the colonies?

Section 2
What were the characteristics of colonial society?

Chapter 4 Essential Question
How did colonial life take shape?

Section 4
How did ideas about religion and government influence colonial life?

Section 3
How did slavery develop in the colonies and affect colonial life?

Key Terms

Complete each of the following sentences so that the second part further explains the first part and clearly shows your understanding of the key term.

1. All colonies in British North America had legislatures, _____.

2. The English Bill of Rights guaranteed habeas corpus, _____.

3. On colonial farms, it was important to have an extended family because _____.

4. Many people came to the colonies from Europe as indentured servants, _____.

5. After a time, slave owners enforced slave codes _____.

Comprehension and Critical Thinking

6. **(a) Identify** What rights did the Magna Carta and the English Bill of Rights guarantee?
(b) Draw Conclusions Why do you think colonists believed they were entitled to the rights guaranteed by the Magna Carta and the English Bill of Rights?
(c) Link Past and Present Which of these rights do Americans still enjoy today?

7. **(a) Describe** What was life like on a colonial farm?
(b) Compare and Contrast How were the responsibilities of men and women similar? How were they different?

8. **(a) Identify** What were the various classes into which colonial society was divided?
(b) Compare In what ways were the poor better off in America than in Europe?
(c) Explain Problems What were some of the limitations placed on free African Americans? Explain.

9. **(a) Recall** What was the triangular trade?
(b) Identify Benefits Which groups benefited from this trade?
(c) Identify Costs Which groups experienced hardships because of this trade?

10. **(a) Describe** What were colonial schools like?
(b) Frame Questions List at least three questions you would ask a colonial school-age child.

History Reading Skill

11. **Determine Meaning From Context** Find an unfamiliar word in Chapter 4 and use context clues to analyze its meaning. Explain the clues you used.

Writing

12. Write two paragraphs summarizing how the ideas and customs that the colonists brought from England began to change once they left their homeland. Focus on the social and political changes.

Your paragraphs should:
- begin with a thesis statement that expresses a main idea;
- include the ideas that the colonists brought from England;
- list and discuss the changes that resulted in the colonists changing their views;
- end by stating how the colonists changed.

13. **Write a Narrative:**
You are a teacher in a colonial school. Name the colony in which you teach. Describe the school. How many students do you have? What are your goals for your students?

Skills for Life

Compare and Contrast
Review what you have learned about the lives of indentured servants and the lives of enslaved Africans in colonial America. Create a Venn diagram showing some of the similarities and differences. Then, answer the following questions.

14. Identify two differences between enslaved Africans and indentured servants.

15. What was one way in which the life of an indentured servant was similar to the life of an enslaved person?

16. Agree or disagree with the following conclusion: The life of an indentured servant was just as harsh as the life of an enslaved African. Give reasons for your answer.

Test Yourself

1. **The colonies offered the right to vote to**

   A Native Americans.

   B African Americans.

   C white male property owners.

   D any colonist born in England.

2. **One reason that colonists disliked the Navigation Acts was that the laws**

   A prevented colonial merchants from selling their goods in England.

   B led to a decline in the shipbuilding industry.

   C created manufacturing jobs in England.

   D cut colonial merchants off from profitable foreign markets.

3. **What was one result of the Great Awakening in the 13 colonies?**

   A It reinforced the principle of freedom of the press.

   B It led to the decline of the Puritan Church in New England.

   C It led to the formation of new churches.

   D It encouraged colonists to accept royal authority.

4. **According to John Locke, natural rights**

   A cannot be taken away.

   B are granted by the king or queen.

   C apply only to English citizens.

   D apply only to the gentry.

Document-Based Questions

Task: Look at Documents 1 and 2, and answer their accompanying questions. Then, use the documents and your knowledge of history to complete the following writing assignment:

   Write an essay about the treatment of enslaved Africans on the journey to America. How does Document 1 support Equiano's statements about conditions during the journey?

Document 1: These diagrams show the loading plan of a slave ship during the Middle Passage from Africa to the Americas. *Based on this picture, describe the way enslaved Africans were treated on the journey.*

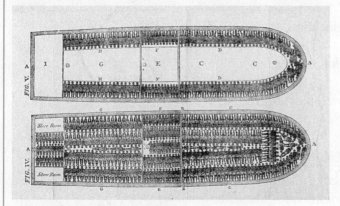

Document 2: Olaudah Equiano, an African who survived the voyage, wrote this description of his experiences. *What were two causes of suffering on the ship?*

"The closeness of the place and the heat of the climate, added to the number in the ship, which was so crowded that each had scarcely room to turn himself, almost suffocated us. . . . The air soon became unfit for respiration . . . and brought on a sickness among the slaves, of which many died. The shrieks of the women, and the groans of the dying, rendered the whole a scene of horror almost inconceivable. Happily perhaps for myself I was soon reduced so low here that it was thought necessary to keep me almost always on deck; and from my extreme youth I was not put in fetters. In this situation I expected every hour to share the fate of my companions, some of whom were almost daily brought upon deck at the point of death, which I began to hope would soon put an end to my miseries. Often did I think many of the inhabitants of the deep much more happy than myself; I envied them the freedom they enjoyed, and as often wished I could change my condition for theirs.

   Every circumstance . . . served only to render my state more painful, and heighten my . . . opinion of the cruelty of the whites. One day they had taken a number of fishes, and when they had killed and satisfied themselves with as many as they thought fit . . . they tossed the remaining fish into the sea again, although we begged and prayed for some."

How did the colonists, with strong roots in the past, develop their own way of life?

DIRECTIONS: Analyze the following documents on the colonial period. Answer the questions that accompany each document or set of documents. You will use your answers to build an answer to the unit question.

HISTORIAN'S CHECKLIST

WHO produced the document?

WHERE was it made?

WHEN was it produced?

WHY was it made and for what audience?

WHAT is its viewpoint?

HOW does it connect to what I've learned?

WHY is the document important?

1 Religion

document

"No person or persons whatsoever within this province . . . professing to believe in Jesus Christ, shall from henceforth be in any way troubled, molested, or discountenanced for or in respect of his or her religion, nor in the free exercise thereof within this province . . . nor in any way compelled to the belief or exercise of any other religion against his or her consent."

—*Maryland, Toleration Act, 1649*

How did religion influence the colonies?

2 Ancient Greece and Rome

document

"Greek and Latin . . . literatures informed the educations . . . of 18th-century Americans, [but] few studies have fully attempted to describe and explore the formative role of the classics for the leaders of the American Revolution and the framers of the Constitution. . . . Historian Richard argues compellingly that the classics played a definitive role in the minds of figures such as Jefferson, Adams, Madison, Washington, and many others, providing not only theories of constitutional government, human nature, and virtue but even models for emulation"

—*T.L. Cooksey, reviewing* The Founders and the Classics: Greece, Rome, and the American Enlightenment *by Carl Richard*

What did 18th century Americans learn from ancient Greece and Rome?

3 Interaction With Native Americans

document

> "Afterwards they ... began to plant their corn, in which service Squanto stood them in great stead, showing them both the manner how to set it, and after how to [cultivate] and tend it. Also he told them, [unless] they got fish and set with it in these old grounds it would come to nothing. **"**
>
> —*William Bradford,*
> Of Plymouth Plantation, 1630

How did Europeans and Native Americans both benefit from their encounter with each other? What problems arose as a result of their meeting?

4 Spanish Texas

document

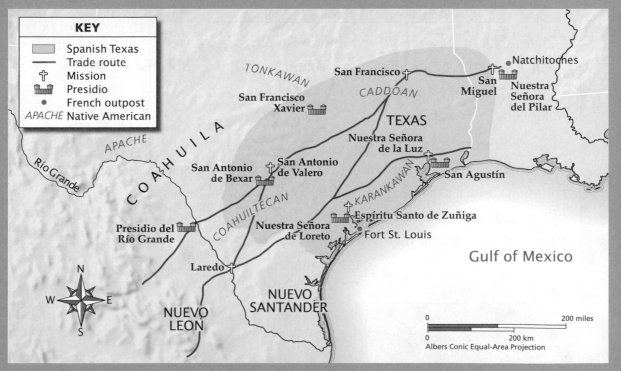

KEY
- Spanish Texas
- Trade route
- † Mission
- Presidio
- • French outpost
- *APACHE* Native American

TONKAWAN · San Francisco † · Natchitoches
CADDOAN · San Miguel · Nuestra Señora del Pilar
San Francisco Xavier
TEXAS
San Antonio de Bexar · San Antonio de Valero · Nuestra Señora de la Luz · San Agustín
APACHE
Río Grande
COAHUILA
COAHUILTECAN
KARANKAWAN
Presidio del Río Grande · Nuestra Señora de Loreto · Espíritu Santo de Zuñiga · Fort St. Louis
Laredo †
NUEVO LEON
NUEVO SANTANDER
Gulf of Mexico

0 — 200 miles
0 — 200 km
Albers Conic Equal-Area Projection

Why did the Spanish build missions and presidios in their colonies?

☞ **Go On**

131

Rights of the English

"Those rights and privileges which I call English, and which are the proper birth-right of Englishmen . . . may be reduced to these three.

I. An ownership, and undisturbed possession: that what they have is rightly theirs, and no body's else.

II. A voting of every law that is made, whereby that ownership or propriety may be maintained.

III. An influence upon, and a real share in, that judicatory power that must apply every such law; which is the ancient, necessary and laudable use of juries. . . . That these have been the ancient and undoubted rights of Englishmen, as three great roots, under whose spacious branches the English people have been wont to shelter themselves against the storms of arbitrary government, I shall endeavor to prove."

—William Penn, "England's Present Interest Considered," 1675

What were some rights that colonists expected as British citizens?

Self-Government

"There shall be in every colony one constable to be chosen annually, by the freeholders of the colony. . . . The election of the subordinate annual officers shall be also in the free-holders of the colony.

All towns incorporate shall be governed by a mayor, twelve aldermen, and twenty-four of the common council. The said common council shall be chosen by the present householders of the said town; the aldermen shall be chosen out of the common council; and the mayor out of the aldermen."

—The Fundamental Constitutions of Carolina, 1669

How did the colonists begin the tradition of self-government?

document 7 Slavery

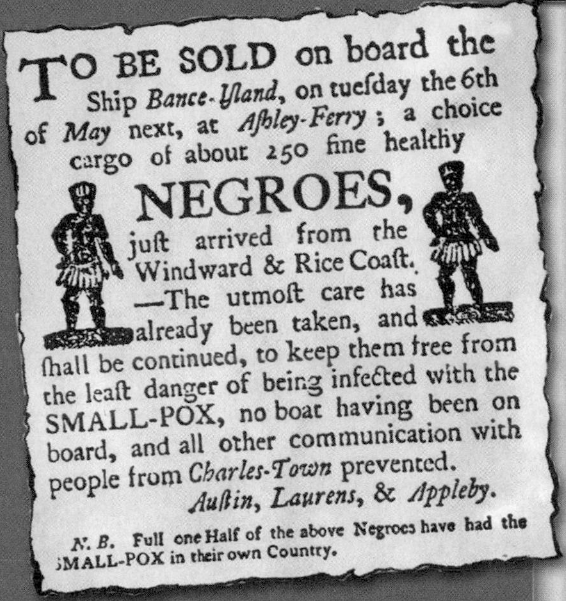

TO BE SOLD on board the Ship *Bance-Yland*, on tueſday the 6th of *May* next, at *Aſhley-Ferry*; a choice cargo of about 250 fine healthy

NEGROES,

juſt arrived from the Windward & Rice Coaſt. —The utmoſt care has already been taken, and ſhall be continued, to keep them free from the leaſt danger of being infected with the SMALL-POX, no boat having been on board, and all other communication with people from *Charles-Town* prevented.

Auſtin, Laurens, & Appleby.

N. B. Full one Half of the above Negroes have had the SMALL-POX in their own Country.

How did slavery affect society in the southern colonies?

document 8 Enlightenment

"The people, in whom the supreme power resides, ought to have the management of everything within their reach: that which exceeds their abilities must be conducted by their [representatives]. But they cannot . . . have their [representatives] without the power of [choosing] them. . . . The people are extremely well qualified for choosing those whom they are to entrust with part of their authority."

—*Baron de Montesquieu,* The Spirit of Laws, 1748

What impact did Enlightenment ideas have on the colonists?

ACTIVITY

Work in pairs or small groups to create a skit or short story that addresses the unit question:

ESSENTIAL QUESTION **How did the colonists, with strong roots in the past, develop their own way of life?**

Review the documents and other information in this unit. Then outline your answer to the unit question. Use your outline to create a skit or short story that captures some portion of your answer to the unit question. Use your imagination to create historically realistic characters or situations. But remember to address both elements of the unit question—the colonists' strong roots in the past and their way of life in America.

Unit 2

How did the colonists break away from Britain and create a republican form of government?

History *Interactive*
Explore Historian's Apprentice Online
Visit: PHSchool.com
Web Code: mvp-2000

Declaration of Independence In unforgettable phrases, the Declaration expressed the conviction of American leaders that the colonies should be independent of the rule of Great Britain.

1776

Writing the Constitution All through the hot summer of 1787, delegates from the states debated the new shape of the U.S. government. The Constitution created a framework for the government of the United States we enjoy today.

1787

Forming a New Nation

The Final Battle Trapped by American and French forces, the British were forced to surrender at the Battle of Yorktown. The British defeat marked the end of the fighting in the American Revolution.

1781

A Bill of Rights The Bill of Rights was intended to prevent the kind of abuses Americans had suffered under English rule. One of the rights protected was the right of the people peaceably to assemble.

1791

The Road to Revolution

1745-1776

"We profess to be his loyal and dutiful subjects.... Nevertheless, to the persecution and tyranny of his cruel ministry, we will not tamely submit."

—Massachusetts Provincial Congress, regarding King George III, 1775

Massachusetts colonists and British soldiers exchange fire across the green at Lexington, April 19, 1775.

What You Will Learn

Section 1
TROUBLE ON THE FRONTIER
A struggle on the western frontier draws France and Britain into a worldwide struggle.

Section 2
THE COLONISTS RESIST TIGHTER CONTROL
Efforts to solve Britain's financial problems raise the anger of people in the colonies.

Section 3
FROM PROTEST TO REBELLION
By 1775, many Americans were so enraged by British tax policies that they were ready to break away from Britain.

Section 4
THE WAR BEGINS
In the first days of the war, both sides expected the struggle to be short. They never expected to fight for seven years.

Reading Skill
Draw Inferences and Conclusions
In this chapter, you will learn how to use details from primary and secondary sources to draw inferences and conclusions.

How did the relationship between

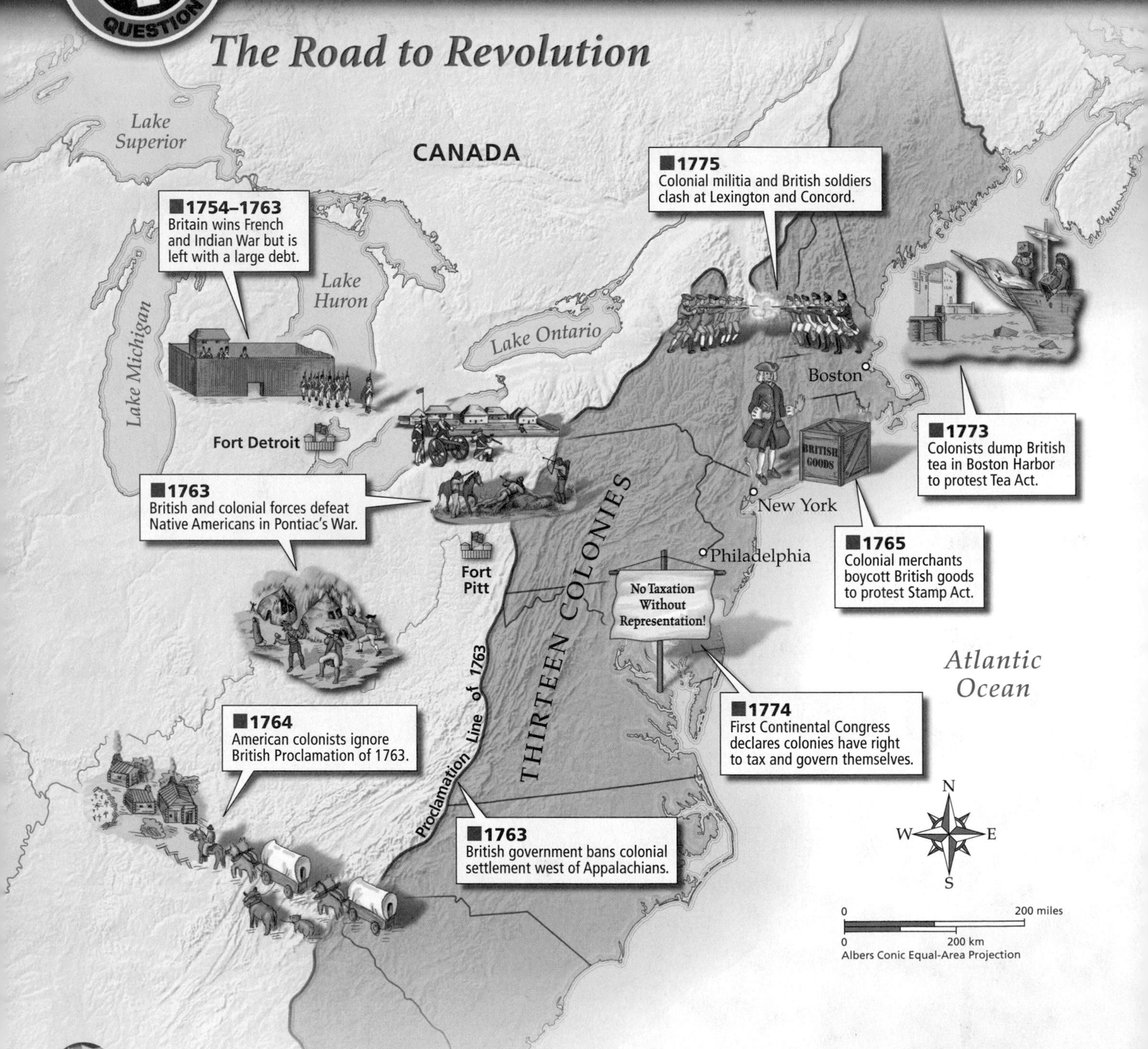

The Road to Revolution

Lake Superior

CANADA

Lake Michigan

Lake Huron

Lake Ontario

■1754–1763
Britain wins French and Indian War but is left with a large debt.

Fort Detroit

■1763
British and colonial forces defeat Native Americans in Pontiac's War.

Fort Pitt

■1775
Colonial militia and British soldiers clash at Lexington and Concord.

Boston

New York

■1773
Colonists dump British tea in Boston Harbor to protest Tea Act.

BRITISH GOODS

Philadelphia

■1765
Colonial merchants boycott British goods to protest Stamp Act.

No Taxation Without Representation!

THIRTEEN COLONIES

Proclamation Line of 1763

■1764
American colonists ignore British Proclamation of 1763.

■1774
First Continental Congress declares colonies have right to tax and govern themselves.

Atlantic Ocean

■1763
British government bans colonial settlement west of Appalachians.

N
W   E
S

| 0 | | 200 miles |
| 0 | | 200 km |

Albers Conic Equal-Area Projection

U.S. Events	**1740s**	English move into Ohio Valley.		French and Indian War begins.	**1754**	**1759**	British capture Quebec.

1740   **1750**   **1760**

World Events			**1748**	Britain and France fight to control trade in India.	**1756**	Seven Years' War breaks out in Europe between France and Britain.

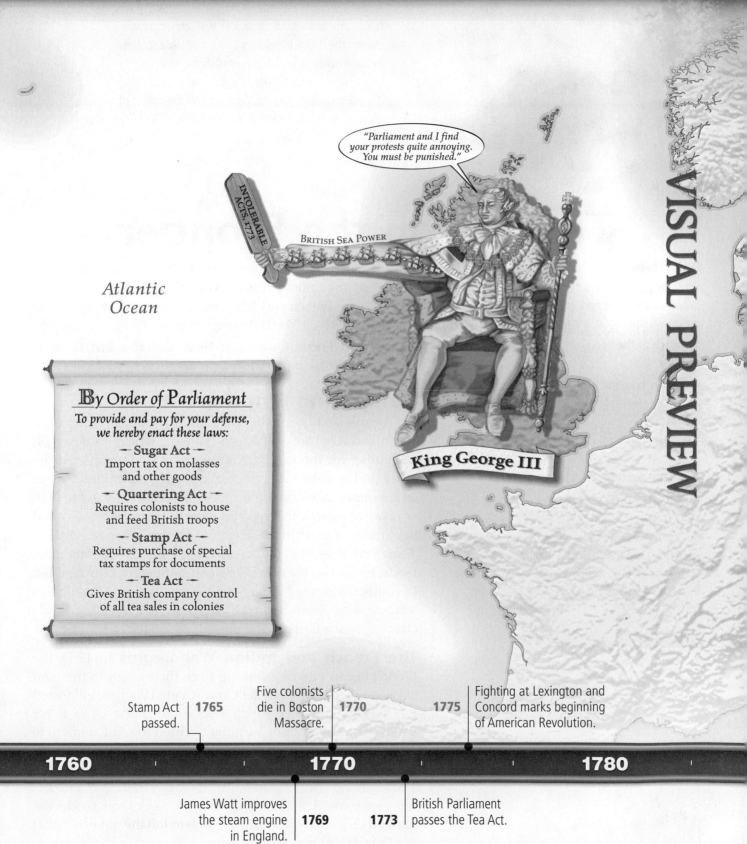

"Parliament and I find your protests quite annoying. You must be punished."

INTOLERABLE ACTS, 1773

BRITISH SEA POWER

King George III

Atlantic Ocean

VISUAL PREVIEW

By Order of Parliament

To provide and pay for your defense, we hereby enact these laws:

— Sugar Act —
Import tax on molasses and other goods

— Quartering Act —
Requires colonists to house and feed British troops

— Stamp Act —
Requires purchase of special tax stamps for documents

— Tea Act —
Gives British company control of all tea sales in colonies

Stamp Act passed. **1765**

Five colonists die in Boston Massacre. **1770**

Fighting at Lexington and Concord marks beginning of American Revolution. **1775**

1760　　　　**1770**　　　　**1780**

James Watt improves the steam engine in England. **1769**

1773 British Parliament passes the Tea Act.

Four Bullets Through My Coat

"We were attacked by a body of French and Indians, whose number (I am certain) did not exceed 300 men. Ours consisted of about 1,300 well-armed troops, chiefly the English soldiers . . . I had four bullets through my coat, and two horses shot under me."

—George Washington, reporting on the defeat of General Braddock's army, 1755

◄ Washington captures French Fort Duquesne, 1758.

Trouble on the Frontier

Objectives

- Identify the reasons why fighting broke out between France and Britain in North America.
- Describe the early defeat of the British by the French at the beginning of the French and Indian War.
- Explain how the British gained victory, and explain the results of the French and Indian War.

Reading Skill

Make Inferences When ideas are not actually stated, readers must infer these ideas by analyzing the details and evidence in the text. As you read about the choices and views of both the Americans and the British in colonial times, think about the inferences you can make from their actions.

Key Terms and People

George
  Washington
militia

alliance
cede

Why It Matters American colonists expanded their settlements. As they pushed further inland, they came into conflict with the French and Indians. In this power struggle, the future of much of North America was at stake.

❓ Section Focus Question: How did the British gain French territory in North America?

Competing Empires

By the middle of the 1700s, France and Britain each controlled large areas of North America which bordered on each other for thousands of miles. Each country feared the other and sought to increase the area it controlled. These ambitions collided on the frontier and eventually led to war.

Native Americans lived on most of the territory claimed by France and Britain. There were few French settlers. Therefore, they did not threaten to seize Native American lands. However, the need of British settlers for farmland led to conflict with the Native Americans. By the 1740s, British settlers were pushing into the Ohio River valley lands claimed by the French. The pressure soon led to trouble.

The French and Indian War Begins In 1753, the French began building forts to back their claim to the land between Lake Erie and the Ohio River. This news alarmed the Virginia Colony, which also claimed the Ohio River valley. The governor of Virginia decided to send soldiers to order the French to leave. He chose a 21-year-old surveyor in the Virginia militia, George Washington, as the leader. The militia is a force made up of civilians trained as soldiers but not part of the regular army. Washington made the dangerous journey, returning home to tell the governor that the French had rejected his warning.

The next year, Washington traveled west again with orders to build a fort where the Allegheny and the Monongahela (muh non goh HEEL uh) rivers meet to form the Ohio River.

Washington arrived in the region too late. The French were there already, building their own fort, which they called Fort Duquesne (du KANE). Learning that a party of French was looking for him, Washington decided to intercept them. His troops, along with some Indian allies, attacked and defeated the French party.

Washington then retreated to an open meadow and built a small fort of his own. He called it Fort Necessity. A larger French army found it, and forced Washington to surrender. Then they allowed Washington and his men to return home to Virginia with the message that the French would never give up the Ohio River valley.

The Albany Congress Expecting war to break out soon, the British government called a meeting of colonial leaders. It took place in Albany, New York. The British wanted the colonies to agree to cooperate in defending themselves against the French. The British also invited the Iroquois tribes to the meeting. They hoped to form an alliance with the Iroquois against the French. An **alliance** is an agreement between nations or groups to help each other against other nations or groups.

The Iroquois refused to make an alliance, in part because they expected the French to defeat the British in a war. The colonial leaders tried to work out a plan to defend themselves. Benjamin Franklin of Pennsylvania believed the colonies had to succeed. To make that point, his newspaper, the *Philadelphia Gazette*, published a picture of a snake chopped into pieces with the warning "Join, or Die."

Make Inferences
How did Virginia's governor view George Washington? Give one detail that supports your inference.

Join, or Die

JOIN, or DIE.

Reading Political Cartoons
Skills Activity

Benjamin Franklin's 1754 cartoon was a plea for unity in defending the colonies during the French and Indian War.

(a) **Distinguish Relevant Information** Identify the eight sets of initials that label the eight pieces of the snake.

(b) **Draw Conclusions** What point is Franklin making about the importance of colonial unity?

Franklin drew up a plan, called the Albany Plan of Union. It called for a council of representatives elected by the colonial assemblies. The council would have authority over western settlements, relations with Native Americans, and other urgent matters. It also could organize armies and collect taxes to pay its expenses.

The Albany Congress approved Franklin's plan, but the colonial assemblies rejected it. The colonies wanted to control their own taxes and armies. Franklin complained that "everyone cries, union is necessary," but they behave like "weak noodles" when the time comes to take action.

☑ **Checkpoint**   **Why were the British concerned about French activity in the Ohio River valley?**

Early British Defeats

Soon after Washington's return, the British government decided it had to push the French out of the Ohio River valley. In 1755, it sent General Edward Braddock to Virginia with orders to capture Fort Duquesne. Braddock arrived with a large force of regular British troops and Virginia militia. Colonel George Washington joined Braddock's force as a volunteer.

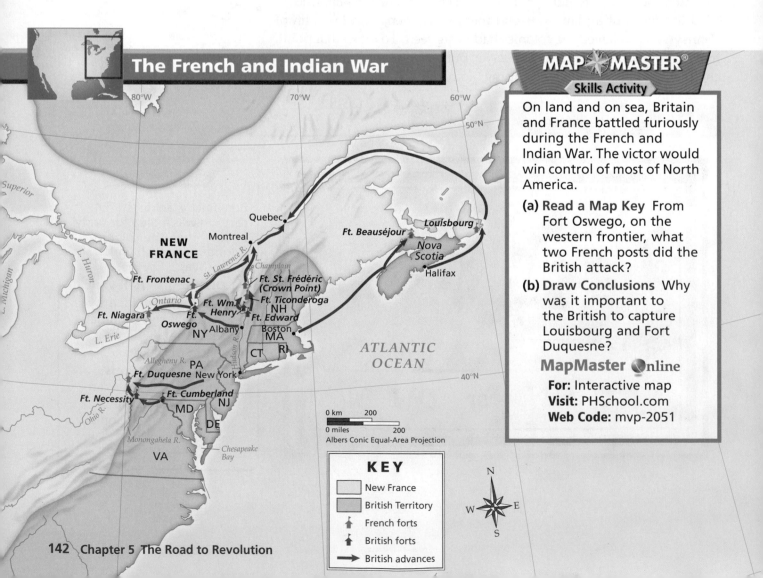

The French and Indian War

MAP MASTER®

Skills Activity

On land and on sea, Britain and France battled furiously during the French and Indian War. The victor would win control of most of North America.

(a) Read a Map Key From Fort Oswego, on the western frontier, what two French posts did the British attack?

(b) Draw Conclusions Why was it important to the British to capture Louisbourg and Fort Duquesne?

MapMaster Online

For: Interactive map
Visit: PHSchool.com
Web Code: mvp-2051

KEY

☐ New France
☐ British Territory
⚑ French forts
⚑ British forts
➜ British advances

Disaster at Fort Duquesne General Braddock understood military tactics used in Europe, where armies fought in formation on open fields. But he knew nothing about fighting in North America, where conditions were very different. Braddock did not respect colonial soldiers. He did not listen to warnings that soldiers marching down a narrow road through a dense forest in red uniforms were perfect targets for an enemy fighting from behind trees and bushes. When Benjamin Franklin warned him about the danger of ambushes, Braddock said they were no threat to his well-trained troops.

As Braddock's force neared Fort Duquesne in early July, it was ambushed by French troops and their Native American allies. More than half of Braddock's men were killed or wounded, with the general himself among the dead.

General Edward Braddock

More British Defeats The British had other setbacks during 1755. An army led by the governor of Massachusetts failed to take Fort Niagara on Lake Ontario. Further east, an army of British colonists and Native Americans was ambushed and suffered heavy losses near Lake George. These defeats may have strengthened Iroquois leaders' <u>resolve</u> not to ally with Britain.

In May 1756, Britain declared war on France, marking the official beginning of the Seven Years' War between the two countries. Shortly thereafter, French troops led by General Louis de Montcalm captured and destroyed Britain's Fort Oswego on Lake Ontario. In 1757, Montcalm captured Fort William Henry on Lake George.

Vocabulary Builder
<u>resolve</u> (ree SAHLV) **n.** strong determination to succeed in doing something

☑ **Checkpoint** **What fatal errors did General Edward Braddock make?**

The British Turn the Tide

The situation improved for Britain during 1757 when William Pitt became prime minister. Pitt sought top generals who had genuine military talent. He chose James Wolfe, who was only 30 years old when he became one of Britain's top generals.

With Pitt's generals in command, the war entered a new <u>phase</u>. In the summer of 1758, Britain scored its first major victory in the war. It captured the fort at Louisbourg. In the fall, the British took Fort Duquesne. The British renamed the post Fort Pitt, in William Pitt's honor. It later became the city of Pittsburgh.

Vocabulary Builder
<u>phase</u> (fayz) **n.** stage of development

These and other victories led the Iroquois to side with the British. More victories in 1759 set the stage for the British attack on Quebec and the key battle of the war.

Quebec, the capital of New France, was located on a high cliff, overlooking the St. Lawrence River. General Montcalm commanded the French defenders, and General Wolfe led the British attack. At first, the British made little progress. Then, at night, they found an unguarded trail that allowed them to climb the cliffs protecting the city without being discovered. In September 1757, approximately 4,000 British soldiers defeated 4,500 French soldiers on the plains in

The British attack Quebec.

front of the city. More than 2,000 soldiers were killed or wounded in the battle, including both Wolfe and Montcalm.

After losing Quebec, France could no longer defend the rest of its North American territory. Montreal, the other major French city in Canada, fell in 1760. In February 1763, Britain and France signed the Treaty of Paris. France lost almost all of its North American possessions. France ceded, or surrendered, French Canada to Great Britain. Great Britain also gained all other French territory east of the Mississippi, with the exception of New Orleans. Britain also received Spanish Florida. New Orleans, along with all French territory west of the Mississippi, went to Spain.

Native Americans also lost a great deal. Without French help, the Native Americans could not stop British settlers from moving on their lands.

✓**Checkpoint** What was the outcome of the Battle of Quebec?

⭐ **Looking Back and Ahead** The defeat of the French left the British in control of a vast area in North America. However, whatever sense of triumph British leaders felt at the war's outcome was soon replaced by a nagging realization. The victory had substituted one set of problems for another.

Section 1 | Check Your Progress

Progress Monitoring Online
For: Self-test with instant help
Visit: PHSchool.com
Web Code: mva-2051

Comprehension and Critical Thinking

1. (a) **Summarize** How did the French and Indian War affect the 13 colonies?
   (b) **Detect Points of View** How did most colonists feel about helping the British? Explain.

2. (a) **Recall** How did the war go for the British before 1757? After 1757?
   (b) **Make Predictions** How might the outcome influence relations between the British and the American colonists?

Reading Skill

3. **Make Inferences** Think about how the Iroquois felt about the Ohio River valley. Why do you think the Iroquois may have preferred to be neutral in the conflict between France and England? What can you infer about how the Iroquois felt about European conflicts in North America?

Key Terms

4. Write two definitions for each key term: militia, alliance. First, write a formal definition for your teacher. Second, write a definition in everyday English for a classmate.

Writing

5. Write two or three sentences identifying the problems facing the Albany Congress. Were these problems solved? Explain your answer in three or four sentences.

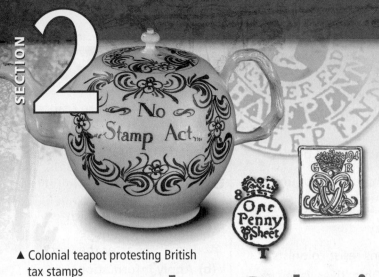

▲ Colonial teapot protesting British tax stamps

A Burdensome Tax

❝We have called this a burdensome tax, because the duties are so numerous and so high, and the embarrassments to business in this infant, sparsely settled country so great, that it would be totally impossible for the people to subsist under it. ❞

—John Adams, speaking against the Stamp Act, 1765

The Colonists Resist Tighter Control

Objectives
- Explain the conflict between Native Americans and British settlers in 1763.
- Describe how the colonists responded to British tax laws.
- Describe what happened during the Boston Massacre.

🕐 Reading Skill

Support Inferences With Details
Inferences must be based on information. This information may be details stated in the text. First, make the logical inference, then read the text and identify support for your inference. If you cannot support the inference, adjust it until the evidence will support it.

Key Terms and People
duty
boycott
petition

writ of assistance
John Adams
Samuel Adams

Why It Matters American colonists enjoyed a large degree of self-government. They were proud of their rights and loyal to the British monarch. But the French and Indian War strained this loyalty.

❓ **Section Focus Question: How did the French and Indian War draw the colonists closer together but increase friction with Britain?**

Conflict With Native Americans

By 1763, Britain controlled almost all of North America east of the Mississippi River. This enormous territory promised endless room for settlement. However, Native Americans living west of the Appalachian Mountains were desperately trying to keep their lands. Fighting between Native Americans and white settlers began as soon as the French and Indian War ended.

Pontiac's War In the last days of the French and Indian War, the leader of the Ottawa nation, Pontiac, formed an alliance of western Native Americans. In May 1763, Pontiac and his allies attacked British forts and settlements throughout the area. Nearly half a dozen western British forts were destroyed and at least 2,000 backcountry settlers were killed. British settlers reacted with equal viciousness. They killed Native Americans who had not attacked them.

The British finally defeated Pontiac's forces in early August at a battle near Fort Pitt. Pontiac continued to fight for another year, but by the fall of 1764, the war was over.

The Proclamation of 1763 Britain wanted to avoid further wars with Native Americans on the frontier. Therefore, the British government issued the Proclamation of 1763. It banned

Effects of the French and Indian War

THE FRENCH AND INDIAN WAR	■ France loses its North American possessions. ■ Britain is left with a large debt. ■ Colonists develop a sense of unity. ■ Colonists begin settling in the Ohio River valley. ■ Native Americans resist colonists settling in the Ohio River valley.

Reading Charts
Skills Activity

The struggle between France and Great Britain to establish an empire in the Americas ended in 1763. The results brought political, social, and economic change to North America.

(a) Read a Chart Which nation faced huge expenses after the war?

(b) Apply Information How do you think the war impacted relations between Britain and the colonies?

colonial settlement west of a line drawn along the Appalachian Mountains. Settlers were told they had to move to a location east of that line.

The Proclamation of 1763 angered many colonists who believed they had the right to reside wherever they wanted. The proclamation was widely ignored and proved impossible for the British to enforce.

☑**Checkpoint**   **What were the terms of the Proclamation of 1763?**

British Rule Leads to Conflict

The colonists were proud of their contribution toward winning the French and Indian War. Tens of thousands of men had served as soldiers, and many had died in the war. Massachusetts alone lost more than 1,500 men. The colonists expected Britain to be grateful for their assistance. At most, they expected only a <u>minimum</u> rise in taxes.

Although ties between the colonies had begun to grow before the war, the 13 colonies still were divided in many ways. But the people of those colonies also saw themselves as different from people living in Britain. In 1763, the colonists still considered themselves loyal British subjects. Increasingly, however, they identified more with one another than with Britain.

The British saw things differently. The French and Indian War left Britain deeply in debt. Furthermore, these expenses continued. The British government had to keep troops in North America to make sure France did not try to regain its lost territory and to protect settlers against Native American attacks. British leaders believed the colonists should pay part of the debt.

The Sugar Act The British effort to impose new taxes on the colonies began in 1764 when Parliament passed the Sugar Act, which put a **duty**—or import tax—on several products, including molasses. It also called for harsh punishment of smugglers. Colonial merchants, who sometimes traded in smuggled goods, protested.

Vocabulary Builder
<u>minimum</u> (MIHN ah muhm)
adj. smallest quantity possible

The Quartering Act One year later, Parliament passed the Quartering Act. The purpose of the Quartering Act was to save money. To enforce the Proclamation of 1763, Britain kept about 10,000 soldiers in the colonies. The act required colonists to quarter, or house, British troops and provide them with food and other supplies. The colonists protested angrily. Once again, the colonists complained that Parliament was violating their rights.

✓**Checkpoint** **Why did the British impose new taxes on the American colonists?**

The Stamp Act

An even more unpopular law was the Stamp Act, passed by Parliament in early 1765. The Stamp Act required that all colonists buy special tax stamps for all kinds of products and activities. The stamps had to be placed on newspapers, wills, licenses, insurance policies, land titles, contracts, and other documents.

Protests against the Stamp Act were widespread. Virginia's House of Burgesses passed several resolutions declaring that it alone had the right to tax the people of Virginia. Patrick Henry, one of the youngest members of that body, made an emotional speech attacking the law. Henry ended his speech with a reference to the murder of Julius Caesar in ancient Rome. When Henry said that some good American would do the same to King George III, cries of treason were hurled against him. Henry replied, "If this be treason, make the most of it."

Other colonial assemblies followed Virginia's example. Merchants in New York, Boston, and Philadelphia organized a **boycott**—an organized campaign to refuse to buy certain products—of British goods. The protests spread to every colony.

In October, delegates from nine colonies met in New York for the Stamp Act Congress. They sent a **petition**—a written request to a government. Addressed to the king and Parliament, this petition demanded the end of both the Sugar Act and Stamp Act.

The protests worked. In 1766, Parliament repealed the Stamp Act. However, at the same time it passed the Declaratory Act, which said Parliament had total authority over the colonies. That set the stage for further trouble between Britain and her colonies.

✓**Checkpoint** **Why did colonists object to the Stamp Act?**

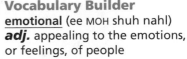

Support Inferences With Details
Use details from the text to support this inference: The British did not expect the colonists to react negatively to new policies after the French and Indian War.

Vocabulary Builder
emotional (ee мон shuh nahl) *adj.* appealing to the emotions, or feelings, of people

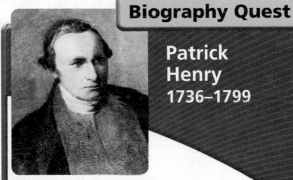

Biography Quest

Patrick Henry
1736–1799

In the days before the American Revolution, the most eloquent spokesperson for independence was Patrick Henry.

Henry gave his famous speech in 1775. He urged Virginians to take up arms in their defense. "I know not what course others may take," he roared, "but as for me, give me liberty or give me death!" He later went on to serve six terms as governor of Virginia.

Biography Quest

How did a salary dispute make Henry famous?

For: The answer to the question about Patrick Henry
Visit: PHSchool.com
Web Code: mvd-2052

Protests Spread

British officials sought a means of taxing the colonists in a way that would not anger them. Under the Townshend Acts of 1767, Britain would no longer tax products or activities inside the colonies. It would only tax products brought into the colonies.

Writs of Assistance The Townshend Acts set up a system to enforce the new import duties. To help customs officers find illegal goods, they were allowed to use **writs of assistance**—court orders that allowed officials to make searches without saying for what they were searching. Many colonists saw these writs and the searches they allowed as yet another violation of their rights.

Charles Townshend, the official in charge of the British treasury, also wanted to weaken the colonial assemblies. When the New York assembly refused to supply money to house and feed soldiers under the Quartering Act, Parliament suspended the assembly. The colonists again reacted by boycotting British goods.

The Boston Massacre Once again, the protests worked. The boycott hurt British merchants and manufacturers, who put pressure on Parliament. On March 5, 1770, Parliament repealed all the Townshend duties—except the one on tea. That tax was left in force to demonstrate Parliament's right to tax the colonies.

Parliament had not acted in time. On March 5, 1770, in Boston, an angry crowd of workers and sailors surrounded a small group of soldiers. They shouted at the soldiers and threw snowballs and rocks at them. The frightened soldiers fired into the crowd, killing five and wounding six. The first to fall for the cause of American independence was Crispus Attucks, an African American sailor.

Governor Thomas Hutchinson tried to calm things down by having the nine soldiers involved in the shooting arrested and tried for murder. John Adams, a well-known Massachusetts lawyer, defended them. Adams also was a leading defender of colonial rights against recent British policies. Yet, he took the unpopular case because he believed that in a free country every person accused of a crime had the right to a lawyer and a fair trial. Only two soldiers were convicted. Their punishment was having their thumbs branded.

Committees of Correspondence As tensions grew, colonial leaders saw the need to keep in closer contact with people in other colonies. After the Boston Massacre, Samuel Adams, a cousin of John Adams, established what he called a Committee of Correspondence. The aim was to keep colonists informed of British actions. Soon, committees were sprouting in other colonies. The committees wrote letters and pamphlets to spread the alarm whenever Britain tried to enforce unpopular acts of Parliament. In this way, the committees helped unite the colonists against Britain.

Samuel Adams

✔**Checkpoint** How did colonists react to the Townshend Acts?

⭐ **Looking Back and Ahead** When colonists heard that the Townshend Acts had been repealed, they were overjoyed. But the dispute over taxes was not settled. Before long, colonists would face other crises that would lead to armed resistance.

Section 2 | **Check Your Progress**

Progress Monitoring Online
For: Self-test with instant help
Visit: PHSchool.com
Web Code: mva-2052

Comprehension and Critical Thinking

1. (a) Recall What was the Proclamation of 1763?
(b) Apply Information Why did the British feel the Proclamation was critical in their relationship with the Native Americans?

2. (a) Describe What happened during the Boston Massacre?
(b) Detect Points of View Why do you think the colonists described this event as a "massacre"?

Reading Skill

3. Support Inferences With Details Read the text following the subheading "Committees of Correspondence." Give a detail from the text to support the following inference: The colonists believed that the strength of unity would help them.

Key Terms

Answer the following questions in complete sentences that show your understanding of the key terms.

4. How did the American boycott affect Great Britain economically?
5. What did the delegates to the Stamp Act Congress hope to achieve by sending a petition to the British king and Parliament?
6. Why did colonists object to writs of assistance?

Writing

7. As a member of Parliament, you vote against repealing the Stamp Act. Brainstorm one or two possible solutions that you think would work better.

A Well-Regulated Militia

❝*Resolved* unanimously, that a well-regulated militia, composed of . . . freemen, is the natural strength and only stable security of a free government, and that such a militia will relieve our mother country from any expense in our protection and defense.❞

—Maryland delegates' resolution, 1774, promoting colonial self-defense

◀ Colonial militiaman

From Protest to Rebellion

Objectives
- Identify the causes of the Boston Tea Party.
- Explain how the colonists protested the Intolerable Acts.
- Describe the events of April 19, 1775, at Lexington and Concord.

Reading Skill

Draw Logical Conclusions Reaching conclusions means analyzing what you have read and forming an opinion about what it means. As with inferences, you can add your own personal knowledge to the information to draw a conclusion. Always ask yourself: Does this conclusion make sense?

Key Terms
monopoly   minuteman
repeal

Why It Matters After the French and Indian War, friction with Britain increased when Britain imposed new taxes and regulations on the colonists. But the colonists' anger had stopped short of armed resistance to the British.

❓ **Section Focus Question: How did British tax policies move the colonists closer to rebellion?**

A Dispute Over Tea

During the early 1770s, the protests in the colonies against British policies quieted down. However, that did not mean the colonists were satisfied with the British government. Although most of the Townshend duties had been repealed, the one on tea remained. Many colonists drank tea. With every cup they drank, they were paying a tax that Parliament had placed on them without their consent.

The Tea Act In 1773, the British Parliament passed the Tea Act. It was intended to help the British East India Company, one of Britain's most important companies. For many years, the company had made money growing tea in India and selling it in Britain and in the colonies. However, the colonial boycott of tea seriously hurt the company.

The Tea Act actually lowered the price of tea by allowing the East India Company to ship tea directly to the colonies. Prior to the Tea Act, the tea first had to be shipped to Britain. Frederick North, the prime minister of England, felt the colonists should not object to the Tea Act since the price of tea was lowered. However, some colonists reacted angrily to the part of the act that gave the East India

Company a monopoly on selling British tea in the colonies. A **monopoly** is total control of a market for a certain product.

The monopoly hurt colonial merchants. Many of them sold Dutch tea that was smuggled into the colonies. Now, they would not be able to compete with the lower-priced East India Company tea. Many colonial leaders also argued that even though the price of tea was lowered, colonists still had to pay the tax on tea.

The Boston Tea Party A group of colonists called the Sons of Liberty soon organized in port cities to stop the East India Company tea from being unloaded. They threatened ship captains who were bringing in the tea and colonial tea merchants who said they would buy it. No tea was unloaded in New York, Philadelphia, or other ports. However, in Boston, Governor Thomas Hutchinson decided to make sure that the tea would be unloaded. He refused to give the arriving tea ships papers that would allow them to return to England. So, when the first tea ships from Britain arrived, Hutchinson ordered the cargo to be unloaded.

For more than two weeks, feelings were tense in Boston. Finally, on the night of December 16, 1773, a large crowd gathered in the harbor. Suddenly, a large group of men disguised as Native Americans boarded the tea ship. During the next three hours, they threw 342 cases of tea into the harbor. As the crowd cheered and shouted, the raiders destroyed 90,000 pounds of tea worth thousands of dollars.

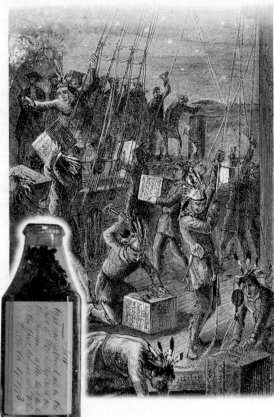

Boston Tea Party
Members of the Sons of Liberty protested the Tea Act by dumping chests of tea into Boston Harbor.
Critical Thinking: *Apply Information* *Why do you think the colonists chose to disguise themselves as Native Americans?*

☑**Checkpoint** **How did Boston colonists show their opposition to the Tea Act?**

The Intolerable Acts

The Boston Tea Party outraged the British government. King George III called for tough action to make examples of the people of Boston and Massachusetts.

In response to the <u>incident</u>, Parliament passed four laws. These laws were so harsh that colonists called them the Intolerable Acts. The first act closed the port of Boston. Two others increased the powers of the royal governor, abolished the upper house of the Massachusetts legislature, and cut the powers of town meetings. Now, anyone accused of murdering a British colonial official could be tried in Britain, rather than in the colonies. Finally, a fourth law strengthened the 1765 Quartering Act.

Parliament also passed the Quebec Act, which set up a government for the territory taken from France in 1763. The Quebec Act claimed land between the Ohio and the Missouri rivers as part of Canada. Quebec's new boundaries took away the western lands claimed by several colonies and blocked colonists from moving west.

Vocabulary Builder
<u>incident</u> (IN suh dunt)
n. happening; occurrence

History *Interactive*

Discover the Events That Led to the Revolution
Visit: PHSchool.com
Web Code: mvl-2054

Roots of the Revolution
Relations between Great Britain and the colonies changed after the French and Indian War. Years of colonial protest against laws passed by Parliament gradually led to open revolt. **Critical Thinking: Explain Problems** *Why did colonists view these laws as attacks on their rights as British citizens?*

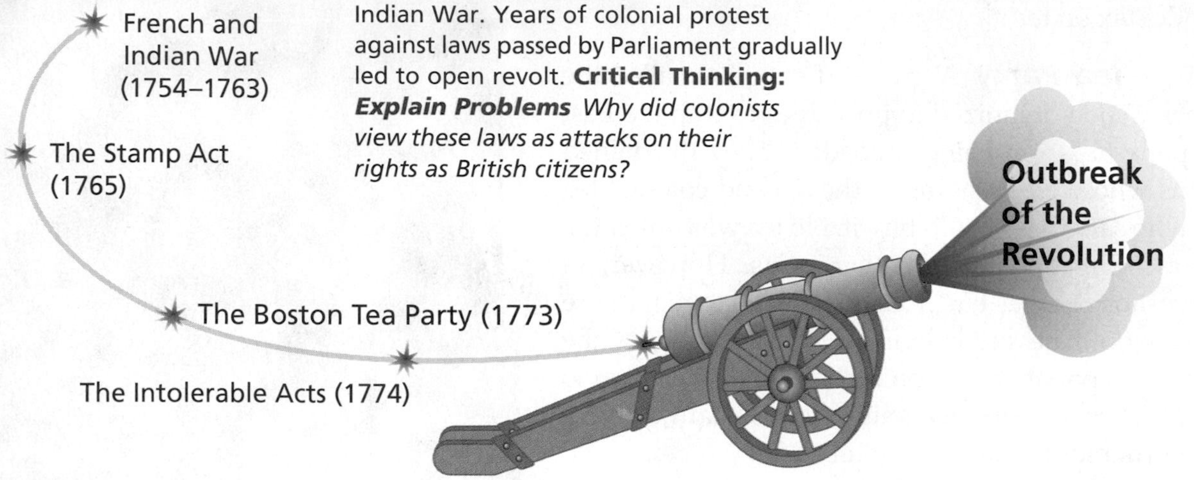

* French and Indian War (1754–1763)

* The Stamp Act (1765)

* The Boston Tea Party (1773)

The Intolerable Acts (1774)

Outbreak of the Revolution

Vocabulary Builder
<u>react</u> (ree AKT) **v.** to act in return

Draw Logical Conclusions
What conclusion can you make about how the Congress felt about independence at this time?

Americans in all the colonies <u>reacted</u> by trying to help the people of Boston. Food and other supplies poured into Boston from throughout the colonies. Meanwhile, the Committee of Correspondence organized a meeting to discuss what to do next.

That meeting, known as the First Continental Congress, took place in Philadelphia in September and October 1774. Twelve of the 13 colonies sent delegates. Only Georgia did not send representatives. Among the delegates were John Adams and Samuel Adams from Massachusetts, John Jay of New York, and George Washington and Patrick Henry from Virginia.

The Congress demanded the **repeal**, or official end, of the Intolerable Acts and declared that the colonies had a right to tax and govern themselves. It also called for the training of militias to stand up to British troops if necessary. The Congress also called for a new boycott of British goods. It then voted to meet again in May 1775 if its demands were not met.

✓**Checkpoint**   **What did the First Continental Congress accomplish?**

The Shot Heard Round the World

The British government had no intention of meeting the demands of the First Continental Congress. It chose, instead, to use force to restore its authority. Meanwhile, the colonists began to arm and form new militia units called **minutemen**—citizen soldiers who could be ready to fight at a minute's notice.

In April, General Thomas Gage, the new governor of Massachusetts, learned the minutemen were storing arms in Concord, about 20 miles from Boston. On April 18, 1775, he sent 700 troops to seize the arms and capture some important colonial leaders. As the troops set out, a signal sent by the Patriots appeared in the steeple of Boston's Old North Church. Two men, Paul Revere and William Dawes, then rode through the night to warn the minutemen.

Five miles from Concord in the town of Lexington, about 77 minutemen were waiting when the British arrived. The British commander ordered the minutemen to go home. They refused. Suddenly, a shot rang out. Nobody knows who fired it, but it turned out to be the first shot of the American Revolution—"the shot heard round the world." The British then opened fire, killing eight Americans.

A larger battle took place in nearby Concord. This time, 400 minutemen fought the British, killing three of them. As the British retreated toward Boston, about 4,000 Americans fired at them from behind trees and fences. By the time the British reached Boston, almost 300 of them had been killed or wounded.

✓**Checkpoint** **What led to the conflict at Lexington and Concord?**

☆ **Looking Back and Ahead** News of the battles at Lexington and Concord traveled fast through the colonies. Many colonists saw their hopes of reaching an agreement with Britain fade. For many, the battles were proof that only war would decide the future of the 13 colonies.

Statue of a minuteman

Section 3 | Check Your Progress

Progress Monitoring ⊘nline
For: Self-test with instant help
Visit: PHSchool.com
Web Code: mva-2053

Comprehension and Critical Thinking

1. (a) Recall Why did Britain pass the Tea Act?
(b) Identify Alternatives What other ways, besides the Boston Tea Party, might colonists have protested the Tea Act?

2. (a) Summarize What were the Intolerable Acts?
(b) Apply Information How did the Intolerable Acts affect colonial unity?

3. (a) Describe How did the American Revolution begin?
(b) Draw Conclusions Why do you think the first shot fired at Lexington was called "the shot heard round the world"?

⊙ Reading Skill

4. Draw Logical Conclusions Based on the battles of Lexington and Concord, what can you conclude about the colonists' advantage in fighting?

Key Terms

Fill in the blanks with the correct key terms.
5. The _____ were colonists who could prepare to fight in a very short time.
6. Because the East India Company had a _____ on selling British tea in the colonies, other countries could not sell their tea there.

7. The First Continental Congress provided for the training of _____ that could fight the British troops.

Writing

8. One of the decisions of the First Continental Congress was to boycott British goods. In a paragraph, identify the problem that Congress was trying to solve by boycotting British goods. Did the boycott solve the problem? Explain.

A Spirit of Protest

From the Stamp Act to the Boston Tea Party to the outbreak of fighting at Lexington and Concord, a spirit of protest steadily grew in the colonies. This defiant mood expressed itself in many ways.

Boycotting British Goods

Women took a leading role in refusing to buy British goods. In October 1774, a group of women in Edenton, North Carolina, signed a pledge. They promised "not to conform to the Pernicious Custom of Drinking Tea." Above, the women of Edenton pour away tea.

A Warning of Danger

Benjamin Franklin was the first to use a serpent as a symbol of the colonies. (See Section 1.) By 1775, the serpent had become a rattlesnake, which stood for the idea that the colonists would ▼ fight back against tyranny.

DONT TREAD ON ME

The Pen as a Weapon

Mercy Otis Warren of Boston wrote plays that made fun of the British. The plays were not acted in theaters but were circulated privately. In *The Blockheads*, Warren shows how the Patriots made fools of the ▼ British troops after Lexington and Concord. One British soldier says:

Mercy Otis Warren

❝Ha, ha, ha,—yankee doodle forever. . . . We were sent here to ransack the country and hang up a parcel of leading fellows for the crows to pick, and awe all others into *peace* and *submission*—instead of this, in our first attempt, we were drove thro' the country, like a pack of *jackasses*.❞

—Mercy Otis Warren, *The Blockheads*

Violent Protests

The spirit of protest sometimes took a violent turn. The British cartoon below shows a tax official in Boston being tarred and feathered by members of the Sons of Liberty. Hot tar was poured over the body of the victim, who was then covered with chicken feathers. Tarring and feathering was not fatal, but it was painful and humiliating. In the background, colonists pour tea into Boston Harbor.

The first Liberty Tree was an elm in Boston, where dummies representing tax collectors were hanged. Patriots in many colonies raised Liberty Trees or Liberty Poles as symbols of protest.

In addition to being tarred and feathered, the unfortunate tax collector has tea poured down his throat.

Analyze LIFE AT THE TIME

Choose a person pictured on these pages. As that person, write a letter to a friend describing how you feel about the new mood of protest in the colonies.

In the Heat of Action

❝We were then very soon in the heat of action. Before we reached the summit of Bunker Hill, and while we were going over the Neck, we were in imminent danger from the cannon shot, which buzzed around us like hail.❞

—American Captain John Chester, describing the Battle of Bunker Hill, 1775

▲ American soldiers prepare for British attack.

The War Begins

Objectives

- Identify the issues facing the Second Continental Congress.
- Describe the differences between Patriots and Loyalists.
- Identify the Olive Branch Petition, and explain why it failed.
- Explain the significance of the Battle of Bunker Hill.

🔄 Reading Skill

Identify Supporting Evidence Readers often draw conclusions without even realizing that they are doing so. However, like inferences, conclusions should be supported and challenged and the evidence identified. This ensures that your conclusions are logical and reliable. Remember, you may need to use evidence from prior reading to reach your conclusions.

Key Terms

blockade
mercenary

Why It Matters After the battles at Lexington and Concord, many colonists hoped that the British would give in quickly to the colonists' demands. The British did not. Instead, a long and difficult struggle lay ahead.

❓ **Section Focus Question: How did the American Revolution begin?**

The Second Continental Congress

Even after the battles of Lexington and Concord, most colonists still did not favor independence. At the same time, many of them were ready to use force, if necessary, to defend their rights against the British.

As the crisis with Britain deepened, the Second Continental Congress came together in Philadelphia in May 1775. The delegates included Thomas Jefferson, a young lawyer from Virginia; Boston merchant John Hancock; and Benjamin Franklin of Philadelphia.

The Congress, at first, was divided about what to do. A group of delegates from New England wanted to declare independence. A more moderate group from the Middle Colonies favored less drastic action. However, nearly all delegates felt they needed to prepare for war. The first step was to form an army.

The Congress chose George Washington as the commander of the newly formed Continental army. He had military experience and was well respected.

The Congress also took steps to pay for its army by printing paper money. The Second Continental Congress was starting to act like a government.

Patriots Against Loyalists By 1775, a split was developing in the American colonies. Colonists who favored independence and were willing to fight for it took the name Patriots. Those who remained loyal to Britain and the king called themselves Loyalists. Most colonists were Patriots. However, as many as one third of the colonists may have had Loyalist sympathies.

The Loyalists came from every colony and all sections of the population. Everywhere, however, they were a minority. During 1774 and 1775, the Patriots took control of local governments.

The Loyalists included some people from the wealthiest families in the colonies. Many leading merchants and large landowners were Loyalists. They feared a rebellion would lead to a change in government and that they would lose their property. Government officials who owed their jobs and place in society to the British Crown often were Loyalists.

At the same time, many enslaved African Americans sided with the British, hoping to win their freedom. So did most Native Americans, who feared they would lose their lands if the colonists won independence.

During the Revolution, thousands of Loyalists fought on the British side. During and after the Revolutionary War, about 100,000 Loyalists left the country forever. Many settled in Canada.

Identify Supporting Evidence
Give evidence to support the conclusion that Loyalists strongly supported social order.

Lord Dunmore's Declaration

Lord Dunmore sent this declaration to the rebel Patriots in Virginia:

> ❝I do require every person capable of bearing arms to resort to His Majesty's standard, or be looked upon as traitors to His Majesty's Crown and government, and [be subject to] penalty . . . such as [loss] of life, confiscation of lands, etc. And I do hereby further declare all indentured servants, negroes, or others [in service to rebels] free that are able and willing to bear arms, they joining His Majesty's troops as soon as may be. . . .❞

—from Proclamation of Lord Dunmore, November 1775

Boys laughing at a Loyalist

Reading Primary Sources
Skills Activity

In 1775, Patriots had taken over Virginia. In desperation, Lord Dunmore, the Loyalist governor, issued a declaration against the rebel Patriots.

(a) Apply Information How does Lord Dunmore encourage indentured servants and black slaves to join the British army?

(b) Evaluate Arguments How could American Patriots accuse Lord Dunmore of being unfair?

Vocabulary Builder
restore (ree STOR) **v.** to bring back
to a normal state; to put back; to
reestablish

Petitioning the King Even months after Lexington and Concord, many delegates at the Second Continental Congress hoped that peace could be <u>restored</u> between Britain and its American colonies. Two resolutions passed in July showed the uncertainty of Congress. The first resolution was called the Olive Branch Petition and was sent to King George. The petition stated that the colonists were loyal to the king. It asked George to stop the fighting so all disputes between the colonists and Britain could be solved peacefully. The petition got its name from the olive branch, a symbol of peace since ancient times.

The next day, the Congress passed a tougher statement called the Declaration of the Causes and Necessities of Taking Up Arms. Written in part by Thomas Jefferson, the document stated that the colonists were ready "to die freemen rather than to live as slaves."

The effort to make peace failed. King George did not bother to answer the Olive Branch Petition. Instead, he declared the colonies were "in open . . . rebellion." Parliament, meanwhile, voted to send 20,000 soldiers to the colonies to end the revolt.

An Important American Victory On May 10, 1775, the same day the Second Continental Congress began meeting, an important battle took place in northern New York. A daring band of colonists made a surprise attack on Fort Ticonderoga (ti kahn duh ROH guh).

Ethan Allen demanding the surrender of Fort Ticonderoga

The fort stood at the southern end of Lake Champlain and protected the water route to Canada. Leading the force was Ethan Allen, a blacksmith. Most of his followers came from the nearby Green Mountains of today's Vermont. Because of that, they were known as the Green Mountain Boys.

Allen's force of 83 men reached the fort by crossing the lake at night and surprising the British in the early morning. Only 42 British troops guarded the fort, and they surrendered almost immediately.

Fort Ticonderoga was important for two reasons. It controlled the main route between Canada and the Hudson River valley. It also held valuable weapons, especially cannons. The Americans needed the cannons to match the powerful British weapons. When the Green Mountain Boys took the fort, they seized several dozen cannons. Later, those cannons were moved to Boston, where George Washington used them to drive the British from the city.

☑ **Checkpoint** How did the divided loyalties of the colonists affect the Second Continental Congress?

Early Battles

By June 1775, the British had 6,500 troops in Boston. The Americans had about 10,000 surrounding the city. About 1,600 of these troops <u>occupied</u> Breed's Hill overlooking the city. From this position, they could fire on British ships in Boston Harbor. Nearby was Bunker Hill, also controlled by the Americans.

Delivering the Cannons

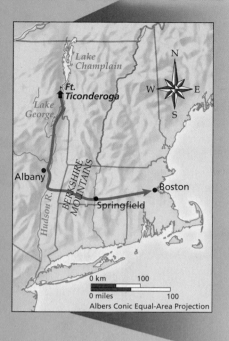

From Fort Ticonderoga to Boston

The difficulty of dragging cannons from Fort Ticonderoga to Boston is evident in this painting of the event. **Critical Thinking: *Apply Information*** *What does this effort indicate about the Continental army's military forces?*

Battle of Bunker Hill The Americans surrounding Boston were farmers and workers, not trained soldiers. Nobody knew if they would stand and fight against tough British troops.

British General William Howe decided to attack straight up Breed's Hill. The American commander, Israel Putnam, knew his soldiers did not have much ammunition. The Americans waited until the British were only about 150 feet away. When they opened fire, hundreds of British soldiers fell dead and wounded.

The first British attack failed. So did the second. The third attack succeeded, only because the Americans ran out of ammunition and had to retreat. The British won the battle but at a terrible cost. More than 1,000 were killed or wounded. American losses were about 400 killed or wounded. The Americans had proved they could fight and stand up to professional British soldiers.

The fighting, called the Battle of Bunker Hill, did not solve Britain's problem. Boston still was surrounded by American forces. In July 1775, George Washington arrived and took charge of the army.

Washington knew he had to build a regular army. Washington also needed powerful weapons to drive the British from Boston. He had the British cannons, which had been seized at Fort Ticonderoga, dragged on sleds across mountains and forests to Boston. That difficult 300-mile journey took three months.

In March, Washington placed the cannons on high ground overlooking Boston. The British could no longer defend the city. On March 17, 1776, they withdrew from Boston by sea and never returned.

The Battle of Bunker Hill

On June 16, 1775, the colonists occupied Bunker Hill and Breed's Hill, two high points near Charles Town, which was across the harbor from Boston. The battle that took place there the following morning fueled the colonists' determination to fight. After this battle, it is said that "a frenzy of revenge" gripped the colonists. **Critical Thinking:** *Understand Sequence Based on the information on this page and on your reading, describe the sequence of events before, during, and after the battle.*

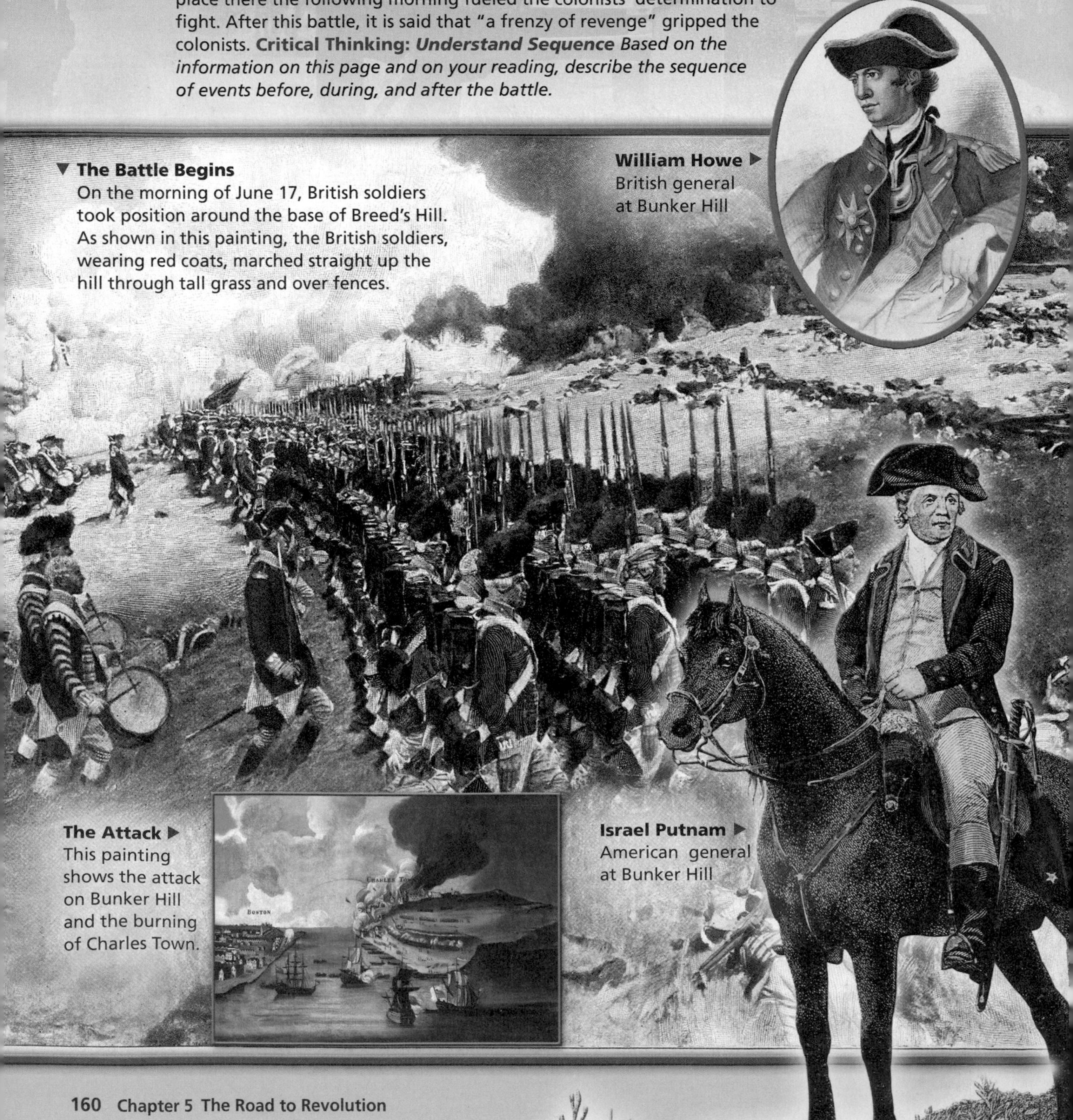

▼ **The Battle Begins**

On the morning of June 17, British soldiers took position around the base of Breed's Hill. As shown in this painting, the British soldiers, wearing red coats, marched straight up the hill through tall grass and over fences.

William Howe ▶
British general
at Bunker Hill

The Attack ▶
This painting shows the attack on Bunker Hill and the burning of Charles Town.

Israel Putnam ▶
American general
at Bunker Hill

Although the Americans won in Boston, Washington knew that the war was far from over. Britain still held most of the advantages. They had the most powerful navy in the world. They used it to transport troops and supplies and to blockade American ports. A **blockade** is the shutting off of a port by ships to keep people or supplies from moving in or out. The British also strengthened their army by hiring **mercenaries**—soldiers who serve another country for money.

Invading Canada While Washington was training one army outside Boston, two other American armies were moving north into Canada. One, led by Richard Montgomery, left from Fort Ticonderoga. The other, led by Benedict Arnold, moved north through Maine.

Arnold had a terrible journey through the Maine woods in winter. His troops were forced to boil candles, bark, and shoe leather for food. In late December 1775, the Americans attacked Quebec during a severe snowstorm. The attack was turned back. Montgomery was killed, and Arnold was wounded. The Americans stayed outside Quebec until May 1776, when the British landed new forces in Canada. Weakened by disease and hunger, the Americans withdrew, leaving Canada to the British.

✓**Checkpoint** **What did the Battle of Bunker Hill show about the American and British forces?**

⭐ **Looking Back and Ahead** After Bunker Hill, King George III was confident that he could soon restore order in the colonies. Meanwhile, colonists wondered what chance they had of defeating a well-armed, powerful nation such as Britain.

Section 4 | **Check Your Progress**

Progress Monitoring Online
For: Self-test with instant help
Visit: PHSchool.com
Web Code: mva-2054

Comprehension and Critical Thinking

1. **(a) Recall** What were the major achievements of the Second Continental Congress?
   (b) Apply Information How did the Second Continental Congress influence the conflict between the colonists and Britain?

2. **(a) Recall** What did the Patriots want?
   (b) Apply Information Why do you think Loyalists were described as "having their heads in England . . . but their bodies in America"?

Reading Skill

3. **Identify Supporting Evidence** Give evidence to support the conclusion that the war's momentum shifted after the Battle of Bunker Hill.

Key Terms

Read each sentence below. If the sentence is true, write YES. If the sentence is not true, write NO and explain why.

4. Countries set up blockades to help strengthen trade relations.

5. Most mercenaries are hired to fight for their own countries.

Writing

6. In a few sentences, describe how a Loyalist might have reacted to the Olive Branch Petition and to the Declaration of the Causes and Necessities of Taking Up Arms as possible solutions to the feud between Britain and the colonies. Then, write a brief response reflecting how a Patriot might have reacted to these documents as a solution to the feud.

21st Century Learning You can increase your understanding of history by asking questions about what you see and read. Formulating, or asking, questions helps you become a more effective learner. The better your questions, the more you will learn.

Patrick Henry presented his views in this excerpt from a speech to the convention that gathered after the Virginia Assembly was suspended.

Primary Source

"Sir, we have done everything to avert the storm which is now coming on. We have petitioned; we have remonstrated; we have supplicated; we have prostrated ourselves before the throne. Our petitions have been slighted; our remonstrances have produced additional violence and insult; our supplications have been disregarded. . . .

There is no longer any room for hope. If we wish to be free; if we mean to preserve inviolate those inestimable privileges for which we have been so long contending; . . . we must fight! I repeat it, sir, we must fight! An appeal to arms and to the God of hosts is all that is left us!

—I know not what course others may take; but as for me,—give me liberty, or give me death!"

—Patrick Henry, March 23, 1775

Learn the Skill
Use these steps to formulate questions.

❶ **Examine the material.** Ask basic questions to summarize what you are reading. Formulate questions that begin with *who, what, when, where,* and *how much.*

❷ **Think of analytical questions.** These are questions that reflect a thoughtful approach to the information. They might begin with *how* or *why.*

❸ **Ask questions that evaluate.** These call for judgments and opinions based on evidence.

❹ **Formulate hypothetical questions.** Hypothetical questions involve the word *if.* They suggest possible outcomes: *if this happens, would such and such occur?*

Practice the Skill
Answer the following questions about the primary source.

❶ **Examine the material.** What is Patrick Henry's view of the American Revolution?

❷ **Think of analytical questions.** (a) How would you describe the tone or feeling? (b) Formulate an analytical question.

❸ **Ask questions that evaluate.** (a) Why is this primary source persuasive? Explain. (b) Formulate a question to evaluate the source.

❹ **Formulate hypothetical questions.** If the British had won the Revolution, what do you think would have happened to Patrick Henry and those who supported his views?

Apply the Skill
See the Review and Assessment at the end of this chapter.

How did the relationship between Britain and the colonies fall apart?

Section 1
Trouble on the Frontier

- British settlers moved into lands claimed by the French in the Ohio River valley.
- After early British defeats at Fort Duquesne, Fort Niagara, and Lake George, France was defeated.
- Under the 1763 Treaty of Paris, Britain and Spain took control of almost all of France's North American possessions.

Section 2
The Colonists Resist Tighter Control

- To avoid conflict with Native Americans, Britain issued the Proclamation of 1763.
- After the end of the war, Britain strengthened its control over the American colonies by imposing a series of new taxes.
- Colonists protested Britain's actions by boycotting British goods.

Section 3
From Protest to Rebellion

- After Parliament passed the Tea Act, American colonists dumped cases of British tea into Boston Harbor.
- The Intolerable Acts further tightened Britain's control over the American colonies.
- The first major conflict between American colonists and British soldiers took place at Lexington and Concord on April 18, 1775.

Section 4
The War Begins

- The Second Continental Congress met in Philadelphia in May 1775 to deal with the deepening crisis with Great Britain.
- The British surrendered Fort Ticonderoga to a small American force led by Ethan Allen.
- When the Olive Branch Petition failed, the Continental Congress approved a more militant statement of purpose.
- Although the Patriots lost the Battle of Bunker Hill, George Washington finally drove the British from Boston.

(?) Exploring the Essential Question

Use the online study guide to explore the essential question.

Section 1
How did the British gain French territory in North America?

Chapter 5 Essential Question
How did the relationship between Britain and the colonies fall apart?

Section 2
How did the French and Indian War draw the colonists closer together but increase friction with Britain?

Section 4
How did the American Revolution begin?

Section 3
How did the British tax policies move the colonists closer to rebellion?

Key Terms

Answer the following questions in complete sentences that show your understanding of the key terms.

1. Why did the British want to form an alliance with the Iroquois during the French and Indian War?

2. How did the role of the militia change after the battles of Lexington and Concord?

3. What did Britain hope to achieve by a blockade of American ports?

4. How did the English king react to the colonists' petition about the Sugar and Stamp Acts?

Comprehension and Critical Thinking

5. **(a) Identify** What were three results of the French and Indian War?
   (b) Make Predictions What would have happened if the French had won the French and Indian War?

6. **(a) Recall** What was Pontiac's War?
   (b) Draw Conclusions What happened to the relationship between Native Americans and colonists after the French and Indian War? Explain your answer.

7. **(a) Recall** What did the First Continental Congress do?
   (b) Recall What did the Second Continental Congress do?
   (c) Compare and Contrast Compare and contrast the achievements of the First and Second Continental Congress.

8. **(a) Recall** What were the terms of the Olive Branch Petition?
   (b) Identify What was the Declaration of the Causes and Necessities of Taking Up Arms?
   (c) Apply Information Given the terms of each document, why might British leaders have felt the colonists were sending mixed messages about independence?

9. **(a) Describe** How did colonists react to the Battle of Bunker Hill?
   (b) Make Predictions How do you think this reaction would help colonial forces during the war?

History Reading Skill

10. **Make Inferences and Draw Conclusions** Draw a conclusion about George Washington as a military leader. Use evidence from throughout this chapter to support your conclusion.

Writing

11. **Write two paragraphs on the following topic:** How did the French and Indian War affect the relationship between the 13 colonies and Britain?
    Your paragraphs should:
    • include a thesis statement that expresses your main idea;
    • develop that main idea with facts, examples, and other information;
    • conclude by describing the lasting impact of what happened.

12. **Write a Narrative:**
    Since 1766, you have been a colonial merchant living in Boston. Write a letter to a friend explaining why you feel it is important to serve on the correspondence committee in your town.

Skills for Life
Formulate Questions
Use the quotation below to answer the questions.

> "As to government matters, it is not in the power of Britain to do this continent justice; the business of it will soon be too weighty and intricate to be managed with any tolerable degree of convenience, by a power so distant from us, and so very ignorant of us; for if they cannot conquer us, they cannot govern us. . . .
> . . . Freedom has been hunted round the globe. . . . O receive the fugitive, and prepare in time an asylum for mankind."
>
> —Thomas Paine, *Common Sense*, January 1776

13. How does Thomas Paine feel about the American Revolution?

14. **(a)** Why does Thomas Paine compare "freedom" to a "fugitive"?
    (b) How would this comparison affect his readers?

Test Yourself

1. **How did the Battle at Bunker Hill affect the colonists?**

   A They needed to train their militia.

   B They were proud of having stood their ground against the British soldiers.

   C They were proud of their victory.

   D They decided to call for a new commanding general.

Refer to the quotation below to answer Question 2.

> "Drive from the Ohio River any European foreigners, and do it in a way that will make them lose all taste for trying to return."

2. **The result of this policy by the French government**

   A ended relations between France and Spain.

   B increased tensions between France and Native Americans.

   C increased tensions between France and England.

   D pushed French colonists farther west.

Refer to the map below to answer Question 3.

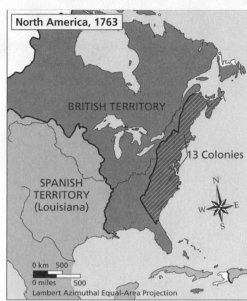

3. **How did the boundaries after 1763 affect the British?**

   A Britain could not expand farther west.

   B Britain gave up control of the 13 Colonies.

   C British colonists settled in Canada.

   D Britain offered to buy Louisiana from Spain.

Document-Based Questions

Task: Look at Documents 1 and 2, and answer their accompanying questions. Then, use the documents and your knowledge of history to complete this writing assignment:

   Use the evidence in the documents to write a two-paragraph essay explaining the causes and degree of colonial anger.

Document 1: Angered by the Stamp Act, in October 1765, representatives from nine colonies met in the Stamp Act Congress. Challenging Britain's right to tax the colonists, they issued a Declaration of Rights, excerpted in the box. *According to the delegates, why did Britain not have the right to tax the colonies?*

> "The members of this congress . . . make the following declarations. . . .
>
>   That His Majesty's . . . subjects in these colonies are entitled to all the . . . rights and privileges of his natural born subjects [in] Great Britain.
>
>   That the people of these colonies are not . . . represented in the House of Commons in Great Britain. . . .
>
>   That the only representatives of the people of these colonies are persons chosen . . . by themselves; and that no taxes ever have been or can be constitutionally imposed on them but by their respective legislatures. . . ."

Document 2: Look at the 1774 engraving of the tarring and feathering of a British tax collector in the Life at the Time feature in this chapter. *The fury of the colonists surprised the British. Why do you think this was so?*

The American Revolution

1776–1783

"These United Colonies are, and of Right ought to be Free and Independent States... all political connection between them and the State of Great Britain, is and ought to be totally dissolved...."

—Declaration of Independence, 1776

This painting by Don Troiani shows an American attack at the 1781 Battle of Cowpens, South Carolina.

What You Will Learn

Section 1
A NATION DECLARES INDEPENDENCE
The Declaration of Independence proclaimed that the colonies were separating from Britain.

Section 2
A CRITICAL TIME
The American army faced many difficulties in the early years of the war.

Section 3
THE WAR WIDENS
The impact of the war was felt by all Americans in every part of the nation.

Section 4
WINNING INDEPENDENCE
After a final victory, the Americans at last achieved independence from British rule.

Reading Skill

Analyze Word Parts In this chapter, you will learn to analyze words by their parts or origins to determine meanings.

The American Revolution

The American Revolution, 1775–1781

1 Declaration of Independence
July 1776: Second Continental Congress approves Declaration of Independence

2 British Capture New York
August 1776: British troops drive Americans off Long Island and out of New York City

3 Battle of Trenton
December 1776: Americans attack at Trenton; defeat German troops fighting for British

4 Turning Point at Saratoga
October 1777: Americans force the surrender of a large British force at Saratoga

5 Valley Forge
Winter 1777–78: At Valley Forge, Washington's army suffers cold winter with few supplies

6 Clark Wins in the West
Spring 1778: Patriot militia under George Rogers Clark capture British and Native American outposts in the West

7 Spain Joins the Fight
1779–1781: Spanish forces attack British forts along the Mississippi and in the Gulf of Mexico

8 Americans Slow British Attack
1780: Americans use guerrilla warfare to slow British advance in the South

9 Battle of Cowpens
January 1781: Americans inflict heavy losses on the British at Battle of Cowpens

10 Victory at Yorktown
October 1781: British trapped by Americans and French at Yorktown; British commander surrenders

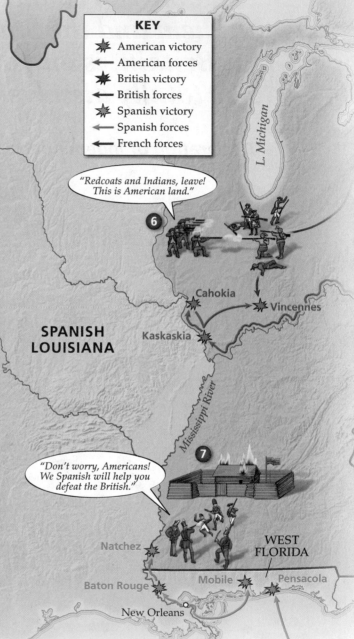

KEY

✹	American victory
←	American forces
✹	British victory
←	British forces
✹	Spanish victory
←	Spanish forces
←	French forces

L. Michigan

"Redcoats and Indians, leave! This is American land."

SPANISH LOUISIANA

Cahokia
Vincennes
Kaskaskia

Mississippi River

"Don't worry, Americans! We Spanish will help you defeat the British."

Natchez

WEST FLORIDA

Baton Rouge
Mobile
Pensacola

New Orleans

U.S. Events

1776 Continental Congress issues Declaration of Independence.

1777 American victory at Saratoga marks turning point in war.

1779 American ship *Bonhomme Richard* defeats British ship in naval battle.

1776 | **1778** | **1780**

World Events

1778 France recognizes the United States.

1779 Spain enters war against Britain.

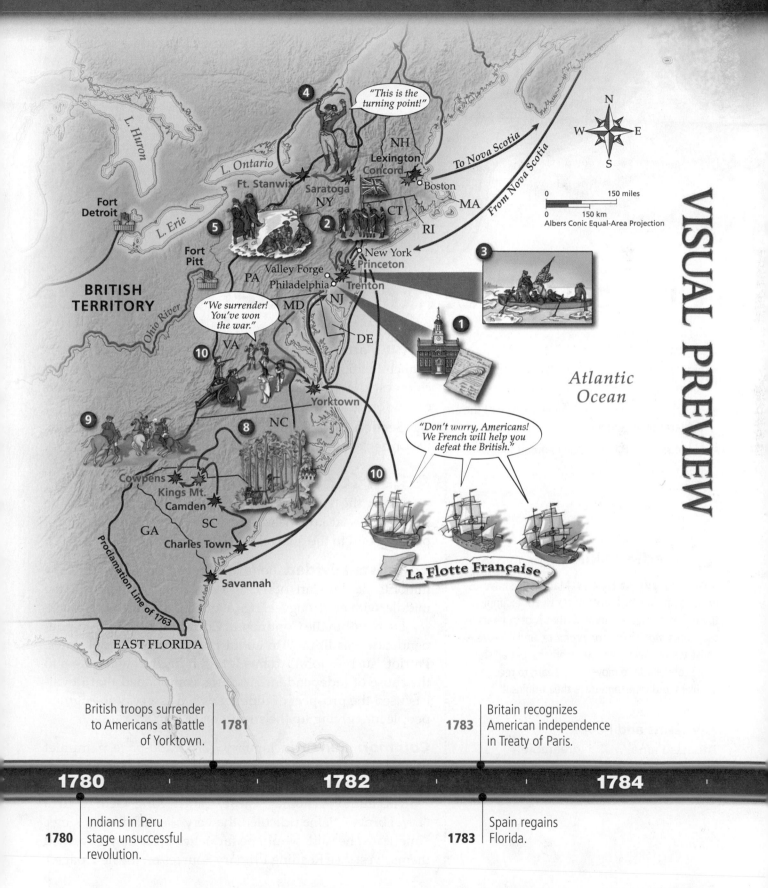

VISUAL PREVIEW

Let Us Separate

❝I could not join to day in the [prayers] of our worthy parson, for a reconciliation between our, no longer parent state, but tyrant state, and these colonies. —Let us separate, they are unworthy to be our brethren. Let us renounce them.❞

—Abigail Adams, letter to husband John Adams at the Continental Congress, 1775

◄ Benjamin Franklin, John Adams, and Thomas Jefferson reviewing the Declaration of Independence

A Nation Declares Independence

Objectives
- Find out how Thomas Paine stirred support for independence.
- Understand the meaning and structure of the Declaration of Independence.
- Learn how Congress finally agreed to separate from England.

Reading Skill

Analyze Word Roots Many English words have common word roots or parts. For example, the root *mot* means "move." That root appears in the words *motion, motor, promote,* and *demote.* Those words have different meanings, but all share some connection to movement. Learn to recognize familiar word roots and trace their origins.

Key Terms and People

Thomas Paine
Richard Henry Lee
resolution

preamble
grievance

Why It Matters After King George rejected the Olive Branch Petition, thousands of British troops were sent to the colonies. As the fighting continued, American Patriots called for independence.

❓ **Section Focus Question: Why did many colonists favor declaring independence?**

A Call for Independence

When the year 1776 began, few colonists could have predicted what lay ahead. Most colonists still hoped for a peaceful end to the quarrel with Britain.

Colonists Divided Both Patriots and Loyalists were in a minority at the start of 1776. Many colonists were in the middle, with no strong feelings about the dispute with Britain.

Even within the Continental Congress, support for independence was limited to about one third of the delegates. Patriots such as John Adams found it hard to win others to the cause of independence. Adams complained that Loyalists used the prospect of independence as a way to frighten people into giving up the struggle.

Common Sense In January 1776, a 50-page pamphlet titled *Common Sense* was published in Philadelphia. The pamphlet stimulated broad support for independence.

The author, Thomas Paine, called King George III a "royal brute." Paine ridiculed the very idea of rule by kings. Americans, he said, would be far better off if they governed themselves. (See Reading Primary Sources on the next page.)

Paine's strong <u>logic</u> and powerful words inspired people in all the colonies. Some 500,000 copies of the pamphlet were sold between January and July of 1776. George Washington wrote, "*Common Sense* is working a powerful change in the minds of men."

Vocabulary Builder
<u>logic</u> (LAH jihk) **n.** reason; careful thought

Virginia's Resolution Paine's pamphlet increased support for independence within the Continental Congress. In May 1776, Virginia authorized its delegates to support independence. Soon after, **Richard Henry Lee** introduced a **resolution,** or formal statement of opinion, to Congress. The Virginia resolution proclaimed that "these United Colonies are, and of right ought to be, free and independent States."

Before voting on Lee's resolution, Congress appointed a committee to draw up a statement stating the reasons for separation from Britain. Thomas Jefferson, a 33-year-old delegate from Virginia, was given the task of composing the declaration. Highly educated but shy, Jefferson spoke little in Congress. However, he was known for his graceful writing style.

In the heat of the Philadelphia summer, Jefferson struggled to find the words that would convince Americans and the world of the rightness of independence. The result was masterful. John Adams and Benjamin Franklin, who were also on the committee, suggested only minor changes.

☑**Checkpoint** **What proposal did Richard Henry Lee make to Congress?**

Common Sense

"I challenge the warmest advocate for reconciliation, to show a single advantage that this continent can reap, by being connected with Great Britain. I repeat the challenge, not a single advantage is derived. Our corn will fetch its price in any market in Europe, and our imported goods must be paid for, buy them where we will. . . . Whenever a war breaks out between England and any foreign power, the trade of America goes to ruin, because of her connection with Britain. . . . Every thing that is right or natural pleads for separation. The blood of the slain, the weeping voice of nature cries, 'TIS TIME TO PART."

—Thomas Paine, *Common Sense*

Thomas Paine

Reading Primary Sources
Skills Activity

In *Common Sense*, Thomas Paine gives political, military, and moral arguments for breaking away from Britain. In the excerpt above, Paine discusses some economic reasons.

(a) Identify Costs Why does Paine think that association with Britain hurts American trade?

(b) Make Inferences What do you think Paine means by "the blood of the slain"?

The Declaration of Independence

The Declaration of Independence is a brilliant piece of writing. Building on the ideas of the Enlightenment, it uses step-by-step logic to explain why the colonists wanted to break away from British rule. (See the Declaration of Independence following this section.)

The Declaration begins with a preamble, or introduction. It says that "a decent respect to the opinions of mankind" requires that Americans explain why they are breaking away from Britain.

Analyze Word Roots
Determine the meaning of the word *respect*. The root *spec* means "see." Also read how the word is used in context.

Natural Rights Following the preamble, the Declaration has three main sections. The first section states some general ideas about society and government. "We hold these truths to be self-evident," or obvious to all. First among these truths is that "all men are created equal." Jefferson goes on to state that everyone is "endowed by their Creator with certain unalienable rights." This statement is based on John Locke's ideas about natural rights. (See Chapter 4.)

Like Locke, Jefferson goes on to state that governments are created in order to protect people's rights. And, like Locke, he concludes that, if a government <u>violates</u> those rights, the people have a right to abolish their government and create another.

Vocabulary Builder
<u>violate</u> (VY uh layt) **v.** fail to keep or observe; infringe on

List of Grievances Jefferson's next task was to prove that the British government had, in fact, violated the rights of the colonists. So the next section details a long list of specific grievances, or formal complaints, against King George III of England.

Many grievances accuse the king of ignoring rights that English citizens had enjoyed since the time of the Magna Carta. For example, the Magna Carta had established trial by jury as a basic right. The Declaration thus condemns the king "for depriving us, in many cases, of trial by jury." The Declaration also charges the king with "imposing taxes on us without our consent"—another violation of traditional English rights.

Time after time, says the Declaration, colonists have appealed to the king. But King George has ignored the petitions they sent. He must, therefore, be considered "unfit to be the ruler of a free people."

King George III

Dissolving the Bonds After stating the basic principle that the people have a right to abolish an unjust government and showing that the king has violated the rights of the colonists, the Declaration reaches a logical conclusion. It asserts that the colonies are "free and independent states . . . and that all political connection between them and the state of Great Britain is, and ought to be totally dissolved."

The document ends with a solemn pledge: "With a firm reliance on the protection of Divine Providence, we mutually pledge to each other our Lives, our Fortunes, and our sacred Honor."

The serious tone shows that, to the Patriots, declaring independence was a serious and deeply felt step.

✓ **Checkpoint** What does the Declaration of Independence say about people's rights?

Impact of the Declaration

When Congress met to debate Lee's resolution, it still was not certain that they would declare independence. But on July 4, 1776, Congress approved the Declaration of Independence. Since then, Americans have celebrated July 4th as Independence Day.

The actual signing of the Declaration took place on August 2. According to tradition, as he stepped up to sign the document, Benjamin Franklin commented, "We must all hang together, or most assuredly we shall all hang separately." Indeed, for the delegates who signed, the personal risk was great. If captured by the British, they could be hanged.

The Declaration of Independence changed the nature of the Revolution. No longer were the Patriots fighting for fairer treatment from Britain. Now, they were fighting to create a new nation. There was no turning back.

Since then, the Declaration of Independence has become one of the world's enduring documents. The statement that "all men are created equal" still inspires Americans and people in other nations. In 1776, these words applied primarily to white, male property owners. Over the years, Americans worked to expand the notion of equality and natural rights.

☑**Checkpoint** **How did the Declaration change the nature of the American Revolution?**

⭐ **Looking Back and Ahead** Declaring independence from Britain was only a first step. For the Declaration to have real meaning, the Americans would have to win their liberties on the battlefield. In the next section, you will read about the progress of the war for independence.

Thomas Jefferson

Section 1 | **Check Your Progress**

Progress Monitoring Online
For: Self-test with instant help
Visit: PHSchool.com
Web Code: mva-2061

Comprehension and Critical Thinking

1. (a) Recall What was the main idea of Thomas Paine's *Common Sense*?
(b) Draw Conclusions Why do you think *Common Sense* had such an impact on colonists?

2. (a) Identify What are the major parts of the Declaration of Independence?
(b) Apply Information Why is the list of grievances against the king an important part of the Declaration?

🔄 Reading Skill

3. Analyze Word Roots Use the word root *spir*, meaning "breathe," to determine the meaning of the word *inspire* in this sentence: The statement that "all men are created equal" still *inspires* Americans and people in other nations.

Key Terms

Complete each sentence so that the second part further explains the first part and clearly shows your understanding of the key term.

4. The Declaration of Independence began with a preamble, or _____.
5. Congress took a step toward independence when Lee introduced Virginia's resolution, or _____.
6. The Declaration includes a list of grievances, or _____.

Writing

7. List two challenges you think Thomas Jefferson faced in writing the Declaration of Independence. Do you think he met these challenges? Explain.

# of Independence

By signing the Declaration of Independence, members of the Continental Congress sent a clear message to Britain that the American colonies were free and independent states. Starting with its preamble, the document spells out all the reasons the people of the United States have the right to break away from Britain. Critical Thinking: *Detect Points of View How would a Loyalist react to the Declaration of Independence?*

Preamble
The document first lists the reasons for writing the Declaration.

Protection of Natural Rights
If a government fails to protect people's natural rights, the people have a right to reject it and create another.

Grievances Against the King
King George has violated colonists' rights and ignored their petitions.

Declaring Independence
Therefore, the colonies declare their independence from Great Britain.

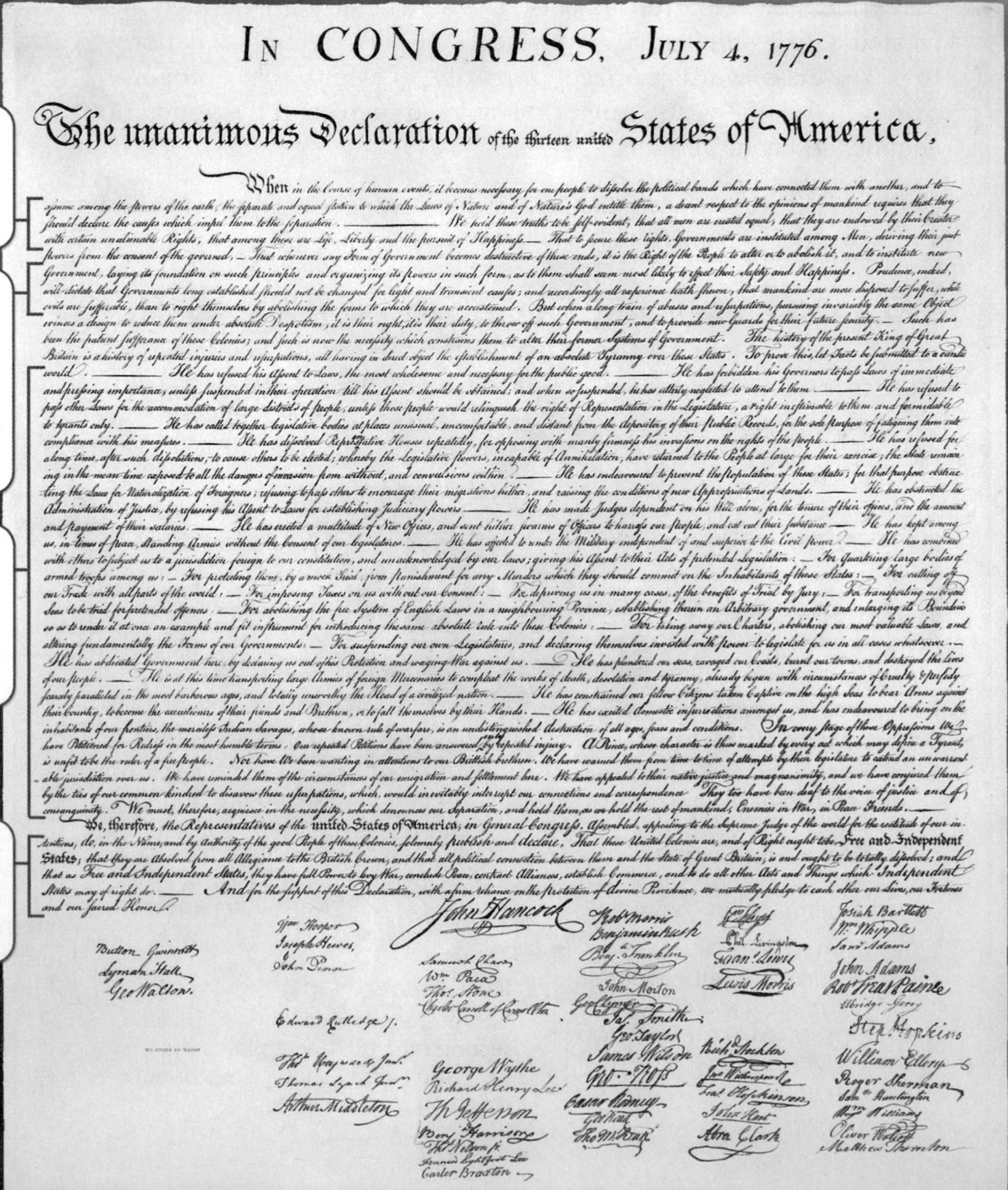

IN CONGRESS, JULY 4, 1776.

The unanimous Declaration of the thirteen united States of America,

When in the Course of human events, it becomes necessary for one people to dissolve the political bands which have connected them with another, and to assume among the powers of the earth, the separate and equal station to which the Laws of Nature and of Nature's God entitle them, a decent respect to the opinions of mankind requires that they should declare the causes which impel them to the separation. — We hold these truths to be self-evident, that all men are created equal, that they are endowed by their Creator with certain unalienable Rights, that among these are Life, Liberty and the pursuit of Happiness. — That to secure these rights, Governments are instituted among Men, deriving their just powers from the consent of the governed, — That whenever any Form of Government becomes destructive of these ends, it is the Right of the People to alter or to abolish it, and to institute new Government, laying its foundation on such principles and organizing its powers in such form, as to them shall seem most likely to effect their Safety and Happiness. Prudence, indeed, will dictate that Governments long established should not be changed for light and transient causes; and accordingly all experience hath shewn, that mankind are more disposed to suffer, while evils are sufferable, than to right themselves by abolishing the forms to which they are accustomed. But when a long train of abuses and usurpations, pursuing invariably the same Object evinces a design to reduce them under absolute Despotism, it is their right, it is their duty, to throw off such Government, and to provide new Guards for their future security. — Such has been the patient sufferance of these Colonies; and such is now the necessity which constrains them to alter their former Systems of Government. The history of the present King of Great Britain is a history of repeated injuries and usurpations, all having in direct object the establishment of an absolute Tyranny over these States. To prove this, let Facts be submitted to a candid world. — He has refused his Assent to Laws, the most wholesome and necessary for the public good. — He has forbidden his Governors to pass Laws of immediate and pressing importance, unless suspended in their operation till his Assent should be obtained; and when so suspended, he has utterly neglected to attend to them. — He has refused to pass other Laws for the accommodation of large districts of people, unless those people would relinquish the right of Representation in the Legislature, a right inestimable to them and formidable to tyrants only. — He has called together legislative bodies at places unusual, uncomfortable, and distant from the depository of their Public Records, for the sole purpose of fatiguing them into compliance with his measures. — He has dissolved Representative Houses repeatedly, for opposing with manly firmness his invasions on the rights of the people. — He has refused for a long time, after such dissolutions, to cause others to be elected; whereby the Legislative powers, incapable of Annihilation, have returned to the People at large for their exercise; the State remaining in the mean time exposed to all the dangers of invasion from without, and convulsions within. — He has endeavoured to prevent the population of these States; for that purpose obstructing the Laws for Naturalization of Foreigners; refusing to pass others to encourage their migrations hither, and raising the conditions of new Appropriations of Lands. — He has obstructed the Administration of Justice, by refusing his Assent to Laws for establishing Judiciary powers. — He has made Judges dependent on his Will alone, for the tenure of their offices, and the amount and payment of their salaries. — He has erected a multitude of New Offices, and sent hither swarms of Officers to harrass our people, and eat out their substance. — He has kept among us, in times of peace, Standing Armies without the Consent of our legislatures. — He has affected to render the Military independent of and superior to the Civil power. — He has combined with others to subject us to a jurisdiction foreign to our constitution, and unacknowledged by our laws; giving his Assent to their Acts of pretended Legislation: — For Quartering large bodies of armed troops among us: — For protecting them, by a mock Trial, from punishment for any Murders which they should commit on the Inhabitants of these States: — For cutting off our Trade with all parts of the world: — For imposing Taxes on us without our Consent: — For depriving us in many cases, of the benefits of Trial by Jury: — For transporting us beyond Seas to be tried for pretended offences — For abolishing the free System of English Laws in a neighbouring Province, establishing therein an Arbitrary government, and enlarging its Boundaries so as to render it at once an example and fit instrument for introducing the same absolute rule into these Colonies: — For taking away our Charters, abolishing our most valuable Laws, and altering fundamentally the Forms of our Governments: — For suspending our own Legislatures, and declaring themselves invested with power to legislate for us in all cases whatsoever. — He has abdicated Government here, by declaring us out of his Protection and waging War against us. — He has plundered our seas, ravaged our Coasts, burnt our towns, and destroyed the lives of our people. — He is at this time transporting large Armies of foreign Mercenaries to compleat the works of death, desolation and tyranny, already begun with circumstances of Cruelty & perfidy scarcely paralleled in the most barbarous ages, and totally unworthy the Head of a civilized nation. — He has constrained our fellow Citizens taken Captive on the high Seas to bear Arms against their Country, to become the executioners of their friends and Brethren, or to fall themselves by their Hands. — He has excited domestic insurrections amongst us, and has endeavoured to bring on the inhabitants of our frontiers, the merciless Indian Savages, whose known rule of warfare, is an undistinguished destruction of all ages, sexes and conditions. In every stage of these Oppressions We have Petitioned for Redress in the most humble terms: Our repeated Petitions have been answered only by repeated injury. A Prince, whose character is thus marked by every act which may define a Tyrant, is unfit to be the ruler of a free people. Nor have We been wanting in attentions to our Brittish brethren. We have warned them from time to time of attempts by their legislature to extend an unwarrantable jurisdiction over us. We have reminded them of the circumstances of our emigration and settlement here. We have appealed to their native justice and magnanimity, and we have conjured them by the ties of our common kindred to disavow these usurpations, which, would inevitably interrupt our connections and correspondence. They too have been deaf to the voice of justice and of consanguinity. We must, therefore, acquiesce in the necessity, which denounces our Separation, and hold them, as we hold the rest of mankind, Enemies in War, in Peace Friends. —

We, therefore, the Representatives of the united States of America, in General Congress, Assembled, appealing to the Supreme Judge of the world for the rectitude of our intentions, do, in the Name, and by Authority of the good People of these Colonies, solemnly publish and declare, That these United Colonies are, and of Right ought to be Free and Independent States; that they are Absolved from all Allegiance to the British Crown, and that all political connection between them and the State of Great Britain, is and ought to be totally dissolved; and that as Free and Independent States, they have full Power to levy War, conclude Peace, contract Alliances, establish Commerce, and to do all other Acts and Things which Independent States may of right do. — And for the support of this Declaration, with a firm reliance on the protection of divine Providence, we mutually pledge to each other our Lives, our Fortunes and our sacred Honor.

John Hancock

The Unanimous Declaration of the Thirteen United States of America

When in the Course of human events, it becomes necessary for one people to dissolve the political bands which have connected them with another, and to assume among the powers of the earth, the separate and equal station to which the Laws of Nature and of Nature's God entitle them, a decent respect to the opinions of mankind requires that they should declare the causes which impel them to the separation.

We hold these truths to be self-evident, that all men are created equal, that they are endowed by their Creator with certain unalienable Rights, that among these are Life, Liberty and the pursuit of Happiness. That to secure these rights, Governments are instituted among Men, deriving their just powers from the consent of the governed. That whenever any Form of Government becomes destructive of these ends, it is the Right of the People to alter or to abolish it, and to institute new Government, laying its foundation on such principles and organizing its powers in such form, as to them shall seem most likely to effect their Safety and Happiness. Prudence, indeed, will dictate that Governments long established should not be changed for light and transient causes; and

The Declaration of Independence has four parts: the Preamble, the Declaration of Natural Rights, the List of Grievances, and the Resolution of Independence. The Preamble states why the Declaration was written. The document will explain to the world the reasons why the colonists feel **impelled** to separate from Great Britain.

People set up governments to protect their basic rights. These rights are **unalienable**; they cannot be taken away. The purpose of government is to protect these natural rights. When a government does not protect the rights of the people, the people must change the government or create a new one. The colonists feel that the king's repeated **usurpations**, or unjust uses of power, are a form of **despotism** accordingly all experience hath shown that mankind are more disposed to suffer, while evils are sufferable, than to right themselves by abolishing the forms to which they are accustomed. But when a long train of abuses and usurpations, pursuing invariably the same Object evinces a design to reduce them under absolute Despotism, it is their right, it is their duty, to throw off such Government, and to provide new Guards for their future security. Such has been the patient sufferance of these Colonies; and such is now the necessity which constrains them to alter their former Systems of Government. The history of the present King of Great Britain is a history of repeated injuries and usurpations, all having in direct object the establishment of an absolute Tyranny over these States. To prove this, let Facts be submitted to a candid world.

He has refused his Assent to Laws, the most wholesome and necessary for the public good.

He has forbidden his Governors to pass Laws of immediate and pressing importance, unless suspended in their operation till his Assent should be obtained; and when so suspended, he has utterly neglected to attend to them.

He has refused to pass other Laws for the accommodation of large districts of people, unless those people would relinquish the right of Representation in the Legislature, a right inestimable to them and formidable to tyrants only.

He has called together legislative bodies at places unusual, uncomfortable, and distant from the depository of their public Records, for the sole purpose of fatiguing them into compliance with his measures.

He has dissolved Representative Houses repeatedly, for opposing with manly firmness his invasions on the rights of the people.

He has refused for a long time, after such dissolutions, to cause others to be elected; whereby the Legislative powers, incapable of Annihilation, have returned to the People at large for their exercise; the State remaining in the mean time exposed to all the dangers of invasion from without, and convulsions within.

He has endeavoured to prevent the population of these States; for that purpose obstructing the Laws for Naturalization of Foreigners; refusing to pass others to encourage their migrations hither, and raising the conditions of new Appropriations of Lands.

He has obstructed the Administration of Justice by refusing his Assent to Laws for establishing Judiciary powers.

He has made Judges dependent on his Will alone, for the tenure of their offices, and the amount and payment of their salaries.

He has erected a multitude of New Offices, and sent hither swarms of Officers to harass our people, and eat out their substance.

He has kept among us, in times of peace, Standing Armies without the Consent of our legislatures.

The List of Grievances details the colonists' complaints against the British government, and King George III in particular. The colonists have no say in determining the laws that govern them and they feel King George's actions show little or no concern for the well being of the people.

The colonists refuse to **relinquish**, or give up, the right to representation, which they feel is **inestimable**, or priceless.

The king has refused to allow new legislators to be elected. As a result, the colonies have not been able to protect themselves against foreign enemies and **convulsions**, or riots, within the colonies.

The king has tried to stop foreigners from coming to the colonies by refusing to pass naturalization laws. Laws for naturalization of foreigners are laws that set up the process for foreigners to become legal citizens.

The king alone has decided a judge's **tenure**, or term. This grievance later would result in Article 3, Section 1, of the Constitution, which states that federal judges hold office for life.

He has affected to render the Military independent of and superior to the Civil power.

He has combined with others to subject us to a jurisdiction foreign to our constitution, and unacknowledged by our laws; giving his Assent to their Acts of pretended Legislation:

For quartering large bodies of armed troops among us:

For protecting them, by a mock Trial, from punishment for any Murders which they should commit on the Inhabitants of these States:

For cutting off our Trade with all parts of the world:

For imposing Taxes on us without our Consent:

For depriving us in many cases, of the benefit of Trial by Jury:

For transporting us beyond Seas to be tried for pretended offences:

For abolishing the free System of English Laws in a neighbouring Province, establishing therein an Arbitrary government, and enlarging its Boundaries so as to render it at once an example and fit instrument for introducing the same absolute rule into these Colonies:

For taking away our Charters, abolishing our most valuable Laws, and altering fundamentally the Forms of our Governments:

For suspending our own Legislatures, and declaring themselves invested with power to legislate for us in all cases whatsoever.

He has abdicated Government here, by declaring us out of his Protection and waging War against us.

He has plundered our seas, ravaged our Coasts, burnt our towns, and destroyed the lives of our people.

He is at this time transporting large Armies of foreign Mercenaries to complete the works of death, desolation, and tyranny, already begun with circumstances of Cruelty and perfidy scarcely paralleled in the most barbarous ages, and totally unworthy the Head of a civilized nation.

He has constrained our fellow Citizens taken Captive on the high Seas to bear Arms against their Country, to become the executioners of their friends and Brethren, or to fall themselves by their Hands.

He has excited domestic insurrections amongst us, and has endeavoured to bring on the inhabitants of our frontiers, the merciless Indian Savages whose known rule of warfare, is an undistinguished destruction of all ages, sexes and conditions.

In every stage of these Oppressions We have Petitioned for Redress in the most humble terms: Our repeated Petitions have been answered only by repeated injury. A Prince, whose character is thus marked by every act which may define a Tyrant, is unfit to be the ruler of a free People.

Forced by the king, the colonists have been **quartering**, or lodging, troops in their homes. This grievance found its way into the Constitution in the Third Amendment.

The king has taken away the rights of the people in a nearby province (Canada). The colonists feared he could do the same to the colonies if he so wished.

The king has hired foreign **mercenaries**, or soldiers, to bring death and destruction to the colonists. The head of a civilized country should never act with the cruelty and **perfidy**, or dishonesty, that the king has.

The colonists have tried repeatedly to petition the king to **redress,** or correct, these wrongs. Each time, they have been ignored by the king or punished by new laws. Because of the way he treats his subjects, the king is not fit to rule a free people.

Nor have We been wanting in attentions to our British brethren. We have warned them from time to time of attempts by their legislature to extend an unwarrantable jurisdiction over us. We have reminded them of the circumstances of our emigration and settlement here. We have appealed to their native justice and magnanimity, and we have conjured them by the ties of our common kindred, to disavow these usurpations, which would inevitably interrupt our connections and correspondence. They too have been deaf to the voice of justice and of consanguinity. We must, therefore, acquiesce in the necessity, which denounces our Separation, and hold them, as we hold the rest of mankind, Enemies in War, in Peace Friends.

We, therefore, the Representatives of the United States of America, in General Congress, Assembled, appealing to the Supreme Judge of the world for the rectitude of our intentions, do, in the Name, and by Authority of the good People of these Colonies, solemnly publish and declare, That these United Colonies are, and of Right ought to be Free and Independent States; that they are Absolved from all Allegiance to the British Crown, and that all political connection between them and the State of Great Britain, is and ought to be totally dissolved; and that as Free and Independent States, they have full Power to levy War, conclude Peace, contract Alliances, establish Commerce, and to do all other Acts and Things which Independent States may of right do. And for the support of this Declaration, with a firm reliance on the protection of Divine Providence, we mutually pledge to each other our Lives, our Fortunes and our sacred Honor.

John Hancock, *President*
Charles Thomson, *Secretary*

Georgia
Button Gwinnett
Lyman Hall
George Walton

North Carolina
William Hooper
Joseph Hewes
John Penn

South Carolina
Edward Rutledge
Thomas Heyward, Jr.
Thomas Lynch, Jr.
Arthur Middleton

Maryland
Samuel Chase
William Paca
Thomas Stone
Charles Carroll

Virginia
George Wythe
Richard Henry Lee
Thomas Jefferson
Benjamin Harrison
Thomas Nelson, Jr.
Francis Lightfoot Lee
Carter Braxton

Pennsylvania
Robert Morris
Benjamin Rush
Benjamin Franklin
John Morton
George Clymer
James Smith
George Taylor
James Wilson
George Ross

Delaware
Caesar Rodney
George Read
Thomas McKean

New York
William Floyd
Philip Livingston
Francis Lewis
Lewis Morris

New Jersey
Richard Stockton
John Witherspoon
Francis Hopkinson
John Hart
Abraham Clark

New Hampshire
Josiah Bartlett
William Whipple
Matthew Thornton

Massachusetts
Samuel Adams
John Adams
Robert Treat Paine
Elbridge Gerry

Rhode Island
Stephen Hopkins
William Ellery

Connecticut
Samuel Huntington
William Williams
Oliver Wolcott
Roger Sherman

The Enemy Surrounded Them

❝O doleful! doleful! doleful!—Blood! Carnage! Fire! . . . Many battalions, of excellent men, went out into the woods on the right and left wing of the enemy;—Alas! numbers went never to return!—The enemy surrounded them. . . . Many, many we fear are lost.❞

—American soldier Philip Fithian, describing fighting in New York, 1776

◀ At Saratoga, American General Benedict Arnold won a key victory over the British.

A Critical Time

Objectives

- Discover the results of fighting in the Middle States.
- Understand why the Battle of Saratoga was a turning point in the American Revolution.
- Learn how foreign nations and volunteers helped the Americans.

🎯 Reading Skill

Apply the Meanings of Prefixes

Prefixes—word parts added to the beginning of words or word roots—can dramatically affect a word's meaning. Applying the meanings of common prefixes will help you define unfamiliar words. Piece together a likely meaning. Check how the word is used within the content of the surrounding text. If necessary, use a dictionary.

Key Terms and People

Nathan Hale
mercenary
alliance
Marquis de
  Lafayette
cavalry
Friedrich von
  Steuben

Why It Matters The thirteen colonies had proclaimed their independence. But this declaration would have lasting meaning only if Washington and his army of poorly trained troops could win victories over the powerful British army.

❓ **Section Focus Question: How were the early years of the war a critical time?**

Retreat From New York

In mid-1776, the heavy fighting shifted from New England to the Middle States. There, the Continental army suffered through the worst days of the war.

Attack and Retreat In June 1776, just as the Continental Congress was considering independence, a large British fleet arrived off New York. Sir William Howe, the British commander, gathered his forces on Staten Island, at the southern edge of New York harbor.

Washington expected Howe's attack. He already had led his forces south from Boston to Brooklyn on Long Island. However, his army was no match for the British. Howe had about 34,000 well-trained troops and 10,000 sailors, as well as ships to ferry them ashore. Washington had fewer than 20,000 poorly trained troops and no navy.

That summer saw a long series of battles and American retreats. In the Battle of Long Island, in August 1776, the British drove Washington's troops out of Brooklyn. The following month, Washington had to abandon New York City. The British pursued the Americans north to White Plains, then west and south across New Jersey.

Nathan Hale During the fight for New York, Nathan Hale became an American legend. Hale was a Connecticut officer, and he volunteered for dangerous spy duty. His mission was to collect information about British battle plans on Long Island.

Caught behind British lines, Hale was tried and condemned to death. He was hanged the next morning. Later, it was reported that his last words had been, "I only regret that I have but one life to lose for my country."

✓**Checkpoint** **What was the result of the Battle of Long Island?**

Surprises for the British

Under relentless British pursuit, the Continental army kept retreating. In December, it crossed the Delaware River into Pennsylvania. The British now threatened Philadelphia. Patriot spirits were low. Many soldiers deserted. Others seemed ready to go home as soon as their terms of service ended.

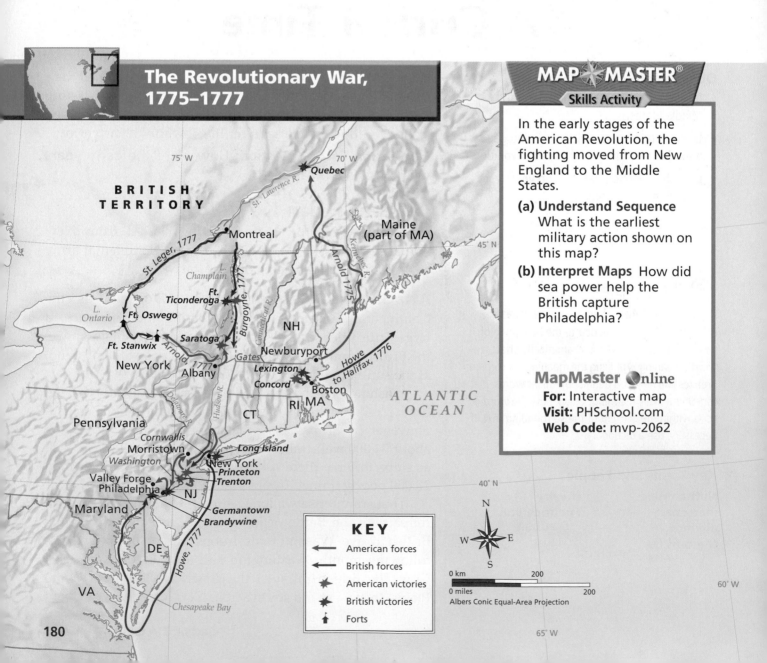

The Revolutionary War, 1775–1777

MAP★MASTER®

Skills Activity

In the early stages of the American Revolution, the fighting moved from New England to the Middle States.

(a) Understand Sequence What is the earliest military action shown on this map?

(b) Interpret Maps How did sea power help the British capture Philadelphia?

MapMaster ●nline
For: Interactive map
Visit: PHSchool.com
Web Code: mvp-2062

KEY

→ American forces
→ British forces
✦ American victories
✸ British victories
⬧ Forts

0 km   200
0 miles   200
Albers Conic Equal-Area Projection

Thomas Paine had retreated with the army through New Jersey. To raise morale, he wrote another pamphlet, *The Crisis*. Paine urged Americans to support the army, despite hard times. He wrote:

> **"**These are the times that try men's souls. The summer soldier and the sunshine patriot will, in this crisis, shrink from the service of his country; but he that stands it now deserves the love and thanks of man and woman.**"**
>
> —Thomas Paine, *The Crisis*

Washington had *The Crisis* read aloud to his troops. At the same time, he made plans for a bold attack.

Crossing the Delaware On Christmas night, 1776, Washington led 2,400 men across the river in small boats. Soldiers huddled in the boats as the spray from the river froze on their faces. So poorly supplied were the troops that some had no shoes. Once across the river, the soldiers marched in the swirling snow. To keep their feet from freezing, the soldiers bound them in rags.

On the far bank, the men trudged several miles with Washington urging them on. Early on December 26, they attacked Trenton from two sides, achieving complete surprise.

An American Victory The attack brought a ringing American victory. The soldiers in Trenton were Hessians (men from Hesse, a small German state). They were among thousands of German mercenaries who were fighting for the British. Mercenaries are soldiers who are paid to fight for a country other than their own. Washington's army captured almost a thousand Hessian mercenaries.

Pursued by the British, Washington used a clever trick to escape. His soldiers made camp near Trenton and lit campfires. After dark, most of the men packed up and quietly withdrew. The British did not discover the trick until daylight, when the main body of soldiers attacked and heavily damaged a British force near Princeton.

☑**Checkpoint** How did Washington attack Trenton?

Saratoga: A Turning Point

British general John Burgoyne came up with a plan he hoped would quickly end the rebellion. His goal was to cut New England off from the rest of the states.

Washington at Trenton
During Washington's surprise attack on Trenton, the commander of the Hessian mercenaries was seriously wounded. In this picture, Washington orders his men to help the dying Hessian officer to his bed. **Critical Thinking: *Apply Information*** *Why was Washington able to win the battle at Trenton?*

The British Plan Burgoyne's plan called for British forces to drive toward Albany, New York, from three directions. From Canada, an army of 8,000 would move south to capture the forts on Lake Champlain, Lake George, and the upper Hudson River. From the west, a smaller British force would drive through the Mohawk Valley toward Albany. And from the south, General Howe would lead a large army up the Hudson River from New York City.

Burgoyne's plan ran into trouble almost immediately. George III ordered Howe to move south from New York in a misguided attempt to attack Philadelphia. Not until November were Howe's forces ready to march north again. At the same time, American forces cut off the British troops coming through the Mohawk Valley.

An American Victory Burgoyne led the main British force from Canada in June. After recapturing Fort Ticonderoga, they slowly pushed south, dragging a large train of baggage carts through the woods. Supplies were running short.

Americans were rushing to block the British. By September, the American commander in New York, General Horatio Gates, had 6,000 men ready to fight. At the village of Saratoga, New York, the Americans surrounded the British. After suffering heavy casualties, Burgoyne surrendered on October 17, 1777.

Apply the Meanings of Prefixes

Reading Skill

The prefix *mis-* means "badly" or "wrongly." What does the word *misguided* mean?

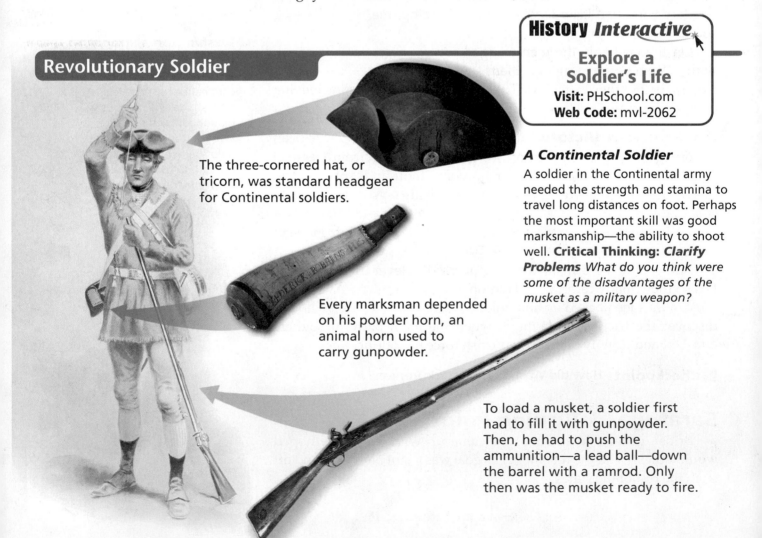

Revolutionary Soldier

History *Interactive*

Explore a Soldier's Life
Visit: PHSchool.com
Web Code: mvl-2062

The three-cornered hat, or tricorn, was standard headgear for Continental soldiers.

Every marksman depended on his powder horn, an animal horn used to carry gunpowder.

To load a musket, a soldier first had to fill it with gunpowder. Then, he had to push the ammunition—a lead ball—down the barrel with a ramrod. Only then was the musket ready to fire.

A Continental Soldier

A soldier in the Continental army needed the strength and stamina to travel long distances on foot. Perhaps the most important skill was good marksmanship—the ability to shoot well. **Critical Thinking:** *Clarify Problems What do you think were some of the disadvantages of the musket as a military weapon?*

Results of the Battle The Battle of Saratoga marked a major turning point in the war. The American victory ended the British threat to New England and destroyed British hopes of an easy victory. It also lifted Patriot spirits at a time when Washington's army was suffering defeats. Perhaps most important, the Battle of Saratoga helped convince Europeans that the Americans had a sound chance of winning.

☑**Checkpoint** List two results of the Battle of Saratoga.

Help From Overseas

Soon after Saratoga, France agreed to openly support American independence. In February 1778, France officially formed an alliance with the United States. An **alliance** is a formal agreement between two powers to work together toward a common goal.

The French Alliance France was eager to weaken Britain. Even before Saratoga, the French had secretly supplied money and arms to the Americans. But the French did not want to take an open stand until it seemed the Americans might win. The Battle of Saratoga convinced the French government to help the struggling young nation. In February 1778, France became the first nation to sign a treaty with the United States.

France and its allies in the Netherlands and Spain also went to war with Britain. By carrying the fight to Europe and the Caribbean, the allies forced Britain to wage war on many fronts. This helped the American cause, because the British could spare fewer troops to fight in North America.

European Volunteers A number of Europeans volunteered to serve with the American forces. They were inspired by the American struggle for liberty.

A French noble, the **Marquis de Lafayette** (lah fay YET), became a high-ranking officer in Washington's army. He and Washington became close friends. When Lafayette was wounded in battle, Washington told a surgeon, "Treat him as though he were my son."

Volunteers from Poland also made <u>vital</u> contributions to the Patriot war effort. Thaddeus Kosciusko (kawsh CHUSH koh) was an engineer who took charge of building fortifications at West Point. Casimir Pulaski led and trained **cavalry,** or units of troops on horseback.

Baron von Steuben A German baron, Friedrich von Steuben (STOO buhn), helped train the Continental army. Steuben had served in the Prussian army, which was considered the best in Europe.

Before Steuben arrived in early 1778, American troops were often poorly trained and undisciplined. Steuben taught the soldiers how to march, how to improve their aim, and how to attack with bayonets. His methods helped to <u>transform</u> raw recruits into soldiers and shaped the Continental army into a more effective force.

☑**Checkpoint** How did France aid the Patriot cause?

Medals commemorating the American-French alliance

Vocabulary Builder
<u>vital</u> (vī tuhl) **adj.** necessary; of great importance

Vocabulary Builder
<u>transform</u> (trans FORM) **v.** to change from one thing or condition to another

Valley Forge

Washington's Continental army suffered through the cruel winter of 1777–1778 in a hastily built camp at Valley Forge in Pennsylvania. Meanwhile, some 22 miles away, British officers in Philadelphia danced the winter away in a merry round of parties and balls.

The 11,000 Continental soldiers were not sufficiently fed, clothed, or housed. Many lacked socks, shoes, and even trousers. Throughout the winter, they shivered in drafty huts. At any one time, about one soldier in four was sick with chills, fever, or worse.

Because food was so scarce, the soldiers mainly ate thin soup and dry bread patties. One private later recalled that he went without food for two days. He was so hungry he would have grabbed food away from anyone, even his best friend. Finally, he found half a pumpkin. He cooked it "upon a rock, the skin side up, by making a fire on it."

When Americans learned about conditions at Valley Forge, they sent help. Women collected food, medicine, warm clothes, and ammunition. Some women, including George Washington's wife, Martha, went to Valley Forge to tend the sick and wounded.

Despite its woes, the Continental army used that winter to gather its strength for the battles that lay ahead. Steuben's drills sharpened the soldiers' skills and discipline.

✓**Checkpoint** **Why was the winter at Valley Forge so difficult?**

☆ **Looking Back and Ahead** By the spring of 1778, the army at Valley Forge was ready to resume the fight. "The army grows stronger every day," wrote one New Jersey soldier. While soldiers drilled, Washington and his staff planned new campaigns against the British.

Washington at Valley Forge

Section 2 | **Check Your Progress**

> **Progress Monitoring** ❂nline
> **For:** Self-test with instant help
> **Visit:** PHSchool.com
> **Web Code:** mva-2062

Comprehension and Critical Thinking

1. (a) Recall What happened at Trenton in December 1776?
(b) Draw Inferences What did Washington's actions at the Battle of Trenton show about his character and leadership?

2. (a) List What were three important results of the American victory at Saratoga?
(b) Make Predictions What do you think would have happened if the Americans had lost the battle?

⟳ Reading Skill

3. Apply the Meanings of Prefixes The prefix *trans-* means "change." The word root *form* means "shape" or "structure." Use this information to explain the meaning of *transform* in this sentence: His methods helped to *transform* raw recruits into soldiers.

Key Terms

Read each sentence below. If the sentence is true, write YES. If the sentence is not true, write NO and explain why.

4. German mercenaries helped the British because they believed the king should rule the Americans.
5. After making an alliance with the Americans, France contributed money and arms to the Patriots.
6. The cavalry soldiers fired at the British soldiers from the ground before running away.

Writing

7. In order to gather enough soldiers to fight the battle in America, the British had to hire German mercenaries. List one strong argument for and one strong argument against this solution.

Valley Forge
by Maxwell Anderson

Prepare to Read

Introduction

Maxwell Anderson's play *Valley Forge* depicts the hardships faced by Washington's army in the winter of 1778. One problem the army faced was men trying to go home. Here, Washington hears the complaints of a soldier named Teague.

Reading Skill

Analyze Dramatic Conflict An important element in any drama is conflict, when two characters want different things. As you read this scene, try to identify the source of the conflict between Washington and Teague.

Vocabulary *Builder*

As you read this literature selection, look for the following underlined words:

commissary (KAH muh sehr ee) *n.* food supplies

munitions (myoo NIH shuhns) *n.* weapons and ammunition

TEAGUE: I'm going hungry here and my woman's going hungry at home. You let me go home for the winter, and you won't have to feed me, and that relieves the <u>commissary</u>. I rustle some wild meat for the younguns and the old woman, and they don't starve and I don't starve. More'n that, everybody knows there's two or three thousand men gone home already for that same reason, and if they was here now they'd be chewing the bark off the second-growth birch like so many cottontails. I don't hold it against you and I don't hold it against anybody because I don't know who in thunder to hold it against, but there's nothing to eat here. . . .

WASHINGTON: Well, Master Teague, if they catch you they'll give you seventy-five lashes, and that's a good deal to take and live. On the other hand, you're quite right from your own angle, and if I were you I'd feel as you do. If you go home, and we all go home this winter, you won't need to bother about coming back in the spring. There'll be not fighting to come back to. General Howe will march out of Philadelphia and take over these states of ours. If he knew now how many have deserted, how many are sick, how many unfit for duty on account of the lack of food and clothes and <u>munitions</u>, he'd come back in force and wring our necks one by one, and the neck of our sickly little revolution along with us.

From *America On Stage: Ten Great Plays of American History,*
ed. Stanley Richards. Doubleday & Co., 1976.

Analyze Dramatic Conflict

What does Teague want? What does Washington want? How are their wishes in conflict?

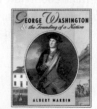

If you liked this excerpt and want to learn more about George Washington, you might want to read *George Washington and the Founding of a Nation* by Albert Marrin. Dutton Books, 2001.

Analyze LITERATURE

Do you think that Washington should permit Teague to go home without punishment? Write a paragraph explaining the reasons for your opinion.

Most Daring Conduct

❝Our situation was now truly critical—no possibility of retreating in case of defeat—and in full view of a town that had . . . six hundred men in it, troops, inhabitants and Indians. . . . We knew that nothing but the most daring conduct would insure success. ❞

—George Rogers Clark, describing the battle against British and Indians at Vincennes, 1779

◄ Clark led his army through western wilderness.

The War Widens

Objectives

- Discover the role that African Americans played in the American Revolution.

- Find out how the war affected women and other civilians.

- Learn about the progress of the fighting on the western frontier and at sea.

Reading Skill

Analyze Word Roots Word roots can do more than help you define unfamiliar words. They can help you expand your vocabulary. As you read Section 3, use word roots to determine meanings. Then, list other words you know that come from the same word roots. Think about how they share meanings with the text words—and how the meanings differ. Notice the shades of meaning that can derive from a single word root.

Key Terms and People

enlist
civilian
continental
George Rogers
  Clark

Bernardo de
  Gálvez
John Paul Jones
privateer

Why It Matters Many early battles of the American Revolution were fought in the Northeast. But the struggle for independence was waged on many fronts and affected Americans in all parts of the country.

❓ **Section Focus Question: How did the effects of the war widen?**

African Americans in the War

African Americans fought on both sides of the American Revolution. For them, the war meant both danger and opportunity.

Free and Slave From the beginning, free African Americans took part in the war. At least nine served as minutemen at Lexington and Concord. Peter Salem fought at Bunker Hill and Saratoga.

Enslaved people served as well. After fleeing his master in Rhode Island, Jehu Grant served in the American army for nine months. He later recalled:

❝When I saw liberty poles and the people all engaged for the support of freedom, I could not but like and be pleased with such thing. . . . The songs of liberty . . . thrilled through my heart.❞
—Jehu Grant, letter, December 1, 1836

The British offered freedom to enslaved people who deserted and joined the British. Many thousands did so. They served mainly in support roles as cooks, blacksmiths, and teamsters. However, some people who had formerly been enslaved fought for the British.

On the American side, Washington at first refused to accept African American soldiers. But the British offer of freedom to enslaved people made Washington change his policy. By the end of the war, some 7,000 African Americans had served on the American side, including 2,000 in the navy. African Americans also served in northern militias and state armies. Most southern states, however, refused to accept African American soldiers. Slave owners feared armed slave revolts.

Freedom Beckons During the Revolution, a number of northern states took steps to end slavery. For example, a Pennsylvania law of 1780 provided for a gradual end to slavery. It allowed slaveholders to keep their existing slaves but barred them from getting more.

✓**Checkpoint** Why did some enslaved African Americans choose to fight for the British?

The War at Home

Many men **enlisted,** or signed up for duty, in the military. After a set term, usually one year, they were free to leave. Thus, Washington had to struggle constantly to keep the ranks of his army filled.

Civilians, or people not in the military, also faced hardships. They were often subject to food shortages and military attack.

Analyze Word Roots
The word root *port* means "to carry." The prefix *sub-* means "under," and *sub-* becomes *sup-* when used before the letter *p*. Use these word parts to explain the meaning of *support*. List three other words that build on the root *port*.

Links Across Time

African American Soldiers

1777 Reversing his earlier policy, Washington permits free African Americans to enlist in the Continental army.

1863 During the last half of the Civil War, African Americans were allowed to join the Union army. Black and white soldiers served in separate units.

1948 President Harry Truman ended racial separation in the military. Two years later, black and white troops served side by side in the Korean War.

Link to Today

The Military Today In today's all-volunteer military, African Americans make up 21 percent of all military personnel.

For: U.S. military in the news
Visit: PHSchool.com
Web Code: mvc-2063

A Woman in Battle
When her husband was wounded at the Battle of Monmouth, Mary Ludwig Hays dropped her water bucket and took up his cannon. Her heroic actions made her a legendary American hero, known as Molly Pitcher. **Critical Thinking: Evaluate Information** *Why do you think Molly Pitcher has become a popular subject for American artists? What image of women does she represent?*

Vocabulary Builder
confine (kuhn FĪN) *v.* to keep within certain limits

Vocabulary Builder
resource (REE sors) *n.* supply of something to meet a particular need

Women As men went to war, women took over many of their duties. On farms, women planted crops and cared for livestock. In towns, women often ran their husbands' businesses.

Some women accompanied their husbands to military camps. In battles, they cared for the wounded. One woman, Deborah Sampson, joined the army, disguised as a man. Wounded in battle, Sampson tended her own wounds in order to keep her secret.

The added responsibilities of wartime gave many women a new confidence. At a time when women's roles were largely <u>confined</u>, the war opened up new opportunities for many women.

Financial Burdens Paying for the war was a difficult task. Congress had limited <u>resources</u>. With no power to tax, Congress had to plead with the states for money. However, the states had little money themselves.

To pay and supply troops, Congress printed continentals, or paper money. But the more money Congress printed, the less the money was worth. By the end of the war, paper money had lost almost all its value.

✓**Checkpoint** **What roles did women play in the Revolution?**

Fighting in the West

Throughout most of the American Revolution, attention was mainly focused on the 13 states along the Atlantic coast. However, skirmishes and battles occurred on the western frontier as well.

Native Americans Take Sides Americans tried to keep the Native Americans neutral. They offered payments to groups willing to remain at peace. Still, most Native American groups sided with Britain. They feared that an American victory would mean more settlers moving west or south onto Native American lands.

The turmoil of war hurt many Indian groups. Sometimes tribes split into warring factions when they could not agree which side to join. Thousands of Indians were driven west by raids. Sometimes whole villages picked up and moved to avoid the fighting. Other Native Americans responded by attacking white settlements.

A smallpox epidemic made matters even worse. The disease first spread among American soldiers in Quebec in 1775, and then along the east coast of the colonies. By 1779, it had reached New Orleans. Soon after, it spread to Native American groups all across North America. Smallpox deaths far outnumbered casualties during the American Revolution. By 1782, more than 130,000 whites and Indians had died from smallpox. In contrast, about 8,000 soldiers had died in battle during the same period.

Defending the Frontier Seeking to defend against attacks on the frontier, Virginia sent George Rogers Clark and a militia force to strike British forts beyond the Appalachian Mountains in 1778. Clark's forces easily captured two Mississippi River outposts, Kaskaskia and Cahokia.

Early in 1779, Clark and his men trudged across 200 miles, at times splashing through icy floodwaters up to their chests. Their midwinter attack on the fort at Vincennes caught the British by surprise. The British and their Native American allies surrendered.

Clark's victories allowed settlers to remain on the frontier. This strengthened the American claim on the Ohio Valley area.

Help From the Spanish The Americans got unofficial help from Spain. At the time, Spain governed Louisiana, the land west of the Mississippi stretching as far north as Canada. The Spanish were eager to get back Florida, which they had lost to Britain at the end of the French and Indian War.

Even before Spain declared war against Britain in 1779, Louisiana governor Bernardo de Gálvez began helping the Americans. He secretly provided money and munitions to George Rogers Clark and other Americans. He also gave American ships safe refuge in New Orleans harbor. From 1779 to 1781, Gálvez played a key role in Spanish attacks that captured British forts on the Mississippi River and the Gulf of Mexico. Financial help also came from the Spanish colony of Cuba.

☑Checkpoint What was the result of the fighting in the West?

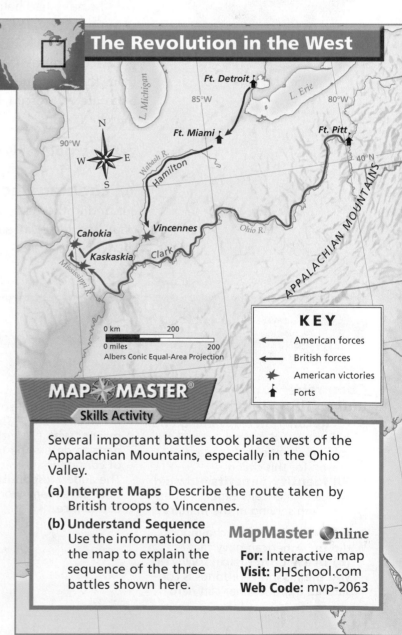

The Revolution in the West

KEY

⟵ American forces
⟵ British forces
✴ American victories
↑ Forts

MAP✪MASTER®

Skills Activity

Several important battles took place west of the Appalachian Mountains, especially in the Ohio Valley.

(a) Interpret Maps Describe the route taken by British troops to Vincennes.

(b) Understand Sequence Use the information on the map to explain the sequence of the three battles shown here.

MapMaster ●nline

For: Interactive map
Visit: PHSchool.com
Web Code: mvp-2063

The War at Sea

Congress had voted to create a Continental navy as early as 1775. But American shipyards were able to build only a few warships. With only a small navy to go against the powerful British fleet, the Americans became skilled at making hit-and-run attacks on British shipping. Still, Britain dominated the seas. The British fleet blocked most ships from entering or leaving American ports.

The most famous naval battle took place off the coast of England in 1779. The American ship *Bonhomme Richard* (bon ohm ree CHARD), under the command of John Paul Jones, fought side by side with the larger British warship *Serapis.* Cannon and musket fire ripped the sails of both ships to shreds and blasted holes in their wooden sides. Though his ship was in tatters, Jones refused to give up. "I have not yet begun to fight," he vowed. Finally, with dozens of sailors dead on each side, the captain of the *Serapis* surrendered.

The navy had help from some 800 privateers that harassed British shipping. Privateers were armed civilian ships that had their government's permission to attack enemy ships and keep their goods. Operating like pirate ships, privateers seized cargoes of rum from the West Indies, wool from England, and furs from Canada. Such attacks forced Britain to spend valuable resources protecting merchant ships.

John Paul Jones

✔**Checkpoint** **How did privateers help the American war effort?**

⭐ **Looking Back and Ahead** Despite important battles at sea and in the West, the main war effort was concentrated in the colonies. In the next section, you will read about the final phase of the war.

Section 3 | **Check Your Progress**

Progress Monitoring ⦿nline
For: Self-test with instant help
Visit: PHSchool.com
Web Code: mva-2063

Comprehension and Critical Thinking

1. **(a) Recall** How did Washington's policy toward African American soldiers change? What was the reason for this change?
   (b) Identify Benefits How did African Americans expect to benefit from serving in the military?

2. **(a) Describe** What challenges did the American navy face?
   (b) Draw Conclusions Why do you think John Paul Jones is considered a great American hero?

⟳ Reading Skill

3. **Analyze Word Roots** The root *fid* means "faith." The prefix *con-* means "with." Use these word parts to determine the meaning of *confidence* in this sentence: The added responsibilities of wartime gave many women a new *confidence.*

Key Terms

4. Draw a table with four rows and three columns. In the first column, list the key terms from this section: enlist, civilian, continental, privateer. In the next column, write the definition of each word. In the last column, make a small illustration that shows the meaning of the word.

Writing

5. Identify the problems facing the Continental Congress during the war. Then, brainstorm one or two possible solutions.

Lord Cornwallis's Catastrophe

❝What we are to do after Lord Cornwallis's catastrophe, God Knows, or how anybody can think there is the least glimmering of hope for this nation surpasses my comprehension. ❞

—Anthony Storer, letter to a British lord after the American victory at Yorktown, 1781

◀ General Washington looks on as the British surrender at Yorktown.

Winning Independence

Objectives

- Find out how the Americans won the final battle of the Revolution.
- Learn the terms of the peace treaty with England.
- Explore the reasons that the Americans were victorious.
- Examine the effects of the American Revolution.

🔄 Reading Skill

Apply the Meanings of the Prefix *re-*
Prefixes sometimes have more than one meaning. For example, the prefix *re-* can mean "again" or "anew," but it can also mean "back" or "backward." You must think about the surrounding words and context in which the word is used before deciding which meaning of the prefix to apply.

Key Terms and People

Charles Cornwallis
guerrilla
Francis Marion
Nathanael Greene
traitor

Why It Matters After the American victory at Saratoga, the British threat to New England had ended. The British next tried to win the war by invading and capturing the South. The attempt failed and the Americans won their independence.

❓ **Section Focus Question: How did the Americans win the war and make peace?**

Fighting Moves South

The British turned to the South late in 1778. Their aim was to capture some key cities, win over the local population, and then march north, acquiring one state after another.

British Advance At first, the plan seemed to work. British soldiers moved north from Florida to Georgia. In December 1778, the British took the city of Savannah. Within a month, they controlled most of Georgia.

Moving on to South Carolina, the British captured the main port, Charles Town, and then the rest of the state. The British commander, Lord Charles Cornwallis, then carried the war into North Carolina. It looked as if the British might be unstoppable.

To slow the British advance, Americans used guerrilla tactics. Guerrillas are fighters who work in small bands to make hit-and-run attacks. In South Carolina, Francis Marion led his men silently through the swamps. They attacked without warning, then escaped. Marion's guerrilla attacks were so efficient that he won the nickname the Swamp Fox. Other bands of guerrillas were also active.

Elsewhere in the South, Loyalist bands roamed the back-country. They plundered and burned Patriot farms, killing men, women, and children. "If a stop cannot be put to these massacres," wrote one Continental general, "the country will be depopulated in a few months more."

Biography Quest

Benedict Arnold
1741–1801

Why did Benedict Arnold betray the American army? Perhaps he was angry when Congress promoted several less experienced officers ahead of him. Arnold's wife also may have played a role. During the Revolution, Arnold married a woman whose family members were strong Loyalists.

Whatever the reason, if you hear someone called a "Benedict Arnold," you know that person is seen as a traitor.

Biography Quest Online

What happened to Arnold after the American Revolution?

For: The answer to the question about Arnold

Visit: PHSchool.com

Web Code: mvd-2064

Vocabulary Builder
fateful (FAYT fuhl) **adj.** having important consequences; decisive

Vocabulary Builder
option (AHP shuhn) **n.** choice; possible course of action

Brighter Days Patriot fortunes began to improve in October 1780. Some 900 frontier fighters defeated a larger force of British troops and Loyalists atop Kings Mountain in South Carolina.

In December 1780, General Nathanael Greene took over command of the Continental army in the South. Greene split his small army in two. He led 1,200 men into eastern South Carolina, leaving General Daniel Morgan with 800 men in the west.

In January 1781, Morgan won a clear victory at the Battle of Cowpens. He put a small militia force in front, telling the men to fire three shots and then retreat. The British rushed forward, only to be met by charging cavalry and a line of skilled riflemen.

American Traitor Still, the British seemed to have the upper hand in the South. In addition to Cornwallis's forces, the British had troops under the command of an American traitor, Benedict Arnold. A **traitor** is a person who betrays his or her country or cause and helps the other side.

Early in the war, Arnold had fought bravely for the Patriots. But Arnold felt Congress undervalued him. He plotted to turn West Point, a key fort on the Hudson River in New York, over to the British. When the plot was discovered in September 1780, Arnold escaped. He and his Loyalist soldiers then staged a series of destructive raids in Virginia.

Final Battle Weakened by battles like Cowpens, Cornwallis headed to Virginia. That gave Greene an excellent opportunity. Over a five-month period, Patriot forces swept through the Deep South. By late summer, only Charles Town and Savannah remained in British hands.

Cornwallis then made a <u>fateful</u> mistake. He moved his main army to the Yorktown peninsula, a tongue of Virginia land poking into Chesapeake Bay. There, he thought, the British fleet could reinforce his position. But at the end of August, the French fleet arrived off Yorktown and chased off British ships.

At the same time, Washington rushed toward Virginia with American and French troops. Cornwallis found himself in a trap. American and French soldiers barred escape by land, while the French fleet blocked escape by sea. After three weeks, Cornwallis had no <u>option</u> but to surrender.

On October 19, 1781, the Americans and French lined up in two facing columns. The British marched glumly between the two columns and tossed their weapons into a large pile on the ground. The victory at Yorktown was the last major battle of the war.

 Checkpoint How were Cornwallis and his troops trapped at Yorktown?

Making Peace With Britain

The news from Yorktown caused shockwaves in Britain. Although the king wanted to keep fighting, Parliament voted in favor of peace.

Peace talks began in Paris in 1782. The American delegation included Benjamin Franklin and John Adams. Britain was eager for peace, so the Americans got most of what they wanted.

Treaty of Paris The talks led to an agreement, the Treaty of Paris. Britain recognized the independence of the United States. The boundaries of the new nation were set at the Atlantic on the east, Canada on the north, the Mississippi River on the west, and Florida on the south. Florida itself was returned to Spain.

For its part, the United States agreed to "earnestly recommend" that the states restore rights and property taken from Loyalists during the war. However, most states ignored this pledge.

On April 15, 1783, Congress approved the treaty. The war was officially over. It had been almost exactly eight years since the "shot heard round the world" started the fighting at Lexington.

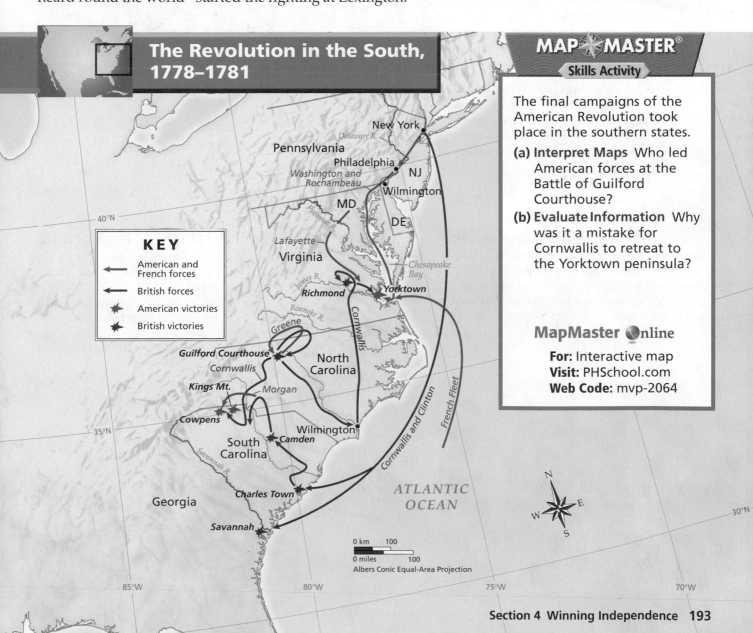

The Revolution in the South, 1778–1781

KEY

→ American and French forces
← British forces
✦ American victories
✦ British victories

MAP MASTER®
Skills Activity

The final campaigns of the American Revolution took place in the southern states.

(a) Interpret Maps Who led American forces at the Battle of Guilford Courthouse?

(b) Evaluate Information Why was it a mistake for Cornwallis to retreat to the Yorktown peninsula?

MapMaster Online

For: Interactive map
Visit: PHSchool.com
Web Code: mvp-2064

Why Did the Americans WIN?

Many factors contributed to the American victory. They fell into four main groups: geographic advantages, help from abroad, patriotic spirit, and skilled leadership.
Critical Thinking: *Evaluate Information What do you think was the most important reason for the American victory?*

Geography

Americans, such as Francis Marion (pictured below), were on their home ground. They knew the forests, hills, and swamps. But British forces were far from their home country. They had to depend on longer supply lines, stretching across the Atlantic Ocean. ▼

Patriotic Spirit ▲

A key asset of the Americans was patriotism. Americans were fighting to create a new nation. Many soldiers stayed in the army for years, at great financial and personal sacrifice. Leaders such as Jefferson and Adams risked their lives and fortunes to champion independence.

Skilled Leadership ▶

Despite great odds, George Washington (left) never gave up. Although he faced criticism in Congress, his courage and knowledge won him broad support in the army. And though his troops suffered at Valley Forge, Washington led them through hardship to victory. ▼

◀ Help From Abroad

The Americans might never have won without help from Europe. Men such as Lafayette (right) and von Steuben (below) provided military leadership and support. Money from such countries as Spain and the Netherlands was also crucial. ▼

Washington's Farewell On December 4, 1783, Washington and his ranking officers were reunited for one last meal together at Fraunces Tavern in New York City. In parting, each man, in turn, embraced Washington. One officer wrote, "Such a scene of sorrow and weeping I had never before witnessed."

Washington wished to retire to his plantation. Soon, though, he would again be called to the aid of the nation he had helped create.

✓ **Checkpoint** What was the Treaty of Paris?

Impact of the Revolution

The immediate effect of the American Revolution was to create a new nation of 13 independent states, linked by ties of custom and history. The long-term effects are still being felt today. The Declaration of Independence cemented ideas like equality and liberty in the American mind. Over time, those concepts have gained broader meanings.

The impact of American independence reached beyond the borders of the infant nation. In 1789, French citizens rebelled. Leaders of the French Revolution, including Lafayette, looked to the American example. They issued the Declaration of the Rights of Man and the Citizen, modeled in part on the Declaration of Independence. The American Revolution also inspired later independence movements in Latin America.

✓ **Checkpoint** How did the American Revolution affect France?

⭐ **Looking Back and Ahead** The United States emerged from the American Revolution as a proud nation—but also weak and deeply in debt. In the next chapter, you will read how the new nation met the challenge of forming a democratic government.

> **Apply the Meaning of the Prefix re-**
> The word root *belli* means "war." Apply a meaning of *re-* to determine the meaning of *rebelled*. Identify the prefix meaning that you applied.

Section 4 | Check Your Progress

Progress Monitoring Online
For: Self-test with instant help
Visit: PHSchool.com
Web Code: mva-2064

Comprehension and Critical Thinking

1. (a) Recall What military strategy defeated Cornwallis at Yorktown?
(b) Apply Information What was one important factor that contributed to the American victory at Yorktown?

2. (a) Describe What were the provisions of the Treaty of Paris?
(b) Identify Benefits Why was setting the nation's western border important economically to the new country?

🔊 Reading Skill

3. Apply the Meanings of the Prefix re- Read the text under the heading "Making Peace With Britain," and find at least two words that use the prefix *re-*. Apply the meanings of the prefix to define those words.

Key Terms

Answer the following questions in complete sentences that show your understanding of the key terms.
4. What advantages did guerrillas have against larger forces?

5. Why did Americans consider Benedict Arnold to be a traitor?

Writing

6. Once the Treaty of Paris was signed, the Americans had to address a new set of problems. Prepare a thesis statement for an essay about the challenges facing the new nation.

21st Century Learning By comparing maps from different time periods, you can see how historical changes affected an area. The two maps below show North America before and after the Revolutionary War.

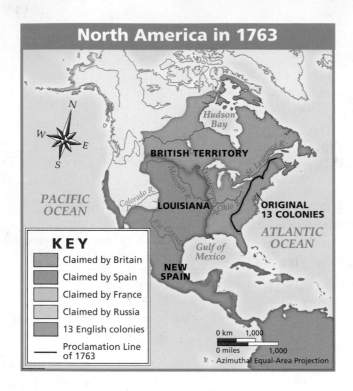

North America in 1763

PACIFIC OCEAN

Hudson Bay

BRITISH TERRITORY

St. Lawrence R.

Missouri R.

Mississippi R.

Colorado R.

LOUISIANA

Ohio

ORIGINAL 13 COLONIES

Rio Grande

ATLANTIC OCEAN

Gulf of Mexico

NEW SPAIN

KEY
- Claimed by Britain
- Claimed by Spain
- Claimed by France
- Claimed by Russia
- 13 English colonies
- Proclamation Line of 1763

0 km 1,000
0 miles 1,000
Azimuthal Equal-Area Projection

North America in 1783

PACIFIC OCEAN

Hudson Bay

BRITISH TERRITORY

St. Lawrence R.

Missouri R.

Colorado R.

LOUISIANA

Ohio

UNITED STATES

Rio Grande

ATLANTIC OCEAN

Gulf of Mexico

NEW SPAIN

KEY
- United States
- British colonies
- French colonies
- Spanish colonies
- Russian territory
- Disputed territory

0 km 1,000
0 miles 1,000
Azimuthal Equal-Area Projection

Learn the Skill
Use these steps to compare maps.

1 **Check the subject and area shown on each map.** What do the map titles and labels tell you? Is the same geographical area shown on each map?

2 **Study the map key.** Determine what symbols are used to present specific information that you can compare.

3 **Compare the maps.** Use the data on the maps to make comparisons and note changes over time.

4 **Interpret the maps.** Think over what you already know about this period from other sources. Draw conclusions or make predictions based on your own knowledge and the information on the maps.

Practice the Skill
Answer the following questions about the two maps on this page.

1 **Check the subject and area shown on each map.** (a) What area is shown on both maps? (b) What is the date of each map?

2 **Study the map key.** (a) What do the colors on the 1763 map key represent? (b) What color was added to the map key on the 1783 map?

3 **Compare the maps.** (a) What was the major difference between North America in 1763 and in 1783? (b) How was North America the same in 1763 and in 1783?

4 **Interpret the maps.** How did the 1783 Treaty of Paris affect the distribution of land in North America?

Apply the Skill
See the Review and Assessment at the end of this chapter.

Quick Study Guide

How did American colonists gain their independence?

Section 1
A Nation Declares Independence

- Thomas Paine's pamphlet *Common Sense* convinced more Americans to support independence from Britain.
- The Declaration of Independence used Enlightenment ideas and careful logic to show why Americans wanted to be free of British rule.

Section 2
A Critical Time

- As fighting moved from New England to the Middle States, American troops faced many setbacks.
- The Battle of Saratoga was a turning point in the war.
- As a result of the American victory at Saratoga, France decided to aid the American cause.

Section 3
The War Widens

- African Americans fought on both sides of the Revolution, often in the hope of gaining freedom.
- As men went to war, women took on added responsibilities.
- Important battles took place on the western frontier and at sea.

Section 4
Winning Independence

- In the final stages of the war, fighting shifted to the South, ending in the British surrender at Yorktown.
- In the Treaty of Paris, Britain recognized American independence.
- The American Revolution and the Declaration of Independence have inspired people in other nations who sought freedom.

? Exploring the Essential Question

Use the online study guide to explore the essential question.

Section 1
Why did many colonists favor declaring independence?

Section 2
How were the early years of the war a critical time?

Chapter 6 Essential Question
How did American colonists gain their independence?

Section 4
How did the Americans win the war and make peace?

Section 3
How did the effects of the war widen?

Key Terms

Complete each of the following sentences so that the second part explains the first part and shows your understanding of the key term.

1. Congress decided to pay the soldiers and buy their food and equipment by printing continentals _____.

2. The Declaration of Independence declared that people have unalienable rights _____.

3. One of the reasons that America won the war was because of its French and Spanish alliances _____.

4. During the Revolution, the small American navy had help from privateers _____.

5. A Polish volunteer led the American cavalry _____.

Comprehension and Critical Thinking

6. (a) **Recall** Why was the publication of *Common Sense* so important?
   (b) **Describe** What was the political importance of the Declaration of Independence?
   (c) **Draw Conclusions** How do you think that *Common Sense* influenced people's reaction to the Declaration of Independence?

7. (a) **Review** How did the course of the war change from June to the end of December 1776?
   (b) **Analyze Cause and Effect** What effect do you think this change had on the Patriots?

8. (a) **Summarize** How did France help America during the Revolution?
   (b) **Make Predictions** What do you think might have happened if France had not come to the aid of America during the Revolution?

9. (a) **Summarize** What financial problems faced Congress during the Revolution?
   (b) **Identify Alternatives** What are some ways the new American government might avoid these same financial problems in the future?

10. (a) **Recall** How did the victories of the militia led by George Clark in the West benefit the frontier settlers?
    (b) **Identify Benefits** What were the economic benefits of these victories for the new nation?

History Reading Skill

11. **Analyze Word Parts** Choose a word that contains any of the word parts discussed in this chapter. Use the word part to define the word. Then, write a sentence that contains the word and clarifies its meaning.

Writing

12. **Write two paragraphs discussing the problem of winning support from other nations for the Patriot cause. Your paragraph should:**
    - include a thesis statement that expresses your main idea;
    - develop the main idea with facts, examples, and other information;
    - conclude by describing the lasting impact of what happened.

13. **Write a Dialogue:**
    It is May 1775. Your family is seriously divided over which course to take. Choose one of the following roles: a parent concerned about the safety of the children, a Loyalist supporter, a Patriot supporter. Write one page of conversation about the situation.

Skills for Life
Compare Maps

Use the maps in Sections 3 and 4 to answer the following questions.

14. (a) What areas are shown on both maps?
    (b) What is the date of the map in Section 4?

15. What information is provided in the map key for "The Revolution in the West" that is not included in the map key for "The Revolution in the South"?

16. Based on the information in the maps, how would you compare the success of the British troops in the South and the West?

Test Yourself

1. **Which statement best describes the effects of the American Revolution on women?**

   A The political rights of women were reduced.

   B Women had to take on many new responsibilities.

   C Many women were forced to serve in the army.

   D The Declaration of Independence granted equal rights to women.

2. **One effect of the Treaty of Paris was that Britain**

   A gave up all its colonies in North America.

   B surrendered to the Patriots.

   C recognized American independence.

   D formed an alliance with the United States.

Refer to the map below to answer Question 3.

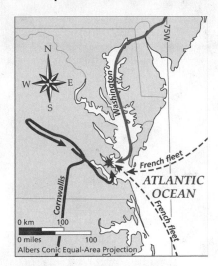

3. **What battle is shown on the map?**

   A Battle of Saratoga

   B Battle of Cowpens

   C Battle of Yorktown

   D Battle of Trenton

Document-Based Questions

Task: Look at Documents 1 and 2, and answer their accompanying questions. Then, use the documents and your knowledge of history to complete this writing assignment:

> Write an essay comparing the ways in which these two documents proclaim people's basic rights. How do they reflect the Enlightenment ideas of John Locke?

Document 1: This excerpt describes the basic principles behind the Declaration of Independence. *According to the Declaration, what basic rights do people have?*

> "We hold these truths to be self-evident, that all men are created equal, that they are endowed by their Creator with certain unalienable Rights, that among these are Life, Liberty, and the pursuit of Happiness. That to secure these rights, Governments are instituted among Men, deriving their just powers from the consent of the governed."
>
> —Declaration of Independence

Document 2: In 1789, on the eve of the French Revolution, the French Assembly issued the Declaration of the Rights of Man and the Citizen. As you can see from the excerpt below, this document was modeled in part on the American Declaration of Independence. *According to the Declaration of the Rights of Man and the Citizen, what is the aim of government?*

> "The representatives of the French people . . . have determined to set forth in a solemn declaration the natural, unalienable, and sacred rights of man.
>
> 1. Men are born and remain free and equal in rights. . . .
> 2. The aim of all political association is the preservation of the natural and imprescriptible rights of man. These rights are liberty, property, security, and resistance to oppression."
>
> —Declaration of the Rights of Man and the Citizen

Creating the Constitution

1776-1790

> "They were fully impressed with the necessity of forming a great consolidated government, instead of a confederation."

—Patrick Henry,
on the Constitutional Convention, 1788

Convention delegates sign the new Constitution in Philadelphia, 1787.

What You Will Learn

Section 1
GOVERNING A NEW NATION
Weaknesses in the Articles of Confederation convinced leading Americans that the country needed a strong central government.

Section 2
THE CONSTITUTIONAL CONVENTION
After months of intense debate, delegates to the Constitutional Convention agreed on a new plan of government.

Section 3
DEBATING THE CONSTITUTION
The states approved the Constitution, but many of the states insisted that it also include a bill of rights.

Reading Skill
Analyze Propositions and Support
In this chapter, you will learn how to identify and study arguments and research the evidence used to support them.

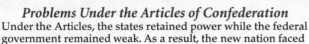

How did the United States Constitution of Confederation and provide for the

Creating the Constitution, 1776–1790

Problems Under the Articles of Confederation

Under the Articles, the states retained power while the federal government remained weak. As a result, the new nation faced many problems.

Economic Weakness
Each state printed its own money and put taxes on goods from other states. This discouraged interstate trade.

"We Spanish will not allow American shipping on the Mississippi River."

"I wish I was stronger!"

"We British will not abandon our forts."

Military Weakness
Believing the United States to be weak, European powers bullied the new nation.

Popular Unrest
After an uprising led by Daniel Shays, many Americans wanted a stronger central government to protect against civil unrest.

SPANISH LOUISIANA

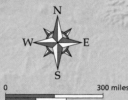

0 | 300 miles
0 | 300 km
Albers Conic Equal-Area Projection

U.S. Events

1777 Congress adopts Articles of Confederation.

1781 Articles of Confederation approved by last of 13 states.

1776   **1780**   **1784**

World Events

1778 France and United States sign treaty of alliance.

overcome the weaknesses of the Articles organization of the new government?

CHAPTER
7

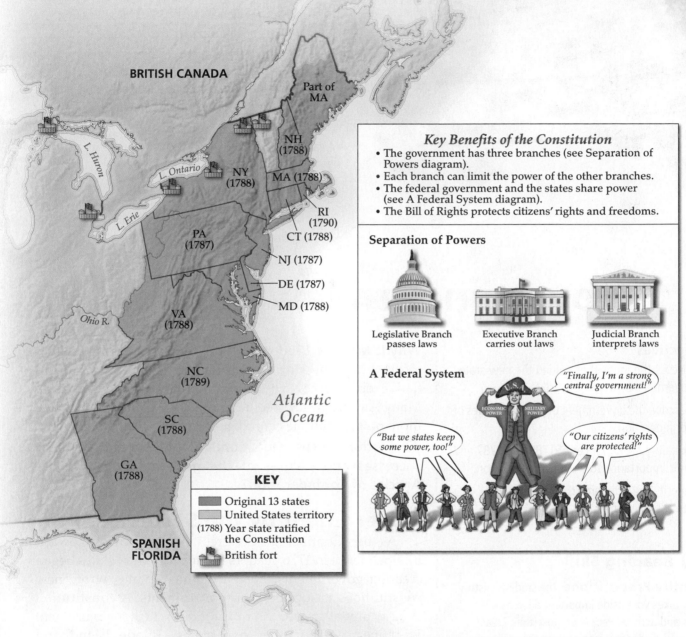

Key Benefits of the Constitution
- The government has three branches (see Separation of Powers diagram).
- Each branch can limit the power of the other branches.
- The federal government and the states share power (see A Federal System diagram).
- The Bill of Rights protects citizens' rights and freedoms.

Separation of Powers

Legislative Branch passes laws

Executive Branch carries out laws

Judicial Branch interprets laws

A Federal System

"Finally, I'm a strong central government!"

U.S.A
ECONOMIC POWER   MILITARY POWER

"But we states keep some power, too!"

"Our citizens' rights are protected!"

KEY
- Original 13 states
- United States territory
- (1788) Year state ratified the Constitution
- British fort

BRITISH CANADA

Part of MA

NH (1788)

NY (1788)

MA (1788)

RI (1790)

CT (1788)

PA (1787)

NJ (1787)

DE (1787)

MD (1788)

VA (1788)

NC (1789)

SC (1788)

GA (1788)

L. Huron

L. Ontario

L. Erie

Ohio R.

Atlantic Ocean

SPANISH FLORIDA

VISUAL PREVIEW

Shays' Rebellion breaks out in Massachusetts. **1786** **1787**

Constitutional Convention creates new plan of government.

1791 Bill of Rights goes into effect.

1784

1788

1792

1789 French Revolution begins.

Emperor of China rejects British trade. **1793**

Our Weak Federal Government

66 The weakness of our federal government . . . prevents the adoption of any measures that are requisite for us as a nation; it keeps us from paying our honest debts; it also throws out of our power all the profits of commerce, and this drains us of cash. 99

—Noah Webster, complaining about national government, 1786

◀ A variety of state currencies weakened the nation's economy.

Governing a New Nation

Objectives

- Discuss the ideas that guided the new state governments.
- Describe the government under the Articles of Confederation.
- Explain the Ordinances of 1785 and 1787 and their importance to westward expansion.
- Identify the problems created by a weak central government.

Reading Skill

Identify Propositions The study of history often takes you inside important debates over ideas and actions. People propose their ideas and then give reasons to support those ideas. Identifying those propositions will help you to understand the beliefs and experiences of people in an earlier time. One way to identify propositions is to ask yourself what problems people had and how they proposed solving those problems.

Key Terms and People

constitution
executive

economic depression
Daniel Shays

Why It Matters Leaders of the new American nation recalled how the king and Parliament in faraway England had exerted excessive power over colonial legislatures. Many Americans favored a republic in which the states had more power than the central government.

❷ **Section Focus Question: What were the major successes and failures of the government under the Articles of Confederation?**

Government by the States

As the Continental Congress began moving toward independence in 1776, leaders in the individual states began creating governments. Eleven of the 13 states wrote new constitutions to support their governments. A constitution is a document stating the rules under which a government will operate. The other two states—Rhode Island and Connecticut—kept using their colonial charters. However, they removed all references to the British king.

Writing State Constitutions In writing state constitutions, Americans were well aware of the problems that had led to the Revolution. Colonists had been unhappy with governors appointed by the British Crown. Thus, the new constitutions minimized the powers of state governors. Instead, they gave most of the power to state legislatures elected by the people.

The governor served as the state's executive. In a government, the **executive** is the person who runs the government and sees that the laws are carried out. Governors appointed key state officials, but usually the legislature had to approve the appointments.

The new constitutions allowed more people to vote than in colonial times. Nonetheless, all but a few states barred African Americans (including those who were free) from voting. New Jersey allowed some women to vote until 1807, but women could not vote in any other state. In order to vote, white males had to be 21 or older. In most states, they also had to own a certain amount of property.

Protecting Rights The Declaration of Independence listed ways that Britain had violated the rights of colonists. To prevent such abuses, states sought to protect <u>individual</u> rights. Virginia was the first state to include a bill of rights in its constitution. Virginia's list included freedom of the press and the right to trial by jury, and it also barred "cruel and unusual punishments." The final clause guaranteed freedom of religion:

> **❝** That religion, or the duty which we owe to our Creator, and the manner of discharging it, can be directed only by reason and conviction, not by force or violence; and therefore all men are equally entitled to the free exercise of religion, according to the dictates of conscience. **❞**
>
> —Virginia Bill of Rights, 1776

Many other states followed Virginia's lead. For example, the New York state constitution also included a bill of rights that guaranteed freedom of religion:

> **❝** This convention doth further, in the name and by the authority of the good people of this State, ordain, determine, and declare, that the free exercise and enjoyment of religious profession and worship, without discrimination or preference, shall forever hereafter be allowed, within this State, to all mankind. **❞**
>
> —New York Constitution of 1777

Massachusetts also included freedom of religion in its bill of rights. However, Massachusetts did retain its official church. Massachusetts's bill of rights declared that people have the freedom to worship as they please, so long as they did not disturb the public peace or interfere with other people's freedom of worship.

☑**Checkpoint** **Why did many state constitutions limit the power of state governors?**

Protecting Rights
Virginia included a bill of rights in its constitution. The Virginia bill of rights became a model for other states and, later, for the national Constitution. **Critical Thinking: Link Past and Present** *Which protections in the Virginia bill of rights are enjoyed by all Americans today?*

Virginia Bill of Rights

- Freedom of Religion
- Freedom of the Press
- Trial by Jury
- Limits on Searches
- Limits on Arrests
- No Cruel and Unusual Punishment

The Articles of Confederation

While the states were writing their constitutions, the Continental Congress created a plan for the nation as a whole. It was called the Articles of Confederation. Congress adopted the Articles in 1777.

Form of Government Instead of having three branches of government like those of most states, the government under the Articles had just one branch—a one-house legislature, called Congress. There was no executive and no system of national courts.

Within Congress, all states would be equal and each had a single vote. Moreover, for the most important matters, nine states had to agree before a law could go into effect.

Identify Propositions
What issues concerned the framers when they were drafting the Articles of Confederation? What did they propose in response?

Limited Government The framers of the Articles of Confederation kept in mind their complaints against Britain. Parliament had passed laws the colonists considered unfair. The new states did not want to risk giving too much power to a central government far from the people. Thus, the Articles provided for a limited central government.

Under the Articles, most power remained in the hands of the states. Congress could not regulate trade or collect taxes. Instead, it had to ask the states for the money it needed.

Congress did have some powers under the Articles. It could deal with foreign nations and with Native Americans outside the 13 states. It could make laws, declare war, coin or borrow money, and run a postal service. However, the national government had no power to enforce the laws that it made. For that, it depended on the states.

☑Checkpoint How did the Articles of Confederation ensure the power of the states?

Settling the Western Lands

The Articles had to be approved by all 13 states. But some states would not give their approval until other states dropped their claims to vast areas of land west of the Appalachian Mountains. It took years to get all the states to give up their claims to western lands. In 1781, Virginia was the final state to agree. Only then did Maryland approve the Articles of Confederation, the final state to do so.

The western lands that the states had given up were turned over to the national government. They proved to be very valuable. Land was in great demand. It could be sold off, piece by piece, to private companies seeking to develop western settlements.

Vocabulary Builder
devise (dee vīz) **v.** to think up an idea for something and figure out how it will work

Land Ordinance of 1785 Congress had to devise a system for land sales and settlement. Under the Land Ordinance of 1785, surveyors were to divide public lands into townships, 6 miles on each side. This would result in a grid of squares. Within each township there would also be a grid, 1 mile on each side. These 36 sections would be sold for no less than $1 an acre.

Within each township, one section was set aside to support schools. This reflected the belief of the nation's leaders that democracy depended on education. Thomas Jefferson later wrote:

❝If a nation expects to be ignorant and free, in a state of civilization, it expects what never was and never will be.**❞**
—Thomas Jefferson, letter to Charles Yancey, 1816

Northwest Ordinance of 1787 Investors were eager to buy land in the Northwest Territory, north of the Ohio River. They pressed Congress to determine how this area would be governed. In response, Congress passed the Northwest Ordinance of 1787. It guaranteed basic rights for settlers and banned slavery there.

The Northwest Ordinance set a three-step process for admitting new states. When a territory was just starting to be settled, Congress would appoint a governor, a secretary, and three judges. Once the territory had 5,000 free adult male settlers, it could elect a legislature. When the free population reached 60,000, the territory could ask to become a state. In time, five states—Ohio, Indiana, Illinois, Michigan, and Wisconsin—were carved out of the Northwest Territory. (For more on the settling of the Northwest Territory, see the Geography and History feature.)

✔Checkpoint **How did the two ordinances turn national land into private holdings?**

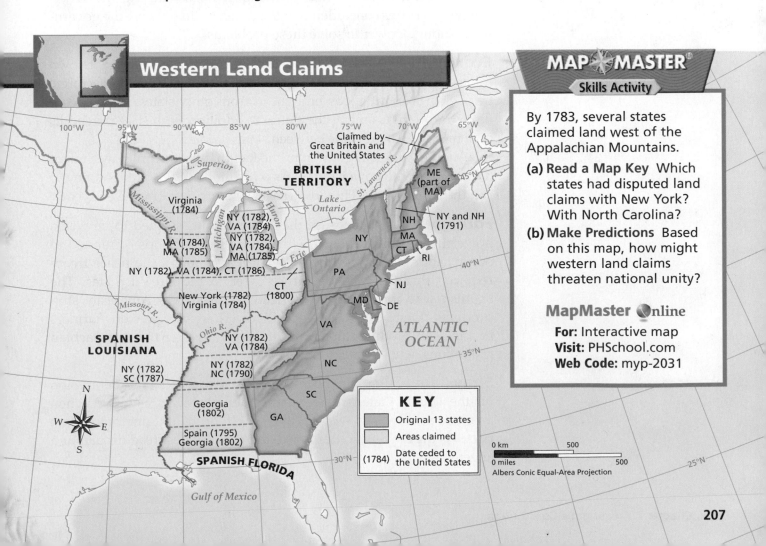

Western Land Claims

MAP MASTER
Skills Activity

By 1783, several states claimed land west of the Appalachian Mountains.

(a) Read a Map Key Which states had disputed land claims with New York? With North Carolina?

(b) Make Predictions Based on this map, how might western land claims threaten national unity?

MapMaster Online

For: Interactive map
Visit: PHSchool.com
Web Code: myp-2031

KEY
- Original 13 states
- Areas claimed
- (1784) Date ceded to the United States

0 km 500
0 miles 500
Albers Conic Equal-Area Projection

Shays' Rebellion
Abigail Adams called the leaders of Shays' Rebellion "ignorant, restless desperadoes without conscience or principles." However, many felt that the Massachusetts farmers had good reason for their anger. Here, farmers attack the Massachusetts statehouse.
Critical Thinking: *Analyze Cause and Effect*
What was the main cause of Shays' Rebellion?

Growing Problems

Under the Articles of Confederation, the United States had many successes. It waged a successful war for independence, negotiated a peace treaty with Britain, and set up rules for settling new territories. But the United States faced growing problems during the 1780s. Many Americans concluded that the Articles did not give the government enough power to solve these problems.

Economic Problems Under the Articles, each state set its own trade policy. Each state tried to help its own farmers and manufacturers by setting taxes on goods brought in from other states. This practice discouraged trade among the states. In addition, each state printed its own money, making trade between states harder.

Another problem grew from the fact that the central government did not have the power to tax. As a result, there was little money to run the government. The situation grew more desperate every year.

Foreign Affairs Because the United States seemed to be weak, powerful nations viewed it with scorn. British troops continued to occupy forts in the Northwest Territory, although the peace treaty required that the forts be turned over to the United States. The Spanish, who controlled New Orleans, refused to let Americans ship products down the Mississippi River. Therefore, western farmers had to send products along the rugged trails over the Appalachian Mountains, which was far more costly.

Shays' Rebellion In the mid-1780s, a severe economic depression hit the United States. An **economic depression** is a period when business activity slows, prices and wages drop, and unemployment rises. As the depression deepened, there was widespread despair and anger.

The depression hit farmers in Massachusetts especially hard. As crop prices declined, many were unable to pay their taxes. The state government then began seizing some farms and selling them in order to get the back taxes. Angry farmers demanded that the legislature stop the farm sales. They also demanded that the state issue more paper money to make it easier to get loans. Still, the legislators took no action.

In August 1786, a former Revolutionary War captain named Daniel Shays led an uprising of about 1,000 Massachusetts farmers. When the farmers tried to seize arms from a state warehouse, the state called out the militia. Shays and other leaders were arrested.

Although Shays' Rebellion fizzled, it had frightened some leading Americans. They believed that a stronger central government would protect against popular unrest. In response, Congress asked the states to send delegates to a convention in Philadelphia in 1787. Their task was to revise the Articles of Confederation.

☑ **Checkpoint** **What did Shays' Rebellion demonstrate about the strength of the national government under the Articles of Confederation?**

☆ **Looking Back and Ahead** After 10 years of independence, some leading Americans had come to the conclusion that the Articles of Confederation needed improvement. The Philadelphia convention was called to revise the Articles. But were the Articles of Confederation worth saving? Or was an entirely new framework required? This decision would be one of the first issues that the delegates at the Philadelphia convention would confront.

Section 1 | Check Your Progress

Progress Monitoring Online
For: Self-test with instant help
Visit: PHSchool.com
Web Code: mya-2031

Comprehension and Critical Thinking

1. **(a) Recall** Why did the Continental Congress make the federal government weak when it drew up the Articles of Confederation?
   (b) Explain Problems Why did foreign powers treat the U.S. government under the Articles of Confederation with scorn?

2. **(a) Recall** Why was a section of public land set aside to support public schools under the Land Ordinance of 1785?
   (b) Analyze Cause and Effect How does education contribute to a successful democracy?

⟳ Reading Skill

3. **Identify Propositions** Reread the text following the heading "Land Ordinance of 1785." What belief did the nation's leaders have about education? What did they propose to further this belief?

Key Terms

Fill in the blanks with the correct key terms.

4. After the break with Britain, each of the states wrote a new _____, a framework for the state government.

5. The _____ is the person in a government responsible for carrying out the laws.

6. In the 1780s, when business slowed and unemployment rose, the nation entered a period of _____.

Writing

7. Identify two problems caused by the creation of a weak national government under the Articles of Confederation. Write a sentence about each problem, explaining why it was important that it be solved.

Settling the Northwest Territory

By the end of the American Revolution, the United States had acquired a vast territory west of the Appalachian Mountains. Congress passed two land ordinances, one in 1785 and another in 1787. The ordinances served as a framework for moving settlers into—and forming states out of—this Northwest Territory. The states of Ohio, Indiana, Illinois, Michigan, Wisconsin, and part of Minnesota were eventually carved out of the expanse.

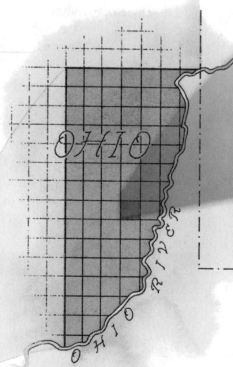

NORTHWEST TERRITORY WITH PRESENT-DAY STATE BOUNDARIES

▲ A New Organization

The Land Ordinance of 1785 established a system for settling the Northwest Territory. Surveyors laid out a grid of lines spaced 6 miles apart. These lines marked off townships. Each township was divided into 36 sections, and these 1-mile square sections could be divided into smaller units for sale to farmers.

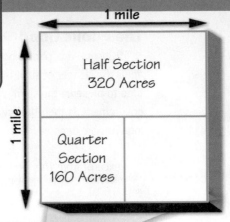

1 mile

1 mile

Half Section
320 Acres

Quarter
Section
160 Acres

6	5	4	3	2	1
7	8	9	10	11	12
18	17	16*	15	14	13
19	20	21	22	23	24
30	29	28	27	26	25
31	32	33	34	35	36

6 miles

6 miles

* Income reserved to support schools

Understand Effects:
Slavery and the Northwest Ordinance

Congress banned slavery in the Northwest Territory in 1787. Eventually, five free states were formed from the territory. Decades later, the balance between free states and slave states would lead to a national crisis.

▼ An Enduring Landscape

The grid established more than 200 years ago remains the basis for land division across the Midwest. Many roads and property lines still follow the straight lines and right angles the original surveyors laid out.

▲ Support for Education

The 1785 ordinance set aside one section in every township to support public schools. Lands were often reserved for school buildings like the one shown here.

Analyze GEOGRAPHY AND HISTORY

Write a pamphlet recruiting settlers to live in the North-west Territory.

The Public Good

❝To secure the public good and private rights against a danger of such faction, and at the same time to preserve the spirit and the form of popular government, is then the great object to which our inquiries are directed.❞

—excerpt from *The Federalist* No. 10, promoting the Constitution, 1787–1788

◄ James Madison, author of several *Federalist Papers*

The Constitutional Convention

Objectives

- Describe the proceedings of the Constitutional Convention.
- Identify the specifics of the Virginia Plan.
- Explain how the Great Compromise satisfied both large and small states.
- Describe the disputes over slavery and the compromises that were reached.
- Discuss the drafting of the new Constitution.

Reading Skill

Identify Support for Propositions As you read about the propositions that people from history made to solve their problems and advance their ideas, look for supporting evidence. How did people try to convince those around them to support these propositions? What reasons did they give to explain their views? Identifying supporting evidence helps you understand and respond to propositions.

Key Terms and People

James Madison
judicial branch
Roger Sherman

James Wilson
compromise
Gouverneur Morris

Why It Matters The weaknesses of the Articles of Confederation prompted the states to call a meeting to revise the Articles. The Constitutional Convention in Philadelphia led to an entirely new framework of government.

❓ **Section Focus Question: What role did compromise play in the creation of the United States Constitution?**

The Constitutional Convention Begins

An air of mystery hung over Philadelphia in the summer of 1787. Every day, the nation's great leaders passed in and out of the statehouse. One Philadelphia resident, Susannah Dillwyn, wrote to her father, "There is now sitting in this city a grand convention, who are to form some new system of government or mend the old one."

Aims of the Convention In fact, members of the convention did not have the authority to "form some new system of government." Congress had called the meeting "for the sole and express purpose of revising the Articles of Confederation." However, many delegates argued that revising the Articles would not be enough.

Early on, the delegates voted to keep their debates secret. Despite the heat, windows remained tightly shut. Guards kept out members of the public. The delegates would be free to speak their minds—even if their discussions took the convention far beyond its original aims.

The Delegates In all, 55 delegates from 12 states took part in the convention. Only Rhode Island did not send any representatives.

Some delegates, such as George Washington and Ben Franklin, had been respected leaders of the Revolution. Washington was quickly voted president of the convention. Most delegates, however, were younger. Alexander Hamilton of New York was only 32. Another influential delegate was 36-year-old James Madison of Virginia. Madison took careful notes on the meetings. Published after his death, Madison's notes became a rich source of historical information.

☑**Checkpoint** **Why did delegates to the Constitutional Convention keep their debates secret?**

The Virginia Plan

On the third day of the convention, Edmund Randolph of Virginia proposed a plan for a new, strong central government. James Madison was the principal author of this Virginia Plan. For the next month, debate focused on this proposal.

Three Branches of Government The Virginia Plan called for the central government to have three separate branches. Congress would continue to be the legislative branch. But two additional branches would be created. The executive branch would carry out the laws. The judicial branch would consist of a system of courts to interpret the law.

Many delegates believed that a strong executive was necessary to correct the weaknesses of the Articles of Confederation. But should the executive be one person or a group of people?

Birthplace of the United States

In 1787, delegates met in this room in Philadelphia's statehouse to debate a new plan of government. Today, the building is known as Independence Hall, in honor of another important event that took place there, the signing of the Declaration of Independence. **Critical Thinking: *Draw Conclusions*** *Why do you think many Americans today visit Independence Hall and other historic places?*

James Wilson

Randolph proposed that Congress appoint three people to serve jointly as chief executive. One person alone, he said, would never be able to win the people's confidence. Others objected. A single executive, they said, could act more quickly when urgent action was required. Eventually, the delegates voted to have one person, called the President, serve as executive.

A Two-House Legislature The Virginia Plan called for a change in the composition of Congress. Rather than a single legislative body, it would consist of two parts—a lower house and an upper house.

Delegates argued long and hard about methods of choosing members of the two houses. Some wanted state legislatures to elect both houses. Roger Sherman of Connecticut said the people "should have as little to do" with the selection process as possible because they can be misled.

On the other hand, James Wilson of Pennsylvania warned against shutting the people out of the process. According to Wilson, election of the legislature by the people was "not only the cornerstone, but the foundation of the fabric."

✓**Checkpoint** How was the national government organized under the Virginia Plan?

The Great Compromise

One part of the Virginia Plan nearly tore the convention apart. The plan called for representation based on population. The more people a state had, the more seats it would have in each house. Naturally, this idea drew support from big states like Virginia, Pennsylvania, and Massachusetts.

New Jersey Plan The smaller states strongly opposed this idea. They wanted each state to have the same number of votes in Congress, as was the case under the Articles of Confederation.

On June 15, William Paterson of New Jersey introduced a modified plan on behalf of the small states. This New Jersey Plan stood in sharp <u>contrast</u> to the Virginia Plan. It called for a single house of Congress, with equal representation for each state. The plan also expanded the powers of Congress to raise money and regulate commerce.

In the summer heat, delegates argued day after day over the great issues at stake. <u>Emotions</u> ran so high that some feared the convention would fail and the Union would break apart.

Terms of the Compromise Finally, Roger Sherman of Connecticut worked out a compromise that he hoped would satisfy both the large and small states. A compromise is an agreement in which each side gives up part of what it wants. On July 16, 1787, delegates narrowly voted to accept Sherman's proposals, which came to be known as the Great Compromise.

Vocabulary Builder
<u>contrast</u> (KAHN trast) *n.* difference

Vocabulary Builder
<u>emotion</u> (ee MOH shuhn) *n.* strong feeling about something or someone

The key to Sherman's plan was a two-house Congress. To please the large states, the lower house, called the House of Representatives, was to be based on population. Bigger states would thus have more votes. Representatives would be chosen by a vote of the people to serve two-year terms. To please the small states, each state would have two seats in the upper house, or Senate. State legislatures would choose senators, who would serve six-year terms.

The Great Compromise was a vital step in creating a new Constitution. Now, small-state delegates were willing to support a strong central government.

☑Checkpoint **What was the main difference between the Virginia Plan and the New Jersey Plan?**

Identify Support for Propositions
Roger Sherman proposed a two-house Congress, hoping to satisfy both small and large states. What support did he give to show how this solution would meet the needs of all states?

Debates Over Slavery

Other issues also divided the delegates—none more so than the question of slavery. The issue touched off bitter debates between northerners and southerners.

Three-Fifths Compromise Southern delegates said that enslaved people should be counted in calculating how many representatives a state should have in Congress. Northern delegates said that because enslaved people could not vote, they should not be counted toward a state's representation.

Finally, Congress agreed to a plan called the Three-Fifths Compromise. Each enslaved person would be counted as three fifths of a free person. Thus, 500 enslaved people would count as 300 free people. The Three-Fifths Compromise was a gain for the South, which got more seats in the House. Northern delegates reluctantly agreed in order to keep the South in the Union.

The Three-Fifths Compromise was a blow to African Americans. It helped preserve slavery in the new Constitution by making a distinction between "free persons" and "all other persons." The compromise was finally overturned when slavery was banned in 1865.

Slave Trade Some northern delegates wanted to ban the buying and selling of people anywhere in the country. Southern delegates protested that a ban would ruin the South's economy.

Once again, a compromise was reached. Ships would be allowed to bring enslaved people into the country for a period of 20 years. After 1808, Congress could bar the importation of enslaved people. But the slave trade *within* the United States was not affected.

☑Checkpoint **What was the Three-Fifths Compromise?**

Links Across Time

Slavery and the Constitution

1787 Slavery was the "unfinished business" of the Constitutional Convention. Compromises postponed the debate over the issue.
1861–1865 Growing disputes between the North and the South finally led to the bloody Civil War. Slavery was banned—and erased from the Constitution—by the Thirteenth Amendment in 1865.

Link to Today

Compromise Today Congress still debates many difficult and troubling issues. What compromises do they reach?

For: Congressional debates in the news
Visit: PHSchool.com
Web Code: myc-2032

Signing THE CONSTITUTION

In his *Signing of the Constitution*, painter Howard Chandler Christy captured the moment on September 17, 1787, when delegates signed the historic document that has guided our government for more than 200 years.

1 **Roger Sherman** helped draft the Great Compromise that determined how states would be represented in Congress. After months of bitter debate, the compromise satisfied both large and small states.

2 **George Washington** was voted president of the meeting. His firm leadership held the convention together when it seemed close to breaking up.

3 **Benjamin Franklin**, though frail and ailing, was one of the convention's most respected delegates. At the end, he wrote a masterful speech supporting the Constitution.

4 **James Madison** wrote much of the Constitution and led the fight to get it approved by the states. He is often called the Father of the Constitution.

The Constitution ▶

Critical Thinking: *Interpret Paintings*
How does the artist draw attention to certain Framers?

A New Constitution

After many more weeks of debate, the delegates agreed on all the terms. A so-called Committee of Style was appointed to draw up the final wording of the new Constitution. Gouverneur Morris, a gifted writer, was largely responsible for writing the Preamble, or introduction.

The Preamble highlights a major difference between the Constitution and the Articles of Confederation. The Articles were a pact between separate states. By contrast, the Constitution opens with the words, "We the People of the United States, in order to form a more perfect union, . . . do ordain and establish this Constitution for the United States of America." The Constitution thus claims to take its authority from the people rather than from the states.

The aging Ben Franklin gave some final advice on the day of the signing. Because he was so ill, Franklin remained seated and another delegate read Franklin's speech. Like many other delegates, Franklin had some doubts about parts of the Constitution. Still, he said, "I agree to this Constitution with all its faults," and he urged others to do the same. At last, the delegates stepped forward to place their signatures on the document.

✓ **Checkpoint** **What is the significance of the Constitution's first phrase: "We the People of the United States"?**

☆ **Looking Back and Ahead** Once the Constitution had been signed, secrecy ended. Public debates began. These debates would stretch over 10 months. And, as the Constitution's supporters soon learned, the battle for approval would be hard-fought and bitter.

Section 2 | Check Your Progress

Progress Monitoring Online
For: Self-test with instant help
Visit: PHSchool.com
Web Code: mya-2032

Comprehension and Critical Thinking

1. (a) Summarize Summarize the arguments for and against having a single executive.
(b) Explain Problems What problems do you think might arise during a crisis if the executive power in the U.S. government was held by three people?

2. (a) Describe How was representation in Congress to be based, according to the terms of the Great Compromise?
(b) Apply Information Why did the small states decide to support a strong central government after the compromise?

🎧 Reading Skill

3. Identify Support for Propositions Reread the text following the heading "Slave Trade." What reason did southerners give to support their position against ending the slave trade?

Key Terms
Fill in the blanks with the correct key terms.
4. The Virginia Plan called for a _____, or system of courts to interpret the law.

5. Under a _____ between northern and southern states, Congress could bar slaves from being imported after 1808.

Writing

6. Choose one of the problems that the delegates at the Constitutional Convention had to solve. List several possible solutions for that problem, and then write a few sentences explaining the solution that the convention eventually chose. What were the advantages and disadvantages of this solution?

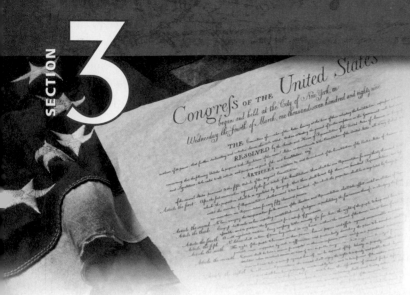

A Bill of Rights

"A bill of rights is what the people are entitled to against every government on earth, general or particular; and what no just government should refuse or rest on inference."

—Thomas Jefferson,
letter to James Madison, 1787

◄ The debate over the Constitution led to the Bill of Rights.

Debating the Constitution

Objectives

- Compare the positions of the Federalists and the Antifederalists.
- Discuss the debate over ratification.
- Describe the Bill of Rights and how it protects the people.

🎯 Reading Skill

Evaluate Support for Propositions

When a person argues a proposition using reasons and support, listeners or readers must evaluate that support—that is, whether the evidence given really supports the proposition. As you read, ask yourself if the propositions are well supported and whether or not they convince you.

Key Terms and People

ratify
Alexander
   Hamilton

John Jay
George Mason

Why It Matters Americans debated whether or not to ratify, or approve, the Constitution. Many states insisted that a bill of rights be added. In the end, the Constitution was ratified and it included the Bill of Rights. The Constitution has successfully served as our framework of government for more than 200 years.

❓ Section Focus Question: How did those in favor of the Constitution achieve its ratification?

Federalists Versus Antifederalists

The convention had set a process for states to ratify, or approve, the Constitution. Each state was to hold a convention. The Constitution would go into effect once it was ratified by nine states.

The Federalist Position Supporters of the new Constitution called themselves Federalists because they favored a strong federal, or national, government. James Madison, Alexander Hamilton, and John Jay published the *Federalist Papers,* a series of 85 newspaper essays in support of the Constitution.

At the heart of the Federalist position was the need for a stronger central government. For the Union to last, they argued, the national government had to have powers denied to it under the Articles of Confederation, including the power to enforce laws. Hamilton wrote:

"Government implies the power of making laws. It is essential to the idea of a law, that it be attended with . . . a penalty or punishment for disobedience. If there be no penalty . . . the resolutions or commands which pretend to be laws will, in fact, amount to nothing more than advice."

—Alexander Hamilton, *The Federalist* No. 15

The Antifederalist Position Opponents of ratification were called Antifederalists. Leading Antifederalists, such as George Mason and Patrick Henry of Virginia, agreed that the Articles of Confederation were not strong enough. However, they felt the Constitutional Convention had gone too far.

Antifederalists were not all united in their reasons for opposing the Constitution. Some of their most frequent arguments included:

- **Weakening the States** Antifederalists argued that the Constitution dangerously weakened the state governments. They feared that a too-strong central government, like that of England, would wipe out state power and individual freedom. "There never was a government over a very extensive country without destroying the liberties of the people," warned Mason.

- **No Bill of Rights** Some Antifederalists pointed out that the proposed Constitution offered no protections for basic freedoms. Unlike the constitutions of many states, it had no bill of rights.

- **President or King?** Another objection was that the Constitution provided for a President who could be reelected again and again. Said Henry, "Your President may easily become a king."

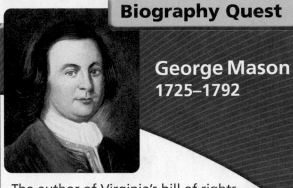

The author of Virginia's bill of rights, George Mason, went to the Constitutional Convention with hopes of forming "a wise and just government." But Mason quickly became dissatisfied. Though a slave owner himself, he favored an end to slavery and disliked the Three-Fifths Compromise. Mason was even more upset when the convention voted against his proposal to add a bill of rights. In the end, he refused to sign his name to the new Constitution.

Biography Quest

Why is Mason called "the father of the Bill of Rights"?

For: The answer to the question about Mason

Visit: PHSchool.com

Web Code: myd-2033

☑**Checkpoint** **Why did Antifederalists believe that the Constitutional Convention had gone too far?**

The Ratification Debate

The debate between Federalists and Antifederalists heated up as states held their ratification conventions. Without the approval of nine states, the Constitution would not go into effect.

Delaware acted first. Its convention unanimously approved the Constitution on December 7, 1787. Pennsylvania, New Jersey, Georgia, and Connecticut quickly followed.

Antifederalists hoped to win in Massachusetts. Opposition to the Constitution was strong in the rural areas from which Shays' Rebellion had drawn its strength. Only a major campaign by Constitution supporters won ratification by the state.

All eyes moved to Virginia. By then, Maryland and South Carolina had ratified, which made a total of eight state ratifications. Only one more was needed. But if large and powerful Virginia rejected the pact, New York and other remaining states might do so, too.

Evaluate Support for Propositions
How do Antifederalists support the proposition that the national government needed fewer powers?

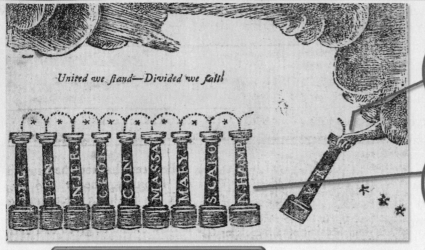

United we stand—Divided we fall

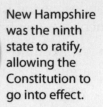

A hand reaches from the heavens to put Virginia in place.

New Hampshire was the ninth state to ratify, allowing the Constitution to go into effect.

Reading Political Cartoons
Skills Activity

The cartoon above appeared in an American newspaper in 1788—at a time when the states were debating whether or not to ratify the Constitution.

(a) Identify Main Ideas What do the pillars represent? Which pillar is first? What pillars are missing?

(b) Detect Points of View Do you think the cartoonist favored the Federalists or the Antifederalists?

Patrick Henry led the attack on the Constitution in Virginia. "There will be no checks, no real balances, in this government," he said. James Madison supported the Constitution and warned of the possible breakup of the Union. In the end, the Federalist view narrowly won out. Virginia's convention approved the Constitution by a vote of 89 to 79.

Meanwhile, in June 1788—while Virginia was still debating— New Hampshire became the ninth state to ratify. The Constitution could now go into effect. In time, New York and North Carolina followed. Finally, in May 1790, Rhode Island became the last of the original 13 states to ratify the Constitution.

On July 4, 1788, Philadelphia celebrated the ratification of the Constitution. A huge parade snaked along Market Street, led by soldiers who had served in the Revolution. Benjamin Rush, a Philadelphia doctor and strong supporter of the Constitution, wrote to a friend, "Tis done. We have become a nation."

✓**Checkpoint** Why was the vote in Virginia so important?

The Bill of Rights

Once the ninth state had ratified the Constitution, Congress took steps to prepare for a new government. George Washington was elected the first President, with John Adams as Vice President.

During the debate on the Constitution, many of the states had insisted that a bill of rights be added. This became one of the first tasks of the new Congress that met in March 1789.

The Framers had provided a way to amend the Constitution. They wanted to make the Constitution <u>flexible</u> enough to change. But they did not want changes made lightly. So, they made the process fairly difficult. (You will read more about the amendment process in the Citizenship Handbook.)

In 1789, the first Congress passed a series of <u>amendments</u>. By December 1791, three fourths of the states had ratified 10 amendments. These amendments are known as the Bill of Rights. The Bill of Rights aims to protect people against abuses by the federal government. Many of them came out of the colonists' struggle with Britain.

The First Amendment guarantees freedom of religion, speech, and the press. The Second Amendment deals with the right to bear arms. The Third Amendment bars Congress from forcing citizens to keep troops in their homes, as Britain had done.

The Fourth Amendment protects citizens from unreasonable searches of their homes or seizure of their property. Amendments Five through Eight protect citizens who are accused of crimes and are brought to trial. The last two amendments limit the powers of the federal government to those that are granted in the Constitution.

☑Checkpoint **Why did Congress move quickly to pass the Bill of Rights?**

⭐ **Looking Back and Ahead** The delegates to the Constitutional Convention are often called the Framers because they framed, or shaped, our form of government. The Constitution they wrote established a republic that has thrived for more than 200 years. On the following pages, you will read the actual text of the Constitution and study its meaning in more detail.

Vocabulary Builder
flexible (FLEHKS ah bahl) **adj.** able to change

<u>amendment</u> (ah MEHND mehnt) **n.** addition or alteration to a document

---

Section 3 | **Check Your Progress**

Progress Monitoring ⬤nline
For: Self-test with instant help
Visit: PHSchool.com
Web Code: mya-2033

Comprehension and Critical Thinking

1. **(a) Summarize** In complete sentences, list three arguments of the Antifederalists against the Constitution.
   (b) Draw Conclusions Why might the Antifederalists think the Constitution would reduce the power of the states?

2. **(a) Recall** Compare the attitudes of Patrick Henry and James Madison toward ratification.
   (b) Apply Information How did the passage of the Bill of Rights help deal with Patrick Henry's concerns?

⟳ Reading Skill

3. **Evaluate Support for Propositions** Patrick Henry led the attack on the Constitution. "There will be no checks, no real balances, in this government," he said. Evaluate his supporting argument. Do you think it is an effective argument?

Key Terms

Answer the following question in a complete sentence that shows your understanding of the key term.
4. Why was it important that Virginia ratify the Constitution?

Writing

5. Write a paragraph discussing the Bill of Rights as the solution to a problem faced by the early U.S. government after the Constitution was ratified. Complete the following topic sentence, and then write four more sentences developing this idea with specific information. **Topic sentence:** In 1789, the first Congress passed 10 amendments to the Constitution, known as the Bill of Rights, in order to protect _____.

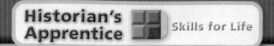
21st Century Learning Major historical events have both causes and effects. Sometimes causes and effects are short term. They take place shortly before or after the major event. Causes and effects can also be long term. They build up over a period of time.

CAUSES
- King George III had limited colonists' liberty.
- America had fought a revolution to protect freedoms.
- Antifederalists wanted a specific list of rights that protected citizens' basic liberties.
- Some states refused to ratify the Constitution unless a bill of rights was added later.

BILL OF RIGHTS ADDED TO CONSTITUTION IN 1791

EFFECTS
- First 10 amendments identify and guarantee basic rights and freedoms.
- The federal government cannot take away rights spelled out in the Bill of Rights.

Learn the Skill
Use these steps to analyze cause-and-effect relationships.

1 Read labels. The labels on the chart tell which event is the focus of study and which statements are the causes and which are the effects.

2 Identify causes. Causal statements give reasons why an event occurred. Major events have both long- and short-term causes.

3 Identify effects. Effect statements tell what happened because of the events. Major events have both long- and short-term effects.

4 Analyze cause-and-effect relationships. Think about why certain causes led to the event and why the event in turn had the results it did.

Practice the Skill
Answer the following questions about cause and effect based on the chart above.

1 Read labels. To what event do the causes lead?

2 Identify causes. (a) What was one cause of the Bill of Rights? (b) Was this a long- or short-term cause? Explain.

3 Identify effects. (a) What was one effect of the Bill of Rights? (b) Was this a long- or short-term effect? Explain.

4 Analyze cause-and-effect relationships. How did colonial history lead to a concern about protecting citizens' rights?

Apply the Skill
See the Review and Assessment at the end of this chapter.

Quick Study Guide

How did the United States Constitution overcome the weaknesses of the Articles of Confederation and provide for the organization of the new government?

Section 1
Governing a New Nation

- Many states added a bill of rights to their constitutions to protect individual freedoms.
- The Northwest Ordinance established a three-stage process for transforming a territory into a state.
- An increasing number of Americans came to believe that a stronger federal government was needed to deal with the country's pressing problems.

Section 2
The Constitutional Convention

- The Virginia Plan, calling for a strong central government with three branches, formed the basis of the U.S. Constitution.
- The Great Compromise set up a Congress with two houses, which pleased both the large and small states.

- As part of the compromise that won support for the Constitution, northern and southern delegates agreed that each enslaved person would count as three fifths of a free person.

Section 3
Debating the Constitution

- Federalists believed that three competing branches of government would keep any one part of the federal government from becoming too strong.
- Antifederalists were concerned that a strong federal government threatened states' rights and individual freedoms.
- A bill of rights was added to the Constitution to protect the people against abuses by the federal government.

? Exploring the Essential Question

Use the online study guide to explore the essential question.

Section 1
What were the major successes and failures of the government under the Articles of Confederation?

Chapter 7 Essential Question
How did the United States Constitution overcome the weaknesses of the Articles of Confederation and provide for the organization of the new government?

Section 2
What role did compromise play in the creation of the United States Constitution?

Section 3
How did those in favor of the Constitution achieve its ratification?

Key Terms

Answer the questions in complete sentences that show your understanding of the key terms.

1. How did the economic depression of the mid-1780s impact farmers?

2. What is the role of the judicial branch in government?

3. What process did the Constitutional Convention set forth for states to ratify the Constitution?

Comprehension and Critical Thinking

4. (a) **Recall** Which powers did the Congress not have under the Articles of Confederation?
(b) **Apply Information** How did not having these powers make the national government weak?

5. (a) **Recall** List the three stages a territory had to go through to become a state under the Northwest Ordinance of 1787.
(b) **Draw Conclusions** How did this process help a territory prepare for statehood?

6. (a) **Describe** What were the causes of Shays' Rebellion of 1786?
(b) **Detect Points of View** Thomas Jefferson called Shays' Rebellion "a medicine necessary for the sound health of government." What do you think he meant?

7. (a) **Contrast** How did the New Jersey Plan differ from the Virginia Plan?
(b) **Link Past and Present** Which key part of the New Jersey Plan is not part of our Constitution today? Why not?

8. (a) **Recall** Describe one contribution made by each of the following to the writing and ratification of the Constitution: George Washington; James Madison; Roger Sherman; Gouverneur Morris.
(b) **Evaluate Information** Whose contribution do you think was most important? Give reasons for your answer.

9. (a) **Summarize** Which freedoms and rights are protected in the Bill of Rights?
(b) **Draw Conclusions** The Bill of Rights limited the powers of the federal government to those granted in the Constitution. Why do you think these limits were included?

History Reading Skill

10. **Analyze Propositions and Support** Reread the text under the heading "The Great Compromise." What did the Virginia Plan propose about representation in Congress? How did delegates from smaller states respond? What support did they give for their different responses? Evaluate that support.

Writing

11. **Write two paragraphs on the following topic:** Explain how the Constitution addressed weaknesses in the Articles of Confederation.
Your paragraphs should:
- include a thesis statement that expresses your main idea;
- develop that main idea with facts, examples, and other information;
- conclude by describing the lasting impact of what happened.

12. **Write a Narrative:**
You are a delegate who has just arrived in Philadelphia in May 1787. Write a letter home explaining your feelings about the upcoming convention.

Skills for Life

Analyze Cause and Effect

Use the information below to answer the questions that follow.

> **Cause:** In 1774, the British Parliament passes an act that forces American colonists to house British troops in their homes.
>
> **Event:** Bill of Rights, Third Amendment
>
> "No soldier shall, in time of peace, be quartered in any house without the consent of the owner; nor in time of war, but in a manner to be prescribed by law."

13. What right does the Third Amendment protect?

14. (a) What was one cause of the Third Amendment?
(b) Was this cause long term or short term? Explain.

15. How did the colonists' experiences under British rule influence their decision to change the Constitution?

Test Yourself

1. **The Great Compromise settled a dispute between**

   A the North and the South.

   B Britain and the new United States.

   C the large states and the small states.

   D the President and Congress.

2. **Antifederalists opposed the Constitution because it**

   A did not give the President enough power.

   B weakened the state governments.

   C contained a bill of rights.

   D could not be amended.

Study the political cartoon below to answer Question 3. Consider how it is similar to and different from the cartoon in Section 3.

3. **What event is the creator of this political cartoon celebrating?**

   A the approval of the Constitution

   B the abolition of the slave trade

   C the failure of Shays' Rebellion

   D the passage of the Northwest Ordinance

Document-Based Questions

Task: Look at Documents 1 and 2, and answer their accompanying questions. Then, use the documents and your knowledge of history to complete this writing assignment:

> Write an essay explaining why the writers of the Constitution felt it was necessary to create a new plan of government.

Document 1: This excerpt from the Articles of Confederation defines the limitations on the powers of the national Congress. *According to this excerpt, what is Congress not allowed to do without the consent of the states?*

"The United States in Congress assembled shall never engage in a war . . . nor coin money, nor regulate the value thereof, nor [spend] the sums and expenses necessary for the defense and welfare of the United States . . . nor borrow money on the credit of the United States . . . nor agree upon the number of vessels of war, to be built or purchased, or the number of land or sea forces to be raised, nor appoint a commander in chief of the army or navy, unless nine States [agree] to the same. . . ."

Document 2: This excerpt from the Constitution defines some of the powers granted to Congress. *Why do you think the Framers of the Constitution gave Congress the power to set standards for weights and measures, rather than leaving it up to each state?*

"The Congress shall have power:
1. To lay and collect taxes . . . to pay the debts and provide for the common defense and general welfare of the United States. . . .
2. To borrow money on the credit of the United States. . . .
3. To coin money, regulate the value thereof, and of foreign coin, and for the standard of weights and measures. . . .
4. To declare war. . . .
5. To raise and support armies. . . .
6. To provide and maintain a navy."

The Constitution of the United States: An Outline

Original Constitution

Preamble

Article I	Legislative Branch
Section 1	A Two-House Legislature
Section 2	House of Representatives
Section 3	Senate
Section 4	Elections and Meetings
Section 5	Legislative Proceedings
Section 6	Compensation, Immunities, and Disabilities of Members
Section 7	Law-Making Process
Section 8	Powers of Congress
Section 9	Powers Denied to Congress
Section 10	Powers Denied to the States

Article II	Executive Branch
Section 1	President and Vice President
Section 2	Powers of the President
Section 3	Duties of the President
Section 4	Impeachment

Article III	Judicial Branch
Section 1	Courts, Terms of Office
Section 2	Jurisdiction
Section 3	Treason

Article IV	Relations Among the States
Section 1	Full Faith and Credit
Section 2	Privileges and Immunities of Citizens
Section 3	New States and Territories
Section 4	Protection Afforded to States by the Nation

Article V	Provisions for Amendment

Article VI National Debts, Supremacy of National Law, Oath

Section 1 Validity of Debts
Section 2 Supremacy of National Law
Section 3 Oaths of Office

Article VII Ratification of Constitution

Amendments

Bill of Rights

1 Freedom of Religion, Speech, Press, Assembly, and Petition
2 Bearing Arms
3 Quartering of Troops
4 Searches and Seizures
5 Criminal Proceedings; Due Process; Eminent Domain
6 Criminal Proceedings
7 Civil Trials
8 Punishment for Crimes
9 Unenumerated Rights
10 Powers Reserved to the States

Additional Amendments

11 Suits Against States
12 Election of President and Vice President
13 Slavery and Involuntary Servitude
14 Rights of Citizens
15 Right to Vote—Race, Color, Servitude
16 Income Tax
17 Popular Election of Senators
18 Prohibition of Alcoholic Beverages
19 Women's Suffrage
20 Presidential Terms; Sessions of Congress; Death or Disqualification of President-Elect
21 Repeal of Prohibition
22 Presidential Tenure
23 Presidential Electors for the District of Columbia
24 Right to Vote in Federal Elections—Tax Payment
25 Presidential Succession, Vice Presidential Vacancy, Presidential Inability
26 Right to Vote—Age
27 Congressional Pay

The Constitution of the United States

A Note on the Text of the Constitution

The complete text of the Constitution, including amendments, appears on the pages that follow. Spelling, capitalization, and punctuation have been modernized, and headings have been added. Portions of the Constitution altered by later amendments or that no longer apply are printed in blue. Commentary appears in the outside column of each page.

The Preamble The Preamble describes the purpose of the government as set up by the Constitution. Americans expect their government to defend justice and liberty and provide peace and safety from foreign enemies.

Preamble

We the people of the United States, in order to form a more perfect union, establish justice, insure domestic tranquillity, provide for the common defense, promote the general welfare, and secure the blessings of liberty to ourselves and our posterity, do ordain and establish this Constitution for the United States of America.

Article I ★ Legislative Branch

Section 1. A Two-House Legislature

Section 1 The Constitution gives Congress the power to make laws. Congress is divided into the Senate and the House of Representatives.

All legislative powers herein granted shall be vested in a Congress of the United States, which shall consist of a Senate and House of Representatives.

Section 2. House of Representatives

1. Election of Members The House of Representatives shall be composed of members chosen every second year by the people of the several states, and the electors in each state shall have the qualifications requisite for electors of the most numerous branch of the state legislature.

2. Qualifications No person shall be a representative who shall not have attained to the age of twenty-five years, and been seven years a citizen of the United States, and who shall not, when elected, be an inhabitant of that state in which he shall be chosen.

3. Apportionment Representatives and direct taxes shall be apportioned among the several states which may be included within this Union, according to their respective numbers, which shall be determined by adding to the whole number of free persons, including those bound to service for a term of years and excluding Indians not taxed, three fifths of all other persons. The actual enumeration shall be made within three years after the first meeting of the Congress of the United States, and within every subsequent term of ten years, in such manner as they shall by law direct. The number of representatives shall not exceed one for every thirty thousand, but each state shall have at least one representative; and until such enumeration shall be made, the state of New Hampshire shall be entitled to choose three, Massachusetts eight, Rhode Island and Providence Plantations one, Connecticut five, New York six, New Jersey four, Pennsylvania eight, Delaware one, Maryland six, Virginia ten, North Carolina five, South Carolina five, and Georgia three.

4. Filling Vacancies When vacancies happen in the representation from any state, the executive authority thereof shall issue writs of election to fill such vacancies.

5. Officers; Impeachment The House of Representatives shall choose their Speaker and other officers; and shall have the sole power of impeachment.

Section 3. Senate

1. Composition; Term The Senate of the United States shall be composed of two senators from each state chosen by the legislature thereof, for six years, and each senator shall have one vote.

2. Classification; Filling Vacancies Immediately after they shall be assembled in consequence of the first election, they shall be divided as equally as may be into three classes. The seats of the senators of the first class shall be vacated at the expiration of the second year, of the second class at the expiration of the fourth year, and of the third class at the expiration of the sixth year, so that one third may be chosen every second year; and if vacancies happen by resignation, or otherwise, during the recess of the legislature of any State, the executive thereof may make temporary appointments until the next meeting of the legislature, which shall then fill such vacancies.

Clause 1 Electors refers to voters. Members of the House of Representatives are elected every two years. Any citizen allowed to vote for members of the larger house of the state legislature can also vote for members of the House.

Clause 3 The number of representatives each state elects is based on its population. An enumeration, or census, must be taken every 10 years to determine population. Today, the number of representatives in the House is fixed at 435. Clause 3 contains the Three-Fifths Compromise worked out at the Constitutional Convention. Persons bound to service meant indentured servants. All other persons meant slaves. All free people in a state were counted. However, only three fifths of the slaves were included in the population count. This three-fifths clause became meaningless when slaves were freed by the Thirteenth Amendment.

Clause 4 Executive authority means the governor of a state. If a member of the House leaves office before his or her term ends, the governor must call a special election to fill the seat.

Clause 5 The House elects a Speaker. Only the House has the power to impeach, or accuse, a federal official of wrongdoing.

Clause 2 Every two years, one third of the senators run for reelection. The Seventeenth Amendment changed the way of filling vacancies, or empty seats. Today, the governor of a state must choose a senator to fill a vacancy that occurs between elections.

Clause 5 Pro tempore means temporary. The Senate chooses one of its members to serve as president pro tempore when the Vice President is absent.

Clause 6 The Senate acts as a jury if the House impeaches a federal official. The Chief Justice of the Supreme Court presides if the President is on trial. Two thirds of all senators present must vote for conviction, or finding the accused guilty. No President has ever been convicted. The House impeached President Andrew Johnson in 1868, but the Senate acquitted him of the charges. In 1998–99, President Bill Clinton became the second President to be impeached and acquitted.

Clause 1 Each state legislature can decide when and how congressional elections take place, but Congress can overrule these decisions. In 1842, Congress required each state to set up congressional districts with one representative elected from each district. In 1872, Congress decided that congressional elections must be held in every state on the same date in even-numbered years.

Clause 1 Each house decides whether a member has the qualifications for office set by the Constitution. A quorum is the smallest number of members who must be present for business to be conducted. Each house can set its own rules about absent members.

Portions of the Constitution altered by later amendments or that no longer apply are printed in blue.

3. Qualifications No person shall be a senator who shall not have attained to the age of thirty years, and been nine years a citizen of the United States, and who shall not, when elected, be an inhabitant of that state for which he shall be chosen.

4. President of the Senate The Vice President of the United States shall be president of the Senate, but shall have no vote, unless they be equally divided.

5. Other Officers The Senate shall choose their other officers, and also a president pro tempore, in the absence of the Vice President, or when he shall exercise the office of the President of the United States.

6. Impeachment Trials The Senate shall have the sole power to try all impeachments. When sitting for that purpose, they shall be on oath or affirmation. When the President of the United States is tried, the Chief Justice shall preside; and no person shall be convicted without the concurrence of two thirds of the members present.

7. Penalty on Conviction Judgment in cases of impeachment shall not extend further than to removal from office, and disqualification to hold and enjoy any office of honor, trust or profit under the United States: but the party convicted shall nevertheless be liable and subject to indictment, trial, judgment, and punishment, according to law.

Section 4. Elections and Meetings

1. Election of Congress The times, places, and manner of holding elections for senators and representatives, shall be prescribed in each state by the legislature thereof; but the Congress may at any time by law make or alter such regulations, except as to the places of choosing senators.

2. Sessions The Congress shall assemble at least once in every year, and such meeting shall be on the first Monday in December, unless they shall by law appoint a different day.

Section 5. Legislative Proceedings

1. Organization Each house shall be the judge of the elections, returns, and qualifications of its own members, and a majority of each shall constitute a quorum to do business; but a smaller number may adjourn from day to day, and may be authorized to compel the attendance of absent members, in such manner, and under such penalties, as each house may provide.

2. Rules Each house may determine the rules of its proceedings, punish its members for disorderly behavior, and with the concurrence of two thirds, expel a member.

3. Record Each house shall keep a journal of its proceedings, and from time to time publish the same, excepting such parts as may in their judgment require secrecy; and the yeas and nays of the members of either house on any question shall, at the desire of one fifth of those present, be entered on the journal.

4. Adjournment Neither house, during the session of Congress, shall, without the consent of the other, adjourn for more than three days, nor to any other place than that in which the two houses shall be sitting.

Section 6. Compensation, Immunities, and Disabilities of Members

1. Salaries; Immunities The senators and representatives shall receive a compensation for their services, to be ascertained by law, and paid out of the Treasury of the United States. They shall in all cases, except treason, felony, and breach of the peace, be privileged from arrest during their attendance at the session of their respective houses, and in going to and returning from the same; and for any speech or debate in either house, they shall not be questioned in any other place.

2. Restrictions on Other Employment No senator or representative shall, during the time for which he was elected, be appointed to any civil office under the authority of the United States, which shall have been created, or the emoluments whereof shall have been increased during such time; and no person holding any office under the United States shall be a member of either house during his continuance in office.

Section 7. Law-Making Process

1. Revenue Bills All bills for raising revenue shall originate in the House of Representatives; but the Senate may propose or concur with amendments as on other bills.

2. How a Bill Becomes Law; the Veto Every bill which shall have passed the House of Representatives and the Senate shall, before it become a law, be presented to the President of the United States; if he approve, he shall sign it, but if not, he shall return it, with his objections, to that house in which it shall have originated, who shall enter the objections at large on their journal, and proceed to reconsider it. If after such reconsideration two thirds of that house shall agree to pass the bill, it shall be sent, together with the objections, to the other house, by which it shall likewise be reconsidered, and if approved by two thirds of that house, it shall become a law. But in all such cases the votes of both houses shall be determined by yeas and nays, and the names of the persons voting for and against the bill shall be entered on the journal of each house respectively. If any bill shall not be returned by the President within ten days (Sundays excepted) after it shall have been presented to him, the same shall be a law, in like manner as if he had signed it, unless the Congress by their adjournment prevent its return, in which case it shall not be a law.

3. Resolutions Passed by Congress Every order, resolution, or vote to which the concurrence of the Senate and House of Representatives may be necessary (except on a question of adjournment) shall be presented to the President of the United States; and before the same shall take effect, shall be approved by him, or being disapproved by him, shall be repassed by two thirds of the Senate and House of Representatives, according to the rules and limitations prescribed in the case of a bill.

Clause 4 Neither house can adjourn, or stop meeting, for more than three days unless the other house approves. Both houses must meet in the same city.

Clause 1 Congress decides the salary for its members. While Congress is in session, a member is free from arrest in civil cases and cannot be sued for anything he or she says on the floor of Congress. This allows for freedom of debate. However, a member can be arrested for a criminal offense.

Clause 2 Emolument means salary. A member of Congress cannot hold another federal office during his or her term. A former member of Congress cannot hold an office created while he or she was in Congress. An official in another branch of government cannot serve at the same time in Congress.

Clause 1 Revenue is money raised by the government through taxes. Tax bills must be introduced in the House. The Senate, however, can make changes in tax bills.

Clause 2 A bill, or proposed law, that is passed by a majority of the House and Senate is sent to the President. If the President signs the bill, it becomes law.

A bill can also become law without the President's signature. The President can refuse to act on a bill. If Congress is in session at the time, the bill becomes law 10 days after the President receives it.

The President can veto, or reject, a bill by sending it back to the house where it was introduced. If the President refuses to act on a bill and Congress adjourns within 10 days, then the bill dies. This way of killing a bill without taking action is called the pocket veto.

Congress can override the President's veto if each house of Congress passes the bill again by a two-thirds vote.

Congress's power is expressed directly in the Constitution. Numbered from 1 to 18, these powers are also known as enumerated powers.

Clause 1 Duties are tariffs. Imposts are taxes in general. Excises are taxes on the production or sale of certain goods.

Clause 3 Only Congress has the power to regulate foreign and interstate commerce. This allows a "common market" with a unified set of laws governing trade. This clause has also been interpreted as giving the federal government authority over Native American nations.

Clause 4 Naturalization is the process whereby a foreigner becomes a citizen. Bankruptcy is the condition in which a person or business cannot pay its debts.

Clause 5 Congressional power to coin money and set its value is one of the keys to creating a stable economy.

Clause 6 Counterfeiting is the making of imitation money. Securities are bonds. Congress can make laws to punish counterfeiters.

Clause 11 Only Congress can declare war. Declarations of war are granted at the request of the President. Letters of marque and reprisal were documents issued by a government allowing merchant ships to arm themselves and attack ships of an enemy nation. They are no longer issued.

Clauses 15, 16 The militia is a body of citizen soldiers. Each state has its own militia, today called the National Guard. Normally, the militia is under the command of a state's governor. However, it can be placed under the command of the President.

Portions of the Constitution altered by later amendments or that no longer apply are printed in blue.

Section 8. Powers of Congress

The Congress shall have power

1. To lay and collect taxes, duties, imposts, and excises, to pay the debts and provide for the common defense and general welfare of the United States; but all duties, imposts and excises shall be uniform throughout the United States;

2. To borrow money on the credit of the United States;

3. To regulate commerce with foreign nations, and among the several states, and with the Indian tribes;

4. To establish an uniform rule of naturalization, and uniform laws on the subject of bankruptcies throughout the United States;

5. To coin money, regulate the value thereof, and of foreign coin, and fix the standard of weights and measures;

6. To provide for the punishment of counterfeiting the securities and current coin of the United States;

7. To establish post offices and post roads;

8. To promote the progress of science and useful arts by securing for limited times to authors and inventors the exclusive right to their respective writings and discoveries;

9. To constitute tribunals inferior to the Supreme Court;

10. To define and punish piracies and felonies committed on the high seas and offenses against the law of nations;

11. To declare war, grant letters of marque and reprisal, and make rules concerning captures on land and water;

12. To raise and support armies, but no appropriation of money to that use shall be for a longer term than two years;

13. To provide and maintain a navy;

14. To make rules for the government and regulation of the land and naval forces;

15. To provide for calling forth the militia to execute the laws of the Union, suppress insurrections, and repel invasions;

16. To provide for organizing, arming, and disciplining the militia, and for governing such part of them as may be employed in the service of the United States, reserving to the states, respectively, the appointment of the officers, and the authority of training the militia according to the discipline prescribed by Congress;

17. To exercise exclusive legislation in all cases whatsoever, over such district (not exceeding ten miles square) as may, by cession of particular states, and the acceptance of Congress, become the seat of the government of the United States, and to exercise like authority over all places purchased by the consent of the legislature of the state in which the same shall be, for the erection of forts, magazines, arsenals, dock-yards, and other needful buildings; —and

18. To make all laws which shall be necessary and proper for carrying into execution the foregoing powers, and all other powers vested by this Constitution in the government of the United States, or in any department or officer thereof.

Section 9. Powers Denied to Congress

1. The Slave Trade The migration or importation of such persons as any of the states now existing shall think proper to admit, shall not be prohibited by the Congress prior to the year one thousand eight hundred and eight, but a tax or duty may be imposed on such importation, not exceeding ten dollars for each person.

2. Writ of Habeas Corpus The privilege of the writ of habeas corpus shall not be suspended, unless when in cases of rebellion or invasion the public safety may require it.

3. Bills of Attainder; Ex Post Facto Laws No bill of attainder or ex post facto law shall be passed.

4. Apportionment of Direct Taxes No capitation, or other direct, tax shall be laid, unless in proportion to the census or enumeration herein before directed to be taken.

5. Taxes on Exports No tax or duty shall be laid on articles exported from any state.

6. Special Preference for Trade No preference shall be given by any regulation of commerce or revenue to the ports of one state over those of another; nor shall vessels bound to, or from, one state, be obliged to enter, clear, or pay duties in another.

7. Spending No money shall be drawn from the Treasury, but in consequence of appropriations made by law; and a regular statement and account of the receipts and expenditures of all public money shall be published from time to time.

8. Titles of Nobility No title of nobility shall be granted by the United States; and no person holding any office of profit or trust under them, shall, without the consent of the Congress, accept of any present, emolument, office, or title, of any kind whatever, from any king, prince or foreign state.

Section 10. Powers Denied to the States

1. Unconditional Prohibitions No state shall enter into any treaty, alliance, or confederation; grant letters of marque and reprisal; coin money; emit bills of credit; make any thing but gold and silver coin a tender in payment of debts; pass any bill of attainder, ex post facto law, or law impairing the obligation of contracts, or grant any title of nobility.

2. Powers Conditionally Denied No state shall, without the consent of the Congress, lay any imposts or duties on imports or exports, except what may be absolutely necessary for executing its inspection laws; and the net produce of all duties and imposts, laid by any state on imports or exports, shall be for the use of the Treasury of the United States; and all such laws shall be subject to the revision and control of the Congress.

Clause 18 Clause 18 gives Congress the power to make laws as needed to carry out the first 17 clauses. It is sometimes called the elastic clause because it lets Congress stretch the meaning of its power.

Clause 1 "Such persons" means slaves. In 1808, as soon as Congress was permitted to abolish the slave trade, it did so.

Clause 2 A writ of habeas corpus is a court order requiring government officials to bring a prisoner to court and explain why he or she is being held. A writ of habeas corpus protects people from unlawful imprisonment. The government cannot suspend this right except in times of rebellion or invasion.

Clause 3 A bill of attainder is a law declaring that a person is guilty of a particular crime. An ex post facto law punishes an act which was not illegal when it was committed. Congress cannot pass a bill of attainder or ex post facto laws.

Clause 7 The federal government cannot spend money unless Congress appropriates it, or passes a law allowing it. The government must publish a statement showing how it spends public funds.

Clause 1 The writers of the Constitution did not want the states to act like separate nations, so they prohibited states from making treaties or coining money. Some powers denied to the federal government are also denied to the states.

Clauses 2, 3 Powers listed here are forbidden to the states, but Congress can pass laws that give these powers to the states. **Clause 2** forbids states from taxing imports and exports without the consent of Congress. States may charge inspection fees on goods entering the states. Any profits go to the United States Treasury.

3. Other Denied Powers No state shall, without the consent of Congress, lay any duty of tonnage, keep troops, or ships of war in time of peace, enter into any agreement or compact with another state, or with a foreign power, or engage in war, unless actually invaded, or in such imminent danger as will not admit of delay.

Article II ★ Executive Branch

Section 1. President and Vice President

1. Chief Executive; Term The executive power shall be vested in a President of the United States of America. He shall hold his office during the term of four years, and, together with the Vice President, chosen for the same term, be elected as follows:

2. Electoral College Each state shall appoint, in such manner as the legislature thereof may direct, a number of electors, equal to the whole number of senators and representatives to which the state may be entitled in the Congress: but no senator or representative, or person holding an office of trust or profit under the United States, shall be appointed an elector.

3. Former Electoral Method The electors shall meet in their respective states, and vote by ballot for two persons, of whom one at least shall not be an inhabitant of the same state with themselves. And they shall make a list of all the persons voted for, and of the number of votes for each; which list they shall sign and certify, and transmit sealed to the seat of the government of the United States, directed to the president of the Senate. The president of the Senate shall, in the presence of the Senate and House of Representatives, open all the certificates, and the votes shall then be counted. The person having the greatest number of votes shall be the President, if such number be a majority of the whole number of Electors appointed; and if there be more than one who have such majority, and have an equal number of votes, then the House of Representatives shall immediately choose by ballot one of them for President; and if no person have a majority, then from the five highest on the list the said House shall in like manner choose the President. But in choosing the President, the votes shall be taken by states, the representation from each state having one vote; a quorum for this purpose shall consist of a member or members from two thirds of the states, and a majority of all the states shall be necessary to a choice. In every case, after the choice of the President, the person having the greatest number of votes of the electors shall be the Vice President. But if there should remain two or more who have equal votes, the Senate shall choose from them by ballot the Vice President.

4. Time of Elections The Congress may determine the time of choosing the electors, and the day on which they shall give their votes; which day shall be the same throughout the United States.

5. Qualifications for President No person except a natural-born citizen, or a citizen of the United States at the time of the adoption of this Constitution, shall be eligible to the office of President; neither shall any person be eligible to that office who shall not have attained to the age of thirty-five years, and been fourteen years a resident within the United States.

6. Presidential Succession In case of the removal of the President from office, or of his death, resignation, or inability to discharge the powers and duties of the said office, the same shall devolve on the Vice President, and the Congress may by law provide for the case of removal, death, resignation or inability, both of the President and Vice President, declaring what officer shall then act as President, and such officer shall act accordingly, until the disability be removed, or a President shall be elected.

7. Salary The President shall, at stated times, receive for his services, a compensation, which shall neither be increased nor diminished during the period for which he shall have been elected, and he shall not receive within that period any other emolument from the United States, or any of them.

8. Oath of Office Before he enter on the execution of his office, he shall take the following oath or affirmation:—"I do solemnly swear (or affirm) that I will faithfully execute the office of the President of the United States, and will to the best of my ability, preserve, protect, and defend the Constitution of the United States."

Section 2. Powers of the President

1. Military Powers The President shall be commander in chief of the army and navy of the United States, and of the militia of the several states, when called into the actual service of the United States; he may require the opinion, in writing, of the principal officer in each of the executive departments, upon any subject relating to the duties of their respective offices, and he shall have power to grant reprieves and pardons for offenses against the United States, except in cases of impeachment.

2. Treaties; Appointments He shall have power, by and with the advice and consent of the Senate, to make treaties, provided two thirds of the senators present concur; and he shall nominate, and by and with the advice and consent of the Senate, shall appoint ambassadors, other public ministers and consuls, judges of the Supreme Court, and all other officers of the United States, whose appointments are not herein otherwise provided for, and which shall be established by law: but the Congress may by law vest the appointment of such inferior officers, as they think proper, in the President alone, in the courts of law, or in the heads of departments.

3. Temporary Appointments The President shall have power to fill up all vacancies that may happen during the recess of the Senate, by granting commissions which shall expire at the end of their next session.

Clause 6 The powers of the President pass to the Vice President if the President leaves office or cannot discharge his or her duties. The Twenty-fifth Amendment replaced this clause.

Clause 7 The President is paid a salary. It cannot be raised or lowered during his or her term of office. The President is not allowed to hold any other federal or state position while in office.

Clause 1 The President is the head of the armed forces and the state militias when they are called into national service. So the military is under civilian, or nonmilitary, control. The President can get advice from the heads of executive departments. In most cases, the President has the power to grant reprieves and pardons. A reprieve suspends punishment ordered by law. A pardon prevents prosecution for a crime or overrides the judgment of a court.

Clause 2 The President has the power to make treaties with other nations. Under the system of checks and balances, all treaties must be approved by two thirds of the Senate.

The President has the power to appoint ambassadors to foreign countries and to appoint other high officials. The Senate must confirm, or approve, these appointments.

Section 3. Duties of the President

He shall from time to time give to the Congress information of the state of the Union, and recommend to their consideration such measures as he shall judge necessary and expedient; he may, on extraordinary occasions, convene both houses, or either of them, and in case of disagreement between them, with respect to the time of adjournment, he may adjourn them to such time as he shall think proper; he shall receive ambassadors and other public ministers; he shall take care that the laws be faithfully executed, and shall commission all the officers of the United States.

Section 4. Impeachment

Section 4
Civil officers include federal judges and members of the Cabinet. High crimes are major crimes. Misdemeanors are lesser crimes. The President, Vice President, and others can be forced out of office if impeached and found guilty of certain crimes.

The President, Vice President and all civil officers of the United States, shall be removed from office on impeachment for, and conviction of, treason, bribery, or other high crimes and misdemeanors.

Article III ★ Judicial Branch

Section 1. Courts, Terms of Office

The judicial power of the United States shall be vested in one Supreme Court, and in such inferior courts as the Congress may from time to time ordain and establish. The judges, both of the Supreme and inferior courts, shall hold their offices during good behavior, and shall, at stated times, receive for their services, a compensation, which shall not be diminished during their continuance in office.

Section 2. Jurisdiction

Clause 1 Jurisdiction refers to the right of a court to hear a case. Federal courts have jurisdiction over cases that involve the Constitution, federal laws, treaties, foreign ambassadors and diplomats, naval and maritime laws, disagreements between states or between citizens from different states, and disputes between a state or citizen and a foreign state or citizen.

1. Scope of Judicial Power The judicial power shall extend to all cases, in law and equity, arising under this Constitution, the laws of the United States, and treaties made, or which shall be made, under their authority;—to all cases affecting ambassadors, other public ministers and consuls;—to all cases of admiralty and maritime jurisdiction;—to controversies to which the United States shall be a party;—to controversies between two or more states; between a state and citizens of another state; —between citizens of different states;—between citizens of the same state claiming lands under grants of different states, and between a state, or the citizens thereof, and foreign states, citizens, or subjects.

Clause 2 Original jurisdiction means the power of a court to hear a case where it first arises. The Supreme Court has original jurisdiction over only a few cases, such as those involving foreign diplomats. More often, the Supreme Court acts as an appellate court. An appellate court does not decide guilt. It decides whether the lower court trial was properly conducted and reviews the lower court's decision.

2. Supreme Court In all cases affecting ambassadors, other public ministers and consuls, and those in which a state shall be a party, the Supreme Court shall have original jurisdiction. In all the other cases before mentioned, the Supreme Court shall have appellate jurisdiction, both as to law and fact, with such exceptions, and under such regulations as the Congress shall make.

Portions of the Constitution altered by later amendments or that no longer apply are printed in blue.

3. Trial by Jury The trial of all crimes, except in cases of impeachment, shall be by jury; and such trial shall be held in the state where the said crimes shall have been committed; but when not committed within any state, the trial shall be at such place or places as the Congress may by law have directed.

Section 3. Treason

1. Definition Treason against the United States shall consist only in levying war against them, or in adhering to their enemies, giving them aid and comfort. No person shall be convicted of treason unless on the testimony of two witnesses to the same overt act, or on confession in open court.

2. Punishment The Congress shall have power to declare the punishment of treason, but no attainder of treason shall work corruption of blood or forfeiture except during the life of the person attained.

> **Clause 1** Treason is clearly defined. An <u>overt act</u> is an actual action.

> **Clause 2** Congress has the power to set the punishment for the traitors. Congress may not punish the children of convicted traitors by taking away their civil rights or property.

Article IV ★ Relations Among the States

Section 1. Full Faith and Credit

Full faith and credit shall be given in each state to the public acts, records, and judicial proceedings of every other state. And the Congress may by general laws prescribe the manner in which such acts, records, and proceedings shall be proved, and the effect thereof.

> Each state must recognize the official acts and records of any other state. For example, each state must recognize marriage certificates issued by another state. Congress can pass laws to ensure this.

Section 2. Privileges and Immunities of Citizens

1. Privileges The citizens of each state shall be entitled to all privileges and immunities of citizens in the several states.

2. Extradition A person charged in any state with treason, felony, or other crime, who shall flee from justice, and be found in another state, shall on demand of the executive authority of the state from which he fled, be delivered up, to be removed to the state having jurisdiction of the crime.

3. Fugitive Slaves No person held to service or labor in one state, under the laws thereof, escaping into another, shall in consequence of any law or regulation therein, be discharged from such service or labor, but shall be delivered up on claim of the party to whom such service or labor may be due.

> **Clause 2** <u>Extradition</u> means the act of returning a suspected criminal or escaped prisoner to a state where he or she is wanted. State governors must return a suspect to another state. However, the Supreme Court has ruled that a governor cannot be forced to do so if he or she feels that justice will not be done.

> **Clause 3** "Persons held to service or labor" refers to slaves or indentured servants. This clause required states to return runaway slaves to their owners. The Thirteenth Amendment replaces this clause.

Section 3. New States and Territories

1. New States New states may be admitted by the Congress into this Union; but no new states shall be formed or erected within the jurisdiction of any other state; nor any state be formed by the junction of two or more states, or parts of states, without the consent of the legislatures of the states concerned as well as of the Congress.

> **Clause 1** Congress has the power to admit new states to the Union. Existing states cannot be split up or joined together to form new states unless both Congress and the state legislatures approve. New states are equal to all other states.

2. Federal Lands The Congress shall have power to dispose of and make all needful rules and regulations respecting the territory or other property belonging to the United States; and nothing in this Constitution shall be so construed as to prejudice any claims of the United States, or of any particular state.

Section 4. Protection Afforded to States by the Nation

Section 4 In a republic, voters choose representatives to govern them. The federal government must protect the states from foreign invasion and from domestic, or internal, disorder if asked to do so by a state.

The United States shall guarantee to every state in this Union a republican form of government, and shall protect each of them against invasion; and on application of the legislature, or of the executive (when the legislature cannot be convened) against domestic violence.

Article V ★ Provisions for Amendment

The Constitution can be amended, or changed, if necessary. An amendment can be proposed by (1) a two-thirds vote of both houses of Congress or (2) a national convention called by Congress at the request of two thirds of the state legislatures. (This second method has never been used.) An amendment must be ratified, or approved, by (1) three fourths of the state legislatures or (2) special conventions in three fourths of the states. Congress decides which method will be used.

Congress has proposed each of the 27 amendments to the Constitution by a vote of two-thirds in both houses. The only amendment ratified by constitutional conventions of the states was the Twenty-first Amendment. State legislatures have ratified all other amendments.

The Congress, whenever two thirds of both houses shall deem it necessary, shall propose amendments to this Constitution, or, on the application of the legislatures of two thirds of the several states, shall call a convention for proposing amendments, which, in either case, shall be valid to all intents and purposes, as part of this Constitution, when ratified by the legislatures of three fourths of the several states, or by conventions in three fourths thereof, as the one or the other mode of ratification may be proposed by the Congress; provided that no amendment which may be made prior to the year one thousand eight hundred and eight shall in any manner affect the first and fourth clauses in the ninth section of the first Article; and that no state, without its consent, shall be deprived of its equal suffrage in the Senate.

Article VI ★ National Debts, Supremacy of National Law, Oath

Section 1. Validity of Debts

All debts contracted and engagements entered into, before the adoption of this Constitution, shall be as valid against the United States under this Constitution, as under the Confederation.

Section 2. Supremacy of National Law

Section 2 The "supremacy clause" in this section establishes the Constitution, federal laws, and treaties that the Senate has ratified as the supreme, or highest, law of the land. Thus, they outweigh state laws. A state judge must overturn a state law that conflicts with the Constitution or with a federal law.

Portions of the Constitution altered by later amendments or that no longer apply are printed in blue.

This Constitution, and the laws of the United States which shall be made in pursuance thereof, and all treaties made, or which shall be made, under the authority of the United States, shall be the supreme law of the land; and the judges in every state shall be bound thereby, anything in the constitution or laws of any state to the contrary notwithstanding.

Section 3. Oaths of Office

The senators and representatives before mentioned, and the members of the several state legislatures, and all executive and judicial officers, both of the United States and of the several states, shall be bound by oath or affirmation, to support this Constitution; but no religious test shall ever be required as a qualification to any office or public trust under the United States.

Article VII ★ Ratification of Constitution

The ratification of the conventions of nine states shall be sufficient for the establishment of this Constitution between the states so ratifying the same.

Done in convention by the unanimous consent of the states present the seventeenth day of September, in the year of our Lord one thousand seven hundred and eighty-seven, and of the independence of the United States of America the twelfth. In Witness whereof, we have hereunto subscribed our names.

Article VII During 1787 and 1788, states held special conventions. By October 1788, the required nine states had ratified the United States Constitution.

Attest: William Jackson, SECRETARY
George Washington, PRESIDENT and deputy from Virginia

New Hampshire
John Langdon
Nicholas Gilman

Massachusetts
Nathaniel Gorham
Rufus King

Connecticut
William Samuel Johnson
Roger Sherman

New York
Alexander Hamilton

New Jersey
William Livingston
David Brearley
William Paterson
Jonathan Dayton

Pennsylvania
Benjamin Franklin
Thomas Mifflin
Robert Morris
George Clymer
Thomas Fitzsimons
Jared Ingersoll
James Wilson
Gouverneur Morris

Delaware
George Read
Gunning Bedford, Jr.
John Dickinson
Richard Bassett
Jacob Broom

Maryland
James McHenry
Dan of St. Thomas Jenifer
Daniel Carroll

Virginia
John Blair
James Madison, Jr.

North Carolina
William Blount
Richard Dobbs Spaight
Hugh Williamson

South Carolina
John Rutledge
Charles Cotesworth Pinckney
Charles Pinckney
Pierce Butler

Georgia
William Few
Abraham Baldwin

The Amendments Amendments are changes. The Constitution has been amended 27 times since it was ratified in 1788. The first 10 amendments are referred to as the Bill of Rights. These amendments give rights to the people and states, thus putting limits on the power of government.

First Amendment The First Amendment protects five basic rights: freedom of religion, speech, the press, assembly, and petition. Congress cannot set up an established, or official, church or religion for the nation. It cannot forbid the practice of religion, nor can it force the practice of religion.

Congress may not abridge, or limit, the freedom to speak and write freely. The government may not censor, or review, books and newspapers before they are printed. This amendment also protects the right to assemble, or hold public meetings. Petition means ask. Redress means to correct. Grievances are wrongs. The people have the right to ask the government for wrongs to be corrected.

Second Amendment Americans debate the exact meaning of the Second Amendment. Some believe that it guarantees the right of individuals to own firearms. Others argue that it guarantees the right of each state to maintain a militia. Gun control, or the passage of laws to regulate the ownership and use of firearms, is one of the most controversial issues today.

Third Amendment In colonial times, the British could quarter, or house, soldiers in private homes without permission of the owners. The Third Amendment prevents such abuses.

Portions of the Constitution altered by later amendments or that no longer apply are printed in blue.

Amendments

First Amendment ★

(1791) Freedom of Religion, Speech, Press, Assembly, and Petition

Congress shall make no law respecting an establishment of religion, or prohibiting the free exercise thereof; or abridging the freedom of speech, or of the press; or the right of the people peaceably to assemble, and to petition the government for a redress of grievances.

Second Amendment ★

(1791) Bearing Arms

A well-regulated militia being necessary to the security of a free state, the right of the people to keep and bear arms shall not be infringed.

Third Amendment ★

(1791) Quartering of Troops

No soldier shall, in time of peace, be quartered in any house, without the consent of the owner; nor in time of war, but in a manner to be prescribed by law.

Fourth Amendment ★

(1791) Searches and Seizures

The right of the people to be secure in their persons, houses, papers, and effects, against unreasonable searches and seizures, shall not be violated, and no warrants shall issue, but upon probable cause, supported by oath or affirmation, and particularly describing the place to be searched, and the persons or things to be seized.

Fifth Amendment ★

(1791) Criminal Proceedings; Due Process; Eminent Domain

No person shall be held to answer for a capital, or otherwise infamous, crime, unless on a presentment or indictment of a grand jury, except in cases arising in the land or naval forces, or in the militia, when in actual service in time of war or public danger; nor shall any person be subject for the same offense to be twice put in jeopardy of life and limb; nor shall be compelled, in any criminal case, to be a witness against himself; nor be deprived of life, liberty, or property, without due process of law; nor shall private property be taken for public use, without just compensation.

Sixth Amendment ★

(1791) Criminal Proceedings

In all criminal prosecutions, the accused shall enjoy the right to a speedy and public trial, by an impartial jury of the state and district wherein the crime shall have been committed, which district shall have been previously ascertained by law, and to be informed of the nature and cause of the accusation; to be confronted with the witnesses against him; to have compulsory process for obtaining witnesses in his favor, and to have the assistance of counsel for his defense.

Fourth Amendment This amendment protects Americans from unreasonable searches and seizures. Search and seizure are permitted only if a judge has issued a warrant, or written court order. A warrant is issued only if there is probable cause. This means an officer must show that it is probable, or likely, that the search will produce evidence of a crime.

Fifth Amendment This amendment protects the rights of the accused. Capital crimes are those that can be punished with death. Infamous crimes are those that can be punished with prison or loss of rights. The federal government must obtain an indictment, or formal accusation, from a grand jury to prosecute anyone for such crimes. A grand jury is a panel of between 12 and 23 citizens who decide if the government has enough evidence to justify a trial.

Double jeopardy is forbidden by this amendment. This means that a person cannot be tried twice for the same crime. However, if a court sets aside a conviction because of a legal error, the accused can be tried again. A person on trial cannot be forced to testify, or give evidence, against himself or herself. A person accused of a crime is entitled to due process of law, or a fair hearing or trial.

Finally, the government cannot seize private property for public use without paying the owner a fair price for it.

Sixth Amendment In criminal cases, the jury must be impartial, or not favor either side. The accused is guaranteed the right to a trial by jury. The trial must be speedy. If the government purposely postpones the trial so that it becomes hard for the person to get a fair hearing, the charge may be dismissed. The accused must be told the charges and be allowed to question all witnesses. Witnesses who can help the accused can be ordered to appear in court. The accused must be allowed a lawyer.

Seventh Amendment ★

(1791) Civil Trials

In suits at common law, where the value in controversy shall exceed twenty dollars, the right of trial by jury shall be preserved, and no fact tried by a jury shall be otherwise re-examined in any court of the United States, than according to the rules of the common law.

Eighth Amendment ★

(1791) Punishment for Crimes

Excessive bail shall not be required, nor excessive fines imposed, nor cruel and unusual punishments inflicted.

Ninth Amendment ★

(1791) Unenumerated Rights

The enumeration in the Constitution, of certain rights, shall not be construed to deny or disparage others retained by the people.

Tenth Amendment ★

(1791) Powers Reserved to the States

The powers not delegated to the United States by the Constitution, nor prohibited by it to the states, are reserved to the states respectively, or to the people.

Eleventh Amendment ★

(1795) Suits Against States

The judicial power of the United States shall not be construed to extend to any suit in law or equity, commenced or prosecuted against one of the United States by citizens of another state, or by citizens or subjects of any foreign state.

Seventh Amendment <u>Common law</u> refers to rules of law established by judges in past cases. This amendment guarantees the right to a jury trial in lawsuits where the sum of money at stake is more than $20. An appeals court can set aside a verdict only if legal errors made the trial unfair.

Eighth Amendment <u>Bail</u> is money that the accused leaves with the court as a pledge to appear for trial. If the accused does not appear, the court keeps the money. This amendment prevents the court from imposing bail or fines that are <u>excessive</u>, or too high. The amendment also forbids cruel and unusual punishments, such as physical torture.

Ninth Amendment The rights of the people are not limited to those listed in the Bill of Rights. In the Ninth Amendment, the government is prevented from claiming these are the only rights people have.

Tenth Amendment Powers not given to the federal government belong to the states. Powers reserved to the states are not listed in the Constitution.

Eleventh Amendment A private citizen from one state cannot sue the government of another state in federal court. However, a citizen can sue a state government in a state court.

Portions of the Constitution altered by later amendments or that no longer apply are printed in blue.

Twelfth Amendment ★

(1804) Election of President and Vice President

The electors shall meet in their respective states, and vote by ballot for President and Vice President, one of whom, at least, shall not be an inhabitant of the same state with themselves; they shall name in their ballots the person voted for as President, and in distinct ballots the person voted for as Vice President, and they shall make distinct lists of all persons voted for as President, and of all persons voted for as Vice President, and of the number of votes for each, which lists they shall sign and certify, and transmit sealed to the seat of the government of the United States, directed to the president of the Senate; the president of the Senate shall, in the presence of the Senate and the House of Representatives, open all the certificates and the votes shall then be counted;—the person having the greatest number of votes for President shall be the President, if such number be a majority of the whole number of electors appointed; and if no person have such a majority, then from the persons having the highest numbers not exceeding three on the list of those voted for as President, the House of Representatives shall choose immediately, by ballot, the President.

But in choosing the President, the votes shall be taken by states, the representation from each state having one vote; a quorum for this purpose shall consist of a member or members from two thirds of the states, and a majority of all states shall be necessary to a choice. And if the House of Representatives shall not choose a President whenever the right of choice shall devolve upon them, before the fourth day of March next following, then the Vice President, shall act as President, as in the case of death or other constitutional disability of the President—The person having the greatest number of votes as Vice President, shall be the Vice President, if such a number be a majority of the whole number of electors appointed, and if no person have a majority, then from the two highest numbers on the list, the Senate shall choose the Vice President; a quorum for the purpose shall consist of two thirds of the whole number of senators, and a majority of the whole number shall be necessary to a choice. But no person constitutionally ineligible to the office of President shall be eligible to that of Vice President of the United States.

Thirteenth Amendment ★

(1865) Slavery and Involuntary Servitude

Section 1. Outlawing Slavery Neither slavery nor involuntary servitude, except as a punishment for crime whereof the party shall have been duly convicted, shall exist within the United States, or any place subject to their jurisdiction.

Section 2. Enforcement Congress shall have power to enforce this article by appropriate legislation.

> **Twelfth Amendment** This amendment changed the way the electoral college voted as outlined in Article II, Clause 3.
>
> This amendment provides that each elector choose one candidate for President and one candidate for Vice President. If no candidate for President receives a majority of electoral votes, the House of Representatives chooses the President. If no candidate for Vice President receives a majority, the Senate elects the Vice President. The Vice President must be a person who is eligible to be President.
>
> This system is still in use today. However, it is possible for a candidate to win the popular vote and lose in the electoral college. This happened in 1888 and in 2000.

> **Thirteenth Amendment** The Emancipation Proclamation (1863) freed slaves only in areas controlled by the Confederacy. This amendment freed all slaves. It also forbids involuntary servitude, or labor done against one's will. However, it does not prevent prison wardens from making prisoners work. Congress can pass laws to carry out this amendment.

Fourteenth Amendment ★

(1868) Rights of Citizens

Section 1. Citizenship All persons born or naturalized in the United States, and subject to the jurisdiction thereof, are citizens of the United States and of the state wherein they reside. No state shall make or enforce any law which shall abridge the privileges or immunities of citizens of the United States; nor shall any state deprive any person of life, liberty, or property, without due process of law; nor deny to any person within its jurisdiction the equal protection of the laws.

Section 2. Apportionment of Representatives Representatives shall be apportioned among the several states according to their respective numbers, counting the whole number of persons in each state, excluding Indians not taxed. But when the right to vote at any election for the choice of electors for President and Vice President of the United States, representatives in Congress, the executive and judicial officers of a state, or the members of the legislature thereof, is denied to any of the male inhabitants of such state, being twenty-one years of age, and citizens of the United States, or in any way abridged, except for participation in rebellion, or other crime, the basis of representation therein shall be reduced in the proportion which the number of such male citizens shall bear to the whole number of male citizens twenty-one years of age in such state.

Section 3. Former Confederate Officials No person shall be a senator or representative in Congress, or elector of President and Vice President, or hold any office, civil or military, under the United States, or under any state, who having previously taken an oath, as a member of Congress, or as an officer of the United States, or as a member of any state legislature, or as an executive or judicial officer of any state, to support the Constitution of the United States, shall have engaged in insurrection or rebellion against the same, or given aid or comfort to the enemies thereof. But Congress may, by a vote of two thirds of each house, remove such disability.

Section 4. Public Debt The validity of the public debt of the United States, authorized by law, including debts incurred for payment of pensions and bounties for services in suppressing insurrection or rebellion, shall not be questioned. But neither the United States nor any state shall assume or pay any debt or obligation incurred in aid of insurrection or rebellion against the United States, or any claim for the loss of emancipation of any slave; but all such debts, obligations and claims shall be held illegal and void.

Section 5. Enforcement The Congress shall have power to enforce, by appropriate legislation, the provisions of this article.

Fifteenth Amendment ★

(1870) Right to Vote—Race, Color, Servitude

Section 1. Extending the Right to Vote The right of citizens of the United States to vote shall not be denied or abridged by the United States or by any state on account of race, color, or previous condition of servitude.

Section 2. Enforcement The Congress shall have power to enforce this article by appropriate legislation.

Sixteenth Amendment ★

(1913) Income Tax

The Congress shall have power to lay and collect taxes on incomes, from whatever source derived, without apportionment among the several states, and without regard to any census or enumeration.

Seventeenth Amendment ★

(1913) Popular Election of Senators

Section 1. Method of Election The Senate of the United States shall be composed of two senators from each state, elected by the people thereof, for six years; and each senator shall have one vote. The electors in each state shall have the qualifications requisite for electors of the most numerous branch of the state legislatures.

Section 2. Vacancies When vacancies happen in the representation of any state in the Senate, the executive authority of such state shall issue writs of election to fill such vacancies: provided, that the legislature of any state may empower the executive thereof to make temporary appointments until the people fill the vacancies by election as the legislature may direct.

Section 3. Those Elected Under Previous Procedure This amendment shall not be so construed as to affect the election or term of any senator chosen before it becomes valid as part of the Constitution.

Fifteenth Amendment, Section 1 Previous condition of servitude refers to slavery. This amendment gave African Americans, both former slaves and free African Americans, the right to vote. In the late 1800s, southern states used grandfather clauses, literacy tests, and poll taxes to keep African Americans from voting.

Fifteenth Amendment, Section 2 Congress can pass laws to carry out this amendment. The Twenty-fourth Amendment barred the use of poll taxes in national elections. The Voting Rights Act of 1965 gave federal officials the power to register voters where there was voting discrimination.

Sixteenth Amendment Congress has the power to collect taxes on people's income. An income tax can be collected without regard to a state's population. This amendment changed Article 1, Section 9, Clause 4.

Seventeenth Amendment, Section 1 This amendment replaced Article 1, Section 2, Clause 1. Before it was adopted, state legislatures chose senators. This amendment provides that senators are directly elected by the people of each state.

Eighteenth Amendment ★

(1919) Prohibition of Alcoholic Beverages

Section 1. Ban on Alcohol After one year from the ratification of this article, the manufacture, sale, or transportation of intoxicating liquors within, the importation thereof into, or the exportation thereof from the United States and all territory subject to the jurisdiction thereof for beverage purposes is hereby prohibited.

Section 2. Enforcement The Congress and the several states shall have concurrent power to enforce this article by appropriate legislation.

Section 3. Method of Ratification This article shall be inoperative unless it shall have been ratified as an amendment to the Constitution by the legislatures of the several states, as provided in the Constitution, within seven years from the date of the submission hereof to the states by Congress.

> **Eighteenth Amendment** This amendment, known as Prohibition, banned the making, selling, or transporting of alcoholic beverages in the United States. Later, the Twenty-first Amendment repealed, or canceled, this amendment.

Nineteenth Amendment ★

(1920) Women's Suffrage

Section 1. The Right to Vote The right of citizens of the United States to vote shall not be denied or abridged by the United States or by any state on account of sex.

Section 2. Enforcement Congress shall have power to enforce this article by appropriate legislation.

> **Nineteenth Amendment** Neither the federal government nor state governments can deny the right to vote on account of sex. Thus, women won suffrage, or the right to vote. Before 1920, some states had allowed women to vote in state elections.

Twentieth Amendment ★

(1933) Presidential Terms; Sessions of Congress; Death or Disqualification of President-Elect

Section 1. Beginning of Terms The terms of the President and Vice President shall end at noon on the 20th day of January, and the terms of senators and representatives at noon on the 3rd day of January, of the years in which such terms would have ended if this article had not been ratified; and the terms of their successors shall then begin.

Section 2. Congressional Sessions The Congress shall assemble at least once in every year, and such meeting shall begin at noon on the 3rd day of January, unless they shall by law appoint a different day.

> **Twentieth Amendment, Section 1.** The date for the inauguration of the President was changed to January 20th, and the date for Congress to begin its term changed to January 3rd. Prior to this amendment, the beginning of term date was set in March. The outgoing officials with little or no influence on matters were not effective in office. Being so inactive, they were called "lame ducks."

> Portions of the Constitution altered by later amendments or that no longer apply are printed in blue.

Section 3. Presidential Succession If, at the time fixed for the beginning of the term of the President, the President-elect shall have died, the Vice President-elect shall become President. If a President shall not have been chosen before the time fixed for the beginning of his term, or if the President-elect shall have failed to qualify, the Vice President-elect shall act as President until a President shall have qualified; and the Congress may by law provide for the case wherein neither a President-elect nor a Vice President-elect shall have qualified, declaring who shall then act as President, or the manner in which one who is to act shall be selected, and such person shall act accordingly until a President or Vice President shall have qualified.

Section 4. Elections Decided by Congress The Congress may by law provide for the case of the death of any persons from whom the House of Representatives may choose a President whenever the right of choice shall have devolved upon them, and for the case of the death of any of the persons from whom the Senate may choose a Vice President whenever the right of choice shall have devolved upon them.

Section 5. Date of Implementation Sections 1 and 2 shall take effect on the 15th day of October following the ratification of this article.

Section 6. Ratification Period This article shall be inoperative unless it shall have been ratified as an amendment to the Constitution by the legislatures of three fourths of the several states within seven years from the date of its submission.

> **Twentieth Amendment, Section 3.** If the President-elect dies before taking office, the Vice President-elect becomes President. If no President has been chosen by January 20 or if the elected candidate fails to qualify for office, the Vice President-elect acts as President, but only until a qualified President is chosen.
>
> Finally, Congress has the power to choose a person to act as President if neither the President-elect nor the Vice President-elect is qualified to take office.

Twenty-first Amendment ★

(1933) Repeal of Prohibition

Section 1. Repeal The eighteenth article of amendment to the Constitution of the United States is hereby repealed.

Section 2. State Laws The transportation or importation into any state, territory, or possession of the United States for delivery or use therein of intoxicating liquors, in violation of the laws thereof, is hereby prohibited.

Section 3. Ratification Period This article shall be inoperative unless it shall have been ratified as an amendment to the Constitution by conventions in the several states, as provided in the Constitution, within seven years from the date of the submission hereof to the states by the Congress.

> **Twenty-first Amendment, Section 1** The Eighteenth Amendment is repealed, making it legal to make and sell alcoholic beverages. Prohibition ended December 5, 1933.

Twenty-second Amendment ★

(1951) Presidential Tenure

Section 1. Two-Term Limit No person shall be elected to the office of the President more than twice, and no person who has held the office of President, or acted as President, for more than two years of a term to which some other person was elected President shall be elected to the office of President more than once. But this article shall not apply to any person holding the office of President when this article was proposed by the Congress, and shall not prevent any person who may be holding the office of President, or acting as President, during the term within which this article becomes operative from holding the office of President or acting as President during the remainder of such term.

Section 2. Ratification Period This article shall be inoperative unless it shall have been ratified as an amendment to the Constitution by the legislatures of three fourths of the several states within seven years from the date of its submission to the state by the Congress.

Twenty-third Amendment ★

(1961) Presidential Electors for the District of Columbia

Section 1. Determining the Number of Electors The district constituting the seat of government of the United States shall appoint in such manner as the Congress may direct:

A number of electors of President and Vice President equal to the whole number of senators and representatives in Congress to which the district would be entitled if it were a state, but in no event more than the least populous state; they shall be in addition to those appointed by the states, but they shall be considered, for the purposes of the election of President and Vice President, to be electors appointed by a state; and they shall meet in the district and perform such duties as provided by the twelfth article of amendment.

Section 2. Enforcement The Congress shall have power to enforce this article by appropriate legislation.

Twenty-fourth Amendment ★

(1964) Right to Vote in Federal Elections—Tax Payment

Section 1. Poll Tax Banned The right of citizens of the United States to vote in any primary or other election for President or Vice President, for electors for President or Vice President, or for senator or representative in Congress, shall not be denied or abridged by the United States or any state by reason of failure to pay any poll tax or other tax.

Section 2. Enforcement The Congress shall have the power to enforce this article by appropriate legislation.

Twenty-second Amendment, Section 1
This amendment provides that no President may serve more than two terms. A President who has already served more than half of someone else's term can serve only one more full term. Before Franklin Roosevelt became President, no President served more than two terms in office. Roosevelt broke with this custom and was elected to four terms. The amendment, however, did not apply to Harry Truman, who became President after Franklin Roosevelt's death in 1945.

Twenty-third Amendment, Section 1
This amendment gives the residents of Washington, D.C., the right to vote in presidential elections. Until this amendment was adopted, people living in Washington, D.C., could not vote for President because the Constitution had made no provision for choosing electors from the nation's capital. Washington, D.C., now has three electoral votes.

Twenty-fourth Amendment, Section 1
A poll tax is a tax on voters. This amendment bans poll taxes in national elections. Some states used poll taxes to keep African Americans from voting. In 1966, the Supreme Court struck down poll taxes in state elections, also.

Portions of the Constitution altered by later amendments or that no longer apply are printed in blue.

Twenty-fifth Amendment ★

(1967) Presidential Succession, Vice Presidential Vacancy, Presidential Inability

Section 1. President's Death or Resignation In case of the removal of the President from office or of his death or resignation, the Vice President shall become President.

Section 2. Vacancies in Vice Presidency Whenever there is a vacancy in the office of the Vice President, the President shall nominate a Vice President who shall take office upon confirmation by a majority vote of both houses of Congress.

Section 3. Disability of the President Whenever the President transmits to the President pro tempore of the Senate and the Speaker of the House of Representatives his written declaration that he is unable to discharge the powers and duties of his office, and until he transmits to them a written declaration to the contrary, such powers and duties shall be discharged by the Vice President as acting President.

Section 4. Vice President as Acting President Whenever the Vice President and a majority of either the principal officers of the executive departments or of such other body as Congress may by law provide, transmit to the President pro tempore of the Senate and the Speaker of the House of Representatives their written declaration that the President is unable to discharge the powers and duties of his office, the Vice President shall immediately assume the powers and duties of the office as acting President.

Thereafter, when the President transmits to the President pro tempore of the Senate and the Speaker of the House of Representatives his written declaration that no inability exists, he shall resume the powers and duties of his office unless the Vice President and a majority of either the principal officers of the executive department or of such other body as Congress may by law provide, transmit within four days to the President pro tempore of the Senate and the Speaker of the House of Representatives their written declaration that the President is unable to discharge the powers and duties of his office. Thereupon Congress shall decide the issue, assembling within forty-eight hours for that purpose if not in session. If the Congress, within twenty-one days after receipt of the latter written declaration, or, if Congress is not in session, within twenty-one days after Congress is required to assemble, determines by two-thirds vote of both Houses that the President is unable to discharge the powers and duties of his office, the Vice President shall continue to discharge the same as acting President; otherwise, the President shall resume the powers and duties of his office.

Twenty-fifth Amendment, Section 1
If the President dies or resigns, the Vice President becomes President. This section clarifies Article 2, Section 1, Clause 6.

Twenty-fifth Amendment, Section 3
If the President declares in writing that he or she is unable to perform the duties of office, the Vice President serves as acting President until the President recovers.

Twenty-fifth Amendment, Section 4
Two Presidents, Woodrow Wilson and Dwight Eisenhower, fell gravely ill while in office. The Constitution contained no provision for this kind of emergency. Section 3 provided that the President can inform Congress he or she is too sick to perform the duties of office. However, if the President is unconscious or refuses to admit to a disabling illness, Section 4 provides that the Vice President and Cabinet may declare the President disabled. The Vice President becomes the acting President until the President can return to the duties of office. In case of a disagreement between the President and the Vice President and Cabinet over the President's ability to perform the duties of office, Congress must decide the issue. A two-thirds vote of both houses is needed to find the President is disabled or unable to fulfill the duties of office.

Twenty-sixth Amendment ★

(1971) Right to Vote—Age

Section 1. Lowering the Voting Age The right of citizens of the United States, who are eighteen years of age or older, to vote shall not be denied or abridged by the United States or by any state on account of age.

Section 2. Enforcement The Congress shall have the power to enforce this article by appropriate legislation.

Twenty-seventh Amendment ★

(1992) Congressional Pay

No law, varying the compensation for the services of the senators and representatives, shall take effect until an election of representatives shall have intervened.

> **Twenty-sixth Amendment, Section 1**
> In 1970, Congress passed a law allowing 18-year-olds to vote. However, the Supreme Court decided that Congress could not set a minimum age for state elections.

> **Twenty-seventh Amendment**
> If members of Congress vote themselves a pay increase, it cannot go into effect until after the next congressional election. This amendment was proposed in 1789. In 1992, Michigan became the thirty-eighth state to ratify it.

> Portions of the Constitution altered by later amendments or that no longer apply are printed in blue.

Independence Hall room where the Constitution was signed

CITIZENSHIP HANDBOOK

Table of Contents

Key Terms

amend, p. 264

appeal, p. 262

bill, p. 259

censorship, p. 267

checks and balances, p. 257

citizen, p. 270

dictatorship, p. 252

dissent, p. 267

federalism, p. 257

habeas corpus, p. 252

interest group, p. 271

jurisdiction, p. 262

libel, p. 267

limited government, p. 256

naturalization, p. 270

override, p. 259

popular sovereignty, p. 256

private property, p. 252

ratify, p. 264

repeal, p. 255

republic, p. 252

separation of powers, p. 253

unconstitutional, p. 263

veto, p. 259

Ideas Behind the Constitution

The delegates to the Constitutional Convention who gathered in Philadelphia were greatly influenced by past experiments with democracy and natural rights. As they debated the new document for American government, the Founders considered a variety of past political ideas.

Ancient Rome

Earlier in this textbook, you read about the ancient Roman Republic. The Framers of the United States Constitution looked to Rome as a model. Like the early Romans, they sought to create a lasting **republic,** or a government in which citizens rule themselves through elected representatives. American leaders also admired what they saw as the independent thinking and public service of Roman citizens. Romans, Americans said, had been willing to serve in public office out of devotion to the republic.

However, Americans also took the fate of Rome as a warning. The Roman Republic eventually collapsed and became a **dictatorship,** a government in which one person or a small group holds complete authority. American leaders believed that the Roman Republic faltered when citizens began to value luxury and comfort more than freedom and public service. The Framers of the Constitution wanted to avoid Rome's fate. They hoped to build a system in which informed, independent citizens played an active role in their own government.

Two Historic Documents

You also learned earlier about the following two important documents in British history: the Magna Carta, which British nobles forced King John to sign in 1215; and the Bill of Rights, which William and Mary issued in 1689 after the Glorious Revolution. These two documents created an English tradition of liberty, which the colonists brought to America.

The following principles found in the these two documents became part of the American system of government:

- Citizens have rights which the government must protect.
- Even the head of the government must obey the law.
- Taxes cannot be raised without the consent of the people.
- Elections should be held frequently.
- People accused of crimes have the right to trial by jury and the right of **habeas corpus,** meaning no person may be held in prison without being charged with a specific crime.
- People have the right to **private property,** or property owned by an individual.

HISTORIAN'S APPRENTICE ACTIVITY PACK

To further explore the topics in this chapter, complete the activity in the Historian's Apprentice Activity Pack to answer this essential question:

How is the rule of law in the Constitution of the United States rooted in the past?

King John signing the Magna Carta

Teachings of the Enlightenment

Many of the Framers were influenced by the works of European Enlightenment thinkers. In his book *Two Treatises on Government*, the English writer John Locke declared that every individual has natural rights to life, liberty, and property. Locke said government is an agreement between the ruler and the ruled. Further, he argued, if a ruler violates the people's natural rights, the people have a right to rebel.

The French thinker Baron de Montesquieu (MOHN tehs kyoo) suggested a concept known as **separation of powers**—the idea that powers of government must be clearly defined and divided into legislative, executive, and judicial branches. This concept was designed to keep one person or group from gaining too much power.

John Locke

Representative Traditions and the Declaration of Independence

Americans enjoyed a long tradition of representative government. The Virginia colonists set up the House of Burgesses, and the Pilgrims drafted the Mayflower Compact in 1620. The compact was the first document of self-government in North America.

Each of the 13 colonies had a written charter that identified the powers and limits of government granted by the British Crown. In addition to these traditions, the Framers of the Constitution drew on the grievances Thomas Jefferson had listed against George III in the Declaration of Independence. In writing the Constitution, they sought to prevent similar abuses in the new American government.

Declaring Independence
Delegates sign the Declaration of Independence.

Assessment

1. Identify two principles of American government that came from the Magna Carta or the English Bill of Rights.

2. How did Montesquieu's ideas affect the crafting of the Constitution?

PART 2

Structure of the Constitution

The principles of the Constitution have guided the United States for more than 200 years. The Constitution is divided into three main parts: the Preamble, or opening statement; the Articles; and the Amendments. The Preamble begins with the words, "We the people of the United States." These words show that the authority of the government comes from its citizens. The Preamble then goes on to outline six basic goals for the new government. They are shown on the chart below.

Goals of the Preamble

Goals	What It Means to Us
■ To form a more perfect union	All states should work together as a unified nation.
■ To establish justice	Everyone should be treated equally and fairly under the law.
■ To ensure domestic tranquillity	The government has the responsibility to ensure peace and order at home.
■ To provide for the common defense	The government has the responsibility to protect its citizens against foreign attack.
■ To promote the general welfare	The government has the responsibility to promote the well-being of all its citizens.
■ To secure the blessings of liberty	The government should value and protect the rights of its citizens.

The Constitution

Articles

The main body of the Constitution is divided into seven sections called articles. Together, they establish the framework for American government. The first three articles describe the three branches of the national government: legislative, executive, and judicial. Article 1 establishes the powers and limits on Congress. Articles 2 and 3 do the same for the President and the courts.

Article 4 deals with relations between states. It requires states to honor one another's laws and also sets out a system for admitting new states. Article 5 provides a process to amend the Constitution. Article 6 states that the Constitution is the "supreme law of the land." States cannot make laws that violate the Constitution and federal laws prevail in all disputes. The final article, Article 7, sets up a procedure for the states to ratify the Constitution.

Amendments

The Amendments are formal changes that have been made to the Constitution. Some of these changes added new ideas to the document. Others **repealed**, or canceled, other parts of the Constitution.

In more than 200 years, only 27 changes have been made to the Constitution. The first 10 amendments, known as the Bill of Rights, were added in 1791. You will read more about the Bill of Rights later in this handbook.

Some later amendments had an immediate and powerful impact on American society. A few of them are illustrated below.

The Thirteenth Amendment ended slavery throughout the United States.

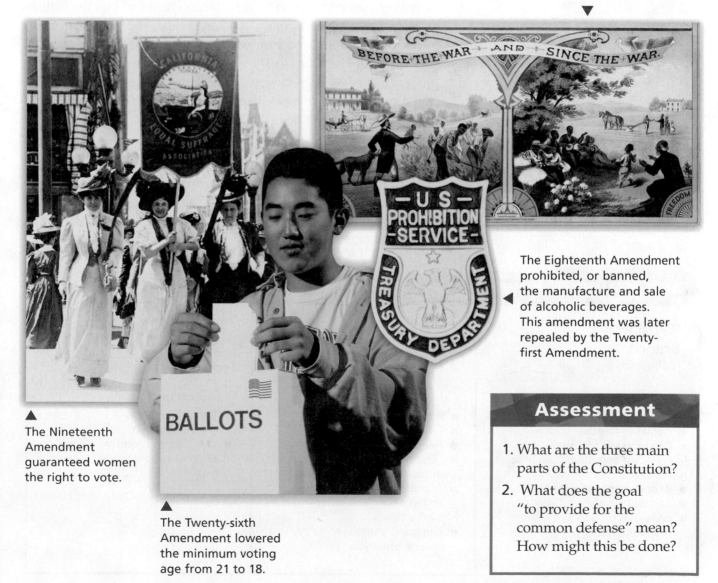

The Nineteenth Amendment guaranteed women the right to vote.

The Twenty-sixth Amendment lowered the minimum voting age from 21 to 18.

The Eighteenth Amendment prohibited, or banned, the manufacture and sale of alcoholic beverages. This amendment was later repealed by the Twenty-first Amendment.

Assessment

1. What are the three main parts of the Constitution?

2. What does the goal "to provide for the common defense" mean? How might this be done?

Principles of the Constitution

The Constitution rests on seven basic principles. They are popular sovereignty, limited government, separation of powers, federalism, checks and balances, republicanism, and individual rights.

- **Popular Sovereignty** The Framers of the Constitution lived at a time when monarchs claimed that their power came from God. The Preamble, which begins "We the people," reflects a revolutionary new idea: a government gets its authority from the people. This principle, known as popular sovereignty, asserts that the people are the primary source of the government's authority.

- **Limited Government** The colonists believed that the British king had ruled them harshly. To avoid a repeat of this rule in their new government, the Framers made limited government a principle of the Constitution. In a limited government, the government has only the powers that the Constitution gives it. Equally important, every citizen of the United States—including the President—must obey the law.

- **Separation of Powers** To further limit the power of the government, the Framers provided for separation of powers. The Constitution divides the government into three branches, and each branch has its own duties. The chart below outlines the duties of each branch of government.

Separation of Powers

Legislative Branch (Congress)	Executive Branch (President) 	Judicial Branch (Supreme Court and Other Federal Courts)
Passes Laws	**Carries Out Laws**	**Interprets Laws**
■ Can override President's veto ■ Approves treaties ■ Can impeach and remove President and other high officials ■ Prints and coins money ■ Raises and supports armed forces ■ Can declare war ■ Regulates foreign and interstate trade	■ Proposes laws ■ Can veto laws ■ Negotiates foreign treaties ■ Serves as commander in chief of armed forces ■ Appoints federal judges, ambassadors, and other high officials ■ Can grant pardons to federal offenders	■ Can declare laws unconstitutional ■ Can declare executive actions unconstitutional

Checks and Balances

Legislative Branch
(Congress makes laws)

Checks on the Executive Branch
- Can override President's veto
- Confirms executive appointments
- Ratifies treaties
- Can declare war
- Appropriates money
- Can impeach and remove President

Checks on the Judicial Branch
- Creates lower federal courts
- Can impeach and remove judges
- Can propose amendments to overrule judicial decisions
- Approves appointments of federal judges

Executive Branch
(President carries out laws)

Checks on the Legislative Branch
- Can propose laws
- Can veto laws
- Can call special sessions of Congress
- Makes appointments
- Negotiates foreign treaties

Checks on the Judicial Branch
- Appoints federal judges
- Can grant pardons to federal offenders

Judicial Branch
(Supreme Court interprets laws)

Check on the Executive Branch
- Can declare executive actions unconstitutional

Check on the Legislative Branch
- Can declare acts of Congress unconstitutional

- **Checks and Balances** A system of checks and balances safeguards against abuse of power. Each branch of government has the power to check, or limit, the actions of the other two. This arrangement guarantees that no branch of government will become too powerful. The chart above describes the specific checks each branch has on the other two. The next six pages of this handbook will detail how each branch of government works.

- **Federalism** The Constitution also establishes the principle of federalism, or division of power between the federal government and the states. The Constitution grants specific powers to the federal government and other powers to the states. Powers that are not clearly given to the federal government belong to the states.

- **Republicanism** The Constitution provides for a republican form of government. Instead of direct participation in government, citizens elect representatives to carry out their will.

- **Individual Rights** The Constitution protects individual rights, such as freedom of speech, freedom of religion, and the right to trial by jury. You will learn more about the rights protected by the Constitution later in this handbook.

Assessment

1. How does the Constitution reflect the principle of separation of powers?

2. How can the judicial branch check the powers of the executive and legislative branches?

The first and longest article of the Constitution deals with the legislative, or lawmaking, branch. Article 1 sets up the Congress to make the nation's laws. Congress is made up of two bodies: the House of Representatives and the Senate.

The Senate

The Senate is based on equal representation, with two senators for each state. Senators are elected to six-year terms. The Vice President of the United States is the president of the Senate. The Vice President presides over the Senate—casting a vote when there is a tie—but cannot take part in Senate debates.

The House of Representatives

The larger of the two bodies is the House of Representatives, which currently has 435 members. Representation in the House is based on population, with larger states having more representatives than smaller states. Every state has at least one representative. Representatives are elected by the people of their district for two-year terms. The leader of the House is called the Speaker. The Speaker, who is chosen by the representatives, regulates debates and controls the agenda.

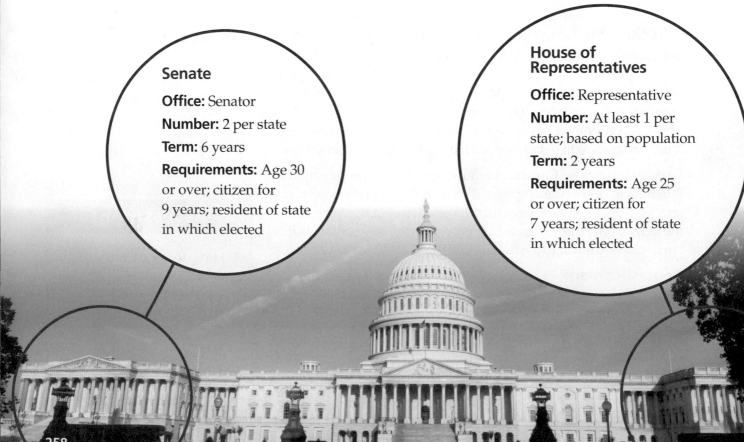

Senate

Office: Senator

Number: 2 per state

Term: 6 years

Requirements: Age 30 or over; citizen for 9 years; resident of state in which elected

House of Representatives

Office: Representative

Number: At least 1 per state; based on population

Term: 2 years

Requirements: Age 25 or over; citizen for 7 years; resident of state in which elected

How a Bill Becomes a Law

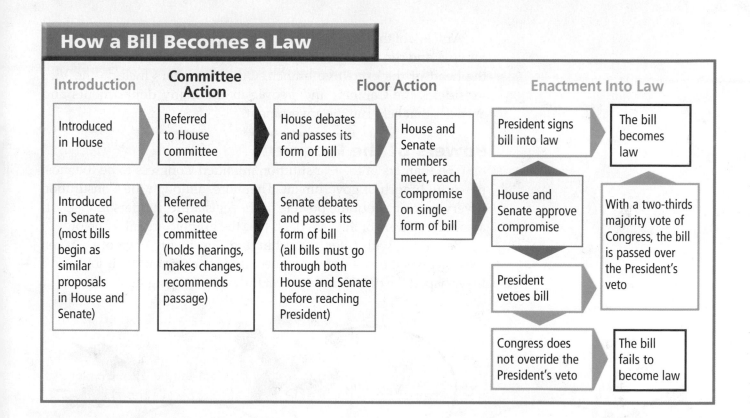

Introduction

Introduced in House

Introduced in Senate (most bills begin as similar proposals in House and Senate)

Committee Action

Referred to House committee

Referred to Senate committee (holds hearings, makes changes, recommends passage)

Floor Action

House debates and passes its form of bill

Senate debates and passes its form of bill (all bills must go through both House and Senate before reaching President)

House and Senate members meet, reach compromise on single form of bill

Enactment Into Law

President signs bill into law

House and Senate approve compromise

President vetoes bill

The bill becomes law

With a two-thirds majority vote of Congress, the bill is passed over the President's veto

Congress does not override the President's veto

The bill fails to become law

Powers of Congress

The most important power of Congress is the power to make the nation's laws. A **bill**, or proposal for a new law, may be introduced either in the House or the Senate. After debate and changes, the bill is voted on. If both houses vote to approve the bill, it then goes to the President to be signed. If the President signs the bill, it becomes a law. The President, however, has the power to **veto**, or reject, the bill. Congress may vote to **override**, or pass a law despite a presidential veto. A two-thirds vote is needed to override. (See flowchart above.)

Other powers of Congress are listed in Article 1, Section 8. These include the power to collect taxes, to coin money, to establish post offices, to fix standard weights and measures, and to declare war.

Congressional Committees

Much of the work in Congress is done through committees. Each committee deals with a specific topic. For example, if someone in Congress introduces a bill to improve the nation's railroad service, the bill would first go to the Transportation Committee for study. Other standing committees deal with such areas as defense, education, taxation, foreign affairs, agriculture, or science.

Assessment

1. What are the major differences between membership in the Senate and membership in the House?

2. How can Congress pass a bill over a presidential veto?

Article 2 of the Constitution sets up an executive branch to carry out the laws and run the affairs of the national government. The President is the head of the executive branch. Other members include the Vice President, the Cabinet, and people in the many departments and agencies that help run the government.

Powers of the President

The Framers of the Constitution intended Congress to be the most powerful branch of government. Therefore, although the Constitution is very specific about the powers of the legislature, it offers few details about the powers of the President. (See the graphic organizer below.)

Beginning with George Washington, Presidents have often taken those actions they thought were necessary to carry out their job. Thus, they shaped the presidency to meet the nation's changing needs.

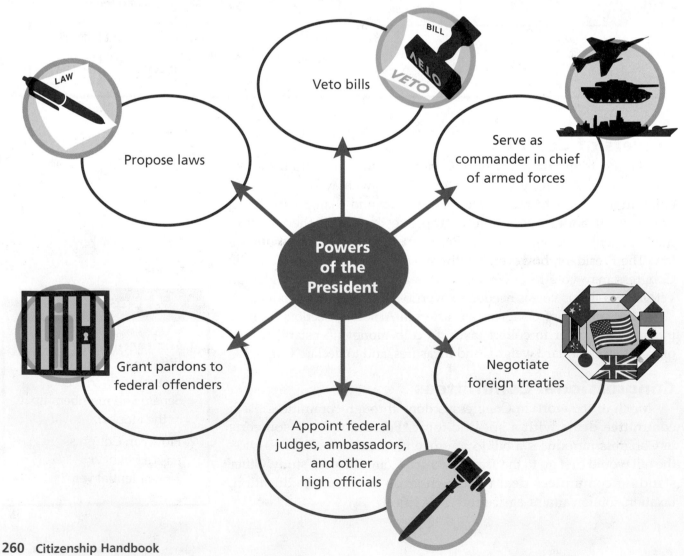

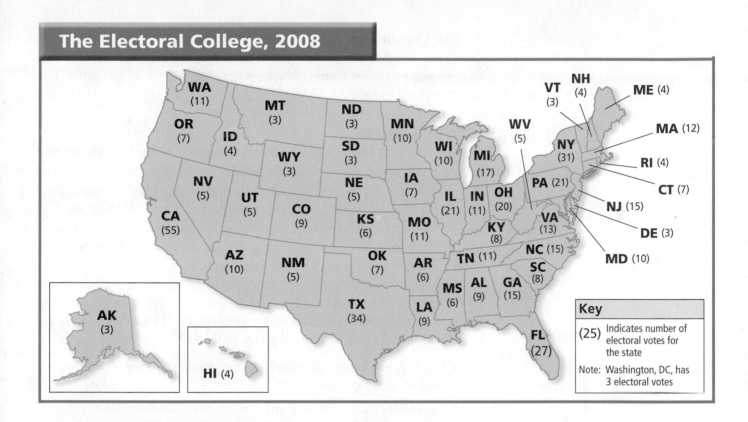

The Electoral College, 2008

Key
(25) Indicates number of electoral votes for the state

Note: Washington, DC, has 3 electoral votes

Electing the President

The President is elected for a four-year term. As a result of the Twenty-second Amendment, adopted in 1951, no President may be elected to more than two complete terms.

The Framers set up a complex system for electing the President, known as the electoral college. When Americans vote for President, they do not vote directly for the candidate of their choice. Rather, they vote for a group of "electors" who are pledged to the candidate. The number of a state's electors depends on the number of its senators and representatives. (See the map above.)

A few weeks after Election Day, these electors meet in each state to cast their votes for President. In most states, the candidate with the majority of the popular vote receives all that state's electoral votes. The candidate who receives a majority of the electoral votes nationwide becomes President. Although electors are not required by federal law to vote for their pledged candidate, only a few have broken their pledges and voted for other candidates in past elections.

Assessment

1. Why do you think the Framers chose not to give the President the power to declare war?

2. How many electors does your state have?

PART 6

How the Federal Government Works: The Judicial Branch

The Constitution establishes a Supreme Court and authorizes Congress to establish any other courts that are needed. Under the Judiciary Act of 1789, Congress set up the system of federal courts that is still in place today.

Lower Courts

Most federal cases begin in district courts. Evidence is presented during trials, and a jury or a judge decides the facts of the case. A party that disagrees with the decision of the judge or jury may **appeal** it, that is, ask that the decision be reviewed by a higher court. The next level of court is the appellate court, or court of appeal. Appellate court judges review decisions of district courts to decide whether the lower court judges interpreted and applied the law correctly.

Court cases can be filed under federal or state jurisdiction. **Jurisdiction** is the power to hear and decide cases. Most cases are tried under state jurisdiction because they involve state laws. A case may be placed under federal jurisdiction if any of the following apply:

- The United States is either suing another party or being sued by another party.
- The case is based on the Constitution or on a federal law.
- The case involves disputes between different states.

Federal Court System

State Route → **United States Supreme Court** ← **Federal Route**

State Supreme Court
- Highest state court
- Hears appeals of appellate court cases

Appellate Court
- Hears appeals of trial court cases

Trial Court
- Handles civil and criminal cases

United States Supreme Court
- Nation's highest court
- Reviews the decisions of lower courts
- Decides cases involving U.S. Constitution and federal laws

Court of Appeal
- Hears appeals of cases originating in U.S. district courts
- Can review decisions by federal administrative agencies

District Court
- Federal trial court
- Handles civil and criminal cases

The Supreme Court
The nine members of the Supreme Court pose for their annual portrait. Chief Justice John G. Roberts, Jr., is seated, center.

The Supreme Court

At the top of the American judicial system is the Supreme Court. (See the chart on the facing page.) The Court is made up of a chief justice and eight associate justices. The President appoints the justices, but Congress must approve the appointments. Justices serve until they resign, retire, or die. However, like other federal officials, Supreme Court justices may be impeached and removed from office.

The main job of the Supreme Court is to serve as the nation's final court of appeal. It hears the cases that have been tried and appealed in lower federal and state courts. The Court hears and decides fewer than 100 cases each year.

Decisions rest on a majority vote of at least five justices. One justice then writes a majority opinion, a document that explains the constitutional reasons for the decision. A justice who voted against the majority may submit a dissenting opinion, explaining his or her reasons for disagreeing with the majority opinion.

There is no court of appeal beyond the Supreme Court. However, if another case dealing with the same issues comes up, the Supreme Court may sometimes reverse its own past decisions.

Judicial Review

The most important power of the Supreme Court is the power to decide what the Constitution means. At the beginning of the 1800s, the Court asserted the right to declare whether acts of the President or laws passed by Congress are **unconstitutional,** that is, not allowed under the Constitution. The landmark 1803 case of *Marbury* v. *Madison* established this power of judicial review for the Supreme Court.

Assessment

1. How does a case reach the United States Supreme Court?
2. What is judicial review?

Amending the Constitution

Although the Framers were pleased with the government they had established through the Constitution, some were dissatisfied with the final document. For one thing, while establishing the powers of the state and federal governments, the document said nothing about the rights of the American people. In 1791, the new nation would do something about this omission when it added the Bill of Rights, the first 10 amendments to the Constitution.

This addition was possible because the founders had written a Constitution that allowed for change. The Constitution was flexible enough to be changed but not so flexible that it could be *easily* changed. Article 5 laid out the method for amending, or changing, the Constitution. The flowchart below shows the amendment process.

The Amendment Process

The Constitution can be changed in one of four ways. There are two different procedures for proposing amendments to the Constitution. There are also two different procedures for ratifying, or approving, amendments to the Constitution, the second step in the process.

Proposing an Amendment Congress can propose an amendment if both the House and Senate vote for a change to the Constitution. Each of the Constitution's 27 amendments has been proposed in this way.

The second way to propose an amendment begins at the state level. Currently, the legislatures of 34 states must call for a national convention. It is then up to the national convention to formally propose an amendment.

Ratifying an Amendment An amendment can be ratified through the action of state legislatures. Currently, the yes vote of 38 states is needed. Twenty-six of the 27 amendments to the Constitution have been ratified in this way.

An amendment can also be ratified through the action of state conventions rather than through state legislatures. Conventions, are special meetings that are called to address a specific issue. Only the Twenty-first Amendment was added through the process of state conventions.

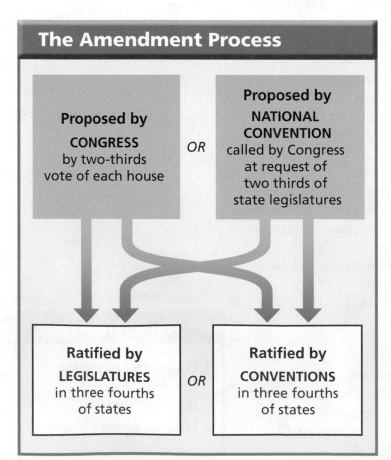

The Amendment Process

Proposed by CONGRESS by two-thirds vote of each house

OR

Proposed by NATIONAL CONVENTION called by Congress at request of two thirds of state legislatures

Ratified by LEGISLATURES in three fourths of states

OR

Ratified by CONVENTIONS in three fourths of states

The Sixth Amendment
The right to trial by jury in a criminal case is guaranteed by the Sixth Amendment. It also ensures that a person accused of a crime has the right to be represented by a lawyer and to hear the testimony given by witnesses in the trial.

The Bill of Rights

The Preamble of the Constitution begins with the words, "We the People of the United States." However, the seven articles of the original document deal mostly with issues involving the structure and powers of the branches of government, not with the rights of individuals. The Bill of Rights, the name given to the first 10 amendments to the Constitution, addresses the freedoms guaranteed to citizens.

- *First Amendment:* freedom of religion, speech, and the press; right of petition and assembly (See the following page.)
- *Second Amendment:* right to bear arms
- *Third Amendment:* government cannot force people to quarter troops in their homes
- *Fourth Amendment:* protects against unreasonable search and seizure
- *Fifth Amendment:* rights of people accused of crimes
- *Sixth Amendment:* right to trial by jury in criminal cases
- *Seventh Amendment:* right to trial by jury in civil cases
- *Eighth Amendment:* forbids excessive bail and cruel or unusual punishment
- *Ninth Amendment:* people's rights are not limited to those listed in the Constitution
- *Tenth Amendment:* states or people have all powers not denied or given to federal government by the Constitution

Assessment

1. Which one of the four different two-step processes has most often been used to add amendments to the Constitution?
2. Why do you think the Founders added the Ninth Amendment to the Bill of Rights?

The First Amendment

The colonial past was very much on the minds of American leaders when they set out to write the Bill of Rights in the early 1790s. It is not surprising, therefore, that the colonial experience inspired the very first amendment to the Constitution.

First Amendment

Congress shall make no law respecting an establishment of religion, or prohibiting the free exercise thereof; or abridging the freedom of speech, or of the press; or the right of the people peaceably to assemble, and to petition the government for a redress of grievances.

Freedom of Religion As you have learned, Pilgrims, Puritans, Quakers, Catholics, and Jews had come to North America because they wanted to practice their religion freely. Yet, colonial religious leaders such as Thomas Hooker, Roger Williams, and Anne Hutchinson were later driven from Massachusetts after clashing with community leaders over religious questions. The Founders wanted to avoid such church-versus-state disputes. Thus, the First Amendment affirms freedom of religion as a basic right. Americans are free to follow any religion or no religion, as they choose.

This part of the First Amendment was inspired by the Virginia Statute on Religious Freedom, written by Thomas Jefferson. Jefferson later spoke of a "wall of separation between Church and State." However, not everyone agrees on the nature of that separation. Some people believe that the First Amendment means that religion should play no role in government. Others argue that the Amendment merely says that Congress cannot establish an official, state-supported church or make any laws that interfere with freedom of worship.

Freedom of the Press American reporters do their jobs without fear of government interference.

Peaceful Assembly
These striking workers are exercising their right of peaceful assembly.

Freedom of Speech and Freedom of the Press

Dictators understand that their power depends on silencing dissent, or disagreement. They will often shut down newspapers and jail people who criticize the government. By contrast, the First Amendment protects the right of Americans to speak without fear of punishment.

The First Amendment also protects the press from government censorship. Censorship is the power to review, change, or prevent the publication of news. Freedom of the press also means that journalists cannot be arrested for criticizing the government or public officials. (As you have read, this principle was established in the colonies by the case of John Peter Zenger.)

The Framers knew that a free flow of ideas is vital to a democratic government. Still, freedom of the press is not unlimited. The press has a responsibility to present the news fairly and accurately. Individuals may sue journalists for libel, or the publication of false and malicious information that damages a person's reputation.

Peaceful Assembly and Petition

As you have read, King George III and Parliament ignored the colonists' petition protesting the Stamp Act. Such experiences had a powerful effect on the leaders who wrote the Bill of Rights. The First Amendment thus guarantees the right of Americans to assemble in peaceful protest. It also protects their right to petition the government for a change in policy.

Assessment

1. What does the First Amendment say about freedom of religion?
2. Identify two rights of a free press.

State and Local Governments

As you have learned, under the principle of federalism, the Constitution assigns some powers to the government in Washington, D.C., and other powers to the states. You have already read about the role of the federal government in our nation's life. Now you will learn about the role played by state and local governments.

State Governments

In general, the federal government deals with national issues. The states concern themselves with needs within each state.

State governments resemble the federal government in many ways. Each state has a constitution of its own, for example, and each state constitution can be amended. In addition, every state is divided into three branches of government. Each state has a legislature, a governor who serves as the chief executive, and a judiciary. But there are some differences between the state and federal governments. Nebraska, for instance, is the only state in the Union with a one-house legislature.

The Federal System

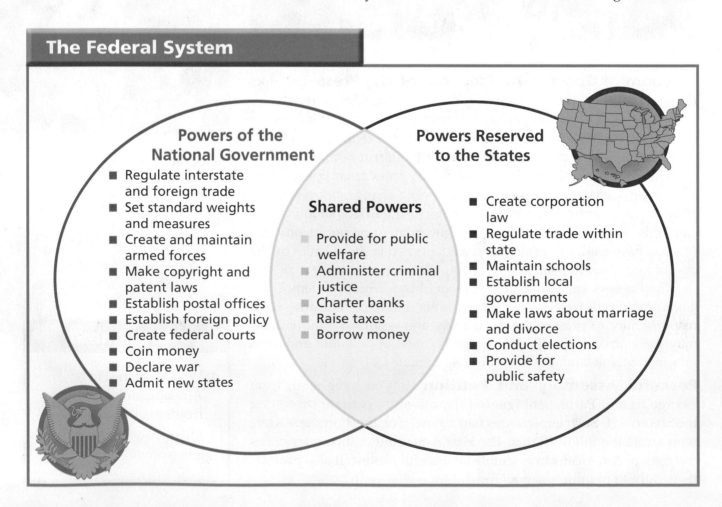

Powers of the National Government

- Regulate interstate and foreign trade
- Set standard weights and measures
- Create and maintain armed forces
- Make copyright and patent laws
- Establish postal offices
- Establish foreign policy
- Create federal courts
- Coin money
- Declare war
- Admit new states

Shared Powers

- Provide for public welfare
- Administer criminal justice
- Charter banks
- Raise taxes
- Borrow money

Powers Reserved to the States

- Create corporation law
- Regulate trade within state
- Maintain schools
- Establish local governments
- Make laws about marriage and divorce
- Conduct elections
- Provide for public safety

Local Government
City or town governments
usually set up and fund
fire departments.

State Services

Enforcing the law, protecting property, regulating business, building and maintaining highways, and operating state parks are just a few of the many tasks the state oversees. In addition, states supervise public education by setting standards and by funding school programs.

Local Governments

As we have seen, the Constitution carefully identifies the powers of state and federal governments. However, it says nothing about local government. Local governments administer smaller units, such as counties, cities, and towns.

Local governments have budgets just like the federal government and state government. Most of the money in their budgets is spent on education. Cities, towns, or school districts hire teachers and staff, buy books and supplies, and maintain school buildings. But local governments do not have sole control over the school system. They are required by law to meet the state's education standards.

Local government generally plays a more direct role in our lives than federal or state government does. For example, local governments hire people who interact with us on a regular basis, such as firefighters, police officers, and garbage collectors. In addition, local governments maintain local roads and hospitals, provide sewers and water, run libraries, oversee parks and recreational facilities, and conduct safety inspections of buildings.

Assessment

1. Name two powers the federal goverment and state governments share. Name two powers that are reserved to the states.

2. What permits local governments to function even though they are not mentioned in the Constitution? Explain your answer.

What is a citizen? A **citizen** is someone who is entitled to all the rights and privileges of a particular nation. Not everyone who lives in a certain nation is a citizen of that nation. On the other hand, some citizens live outside the nation to which they belong.

Becoming an American Citizen

To become a citizen of the United States, you must fulfill one of the following three requirements:

- You were born in the United States or have at least one parent who is a citizen of the United States.
- You were naturalized. **Naturalization** is the official legal process of becoming a citizen.
- You were 18 years old or younger when your parents were naturalized.

Each year, millions of people born in other countries and living in the United States become naturalized. To become a naturalized citizen, a person must live legally in the United States for at least five years. The person then applies for citizenship. He or she must take a citizenship examination and undergo a series of interviews. Finally, the applicant takes the citizenship oath before a judge, swearing to "support and defend the Constitution and laws of the United States."

A naturalized citizen enjoys every right of a natural-born citizen except one. Only natural-born citizens may serve as President or Vice President.

Naturalization
New citizens of the United States proudly take the citizenship oath.

Rights of Citizens

As you have seen, the Bill of Rights guarantees certain rights to citizens. You have the right to worship as you please, the right to express your opinion, and the right to consult a lawyer if you are arrested. But the Ninth Amendment states that citizens' rights are not limited to those listed in the Constitution. Over the years, federal and state laws have identified other rights. For example, the Constitution does not mention education. But today, laws in every state guarantee that children have the right to an education.

Responsibilities of Citizens

In addition to rights, citizens have responsibilities. Some actions are required of every citizen. For example, all citizens *must*

- obey federal, state, and local laws;
- pay their fair share of taxes;
- serve on juries if called;
- defend the nation if called.

Citizens have other responsibilities that are not required by law. Good citizens *should*

- vote in federal, state, and local elections;
- stay informed on important issues;
- serve the community;
- help to create a just society.

Some citizens participate in the political process through interest groups. An **interest group** is an organization that represents the concerns of a particular group. The American Association of Retired Persons, the National Rifle Association, and the Sierra Club are examples of interest groups that try to influence lawmakers and raise public awareness of certain issues.

Young people, too, can get involved in the political process. For example, in one California community, poor children could not afford to pay for public transportation to school every day. Some students organized to solve this problem. Using their First Amendment rights, they collected signatures on petitions and held public rallies. As a result, the local transportation board took up the issue. Like thousands of other Americans, these students used their rights as citizens to voice their views and help their communities.

Registering to Vote
Before a U.S. citizen can vote, he or she must register.

Assessment

1. How does a person become an American citizen?

2. Identify three ways that Americans can participate in the political process.

How did the colonists break away from Britain and create a republican form of government?

DIRECTIONS: Analyze the following documents from the years before, during, and after the American Revolution. Answer the questions that accompany each document or set of documents. You will use your answers to build an answer to the unit question.

HISTORIAN'S CHECKLIST

WHO produced the document?

WHERE was it made?

WHEN was it produced?

WHY was it made and for what audience?

WHAT is its viewpoint?

HOW does it connect to what I've learned?

WHY is the document important?

1 Effects of the French and Indian War

document

THE FRENCH AND INDIAN WAR

- Colonists develop a sense of unity.

- Britain gains territory west of the Appalachians.

- To avoid war with Indians, Britain bans colonial settlement west of the Appalachians.

- War leaves Britain in debt.

- Britain raises taxes to pay for the war.

How did the French and Indian War lead to friction between American colonists and Britain?

2 Americans Protest British Taxes

document

" . . . 3. That it is inseparably essential to the freedom of a people, and the undoubted right of Englishmen, that no taxes be imposed on them, but with their own consent, given personally, or by their representatives.

4. That the people of these colonies are not, and from their local circumstances cannot be, represented in the House of Commons in Great-Britain. "

—*Resolutions of the Stamp Act Congress, 1765*

Why did American colonists think that the Stamp Act was unfair?

3 The American Revolution

document

"Our loss was greater than that of the British.... The British were on the march.... Night came on, there was no house we dare go into; we had no tents. I had no blanket even and must make no fire.... We had heavy rains, were exposed to them all, were wet to the skin but we walked, nay marched ourselves dry! We continued in this way for several days longer—near the British through the day—in the leaves and bushes at night."

—*Captain Enoch Anderson, describing American retreat after Battle of Brandywine, 1777*

What challenges did American soldiers face during the American Revolution?

4 George Washington

document

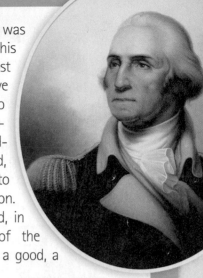

"His integrity was most pure, his justice the most inflexible I have ever known, no motives of interest...of friendship or hatred, being able to bias his decision. He was, indeed, in every sense of the words, a wise, a good, a great man."

—*Thomas Jefferson, describing General Washington*

How do you think Washington's personal characteristics helped the Americans defeat the British?

The Declaration of Independence

document

"We hold these truths to be self-evident, that all men are created equal, that they are endowed by their Creator with certain unalienable Rights, that among these are Life, Liberty, and the pursuit of Happiness. That to secure these rights, Governments are instituted among men, deriving their just powers from the consent of the governed. That whenever any Form of Government becomes destructive of these ends, it is the Right of the People to alter or abolish it, and to institute new Government...."

Why did American patriots feel that they had a right to rebel against British rule?

☞ Go On

6 Foreign Aid

document

"May 6, 1778. This day we fired a grand fue de joy on account of the news . . . which was that the Courts of France and Spain had declared the U States of America to be free and independent . . . and also to assist us in carrying on this just and necessary war. . . . In consequence of this intelligence, this day was set apart for a day of rejoicing throughout the whole army. Accordingly at ten o'clock A.M. a cannon was fired as a signal for the whole to parade."

—*Diary of George Ewing, American patriot and soldier*

How did the offer of French and Spanish assistance mark a turning point in the American war effort?

7 Yorktown

document

"This is to us a most glorious day, but to the English, one of bitter chagrin and disappointment. Preparations are now making to receive as captives that vindictive, haughty commander and that . . . army, who by their robberies and murders, have so long been a scourge to our brethren of the Southern states. . . . The captive troops are to march out with shouldered arms, colors cased and drums beating a British or German march, and to ground their arms at a place assigned for the purpose."

—*Journal of Dr. James Thacher, American soldier, October 19, 1781*

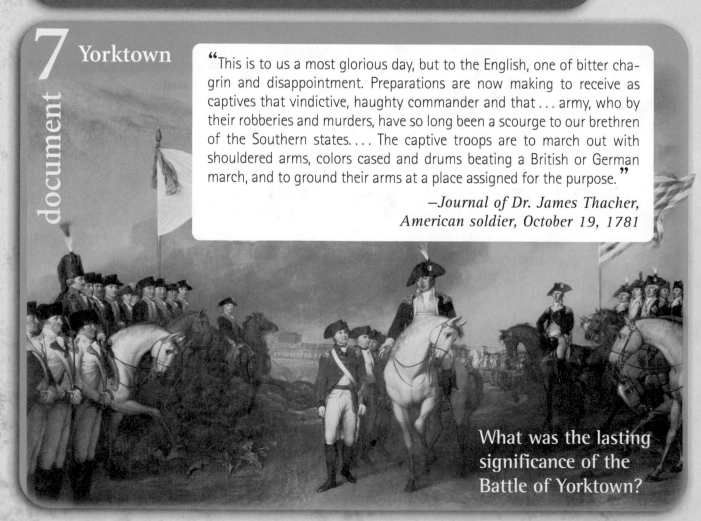

What was the lasting significance of the Battle of Yorktown?

8 Shays' Rebellion

"There are combustibles in every State, which a spark might set fire to.... That Great Britain will be an unconcerned Spectator of the present insurrections (if they continue) is not to be expected. That she is at this moment sowing the Seeds of jealousy and discontent among the various tribes of Indians.... We ought not therefore to sleep nor to slumber. Vigilance in watching, and vigour in acting, is, in my opinion, become indispensably necessary...."

—*George Washington, in a letter to Henry Knox, 1786*

Why did Washington recommend "vigour in acting" against Shays' Rebellion?

9 A More Perfect Union

"We the people of the United States, in order to form a more perfect union, establish justice, insure domestic tranquility, provide for the common defense, promote the general welfare, and secure the blessings of liberty to ourselves and our posterity, do ordain and establish this Constitution for the United States of America."

—*The United States Constitution, September 17, 1787*

How was the new American government different from British colonial government?

ACTIVITY

Review the documents and other information to make political cartoons on the unit question:

 How did the colonists break away from Britain and create a republican form of government?

Create a series of three or more political cartoons about the colonists' breakaway from Britain and their creation of a new republican form of government. Remember that political cartoons express a point of view about a situation. They also often use symbols or exaggeration to make a point. Hang your cartoons in your classroom. Be prepared to explain them to the class and to show how they help to answer the unit question.

What problems might a new nation face?

History *Interactive*
Explore Historian's Apprentice Online
Visit: PHSchool.com
Web Code: mvp-3000

George Washington After leading U.S. troops to victory against the British, Washington led the new nation as its first President. His actions set precedents that future Presidents would follow.

1789

Andrew Jackson A veteran of the War of 1812 and wars against Native Americans, Jackson was the first President from the West.

1828

The New Republic

Exploring the Louisiana Territory
President Thomas Jefferson acquired the Louisiana Territory and sent an expedition to explore lands west of the Mississippi River.

1803

War of 1812 In June 1812, the United States declared war on Great Britain. One reason for war was Britain's refusal to stop seizing U.S. Navy vessels and sailors.

1812

Trail of Tears Forced to move west to Indian Territory under harsh conditions, thousands of Native Americans lost their lives on what became known as the Trail of Tears.

1838

Launching a New Nation

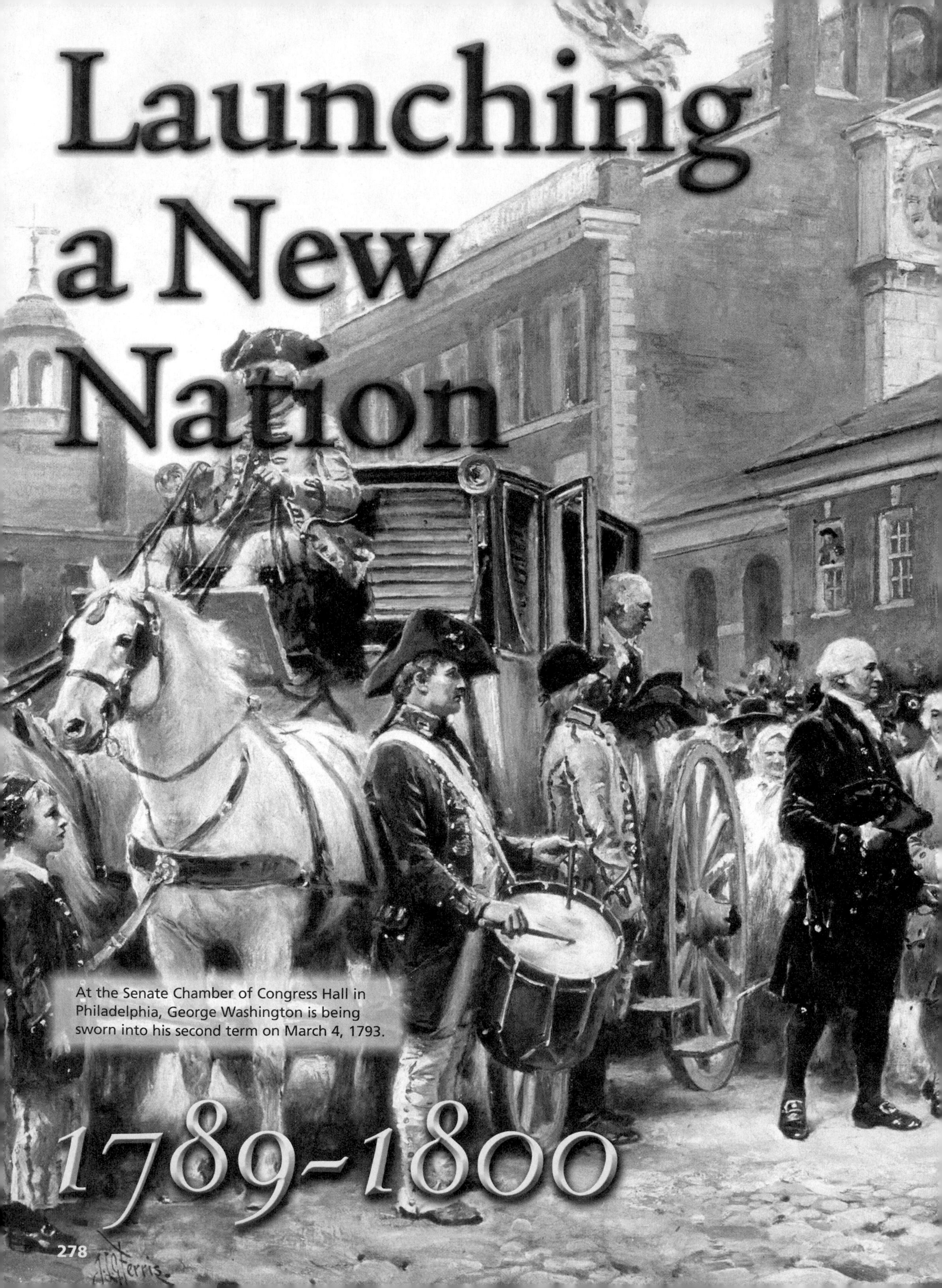

At the Senate Chamber of Congress Hall in Philadelphia, George Washington is being sworn into his second term on March 4, 1793.

1789–1800

"*First in war—first in peace—and first in the hearts of his countrymen...*"

—Congressman Henry Lee,
describing George Washington, 1799

What You Will Learn

Section 1
WASHINGTON TAKES OFFICE

George Washington oversaw the creation of new federal departments and asked Alexander Hamilton to tackle the nation's debt problem.

Section 2
THE BIRTH OF POLITICAL PARTIES

Two political parties began to take shape—the Federalists and the Republicans.

Section 3
TROUBLES AT HOME AND ABROAD

Under Washington, the United States dealt with challenges from Native Americans in the Northwest Territory and from the British navy at sea.

Section 4
THE PRESIDENCY OF JOHN ADAMS

Political divisions grew bitter during the presidency of John Adams, as he struggled to keep peace with France.

Reading Skill

Analyze Comparisons In this chapter, you will learn to identify and study comparisons made through similes, metaphors, and analogies.

How did Americans respond to

Launching a New Nation, 1789–1800

BRITISH CANADA

■Whiskey Rebellion
Pennsylvania farmers revolt when the government imposes a tax on the whiskey they make; Washington sends troops to confront farmers and the rebellion ends.

ME (Part of MA)

L. Superior

NORTHWEST TERRITORY

Mississippi River

L. Huron

Fort Oswego

VT

NH

Fort Niagara

NY

MA

Fort Detroit

L. Erie

CT

RI

New York

Fallen Timbers

Philadelphia ✪

Fort Wayne

PA

NJ

Fort Greenville

Greenville Treaty Line

MD

DE

Washington, D.C.

Vincennes ○

Ohio River

Fort Hamilton

VA

■Trouble at Home
Native Americans attack American settlements in the Northwest Territory; after early defeats, U.S. troops crush Native American resistance at Battle of Fallen Timbers.

SPANISH LOUISIANA

"The Federalist Party knows what the nation needs!"

"The Republican Party has the right ideas!"

NC

■Washington Becomes President
George Washington takes the oath of office at Federal Hall in New York City; the new President works with Congress to put a working government in place.

Fort San Fernando

SC

Atlantic Ocean

MISSISSIPPI TERRITORY

HAMILTON   JEFFERSON

GA

■Political Parties Emerge
Two groups grow out of different ideas of Thomas Jefferson and Alexander Hamilton; Jefferson's supporters become Republicans while Hamilton's supporters become Federalists.

Fort Nogales

Fort Natchez

SPANISH FLORIDA

Gulf of Mexico

N / W E / S

0 ___ 300 miles
0 ___ 300 km
Albers Conic Equal-Area Projection

U.S. Events 1789 — George Washington becomes first President of the United States.

1790 — Alexander Hamilton announces economic plan.

1794 — Whiskey Rebellion is crushed.

1789   1792   1795

World Events 1789 — French Revolution begins.

1793 — France and Britain go to war. "Reign of Terror" occurs in France.

VISUAL PREVIEW

KEY

Original 13 States

United States territory

Lands given up by Indians, 1795

Battle

British fort

American fort

Spanish fort

"But we're neutral!"

"We need your sailors!"

UNITED STATES

BRITAIN

BRITAIN

FRANCE

■**Trouble Abroad**
With Britain and France at war, Washington declares that the United States will not favor either side; both countries seize American cargoes to hurt the other; Britain seizes American sailors to serve on British ships.

"We told you not to trade with Britain!"

"But we're neutral!"

FRANCE

UNITED STATES

Internal Challenges
• The government did not have enough money.
• The nation was in debt.
• Backcountry farmers rebelled against taxes.
• Political parties disagreed on what to do.

External Challenges
• Native Americans and settlers fought over land.
• The British were aiding the Indians.
• War between Britain and France endangered Americans.
• Political parties disagreed on what to do.

1795 | Senate approves Jay Treaty with Britain.

"XYZ Affair" becomes public. Congress passes Alien and Sedition acts. **1798**

1800 | France agrees to stop seizing American ships.

1795   **1798**   **1801**

1799 | Napoleon Bonaparte gains political power in France.

The Sacred Fire of Liberty

❝The preservation of the sacred fire of liberty and the destiny of the republican model of government are . . . staked on the experiment entrusted to the hands of the American people.❞

—George Washington,
First Inaugural Address, 1789

◄ Advisers to President Washington (far right) included (from left) Henry Knox, Thomas Jefferson, Edmund Randolph, and Alexander Hamilton.

Washington Takes Office

Objectives

- Discuss how the new government was organized during Washington's presidency.
- Explain why the new nation faced an economic crisis.
- Identify the three parts of Hamilton's financial plan.
- Describe how Washington responded to the Whiskey Rebellion.

🎯 Reading Skill

Identify Similes Similes use the signal words *like* or *as* to connect two items being compared. The comparison helps the reader to imagine the description more fully. For example, "the gunfire echoed like thunder" creates a mental image of the sound of a battle. Look for similes as you read this section.

Key Terms

inauguration
precedent
bond

speculator
unconstitutional
tariff

Why It Matters In 1789, the American people had a new Constitution. They also had a new Congress and their first President. The United States was one fourth of its size today. All thirteen states were in the East. The nation's western border followed the Mississippi River. In the North, the Great Lakes formed much of the border separating the United States from British-controlled Canada. In the South, the United States bordered on Spanish-controlled Florida and Louisiana.

❓ Section Focus Question: How did President Washington set the course for the new nation?

The First President

In April of 1789, George Washington traveled from Virginia to the nation's capital, New York City, to begin his term as the first President of the United States. Washington's journey along bumpy roads took eight days. Large crowds lined the streets. As one newspaper reported, Americans greatly admired the tall, stately war hero:

❝Many persons in the crowd were heard to say they should now die contented—nothing being wanted to complete their happiness . . . but the sight of the savior of his country.❞

—*Gazette of the United States*, April 1789

Washington's **inauguration**—a ceremony in which the President takes the oath of office—was held on April 30, 1789. Despite all he had achieved, Washington was anxious. The country was divided on many issues. Washington understood how much the new nation depended on him. His actions would set a **precedent**—an example to be followed by others in the future.

The Executive Branch The Constitution of the United States provided only a general outline for organizing the government. When the President took office, the entire federal government was made up of little more than 75 post offices, a few clerks, and a tiny army of 672 soldiers.

The first job of the President and the Congress, therefore, was to put a working government in place. First, Congress passed laws to set up three departments for the executive branch: Treasury, State, and War. Each department was to be headed by a secretary nominated by the President. The President would also appoint an attorney general to advise him on legal matters.

Washington appointed four well-known men to take the new posts. He chose Alexander Hamilton to be secretary of the treasury. Hamilton was considered one of the country's outstanding leaders and an expert on economic affairs. Thomas Jefferson, the author of the Declaration of Independence, became secretary of state. His task was to manage relations with foreign countries. Henry Knox, a former general, was Washington's choice for secretary of war. Edmund Randolph, who had played an important role at the Constitutional Convention, became attorney general.

Washington soon began meeting regularly with these leaders as a group. Over time, this group became known as the Cabinet.

Washington's Inauguration
George Washington took the oath of office on a balcony of Federal Hall in New York City as well-wishers watched from the street below.
Critical Thinking: Link Past and Present Who attended Washington's oath-taking? How would a modern-day President's inauguration be different?

Establishing the Judiciary The Constitution also called for a judiciary, or court system. The Judiciary Act of 1789 provided for a Supreme Court of 6 justices. Under the Supreme Court were 3 circuit courts and 13 district courts. The main job of the federal courts was to hear appeals from the state courts. Washington appointed John Jay of New York as the first Chief Justice of the Supreme Court.

✓**Checkpoint** What were the new executive departments?

The Nation's First Economic Crisis

The American Revolution had left the nation deeply in debt. The federal government owed $52 million. That debt was mainly in the form of bonds. A **bond** is a certificate issued by a government for an amount of money that the government promises to pay back with interest. Both Americans and foreigners had <u>invested</u> in bonds to help the war effort. Would the government pay back this debt?

The issue was complicated because most people who had originally bought the bonds had sold them for less than they were worth. The buyers were **speculators**—people who invest in a risky venture in the hope of making a large profit. It seemed unfair to many Americans that speculators would make a profit after the original bondholders had lost money. Also in dispute was whether or not the federal government should pay back state debts.

The government was operating on a shoestring. It did not even have the money for George Washington's move to New York. Washington had to borrow $3,000 to pay his moving expenses.

✓**Checkpoint** Why was there such a large public debt?

Vocabulary Builder
<u>invest</u> (ihn VEHST) **v.** to purchase something with the hope that its value will grow

The Debt Problem

The U.S. government was collecting enough in taxes to pay its expenses, but hardly enough to pay back the debt. Hamilton's financial plan sought to find new sources of income to repay the debt.
Critical Thinking: *Identifying Economic Costs* *Without the amount of money owed, how much would the government have had left over after paying its costs?*

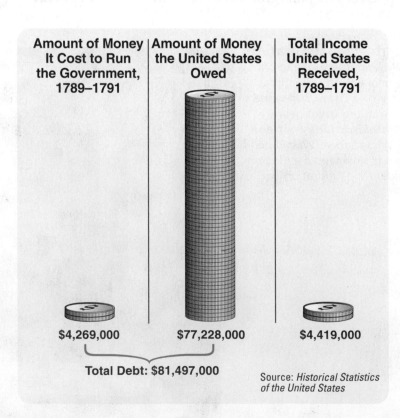

Amount of Money It Cost to Run the Government, 1789–1791	Amount of Money the United States Owed	Total Income United States Received, 1789–1791
$4,269,000	$77,228,000	$4,419,000

Total Debt: $81,497,000

Source: *Historical Statistics of the United States*

Hamilton's Financial Plan

The person responsible for developing a plan to solve the country's financial crisis was Alexander Hamilton, the secretary of the treasury.

Hamilton's program had three parts: (1) The U.S. government would fully assume, or agree to pay, all federal *and* state debts. (2) The U.S. government would charter a national bank for depositing government funds. (3) The government would <u>impose</u> a high tax on goods imported into the country.

Paying the Debt Hamilton knew that paying the debt would be a huge burden on the U.S. government. However, he wanted to prove to people here and abroad that the United States would honor its debts in full. Then, people would be willing to invest again in the future.

Many southerners opposed the plan to repay state debts. Several southern states had paid off their wartime debts on their own. Southerners thought other states should do the same.

Congress debated the plan for six months in 1790. Then, an agreement was reached. Southerners would support Hamilton's plan to have the federal government repay the wartime debt. In return, the government would build its new capital city in the South. The capital would rise along the banks of the Potomac River, between Virginia and Maryland.

A National Bank The second part of Hamilton's plan called for the creation of a privately owned bank of the United States. It would provide a safe place to deposit government funds. The bank would be able to issue paper money that would serve as a national currency.

The debate over the bank of the United States went beyond the bank itself and focused on the powers the government had under the Constitution. Opponents of the bank, such as Thomas Jefferson, insisted that the law establishing the bank was **unconstitutional**—contrary to what is permitted by the Constitution.

Jefferson argued that nowhere in the Constitution was there a provision allowing Congress to set up a national bank. Jefferson's view, that the Constitution permits only what it specifically says, is called a "strict" interpretation of the Constitution. Hamilton argued for a "loose" interpretation. He pointed out that Article 1, Section 8 of the Constitution gave Congress the power to make all laws "necessary and proper" for fulfilling its duties. This suggested that there were things not directly permitted by the Constitution that Congress could do.

Vocabulary Builder
<u>impose</u> (ihm POHZ) **v.** to place a burden on something or someone

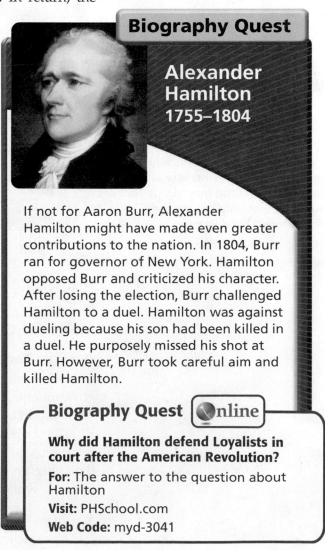

Biography Quest

Alexander Hamilton
1755–1804

If not for Aaron Burr, Alexander Hamilton might have made even greater contributions to the nation. In 1804, Burr ran for governor of New York. Hamilton opposed Burr and criticized his character. After losing the election, Burr challenged Hamilton to a duel. Hamilton was against dueling because his son had been killed in a duel. He purposely missed his shot at Burr. However, Burr took careful aim and killed Hamilton.

Biography Quest **Online**

Why did Hamilton defend Loyalists in court after the American Revolution?

For: The answer to the question about Hamilton

Visit: PHSchool.com

Web Code: myd-3041

THE Whiskey Rebellion

Farmers thought that having to pay a tax on the whiskey they produced from their corn was too heavy a burden. The tax was part of Alexander Hamilton's plan to pay the nation's war debt.
Critical Thinking: *Detect Points of View* *Why did the farmers resist the tax? Why did George Washington think it was important to put down the Whiskey Rebellion?*

Alexander Hamilton ▶

▼ **No Tolerance for Rebellion**
George Washington reviews U.S. troops as they start off to Pennsylvania to put down the rebellion. He said the farmers' actions threatened both "the just authority of government" and "the rights of individuals."

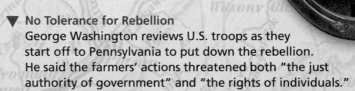

▲ **"We Won't Pay the Tax"**
Angry Pennsylvania farmers and militia members tar and feather a would-be tax collector (second from right). Farmers thought it was unfair to tax their "liquid corn," or whiskey.

In 1791, Congress did pass a law establishing the bank, and the President signed it. However, to this day Americans disagree about whether the Constitution should be interpreted strictly or loosely.

A High Tariff The final part of Hamilton's plan called for a high tariff—a tax on imported goods. It would raise money for the federal government. It would also protect U.S. manufacturers from foreign competition by making imported goods more expensive.

The tariff was the only part of Hamilton's plan that Congress did not pass, and that was because southerners opposed it. They argued that a high tariff would help the North, where most industries were located, while making southerners pay more for the goods they bought.

✓**Checkpoint** How did Congress respond to Hamilton's plan?

The Whiskey Rebellion

In 1791, Congress imposed a tax on all whiskey made and sold in the United States. Hamilton hoped this tax would raise funds for the Treasury. Instead, it led to a revolt that tested the strength of the new government.

Many backcountry farmers made extra money by turning the corn they grew into whiskey. Therefore, they bitterly resented the new whiskey tax. Farmers compared it to the hated taxes that Britain had imposed on the colonies before the Revolution. Many farmers organized protests and refused to pay the tax.

In 1794, officials in western Pennsylvania tried to collect the tax. Farmers rebelled, burning down the home of a tax collector. Soon, a large, angry mob was marching through Pittsburgh like a gathering storm. The violent protest became known as the Whiskey Rebellion.

Washington responded quickly to this challenge to federal authority. He sent the militia to Pennsylvania. When the rebels heard that 13,000 troops were marching against them, they quickly scattered. Washington later pardoned the leaders of the rebellion.

The Whiskey Rebellion tested the will of the new government. Washington's forceful response showed Americans that armed rebellion was not acceptable in a republic.

Identify Similes Find the simile in this paragraph. What two things are being compared?

☑ **Checkpoint** **What was the cause of the Whiskey Rebellion?**

⭐ **Looking Back and Ahead** George Washington set a firm course for the federal government, while Alexander Hamilton began to attack the debt problem. In the next section, you will read how the nation's first political parties developed.

Section 1 | **Check Your Progress**

Progress Monitoring Online
For: Self-test with instant help
Visit: PHSchool.com
Web Code: mya-3041

Comprehension and Critical Thinking

1. (a) Describe How did Washington's inauguration reflect the nation's deep respect for him?
(b) Organize Information Create a chart showing the top posts in the executive branch and judiciary at this time. Define each position and name the first person to occupy each post.

2. (a) Recall What was the nation's first economic crisis? How was it further complicated?
(b) Explain Problems What was Hamilton's plan to solve the crisis? Why was it controversial?

⊙ Reading Skill

3. Identify Similes Identify the simile in this sentence: The new President was as tough as nails. What two things does it compare?

Key Terms

4. Write two definitions for each key term: inauguration, precedent, bond, speculator, unconstitutional, tariff. First, write a formal definition for your teacher. Second, write a definition in everyday English for a classmate.

Writing

5. A newspaper account of George Washington's inauguration referred to him as "the savior of his country." That was a reference to Washington's service as commander in chief during the Revolutionary War. If you were to begin reading an essay about the life of George Washington, list five questions you would like it to answer.

The Arts of Early America

After winning independence, Americans began to develop their own styles in the arts. Often, they deliberately turned away from the model of their former British rulers.

Architecture

American architects of the Federal Period (1790–1830) turned away from the influence of England. They looked instead to two ancient civilizations, Greece and Rome. Domes and pillars were common. Buildings were designed to create a sense of harmony and balance. This picture shows the White House as it looked in 1807.

History *Interactive*

Explore Art and Music of the 1800s
Visit: PHSchool.com
Web Code: myp-3047

Pillars were modeled on Greek style.

Arches were common in Roman architecture.

Equal numbers of doors and windows on each side gave a sense of balance.

▲ The White House, 1807

Folk Art

Folk art is art created by ordinary people rather than trained artists. Common types of American folk art included hand-stitched samplers, weather vanes, ships' figureheads, and tavern signs. Much of the folk art of this time included patriotic images that revealed pride in the new nation. This Pennsylvania Dutch watercolor shows George Washington and his wife, Martha.

Pennsylvania Dutch watercolor ▶

Music

Many early American popular songs— including "Yankee Doodle"(below, right)— were adapted from old English melodies. In 1796, Americans put a new set of words to "Yankee Doodle" (below, left) to show pride in their democracy.

The Right of Free Elections

Should enemies beset us round,
Of foreign, fierce complexions;
Undaunted we will stand our ground,
Upheld by free elections.
We'll never from our duty swerve,
Let who will make objections;
But while we live, unchanged preserve
The freedom of elections.

Yankee Doodle

There was Captain Washington
Upon a slapping stallion
A-giving orders to his men
I guess there was a million.
Yankee Doodle, keep it up
Yankee Doodle dandy
Mind the music and the step
And with the girls be handy.

Early American flute ▲

Analyze LIFE AT THE TIME

Choose one of the examples of art, architecture, or music shown on these pages. Write a paragraph explaining how it shows a sense of pride in being an American.

Violence Erupts in Congress

"Directly before me stood Mr. Griswold laying on blows with all his might upon Mr. Lyon.... Lyon made an attempt to catch his cane, but failed—he pressed towards Griswold and endeavoured to close with him, but Griswold fell back and continued his blows on the head...."

—Federalist Representative George Thacher, describing a fight in Congress, 1798

◄ Fight between Federalist Representative Griswold and Republican Representative Lyon

The Birth of Political Parties

Objectives

- Explain how early political parties emerged.
- Compare the political views of the Republicans and the Federalists.
- Discuss the result of the election of 1796.

Reading Skill

Infer Meanings of Similes Similes compare things that may seem unrelated. The comparison helps you to see things in a new way. When you read a simile, think about how the items being compared are similar. Try to determine what point the writer is making.

Key Terms and People

faction
James Madison
Thomas Jefferson
Alexander Hamilton
John Adams

Why It Matters The arguments over Hamilton's financial plan reflected serious disagreements among the new nation's leaders. Americans also disagreed about the role of their nation's government.

❓ **Section Focus Question: How did two political parties emerge?**

Political Parties Emerge

The Framers of the Constitution did not expect political parties to develop in the United States. Rather, they thought that government leaders would rise above personal or local interests. The leaders, they believed, would work together for the sake of the country.

In those days, people spoke of *factions* rather than *political parties*. A **faction** was an organized political group, and the word was not complimentary. **James Madison** considered factions to be selfish groups, unconcerned with the well-being of the whole nation. Madison argued in the *Federalist Papers* that an effective national government would prevent the growth of factions. As he put it,

"Among the numerous advantages promised by a well-constructed Union, none deserves to be more accurately developed than its tendency to break and control the violence of faction."

—James Madison, *The Federalist* No. 10, 1787

Thomas Jefferson and **Alexander Hamilton**, who were rarely in agreement, both disliked factions. Hamilton warned that the "spirit of faction" might work like a spark to bring mob rule and chaos.

No one was more <u>hostile</u> to factions than George Washington. The President watched unhappily as Jefferson and Hamilton, the leading members of his Cabinet, grew apart. Washington tried to reduce the quarreling. In a letter to Henry Lee, he predicted that factions would destroy the "best fabric of human government and happiness."

Despite Washington's efforts, by the early 1790s two political parties were beginning to form. One group supported Thomas Jefferson and his close ally, James Madison. The other supported Alexander Hamilton and his ideas.

✓Checkpoint Why did many of the nation's leaders dislike political parties?

Republicans Against Federalists

The two parties that took shape during the first half of the 1790s eventually got the names Republicans and Federalists.

The Republicans took their name from political clubs called Democratic-Republican Societies that had been organized in various parts of the country. They argued that the federal government was growing too strong under President Washington. They wanted to keep most power at the state or local level. They feared that a strong central government would act like a monarchy.

Vocabulary Builder
<u>hostile</u> (HAHS tihl) **adj.** unfriendly; adverse or opposed

Infer Meanings of Similes
To what is a strong central government compared to in the final sentence of this paragraph? What does the comparison mean?

Republicans Versus Federalists

Republicans	Federalists
1. Were led by Thomas Jefferson	1. Were led by Alexander Hamilton
2. Believed people should have political power	2. Believed wealthy and educated should lead
3. Favored strong state government	3. Favored strong central government
4. Emphasized agriculture	4. Emphasized manufacturing, shipping, and trade
5. Favored strict interpretation of Constitution	5. Favored loose interpretation of Constitution
6. Were pro-French	6. Were pro-British
7. Opposed national bank	7. Favored national bank
8. Opposed protective tariff	8. Favored protective tariff

Reading Charts

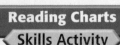

Skills Activity

The nation's first political parties were the Federalists and the Republicans. They took opposing stands on many political issues.

(a) Read a Chart How did the parties differ on federal power?

(b) Apply Information Why did the party that favored strong state governments insist on a strict interpretation of the Constitution?

Links Across Time

Political Parties Then and Now

1790s Political differences between Thomas Jefferson and Alexander Hamilton led to the development of America's first political parties.

1850s By the 1850s, the parties we know today had taken shape. Today's Democratic Party actually traces its roots to Jefferson's Republican Party. The modern Republican Party, which was born during the 1850s over the issue of slavery, has no connection to Jefferson's Republicans.

Link to Today Online

Political Parties Today The two major parties play a leading role in the American political system. How do the parties stand on today's political issues?

For: Political parties in the news
Visit: PHSchool.com
Web Code: myc-3042

The donkey is the modern-day symbol associated with the Democratic Party.

The symbol for today's Republican Party is an elephant.

This early Republican Party drew its main strength from southern planters and northern farmers and artisans. Key leaders were James Madison and Thomas Jefferson. Unhappy with the federal government's policies, Jefferson resigned as secretary of state in 1793.

The Federalists took their name from the people who had supported the adoption of the Constitution after 1787. A prominent leader was Alexander Hamilton. As in the debates over the Constitution, Federalists said the United States needed a strong federal government to hold the country together and deal with its problems.

Federalists drew support mainly from merchants, other property owners, and ordinary workers whose jobs depended on manufacturing and trade. They were especially strong in the North.

Organizing and Arguing At the time that both parties were organizing, the Federalists had an advantage. President Washington usually supported Hamilton and his policies. One Hamilton supporter running for office proudly said, "I am a FEDERALIST, the friend of order, of government, and of the present administration."

A newspaper editor who supported the Republicans saw the situation very differently. In 1792, he printed a series of questions in the *National Gazette* implying that the Federalists wanted to betray the Constitution and bring back a king. "Are not some amongst us . . . advocates for monarchy and aristocracy?" he asked. "Are not the principles of all such [people] hostile to the principles of the constitution?"

Other Disagreements In addition to their <u>fundamental</u> disagreement about the power of the federal government, Federalists and Republicans disagreed about other issues. Federalists favored the national bank and a national tariff. The Republicans opposed both. Federalists favored close ties with England. Republicans were sympathetic to France, where a revolution overthrew the king in 1789. (You will read more about the French Revolution in Section 3.)

☑Checkpoint   **How did Federalists and Republicans differ?**

Vocabulary Builder
<u>fundamental</u> (fuhn duh MEHN tahl)
adj. basic; most important; forming the foundation of an idea or action; essential

The Election of 1796

In 1796, George Washington said he would not seek a third term. This set an important precedent. Not until Franklin Roosevelt ran for and won a third term in 1940 would any President seek more than two terms. (In 1951, the Twenty-second Amendment legally limited the President to two terms.)

The Republican candidate for President in 1796 was Thomas Jefferson. The Federalists nominated John Adams, a New Englander, who had been Washington's Vice President.

In 1796, President and Vice President were not elected together as a ticket, as they are today. Instead, the candidate getting the most votes became President and the second-place candidate became Vice President.

Adams finished first and Jefferson second. The country thus gained a Federalist President and a Republican Vice President. Not surprisingly, this led to serious tensions during the next four years.

☑Checkpoint   **Which party won the presidency in 1796?**

⭐ **Looking Back and Ahead** The Republicans and Federalists had conflicting visions of what the federal government should do. In the next section, you will read how President Washington dealt with challenges at home and abroad.

Section 2 | Check Your Progress

Progress Monitoring ⊙nline
For: Self-test with instant help
Visit: PHSchool.com
Web Code: mya-3042

Comprehension and Critical Thinking

1. **(a) Describe** How did the Framers of the Constitution feel about political parties?
(b) Draw Conclusions Do you believe having political parties helps or hurts the nation? Explain.

2. **(a) Recall** What was the fundamental difference between the two political parties?

(b) Detect Points of View If you were a worker at a northern textile mill during Washington's presidency, would you have supported the Republicans or the Federalists? Explain.

◑ **Reading Skill**
3. **Infer Meanings of Similes** Explain the simile in this sentence: Alexander Hamilton acted like a friend to government.

Key Terms
Complete this sentence so it clearly shows your understanding of the key term.
4. As a result of factions, _____.

Writing
5. Use Internet or library resources to find and read an article giving an overview of the life of George Washington. Then, create a timeline showing the most important events in Washington's life.

Vital to Its Survival

❝ Two hundred years ago the United States, a Confederation of Indian tribes and Great Britain all sought control of the land known as the Northwest Territory, a vast area north of the Ohio and east of the Mississippi rivers. For the young United States, the control of this area was vital to its survival. ❞

—Dr. G. Michael Pratt, address at 1994 commemoration of Battle of Fallen Timbers

▲ General Anthony Wayne (right) led American soldiers to victory at Fallen Timbers.

Troubles at Home and Abroad

Objectives
- Discuss the conflicts with Native Americans in the Northwest Territory.
- Describe how Americans reacted to the French Revolution.
- Identify the main points of Washington's Farewell Address.
- Summarize Washington's accomplishments as President.

🔍 Reading Skill

Infer Meanings of Metaphors As you read, notice metaphors that speak of one item as if it were another. For example, "he is the foundation of our success" means that his work supports our success, as a foundation supports a building. The word *like* is absent but is suggested by the comparison. As you read this section, look for metaphors.

Key Terms and People

Anthony Wayne impressment
neutral John Jay

Why It Matters Political parties emerged because Americans had differing viewpoints about the government and economy. Americans also disagreed on foreign policy issues.

❓ **Section Focus Question: How did the actions of Britain and France affect the United States?**

Conflicts in the Northwest Territory

As a result of the Treaty of Paris that ended the American Revolution, the United States won the vast territory north and west of the Ohio River to the Mississippi River. Although the British still had forts in the region, they promised to withdraw within a "reasonable" time. A decade later, the British soldiers were still there. Moreover, the British were supplying Native Americans with guns and ammunition. The British hoped that this would limit American settlement in the Northwest Territory.

A Struggle Over Lands Native Americans in the Northwest Territory wanted to keep their lands. During the 1780s, they attacked many American settlements. Several Native American groups joined together to oppose settlement.

Many American leaders believed that the country's future depended on settling its western lands. Therefore, the federal government tried to force Native Americans in the territories to sell their lands. By 1790, the United States had succeeded in buying Native American lands in most of Kentucky and in part of Tennessee. North of the Ohio River, Native Americans refused to sell. Even there, though, the flow of white settlement continued.

A Series of Battles In 1790, Washington sent a small force to end the Native American attacks on settlers. Warriors led by Little Turtle of the Miami Nation and Blue Jacket of the Shawnees defeated the soldiers. The next year, Washington sent a larger force. This time, Little Turtle won an even bigger victory. More than 900 soldiers were killed or wounded. It was the worst defeat the army would ever suffer in a battle with Native Americans.

Washington then turned to a Revolutionary War hero, General Anthony Wayne, to lead the forces against the Native Americans. Native Americans gathered for battle at a place where fallen trees covered the ground. They thought the trees would cause trouble for Wayne and his soldiers. But in August 1794, Wayne won a major victory at the Battle of Fallen Timbers.

That battle broke the Native American hold on the Northwest. In the 1795 Treaty of Greenville, leaders of the defeated Native American nations gave up most of their lands from the Ohio River in the south to Lake Erie in the north. Today, that is most of the state of Ohio.

✓Checkpoint How were the conflicting claims of settlers and Native Americans resolved?

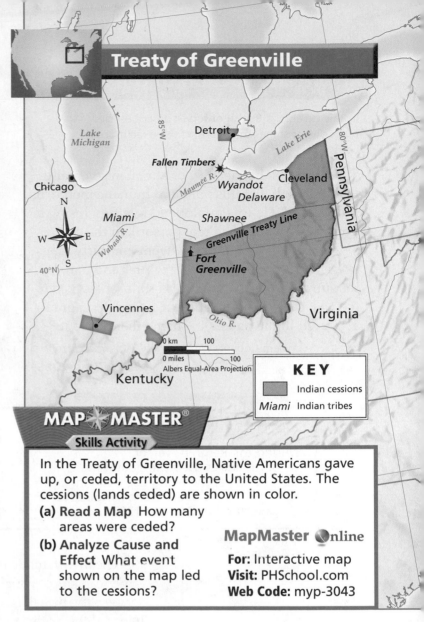

Treaty of Greenville

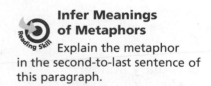
Skills Activity

In the Treaty of Greenville, Native Americans gave up, or ceded, territory to the United States. The cessions (lands ceded) are shown in color.

(a) Read a Map How many areas were ceded?

(b) Analyze Cause and Effect What event shown on the map led to the cessions?

MapMaster ●nline

For: Interactive map
Visit: PHSchool.com
Web Code: myp-3043

The French Revolution

The French Revolution began in 1789. Most Americans at first supported the French revolutionaries. In their eyes, France was following the lead of the United States in fighting monarchy.

Soon, though, the French Revolution became controversial in the United States. One reason was that it became more violent. This process peaked in mid-1793 with a period called the Reign of Terror. The French revolutionaries executed about 17,000 people, including the king and queen. For the Federalists, the Revolution was a bloodthirsty monster. But Jefferson and his supporters argued that in a fight by oppressed people to win freedom, some injustices were to be expected.

Secondly, by early 1793, France and Britain were at war. In that war, said President Washington, the United States would remain neutral—not favoring either side in a dispute.

The United States wanted to trade with both sides. However, each European country feared such trade would benefit the other. Both countries began stopping American ships and seizing their cargoes.

Infer Meanings of Metaphors
Explain the metaphor in the second-to-last sentence of this paragraph.

American Reaction to the Reign of Terror

In this excerpt, a British observer describes the reactions of some Americans to the execution of Louis XVI.

In this illustration, an executioner displays the severed head of Louis XVI.

❝Never was the memory of any man so cruelly insulted as that of this mild and humane monarch [Louis XVI]. He was guillotined in effigy [using a dummy to represent a real person], in the capital of the Union [Philadelphia], twenty or thirty times every day, during one whole winter and part of the summer. Men, women, and children flocked to the tragical exhibition, and not a single paragraph appeared in the papers to shame them from it.❞

—William Cobbett, *History of the American Jacobins* (Philadelphia, 1796)

Reading Primary Sources
Skills Activity

During the Reign of Terror, revolutionaries used the guillotine to behead the French king Louis XVI in January 1793. Queen Marie Antoinette was executed in October 1793.

(a) **Detect Points of View** How did the author view Louis XVI's execution?

(b) **Draw Conclusions** How do you think Philadelphians who attended the "tragical exhibition" felt about the king's execution? Explain.

The British made matters worse by the **impressment** of sailors on American ships, which meant seizing the sailors and forcing them to serve in the British navy. Some of the sailors were British sailors who had fled the British navy, but many were Americans.

As tensions rose, Hamilton urged the President to stay friendly with Britain. He argued that American prosperity depended on trade with Britain. The British purchased 75 percent of American exports and supplied 90 percent of American imports.

Washington agreed and tried to repair relations with Britain. He sent John Jay to London to try to solve the most serious problems.

Jay returned with a treaty in 1795. In it, the United States agreed to pay debts long owed to British merchants. In return, Britain agreed to pay for the ships it had seized. It also agreed to withdraw its troops from the Northwest Territory and stop aiding Native Americans there. However, the British refused to recognize a U.S. right to trade with France. They also refused to <u>cease</u> impressment of U.S. sailors.

The Jay Treaty angered Republicans. They claimed the United States had given away too much and gotten too little. Federalists, in contrast, liked the treaty because it kept peace with Britain. Since Federalists controlled the Senate, the Jay Treaty won approval by a narrow margin.

Vocabulary Builder
<u>cease</u> (sees) **v.** to cause to come to an end; to stop

✔**Checkpoint** How did Americans react to the Jay Treaty?

Washington Retires From Public Life

In 1796, Washington published a letter to fellow Americans that had lasting influence. Washington's Farewell Address made two major points. First, the President warned against political divisions at home. He feared that violent divisions might tear the nation apart.

Washington's second piece of advice concerned foreign policy. In a famous passage, Washington <u>emphasized</u> his belief that the United States must not get entangled in the affairs of Europe. He said:

> **❝**Europe has a set of primary interests which to us have none or a very remote relation. . . . Why . . . entangle our peace and prosperity in the toils [traps] of European ambition? . . . It is our true policy to steer clear of permanent alliances with any portion of the foreign world.**❞**
>
> —George Washington, Farewell Address, 1796

As he left office, Washington could take pride in his accomplishments: (1) The United States now had a functioning federal government. (2) The economy was improving. (3) Washington had avoided war. (4) The British had been forced to leave their forts in the Northwest Territory, an area that was now safe for settlement.

Still, political divisions were growing and challenges remained.

☑Checkpoint **What were Washington's chief accomplishments?**

⭐ **Looking Back and Ahead** As President, George Washington created conditions for a strong federal government. In the next section, you will read how his successor sought to deal with divisions at home and challenges abroad.

Vocabulary Builder
<u>emphasize</u> (EM fuh syz) **v.** to stress; to give more importance to

Section 3 | **Check Your Progress**

Progress Monitoring ⓞnline
For: Self-test with instant help
Visit: PHSchool.com
Web Code: mya-3043

Comprehension and Critical Thinking

1. (a) Describe How did Washington deal with Britain's policy of impressment?
(b) Compare and Contrast How did Washington's policy on matters at home differ from his foreign policy?

2. (a) Recall What were the two main arguments Washington made in his Farewell Address?
(b) Distinguish Facts From Opinions Support the following opinion with facts from the chapter: George Washington was a great first President.

🔄 **Reading Skill**

3. Infer Meanings of Metaphors Identify and explain the metaphor in this sentence: In the heated political atmosphere, this warning had little impact.

Key Terms

Read each sentence that follows. If the sentence is true, write YES. If the sentence is not true, write NO and explain why.
4. As a neutral nation, the United States should trade only with Britain and not France.

5. The Jay Treaty did not end the impressment of American sailors by the British navy.

Writing

6. Based on what you have read about George Washington in this section, write a description of the personality traits he showed as President of the United States. Include at least two specific examples of actions that he took as President.

Make Haste to Wage War

❝We must make haste to *wage war,* or we shall be lost. . . . Something energetic and decisive must be done soon. Congress fiddles while our Rome is burning. America . . . can interdict [prohibit] France the ocean.❞

—Fisher Ames, urging war with France, 1798

◄ French ship attacking an American ship

The Presidency of John Adams

Objectives

- Discuss the reasons for tension between the United States and France.
- Describe the main provisions of the Alien and Sedition acts.
- Explain how controversy arose over states' rights.

🔄 Reading Skill

Identify Analogies In an analogy, two pairs of items are connected with the same sort of comparison. For example, both pairs might compare synonyms, or words with similar meanings. You must understand the comparison between the first pair in order to complete the comparison between the second pair. Some common types of analogies are cause-effect, antonyms, and synonyms.

Key Terms

alien
sedition

nullify
states' rights

Why It Matters John Adams succeeded Washington as President. He struggled to reduce the country's divisions and to steer a neutral course in foreign policy.

❓ **Section Focus Question: How did problems with France intensify the split between the Federalists and Republicans?**

Troubles With France

Adams immediately faced a crisis over relations with France. The French were angered by U.S. neutrality in the war between France and Britain. France had hoped for U.S. support. Had not French assistance been the key to success in the American Revolution? Why didn't Americans show their gratitude by helping the French now?

The Jay Treaty only increased tensions with France. As the French saw it, the treaty put the United States on Britain's side. France reacted late in 1796 by snubbing a U.S. diplomat. Moreover, the French continued to attack American merchant ships.

The XYZ Affair In 1797, Adams sent a new three-person mission to France. Agents of the French government demanded that the United States pay a bribe of $250,000. The agents also wanted the United States to lend France several million dollars.

The Americans said they would pay "not a sixpence [a coin worth six pennies]." Later, that statement led to the slogan, "Millions for defense, but not one sixpence for tribute [a forced payment]."

The bribe attempt was a sensation when it became public. Because the names of the French agents were kept secret, they were called X, Y, and Z. The incident became known as the XYZ Affair.

War Fever The XYZ Affair caused an outbreak of war fever in the United States. Many Federalists demanded that Adams ask Congress to declare war on France.

With war fever rising, Adams asked Congress to increase the size of the army and rebuild the navy. It did both, thus enhancing the power of the central government. Adams also convinced Congress to create a separate department of the navy. Between 1798 and 1800, the United States fought an undeclared naval war with France.

Nonetheless, the President and many other Americans opposed a full-scale war. To avoid war, Adams sent a new mission to France. Napoleon Bonaparte, France's dictator, was busy dealing with war in Europe. In 1800, he agreed to stop seizing American ships.

President Adams had avoided war. But the agreement angered leaders of his own Federalist Party, especially the pro-British Hamilton. This disapproval weakened Adams politically.

Still, Adams was satisfied. He told a friend that he wanted his tombstone to read: "Here lies John Adams, who took upon himself the responsibility of peace with France in the year 1800."

☑**Checkpoint** **How did Adams settle differences with France?**

The Alien and Sedition Acts

The war fever deepened the split between Federalists and Republicans. Federalists' fear of revolutionary France spilled over into a mistrust of immigrants. Federalists suspected them of bringing in dangerous ideas and feared that they would back the Republicans.

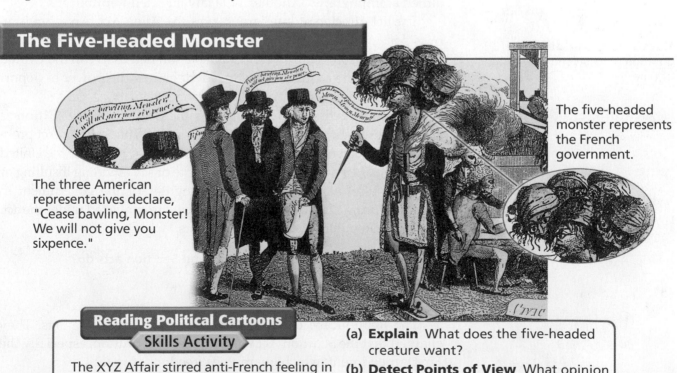

The Five-Headed Monster

The three American representatives declare, "Cease bawling, Monster! We will not give you sixpence."

The five-headed monster represents the French government.

Reading Political Cartoons
Skills Activity

The XYZ Affair stirred anti-French feeling in the United States. This 1798 cartoon shows a five-headed creature demanding a bribe from the three American representatives (at left).

(a) **Explain** What does the five-headed creature want?

(b) **Detect Points of View** What opinion do you think the cartoonist has of the French government? What evidence supports your view?

New Life for a Debate

Passage of the Alien and Sedition acts renewed the debate over federal versus state power. Jefferson and Madison wrote the Kentucky and Virginia resolutions in defense of states' rights. **Critical Thinking: *Detect Points of View*** *According to defenders of states' rights in 1798, what could states do if they disliked a federal law?*

Arguments for States' Rights	Arguments for Federal Power
■ The federal government derives its power from rights given to it by the states. ■ Because the states created the United States, individual states have the power to nullify a federal law.	■ The federal government derives its power from rights given to it by the American people. ■ States have no power to nullify federal laws. ■ States cannot revoke federal powers set forth in the Constitution.

Trouble on the Horizon

Within 25 years of the Alien and Sedition acts, people in New England and South Carolina would threaten to leave the Union because they either disagreed with American foreign policy or opposed laws passed by Congress.

Vocabulary Builder
<u>duration</u> (doo RAY shun) *n.* length of time

Federalist leaders decided that to restore order at home they must destroy their political opponents. Congress passed an act in 1798 aimed at immigrants. Another 1798 law targeted Republicans.

The act directed at immigrants was the Alien Act. An **alien** is an outsider or someone from another country. The Alien Act increased the <u>duration</u> from 5 to 14 years that a person had to live in the United States to become a citizen. The President gained the power to deport or imprison any alien he considered dangerous.

The act targeting Republicans was the Sedition Act. **Sedition** is activity designed to overthrow a government. The Sedition Act probably was the harshest law limiting free speech ever passed in the United States. It made it a crime for anyone to write or say anything insulting or anything false about the President, Congress, or the government in general. During 1798 and 1799, ten people were convicted under the act. Most were Republican editors and printers.

✓**Checkpoint** **What did the Alien and Sedition acts do?**

States' Rights

The Republicans denounced the Alien and Sedition acts. They charged that the Sedition Act violated the Constitution, especially the First Amendment, which guarantees freedom of speech.

However, the Republicans faced a problem opposing the law. At the time, it was not clearly established that the Supreme Court had the power to strike down a law as unconstitutional. Because of this, the Republicans expressed their opposition through the state legislatures.

Republicans James Madison and Thomas Jefferson, both Virginians, led the campaign. Madison wrote a resolution attacking the Alien and Sedition acts. It was passed by the Virginia legislature. Jefferson wrote a similar resolution that was passed by the Kentucky legislature. Together, the Virginia and Kentucky resolutions stated that the Alien and Sedition acts were unconstitutional. They declared that states had the right to declare laws passed by Congress to be unconstitutional.

No other states supported Virginia and Kentucky, so the two resolutions had little immediate impact. As for the Alien and Sedition acts, they were not in force for long. The law that gave the President the power to imprison or deport dangerous aliens expired after two years. The Sedition Act expired in 1801. The waiting period for immigrants to become citizens was restored to five years in 1802.

However, over the long term the Virginia and Kentucky resolutions were far more important than the laws that provoked them. The resolutions claimed that states could nullify—deprive of legal force—a law passed by Congress. The resolutions also boosted the idea of states' rights. This is the idea that the union binding "these United States" is an agreement between the states and that they therefore can overrule federal law. In decades to come, a number of states would refuse to obey certain federal laws. States' rights would become the rallying cry for southern defenders of slavery.

James Madison

Vocabulary Builder
provoke (prah VOHK) *v.* to cause to anger; to excite; to cause an action

☑**Checkpoint** **Why did the issue of states' rights arise at this time?**

⭐ **Looking Back and Ahead** You have read how the United States got up and running under its first two Presidents. The next chapter deals with the next two Presidents, Thomas Jefferson and James Madison, and the challenges they faced.

Section 4 | **Check Your Progress**

Progress Monitoring ⬡nline
For: Self-test with instant help
Visit: PHSchool.com
Web Code: mya-3044

Comprehension and Critical Thinking

1. (a) **Recall** What problem did President Adams face abroad?
(b) **Explain Problems** How did Adams resolve this problem?

2. (a) **Summarize** Why did the Federalist Congress pass the Alien and Sedition acts?
(b) **Analyze Cause and Effect** Explain the following statement: State reaction to the Alien and Sedition acts caused further tension between the political parties.

Reading Skill

3. **Identify Analogies** Explain the analogy in this sentence: As the call for war heated up, John Adams tried to be the nation's firefighter.

Key Terms

Answer the following questions in complete sentences that show your understanding of the key terms.

4. Why did Federalists mistrust aliens?

5. Why did newspaper editors accused of sedition tend to be Republicans?

6. Why did Republicans want to nullify the Alien and Sedition acts?

7. How can states' rights be used to oppose federal laws?

Writing

8. Use Internet or library resources to research the life of John Adams. List the principal events in his life. Then, describe the personality traits he displayed as President of the United States. Write a thesis statement that could be used to introduce a biographical essay about Adams.

21st Century Learning — It is important to be able to tell the difference between facts and opinions when you read historical stories and narratives. A fact is something that can be proved to be true or can be observed. An opinion is a statement that reflects a person's feelings, judgments, or beliefs about a subject.

This diary entry, which is historical fiction, was written by a merchant living in colonial Philadelphia in the 1790s.

February 28

After dinner tonight I finished reading today's edition of the *Gazette of the United States.* The publisher of the newspaper is John Fenno. In my opinion, he is right to favor the Federalist leader, Alexander Hamilton. Of course, I am a merchant and I agree with Hamilton's support of trade and manufacturing. To me it is a more worthwhile policy than Mr. Jefferson's support of the farmers.

I believe that I have Hamilton alone to thank for the National Bank. This Bank, established by Congress in 1791, has the power to make loans to businesses, such as my dry goods store. Of course, the federal Bank is opposed by that friend of the states, Thomas Jefferson, who isn't thinking of our country's future. I only hope that Mr. Hamilton's party wins the next election.

—Isaac Smith

Learn the Skill
Use these steps to identify facts and opinions.

1. **Decide which statements are facts.** Facts are statements that are based on direct evidence and can be proved to be true. Facts tell what really happened. You can look up a statement in a research source to prove it is a fact.

2. **Decide which statements are opinions.** An opinion is a personal interpretation of an event, an idea, or a person. Words such as "I think," "I believe," or "I feel" are often used in a statement of opinion. Look for these words when you read.

3. **Recognize how writers or speakers mix facts and opinions.** Sometimes writers use facts to support their personal opinion. Or, writers use facts and opinions to persuade the reader to support their point of view.

Practice the Skill
Answer the following questions about the journal entry on this page.

1. **Decide which statements are facts.** (a) Find two facts in this journal entry. (b) How can you prove that each statement is a fact?

2. **Decide which statements are opinions.** (a) Find two statements of opinion in this journal entry. (b) How can you tell that each is an opinion?

3. **Recognize how writers or speakers mix facts and opinions.** (a) Find an example of a statement that mixes fact and opinion. What is the fact? What is the opinion? (b) Why do you think the writer mixed fact and opinion in this selection?

Apply the Skill
See the Review and Assessment at the end of this chapter.

Quick Study Guide

How did Americans respond to internal and external challenges?

Section 1
Washington Takes Office

- George Washington was inaugurated as the first President in April of 1789.
- Washington and Congress organized the executive and judiciary branches.
- Alexander Hamilton developed a financial plan to repay the country's large war debt.
- Federal forces put down the Whiskey Rebellion in 1794.

Section 2
The Birth of Political Parties

- Deepening differences between factions led to the first political parties.
- Republicans wanted a limited national government, while Federalists favored a strong federal government.
- John Adams, a Federalist, won the presidency in 1796. Thomas Jefferson, a Republican, won the vice presidency.

Section 3
Troubles at Home and Abroad

- Washington responded forcefully to conflict in the Northwest Territory between settlers and Native Americans.
- The United States remained neutral when France and Britain went to war.
- In his Farewell Address, George Washington warned the nation against disunity and against becoming involved in foreign wars.

Section 4
The Presidency of John Adams

- John Adams was elected President of the United States in 1796.
- The United States and France avoided full-scale war under Adams but fought an undeclared naval war.
- The Federalist-sponsored Alien and Sedition acts provoked a strong reaction by Republicans in favor of states' rights.

? Exploring the Essential Question

Use the online study guide to explore the essential question.

Section 1
How did President Washington set the course for the new nation?

Section 2
How did two political parties emerge?

Chapter 8 Essential Question
How did Americans respond to internal and external challenges?

Section 4
How did problems with France intensify the split between the Federalists and the Republicans?

Section 3
How did the actions of Britain and France affect the United States?

Key Terms
Fill in the blanks with the correct key terms.

1. Many of the customs that Washington started set a _____ for how other Presidents were to act in the future.

2. Jefferson said the national bank was _____ because it was not written in the Constitution that Congress had authority to establish one.

3. Neither France nor Britain agreed that the United States could be a _____ nation and trade with both sides during their war.

4. The _____ Act violated the First Amendment of the Constitution.

Comprehension and Critical Thinking

5. **(a) Recall** What was the purpose of George Washington's Cabinet?
(b) Link Past and Present Why do you think current Presidents have more advisers than the number required in Washington's day?

6. **(a) Describe** What were two internal problems and their resolutions during Washington's second term as President?
(b) Explain Problems What does the picture below indicate about Washington's view of the Whiskey Rebellion?

7. **(a) Recall** In Washington's Farewell Address, he talked about neutrality toward European nations. Why did Washington believe that the United States needed to be neutral in the war between France and Britain?
(b) Draw Conclusions In Washington's Farewell Address, he also talked about national unity. Why was building unity an important goal for Washington?

8. **(a) Recall** Why were the Alien and Sedition acts unpopular with many people?
(b) Apply Information Would you defend or oppose the government's right to silence people who criticize it? Explain.

History Reading Skill

9. **Analyze Comparisons** George Washington is often referred to as the Father of Our Country. What is the meaning of this metaphor? Do you think this is a valid comparison? Explain.

Writing

10. **Write a paragraph about either George Washington or John Adams.**
Include major events and describe your subject's personality.

Your paragraph should:
- begin with a thesis statement;
- expand on that main idea with facts, examples, and other information;
- conclude by stating what you think was your subject's most important contribution to the new nation.

11. **Write a Narrative:**
Study the pictures and text in Section 1 about the Whiskey Rebellion. Write a two-paragraph narrative describing the rebellion. Write from the point of view of either a farmer or a soldier.

Skills for Life
Distinguish Facts From Opinions
Use the fictional journal entry below to answer the questions that follow.

> "I am grateful that at least our Vice President, Thomas Jefferson, is a Republican. I believe that his policies are the only hope for farmers, such as myself and my neighbors. In my opinion, our political leaders don't have to be rich or well-educated. The people can lead as well as follow. Of course, the Federalist Mr. Hamilton, with his fine clothes, favors the wealthy merchants."

12. **(a)** Identify one fact in the journal entry.
(b) How can you prove the statement is a fact?

13. **(a)** What is an example of an opinion?
(b) How can you tell the statement is an opinion?

14. Find a statement that mixes fact and opinion. What is the fact? What is the opinion?

Test Yourself

1. **Which of the following led to tension between France and the United States during Adams's presidency?**

   A Treaty of Greenville

   B Jay Treaty

   C Treaty of Paris

   D Declaration of Independence

Refer to the quotation below to answer Question 2.

> "It is in my judgment necessary under the circumstances of the case to take measures for calling forth the militia in order to . . . cause the laws to be duly executed."

2. **What event is the subject of the quotation?**

   A French Revolution

   B XYZ Affair

   C Battle of Fallen Timbers

   D Whiskey Rebellion

Refer to the chart below to answer Question 3.

The First Political Parties	
Federalists	**Republicans**
Favored strong central government	Favored state government
Emphasized manufacturing, shipping, and trade	Emphasized agriculture
Supported loose interpretation of the Constitution	Supported strict interpretation of the Constitution
Favored national bank	Opposed national bank

3. **Which statement describes a fundamental difference between the two parties?**

   A Federalists believed in a strong central government, and Republicans did not.

   B Federalists believed in a strict interpretation of the Constitution, and Republicans did not.

   C Republicans believed in a strong central government, and Federalists did not.

   D Republicans believed in a loose interpretation of the Constitution, and Federalists did not.

Document-Based Questions

Task: Look at Documents 1 and 2, and answer their accompanying questions. Then, use the documents and your knowledge of history to complete this writing assignment:

> Write a newspaper editorial supporting or attacking President Adams's decision to avoid war with France.

Document 1: In 1797, France began seizing American ships. Enraged Americans called for war, but President John Adams urged a policy of peace. *What action does Adams say he will take toward France?*

> "It is my sincere desire . . . to preserve peace and friendship with all nations; and believing that neither the honor nor the interest of the United States absolutely forbid the repetition of advances for securing these desirable objects with France, I shall institute a fresh attempt at negotiation, and shall not fail to promote and accelerate an accommodation on terms compatible with the rights, duties, interests, and honor of the nation."

Document 2: After the XYZ Affair, newspapers published cartoons such as the one shown below. It depicts the United States as a young woman surrounded by members of the French government. *What is the cartoonist's view of the XYZ Affair?*

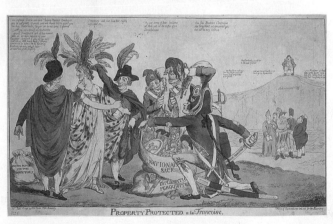

PROPERTY PROTECTED. à la Françoise.

The Era of Thomas Jefferson

1800–1815

> *"The territory acquired, as it includes all the waters of the Missouri and Mississippi, has more than doubled the area of the United States...."*
>
> —Thomas Jefferson, describing the Louisiana Purchase, 1803

Jefferson sent an expedition under Lewis and Clark to explore the Louisiana Purchase. Here, the expedition (left) meets a group of Native Americans on the Colombia River.

CHAPTER 9

What You Will Learn

Section 1
JEFFERSON TAKES OFFICE

Thinking of his election as "the Revolution of 1800," President Jefferson hoped to make far-reaching changes in government.

Section 2
THE LOUISIANA PURCHASE

Having acquired a vast expanse of western territory, Jefferson sent Meriwether Lewis and William Clark to explore the region.

Section 3
A TIME OF CONFLICT

Conflicts with the British at sea and Native Americans in the West led to the War of 1812.

Section 4
THE WAR OF 1812

Although the War of 1812 did not resolve British-American disputes, many Americans considered the war a victory.

 Reading Skill

Relate Events in Time In this chapter, you will learn to relate the chronological order of events and determine their relationships to one another.

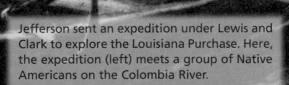

The Era of Jefferson and Madison

The Achievements of Jefferson and Madison

- Replaced most Federalist policies with Republican policies
- Doubled the size of the United States
- Oversaw exploration of new western territories
- Weakened Native American resistance
- Strengthened national unity as result of war with Great Britain
- Showcased America's growing power to European nations

■1804
Meriwether Lewis and William Clark set out to explore the Louisiana Territory and find a water route to the Pacific.

OREGON COUNTRY

LOUISIANA TERRITORY

■1805
Zebulon Pike leads an expedition west across Louisiana Territory to Rocky Mountains and eventually into Spanish New Mexico.

SPANISH TERRITORY

Pacific Ocean

■1803
The United States purchases the Louisiana Territory from France for $15 million.

0 ___ 300 miles
0 ___ 300 km
Albers Conic Equal-Area Projection

KEY
United States and its territories, 1810
Unorganized U.S. territory, 1810
Spanish territory
Disputed area

U.S. Events

United States purchases Louisiana from France. **1803**

1804 Lewis and Clark set out to explore Louisiana.

1809 Embargo Act bans foreign trade.

1800　　　　**1805**　　　　**1810**

World Events

Napoleon becomes emperor of France. **1804**

Mexico declares independence from Spain. **1810**

VISUAL PREVIEW

BRITISH CANADA

■**1807**
Congress forbids all foreign trade; American smugglers illegally import and export goods anyway.

■**1813**
American ships under Oliver Hazard Perry defeat British fleet on Lake Erie and force British retreat into Canada.

■**1800**
Thomas Jefferson is elected President.

■**1812**
After war breaks out between the United States and Britain, USS *Constitution* defeats British warship in major sea battle.

"As President, I will enact a new set of policies!"

■**1811**
Shawnee leader Tecumseh organizes western Native American tribes to resist American expansion.

Washington, D.C.

UNITED STATES

Mississippi River

■**1814**
General Andrew Jackson leads American victory over Native American allies of the British at Battle of Horseshoe Bend.

■**1814**
During the War of 1812, the British attack Washington and burn government buildings, including the White House.

Atlantic Ocean

To Barbary States

■**1815**
Before news of peace treaty ending War of 1812 reaches America, Jackson defeats British at Battle of New Orleans.

°New Orleans

■**1801–1805**
Jefferson sends warships to the Mediterranean Sea to protect American shipping from pirates of the Barbary States.

Gulf of Mexico

| 1811 | Americans defeat Native Americans at Tippecanoe. | 1812 | United States declares war on Britain. | 1815 | Battle of New Orleans is fought. |

1810   **1815**   **1820**

| | Napoleon suffers final defeat at Battle of Waterloo. | 1815 | | 1819 | Simón Bolívar seizes Bogotá from the Spanish. |

◄ Jefferson Memorial statue in Washington, D.C.

Good Government

❝A wise and frugal Government . . . shall restrain men from injuring one another, . . . shall leave them otherwise free to regulate their own pursuits . . . , and shall not take from the mouth of labor the bread it has earned. This is the sum of good government.❞

—Thomas Jefferson, First Inaugural Address, 1801

Jefferson Takes Office

Objectives
- Describe the outcome of the election of 1800.
- Explain Jefferson's policies as President.
- Discuss the importance of *Marbury* v. *Madison.*

🔄 Reading Skill

Understand Sequence of Events A historian must master the sequence of events that make up a historical episode. To understand the sequence, determine what happened first, next, or last. Look for clues such as dates and sequence signal words. Compare when events occurred. This will help you identify connections between events.

Key Terms and People

Thomas Jefferson   John Marshall
Aaron Burr   judicial review
laissez faire

Why It Matters The Federalists had controlled the national government until the election of 1800. As a result of this election, the new Republican administration of Thomas Jefferson reversed some federalist policies. In fact, Jefferson referred to the election as the "Revolution of 1800."

❷ Section Focus Question: How did Jefferson chart a new course for the government?

Republicans Take Charge

Margaret Smith attended the inauguration of Thomas Jefferson as President of the United States in March 1801. After the inauguration, she wrote a letter explaining how proud she was of the United States. In other countries, the transfer of power usually involved "confusion . . . and bloodshed." However, "in our happy country" that transfer was peaceful and orderly.

A Bitter Campaign The presidential election of 1800 was viciously contested. The Federalists raised the prospect of civil war if Jefferson were elected. Republicans accused John Adams of wanting to create a monarchy.

By receiving 73 electoral votes, Jefferson defeated Adams. According to the Constitution, the person who received the next highest total of electoral votes would be Vice President. However, Aaron Burr, Jefferson's running mate, also received 73 votes. It was up to the House of Representatives to decide who would be President. For six days, the House was deadlocked. On the 36th vote, Jefferson won the election.

To avoid this situation in the future, the Twelfth Amendment to the Constitution changed how electors voted. Beginning in 1804, electors would vote separately for President and Vice President.

Jefferson's Inauguration Thomas Jefferson was the first President to be inaugurated in Washington, D.C., the country's new capital. Jefferson believed the government should be less <u>aristocratic</u>. To make the point, he walked to his inauguration instead of riding in a fancy carriage. He also ended the custom of people bowing to the President. Instead, they just shook his hand.

Jefferson used his inaugural address to bring a divided country together. He told the American people:

> **❝**Let us, then, fellow-citizens, unite with one heart and one mind. . . . Every difference of opinion is not a difference of principle. . . . We are all Republicans; we are all Federalists.**❞**
> —Thomas Jefferson, First Inaugural Address, March 4, 1801

☑**Checkpoint** **Why did the election of 1800 have to be decided in the House of Representatives?**

Jefferson Charts a New Course

Jefferson thought of his election as the "Revolution of 1800." Jefferson's first goal as President was to limit the federal government's power over states and citizens. The new President thought that under Washington and Adams the federal government had become too involved in economic affairs. He believed in the idea known as laissez faire (LEHS ay fehr), from the French term for "let alone." **Laissez faire** means that the government should not interfere in the economy.

New Republican Policies Jefferson put his laissez faire ideas into practice when he reduced the number of people in government. He fired all tax collectors and cut the number of U.S. diplomats.

Vocabulary Builder
<u>aristocratic</u> (uh ris tuh KRAT ik)
adj. of an aristocracy or upper class

Thomas Jefferson's Home
Thomas Jefferson designed his home, Monticello. In the design, he included elements of Greek architecture, such as columns, and Roman architecture, such as domes. **Critical Thinking: *Link Past and Present*** *What elements of Greek and Roman culture are still important to us today?*

Goals and Policies of Thomas Jefferson

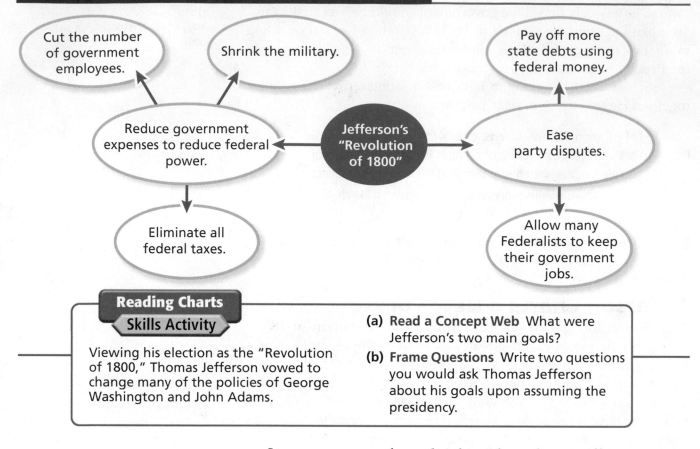

Reading Charts

Skills Activity

Viewing his election as the "Revolution of 1800," Thomas Jefferson vowed to change many of the policies of George Washington and John Adams.

(a) **Read a Concept Web** What were Jefferson's two main goals?

(b) **Frame Questions** Write two questions you would ask Thomas Jefferson about his goals upon assuming the presidency.

Vocabulary Builder
revenue (REV uh noo) **n.** the income from taxes, licenses, etc., as of a city, state, or nation

Larger cuts came from shrinking the military. Jefferson cut the army's budget in half, reducing the army's size from 4,000 to about 2,500 soldiers. At the same time, Jefferson eliminated all federal taxes inside the country. Now, most tax revenue came from the tariff on imported goods.

The Sedition Act was another of Jefferson's targets. As you have read, a number of people had been convicted and fined under the act. Jefferson ordered those fines refunded. Those imprisoned under the Sedition Act were released.

Federalist Policies Remain Jefferson could not reverse all Federalist policies. He believed that the United States had to keep repaying its national debt. He also did not fire most of the Federalist officeholders. He said they could keep their jobs if they did them well and were loyal citizens.

☑ **Checkpoint** **What action did Jefferson take as President to help those convicted under the Sedition Act?**

The Supreme Court and Judicial Review

One Federalist who did not keep his job was Judge William Marbury. Adams had appointed Marbury and several other judges in the last hours before he left office. The Republicans argued that these appointments were aimed at maintaining Federalist power.

When Jefferson took office, he ordered James Madison, his secretary of state, to cease work on the appointments. Marbury then sued Madison, citing the Judiciary Act of 1789. This act gave the Supreme Court the power to review cases brought against a federal official.

The outcome of the case forever changed the relationship of the three branches of government. In his ruling, Chief Justice John Marshall spoke for a unanimous Court. He ruled that the Judiciary Act of 1789 was unconstitutional. Marshall stated that the Court's powers came from the Constitution, not from Congress. Therefore, Congress did not have the right to give power to the Supreme Court in the Judiciary Act. Only the Constitution could do that.

The Court's actual decision—that it could not help Marbury gain his commission—was not highly significant. However, the ruling did set an important precedent. Marshall used the case of *Marbury* v. *Madison* to establish the principle of judicial review—the authority of the Supreme Court to strike down unconstitutional laws. Today, judicial review remains one of the most important powers of the Supreme Court.

☑ **Checkpoint** What is judicial review?

⭐ **Looking Back and Ahead** Thomas Jefferson had long argued that the federal government's powers were limited to what was set down in the Constitution. The Constitution did not specifically give the government the power to buy land from a foreign country. In the next section, you will read about Jefferson's dilemma when France offered to sell the United States the huge territory known as Louisiana.

Understand Sequence of Events
What words in this paragraph are clues to sequence?

Section 1 | Check Your Progress

Progress Monitoring Online
For: Self-test with instant help
Visit: PHSchool.com
Web Code: mya-3051

Comprehension and Critical Thinking

1. **(a) Recall** How did Jefferson's inauguration demonstrate the changes he planned for the U.S. government?
   (b) Apply Information How did Jefferson's policies change the American government?

2. **(a) Identify** What was Chief Justice Marshall's decision in the case of *Marbury* v. *Madison*?
   (b) Make Predictions How did the outcome of *Marbury* v. *Madison* affect the relationship of the three branches of government?

Reading Skill

3. **Understand Sequence of Events** Read the first paragraph under the heading "Jefferson Charts a New Course." What was Jefferson's *first* priority as President?

Key Terms

Read each sentence below. If the sentence is true, write YES. If the sentence is not true, write NO and explain why.

4. Jefferson believed in laissez faire, the idea that the federal government should not interfere in economic affairs.

5. John Marshall cited judicial review as the reason why only the Senate had the right to decide whether acts of Congress are constitutional.

Writing

6. Based on what you have read in this section about Jefferson's early days in office, write a thesis statement about Jefferson's influence on American government. Then, list the kinds of supporting information that would back up your thesis statement.

The Louisiana Territory

❝[The Missouri River] passes through a rich fertile and one of the most beautifully picturesque countries that I ever beheld. . . . Innumerable herds of living animals are seen. . . . Its lofty and open forests are the habitation of myriads of the feathered tribes.❞

—Meriwether Lewis, journal entry describing the Louisiana Territory, 1805

◀ Many Indian nations lived in the Louisiana Territory.

The Louisiana Purchase

Objectives
- Explain the importance of New Orleans and the crisis over its port.
- Describe how the United States gained the Louisiana Purchase.
- Discuss Lewis and Clark's expedition.

🔄 Reading Skill

Distinguish Events in Sequence As you read, it will help you to identify events that occur at about the same time in different locations. Ask yourself if these events share a common cause. Was there any advantage for people to make these events happen at the same time? Would faster communication have changed the sequence at all?

Key Terms and People

expedition	continental divide
Meriwether Lewis	Zebulon Pike
William Clark	

Why It Matters Jefferson focused on reducing the power and size of the federal government. But his foreign policy was more expansive. President Jefferson expanded the country's borders far to the west.

❓ Section Focus Question: What was the importance of the purchase and exploration of the Louisiana Territory?

The Nation Looks West

The tide of westward settlement speeded up in the years after the United States won independence. By 1800, more than one million settlers lived between the Appalachian Mountains and the Mississippi River.

Most western settlers were farmers. Because there were few roads in the West, they relied on the Mississippi River to ship their crops to the port at New Orleans. From there, the goods were loaded on ships and carried to markets in the East.

Spain, which controlled the Mississippi and New Orleans, had several times threatened to close the port to American ships. To prevent this from happening again, in 1795 the United States negotiated a treaty with Spain. The Pinckney Treaty guaranteed the Americans' right to ship their goods down the Mississippi to New Orleans. There, they could be stored until they were transferred to ocean-going ships for the journey east.

For a time, Americans shipped their goods through New Orleans peacefully. Then, in 1801, a crisis developed. Jefferson discovered that Spain had secretly given New Orleans and the rest of its Louisiana Territory to France.

Jefferson was alarmed by this development. The French ruler, Napoleon Bonaparte, had already set out to conquer Europe. Jefferson feared that he now intended to make France the <u>dominant</u> power in America as well. If Napoleon controlled Louisiana, the westward expansion of the United States would be blocked.

✔**Checkpoint** **What important right did the United States gain with the Pinckney Treaty of 1795?**

Buying Louisiana

Even before the actual transfer of Louisiana to France took place, America's position in Louisiana was threatened. In 1802, the Spanish governor of Louisiana withdrew the right of Americans to ship their goods through New Orleans. Westerners exploded in anger. They demanded that Jefferson go to war to win back their rights.

The situation was explosive. What would happen, Jefferson worried, when the French took over New Orleans?

A Surprise Offer The President decided the best approach was to try to buy the city of New Orleans from the French. He sent his friend James Monroe to France to make a deal. Monroe had the help of Robert Livingston, the American minister in Paris. Jefferson instructed the two men to buy New Orleans and a territory to the east called West Florida.

In Paris, the Americans discovered an <u>altered</u> situation. A revolution led by Toussaint L'Ouverture (too SAN loo vehr TYOOR) had driven the French from their Caribbean colony of Haiti. Without Haiti as a base, the French would have trouble defending Louisiana in the event of a war. At the same time, tensions between France and Britain were again on the rise. War was looming and Napoleon needed money to support the war effort. France offered to sell the United States not only New Orleans but the *entire* Louisiana Territory.

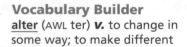

It would take months to get Jefferson's advice. So Livingston and Monroe agreed to buy the whole Louisiana Territory for $15 million— about 4 cents an acre. This included an enormous area stretching from the Gulf of Mexico to Canada and from the Mississippi River to the Rocky Mountains.

Haitian Independence
Toussaint L'Ouverture (right) helped lead the Haitian struggle to expel the French.
Critical Thinking: *Analyze Cause and Effect* *Why would France have trouble defending Louisiana if it did not control Haiti?*

Exploring the Louisiana Purchase

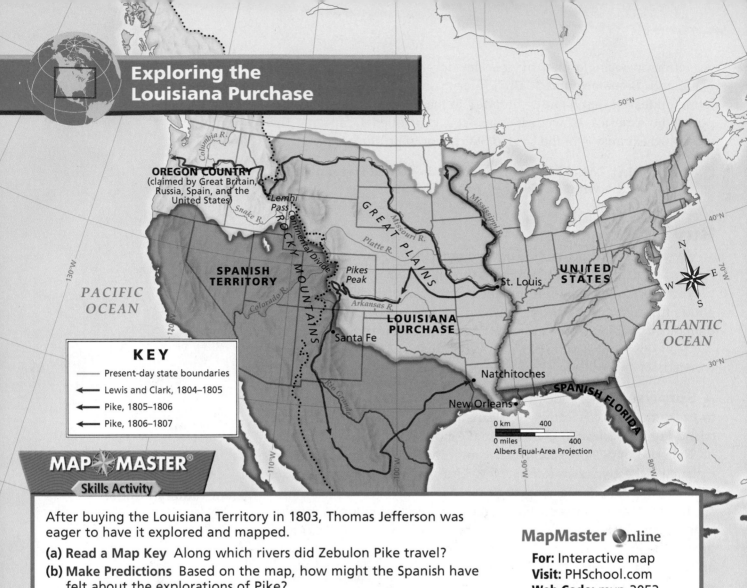

KEY

Present-day state boundaries

Lewis and Clark, 1804–1805

Pike, 1805–1806

Pike, 1806–1807

MAP MASTER®
Skills Activity

After buying the Louisiana Territory in 1803, Thomas Jefferson was eager to have it explored and mapped.

(a) Read a Map Key Along which rivers did Zebulon Pike travel?

(b) Make Predictions Based on the map, how might the Spanish have felt about the explorations of Pike?

MapMaster Online

For: Interactive map
Visit: PHSchool.com
Web Code: myp-3052

The Louisiana Purchase proved an amazing bargain for the United States. Its area almost doubled the size of the country. Although largely unexplored, the region clearly had millions of acres of fertile farmland and other natural resources. Ownership of Louisiana gave the United States control of the Mississippi River. As Livingston put it, "From this day, the United States take their place among the powers of the first rank."

Jefferson's Dilemma Jefferson was delighted with the deal. At the same time, he had a serious problem. The Constitution nowhere states that the President has the power to buy land from a foreign country. Adding the huge Louisiana Territory would dramatically change the character of the nation.

In the end, Jefferson decided that he did have authority to buy Louisiana. The Constitution, he reasoned, allowed the President to make treaties. The Senate approved the treaty and Congress quickly voted to pay for the land.

✓**Checkpoint** Why did President Jefferson hesitate to approve the purchase of the Louisiana Territory?

Lewis and Clark Explore the West

In January 1803, even before the United States had bought Louisiana, Jefferson convinced Congress to spend $2,500 on a western expedition (eks puh DISH uhn). An **expedition** is a long and carefully organized journey.

Jefferson chose army captain Meriwether Lewis to lead the exploration. Lewis chose William Clark, also an army officer, as his coleader. The men were ordered to report back on the geography, plants, animals, and other natural features of the region.

The expedition also had other goals. Jefferson wanted Lewis and Clark to make contact with Native Americans who lived in the Louisiana Territory. The President also wanted Lewis and Clark to find out if a waterway existed between the Mississippi River and the Pacific Ocean.

Into the Unknown In the spring of 1804, Lewis and Clark left St. Louis and headed up the Missouri River. Their three boats carried tons of supplies and about 40 men. Most were Americans, although there were several French Canadians. The expedition also included an enslaved African American named York.

In mid-July, the party reached the mouth of the Platte River, a powerful tributary that flows into the Missouri. In early August, they met Native Americans for the first time. Three weeks later, the expedition reached the eastern edge of the Great Plains.

Links Across Time

1969 American astronauts Buzz Aldrin (shown here) and Neil Armstrong landed on the moon.

Exploration

1804–1806 Lewis and Clark explored the lands of the Louisiana Purchase. Their journals, maps, and drawings inspired the rapid settlement of the West.

1960s American explorers ventured into the "new frontier" of outer space. On July 20, 1969, the United States became the first nation to land a man on the moon. People around the world watched the landing on television.

Link to Today

Exploration Today The United States has sent additional missions to the moon and beyond. What kinds of exploration are going on today?

For: Recent activities of the U.S. space program
Visit: PHSchool.com
Web Code: mvc-3052

**Lewis and Clark:
A Hard Journey**
At times during their travel up
the Missouri River, members
of the Lewis and Clark party
had to carry their boats
around rapids and falls.
*Critical Thinking: Apply
Information* *What other
hazards did Lewis and Clark
face on their river voyages?*

In late October 1804, the expedition reached the territory of the Mandan people, in what is now North Dakota. Lewis and Clark decided to camp there for the winter. They were joined in camp by a French Canadian trader and his wife, a Native American named Sacagawea (sahk uh juh WEE uh). She was a Shoshone (shoh SHOH nee) who would travel with them and serve as translator.

Crossing the Rockies In April 1805, the party set out again. By summer they were in what is now Montana. They began to climb the Rockies. By August, they had reached the Continental Divide. A **continental divide** is the place on a continent that separates river systems flowing in opposite directions. The view to the west was beautiful but also deeply disappointing. Lewis had hoped to see a wide river that would take the group to the Pacific. Instead, all he saw were "immense ranges of mountains still to the west."

The next day, Lewis met a group of Shoshone warriors. When Sacagawea arrived to interpret, she was astonished to see that the Shoshone chief was her brother. She jumped up and threw her arms around him. Thanks to Sacagawea, the Shoshones agreed to sell the expedition horses that were needed to cross the mountains.

At the Pacific On the west side of the Rockies, Lewis and Clark reached the Columbia River. Here, they stopped to build canoes for the downriver voyage. At one point, they had to cross a 55-mile stretch of rapids and rough water. Finally, through a dense early November fog, they saw the Pacific Ocean.

The travelers spent the wet and gloomy winter of 1805–1806 near the point where the Columbia River flows into the Pacific. They began the return journey in March 1806. It took the party half a year to return to St. Louis. Their return, however, brought the American people a new awareness of a rich and beautiful part of the continent.

Pike's Expedition At the same time that Lewis and Clark were trekking back home, other Americans also hoped to learn more about the West. From 1806 to 1807, Zebulon Pike explored the southern part of the Louisiana Territory.

Pike led an expedition due west to the Rocky Mountains. There, he tried to climb a mountain that rose out of the Colorado plains. He made it about two thirds of the way to the top. Standing in snow up to his waist, he was forced to turn back. Today, this mountain is known as Pikes Peak.

Pike's return route took him into Spanish New Mexico. Early in 1807, Spanish troops arrested the members of the party as spies. The Spanish feared Pike was gathering information so that the Americans could take over the region. After several months of captivity, the men were released and escorted back to the United States. As the Spanish had feared, Pike's reports about the Spanish borderlands created great American interest in the region.

✓**Checkpoint** **What goals did President Jefferson set for Lewis and Clark's expedition?**

☆ **Looking Back and Ahead** Lewis and Clark and Pike gave the United States detailed knowledge of the West. However, Americans had little time to digest this information. They soon found themselves caught up again in Europe's conflicts.

Distinguish Events in Sequence
What do the words "at the same time" tell you about the sequence of events? What was happening at the same time?

Section 2 | Check Your Progress

Progress Monitoring Online
For: Self-test with instant help
Visit: PHSchool.com
Web Code: mya-3052

Comprehension and Critical Thinking

1. **(a) Recall** Why was New Orleans important to the United States?
   (b) Identify Benefits What was the significance of the Louisiana Purchase?

2. **(a) Identify** Who was Sacagawea, and how was she important to the success of the Lewis and Clark expedition?
   (b) Compare and Contrast How was Pike's expedition similar to that of Lewis and Clark's? How was it different?

Reading Skill

3. **Distinguish Events in Sequence** Describe how the sequence of Lewis and Clark's expedition related to that of Zebulon Pike.

Key Terms

4. Draw a table with two rows and two columns. In the first column, list the key terms from this section: expedition, continental divide. In the next column, write the definition of each word.

Writing

5. Use this section and the following items to write a thesis statement about the life of Meriwether Lewis. **Items:** Born in 1774; Virginian; family friend of Jefferson; in 1792 asked by Jefferson to lead exploration of the Northwest; with Clark led expedition through Louisiana Territory; was appointed governor of Louisiana Territory in 1808; died mysteriously in 1809.

Exploring the Louisiana Purchase

An atmosphere of eager anticipation filled the air as Meriwether Lewis and William Clark and their men set out to explore the vast lands that lay west of the Mississippi River. Use the map below to follow Lewis and Clark on their journey to the Pacific Ocean.

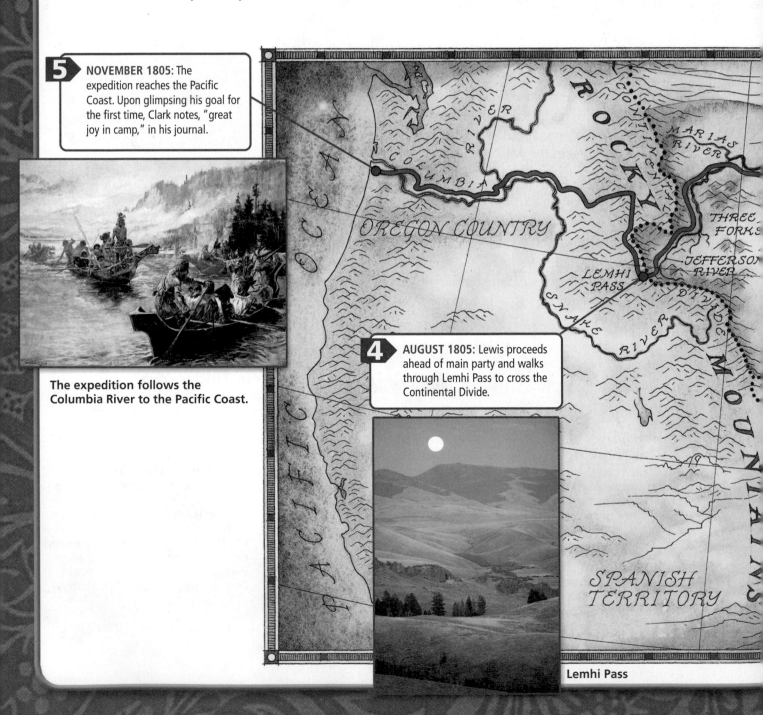

5 NOVEMBER 1805: The expedition reaches the Pacific Coast. Upon glimpsing his goal for the first time, Clark notes, "great joy in camp," in his journal.

The expedition follows the Columbia River to the Pacific Coast.

4 AUGUST 1805: Lewis proceeds ahead of main party and walks through Lemhi Pass to cross the Continental Divide.

Lemhi Pass

William Clark

Clark's compass ▲

Legacy of the Expedition

The explorers returned to St. Louis in 1806. Though the expedition was a success, it failed to excite the majority of Americans. Over time, however, the journey of Lewis and Clark contributed to a national feeling that Americans had a Manifest Destiny, a duty to expand west across the continent.

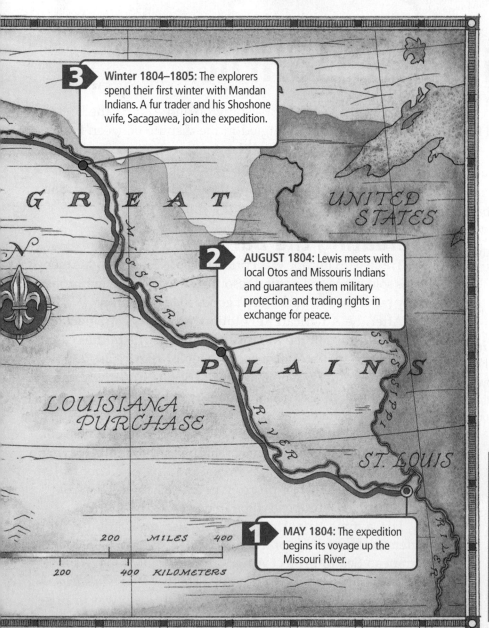

3 Winter 1804–1805: The explorers spend their first winter with Mandan Indians. A fur trader and his Shoshone wife, Sacagawea, join the expedition.

UNITED STATES

G R E A T

MISSOURI

2 AUGUST 1804: Lewis meets with local Otos and Missouris Indians and guarantees them military protection and trading rights in exchange for peace.

P L A I N S

MISSISSIPPI

LOUISIANA PURCHASE

RIVER

ST. LOUIS

200 MILES 400

200 400 KILOMETERS

RIVER

1 MAY 1804: The expedition begins its voyage up the Missouri River.

Meriwether Lewis

A page from Lewis's journal ▲

Analyze GEOGRAPHY AND HISTORY

Write a journal entry that expresses Lewis and Clark's excitement about crossing the Continental Divide. How did the explorers know they were closer to their goal?

This Dreadful Fight

❝The Indians are committing depredations [attacks] upon the white inhabitants located upon our Western frontier.... The British furnish them with arms, ammunition, and rations.... Many... are made widows and orphans by this dreadful fight.❞

—Lydia B. Bacon, wife of U.S. army officer in Indiana Territory, 1811

◀ American troops and Indians clash at the Battle of Tippecanoe.

A Time of Conflict

Objectives

- Discuss how the United States defeated the Barbary pirates.
- Explain how war in Europe hurt American trade.
- Discuss the causes and effects of the Embargo Act.
- Identify the events leading up to the Battle of Tippecanoe.

Reading Skill

Explain How Events Are Related in Time Many events that occur in sequence have cause-and-effect relationships. Explaining how events are related in time will help you find these cause-and-effect links. As you read this section, look for events that have this relationship.

Key Terms and People

tribute
Stephen Decatur
embargo
smuggling
Tecumseh
William Henry
    Harrison

Why It Matters Under Washington and Adams, the United States had become entangled in the dispute between France and Britain. That problem did not go away. It rose again with added fury during the administration of Thomas Jefferson.

❓ **Section Focus Question: How did Jefferson respond to threats to the security of the nation?**

Defeating the Barbary States

Trade with Europe was critical to the U.S. economy. Americans sold crops and natural resources to customers in Europe. They purchased manufactured goods made in Europe.

After the American Revolution, pirates began attacking American ships in the Mediterranean Sea. The pirates came from four small countries on the North African coast—Morocco, Algiers, Tunisia, and Tripoli. Together, these countries were known as the Barbary States.

Barbary pirates raided European and American ships, taking property and enslaving sailors and holding them for ransom. European governments stopped such raids by paying the Barbary States tribute—money paid by one country to another in return for protection. In exchange, their rulers agreed to leave European ships alone.

For a time, the United States also paid tribute. But Jefferson stopped this practice and sent warships to the Mediterranean Sea to protect American merchant ships. At first, these military patrols went badly. The warship *Philadelphia* ran aground near the Tripoli coast and its crew was imprisoned. To keep the pirates from using the ship, American sailors led by Stephen Decatur raided Tripoli harbor in 1804 and burned the *Philadelphia* down to the waterline.

The next year, a small force of American marines marched 600 miles across the Sahara and captured Tripoli. A line in the U.S. Marine Corps anthem—"To the shores of Tripoli"—recalls that victory. It inspired a wave of confidence in the ability of the United States to deal forcefully with foreign powers that threatened American security and prosperity.

✓**Checkpoint** **How did European nations protect themselves against raids by the Barbary pirates?**

American Neutrality Is Challenged

A more serious threat to American overseas trade came from two much more powerful countries, Britain and France. By 1803, the two nations once again were at war. The United States remained neutral.

Because it was neutral, the United States continued trading with both Britain and France. The war in Europe had created opportunities for Americans to sell their products there.

Meanwhile, Britain and France looked for ways to weaken each other. One method was to cut off the other country's foreign trade. British warships started seizing American ships trading with France. French warships did the same to American ships trading with Britain. Between 1803 and 1807, France seized 500 American ships and Britain seized more than 1,000.

Britain badly needed sailors for its war against France. So it turned again to impressment. As a result, thousands of American sailors were forced to serve in the British navy.

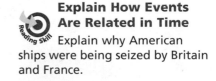

Explain How Events Are Related in Time
Explain why American ships were being seized by Britain and France.

Impressment
A nineteenth-century woodprint shows unfortunate American sailors being impressed by British gangs. Conditions on board British warships were harsh.
Critical Thinking: *Draw Conclusions* *What impact do you think impressment had on the performance of the British navy?*

Carving Up the World

Pitt   Napoleon

Reading Political Cartoons

Skills Activity

Britain's Prime Minister William Pitt and French leader Napoleon Bonaparte are shown dividing the world in this American cartoon. Their rivalry drew the United States into a conflict it did not want to enter.

(a) Identify Main Ideas What portion of the globe is Napoleon taking? What portion is Pitt taking?

(b) Detect Points of View What do you think the cartoonist's opinion is of the two European leaders?

Beginning in 1805, Britain and France increased their efforts to attack trade with their foes. No matter what American merchant ships did, they risked being seized by either Britain or France.

✓**Checkpoint** **Why did Britain and France attack American merchant ships?**

Jefferson Responds With an Embargo

The President looked for peaceful methods to force Britain and France to respect American neutrality. He decided to use an **embargo**—a government order that forbids foreign trade. In 1807, Congress passed the Embargo Act. It imposed a total embargo on American ships sailing to any foreign port. Jefferson predicted that both countries would soon cease attacking American ships.

Things did not turn out as Jefferson expected. Indeed, the big loser proved to be the United States. In just one year, American exports fell from $109 million to $25 million. Prices of American crops <u>declined</u>, hurting farmers and planters. Tens of thousands of Americans lost their jobs.

Vocabulary Builder
<u>decline</u> (dee KLĪN) **v.** to gradually lose strength or power

Many Americans were outraged by the embargo. Anger was greatest in New England, where merchants depended heavily on foreign trade. Thousands of Americans turned to **smuggling**—the act of illegally importing or exporting goods—in order to evade the embargo.

Congress finally repealed the Embargo Act in 1809, just before Jefferson left office. Then, Congress passed a less severe law that reopened foreign trade with every country except Britain and France. The law stated that the United States would reopen trade with those countries when they started respecting America's trading rights as a neutral nation.

☑Checkpoint Why did President Jefferson place an embargo on foreign goods in 1807?

Tecumseh and the Prophet

In the years after the Battle of Fallen Timbers, tens of thousands of settlers moved westward. Ohio became a state in 1803. Americans continued to push into new areas. They settled in the territory of Indiana and other lands farther west.

The tide of settlement had a grave impact on Native Americans. Diseases such as measles, smallpox, and influenza killed thousands of Native Americans who had never been exposed to such diseases before. Settlers took over large parts of the Native American hunting grounds. Deer and other animals the Native Americans depended on were driven away as farmers cleared the forests for planting. The Native American population decreased, and the power of their traditional leaders declined.

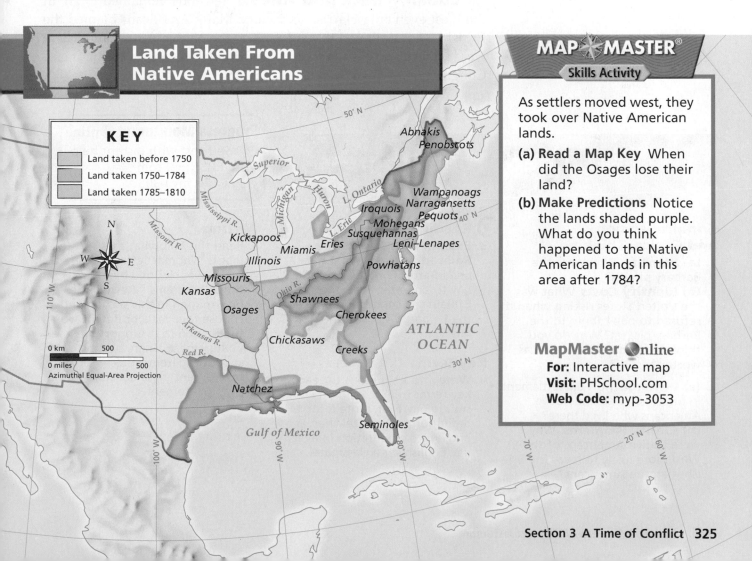

Land Taken From Native Americans

KEY
- Land taken before 1750
- Land taken 1750–1784
- Land taken 1785–1810

MAP☀MASTER®
Skills Activity

As settlers moved west, they took over Native American lands.

(a) Read a Map Key When did the Osages lose their land?

(b) Make Predictions Notice the lands shaded purple. What do you think happened to the Native American lands in this area after 1784?

MapMaster Online
For: Interactive map
Visit: PHSchool.com
Web Code: myp-3053

New Leaders Take Charge The Shawnee people were hard hit by these developments. After 1805, two Shawnee brothers—Tenskwatawa (tehn SKWAH tuh wuh) and Tecumseh (tih KUHM suh)—began urging Native American resistance. Tecumseh and Tenskwatawa, who was also known as the Prophet, called on Native Americans to preserve traditional ways.

Tecumseh organized the western tribes into a league to restore Indian lands. He traveled widely spreading his message.

Harrison's Victory American officials were deeply concerned by Tecumseh's activities. In 1811, William Henry Harrison, governor of the Indiana Territory, decided to take action. While Tecumseh was traveling in search of allies, Harrison marched a thousand soldiers against Shawnee villages on the Tippecanoe River. In the Battle of Tippecanoe, Harrison defeated the Native Americans.

The Battle of Tippecanoe marked the high point of Native American opposition to settlement. Even though the alliance declined in power after the battle, Tecumseh and his warriors continued their struggle during the next several years.

✓**Checkpoint** **What actions did Tecumseh and the Prophet urge on their followers?**

☆ **Looking Back and Ahead** Tensions remained high in the West even after Harrison's victory. Many Americans blamed the British, who continued to send arms to the Native Americans. There were widespread calls for war with Britain. Could the President and Congress resist them?

Section 3 | **Check Your Progress**

Progress Monitoring Online
For: Self-test with instant help
Visit: PHSchool.com
Web Code: mya-3053

Comprehension and Critical Thinking

1. **(a) Identify** Who were the Barbary pirates?
   (b) Identify Costs What was the United States risking when it refused to pay tribute to the Barbary pirates? Why do you think Jefferson believed it was worth the risk?

2. **(a) Describe** How did settlement in the West affect the Native Americans who lived there?
   (b) Clarify Problems Why were Native Americans of the West more likely to favor the British than the Americans?

Reading Skill

3. **Explain How Events Are Related in Time** What happened after Congress passed a law to undo the Embargo Act? Explain the connection between the Embargo Act and the new law.

Key Terms

4. Write two definitions for each key term: tribute, embargo, smuggling. First, write a formal definition for your teacher. Second, write a definition in everyday English for a classmate.

Writing

5. Read the following thesis statement: "Thomas Jefferson's presidency was clouded by international problems." Review the information in this section and choose four facts or details from the section that support this thesis statement. Then, based on the supporting items you chose, write several sentences developing the thesis statement.

I Must Leave This House

❝I am still here within sound of the cannon! . . . I have had [a wagon] filled with the . . . most valuable portable articles. . . . I insist on waiting until the large picture of Gen. Washington is secured. . . . And now, dear sister, I must leave this house.❞

—Dolley Madison, letter describing British attack on the White House, 1814

◄ British soldiers attack Washington, D.C.

The War of 1812

Objectives
- Explain why the United States declared war on Britain.
- Describe what happened in the early days of the war.
- Discuss the American invasion of Canada and the fighting in the South.
- Identify the events leading to the end of the War of 1812.

🎯 Reading Skill

Explain How Events Are Related in Time Events can be related in time in many ways. One event may directly cause another or events may unfold over time. As you read this section, try to relate the many events to one another in time. Use the skills you practiced in Sections 1–3 as tools. Also, use sequence verbs as a tool. These verbs describe how events progress over time.

Key Terms and People

nationalism
war hawk
blockade

Oliver Hazard
Perry
Andrew Jackson
secede

Why It Matters Presidents Washington, Adams, and Jefferson had all worked hard to avoid war with Britain and France. But finally, in 1812, the United States declared war on Britain.

❓ Section Focus Question: What were the causes and effects of the War of 1812?

The Move Toward War

Tension with Britain was high when James Madison took office in 1809. Americans were angry at Britain for arming Native Americans in the Northwest. Americans also resented the continued impressment of American sailors by the British.

To most Americans, the country's honor was at stake. They felt a new sense of American nationalism—pride in one's country. In 1810, two strong nationalists, Henry Clay of Kentucky and John C. Calhoun of South Carolina, became leaders in the House of Representatives.

Clay, Calhoun, and their supporters were called war hawks—those who were eager for war with Britain. Opposition to war was strongest in New England. Many New Englanders believed war with Britain would harm American trade.

Relations with Britain worsened steadily in the early months of 1812. In the spring, the British told the United States they would continue impressing sailors. Meanwhile, Native Americans in the Northwest began new attacks on frontier settlements. In June, Congress declared war on Britain.

☑**Checkpoint** **In what regions of the United States was the support for war with Britain the strongest?**

Early Days of the War

The war did not come at a good time for the British, who were still at war in Europe. However, Britain was not willing to meet American demands to avoid war. Providing Native Americans with support was one way of protecting Canada against an American invasion.

When the war began, Americans were confident that they would win. It soon became apparent that the United States was not prepared for war. Jefferson's spending cuts had weakened American military strength. The navy had only 16 warships ready for action. The army also was small, with fewer than 7,000 men.

In the first days of the war, the British set up a blockade of the American coast. A **blockade** is the action of shutting a port or road to prevent people or supplies from coming into an area or leaving it. By 1814, the British navy had 135 warships blockading American ports. After reinforcing their troops, the British were able to close off all American ports by war's end.

A major sea battle was fought at the beginning of the war. In August 1812, the USS *Constitution* defeated the British warship *Guerrière* (gai ree AIR) in a fierce battle. According to tradition, American sailors nicknamed the *Constitution* "Old Ironsides" because British artillery fire bounced off the ship's thick wooden hull. To the Americans, it seemed as if the *Constitution* were made of iron.

✓Checkpoint **Why was the United States unprepared for war?**

Vocabulary Builder
reinforce (ree ihn FORS) **v.** to strengthen with additional troops

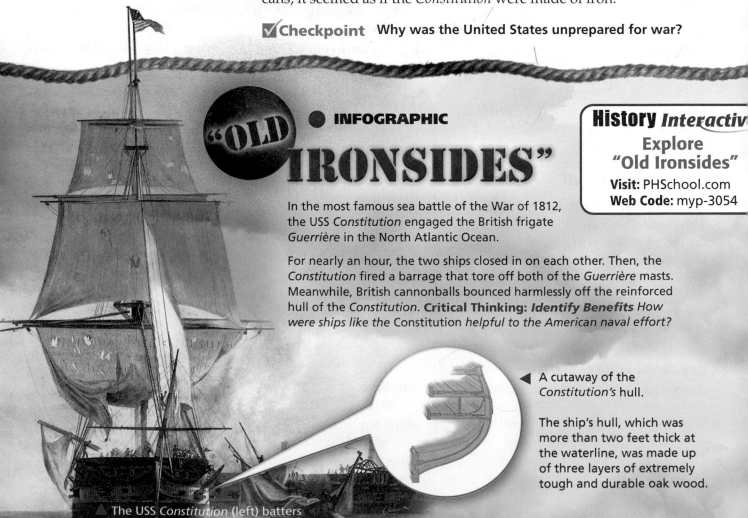

● **INFOGRAPHIC**

"OLD IRONSIDES"

History *Interactiv*
Explore "Old Ironsides"
Visit: PHSchool.com
Web Code: myp-3054

In the most famous sea battle of the War of 1812, the USS *Constitution* engaged the British frigate *Guerrière* in the North Atlantic Ocean.

For nearly an hour, the two ships closed in on each other. Then, the *Constitution* fired a barrage that tore off both of the *Guerrière* masts. Meanwhile, British cannonballs bounced harmlessly off the reinforced hull of the *Constitution*. **Critical Thinking:** *Identify Benefits How were ships like the* Constitution *helpful to the American naval effort?*

◀ A cutaway of the *Constitution's* hull.

The ship's hull, which was more than two feet thick at the waterline, was made up of three layers of extremely tough and durable oak wood.

The USS *Constitution* (left) batters the British ship HMS *Guerrière* (right).

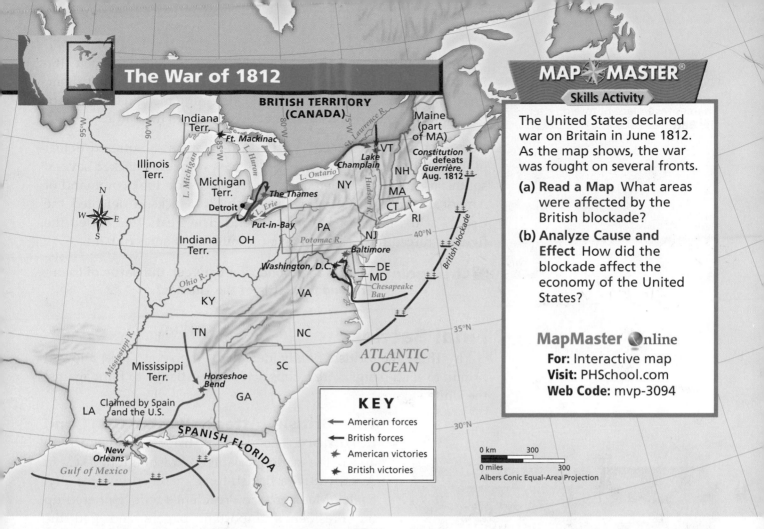

The War of 1812

MAP MASTER®
Skills Activity

BRITISH TERRITORY (CANADA)

Indiana Terr.
Ft. Mackinac
Illinois Terr.
Michigan Terr.
L. Michigan
L. Huron
The Thames
Detroit
L. Erie
Put-in-Bay
Indiana Terr.
OH
Ohio R.
KY
TN
Mississippi Terr.
Horseshoe Bend
GA
Claimed by Spain and the U.S.
LA
SPANISH FLORIDA
New Orleans
Gulf of Mexico

Maine (part of MA)
St. Lawrence R.
VT
Lake Champlain
L. Ontario
NH
NY
MA
Hudson R.
CT
RI
PA
NJ
Potomac R.
Baltimore
Washington, D.C.
DE
MD
Chesapeake Bay
VA
NC
SC
ATLANTIC OCEAN

Constitution defeats Guerrière, Aug. 1812

British blockade

40°N
35°N
30°N

KEY
← American forces
← British forces
★ American victories
★ British victories

The United States declared war on Britain in June 1812. As the map shows, the war was fought on several fronts.

(a) Read a Map What areas were affected by the British blockade?

(b) Analyze Cause and Effect How did the blockade affect the economy of the United States?

MapMaster Online
For: Interactive map
Visit: PHSchool.com
Web Code: mvp-3094

0 km 300
0 miles 300
Albers Conic Equal-Area Projection

The War in the West and South

In the West, the Americans and British fought for control of the Great Lakes and the Mississippi River. Both sides had Native American allies.

Invasion of Canada Even before the war began, war hawks were demanding an invasion of Canada. They expected Canadians to welcome the chance to throw off British rule.

In July 1812, American troops under General William Hull invaded Canada from Detroit. Hull was unsure of himself. Fearing he did not have enough soldiers, he soon retreated.

The British commander, General Isaac Brock, took advantage of Hull's confusion. His army of British soldiers and Native American warriors quickly surrounded Hull's army and forced it to surrender. The British captured more than 2,000 American soldiers. It was a serious defeat for the United States.

American forces had better luck on Lake Erie. Both sides were aware of the importance of controlling the lake. A key three-hour battle took place at Put-In-Bay, in the western part of the lake, in 1813.

During the battle, the American flagship was badly damaged. The American commander, Oliver Hazard Perry, switched to another ship and continued the fight until it was won. Perry announced his victory with a dramatic message: "We have met the enemy and they are ours." With Americans in control of the lake, the British were forced to leave Detroit and retreat back into Canada.

Explain How Events Are Related in Time
Did the Battle of the Thames take place before or after the Battle of Lake Erie?

As the British and their Native American allies retreated, the Americans under General William Henry Harrison pursued them. They followed the British into Canada, defeating them in the Battle of the Thames. Tecumseh was among those killed in the battle.

Conflict in the South Native Americans also suffered defeat in the South. In the summer of 1813, Creek warriors attacked several southern American settlements. Andrew Jackson took command of American forces in Georgia. In March 1814, Jackson defeated the Creeks at the Battle of Horseshoe Bend. The treaty that ended the fighting forced the Creeks to give up millions of acres of land.

✓**Checkpoint** What is the connection between the Battle of Lake Erie and the Battle of the Thames?

Final Battles

In 1814, the British finally defeated Napoleon. This allowed Britain to send many more troops across the Atlantic to fight against the United States.

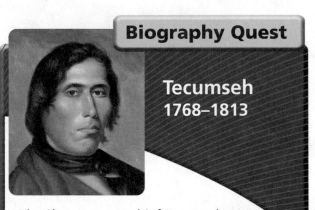

Biography Quest

Tecumseh
1768–1813

The Shawnee war chief Tecumseh challenged the tide of white settlement. Tecumseh visited Native Americans from the Great Lakes to Florida, urging them to unite. He was away recruiting when General Harrison defeated the Shawnee at Tippecanoe. After the battle, Tecumseh allied his forces with the British, hoping that a British victory would mean the return of Native American lands. His death at the Battle of the Thames dealt a blow to Native American resistance.

Biography Quest ⦿nline

Why did Tecumseh issue an angry challenge to his allies, the British?

For: The answer to the question about Tecumseh

Visit: PHSchool.com

Web Code: myd-3054

The British Attack Washington and Baltimore The new British strategy was to attack the nation's capital, Washington, D.C. In August 1814, a British force marched into the city. Dolley Madison, the President's wife, gathered up the President's important papers and fled the White House. The British set fire to several government buildings, including the White House. Americans were shocked to learn that their army could not defend Washington.

The British now moved on to Baltimore. Their first objective was Fort McHenry, which defended the city's harbor. British warships bombarded the fort throughout the night of September 13, 1814. Francis Scott Key, a young American, watched the attack. At dawn, Key saw the American flag still flying over the fort. The Americans had beaten off the attack.

On the back of an old envelope, Key wrote a poem that he called "The Star-Spangled Banner." It told the story of his night's watch. The poem became popular and was set to music. In 1931, Congress made it the national anthem of the United States.

The War Ends By 1814, Britain had tired of war. Peace talks began in Ghent (gehnt), Belgium. On Christmas Eve 1814, the two sides signed the Treaty of Ghent, which ended the war. The treaty returned things to the way they had been before the war.

News of the treaty took several weeks to reach the United States. In that time, the two sides fought one more battle. In January 1815, American forces under General Andrew Jackson won a stunning victory over the British at the Battle of New Orleans.

Protests and Peace From the start, there had been opposition to the War of 1812 within the United States. As the war dragged on, Federalist <u>critics</u> of President Madison spoke out more strongly, criticizing what they called "Mr. Madison's War." New Englanders in particular disliked the war, mainly because the blockade had badly damaged New England trade.

In December 1814, a group of Federalists met in Hartford, Connecticut. Some delegates to the Hartford Convention suggested that the New England states secede, or withdraw, from the United States. While the delegates debated, news of the peace treaty arrived. With the war over, the Hartford Convention quickly ended.

To some Americans, the War of 1812 was the "Second War of Independence." Once and for all, the United States secured its independence from Britain. European nations would now have to treat the young republic with respect. Pride at this achievement brought the confidence of Americans to a new height.

☑**Checkpoint** **What was the purpose of the Hartford Convention?**

☆ **Looking Back and Ahead** After the War of 1812, Americans entered a new era of confidence. Tensions between regions, which had been high during the war, cooled with the coming of peace. In the postwar period, Americans enjoyed a period of calm and unity. As you will read in the next chapter, this era paved the way for a major expansion of American democracy.

Vocabulary Builder
<u>critic</u> (KRIHT ihk) **n.** someone who makes judgments on the value of actions

Section 4 | **Check Your Progress**

Comprehension and Critical Thinking

1. (a) **Identify** Who were the war hawks? Why did they push for war with Britain?
(b) **Draw Conclusions** Were the war hawks overconfident? What did they overlook in their evaluation of British power?

2. (a) **Recall** How did the War of 1812 end?
(b) **Analyze Cause and Effect** What were some results of the war that were not expressly written in the treaty?

Reading Skill

3. **Explain How Events Are Related in Time** What battle was taking place at about the same time that William Hull was invading Canada?

Key Terms

Add a second sentence to each of the following sentences that clearly shows your understanding of the key term.
4. The War of 1812 increased U.S. nationalism. _____.
5. At the Hartford Convention, dissatisfied Federalists made plans for the New England states to secede. _____.

Writing

6. Read the following notes about First Lady Dolley Madison and rearrange them in the best order for a biographical essay. **Notes:** Died in 1849; stylish woman; married James Madison in 1794; served as President Jefferson's official hostess; saved many valuables from White House when British invaded in 1814; turned Washington from a "dull swamp" into lively social city.

21st Century Learning   When reading a historical document, it is important to remember that the writer has a particular point of view, or way of looking at a subject. It is also important to consider how events of the time may have influenced the author's feelings.

The Danbury Baptist Association wrote to President Jefferson, asking why he would not establish national days of fasting and thanksgiving, as previous Presidents had done. Jefferson answered the letter in 1802. His carefully worded reply reflects his opinion about the separation of government and religion in the new nation.

Primary Source

"Believing with you that religion is a matter which lies solely between man & his god, that he owes account to none other for his faith or his worship, that the legitimate powers of government reach actions only, and not opinions, I contemplate with sovereign reverence that act of the whole American people which declared that their legislature should make no law respecting an establishment of religion, or prohibiting the free exercise thereof, thus building a wall of separation between church and state."

—Thomas Jefferson, Jan. 1, 1802

Learn the Skill

Use these steps to put historical points of view in context.

1 **Identify the context.** If you know the history of the period when a document was written, you can better understand the writer's point of view.

2 **Identify the main idea.** What main point does the writer make?

3 **Look for important words or phrases.** The writer may use key words or phrases that sum up the point of view being expressed.

4 **Identify point of view.** How does the writer or speaker feel about the subject?

5 **Relate point of view to context.** How was the point of view affected by historical context?

Practice the Skill

Answer the following questions about the primary source on this page.

1 **Identify the context.** (a) Why was this letter written? (b) How did the Bill of Rights address the issue of an American national church?

2 **Identify the main idea.** What is the main point of this letter?

3 **Look for important words or phrases.** What is an example of a key word or phrase that sums up the writer's point of view?

4 **Identify point of view.** How does the writer feel about the subject of the letter?

5 **Relate point of view to context.** How was Jefferson's point of view influenced by the events of the time?

Apply the Skill

See the Review and Assessment at the end of this chapter.

Quick Study Guide

How did Jefferson and Madison deal with unresolved problems?

Section 1
Jefferson Takes Office

- The Twelfth Amendment was added to the Constitution to prevent the deadlock in government that occurred when Jefferson and Burr received the same number of electoral votes in the election of 1800.
- In *Marbury* v. *Madison,* Chief Justice John Marshall and the Supreme Court established judicial review.

Section 2
The Louisiana Purchase

- In 1803, the United States purchased the Louisiana Territory from France.
- The Louisiana Purchase gave the United States control of the Mississippi River.
- Jefferson sent Lewis and Clark on an expedition to explore the new territory.

Section 3
A Time of Conflict

- In an attempt to punish Britain and France, Jefferson proposed the Embargo Act. The embargo hurt the U.S. economy.
- Native Americans were defeated when they opposed U.S. settlement in the Northwest Territory.

Section 4
The War of 1812

- The war hawks blamed Britain for trouble with the Native Americans and decreased trade.
- The War of 1812 ended without a clear victor, but the United States achieved a new sense of nationalism.

? Exploring the Essential Question

Use the online study guide to explore the essential question.

Section 1
How did Jefferson chart a new course for the government?

Section 2
What was the importance of the purchase and exploration of the Louisiana Territory?

Chapter 9 Essential Question
How did Jefferson and Madison deal with unresolved problems?

Section 4
What were the causes and effects of the War of 1812?

Section 3
How did Jefferson respond to threats to the security of the nation?

Key Terms
Fill in the blanks with the correct key terms.

1. The principle of _____ gave the Supreme Court a central role in American government.

2. Lewis and Clark's _____ inspired many Americans to move west.

3. When Congress repealed Jefferson's _____ on trade, foreign trade was allowed again with every country except Britain and France.

4. During the Embargo Act, thousands of Americans turned to _____.

5. After crossing the _____ in the Rocky Mountains, Lewis and Clark began traveling on rivers that flowed to the Pacific Ocean.

Comprehension and Critical Thinking

6. (a) **Recall** What was Jefferson's view about the powers the federal government should have?
(b) **Clarify Problems** How did he apply these views to the situation of buying Louisiana?
(c) **Draw Conclusions** Use these situations and other information from the chapter to evaluate Jefferson's record as President.

7. (a) **Summarize** Why did Jefferson not want to keep William Marbury and other last-minute appointments of former President Adams on the federal payroll?
(b) **Explain Problems** How did Chief Justice John Marshall deal with the problem created by James Madison's inaction?

8. (a) **Describe** What obstacles did Lewis and Clark's expedition encounter?
(b) **Draw Conclusions** In what ways did Lewis and Clark's expedition help western settlers?
(c) **Link Past and Present** What modern-day explorations compare to Lewis and Clark's and Pike's expeditions?

9. (a) **Recall** What was the Embargo Act of 1807?
(b) **Identify Alternatives** What did Congress do to ease the economic effects of the embargo?

10. (a) **Summarize** What were the goals of Tecumseh and the Prophet?
(b) **Detect Points of View** How did settler views differ from Shawnee views?

11. (a) **Recall** Why were many Native Americans allied with the British during the War of 1812?
(b) **Identify Costs** Do you think siding with the British military helped or hurt the Native American cause? Explain.

History Reading Skill
12. **Relate Events in Time** Read the text under the heading "Lewis and Clark Explore the West." Which of these events happened first: Lewis and Clark headed up the Missouri River, or Lewis and Clark reached the mouth of the Platte River? What signal words offer clues to the sequence?

Writing
13. Write two paragraphs discussing Thomas Jefferson's experiences as President.
Your paragraphs should:
• begin with a thesis statement that expresses your main impressions;
• expand on that main idea with facts, examples, and other information;
• conclude by stating Jefferson's most important contribution to the new nation.

14. **Write a Narrative:**
What would it have been like to be an American sailor impressed by the British? Write a paragraph describing what the experience might have been like. Be sure to describe the conflicting emotions sailors may have felt.

Skills for Life
Detect Historical Points of View
Use the quotation below to answer the questions.

"I consider the government of the United States as [prevented] by the Constitution from intermeddling religious institutions, their doctrines, discipline, or exercise. This results not only from the provision that no law shall be made respecting the establishment, or free exercise, of religion, but from that also which reserves to the states the powers not delegated to the U.S."

—Thomas Jefferson, to Samuel Miller, Jan. 23, 1808

15. What is Jefferson's point of view?

16. How was Jefferson's point of view affected by historical events?

Test Yourself

1. **Which of the following of Jefferson's policies negatively affected the American ability to fight the British in the War of 1812?**

   A the increase of federal taxes

   B the Embargo Act of 1807

   C the purchase of the Louisiana Territory

   D the reduction of the military

2. **Which present-day states were formed from the Louisiana Purchase?**

   A Pennsylvania, New York, Massachusetts, and Maine

   B South Dakota, Nebraska, Kansas, and Oklahoma

   C Washington, Oregon, California, and Nevada

   D South Carolina, Virginia, Florida, and Georgia

Refer to the quotation below to answer Question 3.

"Where are the Narragansett, the Mohican, the Pocanet, and other powerful tribes of our people? They have vanished before the avarice and oppression of the white man. . . . Will we let ourselves be destroyed in our turn?. . . Shall we, without a struggle, give up our homes . . .?"

3. **Who was the likely speaker of this quotation?**

   A President Thomas Jefferson

   B Chief Justice John Marshall

   C Native American leader Tecumseh

   D Secretary of State John Quincy Adams

Document-Based Questions

Task: Look at Documents 1 and 2, and answer their accompanying questions. Then, use the documents and your knowledge of history to complete this writing assignment:

Write a draft of a document explaining New England's opposition to the War of 1812 and expressing the region's views on the rights of states to challenge, or even separate from, the federal government.

Document 1: During the War of 1812, the British blockaded American ports. *Based on this map, how would the blockade affect merchants in New England?*

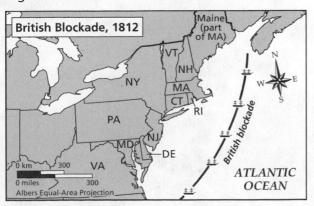

British Blockade, 1812

Document 2: In 1814, New Englanders meeting in the Hartford Convention called for increased states' rights and even considered secession from the Union. *In the portion of the document below, issued by the Hartford Convention, what causes are cited as reasons for separating from the Union?*

"Events may prove that the causes of our calamities are deep and permanent. . . . They may be traced to implacable combinations of individuals, or of states, to monopolize power and office, and to trample without remorse upon the rights and interests of commercial sections of the Union.

Whenever it shall appear that these causes are radical and permanent, a separation, by equitable arrangement, will be preferable to an alliance by constraint, among nominal friends. . . ."

A Changing Nation

1815–1840

"*[President] Jackson is the majority's slave; he yields to its intentions, desires, and half-revealed instincts, or rather he anticipates...them.*"

—Alexis de Tocqueville,
Democracy in America, 1835

This engraving, *Stump Speaking*, captures the energy of an election rally during the era of Jacksonian democracy.

What You Will Learn

Reading Skill

Analyze Cause and Effect In this chapter, you will learn to identify causes and their effects to help connect and understand historical events and issues.

A Changing Nation

Growing National Power, 1815–1840

1. **Building Infrastructure:** Government uses tax revenues to build a network of canals and roads.

2. **Second Bank of the United States:** Congress reestablishes the national bank to issue loans and control the money supply.

3. **Protective Tariffs:** Congress passes taxes on foreign goods to help American manufacturers.

4. **Supreme Court Rulings:** Court promotes national economic growth and the power of the federal government.

5. **Relations With Spain:** Andrew Jackson recaptures runaway slaves in Spanish Florida; attack leads Spain to sell Florida to the United States.

6. **Monroe Doctrine:** United States will not allow European colonies or influence in the Americas.

7. **Relations With Canada:** Border disputes are settled with Britain; United States further stabilizes its northern border.

8. **Indian Removal:** Native Americans are pressured to move west of the Mississippi; some leave Southeast peacefully, others removed by force.

9. **Nullification Crisis:** South Carolina cancels federal tariff laws and threatens to secede; Jackson and Calhoun divided over states' rights.

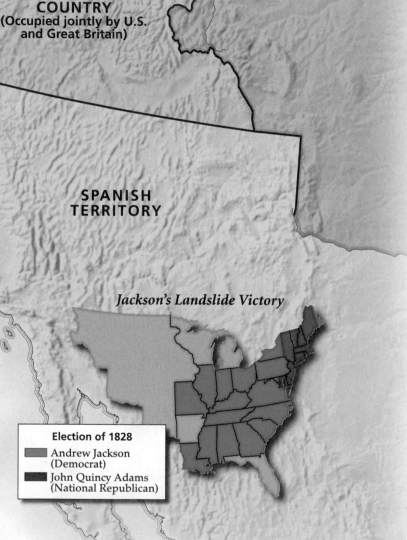

OREGON COUNTRY
(Occupied jointly by U.S. and Great Britain)

SPANISH TERRITORY

Jackson's Landslide Victory

Election of 1828
- Andrew Jackson (Democrat)
- John Quincy Adams (National Republican)

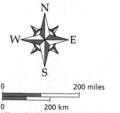

N W E S

0 — 200 miles
0 — 200 km
Albers Conic Equal-Area Projection

U.S. Events

Congress passes Tariff of 1816. | **1816**

| **1819**

McCulloch v. *Maryland* strengthens federal government.

1823 | Monroe Doctrine is issued.

1810   **1818**   **1826**

World Events

Spain cedes Florida to United States. | **1819**

1821 | Spain recognizes independence of Mexico.

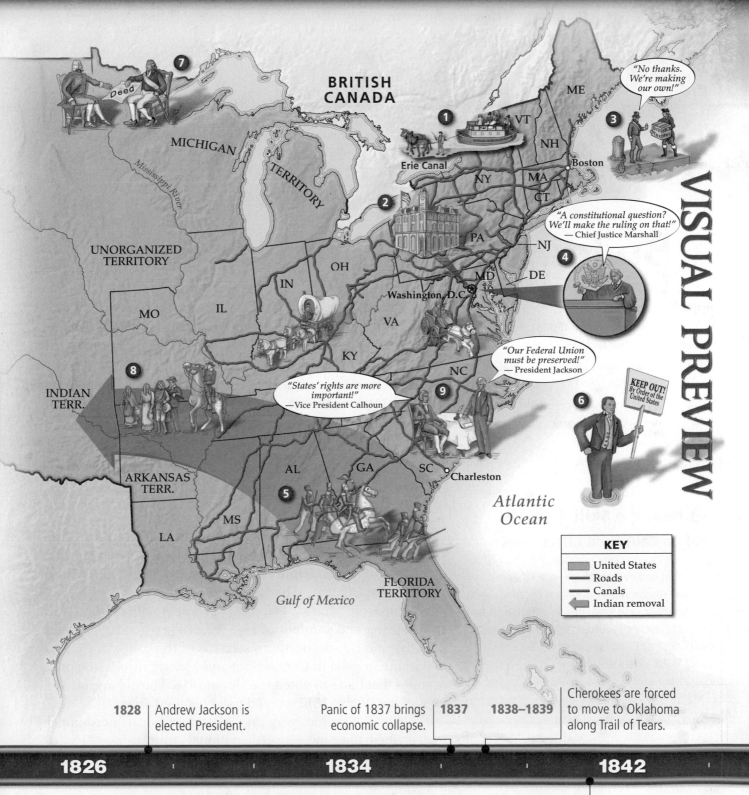

VISUAL PREVIEW

"No thanks. We're making our own!"

"A constitutional question? We'll make the ruling on that!" — Chief Justice Marshall

"Our Federal Union must be preserved!" — President Jackson

"States' rights are more important!" — Vice President Calhoun

KEEP OUT! By Order of the United States

KEY
- United States
- Roads
- Canals
- Indian removal

BRITISH CANADA

MICHIGAN TERRITORY

Erie Canal

Mississippi River

UNORGANIZED TERRITORY

Washington, D.C.

INDIAN TERR.

ARKANSAS TERR.

Gulf of Mexico

FLORIDA TERRITORY

Atlantic Ocean

Charleston

Deed

ME, VT, NH, NY, MA, CT, PA, NJ, MD, DE, OH, IN, IL, MO, VA, KY, NC, SC, AL, GA, MS, LA

1828	Andrew Jackson is elected President.
1837	Panic of 1837 brings economic collapse.
1838–1839	Cherokees are forced to move to Oklahoma along Trail of Tears.

1826　　　　**1834**　　　　**1842**

| Act of Union unites Upper and Lower Canada. | 1841 |

Drawing the Country Together

❝ There are existing powers in Congress to effectuate a comprehensive system of roads and canals, the effect of which would be to draw the different parts of the country more closely together. ❞

—Henry Clay, speech to
House of Representatives, 1818

◀ Seaports like Charleston (left) were vital to America's growing economy.

Building a National Identity

Objectives

- Describe the feeling of national unity that followed the War of 1812.
- Explain how Congress tried to strengthen the national economy.
- Discuss how Supreme Court rulings supported federal power and economic growth.

🔄 Reading Skill

Analyze Cause and Effect Events in history are often linked by cause and effect. This means that one event makes another happen. However, you cannot assume that because events occur together or in sequence they have a cause-and-effect link. Ask yourself: Why did this event or result happen? What happened because of this event? The answers will show if a cause-and-effect relationship exists.

Key Terms and People

Henry Clay
John C. Calhoun
Daniel Webster
charter
dumping
contract
capitalism
interstate
commerce

Why It Matters With peace restored after the War of 1812, the United States focused more on internal affairs. American leaders wanted to build national unity and improve the nation's economy.

❓ **Section Focus Question: How was the power of the federal government strengthened during the Era of Good Feelings?**

The Era of Good Feelings

With the end of the War of 1812, the Republicans took firm control of the government. The presidential election of 1816 resulted in a landslide victory for Republican candidate James Monroe of Virginia. He defeated Rufus King, the Federalist candidate, by 183 to 34 electoral votes. Stung by this defeat, the Federalist Party began to lose power. Within a few years, the party had disappeared.

President Monroe wanted to promote national unity. In the spring and summer of 1817, he made a goodwill circuit of the middle and northern sections of the country. He was warmly greeted in Connecticut and Massachusetts, the only states that had not voted for him in 1816. The old arguments over the War of 1812 seemed to have faded away.

While Monroe was in Boston, a local newspaper described the new sense of national unity as the "Era of Good Feelings." The name stuck and was used to describe Monroe's two terms in office. When he ran for reelection in 1820, no candidate opposed him.

☑ **Checkpoint** What happened to the Federalist Party after the War of 1812?

Building the National Economy

After 1815, many Americans believed the federal government should take action to increase economic prosperity in all regions of the country. Even the Republicans began to see merit in certain federal programs. This was a change, because in previous years Republicans had been known for stressing states' rights. Support for federal measures to promote economic prosperity came from many regions.

These beliefs were expressed by a number of bright young members of Congress from different regions. Outstanding among those who favored federal action were Henry Clay of Kentucky, John C. Calhoun of South Carolina, and Daniel Webster of Massachusetts.

- Clay spoke for people in the West who thought the country needed better roads and canals to transport goods from one region to another.

- Calhoun spoke for the interests of the South. While first a defender of national unity, he later put more emphasis on the idea of states' rights.

- Webster became a spokesperson for the Northeast. At first, he opposed high tariffs, but he later came to support them as a way of protecting industry.

Analyze Cause and Effect

Explain what Americans believed was needed to make national unity grow. What would cause that growth to happen?

Vocabulary Builder
emphasis (EM fuh sis) **n.** special importance or significance

Henry Clay

Daniel Webster

NORTH

WEST

SOUTH

John C. Calhoun

New Leaders Speak for Their Regions

During the Era of Good Feelings, three young members of Congress became spokespersons for their regions.

Daniel Webster - Massachusetts
He supported tariffs because they allowed New England's factories to compete against European manufacturers.

John C. Calhoun - South Carolina
He opposed tariffs because they raised the price of goods that southerners bought.

Henry Clay - Kentucky
He supported the construction of roads and canals because they would enable the three regions of the country to trade with one another.

Critical Thinking: *Apply Information* Which of the three leaders would you expect to be the strongest supporter of slavery? Explain.

341

How Tariffs Work

By increasing the cost of imported goods, tariffs helped U.S. manufacturers to compete with foreign manufacturers. But the higher prices hurt consumers.
Critical Thinking: *Identify Economic Costs* *Why was the cost of cloth higher in the United States than in Britain?*

	United States	Great Britain
Cost of cloth	$6.00	$5.00
Cost to manufacture final product	$0.85	$0.50
Shipping costs	$0.20	$0.25
Tariff	—	$1.50
Total	$7.05	$7.25

The Second Bank of the United States As you have read, Congress passed a law in 1791 creating the first Bank of the United States. In 1811, the Bank ceased to exist. Its charter—a legal document giving certain rights to a person or company—had run out. Without the Bank, the economy suffered. State banks made too many loans and issued too much money. This caused an increase in spending and led to rising prices.

To cure these problems, Congress established the second Bank of the United States in 1816. Like the first Bank, the new Bank was privately owned and had a charter to operate for twenty years. It lent money to individuals and controlled the money supply. This gave a boost to American businesses.

The Tariff of 1816 Another problem the nation faced after the War of 1812 was foreign competition. Most British goods had been kept out of the United States by the Embargo Act and the War of 1812. This helped American industry grow rapidly. New American factories made textiles, smelted iron, and produced many other products.

After the War of 1812, British manufacturers looked to sell their goods in the United States. They could still produce goods more cheaply than the Americans because they had well-established factories and more customers. This gave the British an opportunity to drive their American competitors out of business by dumping their goods in the United States. Dumping is selling goods in another country below market prices.

British dumping caused dozens of New England businesses to fail. As their investments collapsed, angry factory owners turned to Congress for help. They demanded protective tariffs to raise the price of foreign goods.

Congress responded with the Tariff of 1816, which put a tax on foreign textiles, iron, leather goods, paper, and other products. In 1818 and 1824, Congress passed even higher tariffs.

These tariffs were popular in the North, where most factories were located. However, the tariffs were deeply resented in the South, where they forced southerners to pay more for their goods. John C. Calhoun became a bitter foe of tariffs. He argued that they made northern manufacturers rich at the expense of the South.

Clay's American System As the debate over tariffs raged, Henry Clay came up with a plan that he believed would help the economy of each section of the country. He called his plan the American System. It proposed high tariffs and a federal program of public works.

Clay believed that high tariffs helped all regions of the country, not just the North. According to Clay, the wealth produced by tariffs would enable northerners to buy farm products from the West and the South. The tariff also would provide revenue for the federal government. The government could then use the money to build up the infrastructure—roads, bridges, and canals—in the South and West.

Clay's American System never fully became government policy. Presidents Madison and Monroe both refused to support some of Clay's projects. Also, southerners continued to oppose protective tariffs. They were not convinced by Clay's argument that high tariffs would aid the South in the long run.

☑**Checkpoint** According to Henry Clay, how would his American System benefit the economy?

British Leather Boots
The U.S. tariff on imports such as leather goods helped New England manufacturers to compete.

Vocabulary Builder
infrastructure (IHN frah struhk chahr) *n.* basic public works, like bridges and roads, needed for a society to function

Three Important Supreme Court Rulings

The Supreme Court also promoted national economic growth and the power of the federal government during this era. Led by Chief Justice John Marshall, a Federalist sympathizer, the Court issued a series of important rulings between 1819 and 1824.

In *McCulloch* v. *Maryland* (1819), the Court protected the second Bank of the United States. The case grew out of an attempt by the state of Maryland to put a tax on the branch of the Bank operating in that state. The Bank refused to pay the tax.

The Court's 1819 decision, written by Marshall, strengthened the power of the federal government. It ruled that states had no power to interfere with federal institutions. A tax, said the Court, was a dangerous interference because "the power to tax involves the power to destroy." Moreover, according to Marshall, a state cannot pass any law that violates a federal law. This reasoning would be used in future years to expand the power of the federal government.

Interstate Commerce
No individual state could grant a monopoly to a steamboat company to use a river that divides two states, the Supreme Court ruled in *Gibbons* v. *Ogden*.

Two other decisions helped shape American life. In *Dartmouth College* v. *Woodward* (1819), the Court ruled that the charter of Dartmouth College in New Hampshire was a private contract. A **contract** is an agreement between two or more parties that can be enforced by law. Since the Constitution protected private contracts, New Hampshire could not change Dartmouth's charter. In protecting private contracts, the Court was protecting private businesses. In doing that, it helped promote **capitalism**—the economic system in which privately owned businesses compete in a free market.

In *Gibbons* v. *Ogden* (1824), the Court again supported federal power. It ruled that New York State could not give a steamboat company a monopoly to carry passengers on the Hudson River. The Court pointed out that travel on the Hudson River included stops in New Jersey as well as New York. Therefore, it was **interstate commerce**—trade between two or more states. Under the Constitution, only Congress can regulate interstate commerce. Again, the Court had strengthened the federal government at the expense of the states.

✔**Checkpoint** How did the Supreme Court ruling in *Dartmouth College* v. *Woodward* support economic growth?

☆ **Looking Back and Ahead** Americans turned their attention to economic growth after the War of 1812. But while Americans were debating Henry Clay's American System, events in Latin America were drawing the concern of American leaders.

Section 1 | **Check Your Progress**

Progress Monitoring Online
For: Self-test with instant help
Visit: PHSchool.com
Web Code: mya-3061

Comprehension and Critical Thinking

1. (a) **Recall** Which groups supported and which opposed tariffs?
   (b) **Draw Conclusions** Do you think the American System offered a good solution to regional differences? Explain.

2. (a) **Recall** What did *McCulloch* v. *Maryland* decide?
   (b) **Compare** What did the Supreme Court decisions in *McCulloch* v. *Maryland* and *Gibbons* v. *Ogden* have in common?

Reading Skill

3. **Analyze Cause and Effect** Reread the text following the headings "The Tariff of 1816" and "Clay's American System." What did Clay believe would result from high tariffs?

Key Terms
Fill in the blanks with the correct key terms.

4. To set up the Bank of the United States, the government granted it a _____.

5. Private businesses compete in the American economic system called _____.

Writing

6. Decide which is the best closing sentence for an essay on James Monroe. Explain your choice.
   Sentences:
   (a) James Monroe, the fifth President of the United States, won two landslide victories.
   (b) Clearly, James Monroe deserved to have his presidency called the Era of Good Feelings.
   (c) James Monroe is, without a doubt, one of the greatest men ever elected President.

SECTION 2

The Monroe Doctrine

"In the wars of the European powers in matters relating to themselves we have never taken any part. . . . We owe it, therefore, to candor and to the amicable relations existing between the United States and those powers to declare that we should consider any attempt on their part to extend their system to any portion of this hemisphere as dangerous to our peace and safety."

—President James Monroe, address to Congress, 1823

◄ President James Monroe

Dealing With Other Nations

Objectives

- Explain why Spain ceded Florida to the United States.
- Describe how Spanish territories in the Americas gained independence.
- Explain why the Monroe Doctrine was issued.
- Discuss how Canada became self-governing.

Reading Skill

Identify Multiple Effects As you read about historical events, note that some events have multiple, or more than one, effects. Several effects may happen at the same time or one effect may lead to the next. As you read this section, look for multiple effects of each event.

Key Terms and People

cede
Miguel Hidalgo
Simón Bolívar
James Monroe
John Quincy Adams
self-government

Why It Matters After the War of 1812, the United States took a firm position against European influence in the Americas. President Monroe established a policy that would have a lasting impact on U.S. relations with Latin America.

❓ Section Focus Question: How did U.S. foreign affairs reflect new national confidence?

Relations With Spain

At the time of the War of 1812, the United States and Haiti were the only parts of the Americas not under European control. Spain controlled more territory in the Americas than any other European country. However, Spain's power had steadily weakened over several hundred years.

Spain's control was especially weak in Florida. Spain could not stop enslaved African Americans who escaped from plantations in Georgia and Alabama from crossing into Florida. Once in Florida, many of the escapees joined the Seminole Nation. The Seminoles often crossed into the United States to raid American settlements.

In 1817, the U.S. government sent Andrew Jackson to recapture those who had escaped slavery. Jackson attacked and destroyed Seminole villages. He then went far beyond his orders. He seized two important Spanish towns and forced the governor to flee Florida.

Jackson's attack on Florida showed that the United States could take over Florida whenever it wanted. Since Spain could not protect Florida, it decided to give up the territory. In the Adams-Onís Treaty of 1819, Spain ceded, or gave up, Florida to the United States.

✓ Checkpoint What effect did Andrew Jackson's attack on Florida have on the government of Spain?

Spanish Colonies Win Independence

By 1810, opposition to Spanish rule ran strong in Spain's American colonies. The American and French revolutions had inspired Latin Americans to want to control their own affairs. Revolutionary movements were growing in almost all of the Spanish colonies. Spain seemed unable to control the pressure for change in Latin America.

Mexico Breaks Away Mexico's struggle for independence began in 1810. In that year, Father **Miguel Hidalgo** (ee DAHL goh) organized an army of Native Americans that freed several Mexican <u>provinces</u>. However, in 1811, Hidalgo was captured and executed by troops loyal to Spain.

Another revolution broke out in Mexico in 1820. This time, Spain was unable to end the fighting. In 1821, Spain agreed to Mexico's independence.

At first, Mexico was ruled by an emperor. Then, in 1823, the monarchy was overthrown. A new constitution, patterned after the United States Constitution, made Mexico a federal republic of nineteen states and four territories.

Independence for South and Central America South America, too, was affected by revolutionary change. Here, the best-known leader of the struggle for independence from Spain was **Simón Bolívar** (see MOHN boh LEE vahr).

Vocabulary Builder
<u>province</u> (PRAHV ahns)
n. governmental division of a country, similar to a state

Identify Multiple Effects
What other nations were influenced by the American and French revolutions?

New Nations of Latin America

MAP MASTER®
Skills Activity

Wars of independence led to the creation of many new countries in Latin America in the first half of the 1800s.

(a) Read a Map What parts of Latin America remained colonies of European nations?

(b) Apply Information Use the world map in the Atlas in this textbook to identify how the border between the United States and Mexico has changed.

MapMaster Online
For: Interactive map
Visit: PHSchool.com
Web Code: myp-3062

KEY
New nations
European colonies

0 km   2,000
0 miles   2,000
Azimuthal Equal-Area Projection

Bolívar is often called the Liberator for his role in leading independence movements in the northern part of South America. In August 1819, he led an army on a daring march from Venezuela over the ice-capped Andes Mountains and into Colombia. There, he defeated the Spanish and became president of the independent Republic of Great Colombia. It included today's nations of Venezuela, Colombia, Ecuador, and Panama.

Farther north, the people of Central America declared their independence from Spain in 1821. Two years later, they formed the United Provinces of Central America. It included today's nations of Nicaragua, Costa Rica, El Salvador, Honduras, and Guatemala.

In 1822, Brazil announced its independence from Portugal. Soon after, the United States recognized the independence of Mexico and six other former colonies in Central and South America. By 1825, most parts of Latin America had thrown off European rule.

✔Checkpoint **Why was Miguel Hidalgo important to the history of Mexico?**

Links Across Time

Beyond the Monroe Doctrine

1823 The Monroe Doctrine warned European nations not to interfere in Latin America.

1900s U.S. Presidents cited the Monroe Doctrine to justify armed actions in Latin America. The actions often angered Latin Americans.

1930s President Franklin D. Roosevelt launched a Good Neighbor Policy. It stressed cooperation and trade to promote U.S. interests in the hemisphere.

Link to Today

Connection to Today What is the state of our relations with the countries of Latin America today?

For: U.S. relations with Latin America today
Visit: PHSchool.com
Web Code: myc-3062

The Monroe Doctrine

The future of these new countries was soon clouded. Several European powers, including France and Russia, indicated that they might help Spain regain its colonies.

This worried President James Monroe and Secretary of State John Quincy Adams. It also worried the British. Both nations wanted to protect trade with Latin America. In 1823, Britain suggested that the two countries issue a joint statement. The statement would announce their determination to protect the freedom of the new nations of Latin America.

Adams told President Monroe he thought the United States should take action alone. He believed a joint statement would make the United States look like Britain's junior partner. Monroe agreed.

In a message to Congress in December 1823, the President stated what is known as the Monroe Doctrine. The United States would not allow European nations to create American colonies or interfere with the free nations of Latin America. The United States would consider any attempt to do so "dangerous to our peace and safety."

At the time, the United States was not strong enough to block European action. Only the British navy could do that. As U.S. power grew, however, the Monroe Doctrine boosted the influence of the United States in the region.

✔Checkpoint **What was Adams's advice to Monroe?**

Relations With Canada

Canada remained a British colony after the American Revolution. In 1791, the country was divided into two parts. Upper Canada was mainly English, and Lower Canada was mainly French. In 1837, there were rebellions against British rule in both parts of Canada.

Although the British put down the rebellions, they learned a lesson. They could no longer deny rights to Canadians. Britain would have to give Canadians more powers of self-government—the right of people to rule themselves independently. The Act of Union of 1841 was a major step in that direction. It merged Canada's two parts into a single unit governed by a Canadian legislature. Britain, however, still had ultimate control.

Canada and the United States had their own disagreements. Tensions were particularly high when the United States unsuccessfully tried to invade Canada during the War of 1812.

The situation slowly improved after the war. Between 1818 and 1846, the United States and Britain settled several border disputes regarding Canada. Eventually, the United States and Canada established excellent relations. Their relations remain strong to this day.

☑Checkpoint **Why did Britain grant some self-government to Canada?**

☆ **Looking Back and Ahead** The Monroe Doctrine convinced Americans that their southern borders were safe from European expansion. Treaties with Britain lessened the tensions along the northern border with Canada. With a new sense of confidence, Americans prepared to make great strides on the domestic front. The 1820s and 1830s would see an upsurge in the democratic spirit.

Vocabulary Builder
domestic (doh MEHS tihk) **adj.** relating to one's country; internal

---

Section 2 | **Check Your Progress**

Progress Monitoring ⬤nline
For: Self-test with instant help
Visit: PHSchool.com
Web Code: mya-3062

Comprehension and Critical Thinking

1. (a) **Summarize** What was the Monroe Doctrine?
(b) **Clarify Problems** Would the United States have looked weak if it had jointly issued a warning with Britain? Explain.

2. (a) **List** Name six of today's Latin American countries that were independent by 1825.
(b) **Identify Economic Benefits** How did Great Britain and the United States benefit from the independence of Spain's American colonies?

⟳ Reading Skill

3. **Identify Multiple Effects** European powers, such as France and Russia, considered helping Spain regain its South and Central American colonies. What were the effects of this situation? Reread the text under the heading "The Monroe Doctrine."

Key Terms

Answer the following questions in complete sentences that show your understanding of the key terms.

4. What did Spain cede to the United States in the Adams-Onís Treaty?

5. How did Canadians benefit when Britain granted them more self-government?

Writing

6. Revise the following sentences to make them flow better. **Sentences:** The Monroe Doctrine stated that the United States would not allow Spain to take back its former colonies. The doctrine helped the new Latin American states remain free. The doctrine supported the cause of democracy in the Western Hemisphere.

Jackson Forever!
The Hero of Two Wars and of Orleans!
The Man of the People!
PRESIDENCY!

BECAUSE
It should be derived from the
PEOPLE!

KNOCK DOWN

OLD HICKORY
AND THE ELECTORAL LAW.

Election Fever

❝The election fever which is constantly raging through the land . . . engrosses every conservation, it irritates every temper, it substitutes party spirit for personal esteem. . . .❞

—Frances Trollope, comments on the election of 1832

◀ Supporters of Andrew Jackson were proud of his military exploits and elected him President.

The Age of Jackson

Objectives

• Discuss the conflict between Andrew Jackson and John Quincy Adams over the election of 1824.

• Explain how the right to vote expanded in the United States.

• Describe Andrew Jackson's victory in the election of 1828.

🎯 Reading Skill

Identify Short-Term Effects Some events have effects that take place shortly after the event. Other events create changes that last only a short time. Both of these types of effects are short-term effects. As you read Section 3, look for examples of the short-term effects of events.

Key Terms and People

Andrew Jackson
suffrage
caucus

nominating
convention
spoils system

Why It Matters The Constitution had established a system based on representative government. But not all citizens could fully participate in the early American republic. During the Age of Jackson, however, the democratic spirit grew and more Americans played an active role in government.

❓ Section Focus Question: How did the people gain more power during the Age of Jackson?

Adams and Jackson in Conflict

Andrew Jackson served two terms as President, from 1829 to 1837. His presidency marked the opening of a new and more democratic era in American political life. So great was his influence that the twenty-year period after he became President is often called the Age of Jackson.

Andrew Jackson was a wealthy man by the time he became President. However, he began life with very little. Born in a log cabin on the border of North and South Carolina, he was an orphan by the age of 14. Jackson was ambitious, brave, and tough. He survived smallpox as a child and severe gunshot wounds as an adult.

During a difficult march with his troops in 1812, one soldier described him as "tough as hickory." Hickory trees are extremely strong, and their wood is very hard. The description fit Jackson so well that it stuck as a nickname. Jackson became known as Old Hickory.

Jackson stood for the idea that ordinary people should participate in American political life. As a general and later as President, Andrew Jackson was deeply loved by millions of ordinary Americans. They loved him for his humble beginnings and his firm leadership.

The Election of 1824 Jackson first ran for President in 1824. His opponents were John Quincy Adams, Henry Clay, and William H. Crawford of Georgia. Jackson received the most electoral votes, but not a majority. According to the Constitution, the House of Representatives would have to decide the election.

The choice was between Jackson and Adams, the two who had received the most votes. As Speaker of the House, Clay had great influence. He told his supporters to vote for Adams. The House then elected Adams on the first ballot.

Jackson <u>reacted</u> with fury. He had won the most popular votes and the most electoral votes, but still had lost the election. When Adams appointed Clay secretary of state, Jackson's supporters claimed the two men had made a "corrupt bargain."

The Presidency of John Quincy Adams Adams was burdened by the charges of a secret deal. He accomplished little, even though he had ambitious plans for the nation. He supported Clay's American System and wanted the federal government to play a larger role in supporting the American economy.

Adams proposed a national program to build roads and canals and a high tariff to protect industry. He also planned to set up a national university and an observatory for astronomers in Washington, D.C. However, he lacked the political skill to push his programs through Congress. Adams never won the trust of the American people. As a result, he served only one term.

● **INFOGRAPHIC**

Democracy in Action

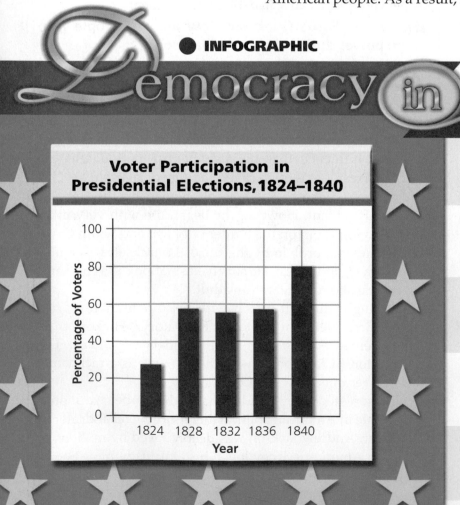

Voter Participation in Presidential Elections, 1824–1840

The Age of Jackson saw the first stirrings of democracy in action in the United States. More men could and did vote, and many more people joined political parties and participated in election campaigns.

It would be many years until women and African Americans also gained the right to vote. However, the kinds of political contests that are familiar to Americans today had their beginnings in the presidential elections of the 1820s and 1830s. **Critical Thinking:** *Draw Conclusions Why would people become more actively involved in political campaigns as the right to vote was extended to new groups?*

Despite his failures, Adams was an eloquent supporter of what he saw as America's special place in the world. He stated his ideas in a Fourth of July speech in 1821. He said the United States had no designs on the territory of other nations:

> **“**Wherever the standard of freedom and independence has been or shall be unfurled, there will her [America's] heart, . . . and her prayers be. But she goes not abroad in search of monsters to destroy. She is the well-wisher to the freedom and independence of all.**”**
>
> —John Quincy Adams, Fourth of July 1821 Address

☑**Checkpoint** **Why did Jackson's supporters claim there had been a "corrupt bargain" in the election of 1824?**

A New Era in Politics

The election of 1824 disappointed Andrew Jackson and his followers. Still, that election began a new era in American politics.

Back in the 1790s, states had begun extending suffrage—the right to vote. Many states dropped the requirement that men had to own property to be able to <u>participate</u> in voting. Voting requirements varied slightly from state to state. However, almost all adult white males now could vote and hold office.

Vocabulary Builder
<u>participate</u> (pahr TIHS ah payt)
v. to take part in; to share in an activity

◀ *The County Election*, George Caleb Bingham

◀ Portrait of Andrew Jackson shown inside a souvenir box from an early presidential campaign.

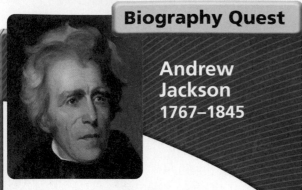

Andrew Jackson
1767–1845

Andrew Jackson was a Tennessee landowner, lawyer, and judge. His military campaigns against the British in the War of 1812 and against Native Americans in Florida made him a war hero. Political opponents called him a country hick. But supporters admired him as a self-made man who spoke out for ordinary people. His election as President was a sign that the United States was becoming a more democratic nation.

Biography Quest

How did Jackson gain a reputation as a supporter of ordinary people?

For: The answer to the question about Jackson

Visit: PHSchool.com

Web Code: myd-3063

Identify Short-Term Effects

What was the immediate effect of using nominating conventions to choose presidential candidates?

States also were changing how they chose presidential electors. Previously, state legislatures chose them. Now, that right went to the voters. In 1824, voters chose the presidential electors in 18 out of 24 states.

Of course, suffrage was still restricted in the United States. Women could not participate in government. Nor could enslaved African Americans, male or female. In most states, even free African Americans could not vote.

Democracy in the Age of Jackson

Extending the right to vote was part of a larger spread of democratic ideas. Supporters of Andrew Jackson believed that ordinary people should vote in elections, hold public office, and do anything else they had the ability to do. Jackson's supporters strongly opposed special privileges for those of high social status.

Wealthy observers were sometimes dismayed by this spirit of equality. One visitor complained, "the rich and the poor, the educated and the ignorant, the polite and the vulgar, all . . . feed at the same table."

Jackson and his supporters did not trust government. They believed it often favored the rich and powerful. The Jacksonians also were suspicious of banks, which they believed favored the rich.

New Political Parties The Age of Jackson brought back the two-party system that had briefly ended during the Era of Good Feelings. During the 1824 election, the Republican Party split. Supporters of Adams called themselves National Republicans. Jackson's supporters used the name Democrats.

In 1831, the National Republicans nominated Henry Clay to run against Jackson. Jackson won easily, with strength in all parts of the country. However, by 1836, the anti-Jackson forces had formed a new party, the Whigs. From then until 1852, the Democrats and the Whigs were the country's two major political parties.

The new parties adopted a new way of choosing their presidential candidates. Previously, a party's members of Congress held a caucus—a meeting of members of a political party. These caucuses involved only a small group of people. Beginning in 1831, political parties started holding national nominating conventions—large meetings of party delegates to choose candidates for office. National conventions opened the nominating process to many more people and made it more democratic.

✓Checkpoint **Which groups did not benefit from increased suffrage in the United States?**

Jackson Becomes President

Three times as many people voted in the election of 1828 as had voted in 1824. Most of these new voters supported Jackson, who easily defeated Adams.

The election revealed growing sectional and class divisions among American voters. Jackson did best in the West and the South, where planters and small farmers supported him. He also did well among small business people, artisans, and workers in cities and towns nationwide. Adams was most popular in his home region of New England.

Jackson's Inauguration Jackson's supporters called the election a victory for the "common man." His inauguration in March 1829 showed what they meant. Thousands of ordinary working people jammed into Washington for the event. After the inauguration at the Capitol, Jackson rode a horse to the White House. A journalist described the scene:

> **❝**As far as the eye could reach, the sidewalks of the Avenue were covered with people on foot . . . with . . . carriages and persons on horseback. . . . For a full half hour, I stood waiting for the stream to run by; but like a never failing fountain people continued pouring forth.**❞**
>
> —Amos Kendall in the *Argus of Western America*,
> March 29, 1829

Jackson's Inauguration
Joyful crowds welcomed Andrew Jackson to the White House upon his inauguration in 1829. The artist who created this picture made sly fun of the celebrants. **Critical Thinking: Apply Information** *Why were some people upset by what happened at Jackson's inauguration?*

Twenty thousand people crowded in and around the White House for a reception in Jackson's honor. They did not all behave well. Some broke furniture, spilled drinks, trampled rugs, and broke several thousand dollars worth of glassware and dishes. Officials finally lured the unruly crowd outside by moving the punch bowl onto the White House lawn.

Jackson's opponents were shocked. One member of the Supreme Court complained about the "reign of King Mob." A Jackson supporter saw things more positively: "It was the People's day, and the People's President, and the People would rule."

The Spoils of Victory Jackson began his term by replacing some government officials with his supporters. Previous Presidents had done the same thing. In fact, during his two terms Jackson replaced only about 20 percent of federal officeholders.

The difference was that Jackson openly defended what he was doing. He claimed putting new people into government jobs furthered democracy. One of his supporters put it more selfishly when he compared the process to a conquering army after a war, saying "to the victors belong the spoils [loot]." People quickly applied the term spoils system to the practice of rewarding government jobs to loyal supporters of the party that wins an election.

☑**Checkpoint** **How did Andrew Jackson justify the spoils system?**

☆ **Looking Back and Ahead** As President, Andrew Jackson supported the right of ordinary people to participate in government. Jackson's belief in equality, however, left out many, including Native Americans. In the next section, you will read how government policies denied basic rights to Native Americans.

Section 3 | **Check Your Progress**

Progress Monitoring ⓞnline
For: Self-test with instant help
Visit: PHSchool.com
Web Code: mya-3063

Comprehension and Critical Thinking

1. (a) **Recall** What was the "corrupt bargain"?
(b) **Evaluate Information** Who benefited from accusations of a "corrupt bargain"?

2. (a) **Recall** How did the United States become more democratic between the 1790s and the 1830s?
(b) **Draw Conclusions** How did these democratic changes contribute to Jackson's election in 1828?

🎯 **Reading Skill**

3. **Identify Short-Term Effects** What was the immediate effect when Henry Clay told his supporters to vote for Adams?

Key Terms

Read each sentence below. If the sentence is true, write YES. If the sentence is not true, write NO and explain why.

4. By 1828, suffrage had been extended to white women and African Americans.

5. In 1824, a nominating convention chose John Quincy Adams to run for President.

6. Tens of thousands of ordinary citizens showed up for the caucus celebrating Jackson's victory.

Writing

7. Using vivid, specific words will make your writing livelier and more accurate. Rewrite these sentences using more specific, colorful words. **Sentences:** Many people liked Andrew Jackson, and he was very popular. People liked Jackson better than John Quincy Adams. They felt Jackson was a man of the people and Adams was not a man of the people.

◄ Seminole woman

Jackson's Viewpoint

❝It will incalculably strengthen the southwestern frontier and render the adjacent states strong enough to repel future invasions without remote aid . . . and enable those states to advance rapidly in population, wealth, and power. ❞

—Andrew Jackson, explaining the benefits of Indian removal, 1830

Indian Removal

Objectives
- Describe the culture of Native Americans in the Southeast.
- Describe the conflict over land occupied by Native Americans in the Southeast.
- Discuss the forced removal of Native Americans.

Reading Skill

Identify Long-Term Effects Many historical events have long-term effects—lasting effects that build up over time. As you read Section 4, look for events that have long-term effects. Think about why these causes have had such a lasting effect.

Key Person
Sequoyah

Why It Matters As a general, Andrew Jackson won great popularity for his victories over Indians in Georgia and Florida. As President, he worked to remove Native Americans from their homelands. This forced migration still affects Native Americans today.

❓ Section Focus Question: Why did Jackson use force to remove Indians from the Southeast?

Native Americans of the Southeast

When Andrew Jackson became President, more than 100,000 Native Americans still lived east of the Mississippi River. Many were farmers or lived in towns.

The Choctaw, Chickasaw, Cherokee, and Creek nations lived in parts of Mississippi, Alabama, Georgia, North Carolina, and Tennessee. The Seminoles, who lived in Florida, had an unusual origin. They were a combination of Creeks who had moved into Florida, Florida Native Americans, and escaped African American slaves.

The Cherokees had adopted some white customs. Aside from farming, they ran successful businesses, such as grain and lumber mills. Some could speak and read English. Many had converted to Christianity.

The Cherokees even had a written alphabet for their language. It had been created by a learned leader named Sequoyah (sih KWOY uh). In 1827, the Cherokees established a government based on a written constitution. They claimed status as a separate nation. The next year, they started a newspaper in both English and Cherokee.

✔**Checkpoint** What were some of the customs and ways of life of the Cherokees?

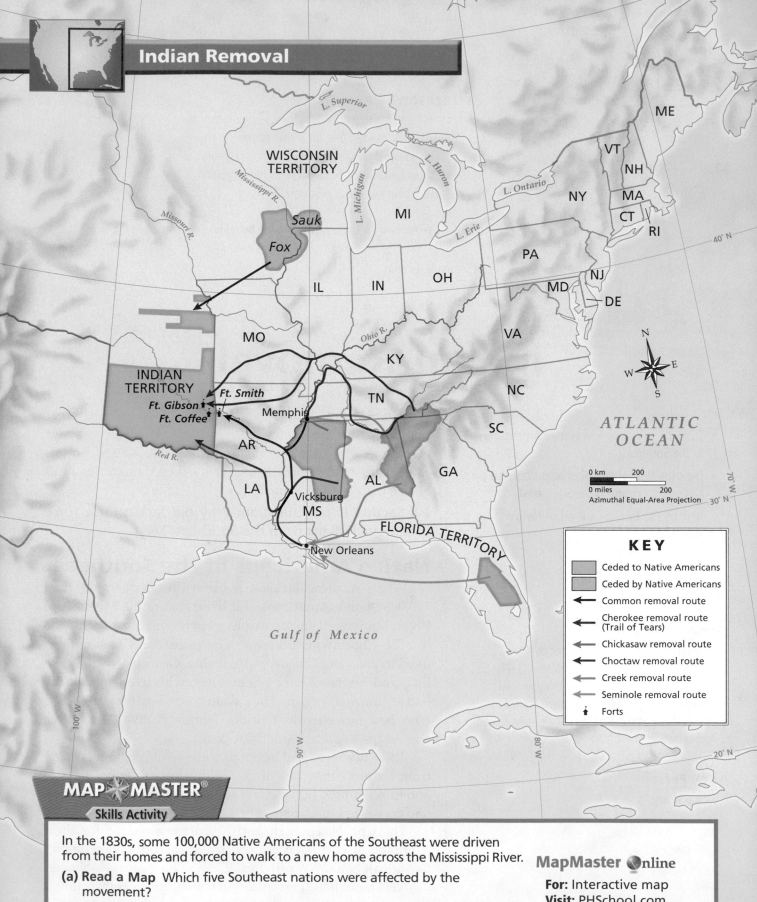

Indian Removal

WISCONSIN TERRITORY

Sauk

Fox

INDIAN TERRITORY

Ft. Smith
Ft. Gibson
Ft. Coffee

Memphis

MO

KY

TN

AR

LA

Vicksburg
MS

New Orleans

AL

GA

SC

NC

VA

MD

DE

NJ

PA

NY

CT
RI
MA
NH
VT
ME

MI

IL

IN

OH

FLORIDA TERRITORY

Gulf of Mexico

ATLANTIC OCEAN

L. Superior

L. Michigan

L. Huron

L. Ontario

L. Erie

Mississippi R.

Missouri R.

Ohio R.

Red R.

0 km 200
0 miles 200
Azimuthal Equal-Area Projection

40° N
30° N
20° N
100° W
90° W
80° W
70° W

KEY

�▪	Ceded to Native Americans
▪lighttone▪	Ceded by Native Americans
→	Common removal route
→	Cherokee removal route (Trail of Tears)
→	Chickasaw removal route
→	Choctaw removal route
→	Creek removal route
→	Seminole removal route
⚑	Forts

MAP⬥MASTER®
Skills Activity

In the 1830s, some 100,000 Native Americans of the Southeast were driven from their homes and forced to walk to a new home across the Mississippi River.

(a) Read a Map Which five Southeast nations were affected by the movement?

(b) Apply Information Use the scale of miles and the map above to answer the following question: About how far did the Seminoles have to travel to get from Florida Territory to New Orleans?

MapMaster Online

For: Interactive map
Visit: PHSchool.com
Web Code: myp-3064

Conflict Over Land

To government leaders, the presence of Native Americans in the Southeast stood in the way of westward expansion of the United States. Furthermore, the Native Americans lived on fertile land. White farmers wanted that land for growing cotton.

Forced Movement Policies to move Native Americans from their lands dated from the presidency of Thomas Jefferson. Jefferson hoped the movement would be <u>voluntary</u>. He believed that moving west was the only way the Native Americans could preserve their cultures.

After the War of 1812, the federal government signed treaties with several Native American groups of the Old Northwest. Under those treaties, the groups gave up their lands and moved west of the Mississippi River.

However, the Native Americans of the Southeast would not move. In 1825, President James Monroe suggested a plan to move all Native Americans living east of the Mississippi to land west of the river. However, nothing came of the plan. Yet, year by year, the pressure on the Native Americans of the Southeast grew. By the 1820s, many white southerners were demanding that Native Americans be removed by force.

In 1825 and 1827, the state of Georgia passed a law forcing the Creeks to give up most of their land. In 1828, Georgia tried to get the Cherokees to do the same. The state said the Cherokees were not a separate nation and they had to move off their land.

Support for Native Americans Georgia's actions were challenged in two suits that reached the Supreme Court. The decision in the first suit went against the Cherokees. In *Cherokee Nation* v. *Georgia* (1831), the Court refused to stop Georgia from enforcing its law. But in *Worcester* v. *Georgia* (1832), the Court declared that Georgia's laws "can have no force" within Cherokee territory.

Chief Justice John Marshall wrote the Court's majority opinion in *Worcester* v. *Georgia*. He <u>quoted</u> treaties that the United States had signed, guaranteeing certain territory to Native Americans. Under the Constitution, treaties are the supreme law of the land. Therefore, Marshall said, Georgia had no say over Cherokee territory.

Like the state of Georgia, President Jackson wanted to remove the Native Americans from their land. He was furious when he heard of the ruling in *Worcester* v. *Georgia*. "John Marshall has made his decision," he is reported to have said. "Now let him enforce it!"

Jackson was already putting into effect a federal law called the Indian Removal Act of 1830. The law gave him authority to offer Native American nations land west of the Mississippi in exchange for their lands in the East. It also provided money so the law could be carried out.

☑**Checkpoint** **According to Marshall, why was Georgia barred from applying its laws to Cherokee territory?**

Vocabulary Builder
<u>voluntary</u> (VAHL ahn tair ee)
adj. done willingly, of one's own free will

Vocabulary Builder
<u>quote</u> (kwoht) ***v.*** to repeat the exact words spoken or written

A Tragic Journey This painting, *Shadow of the Owl*, by Cherokee artist John Guthrie portrays the Trail of Tears. More than 4,000 Cherokees died along the trail. *Critical Thinking: Interpret Art* What do you think the owl in the main picture represents?

On the Trail of Tears

Believing they had no choice, most Native American leaders signed new treaties giving up their lands. They agreed to move to what was called the Indian Territory. Today most of that area is in the state of Oklahoma.

Removal of the Choctaws The Choctaws signed the first treaty in 1830. The Treaty of Dancing Rabbit Creek stated that

> **"**the United States under a grant . . . shall cause to be conveyed to the Choctaw Nation a tract of country west of the Mississippi river . . .**"**
>
> —Article II, Treaty of Dancing Rabbit Creek, 1830

Closely guarded by American soldiers, the Choctaws moved west between 1831 and 1833.

The federal government did not provide enough tents, food, blankets, shoes, winter clothes, or other supplies. Heavy rain and snow caused enormous suffering. An army lieutenant wrote that one group "walked for 24 hours barefoot through the snow and ice" before reaching shelter.

Cherokee Removal The Cherokees held out a few years longer. They were still on their land in 1837 when Jackson left office.

Finally, in 1838, President Martin Van Buren forced the Cherokees to move. In the winter of 1838–39, they went to Indian Territory, guarded by 7,000 soldiers. The route is called the Trail of Tears. A soldier's description helps explain why:

> ❝On the morning of November 17th, we encountered a terrific sleet and snow storm with freezing temperatures, and from that day until we reached the end of the fateful journey on March the 26th, 1839, the sufferings of the Cherokee were awful. The trail of the exiles was a trail of death.❞
> —Memoirs of Private John G. Burnett, December 1890

The Cherokees were forced to march hundreds of miles. They had little food or shelter. Many did not survive. Of 15,000 Cherokees who began the trip, 4,000 died along the way.

One group refused to move. The Seminoles fought three wars against removal. However, in the 1840s most Seminoles were forced to move. In their new homes in the Indian Territory, Native Americans struggled to rebuild their lives under very difficult conditions.

☑️ **Checkpoint** What mistakes in planning did the government make before removing Native Americans?

⭐ **Looking Back and Ahead** Andrew Jackson was determined to be a strong President. He defied the Supreme Court by enforcing the Indian Removal Act. In Section 5, you will learn about his stands against the nation's bankers and his dramatic actions to save the Union.

HISTORIAN'S APPRENTICE ACTIVITY PACK

To further explore the topics in this chapter, complete the activity in the Historian's Apprentice Activity Pack to answer this essential question:
Who owns the land?

Identify Long-Term Effects
President Jackson sent federal agents to finalize treaties for Native American removal. Summarize the long-term effects of this policy. Explain how the policy affected the Native Americans in the region.

Section 4 | Check Your Progress

Progress Monitoring Online
For: Self-test with instant help
Visit: PHSchool.com
Web Code: mya-3064

Comprehension and Critical Thinking

1. **(a) Recall** How did the Supreme Court rule in the case of *Worcester* v. *Georgia*?
   (b) Detect Bias Why do you suppose President Jackson objected to the Court's decision?

2. **(a) Compare and Contrast** Describe the removal of the Choctaws and the Cherokees.
   (b) Identify Economic Benefits Why would the Cherokees be particularly opposed to removal from their land?

Reading Skill

3. **Identify Long-Term Effects** A long-term effect is an effect that lasts over a long period of time. White farmers wanted the lands belonging to Native Americans of the Southeast. Write three sentences summarizing the long-term effects of this desire for land.

Writing

4. A paragraph should focus on a single topic. Rewrite the following paragraph to get rid of any sentences that stray from the topic. **Paragraph:** By the 1830s, Native Americans had fought several legal battles over land. Many Native Americans wore traditional clothing. The states tried to make the Native Americans move. However, the Supreme Court decided that states could not force them from their homes.

Sequoyah and the Cherokee Alphabet
by Robert Cwiklik

Prepare to Read

Introduction

The leader Sequoyah became convinced that the Cherokee needed a system to write in their own language. The following selection is from a biography of Sequoyah. In this excerpt, Sequoyah becomes interested in the "talking leaves" of an English book.

Reading Skill

Analyze Motivation A character's motives are the reason for his or her actions. As you read this excerpt, look for clues that tell why Sequoyah wanted the book.

Vocabulary *Builder*

As you read this literature selection, look for the following underlined words:

leaves (leevz) *n.* pages or sheets

wampum belt (WAHM pum) *n.* belt woven with images made with beads or shells, used to record historic events

pelts (pehltz) *n.* animal skins

bristled (BRIHS ahld) *v.* became angry

Background

The images on the wampum belt were a record of events in Cherokee history. Details like names of people and places were passed down from one medicine man to the next. The medicine men would tell the history of the tribe based on the images on the belt.

Sequoyah picked up the book to examine it. He saw that it was made of thin <u>leaves</u> of paper. Instead of the pictures on a <u>wampum belt</u>, there were marks of some kind on the paper, like the footprints of a crow. And the marks were in neat rows like the rows of corn planted in a garden. When the reader looked at those rows, the leaves of the book "talked" to him. The reader then told his friends what the leaves said. Sequoyah found these talking leaves fascinating.

Sequoyah mentally compared the markings on the talking leaves to the designs on a wampum belt. The colorful belt was much prettier, but the book was filled with many thin leaves, each covered with markings. It must surely "remember" more than the wampum belt. Wu The had told Sequoyah that books made the white people's medicine powerful. She had said that just one of their books of talking leaves could remember more than all the medicine men of Taskigi together. And the white men had many, many such books. This is why Wu The wanted Sequoyah to learn English—so he could learn the secret of the talking leaves, the secret of the white people's powerful medicine.

Sequoyah was so curious about the talking leaves that he bought the book from the hunter for two good deer <u>pelts</u>. The men laughed, thinking they had again cheated an Indian. Sequoyah knew his pelts were worth more in silver than this book. Still he wished to have it. He wanted to ponder the secret of its talking leaves.

Agi Li and Rabbit Eyes kidded Sequoyah as the three hiked home after the rain stopped, "You gave good pelts for a book you cannot even understand," they said, laughing.

Later the boys fell to talking about the talking leaves. "Surely," Rabbit Eyes said, "it was a magic power of the white man to be able to put his speeches into books."

"Surely," Agi Li said, "one must learn the white man's language to gain the power of the talking leaves."

Sequoyah <u>bristled</u> at this. "Bah," he said. "These are mere scratchings, mere crow's prints. It is not magic. I could invent them for the Cherokee language, and we, too, could have our own talking leaves."

The other boys laughed at this. "How can you do such a thing?" asked Agi Li, chuckling.

Sequoyah picked up a flat stone and scratched out a picture of a deer on it with the blade of his knife. "There," he said, showing them the stone. "That means 'deer,' see?" Then Sequoyah drew an arrow through the deer. "And that means 'to hunt a deer,'" he said.

His friends laughed again. "At this rate, you will be scratching on stones until you are an old man, Sequoyah, to make pictures of every word there is in our language. It is impossible. The talking leaves belong to the white man. They are not meant for us."

Sequoyah stood his ground. "You are wrong," he said. "You think the white man has special medicine. That is why you wear his clothes," Sequoyah said, pointing to their trousers and shirts. "Well, our medicine can be just as strong, if we wish it."

From *Sequoyah and the Cherokee Alphabet,* by Robert Cwiklik.
© 1989 Silver Burdett Press.

☑ **Checkpoint** **Why did Wu The want Sequoyah to learn English?**

Analyze Motivation

At the beginning of the excerpt, Sequoyah's curiosity motivates him to buy the book. What is his motivation for wanting to write his language?

If you liked this story about Sequoyah, you might want to read more about the Cherokees in *The Cherokee Dragon: A Novel of the Real People* by Robert J. Conley. St. Martin's Press. 2000.

Sequoyah and his Cherokee alphabet

Analyze LITERATURE

Sequoyah went on to create an alphabet for the Cherokees. Imagine that you are Sequoyah. Write a paragraph explaining to the Cherokees why they should learn to write.

SECTION

5

STATES CUSTOM HOUSE

An Interfering Government

❝We must be blind to the lessons of reason and experience not to see that the more a government interferes with the labor and wealth of a community, the more it exacts from one portion and bestows on another. . . .❞

—Vice President John C. Calhoun, protesting tariffs collected by U.S. Customs agents, 1832

▲ U.S. Custom House in Charleston, South Carolina

States' Rights and the Economy

Objectives

- Describe the disagreement over the Bank of the United States.
- Discuss the differing viewpoints on the balance of federal and state powers.
- Explain why South Carolina threatened to secede from the Union.
- Describe the economic crisis that began in 1837.

🔄 Reading Skill

Identify Multiple Causes Just as events can have multiple effects, so too can they have multiple causes. Major events in history often have many causes. As you read Section 5, look for events that have multiple causes.

Key Terms and People

nullification
Martin Van Buren

William Henry
Harrison

Why It Matters The issue of states' rights versus the power of the federal government had been debated since the founding of the United States. The debate became more urgent when Americans disagreed on important economic measures.

❓ Section Focus Question: How did old issues take a new shape in the conflict over a national bank and tariffs?

The Bank War

Between 1816 and the early 1830s, the second Bank of the United States earned strong support from business people. They liked the fact that the Bank made loans to businesses. Moreover, the Bank was a safe place for the federal government to keep its money. The paper money it issued formed a stable currency. Its careful policies helped create confidence in banks all over the country.

On the other hand, many Americans disliked the Bank. They opposed the way the Bank restricted loans made by state banks. Fearing that state banks were making too many loans, Bank directors often limited the amount of money banks could lend. This angered farmers and merchants who wanted to borrow money to buy land. Many southerners and westerners blamed the Bank for the economic crisis that broke out in 1819. In that crisis, many people lost their farms.

The Bank's most powerful enemy was Andrew Jackson, who called the Bank "the Monster." According to Jackson, the Bank allowed a small group of the wealthy people to enrich themselves at the expense of ordinary people. Jackson believed that the wealthy stood for unfair privilege. Jackson especially disliked Nicholas Biddle, the Bank's president. Biddle, who came from a wealthy Philadelphia family, was skilled at doing favors for powerful politicians.

Biddle got Congress to renew the Bank's charter in 1832, although the charter still had four years to go. The news reached Jackson when he was sick in bed. The President vowed, "The Bank . . . is trying to kill me, but I will kill it!"

Jackson immediately vetoed the bill. The fight over the Bank became a major issue in the 1832 presidential election. Henry Clay, who ran against Jackson, strongly supported the Bank. But most voters stood solidly behind Jackson's veto of the Bank bill. Jackson won reelection by a huge margin.

Jackson's victory over the Bank helped to increase the powers of the presidency. It showed that a determined President could stir up the voters and face down powerful opponents in Congress.

The second Bank ceased to exist when its charter ran out in 1836. Unfortunately for Jackson's successor, an economic crisis struck a few months after Jackson left office. Without a Bank of the United States, it was harder for the new President to end the crisis.

✔ **Checkpoint** **What were the arguments for and against the second Bank of the United States?**

The Question of States' Rights

Since the founding of the United States, Americans had debated what should be the balance between the powers of the states and the powers of the federal government.

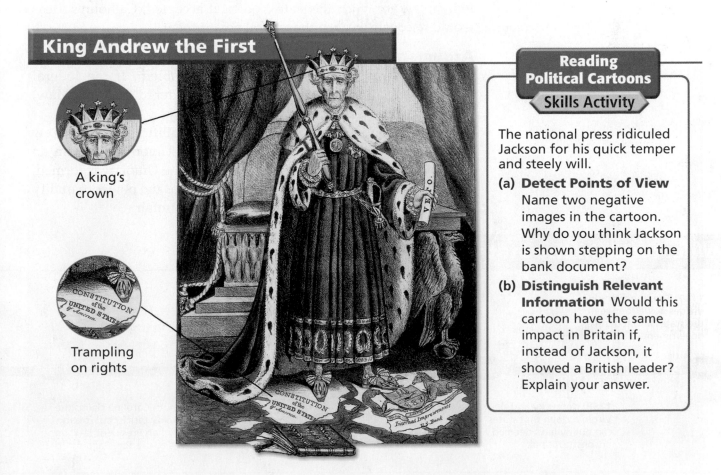

King Andrew the First

A king's crown

Trampling on rights

Reading Political Cartoons

Skills Activity

The national press ridiculed Jackson for his quick temper and steely will.

(a) Detect Points of View Name two negative images in the cartoon. Why do you think Jackson is shown stepping on the bank document?

(b) Distinguish Relevant Information Would this cartoon have the same impact in Britain if, instead of Jackson, it showed a British leader? Explain your answer.

The Constitutional Convention of 1787 had created a government based on federalism, the division of power between the national government and the states. The Constitution gave the federal government many significant powers. At the same time, the Tenth Amendment set limits on federal power. It states that any powers not specifically given to the federal government are "reserved to the States respectively, or to the people."

Over the years, the issue of balancing federal and state power had come up repeatedly. The Alien and Sedition acts had raised the issue. So had the Virginia and Kentucky resolutions and the Hartford convention. The issue could never be fully <u>resolved</u>. During Andrew Jackson's presidency, arguments over federal power and states' rights caused a serious crisis.

Vocabulary Builder
<u>resolve</u> (ree SAHLV) **v.** to decide; to solve

☑**Checkpoint** How does the Tenth Amendment limit federal powers?

The Nullification Crisis

The crisis erupted when Congress passed a law in 1828 raising the tariff on iron, textiles, and other products. The tariff helped manufacturers in the North and some parts of the West. But it made southerners pay more for manufactured goods. It seemed to southerners that the federal government was forcing them to obey an unfair law.

Vice President John C. Calhoun of South Carolina argued that the states had the right of **nullification,** an action by a state that cancels a federal law to which the state objects. If accepted, Calhoun's ideas would seriously weaken the federal government.

Arguments for Nullification To many southerners, the tariff issue was part of a much larger problem. If the federal government could enforce what they considered an unjust law, could it also use its power to end slavery?

John C. Calhoun had based his theory of nullification on his view of how the Union was formed. He said the Union grew from an agreement between the various states. After the Union was formed, each state kept certain powers. One of them was the power to nullify federal laws the people of the state considered unfair.

Milestones in the States' Rights Debate

1787: The Constitution divides power between the states and federal government.

1814–1815: At the Hartford Convention, opponents of the War of 1812 insist that states have the right to secede.

| 1787 | 1802 | 1817 | 1832 |

1798: Kentucky and Virginia claim that states can nullify laws deemed unconstitutional.

1832: South Carolina claims the right to nullify tariffs, but it backs down when President Jackson threatens to use force against it.

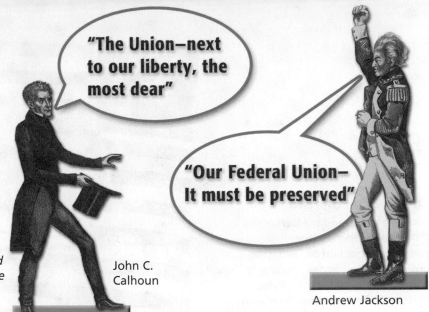

Federal Power Versus States' Rights

President Andrew Jackson and Vice President John C. Calhoun took opposing views on states' rights and nullification. They had once been friends. However, by 1830, the two men were fierce enemies. **Critical Thinking: *Detect Points of View*** *How may Andrew Jackson's views about nullification have been affected by his responsibility as President of the United States?*

"The Union—next to our liberty, the most dear"

John C. Calhoun

"Our Federal Union— It must be preserved"

Andrew Jackson

Arguments Against Nullification The clearest argument against nullification came from Massachusetts Senator Daniel Webster. He argued that the United States had not been formed by the states, but by the entire American people. In a dramatic speech on the floor of the Senate in January 1830, Webster defended his belief, saying "We are all agents of the same supreme power, the people."

A few months later, President Jackson dramatically defended the Union. At a banquet, Jackson stared directly at Vice President Calhoun and said, "Our Federal Union—It must be preserved." Ominously, Calhoun responded: "The Union—next to our liberty, the most dear." The challenge was clear. To Calhoun, states' rights was more important than saving the Union.

South Carolina Threatens to Secede In 1832, Congress passed another tariff law. Although it lowered some tariffs, it passed high tariffs on iron and textiles. South Carolina then called a state convention, which voted to nullify the tariffs. The tariffs of 1828 and 1832, it said, did not apply to South Carolina. The state also warned the federal government not to use force to impose the tariffs. If it did, South Carolina would secede from the Union.

A furious Jackson responded strongly. In December 1832, he put federal troops in South Carolina on alert. Then he issued a "Proclamation to the People of South Carolina." It said that the Union could not be <u>dissolved</u>. It also warned that "disunion by armed force is treason." With tensions running high, Calhoun resigned as Vice President.

Early in 1833, Jackson asked Congress to allow the federal government to collect its tariff in South Carolina by force if necessary. At the same time, he supported a compromise bill that would lower the tariffs. In March 1833, Congress passed both laws.

Unable to win support for its position from other states, South Carolina then repealed its tariff nullification. Many Americans breathed a sigh of relief. The crisis had been settled peacefully.

Vocabulary Builder
<u>dissolve</u> (dih ZAHLV) **v.** break up into smaller parts

The Election of 1840
Both the Whigs and the Democrats tried new methods in the presidential election of 1840. They broadened their appeal, hoping to win the vote of the "common man."
Critical Thinking: *Link Past and Present* How are presidential campaigns today similar to the 1840 campaign? How are they different?

Jackson had successfully defended federal power, while states' rights supporters had suffered a setback. However, the issue of states' rights would not go away. Americans would continue to debate the balance between states' rights and federal powers until the Civil War broke out in 1861.

✓**Checkpoint** **What was the position of Vice President John C. Calhoun on nullification?**

The End of the Jackson Era

A weary Andrew Jackson retired from office after two terms. Martin Van Buren was Andrew Jackson's choice to succeed him. Van Buren, the son of a New York tavern owner, had played a central role in organizing Jackson's first election victory in 1828. He had been secretary of state during Jackson's first term and Vice President during his second term. He had long been a close political adviser to Jackson.

In the election of 1836, the Whigs ran three candidates, each from a different region of the country. Their goal was to prevent any candidate from receiving a majority of electoral votes. This would throw the election into the House of Representatives. However, the strategy did not work. Van Buren received a majority of both the electoral and the popular vote.

The Panic of 1837 Van Buren took office at a time when the American economy was beginning a severe slump. Because Britain was experiencing an economic slowdown, British manufacturers were buying less cotton. This caused cotton prices to fall sharply. American banks could not collect on the loans they had made to cotton growers. As a result, hundreds of banks went bankrupt.

The result was an economic collapse in the United States called the Panic of 1837. The economic hard times that followed lasted six years. The hardships of those years ruined Van Buren's presidency.

The Election of 1840 Van Buren ran for reelection in 1840 against the Whig candidate, William Henry Harrison. This time the Whigs ran a skillful campaign. They used parades, barbecues, and other forms of entertainment to reach ordinary voters. They portrayed Harrison as a "man of the people" who would feel right at home in a simple log cabin. Helped by his "log cabin" campaign, Harrison easily defeated Van Buren. The Whigs were in power and the Age of Jackson was over.

☑ **Checkpoint** What was the main cause of the Panic of 1837?

☆ **Looking Back and Ahead** Throughout the administrations of John Quincy Adams, Andrew Jackson, and Martin Van Buren, Americans continued to push westward. By the 1830s, Americans had settled most of the land east of the Mississippi River. By the 1840s, they were crossing the Mississippi in large numbers. You will read about this movement in the next unit.

Identify Multiple Causes
In 1837, the United States experienced an economic collapse. What were two causes of this collapse?

Section 5 | **Check Your Progress**

Progress Monitoring ⊕nline
For: Self-test with instant help
Visit: PHSchool.com
Web Code: mya-3065

Comprehension and Critical Thinking

1. (a) Recall Why did states' rights become an issue in the 1820s?
(b) Distinguish Relevant Information Agree or disagree with the following statement and provide relevant facts to support your position: "The issue of states' rights had plagued the nation from the time of the Constitutional Convention."

2. (a) Summarize What were John C. Calhoun's and Daniel Webster's positions on nullification?
(b) Detect Points of View What did John C. Calhoun mean when he said, "The Union—next to our liberty, the most dear"?

Reading Skill

3. Identify Multiple Causes After the nullification crisis, South Carolina repealed its nullification of the federal tariffs. What were two causes of the state's action?

Key Terms

4. Write two definitions for the key term nullification. First, write a formal definition for your teacher. Second, write a definition in everyday English for a classmate.

Writing

5. Correct the errors in grammar, spelling, and punctuation in the following passage. **Passage:** The Nullification Crises represent a conflict between the South and the federal government. president Jackson at a banquet said that the Union must be preserved. John Calhoun answered "The Union—next to our liberty, the most dearest."

21st Century Learning Bias is slanted writing that communicates a certain point of view about an idea or event. The writer either leaves out information or purposely changes the facts in order to create a certain impression. Bias is different from objective writing, which presents the facts in a balanced way.

The following excerpt, from Andrew Jackson's seventh annual message to Congress, focuses on his Indian removal policy.

Primary Source

". . . The plan of removing the [native] people to . . . country west of the Mississippi River approaches its [conclusion]. . . . All preceding experiments for the improvement of the Indians have failed. It seems now to be an established fact that they can not live in contact with a civilized community and prosper. . . .

The plan for their removal . . . is founded upon the knowledge we have gained of their character and habits, and has been dictated by a spirit of [generosity]. A territory exceeding in extent that [given up] has been granted to each tribe. Of its climate, fertility, and capacity to support an Indian population the representations are highly favorable. . . .

. . . A country west of Missouri and Arkansas has been assigned to them, into which the white settlements are not to be pushed. . . . A barrier has thus been raised for their protection . . . guarding the Indians as far as possible from those evils which have brought them to their present condition."

—Andrew Jackson, December 7, 1835

Learn the Skill
Use these steps to identify bias.

1. **Identify the source.** Knowing the speaker or writer and the audience helps you understand why the point of view might be biased.

2. **Find the main idea.** Summarize the main point in the primary source.

3. **Compare the primary source with objective writing.** Look for differences between the biased writing and an objective account of the same subject. Does the biased writer leave out information or alter facts? Does the biased writer use broad generalizations that support a particular point of view? Does the biased writer use emotionally charged words?

4. **Draw conclusions.** What does the writer or speaker hope to accomplish?

Practice the Skill
Answer the following questions about the primary source on this page.

1. **Identify the source.** (a) Who is the author? (b) Why might the author's position be biased?

2. **Find the main idea.** What is the main point of the speech?

3. **Compare the primary source with objective writing.** Read the information about the government's Indian removal policy in Section 4. (a) What is one way that this account differs from the account in Section 4? (b) What is an example of a broad generalization that creates a biased view? (c) What information about the real reason for Indian removal is not included?

4. **Draw conclusions.** What message does the author want to present to the audience?

Apply the Skill
See the Review and Assessment at the end of this chapter.

Quick Study Guide

How did the nation reflect a growing sense of national pride and identity?

Section 1
Building a National Identity

- James Monroe's time as President was called the Era of Good Feelings.
- Tariffs protected northern factories but forced the South to pay more for goods.
- Key Supreme Court decisions strengthened the power of the federal government.

Section 2
Dealing With Other Nations

- The United States acquired Florida in 1819.
- Spanish territories in the Americas revolted and gained their independence.
- Britain granted Canadians more rights.

Section 3
The Age of Jackson

- John Quincy Adams served only one term.
- Democratic reforms allowed more white men to vote.

Section 4
Indian Removal

- The government forced Native Americans to move west of the Mississippi River.
- Thousands of Native Americans died resisting removal or along the journey west.

Section 5
States' Rights and the Economy

- Jackson vetoed a bill to renew the charter of the second Bank.
- South Carolina said that states had the right to nullify federal laws.
- Jackson insisted that states could not nullify federal laws.
- Eventually, South Carolina backed down on nullification.

? Exploring the Essential Question

Use the online study guide to explore the essential question.

Section 1
How was the power of the federal government strengthened during the Era of Good Feelings?

Section 5
How did old issues take a new shape in the conflict over a national bank and tariffs?

Chapter 10 Essential Question
How did the nation reflect a growing sense of national pride and identity?

Section 2
How did U.S. foreign affairs reflect new national confidence?

Section 3
How did the people gain more power during the Age of Jackson?

Section 4
Why did Jackson use force to remove Native Americans from the Southeast?

Key Terms

Answer the following questions in complete sentences that show your understanding of the key terms.

1. How would British **dumping** hurt American business?

2. What are the advantages of **suffrage**?

3. Which group of people might hold a **caucus**?

4. Who did John C. Calhoun believe had the right of **nullification**?

Comprehension and Critical Thinking

5. **(a) List** How did Henry Clay believe the United States would benefit from his American System?
   (b) Analyze Cause and Effect Which regions of the country were likely to benefit most from the plan? Why?

6. **(a) Explain** Why did President Monroe issue the Monroe Doctrine?
   (b) Apply Information How might the Monroe Doctrine aid Latin American nations?
   (c) Draw Conclusions How do you think Latin American leaders felt about the Monroe Doctrine?

7. **(a) Describe** Why did Andrew Jackson lose the presidential election in 1824?
   (b) Analyze Cause and Effect What changes occurred between 1824 and 1828 that resulted in Jackson winning the 1828 election?

8. **(a) Identify** What was the Trail of Tears?
   (b) Link Past and Present Why does the state of Oklahoma today have a large Native American population?

9. **(a) Describe** How did the spoils system work?
   (b) Draw Conclusions How would it affect a political party?
   (c) Detect Points of View Why did Jackson say the spoils system furthered democracy?

10. **(a) Identify** What was the Panic of 1837?
    (b) Draw Inferences How might the panic have contributed to the election of William Henry Harrison in 1840?

History Reading Skill

11. **Analyze Cause and Effect** Reread the text in Section 1 under the heading "Three Important Supreme Court Rulings." What was the cause of the Supreme Court's decision in *McCulloch* v. *Maryland*? What were the results of the decision? Which results were short-term? Which were long-term?

Writing

12. **Revise the following paragraph to correct the errors in grammar, spelling, and punctuation:**
    In 1832, congress pass a new law, which lowered some tariffs but continued the high tarriffs on iron and textiles. Generally the South opposed tarifs. South Caroline actually voted to oppose the tariff legislation. Because President Jackson regard this act as a challenge to his authority. He issued a "Proclamation to the People of South Carolina." Which said that leaving the Union would be an act of treeson.

13. **Write a Narrative:**
    Imagine you are a Cherokee in 1838–1839. Write a narrative describing your journey to the Indian Territory.

Skills for Life
Identify Bias

Use the excerpt below to answer the questions.

> "More than eight millions of the stock of this bank are held by foreigners. By this act the American Republic proposes virtually to make them a present of some millions of dollars. . . . If we must have a bank with private stockholders, every consideration of sound policy and every impulse of American feeling admonishes that it should be *purely American*. . . ."
>
> —Andrew Jackson, "Bank Veto Message,"
> July 10, 1832

14. **(a)** Who is the author? **(b)** Why would the author's position be biased?

15. What is the main point of the message?

16. Give an example of emotionally charged words used to support the writer's point of view.

17. What message does the writer want to convey to the audience?

Test Yourself

1. **What was the principal reason Andrew Jackson opposed the second Bank of the United States?**

   A Its policies hurt revenue Jackson expected to get from tariffs.

   B The second Bank refused to loan money to state banks.

   C Jackson believed it gave power to a small group of wealthy people.

   D The second Bank backed John C. Calhoun on the issue of nullification.

2. **Which issue was Andrew Jackson referring to when he said, "John Marshall has made his decision. Now let him enforce it"?**

   A a case about the importance of private contracts

   B a state attempt to apply its laws to Cherokee territory

   C interstate commerce

   D the dumping of goods by Britain in the United States

Refer to the map below to answer Question 3.

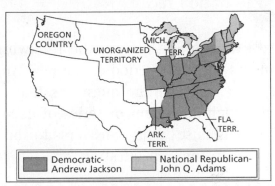

3. **Based on the map above, what was the major reason Jackson won the election of 1828?**

   A Jackson won only the states with large electoral vote totals.

   B New states that joined the Union between 1824 and 1828 voted for Jackson.

   C Many states that had voted for Adams in 1824 switched to Jackson.

   D Jackson swept the electoral votes of states in the South and West.

Document-Based Questions

Task: Look at Documents 1 and 2, and answer their accompanying questions. Then, use the documents and your knowledge of history to complete this writing assignment:

Write a short essay describing how changing political practices reflected new views of democracy that began to take hold during the Age of Jackson.

Document 1: William Henry Harrison's 1840 presidential campaign was filled with advertising, slogans, organized rallies, and campaign songs like this one. *What image of Harrison was this song trying to create?*

"Come swell the throng and join the song,
Make the circle wider
Join the round for Harrison, Log Cabin and Hard Cider.
With Harrison our country's won,
No treachery can divide her.
Thy will be done
With Harrison, Log Cabin and Hard Cider."

Document 2: This campaign poster combines images of a humble log cabin with slogans about Harrison's exploits as a general. *What image of Harrison does this poster create? How does this image compare to Andrew Jackson's image?*

Historian's Apprentice Workshop

What problems might a new nation face?

DIRECTIONS: Analyze the following documents from the period of the new American republic. Answer the questions that accompany each document or series of documents. You will use your answers to build an answer to the unit question.

HISTORIAN'S CHECKLIST

WHO produced the document?

WHERE was it made?

WHEN was it produced?

WHY was it made and for what audience?

WHAT is its viewpoint?

HOW does it connect to what I've learned?

WHY is the document important?

Economic Problems

document 1

PROBLEM	HAMILTON'S SOLUTION
• States owe money on loans made during American Revolution	Federal government repays state debts to restore lenders' confidence
• Government needs income to pay off debts	Government places tariff on imports
• Government needs a safe place to deposit its funds	Government creates national bank

Why did the new government have a debt problem?

Whiskey Rebellion

document 2

"I, George Washington, President of the United States, do hereby command all persons, being insurgents, ... to disperse and retire peaceably to their respective abodes."

—*George Washington, 1794*

Why did Washington's new government have trouble collecting taxes?

3 Party Politics

document

"Let us, then, fellow-citizens, unite with one heart and one mind. Let us restore to social intercourse that harmony and affection without which liberty and even life itself are but dreary things.... Every difference of opinion is not a difference of principle. We have called by different names brethren of the same principle. We are all Republicans, we are all Federalists."

—*Thomas Jefferson,*
First Inaugural Address, 1801

According to Jefferson, what was causing disharmony?

4 The Supreme Court

document

"It is emphatically the province and duty of the judicial department to say what the law is. Those who apply the rule to particular cases, must of necessity expound and interpret that rule. If two laws conflict with each other, the courts must decide on the operation of each."

—*John Marshall,*
Marbury v. *Madison, 1803*

How did Marshall address the problem of some laws being unconstitutional?

The Louisiana Purchase

document 5

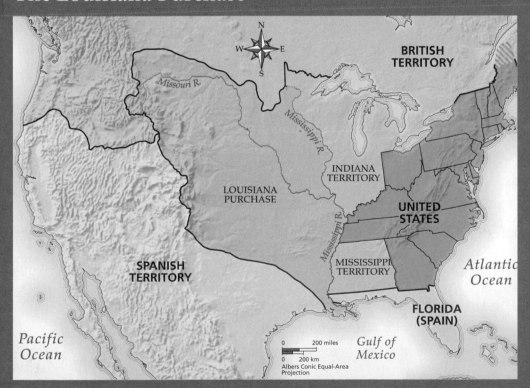

How did the Louisiana Purchase increase the likelihood of wars in the West?

6 The War of 1812

"Oh, say, can you see, by the dawn's early light,
What so proudly we hail'd at the twilight's last gleaming? Whose broad stripes and bright stars, thro' the perilous fight, O'er the ramparts we watch'd, were so gallantly streaming? And the rockets' red glare, the bombs bursting in air,
Gave proof thro' the night that our flag was still there.
O say, does that star-spangled banner yet wave
O'er the land of the free and the home of the brave?"

—Francis Scott Key, "The Star-Spangled Banner," 1814

How do you think Key's words affected American soldiers fighting against the British?

7 Differing Views

"Our federal Union—it must be preserved!"
—President Andrew Jackson, April 13, 1830

"To the Union. Next to our liberty, most dear."
—Vice President John C. Calhoun, April 13, 1830

What were Jackson and Calhoun disagreeing about?

Andrew Jackson ▶

◀ John C. Calhoun

8 Conflict With Native Americans

document

"We wish to remain on the land of our fathers. We have a perfect and original right to remain without interruption or molestation. The treaties with us, and laws of the United States made in pursuance of treaties, guarantee our residence and our privileges, and secure us against intruders. Our only request is, that these treaties may be fulfilled, and these laws executed. But if we are compelled to leave our country, we see nothing but ruin before us."

—Letter from the Cherokee Nation, 1830

Why did the Cherokee write this letter to the federal government?

9 Jacksonian Democracy

document

Jackson Forever!
The Hero of Two Wars and of Or'eans!
The Man of the People!
HE WHO COULD NOT BARTER NOR BARGAIN FOR THE
PRESIDENCY!
Who, although "A Military Chieftain," valued the purity of Elections and of the Electors, MORE than the Office of PRESIDENT itself! Although the greatest in the gift of his countrymen, and the highest in point of dignity of any in the world,
BECAUSE
It should be derived from the
PEOPLE!
No Gag Laws! No Black Cockades! No Reign of Terror! No Standing Army or Navy Officers, when under the pay of Government, to browbeat, or
KNOCK DOWN
Old Revolutionary Characters, or our Representatives while in the discharge of their duty: To the Polls then, and vote for those who will support
OLD HICKORY
AND THE ELECTORAL LAW.

How did politics change in the "Age of Jackson"?

ACTIVITY

Divide into three groups to prepare and stage a mock Congressional hearing on the unit question:

 What problems might a new nation face?

Each group should use the documents and other information from the unit to prepare a report to submit to Congress. One group should focus on the economic problems our new nation faced. The second group should concentrate on the political problems. And the third group should focus on problems in international relations. After the groups have prepared their reports, conduct a Congressional hearing. The class is Congress. One member from each group presents an oral report to Congress. After each report, members of Congress may ask questions regarding the problems and possible solutions.

Unit 4

What forces unite and divide a nation?

History *Interactive*
Explore Historian's Apprentice Online
Visit: PHSchool.com
Web Code: mvp-4000

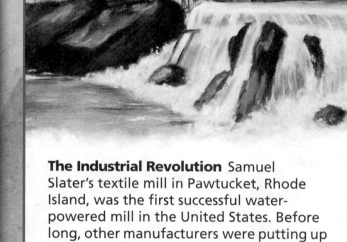

The Industrial Revolution Samuel Slater's textile mill in Pawtucket, Rhode Island, was the first successful water-powered mill in the United States. Before long, other manufacturers were putting up mills alongside northeastern rivers.

1793

Elizabeth Cady Stanton Stanton (shown here) and Lucretia Mott were the driving forces behind the 1848 Seneca Falls Convention in New York, a convention to advance women's rights.

1848

The Nation Expands and Changes

"Am I Not a Man and a Brother?" An emblem of a man in chains became the symbol of the struggle against slavery. In 1827, Samuel Cornish and John Russwurm set up an abolitionist newspaper called *Freedom's Journal.*

1827

Battle of Buena Vista Outnumbered two to one, an American force under General Zachary Taylor (on his white horse) forced General Santa Anna's Mexican army to retreat under cover of night back into central Mexico.

1847

San Francisco Boom Within a few years of the California gold rush, San Francisco had become a thriving town with rows of houses looking out at a busy waterfront.

1850s

North and South Take Different Paths

1800–1845

> *"We behold systematic efforts ...to excite the South against the North and the North against the South...."*
>
> —President Andrew Jackson, *Farewell Address, 1837*

Although scenes like this one spurred American nationalism, sectional differences grew during the first half of the nineteenth century.

What You Will Learn

Section 1
THE INDUSTRIAL REVOLUTION
New inventions brought new ways of making basic products.

Section 2
THE NORTH TRANSFORMED
Differences between the North and the South increased with the growth of industry.

Section 3
THE PLANTATION SOUTH
The invention of the cotton gin increased the South's dependence on the labor of enslaved people.

Section 4
THE CHALLENGES OF GROWTH
As settlement spread westward, debates over slavery increased tensions between North and South.

Reading Skill

Identify and Explain Central Issues In this chapter, you will learn to identify central issues and describe them in the context of the times and places in which they occurred.

Why did Americans take different

North and South Take Different Paths

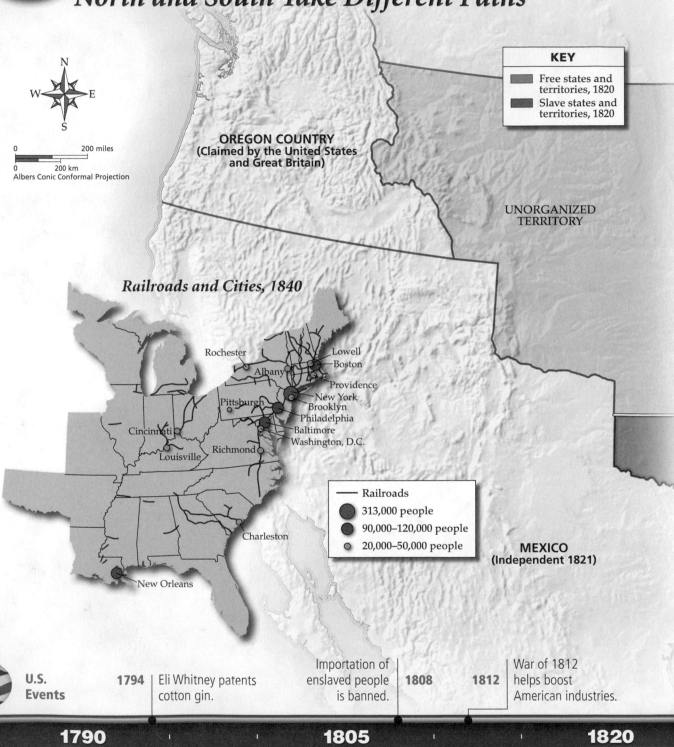

KEY
- Free states and territories, 1820
- Slave states and territories, 1820

OREGON COUNTRY
(Claimed by the United States and Great Britain)

UNORGANIZED TERRITORY

Railroads and Cities, 1840

Rochester
Lowell
Boston
Albany
Providence
Pittsburgh
New York
Brooklyn
Philadelphia
Cincinnati
Baltimore
Washington, D.C.
Louisville
Richmond

Charleston

MEXICO
(Independent 1821)

New Orleans

— Railroads
- 313,000 people
- 90,000–120,000 people
- 20,000–50,000 people

N W E S

0 200 miles
0 200 km
Albers Conic Conformal Projection

U.S. Events | **1794** Eli Whitney patents cotton gin. | Importation of enslaved people is banned. **1808** | **1812** War of 1812 helps boost American industries.

1790   **1805**   **1820**

World Events **1790** Richard Arkwright builds first steam-powered textile factory in England. | Spain cedes Florida to United States. **1819**

380

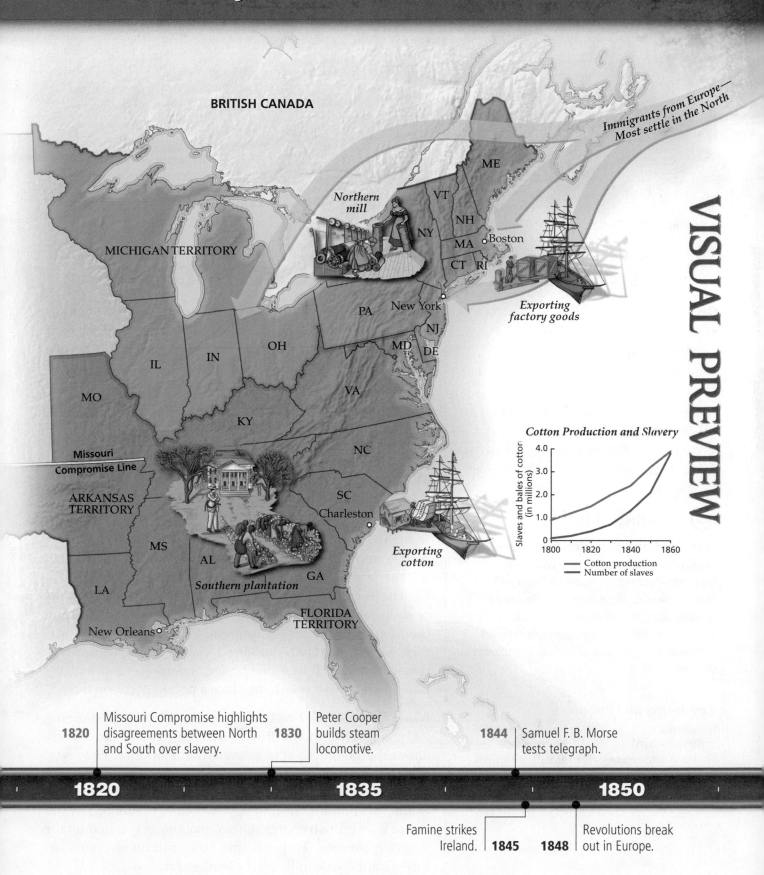

VISUAL PREVIEW

BRITISH CANADA

Immigrants from Europe— Most settle in the North

ME

VT

Northern mill

NH

NY

MA ○ Boston

MICHIGAN TERRITORY

CT RI

PA New York ●

Exporting factory goods

NJ

OH MD

DE

IL IN

VA

MO

KY

Missouri Compromise Line

NC

ARKANSAS TERRITORY

SC

Charleston ○

MS

AL

Exporting cotton

LA

Southern plantation

GA

New Orleans ○

FLORIDA TERRITORY

Cotton Production and Slavery

Slaves and bales of cotton (in millions)

4.0
3.0
2.0
1.0
0

1800   1820   1840   1860

— Cotton production
— Number of slaves

1820 | Missouri Compromise highlights disagreements between North and South over slavery. | **1830** Peter Cooper builds steam locomotive.

1844 | Samuel F. B. Morse tests telegraph.

1820   1835   1850

Famine strikes Ireland. | **1845**   **1848** | Revolutions break out in Europe.

You Will Be Astounded

❝There are more than 5,000 females employed in Lowell; and when you come to see the amount of labor performed by them, in superintending the different machinery, you will be astonished. . . . Everything moves on like clockwork. . . .❞

—Congressman Davy Crockett of Tennessee, after visiting mills in Lowell, Massachusetts, 1834

▲ New England mill town, early 1800s

The Industrial Revolution

Objectives

- Explain the changes that the Industrial Revolution brought to American life.

- Discuss the importance of Samuel Slater's cotton mill.

- Describe the growth of industry in the United States after 1812.

- Identify important developments in factories and the problems that factory life produced.

⊙ Reading Skill

Identify Central Issues From the Past
To effectively study history, you can identify important—or central—issues and then seek to make generalizations from them. To make a generalization, identify main points or ideas in a text. Then, devise a general principle or broad statement that applies to all of them and to other situations.

Key Terms and People

Industrial
  Revolution
factory system
capitalist

Francis Cabot
  Lowell
mass production
interchangeable
  parts

Why It Matters In early America, most people worked as farmers. Men worked in the fields to produce food for their families. Women helped in the fields and made simple goods, like candles and soap, at home. The Industrial Revolution changed all this.

❓ **Section Focus Question: How did the new technology of the Industrial Revolution change the way Americans lived?**

A Revolution in Technology

In the 1700s, a great change began that we now call the **Industrial Revolution.** Gradually, machines took the place of many hand tools. Much of the power once provided by people and horses began to be replaced, first by flowing water and then by steam engines.

The Industrial Revolution began in Britain, in the textile, or cloth-making, industry. For centuries, workers had spun thread in their homes on spinning wheels. The thread was then woven into cloth on hand looms. Making thread was time-consuming. It took one person, spinning one strand at a time, almost two weeks to produce a pound of cotton thread.

Machines and Factories In the 1760s, the spinning jenny speeded up the thread-making process. The jenny allowed a person to spin many strands at once. However, thread still had to be made by hand.

Then, in 1764, Richard Arkwright invented the water frame, a spinning machine powered by running water rather than human energy. Other inventions speeded up the weaving process. To house the large machines, manufacturers built textile mills on the banks of rivers.

The new mills created a new way of working, known as the factory system. The **factory system** brings workers and machinery together in one place. Instead of spinning at home, textile workers had to go to the factories and begin and end work at specific hours. Workers now had to keep up with the machines instead of working at their own pace.

British mill owners soon recognized the potential of the new water frames and the factory system. However, the system required huge amounts of money to be <u>invested</u> in buildings and machines. Thus, the mill owners turned to **capitalists,** people who invest capital, or money, in a business to earn a profit. Factories proved to be a good investment for the capitalists and mill owners. By 1784, British workers were producing 24 times as much thread as they had in 1765.

Steam Power Building factories on riverbanks had some disadvantages. In a dry season, the machines had no power. Also, most factories were far from cities, and labor was hard to find in rural areas.

In 1790, Arkwright built the first steam-powered textile plant. The steam engine was a reliable source of power. Factories no longer had to be built on riverbanks. They could be built in cities, where young women and children provided cheap labor.

Britain tried to guard the secrets of its industrial success. It forbade anyone to take information about textile machinery out of Britain. Skilled workers were forbidden to leave the country.

☑**Checkpoint** How did the Industrial Revolution change the way work was performed?

Vocabulary Builder
<u>invest</u> (ihn VEHST) *v.* to supply money for a project in order to make a profit

A Steam Engine

❶ Cylinder
Steam from boiling water rises into the cylinder.

❸ Flywheel
The other end of the beam goes down, moving gears to turn the flywheel.

❷ Piston rod Pressure from the rising steam pushes the piston rod up and raises one end of the beam.

History *Interactive*
Study a Steam Engine in Action
Visit: PHSchool.com
Web Code: myp-4071

Steam Engine
Steam engines use the energy created by boiling water to push rods and wheels. **Critical Thinking:** *Identify Economic Benefits* What advantage would the steam engine have given to a manufacturer over competitors who depended on water power to operate their machinery?

Signs of Progress
The Industrial Revolution put people to work in large factories like the one shown here. **Critical Thinking: *Distinguish Relevant Information*** *From the evidence in this picture, how might the presence of a factory affect the surrounding communities?*

The American Industrial Revolution

In 1789, a young apprentice in one of Arkwright's factories decided to immigrate to the United States. Samuel Slater knew that his knowledge of Arkwright's machines could be worth a fortune. He studied hard and memorized the plans of Arkwright's machines. Then, he boarded a ship for New York.

In the United States, Slater joined forces with a wealthy merchant, Moses Brown. Brown had rented a textile mill in Pawtucket, Rhode Island. Relying entirely on his memory, Slater constructed a spinning machine based on Arkwright's. Slater's factory began producing cotton thread at a rate never before seen in the United States.

☑ **Checkpoint** **Why did Samuel Slater have to build his machines from memory?**

American Industry Grows

The success of Slater's mill marked the beginning of American industrialization. Industrialization began in the Northeast. The region was home to a class of merchants who had capital to build factories and to buy raw materials.

Still, U.S. industry did not grow significantly until the War of 1812. As the British navy blockaded U.S. ports, Americans had to depend on their own industries to supply goods.

The Lowell Mills Francis Cabot Lowell found a way. Before the war, he had visited England and seen the latest weaving machines. When he returned to the United States, Lowell and an associate built an improved version of the English machines.

With several other capitalists, Lowell opened a mill in Waltham, Massachusetts. The mill was organized in a new way. Instead of obtaining thread from separate spinning mills, Lowell's factory brought together spinning and weaving in one building.

After Lowell died in 1817, his partners expanded the business. Wanting better lives for their workers, the partners built a new town, with boardinghouses, a library, and a hospital. They named their mill town Lowell after their late partner.

Lowell Girls The new factories were staffed with young women from nearby farms. "Lowell girls" lived in boardinghouses under strict supervision. After work, they might attend lectures or visit libraries. As a result, many women gained an education they probably would not have received on their family farms. The British novelist Charles Dickens was amazed when he saw Lowell:

> **“**Firstly, there is a . . . piano in a great many of the boardinghouses. Secondly, nearly all these young ladies subscribe to circulating libraries. Thirdly, they have [created] a periodical called 'The Lowell Offering.' . . .**”**
>
> —Charles Dickens, *American Notes*, 1842

✓**Checkpoint** How was the Lowell factory system different from the European factory system?

Identify Central Issues From the Past

What generalization can you make about the link between war, trade, and inventiveness?

Links Across Time

2000s Office workers and researchers use computers for much of what they do.

Technology and Work

1820s The Industrial Revolution opened the way for new developments in technology, which changed the way people worked.

1981–2000s Since the invention of the personal computer, changes in technology have affected not only *how* people work but also *where* they work. With speedy laptops and hand-held devices, workers are able to work successfully at home or at the office.

Link to Today

Technology's Impact Technology continues to advance. How are technological innovations changing people's lives today?

For: Technology in the workplace
Visit: PHSchool.com
Web Code: myc-4071

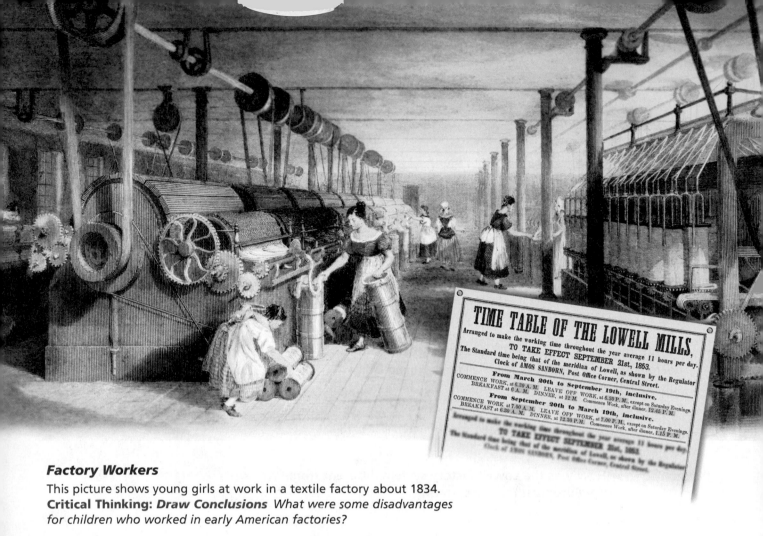

Factory Workers

This picture shows young girls at work in a textile factory about 1834.
Critical Thinking: *Draw Conclusions* *What were some disadvantages for children who worked in early American factories?*

The Revolution Takes Hold

The Lowell system was an example of a unique American outlook. Without a long tradition of doing things a certain way, Americans experimented with new methods. One of the most important developments was **mass production**, or the rapid manufacture of large numbers of identical objects.

Before the 1800s, skilled craftsworkers manufactured clocks, guns, and other mechanical products. Each part of the gun or clock was handcrafted. When a part broke, a craftsworker had to create a unique piece to fit the product. In the 1790s, American inventor Eli Whitney devised a system of **interchangeable parts**, identical pieces that could be assembled quickly by unskilled workers.

Interchangeable parts soon came to be used in the manufacture of other products. Manufacturing became more <u>efficient</u>. The price of many goods dropped. As people bought more goods, U.S. industry expanded to satisfy their needs.

Factory Life As you have read, the Lowell mills treated factory workers in a new and kinder way. However, this was not the general rule. Samuel Slater employed children in his textile mill, as had been done for decades in British factories. As time went on, working conditions for children and adults became harsher.

Vocabulary Builder
efficient (ee FISH ehnt) *adj.* acting effectively, without wasted cost or effort

Child Labor Children routinely worked on family farms in the 1800s. Their labor was often needed to help feed their families. Working on a home farm was different from working in a factory, however. American textile mills, coal mines, and steel foundries employed children as young as 7 or 8. These children had no opportunities for education. They often worked in unsafe conditions. By 1880, more than a million children between the ages of 10 and 15 worked for pay.

Factory Conditions Working conditions were appalling. Factories were poorly lighted. There was little fresh air. Machines were designed to perform a task, not to protect the worker. As a result, many workers were injured on the job. A worker who lost a hand or a foot received no help. He or she needed to depend on family for support. Business owners provided no payments for disabled workers, as they do by law today.

To keep machines running as long as possible, workdays lasted 12 or 14 hours. By 1844, workers were demanding shorter days. "Eight hours for work, eight hours for sleep, and eight hours for God and the brethren" was an early slogan. Conditions gradually improved, but the 8-hour workday was far in the future.

✔**Checkpoint** **How did Eli Whitney's system of interchangeable parts speed up the manufacturing process?**

☆ **Looking Back and Ahead** Although the new factories were hard on workers, industrialization led to vastly increased production and lower prices. In the next section, you will read how the growth of northern industry helped to widen the gap between the North and the South.

Section 1 | Check Your Progress

Progress Monitoring ⓞnline
For: Self-test with instant help
Visit: PHSchool.com
Web Code: mya-4071

Comprehension and Critical Thinking

1. **(a) Describe** How did the War of 1812 affect U.S. industry?
(b) Draw Conclusions Why did advances in industry occur mainly in the North?

2. **(a) Recall** What are interchangeable parts?
(b) Draw Conclusions How did the system of interchangeable parts affect employment in the United States?

Reading Skill

3. **Identify Central Issues From the Past** Based on this section, what generalization can you make about the impact of inventiveness during the early Industrial Revolution?

Key Terms

4. Write two definitions for each key term: factory system, capitalist, interchangeable parts. First, write a formal definition for your teacher. Second, write a definition in everyday English for a classmate.

Writing

5. Rewrite the following lists of causes and effects, so that causes are correctly paired up with their effects.

Causes: Francis Lowell; Arkwright's textile plant; Samuel Slater's emigration; Eli Whitney

Effects: efficiency in mass production; libraries for factory workers; factories built in cities; increased American production of cotton thread

Mill Workers
by Lucy Larcom

Prepare to Read

Introduction

Lucy Larcom was born in Massachusetts in 1824. After her father died when she was 11, Lucy went to work in the Lowell textile mills. Years later, she wrote about her experiences. The following selection is an excerpt from her memoirs.

⊙ Reading Skill

Analyze Setting In literature, a character's actions and attitudes often are affected by his or her surroundings. In the memoir below, we learn how the physical conditions in a textile mill affect Lucy Larcom's outlook on work. As you read, pay attention to her descriptions of the mill.

Vocabulary *Builder*

As you read this literature selection, look for the following underlined words:

bobbin (BAHB ihn) *n.* spool for thread or yarn, used in spinning, weaving, or in a sewing machine

board (bord) *n.* meals provided regularly for pay

drudge (druhj) *n.* person who does hard, menial, or tedious work

⭐ Background

Women and girls who worked in northern mills were educated. Some mills published collections of workers' essays and poetry.

I went to my first day's work in the mill with a light heart. The novelty of it made it seem easy, and it really was not hard just to change the <u>bobbins</u> on the spinning-frames every three-quarters of an hour or so, with half a dozen other little girls who were doing the same thing. When I came back at night, the family began to pity me for my long, tiresome day's work, but I laughed and said, "Why, it is nothing but fun. It is just like play."

And for a while it was only a new amusement. . . . We were not occupied more than half the time. The intervals were spent frolicking around the spinning-frames, teasing and talking to the older girls, or entertaining ourselves with games and stories in the corner, or exploring, with the overseer's permission, the mysteries of the carding-room, the dressing-room, and the weaving-room.

I never cared much for machinery. The buzzing and hissing of pulleys and rollers and spindles and flyers around me often grew tiresome. I could not see into their complications, or feel interested in them. But in a room below us we were sometimes allowed to peer in through a sort of blind door at the great waterwheel that carried the works of the whole mill. It was so huge that we could only watch a few of its spokes at a time, and part of its dripping rim, moving with a slow, measured strength through the darkness that shut it in. It impressed me with something of the awe which comes to us in thinking of the great Power which keeps the mechanism of the universe in motion. . . .

When I took my next three months at the grammar school, everything there was changed, and I too was changed. . . . It was a great delight to me to study, and at the end of the three months the master told me that I was prepared for the high school.

Lowell girls weaving in a Massachusetts textile mill in the 1850s

But alas! I could not go. The little money I could earn—one dollar a week, besides the price of my <u>board</u>—was needed in the family, and I must return to the mill. . . .

At this time I had learned to do a spinner's work, and I obtained permission to tend some frames that stood directly in front of the windows, with only them and the wall behind me, extending half the length of the mill. . . .

The last window in the row behind me was filled with flourishing houseplants—fragrant-leaved geraniums, the overseer's pets. . . . T[he] perfume and freshness tempted me there often. . . . On the whole, it was far from being a disagreeable place to stay in. The girls were bright looking and neat, and everything was kept clean and shining. The effect of the whole was rather attractive to strangers. . . .

Still, we did not call ourselves ladies. We did not forget that we were working girls, wearing coarse aprons suitable to our work, and that there was some danger to our becoming <u>drudges</u>. I know that sometimes the confinement of the mill became very wearisome to me. In the sweet June weather I would lean far out of the window, and try not to hear the unceasing clash of the sound inside. Looking away to the hills, my whole stifled being would cry out, "Oh that I had wings!"

From *A New England Girlhood,* by Lucy Larcom.
Peter Smith, 1973. First published in 1887 by Macmillan.

Checkpoint **Why did Larcom return to the mill after finishing three months at grammar school?**

Analyze LITERATURE

Lucy Larcom's words describe a mill in New England during the 1800s. Consider the sights and sounds around her, and how working in the mill made her feel. Write a paragraph in which you describe what it is like to work in a mill.

Background

The wages paid for millwork offered new opportunities to many women and girls, but workers lived apart from their families and often felt lonely.

Analyze Setting

Reading Skill

Lucy's attitude toward the mill changes somewhat over the course of this excerpt. How does setting contribute to this change?

If you liked this passage from *A New England Girlhood,* you might want to read more first-person accounts in *Ordinary Americans: U.S. History Through the Eyes of Everyday People,* edited by Linda R. Monk. Close Up Foundation. 2003.

Plenty of Work to Be Had

❝Now I will tell you something about . . . New York. Provisions are very cheap; plenty of work to be had; clothes are dear, but men paid well for their work; house rent is very dear in New York, it is a very healthy place. . . .❞

—English immigrant boy's letter to his mother, 1850

▲ New York harbor, 1840

The North Transformed

Objectives

- Explain why American cities grew in the 1800s.
- List the new inventions and advances in agriculture and manufacturing.
- Describe the improvements in transportation during the early 1800s.
- Discuss the wave of immigration to the United States in the 1840s and 1850s.
- Describe the problems African Americans faced in the North.

🎯 Reading Skill

Explain Central Issues From the Past As you read about the events of the past, you'll discover that people struggled with issues, much as they do today. Explain those issues to yourself—try to identify what people's concerns were, how they felt about issues, what the issues were about. This will make issues more real and understandable for you.

Key Terms and People

urbanization
telegraph
Samuel F.B. Morse

famine
nativist
discrimination

Why It Matters From colonial times, the North and South developed as distinct regions. At first these differences were small. But during the Industrial Revolution, the differences between the North and South widened dramatically.

❓ **Section Focus Question: How did urbanization, technology, and social change affect the North?**

Northern Cities

American cities had long been the centers of commerce and culture. By today's standards, these early cities were small. New York, the largest, had a population of slightly more than 33,000 in 1790. Compared to the major cities of Europe, or even the ancient Aztec capital of Tenochtitlán, New York was hardly more than a town.

Growth of Cities In the 1800s, however, U.S. cities grew larger. The Industrial Revolution spurred urbanization, or the growth of cities due to movement of people from rural areas to cities. As capitalists built more factories, agricultural workers were attracted to the new types of work available in the cities.

As cities along the eastern coast became crowded, newly arrived immigrants headed west. Pittsburgh, Pennsylvania, had about 23,000 people in 1840. Ten years later, the city had more than doubled in population. Farther west, the Kentucky city of Louisville was also growing. German and Irish immigrants increased the city's population to more than 43,000 by 1850, making Louisville larger than Washington, D.C.

Urban Problems Growing cities faced many problems. Filthy streets, the absence of good sewage systems, and a lack of clean drinking water encouraged the spread of disease.

> "One finds in the streets [of New York] dead cats and dogs, which make the air very bad; dust and ashes are thrown out into the streets, which are swept perhaps once every [two weeks]."
>
> —Baron Axel Klinckowstrom of Sweden

Citywide fires were another common problem. Most structures were made of wood. Volunteer firefighters were often poorly trained and equipped. Insurance companies paid firefighters for saving an insured building. Racing to fire scenes to earn the insurance money, rival fire companies sometimes ended up fighting one another instead of the fire.

✓**Checkpoint** **What problems did cities face in the early 1800s?**

The Growth of Northern Industry

New inventions revolutionized communications. The most important was the telegraph, a device that used electrical signals to send messages quickly over long distances.

The Telegraph Samuel F.B. Morse's invention worked by sending electrical signals over a wire. A code devised by Morse used shorter and longer bursts of electricity. In his system, known as the Morse code, each letter of the alphabet is represented by its own mix of short signals ("dots") and long signals ("dashes").

Explain Central Issues From the Past
Explain the link between industrialization and urban problems.

Growing Cities
American cities became bustling centers of enterprise during the 1800s. This is a view along State Street in Boston. **Critical Thinking: *Explain Problems*** *What problems did the rapid growth of cities pose for city dwellers?*

In 1844, Morse tested his system. He wired a message from Washington, D.C., to his assistant in Baltimore: "What hath God wrought?" A few minutes later, a response came back from Baltimore.

The telegraph soon became part of American life. Thousands of miles of wires were strung across the nation. Factories in the East could communicate with their markets in the West in a matter of hours rather than weeks.

Advances in Agriculture The mechanical reaper, invented by Cyrus McCormick, made it easier for farmers to settle the prairies of the Midwest. The reaper cut stalks of wheat many times faster than a human worker could. This enabled farmers to cultivate more land and harvest their crops with fewer workers.

Improvements in threshers also speeded up the harvesting of grain. Threshers separate the grains of wheat from their stalks. The wheat grains are then ground into flour. Eventually, the mechanical reaper and the thresher were put together into one machine called a combine.

These advances in agriculture also affected industry. Farm laborers who had been replaced by machines went to cities to work in shops and factories. Cities like Cincinnati grew as both agricultural and industrial centers.

Advances in Manufacturing Other inventions revolutionized the way goods were made. In 1846, Elias Howe patented a machine that could sew seams in fabric. A few years later, Isaac Singer improved on Howe's design. The sewing machine made it much more efficient to produce clothing in quantity. As clothes became less expensive, people of modest means began to dress almost as well as wealthier Americans.

By 1860, factories in New England and the Middle Atlantic states were producing most of the nation's manufactured goods. That year, Americans had over $1 billion invested in businesses. Of that total, more than 90 percent was invested in businesses in the North.

✓**Checkpoint** **What new inventions helped northern industry to grow?**

A Transportation Revolution

Improvements in transportation spurred the growth of American industry. As transportation became faster and easier, factories could make use of raw materials from farther away. Improved transportation also allowed factory owners to ship their goods to distant markets.

Steamboats and Clipper Ships In 1807, Robert Fulton, an American inventor, used a steam engine to power a boat. Fulton's *Clermont* was the first practical steamboat. It was 133 feet long and had wooden side paddles that pulled it through the water.

Although side-paddle steamboats were ideal for traveling on rivers, they were not suited to ocean travel. In 1850, a new type of American-built ship appeared, the clipper ship. Long and slender, with tall masts, the clipper ships were magnificent, swift vessels. The Yankee clippers, as they were called, were the world's fastest ships. Their reign was brief, however. By the 1850s, Great Britain was producing oceangoing steamships. These ironclad steamships were faster and could carry more cargo.

Vocabulary Builder
reign (rayn) *n.* period of dominance or rule

Railroads Of all forms of transportation, railroads did the most to tie together raw materials, manufacturers, and markets. Steamboats had to follow the paths of rivers, which sometimes froze in winter. Railroads, however, could be built almost anywhere.

America's first railroad, the Baltimore and Ohio, was begun in 1828. As with most European railroads, its cars were drawn along the track by horses. Then, in 1830, Peter Cooper built the first American-made steam locomotive. By 1840, about 3,000 miles of railway track had been built in the United States.

☑ **Checkpoint** **Why were railroads a better means of transportation than steamboats?**

A New Wave of Immigrants

The American population grew rapidly in the 1840s. Millions of immigrants entered the United States, mostly from western Europe. Some came because they had heard of opportunities to buy cheap land. Others believed their skills would serve them well in the United States. Still others had little choice, because they could not survive at home.

Fulton's Steamboat
Robert Fulton's steamboat, the *Clermont*, carried passengers between New York and Albany on the Hudson River. **Critical Thinking: *Interpret Pictures*** *Why would the* Clermont *not be suitable for ocean travel?*

Irish Immigration, 1845–1853

Number of Immigrants (in thousands)

240
200
160
120
80
40
0

1845 1847 1849 1851 1853

Year

Source: *Historical Statistics of the United States*

Fleeing the Famine

A famine in the 1840s drove many Irish to the United States. They contributed to a sharp rise in immigration. **Critical Thinking: Draw Inferences** *Why do you suppose the peak did not come immediately after the famine started in 1845?*

The Great Hunger Ireland had long been under British rule. While the best farmland was owned by British landlords, the potato was the staple, or basic, food for most of the population. Then, in 1845, a fungus destroyed the potato crop, leading to famine, or widespread starvation. The years that followed are often called the Great Hunger. More than a million people starved to death. About a million more left Ireland.

Most of the Irish immigrants who came to the United States during this period had been farm laborers at home. The men found work doing the lowliest jobs in construction or laying railroad track in the East and Midwest. Young Irish women were often employed as household workers.

German Newcomers Germans came to America during this period as well. Many had taken part in revolutions against harsh rulers. When the revolutions failed, the Germans fled to the United States.

Unlike the Irish, German immigrants came from many different levels of society. After arriving in the United States, most Germans moved west. Many settled in the Ohio Valley and the Great Lakes region.

Reaction Against Immigrants Some Americans worried about the growing foreign population. These were nativists, or people who wanted to preserve the country for white, American-born Protestants. Nativists especially opposed Irish immigration because most of the Irish were Roman Catholics.

One group of nativists in New York formed a secret group. When asked about their secret order, members replied, "I know nothing." In time, the Know-Nothings became a political party. In 1856, the Know-Nothing candidate for President won 21 percent of the vote. Soon after, the party split over the issue of slavery and dissolved.

✓**Checkpoint** Why did Irish and German immigration to the United States increase in the 1840s?

African Americans in the North

Even more than immigrants, African Americans in the North faced discrimination. Discrimination is the denial of equal rights or equal treatment to certain groups of people.

Slavery had largely ended in the North by the early 1800s. Free African Americans there were joined by new arrivals from the South. Freedom, however, did not grant equal treatment. African Americans were often denied the right to vote. They were not allowed to work in factories or in skilled trades. Even when they sought the least desirable jobs, they were at a disadvantage. Many employers preferred to hire white immigrants rather than African Americans.

Prejudice against African Americans led to the racial segregation of schools and public facilities. Turned away by white congregations, African Americans formed their own churches. For example, people who had been freed from slavery started the African Methodist Episcopal Church in Philadelphia in 1816.

White newspapers often portrayed African Americans as <u>inferior</u>. African Americans responded by starting their own publications. The first newspaper owned and run by African Americans was *Freedom's Journal*, which was established in 1827 in New York. Its editor, John B. Russwurm, had been one of the first African Americans to graduate from an American college.

Vocabulary Builder
<u>inferior</u> (ihn FIR ee uhr) *adj.* less worthy; less valuable; of lower rank

✓**Checkpoint** **What obstacles did African Americans face in the North?**

⭐ **Looking Back and Ahead** Northern cities grew with the arrival of immigrants from abroad and African Americans from rural areas. Meanwhile, as you will read in the next section, the South depended more and more on cotton and slavery.

Section 2 | **Check Your Progress**

Progress Monitoring ⊙nline
For: Self-test with instant help
Visit: PHSchool.com
Web Code: mya-4072

Comprehension and Critical Thinking

1. **(a) Recall** What factors led to the growth of cities?
   (b) Evaluate Information How did the rapid growth of cities affect urban living conditions?

2. **(a) Recall** How did the telegraph improve communication?
   (b) Identify Economic Benefits How might improved communication help the growing economy?

⊙ **Reading Skill**

3. **Explain Central Issues From the Past** Reread the text following the heading "Advances in Agriculture." Explain how changes in agriculture affected workers in the nineteenth century.

Key Terms

Read each sentence below. If the sentence is true, write YES. If the sentence is not true, write NO and explain why.

4. Urbanization is the movement of people from urban areas to farms.

5. More than a million people died in a famine during the Great Hunger that started in Ireland in 1845.

6. Even though many African Americans living in the North were legally free, they still suffered from discrimination.

Writing

7. Based on what you have read in this section, list as many causes as you can for the growth of industry in the North. Put stars next to the causes that you think are most important.

The Slaves' Quarters

"As to beds to sleep on, they were known to none of the field hands; nothing but a coarse blanket . . . was given them, and this only to the men and women. The children stuck themselves in holes and corners, about the quarters; often in the corner of the huge chimneys, with their feet in the ashes to keep them warm."

—Frederick Douglass, *My Bondage and My Freedom*, describing his early life as a slave

▲ The plantation owner's house was very different from the slaves' quarters.

The Plantation South

Objectives
- Explain the significance of cotton and the cotton gin to the South.
- Describe what life was like for free and enslaved African Americans in the South.

Reading Skill

Explain Problems From the Past Why did problems occur in the past? Try to answer this question as you read. It will help you connect events and understand people's beliefs and actions. Put yourself in the shoes of the people about whom you read. What problems would you have with these same issues? Explain these problems to clarify them.

Key Terms and People
cotton gin   spiritual
slave code   Nat Turner

Why It Matters The Industrial Revolution brought change to both the North and South. In the North, industry, immigration, and cities all grew. But in the South, the economy became more dependent on cotton and slave labor.

❓ Section Focus Question: How did cotton affect the social and economic life of the South?

The Cotton Kingdom

As the North became more urban and industrialized, the South remained largely rural. Two events changed life in the South. First, a boom in textiles caused by the Industrial Revolution created a huge demand for cotton. Second, a new invention allowed the South to satisfy that demand.

The Cotton Gin In 1793, Eli Whitney devised a simple machine that speeded the processing of cotton. His cotton gin used a spiked cylinder to remove seeds from cotton fibers.

Before the introduction of the cotton gin, the seeds had to be picked out of the cotton fibers by hand. This was a slow process. Working by hand, a laborer could clean only a pound of cotton a day.

The cotton gin was revolutionary technology. A worker could process fifty times more cotton fiber with the gin than by hand. Cotton growing became far more profitable.

Slave Labor To grow more cotton, planters used more slave labor. In 1790, there were about 698,000 enslaved African Americans in the United States. By 1860, the census recorded nearly 4 million. During that time, the price of a slave increased ten or twenty times.

Cotton became the greatest source of wealth for the United States. It enriched planters in the South, as well as bankers and shipowners in the North. Cotton production rose at an astonishing rate. Planters grew one and a half millon pounds of cotton in 1790. In 1820, they grew ten times as much.

Southern states were not all alike. States like Alabama and Mississippi, which depended on cotton, had large populations of enslaved people. Other states, such as Kentucky, <u>devoted</u> less attention to cotton. Fewer enslaved people lived there.

In the southern "Cotton Kingdom," society was dominated by owners of large plantations. This small but wealthy class lived in luxury and sent their children to the finest schools. But more than half of all southern farmers did not have slaves. They grew corn and raised hogs and chickens.

Defending Slavery Most southern whites accepted the system of slavery. Many feared that any weakening of controls over African Americans might encourage violent uprisings. By the 1830s, some people in the North were urging that slavery be banned. (You will read about the movement to end slavery in the next chapter.) In response, southern whites hardened their support for slavery.

Supporters of slavery said it was more humane than the free labor system of the North. Unlike northern factory workers, they argued, enslaved African Americans did not worry about unemployment.

Vocabulary Builder
devote (dee VOHT) **v.** to commit; to apply (time and energy, for example)

Explain Problems From the Past
Explain the disagreements between supporters and critics of slavery.

Cotton Production and Slavery

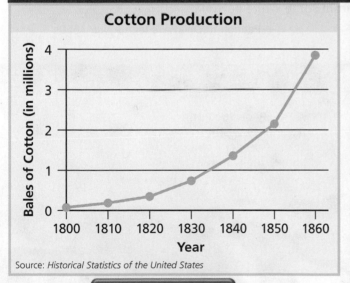

Cotton Production

Source: *Historical Statistics of the United States*

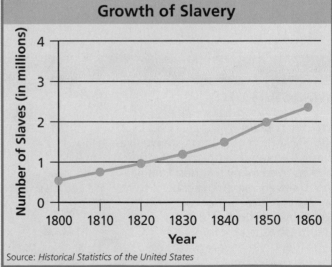

Growth of Slavery

Source: *Historical Statistics of the United States*

Reading Charts
Skills Activity

The rise in cotton production in the South was paralleled by a rise in the number of enslaved African Americans.

(a) Read Graphs How much did cotton production increase between 1800 and 1850? In what 10-year period did slavery grow the fastest?

(b) Make Predictions If cotton production had decreased, would the number of slaves have declined? Explain your reasoning.

Critics of slavery, however, challenged this reasoning. They argued that northern workers were free to quit a job and take another if conditions became too harsh. Also, the critics said, people held in slavery often suffered physical or other abuse from white owners. There was no satisfactory substitute for freedom.

☑**Checkpoint** How widespread was slave ownership?

African Americans in the South

Not all of the 4 million African Americans in the South were enslaved. About 253,000 (or 6 percent) were free. Many had purchased their freedom. A few did well, especially in cities like New Orleans. But most did not share in the prosperity around them.

Restrictions on Free African Americans Laws denied basic rights even to African Americans who were free. By law, they were excluded from all but the most menial jobs. Their children were denied the right to attend public schools. African Americans could not vote, serve on juries, or testify against white defendants in court.

Free African Americans were discouraged from traveling. In a petition, some described the conditions they faced:

❝[When] we have occasion to . . . Travel . . . [b]y Steem boat or Stage, we have been exceedingly anoyd And put to very considerable inconvenience and eaven compeled to Leave the boat and thereby entirely defeated from accomplishing our just and lawful business because we have not [had] a certificate from some White person.❞

—Petition to Delaware legislature, 1850s

● **INFOGRAPHIC**

Plantation Life
Life on a southern plantation showed vast contrasts. The families of large plantation owners enjoyed many luxuries. Families bound to slavery experienced hard work and many cruelties.
Critical Thinking: *Compare and Contrast How do these pictures support the view that plantation owners and enslaved African Americans lived very different lives?*

Keeping Cool
Refreshing breezes from fans like this kept wealthy women cool. ▼

▼ **A Family on the Patio**
A wealthy southern family relaxes on their patio as they survey their estate.

The freedom of African Americans in the South was never secure. Slave catchers prowled the streets looking for escapees. They often kidnapped free African Americans and sold them into slavery.

In spite of all the restrictions placed upon them, many free African Americans made valuable contributions to southern life. Norbert Rillieux revolutionized the sugar industry. His method of refining sugar made the process faster, safer, and less costly. Another African American inventor, Henry Blair, developed a seed-planting device that reduced the time a farmer spent sowing a crop.

Life Under Slavery For all the problems faced by free African Americans, those who were enslaved faced much greater trials. They had no rights at all. Laws known as **slave codes** controlled every aspect of their lives. As a Kentucky court ruled in 1828, ". . . a slave by our code is not treated as a person but as a . . . thing. . . ."

Many enslaved African Americans became skilled workers. Their skills kept the plantations operating efficiently. Others worked in the owners' homes as housekeepers, butlers, or nannies and became trusted house servants.

The vast majority did heavy farm labor. Most slaveholders stopped short of working a laborer to death. Some came close, however. On the large plantations, white overseers administered punishment—often a whipping—for many offenses.

Enslaved African Americans had only one real protection against mistreatment: Owners looked on them as valuable property that they needed to keep healthy and productive.

Families of enslaved African Americans were often broken apart when slave owners sold one or more of their family members. Many children had only the slightest memory of their parents.

HISTORIAN'S APPRENTICE ACTIVITY PACK

To further explore the topics in this chapter, complete the activity in the Historian's Apprentice Activity Pack to answer this essential question:

How can a nation be united and divided at the same time?

▼ **A Family in the Fields**
Children worked in the fields with their enslaved parents. This Georgia family was picking cotton.

▼ **Bonds of Slavery**
Shackles such as these were used to restrain slaves who tried to escape or who otherwise displeased a master.

Nat Turner captured

Vocabulary Builder
revolt (ree VOHLT) *n.* uprising; rebellion

After 1808, it was illegal to import enslaved Africans to the United States. As a result, African Americans had little direct contact with Africa. Nevertheless, African customs, music, and dance survived in their daily lives from one generation to another.

Many African Americans found a message of hope in the Bible. African Americans composed spirituals, religious folk songs that blended biblical themes with the realities of slavery.

Resistance to Slavery Many African Americans did what they could to resist the slaveholders. Some worked slowly or pretended not to understand what they were told to do. Others deliberately broke farm equipment. The most daring fled north to freedom.

Sometimes, resistance became rebellion. Nat Turner led the most famous slave revolt in 1831. Turner said he had a vision that told him to kill whites. He and others killed about 60 whites. In reprisal, many innocent African Americans were executed.

✓**Checkpoint** How did enslaved African Americans adapt to slavery and resist it?

☆ **Looking Back and Ahead** The more cotton they grew, the more southern planters depended on the labor of enslaved African Americans. At the same time, African Americans in the South struggled to endure or resist slavery. In the next section, you will read how the settling of western areas caused new tensions between North and South.

Section 3 | **Check Your Progress**

Progress Monitoring Online
For: Self-test with instant help
Visit: PHSchool.com
Web Code: mya-4073

Comprehension and Critical Thinking

1. (a) **Summarize** How were northern textile mills and southern cotton plantations linked? What key invention deepened this connection?
(b) **Understand Sequence** Place the following events in the order in which they happened: population of cotton-producing states triples; Whitney invents the cotton gin; Nat Turner leads slave revolt; the need for slaves increases; northern textile factories have need for cotton; support for slavery hardens among southern whites.

2. (a) **Describe** What might a typical workday be like for an enslaved African American on a southern cotton plantation?
(b) **Draw Conclusions** Why do you think enslaved people rebelled, even though the risk was so great and the likelihood of success so small?

Reading Skill
3. **Explain Problems From the Past** Connect the problems facing southern planters and southern African Americans.

Key Terms
Answer the following questions in complete sentences that show your understanding of the key terms.

4. How does the cotton gin work?
5. How did slave codes control every aspect of the lives of enslaved African Americans?
6. What would be a common theme of an African American spiritual?

Writing
7. Based on what you have read in this section, list as many effects as you can that resulted from the invention of the cotton gin by Eli Whitney. List the effects in the order in which they happened. If one effect led to another effect, draw an arrow between those two developments.

The Wagons Were So Numerous

❝ The wagons were so numerous that the leaders of one team had their noses in the trough at the end of the next wagon ahead. . . . Besides the coaches and wagons, there were gentlemen travelling singly in the saddle, with all their luggage stuffed into their saddlebags. There were enormous droves of sheep and herds of cattle, which raised the dust like a cloud along their path. ❞

—A traveler's recollection of traffic on the National Road, early 1800s

▲ Settlers heading West.

The Challenges of Growth

Objectives
- Identify the problems Americans moving westward faced.
- Describe the impact of the building of the Erie Canal.
- Discuss the debate over slavery and the Missouri Compromise.

🔄 Reading Skill

Place Events in a Matrix of Time and Place Each event in history takes place in the context of a specific time and place. As you read this textbook or other history textbooks, try to remember additional events from the same time or place. Then, look for possible connections among the events discussed in the different parts of a chapter or unit.

Key Terms and People

Daniel Boone   canal
turnpike   Henry Clay
corduroy road

Why It Matters Americans kept moving westward. As northerners and southerners migrated and settled in new lands, they brought their differing ways of life with them.

❓ **Section Focus Question: How did Americans move west, and how did this intensify the debate over slavery?**

Moving West

During colonial times, Americans looked on the back-country between the Atlantic Coast and the Appalachian Mountains as the western frontier. By the 1750s, the Scotch-Irish and the Germans of Pennsylvania had begun to settle the backcountry.

The most famous early pioneer was Daniel Boone. In 1775, Boone and a party of 30 men cleared a new route to the West—the Wilderness Road. It crossed the Appalachian Mountains through the Cumberland Gap into Kentucky. The Wilderness Road became the main route across the Appalachians. In time, pioneers created many other routes for westward travel. (See the map on the next page.)

A Growing Population By the early 1800s, the flow of immigrants to the West had become a flood. As western populations grew, many areas applied to become states. From 1792 to 1819, eight states joined the Union: Kentucky (1792), Tennessee (1796), Ohio (1803), Louisiana (1812), Indiana (1816), Mississippi (1817), Illinois (1818), and Alabama (1819).

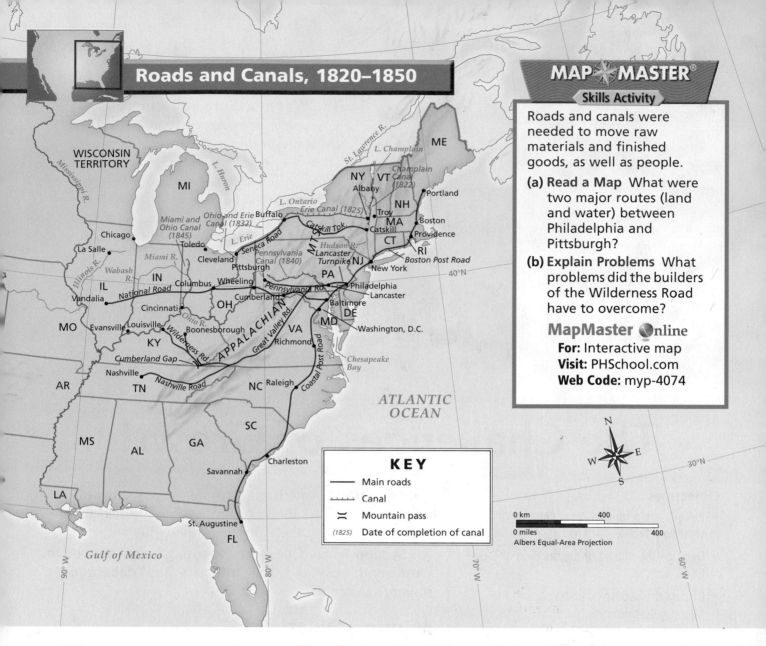

Roads and Canals, 1820–1850

MAP MASTER®
Skills Activity

Roads and canals were needed to move raw materials and finished goods, as well as people.

(a) Read a Map What were two major routes (land and water) between Philadelphia and Pittsburgh?

(b) Explain Problems What problems did the builders of the Wilderness Road have to overcome?

MapMaster Online
For: Interactive map
Visit: PHSchool.com
Web Code: myp-4074

KEY
— Main roads
⊢⊢⊢⊢ Canal
⊰ Mountain pass
(1825) Date of completion of canal

0 km 400
0 miles 400
Albers Equal-Area Projection

Vocabulary Builder
pursue (per SYOO) **v.** to chase after; to try to capture

Traveling west was not easy. Many early roads began as paths for deer or bison. Indians used these well-worn paths to **pursue** game. Then, white settlers began to drive their wagons over these paths. Not surprisingly, the roads were terrible. They were unpaved, dotted with tree stumps, and easily washed out by rain.

✓**Checkpoint** How did American settlers heading west reach their new homes?

Place Events in a Matrix of Time and Place
Name two important events from the early nineteenth century that contributed to America's growth as a nation. Consider the topics covered in this chapter and in previous chapters.

Roads and Turnpikes

Clearly the nation needed better roads. Farmers and merchants had to have a way to move their goods to market quickly and cheaply. Some capitalists decided to provide that way.

Private companies began to build turnpikes, or toll roads. At certain points, a bar on a hinge swung out across the road. The bar resembled a spear, or pike. Travelers would have to stop and pay a toll in order to pass.

In 1795, a private company in Pennsylvania built a turnpike between Lancaster and Philadelphia. The Lancaster Turnpike was the first long-distance stone road in the United States. The road provided cheap, reliable transportation to <u>isolated</u> agricultural areas.

In marshy areas, wagons traveled on **corduroy roads,** roads made of sawed-off logs, laid side by side. This meant a bumpy ride as wagons bounced over each log. Corduroy roads were a hazard to horses, because they could break their legs if they slipped through the logs.

The National Road was the first federally funded road. Begun in 1811 in Cumberland, Maryland, it stretched to Wheeling, in western Virginia, by 1818 and reached Vandalia, Illinois, in 1850. The road crossed hundreds of miles of varying terrain. Bridges carried it over many rivers and streams.

✔**Checkpoint** What was the National Road?

Canals

Slow road travel isolated western farmers from eastern markets. The fastest, cheapest way to ship goods was by water. However, the major rivers ran north and south. The solution was to build canals from east to west. A **canal** is a channel that is dug across land and filled with water. Canals allow boats to reach more places.

In 1816, New York Governor DeWitt Clinton proposed a canal from the Hudson River to Lake Erie. Critics scoffed at the idea. Still, work began on "Clinton's Ditch" in 1817.

Building the canal was a challenge for canal engineers—and for workers, who were mostly Irish immigrants. The land in upstate New York is not level. Locks had to be built to raise or lower boats in the canal. Locks are chambers just big enough to hold a boat. When a boat enters a lock, gates close at both ends of the chamber. If the boat is to be raised, water flows into the lock. If the boat must be lowered, water drains out.

At Lockport, five double locks raised the canal 50 feet. One canal traveler wrote:

> **"**As one passes along this deep cavern and sees . . . the rough perpendicular walls pierced in every part with drill-holes used for blasting the rock, he is astonished at the perseverance, labor, and expense which it cost.**"**
> —from the *Diary of Jonathan Pearson,* 1833

Within two years of its opening in 1825, the canal had paid for itself. Produce from the Midwest came across Lake Erie, passed through the Erie Canal, and was carried down the Hudson River to New York City. Because of its location at the end of the river, New York soon became the richest city in the nation.

Vocabulary Builder
<u>isolated</u> (ī sah lay tehd) *adj.* set apart

Crazy Over Canals

American popular culture celebrated the new canals with songs, stories, and even jokes.

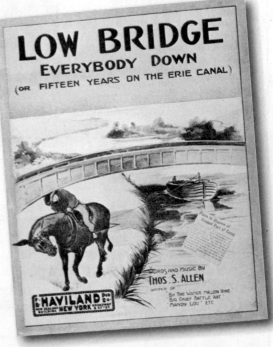

The success of the Erie Canal sparked a surge of canal building. In 1829, a canal was built through Delaware. Canals were soon underway in Virginia, Pennsylvania, Ohio, Indiana, and Illinois.

☑Checkpoint **How did the building of the Erie Canal help farmers in the interior of the country?**

The Extension of Slavery

Westward expansion strengthened the nation. It also caused problems. The most serious problem was the extension of slavery.

Slave and Free States In 1819, the nation consisted of 11 "slave states," which permitted slavery, and 11 "free states," which prohibited slavery. However, Missouri had been seeking admission as a slave state since 1817.

Northerners had reacted strongly. Adding another slave state would upset the balance in the Senate, where each state had two votes. Adding two more senators from a slave state would make the South more powerful than the North.

In 1819, Representative James Tallmadge of New York proposed that Missouri be admitted as a slave state. However, once it was admitted, no more slaves could be brought into the state.

The bill passed the House of Representatives, but it failed in the Senate. Southern senators feared that slavery itself—and thus the South's economic well-being—was being threatened.

The Missouri Compromise In the next session of Congress, Maine applied for admission to the Union. Unlike Missouri, Maine prohibited slavery. The admission of both a free state and a slave state would maintain the balance in the Senate.

In 1820, Senator Henry Clay persuaded Congress to adopt the Missouri Compromise. It permitted Maine to be admitted to the Union as a free state and Missouri to be admitted as a slave state. In addition, the compromise provided that the Louisiana Territory north of the southern border of Missouri would be free of slavery. The compromise had one other important feature. It gave southern slave owners a clear right to pursue escaped fugitives into "free" regions and return them to slavery.

Free and Slave States

Free States	Slave States
Maine	Missouri
Illinois	Alabama
Indiana	Mississippi
Ohio	Louisiana
Vermont	Tennessee
Rhode Island	Kentucky
New York	Virginia
New Hampshire	North Carolina
Massachusetts	South Carolina
Connecticut	Maryland
New Jersey	Georgia
Pennsylvania	Delaware

Original 13 States

Reading Charts
Skills Activity

The addition of Missouri to the Union threatened to upset the balance between free states and slave states.

(a) Read a Chart Which of the following was a free state: Kentucky, Tennessee, or Ohio?

(b) Explain Problems Why did northern states wish to have Missouri and Maine enter the Union at the same time?

A Continuing Problem The Missouri Compromise revealed how much sectional rivalries divided the states of the Union. The compromise seemed to balance the interests of the North and the South. However, white southerners were not happy that Congress had given itself the power to make laws regarding slavery. Many northerners, in turn, were angry that Congress had allowed slavery to expand into another state.

Thomas Jefferson was alarmed by the fierce debate over the Missouri Compromise. The former President, much older now, saw that the issues raised by the compromise could tear the nation apart. He wrote to a friend:

“This momentous question, like a firebell in the night, awakened and filled me with terror. I considered it at once as the knell of the Union. . . . [W]e have the wolf by the ears, and we can neither hold him, nor safely let him go.”
—Thomas Jefferson, letter of April 22, 1820

As Jefferson observed, the bitterness of feelings about slavery posed a serious threat to national unity. In time, the issue of slavery would indeed split the nation in two.

✓Checkpoint **Why was Jefferson alarmed at the bitterness of the debate over the extension of slavery?**

⭐ Looking Back and Ahead In this chapter, you learned about increasing differences between North and South. In the next chapter, you will read about the movement to end slavery and other efforts to bring social change.

Section 4 | Check Your Progress

Progress Monitoring Online
For: Self-test with instant help
Visit: PHSchool.com
Web Code: mya-4074

Comprehension and Critical Thinking

1. **(a) Recall** How did building better roads and canals transform the United States?
   (b) Identify Economic Benefits How did improved transportation lead to economic growth?

2. **(a) List** What were the main points of the Missouri Compromise?
   (b) Make Predictions Why would the issues addressed by the Missouri Compromise continue to tear the nation apart?

💡 Reading Skill

3. **Place Events in a Matrix of Time and Place** What event in the early nineteenth century led to the creation of the Missouri Territory and later to the state of Missouri? Describe this event.

Key Terms

4. Draw a table with three rows and three columns. In the first column, list the key terms from this section: turnpike, corduroy road, canal. In the next column, write the definition of each term. In the last column, make a small illustration that shows the meaning of the term.

Writing

5. Based on what you have read in this section, write a thesis statement about the most important change caused by the development of new routes to the West.

21st Century Learning Political cartoons have been used throughout American history to comment on events and issues. Cartoonists often use symbols and exaggeration to make their points. Learning to analyze cartoons can help you better understand viewpoints on current and historical events.

Learn the Skill

Use these steps to learn how to read a political cartoon.

1 **Identify common symbols.** A symbol is an object that represents something other than itself. Sometimes, symbols are labeled to make the connection clear.

2 **Determine the main idea.** What issue is being portrayed? What clues convey the issue?

3 **Investigate point of view.** Is the cartoon pointing out a problem? What is the cartoonist's attitude toward the problem?

4 **Draw conclusions.** Use the symbols, main ideas, and point of view to identify meaning: What is this cartoon saying?

Practice the Skill

Use the political cartoon above to answer the following questions.

1 **Identify common symbols.** What symbols are used in this cartoon?

2 **Determine the main idea.** What issue from this chapter is being portrayed in the cartoon?

3 **Investigate point of view.** What point of view on the issue does the cartoon suggest?

4 **Draw conclusions.** Explain the cartoon's meaning in your own words. What is your opinion of its message?

Apply the Skill

See the Review and Assessment at the end of this chapter.

Why did Americans take different paths in the early 1800s?

Section 1
The Industrial Revolution

- By the end of the 1700s, advances in technology allowed goods to be produced cheaply and quickly by machines.
- In the United States, the Industrial Revolution centered in the Northeast, which had an ample supply of labor and raw materials.
- Factory conditions became increasingly dangerous, and laborers fought for better working conditions.

Section 2
The North Transformed

- Cities grew rapidly during the 1800s, and crowding, disease, and fast-spreading fires were common problems.
- Northern industries grew due to advances in technology.

Section 3
The Plantation South

- Eli Whitney's cotton gin made possible a huge increase in cotton production.
- As cotton production grew, the number and value of enslaved African Americans increased dramatically.
- In the face of cruel conditions, many enslaved African Americans resisted slavery.

Section 4
The Challenges of Growth

- By the early 1800s, a flood of settlers westward helped many territories qualify for statehood.
- Better roads and canals further increased the rate of western settlement.
- Tension arose over slavery in the territories, but the Missouri Compromise settled the issue temporarily.

(?) Exploring the Essential Question

Use the online study guide to explore the essential question.

Section 1
How did the new technology of the Industrial Revolution change the way Americans lived?

Section 2
How did urbanization, technology, and social change affect the North?

Chapter 11 Essential Question
Why did Americans take different paths in the early 1800s?

Section 4
How did Americans move west, and how did this intensify the debate over slavery?

Section 3
How did cotton affect the social and economic life of the South?

Key Terms
Fill in the blanks with the correct key terms.

1. The _____ was the change in the way people made goods beginning in the late 1700s.

2. People who wanted to keep immigrants out of the country were called _____.

3. African Americans sang _____ to keep hope during their difficult lives.

4. Travelers had to pay tolls on _____ in order to pass.

Comprehension and Critical Thinking

5. **(a) Describe** Who were the Lowell girls?
   (b) Apply Information How do you think the Lowell system affected production?

6. **(a) Identify** What contribution did Eli Whitney make to manufacturing?
   (b) Identify Economic Benefits How did this contribution benefit consumers?

7. **(a) Summarize** How did the physical limitations of steamboats differ from those of railroads?
   (b) Draw Conclusions Why were both means of transportation important to the growth of industry?

8. **(a) Summarize** How did the cotton gin benefit southern planters? How did it benefit northern textile manufacturers?
   (b) Analyze Cause and Effect How did the cotton gin change life for enslaved people?

9. **(a) Contrast** What arguments did some southerners use to defend slavery? What were some points raised by northern critics of slavery to challenge those arguments?
   (b) Apply Information What were some tactics that enslaved African Americans employed in order to endure or resist slavery?

10. **(a) Describe** What were some of the difficulties Americans faced as they traveled west?
    (b) Analyze Cause and Effect How did improved transportation affect western settlement? How did it affect industry?
    (c) Draw Conclusions How were immigrants important to the transportation revolution?

11. **(a) Recall** How was slavery an issue in the debate over Missouri's statehood?
    (b) Detect Points of View Why did northerners believe that it would be damaging to the North if the South became more powerful in the Senate?

History Reading Skill
12. **Identify and Explain Central Issues** Write a paragraph that explains the issues central to the Missouri Compromise. Orient the issues in the context of the times and places in which they occurred.

Writing
13. Write a paragraph explaining *either* the causes *or* the effects of one of the following developments:
    - Industrialization of the North
    - The cotton empire of the South

    Your paragraph should:
    - begin with a sentence that expresses your main idea;
    - indicate whether you will focus on the subject's causes or its effects;
    - expand on your main idea with facts, examples, and other information.

14. **Write a Narrative:**
    Choose one of the inventions developed during the first half of the nineteenth century. Write a narrative that describes how people were affected by the invention.

Skills for Life
Build Political Cartoon Skills
Use the political cartoon on page 363 (Chapter 10) to answer the following questions.

15. What symbols are used in this cartoon?

16. What issue from this chapter is portrayed in the cartoon?

17. What is the main idea of this cartoon?

18. What does this cartoon say about the time period?

Test Yourself

1. **Which of the following inventions did the most to advance the connection between goods, raw materials, and markets?**

   A interchangeable parts

   B steamboats

   C telegraphs

   D railroads

2. **In the mid-1800s, many immigrants came to the United States from Ireland to escape**

   A revolutions.

   B famine.

   C political unrest.

   D religious persecution.

Refer to the quotation below to answer Question 3.

> "This momentous question, like a firebell in the night, awakened and filled me with terror. I considered it at once as the knell of the Union. . . ."

3. **To which issue does this quotation refer?**

   A transportation

   B slavery

   C immigration

   D mass production

Document-Based Questions

Task: Look at Documents 1 and 2, and answer their accompanying questions. Then, use the documents and your knowledge of history to complete this writing assignment:

> Write an essay describing what life was like for enslaved African Americans in the South. Use information from the graph to explain why slaveholders felt restrictive measures were necessary.

Document 1: This graph gives information about the population of some slave-holding states in 1840. *Use the graph to make a generalization about the South's slave population.*

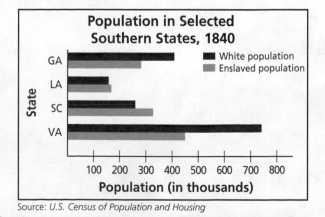

Population in Selected Southern States, 1840

■ White population
■ Enslaved population

State: GA, LA, SC, VA

Population (in thousands): 100 200 300 400 500 600 700 800

Source: *U.S. Census of Population and Housing*

Document 2: The excerpt below is from a 1930s interview with Fountain Hughes, born a slave in 1848 near Charlottesville, Virginia. *How does Fountain Hughes describe what it meant to be a slave?*

> "Well, I belonged to B., when I was a slave. My mother belonged to B. But we was all slave children. . . .
>
> Now I couldn' go from here across the street . . . [with]out I have a note, or something from my master. . . . Whoever he sent me to, they'd give me another pass an' I'd bring that back so as to show how long I'd been gone. . . . An' when I come back, why I carry it to my master an' give that to him, that'd be all right. But I couldn' jus' walk away like the people does now. . . .
>
> We belonged to people. They'd sell us like they sell horses an' cows an' hogs an' all like that. Have a auction bench, an' they'd put you on, up on the bench an' bid on you jus' same as you bidding on cattle."

An Age of Reform

1820-1860

"*For while the man is born to do whatever he can, to the woman and the negro there is no such privilege.*"

—Elizabeth Cady Stanton, speech to the American Anti-Slavery Society, 1860

In this painting, a suffragist lobbies male politicians.

What You Will Learn

Section 1
IMPROVING SOCIETY
By the mid-1800s, people were seeking reform in many areas of American life, including education.

Section 2
THE FIGHT AGAINST SLAVERY
Abolitionists sought an end to slavery in the United States.

Section 3
A CALL FOR WOMEN'S RIGHTS
Some reformers sought to win political and economic equality for women.

Section 4
AMERICAN LITERATURE AND ARTS
In the early 1800s, American artists, writers, and musicians began to develop a distinct style.

⤶ Reading Skill
Draw Conclusions From Sources In this chapter, you will learn how to use details from primary and secondary sources to draw conclusions.

How did reformers and writers inspire

An Age of Reform, 1820–1860

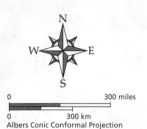

0   300 miles
0   300 km
Albers Conic Conformal Projection

Pacific Ocean

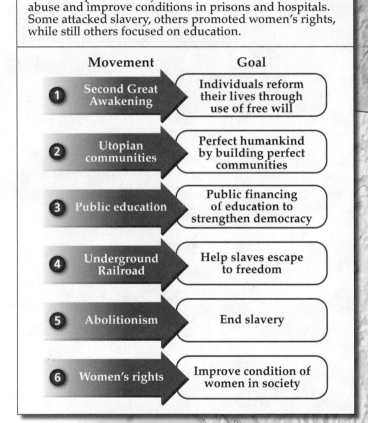

Major Reform Movements
Driven by religious fervor and high morals, reformers tried to improve society. Reformers wanted to end alcohol abuse and improve conditions in prisons and hospitals. Some attacked slavery, others promoted women's rights, while still others focused on education.

Movement	Goal
1 Second Great Awakening	Individuals reform their lives through use of free will
2 Utopian communities	Perfect humankind by building perfect communities
3 Public education	Public financing of education to strengthen democracy
4 Underground Railroad	Help slaves escape to freedom
5 Abolitionism	End slavery
6 Women's rights	Improve condition of women in society

TEXAS ANNEXATION (1845)

MEXICO

 **U.S. Events**

Charles Finney begins holding religious revival meetings. **1826**

William Lloyd Garrison founds antislavery newspaper. **1831**

Horace Mann begins campaign to improve public schools. **1837**

1820   **1830**   **1840**

World Events

1822 Colony of Liberia is founded in West Africa.

1833 Slavery is banned in all British colonies.

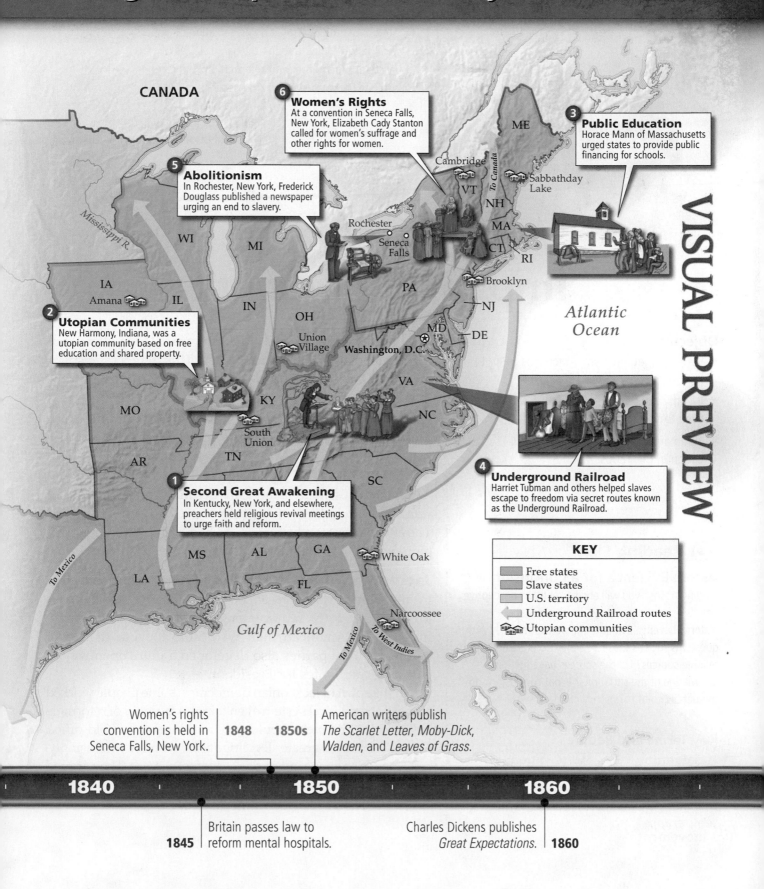

CANADA

VISUAL PREVIEW

6 Women's Rights
At a convention in Seneca Falls, New York, Elizabeth Cady Stanton called for women's suffrage and other rights for women.

3 Public Education
Horace Mann of Massachusetts urged states to provide public financing for schools.

5 Abolitionism
In Rochester, New York, Frederick Douglass published a newspaper urging an end to slavery.

2 Utopian Communities
New Harmony, Indiana, was a utopian community based on free education and shared property.

1 Second Great Awakening
In Kentucky, New York, and elsewhere, preachers held religious revival meetings to urge faith and reform.

4 Underground Railroad
Harriet Tubman and others helped slaves escape to freedom via secret routes known as the Underground Railroad.

Mississippi R.

ME

Cambridge
Sabbathday
Lake

VT
NH

Rochester
MA

Seneca
Falls

CT
RI

WI
MI

IA

Amana

IL

IN

OH

Brooklyn

PA

NJ

MO

KY

Union
Village

Washington, D.C.

MD
DE

VA

NC

*Atlantic
Ocean*

South
Union

TN

AR

SC

To Mexico

MS
AL
GA

White Oak

LA

FL

Narcoossee

Gulf of Mexico

To Mexico

To West Indies

KEY

Free states
Slave states
U.S. territory
Underground Railroad routes
Utopian communities

Women's rights
convention is held in
Seneca Falls, New York.

1848   **1850s**

American writers publish
*The Scarlet Letter, Moby-Dick,
Walden,* and *Leaves of Grass.*

1840   **1850**   **1860**

1845 | Britain passes law to
reform mental hospitals.

Charles Dickens publishes
Great Expectations. | **1860**

◄ Charles Finney

Their Hearts Will Be Changed

❝When the churches are thus awakened and reformed, the reformation and salvation of sinners will follow, going through the same stages of conviction, repentance, and reformation. Their hearts will be broken down and changed. ❞

—Charles Finney, a religious revival preacher, 1834

Improving Society

Objectives

- Discuss what led many Americans to try to improve society in the 1800s.
- Identify the social problems that reformers tried to solve.
- Summarize the improvements in public education in the 1800s.

Reading Skill

Assess Evidence for a Conclusion In reading history, you will encounter many descriptive details that help you draw conclusions about historical events. Evaluate the details carefully with questions such as these: Are they accurate and from reliable sources? Do the sources have firsthand knowledge of the situations? What conclusions do the details point to?

Key Terms and People

social reform
predestination
Charles Finney
revival
temperance
  movement
prohibition
Dorothea Dix
public school
Horace Mann

Why It Matters The Age of Jackson was a time of expanding democracy in the United States. This democratic spirit, combined with religious ideas, inspired people to improve American society.

❓ **Section Focus Question: How did key people bring about reform in education and society?**

The Reforming Spirit

In the 1830s, many Americans became interested in social reform, or organized attempts to improve conditions of life. The effort to create a better society had both political and religious roots.

Jacksonian Democracy The expansion of democracy in the Age of Jackson encouraged reform. Most states dropped property requirements for voting. As a result, more white American men were able to vote than ever before. Political parties also developed a more open way of choosing candidates for President.

In the spirit of Jacksonian democracy, some people worked to make the political system even fairer. A number of reformers believed that all men should vote and be able to hold office. Others supported greater legal rights for women. Increasingly, reformers also spoke out strongly against slavery. They argued that no society that allowed one human being to own another could call itself democratic.

The Second Great Awakening Religious feelings and ideas also sparked the reforming <u>impulse</u>. Beginning in the early 1800s, a new generation of ministers challenged some traditional views. This movement became known as the Second Great Awakening.

Changing religious ideas sparked the Second Great Awakening. In colonial days, many American Protestants believed in **predestination**, the idea that God decided the fate of a person's soul even before birth. But leaders of the Second Great Awakening preached that people's own actions determined their salvation. This "doctrine of free will" blended easily with political ideas about democracy and independence.

The most important of this new generation of preachers was **Charles Finney**. Finney held the first of many religious revivals in 1826. A **revival** is a huge outdoor religious meeting. Before long, Finney and other preachers were conducting revivals across the nation. A single revival might go on for several days or even a week. Ministers of different faiths preached day and night, trying to <u>convert</u> sinners and urging people to reform their lives.

Finney believed that the emotion of a revival could touch even the most hopeless sinner. "All sorts of abandoned characters are awakened and converted," he wrote. "The worst part of human society is softened and reclaimed, and made to appear as a lovely specimen of the beauty of holiness."

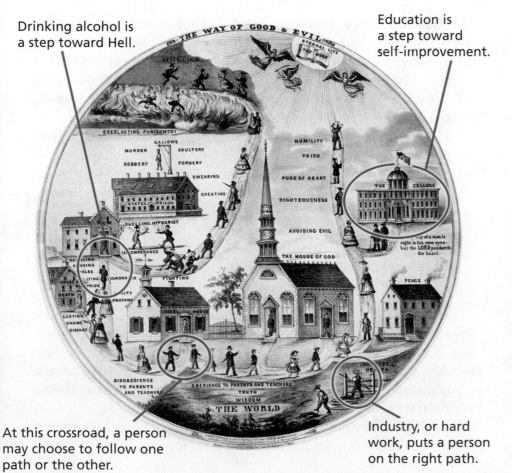

Drinking alcohol is a step toward Hell.

Education is a step toward self-improvement.

At this crossroad, a person may choose to follow one path or the other.

Industry, or hard work, puts a person on the right path.

The Way to Salvation
This symbolic painting, *The Way of Good and Evil*, shows two paths a person can take. One path leads to Hell and the other leads to Heaven. **Critical Thinking: *Apply Information*** *How does this painting reflect the doctrine of free will that was part of the Second Great Awakening?*

Preaching at a revival meeting

Thus, the religious revivals of the Second Great Awakening encouraged reform. People came to believe that, if they had the power to improve themselves, they could improve society as well.

Utopian Communities The desire to create a more perfect society spurred some reformers to found utopian communities. (*Utopia* was a book about a fictional ideal society.) Utopian reformers hoped their communities would become models for others to follow.

Robert Owen founded a utopian community in Indiana in 1825. He called this colony New Harmony. New Harmony was based on common ownership of property. Residents were to raise their own food and manufacture their own goods. However, New Harmony turned out to be anything but harmonious. Members argued among themselves about goals and actions. The colony dissolved after about two years. Indeed, most utopian communities did not last very long.

☑ **Checkpoint** **What was the goal of the Second Great Awakening?**

Social Reformers at Work

Utopian reformers tried to create perfect, separate communities. However, most reform-minded Americans chose to work within the existing society. The reforming impulse took many forms.

The Temperance Movement Many reformers supported the temperance movement, an organized effort to end alcohol abuse and the problems created by it. Alcohol was widely used in the United States. Whiskey was cheaper than milk or beer. Often, it was safer to drink than water, which was frequently contaminated. As a result, alcohol abuse reached epidemic proportions.

Many women were drawn to the temperance movement. They pointed out how many women and children suffered at the hands of husbands and fathers who drank too much. Such organizations as the American Temperance Society published pamphlets denouncing "strong drink."

Most reformers favored temperance, or moderation in drinking. But others called for prohibition, a total ban on the sale and consumption of alcohol. During the 1850s, supporters of prohibition got nine states to pass laws banning the sale of alcohol. The movement was interrupted by the Civil War but reemerged later.

Prison Reform Other reformers sought to improve the nation's prison system. Prisons had traditionally been harsh places, designed to make people want to stay out of them. Poorly heated buildings, inadequate food, and cramped conditions were typical. Many people in prison were not criminals at all but were people who owed money they could not pay back. Because debtors could seldom earn money while in jail, they often remained locked up for years.

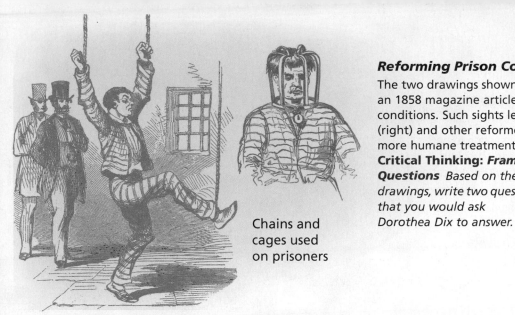

Reforming Prison Conditions
The two drawings shown at left are from an 1858 magazine article about prison conditions. Such sights led Dorothea Dix (right) and other reformers to call for more humane treatment of prisoners.
Critical Thinking: *Frame Questions* *Based on these drawings, write two questions that you would ask Dorothea Dix to answer.*

Chains and cages used on prisoners

Dorothea Dix

Social reformers began investigating conditions in jails. Dorothea Dix, a Massachusetts schoolteacher, was one of those who took up the cause of prison reform. Over the years, she worked to convince state legislatures to build new, more sanitary, and more humane prisons. In addition, debtors were no longer sent to jail.

Reforms for the Mentally Ill Dix was outraged to find that prisons were also used to house individuals with mental illnesses. After a careful investigation, she reported to the Massachusetts legislature on the horrifying conditions she had witnessed: "A woman in a cage . . . [One man] losing the use of his limbs from want of exercise . . . One man and one woman chained."

Dix's shocking report helped persuade the Massachusetts legislature to fund a new mental hospital. She then continued her efforts in other states. She urged city and state governments around the country to create separate institutions, called asylums, for those with mental illnesses. The new asylums provided treatment, rather than punishment.

☑ **Checkpoint** How did Dorothea Dix contribute to social reform?

Education Reform

Education was another area of concern to reformers. The first American schools were set up for religious purposes. The Puritans of Massachusetts believed that all people needed to be able to read and understand the Bible. In 1642, they passed a law requiring all large towns to hire teachers and build schools. In this way, Massachusetts set up the first public schools, or free schools supported by taxes.

Need for Better Education By the early 1800s, Massachusetts was still the only state to require public schools. In other states, children from wealthy families were educated privately, whereas poor children generally received no education outside the home. Under these circumstances, many Americans could not read or write.

Links Across Time

Public Education

1852 Massachusetts became the first state to pass a law that required all children to attend school up to a certain age. This was known as compulsory education.

1918 By this date, compulsory education laws had been passed in every state in the Union. As a result, for the first time, every state required children to attend school at least up to the tenth grade.

Link to Today Online

Education Today Today, billions of dollars in federal, state, and local taxes go to support public education. But not everybody agrees on the best way to spend that money and to educate American children.

For: Education in the news
Visit: PHSchool.com
Web Code: myc-4081

Public school classroom, around 1920

The reforms of the Jacksonian Era increased the number of eligible voters. Reformers grew concerned that the education system was not keeping up with the political system. They argued that education was necessary to ensure that voters were intelligently informed. With immigration on the rise, reformers also pointed out that better schools would help immigrants assimilate, or become part of, American culture.

Mann and Public Education Horace Mann of Massachusetts took the lead in education reform. To Mann, public financing of education was essential for democracy to work. He said:

> **❝**If we do not prepare children to become good citizens; if we do not develop their capacities, if we do not enrich their minds with knowledge . . . then our republic must go down to destruction as others have gone before it.**❞**
>
> —Horace Mann, quoted in *A Century of Childhood* (Heininger)

After becoming head of the state board of education in 1837, Mann convinced Massachusetts to improve its public school system. It created colleges to train teachers, raised the salaries of teachers, and lengthened the school year. (To learn more about public education in the 1800s, see the Life at the Time feature.)

Assess Evidence for a Conclusion

Read the quotation by Horace Mann. Assess the credibility of this source in supporting the following conclusion: Mann believed that strong character, moral behavior, and wide knowledge were equally important qualities. List three examples from the quotation that support this conclusion.

Other states soon followed Massachusetts's example. By the 1850s, public schools had gained much acceptance in the Northeast. Southern and western states lagged behind, however. They would not create their own public school systems until many decades later.

Education for African Americans The improvements in public education did little for African Americans. Southern states prohibited teaching enslaved persons to read. In the North, free black children were seldom admitted to the same schools as white children.

Reformers who tried to improve educational opportunities for African Americans often met with resistance. Prudence Crandall, a Quaker teacher, opened a school for African American girls in Connecticut. Hostile neighbors attacked and destroyed the school.

Still, some opportunities did open up. In major northern cities, free African American educators opened their own schools. In 1855, Massachusetts became the first state to admit African American students to public schools. Some African Americans attended private colleges such as Harvard and Oberlin. In 1854, Pennsylvania chartered Ashmun Institute (later called Lincoln University), the nation's first college for African American men.

☑**Checkpoint**   **How did public education improve in the mid-1800s?**

☆ **Looking Back and Ahead** Inspired by political or religious ideals, reformers tackled many social problems. But one issue towered above all others in the minds of reformers. In the next section, you will read about the growing efforts to end slavery.

Section 1 | **Check Your Progress**

Progress Monitoring ⓞnline
For: Self-test with instant help
Visit: PHSchool.com
Web Code: mya-4081

Comprehension and Critical Thinking

1. (a) Identify What were the ideas of predestination and the doctrine of free will?
(b) Draw Conclusions How might the doctrine of free will promote democracy?

2. (a) Recall Which reforms did Horace Mann convince the state of Massachusetts to make?
(b) Detect Points of View According to Mann, why is it important for a democracy to have educated citizens?

ⓞ Reading Skill

3. Assess Evidence for a Conclusion Assess the quotation that follows by Dorothea Dix. Is the evidence reliable? Does it support the conclusion that the mentally ill were poorly treated? **Quotation:** "[T]wo females . . . lie in wooden bunks filled with straw; always shut up. . . . The use of cages [is] all but universal."

Key Terms

Answer the following questions in complete sentences that show your understanding of the key terms.
4. What did the temperance movement seek?

5. What was the goal of social reform in the 1830s?
6. What is a religious revival?

Writing

7. A topic sentence sets the focus for a single paragraph. A thesis statement expresses a broader idea to be developed in an entire essay. Write three topic sentences for paragraphs that would support and develop the following thesis statement: A powerful reforming spirit swept through this country in the 1830s.

Going to School

Following the lead of Massachusetts, other states in the North began to fund public schools. Not all children were able to attend school, and most of those who did only got as far as the eighth grade. What were these early American classrooms like?

The Classroom

Schools in the early 1800s were not like the large public buildings we know today. In rural areas especially, many children went to one-room schoolhouses, where children of all ages were taught together. Students wrote on chalk slates and were expected to recite their lessons when called upon by the teacher.

History *Interactive*

Explore an Early American Classroom

Visit: PHSchool.com
Web Code: myp-4081

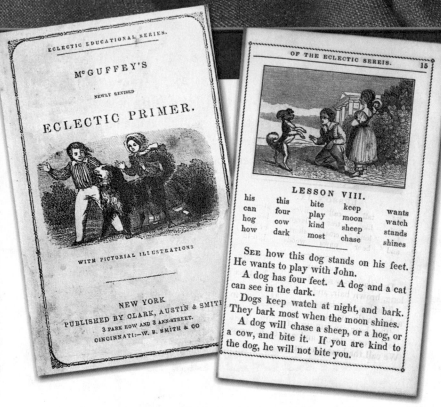

A Popular Textbook ▲

In elementary schools, the most popular text-books were *McGuffey's Eclectic Readers* (Primer through Sixth). First published in 1836, the Readers offered moral lessons along with the "three Rs"—reading, 'riting, and 'rithmetic. The lesson shown above was used to teach children how to read and how to treat pets.

Rewards and Punishments ▶

Discipline was strict in early classrooms. Students who failed to learn their lessons might have to sit in a corner wearing a "dunce cap" (right). But there were also rewards. Students might get certificates for learning their lesson well, for good behavior, or just for coming to school on time (below).

▼

Analyze LIFE AT THE TIME

Look at the pages from *McGuffey's Eclectic Primer* shown at the top of this page. Then, write a lesson for the Primer about the importance of going to school. Use simple language that can be understood by elementary school students.

An Abolitionist's Plea

❝Cease to oppress. . . . Bind him no longer by the cords of slavery, but with those of kindness and brotherly love.❞

—John Greenleaf Whittier,
1833 pamphlet opposing slavery

◀ Antislavery medallion.

The Fight Against Slavery

Objectives

- Describe efforts in the North to end slavery.
- Discuss the contributions of William Lloyd Garrison, Frederick Douglass, and other abolitionists.
- Describe the purpose and risks of the Underground Railroad.
- Explain why many people in the North and South defended slavery.

Reading Skill

Form an Opinion Based on Evidence
You can use details and evidence in primary and secondary sources to help you form opinions about history. Remember that primary sources come from people who saw or experienced events, whereas secondary sources (such as this textbook) build on many sources to recount historical information.

Key Terms and People

abolitionist
William Lloyd
   Garrison

Frederick Douglass
Harriet Tubman

Why It Matters Since colonial times, some Americans had opposed the enslavement of people. They condemned slavery on religious and moral grounds. In the mid-1800s, the reforming spirit spurred a vigorous new effort to end slavery.

❓ **Section Focus Question: How did abolitionists try to end slavery?**

Roots of the Antislavery Movement

A number of prominent leaders of the early republic, such as Alexander Hamilton and Benjamin Franklin, opposed slavery. They believed that slavery violated the most basic principle of the Declaration of Independence, "that all men are created equal."

Slavery Ends in the North In 1780, Pennsylvania became the first state to pass a law that gradually eliminated slavery. By 1804, every northern state had ended or pledged to end slavery. Congress also outlawed slavery in the Northwest Territory. As a result, when Ohio entered the Union in 1803, it became the first state to ban slavery in its state constitution.

The Colonization Movement The American Colonization Society, established in 1817, was an early antislavery organization. This society proposed that slaves be freed gradually and transported to Liberia, a colony founded in 1822 on the west coast of Africa.

The colonization movement did not work. Most enslaved people had grown up in the United States and did not desire to leave. By 1830 only about 1,400 African Americans had migrated to Liberia.

☑**Checkpoint** How did slavery end in the North?

Growing Opposition to Slavery

The Second Great Awakening inspired further opposition to slavery. Many people were influenced by the preaching of Charles Finney, who condemned slavery. By the mid-1800s, a small but growing number of people were **abolitionists,** reformers who wanted to abolish, or end, slavery. Rejecting gradual emancipation, abolitionists called for a complete and immediate end to slavery.

Garrison One of the most forceful voices for abolition was **William Lloyd Garrison.** A Quaker, he strongly opposed the use of violence to end slavery. Still, Garrison was more <u>radical</u> than many others, because he favored full political rights for all African Americans.

In 1831, Garrison launched an abolitionist newspaper, the *Liberator.* It became the nation's leading antislavery publication for 34 years, ending only when slavery itself ended.

Garrison cofounded the New England Anti-Slavery Society, which later became the American Anti-Slavery Society. Leaders of this group included Theodore Weld, a minister who had been a pupil of Charles Finney. Weld brought the zeal of a religious revival to anti-slavery rallies. Other members included Sarah and Angelina Grimke, daughters of a South Carolina slaveholder.

African American Abolitionists Prominent African Americans in the North took a leading role in the abolitionist movement. In 1829, David Walker published his *Appeal: to the Coloured Citizens of the World.* This strongly worded pamphlet urged enslaved people to rebel, if necessary, to gain their freedom.

Vocabulary Builder
<u>radical</u> (RAD ih kul) *adj.* favoring extreme change

The Liberator

"Let Southern oppressors tremble—let all the enemies of the persecuted blacks tremble. . . . On this subject, I do not wish to think, or to speak, or to write, with moderation. No! No! Tell a man whose house is on fire to give a moderate alarm . . . but urge me not to use moderation in a cause like the present. I am in earnest—I will not equivocate—I will not excuse—I will not retreat a single inch—AND I WILL BE HEARD."

—William Lloyd Garrison, *Liberator,* January 1831

William Lloyd Garrison

Reading Primary Sources
Skills Activity

In the above excerpt from the first issue of the *Liberator,* William Lloyd Garrison vows to take a firm stand against slavery.

(a) Detect Points of View What is Garrison's attitude toward slaveholders?

(b) Draw Conclusions What does Garrison mean when he writes, "Tell a man whose house is on fire to give a moderate alarm"?

Perhaps the most powerful speaker for abolitionism was Frederick Douglass. Born into slavery, Douglass had broken the law by learning to read. He later escaped to freedom in the North. Garrison and other abolitionists encouraged Douglass to describe his experiences at antislavery rallies. Douglass told one crowd:

> **❝**I appear this evening as a thief and a robber. I stole this head, these limbs, this body from my master, and ran off with them.**❞**
>
> —Frederick Douglass, speech, 1842

By appearing in public, Douglass risked being sent back into slavery. Yet, he continued to speak before larger and larger audiences. He also published his own antislavery newspaper, the *North Star*.

A Former President Takes a Stand Abolitionists won the support of a few powerful people. Former President John Quincy Adams, now a member of Congress, read antislavery petitions from the floor of the House of Representatives. In 1839, Adams proposed a constitutional amendment that would ban slavery in any new state joining the Union. However, the amendment was not passed.

Two years later, Adams made a dramatic stand against slavery. Captive Africans aboard the slave ship *Amistad* had rebelled, killing the captain and ordering the crew to sail back to Africa. Instead, the crew sailed the ship to America. The 73-year-old Adams spoke to the Supreme Court for nine hours and helped the captives regain their freedom.

✓**Checkpoint** What role did Frederick Douglass play in the abolitionist movement?

The Underground Railroad

Some courageous abolitionists dedicated themselves to helping people escape from slavery. They established a system known as the Underground Railroad. Despite its name, it was neither underground nor a railroad. It was a network of people—black and white, northerners and southerners—who secretly helped slaves reach freedom.

Working for the Underground Railroad was illegal and dangerous. "Conductors" led fugitive slaves from one "station" to the next. Stations were usually the homes of abolitionists, but might be churches or caves. Supporters helped by donating clothing, food, and money to pay for passage on trains and boats. Many people risked their lives to help runaway slaves. Levi Coffin, an Indiana Quaker, assisted more than 3,000 fugitives.

Harriet Tubman, who had herself escaped from slavery, escorted more than 300 people to freedom via the Underground Railroad. Tubman was nicknamed the Black Moses after the biblical leader who led the Israelites out of slavery in Egypt. She proudly told Frederick Douglass that, in 19 trips to the South, she "never lost a single passenger." Slave owners promised a $40,000 reward for her capture.

Form an Opinion Based on Evidence
What is your opinion of Frederick Douglass's speech? Do you think it was an effective statement against slavery? Use evidence to support your opinion.

Frederick Douglass

Vocabulary Builder
via (VEE ah) *prep.* by way of

INFOGRAPHIC
The UNDERGROUND RAILROAD

As many as 50,000 African Americans escaped from slavery in the South to freedom in the North or in Canada via the Underground Railroad.
Critical Thinking: *Identify Costs and Benefits* *What were the risks of helping fugitive slaves escape? Why do you think conductors on the Underground Railroad chose to take those risks?*

This song contained ▶ directions for escaping slaves. The "drinking gourd" is the Big Dipper.

"The riverbank makes a very good road.
The dead trees will show you the way.
Left foot, peg foot, traveling on,
If you follow the drinking gourd."

KEY
RAILROAD ROUTES
FREE STATES
SLAVE STATES
TERRITORIES

CANADA
(BRITISH TERRITORY)

0   200   400 MILES
KILOMETERS 0   200   400

Milton
Davenport
Des Moines
St. Louis
Indianapolis
New York
Atlantic Ocean
Washingon, D.C.
Richmond
Charleston
Savannah
New Orleans
Gulf of Mexico
MEXICO

N

Harriet Tubman, the ▶ most famous conductor on the Underground Railroad

Each year, hundreds of slaves moved along the Underground Railroad to freedom in the North or in Canada. In total, perhaps as many as 50,000 gained their freedom in this way.

☑**Checkpoint** **How did the Underground Railroad work?**

Opposing Abolition

Abolitionists faced powerful obstacles in the North as well as in the South. Many northerners profited from the existence of slavery. Northern textile mill owners and merchants relied on the cotton produced by southern slave labor. Northern workers feared that freed slaves might come north and take their jobs.

Such fears sometimes prompted violence against abolitionists. Mobs attacked antislavery meetings. In 1835, William Lloyd Garrison was dragged through the streets of Boston with a rope around his neck.

As you have read, southerners had long defended slavery as a positive force. Now, as support for abolition grew louder, they went on the offensive. The state of Georgia offered a $5,000 reward for the arrest and conviction for libel of William Lloyd Garrison. Southerners in Congress won passage of a "gag rule" that blocked discussion of antislavery petitions. John Quincy Adams unsuccessfully fought for the repeal of the gag rule.

☑**Checkpoint** **Why did some northerners oppose abolition?**

⭐ **Looking Back and Ahead** By the 1840s, the North and the South were increasingly divided by the issue of slavery. Abolitionists succeeded in making converts in the North. Slavery was spreading along with the cotton boom in the South.

Section 2 | **Check Your Progress**

Progress Monitoring ⏼nline
For: Self-test with instant help
Visit: PHSchool.com
Web Code: mya-4082

Comprehension and Critical Thinking

1. **(a) List** What solutions did the American Colonization Society propose to end slavery?
   (b) Explain Problems Why did most African Americans reject the society's goals?

2. **(a) Identify** Which groups in the North were opposed to abolition? Why?
   (b) Identify Alternatives How might the concerns of these groups have been calmed?

⟳ Reading Skill

3. **Form an Opinion Based on Evidence** Henry Brown mailed himself to freedom in a crate. What do you think was important to him? Use evidence quoted from his own narrative to form your opinion: "I was . . . placed on my head. . . . In this dreadful position, I remained the space of an hour and a half . . . my eyes were almost swollen out of their sockets, and the veins on my temples seemed ready to burst. I made no noise, however, determining to obtain *'victory or death.'*"

Key Terms

4. Write two definitions for the key term abolitionist. First, write a formal definition for your teacher. Second, write a definition in everyday English for a classmate.

Writing

5. Choose three details from Section 2 that support the topic sentence that follows. Then, write a paragraph developing the topic based on these details.
   Topic sentence: Abolitionists used a variety of tactics to oppose slavery.

The Improvement of Women

❝As a general rule, men do not desire the improvement of women. . . . As *they* have determined that Jehovah has placed woman on a lower platform than man, they of course wish to keep her there; and hence the noble faculties of our minds are crushed, and our reasoning powers are almost wholly uncultivated. . . .❞

—Sarah Grimke, protesting against poor educational opportunities, 1838

◀ Statue of women's rights leaders (from left) Lucretia Mott, Susan B. Anthony, and Elizabeth Cady Stanton

A Call for Women's Rights

Objectives

- Explain how the women's suffrage movement began.
- Describe the goals of the Seneca Falls Convention in 1848.
- Identify the new opportunities that women gained in the mid-1800s.

🔎 Reading Skill

State the Meaning of Evidence One way to draw conclusions from source material is to make a statement about the meaning of the evidence. This statement will be a conclusion drawn from the details of the evidence. Your statement should use your own words, fit with all the details, and make sense to you.

Key Terms and People

Sojourner Truth
Lucretia Mott
Elizabeth Cady
  Stanton

women's suffrage
women's rights
  movement
Susan B. Anthony

Why It Matters Women participated in abolitionism and other reform efforts. Some women activists also began to focus on equal rights for themselves. They hoped to win the right to vote as well as other advances.

❓ Section Focus Question: How did the women's suffrage movement begin?

The Struggle Begins

In 1820, the rights of American women were limited. They could not vote, serve on juries, attend college, or enter such professions as medicine or law. Married women could not own property or keep their own wages. Most Americans—both men and women—believed that a woman's place was in the private world of the home.

Women who were active in abolition or other social reform movements believed that they had important contributions to make to American society. They began to demand rights as equal citizens. Among these women was Sojourner Truth. Born into slavery in New York State, she was illiterate, but her words inspired the crowds that heard her. Truth became a powerful voice on behalf of both enslaved African Americans and women.

Lucretia Mott, a Quaker, had spent years working in the antislavery movement. Quakers allowed women to take public roles that other religions prohibited. Mott thus had organizing skills and public speaking experience that most women of her day did not.

✅ **Checkpoint** Why did some reformers turn to the issue of women's rights?

Seneca Falls Convention

In 1840, Mott traveled to London to attend an international anti-slavery convention. There, she met another abolitionist, **Elizabeth Cady Stanton.** Stanton was honeymooning in London with her husband, a delegate to the conference. But when Mott and Stanton tried to attend a meeting, they were told that women were not permitted to take an active role in the proceedings.

Mott and Stanton were infuriated at being <u>excluded</u>. Sitting outside the convention hall, they agreed on the need for a convention to advance women's rights. They followed through on that idea in the summer of 1848. Their convention met in Seneca Falls, New York, "to discuss the social, civil, and religious rights of women." The Seneca Falls Convention attracted over 300 men and women.

Declaration of Sentiments Stanton wrote a Declaration of Sentiments, modeled on the Declaration of Independence. It began, "We hold these truths to be self-evident: that all men and women are created equal. . . ." The declaration then listed injustices women suffered, including being shut out from educational opportunities and good jobs. The Declaration of Sentiments demanded full equality for women in every area of life.

Like the colonial Patriots, Stanton opposed "taxation without representation." In a speech just before the convention, she declared:

> ❝[W]e are assembled to protest against a form of government existing without the consent of the governed—to declare our right to be free as man is free, to be represented in the government which we are taxed to support.❞
>
> —Elizabeth Cady Stanton, speech, July 19, 1848

Call for Suffrage Stanton's argument was the beginning of the long battle for **women's suffrage,** or the right of women to vote. However, not all of the delegates agreed when Stanton included a call for women's suffrage in the Declaration of Sentiments. Some, such as Frederick Douglass, strongly supported it. Others, including Lucretia Mott, feared that the call for women's suffrage would be so controversial that it would harm their other causes. Still, the convention narrowly voted to support the demand for women's suffrage.

✔**Checkpoint** What was the purpose of the Declaration of Sentiments?

Vocabulary Builder
<u>exclude</u> (ehks KLYOOD) **v.** to keep out or expel; to reject

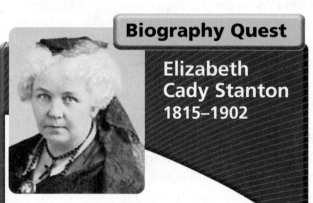

Biography Quest

Elizabeth Cady Stanton
1815–1902

With seven children to care for, Elizabeth Cady Stanton still found time to try to change the world. She began her long political partnership with Susan B. Anthony in 1851. For much of the next 50 years, the two women pooled their talents to try to win women the right to vote. "[I am] a fine writer," Stanton noted. "Miss Anthony is a thorough manager." Sadly, Stanton died 18 years before women finally won the vote.

Biography Quest

Why was Stanton's wedding ceremony unusual for its day?

For: The answer to the question about Stanton

Visit: PHSchool.com

Web Code: myd-4083

New Opportunities for Women

The Seneca Falls Convention launched the women's rights movement in the United States. The **women's rights movement** was an organized effort to improve the political, legal, and economic status of women in American society.

Political Victories In the years after the Seneca Falls Convention, Susan B. Anthony became a close <u>ally</u> of Stanton. The two made a dynamic team. As an unmarried woman, Anthony was free to travel and devote herself to reform work. Stanton, the mother of a growing family, more often wrote speeches from her home. Together, they founded the National Woman Suffrage Association in 1869.

The fight for women's suffrage made little progress at first. Yet the women's rights movement won some victories. In 1860, Stanton and Anthony convinced New York to pass a law protecting women's property rights. Many other states followed. Some states revised their laws to allow married women to keep their wages.

Education for Women The women's rights movement focused much attention on education. American schools emphasized education for boys, who would grow up to be voters, citizens, and professionals. Girls seldom studied advanced subjects like math and science.

Even before the Seneca Falls Convention, reformers worked to give girls a chance for a better education. In 1821, Emma Willard started an academy in Troy, New York, that soon became the model for girls' schools everywhere. The Troy Female Seminary attracted the daughters of lawyers and doctors. The first year, 90 students enrolled. By 1831, the seminary had more than 300 students. Many female reformers of this era attended Willard's school.

Mary Lyon began an even bolder experiment when she opened Mount Holyoke Female Seminary in Massachusetts, in 1837. Lyon did not call her school a college. However, Mount Holyoke was, in fact, the first college for women in the United States. The school showed that women could indeed learn subjects like Latin, geometry, and chemistry.

Vocabulary Builder
<u>ally</u> (AL ī) **n.** a person joined with another for a common purpose

Cause and Effect

CAUSES
- Women could not vote, serve on juries, own property, or divorce abusive husbands.
- Many abolitionists believed that women also deserved equal rights.
- Women were denied equal educational opportunities.
- Seneca Falls Convention launched the women's rights movement.

THE WOMEN'S RIGHTS MOVEMENT

EFFECTS
- Suffragist movement demanded that women get the right to vote.
- States passed laws that protected women's property rights.
- Private schools for women opened, and some colleges accepted women as students.
- Women entered careers once closed to them.

Reading Charts
Skills Activity

The Seneca Falls Convention marked the start of an organized women's rights movement in the United States.

(a) Read a Chart Identify two effects of the women's rights movement.

(b) Analyze Cause and Effect Why is the abolition movement shown as a cause of the women's rights movement?

State the Meaning of Evidence

Make a general statement that is supported by the evidence in these three paragraphs.

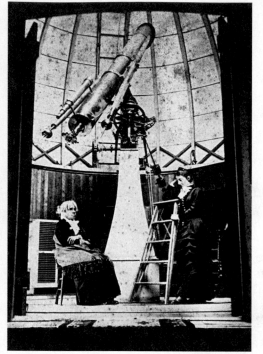

Maria Mitchell (left) at her telescope

New Careers Gradually, American society came to accept that girls could be educated and that women could be teachers. More and more schools began hiring women teachers who had been trained at one of the new academies or colleges for women. Some women began trying to enter other professions as well.

Margaret Fuller made a career as a journalist, scholar, and literary critic. She spoke in public for pay at a time when it was illegal for women to do so. In 1845, Fuller published an influential book, *Women in the Nineteenth Century.* "We would have every . . . barrier thrown down. We would have every path laid open to Woman as freely as to Man," she wrote.

Other women excelled in science. Elizabeth Blackwell was admitted to Geneva Medical College in New York. Blackwell graduated first in her class in January 1849, becoming the first woman to graduate from an American medical school. The astronomer Maria Mitchell was the first professor hired at Vassar College. She was also the first woman elected to the American Academy of Arts and Sciences in 1848. A crater on the moon was later named in her honor.

✓ **Checkpoint** Give two examples of advances in education for women.

☆ **Looking Back and Ahead** The delegates at the Seneca Falls Convention hesitated to demand women's suffrage. As it turned out, getting the vote was a long struggle. Not until 1920 did a constitutional amendment guarantee women's right to vote. You will read more about the women's suffrage movement in a later chapter.

Section 3 | **Check Your Progress**

Progress Monitoring Online
For: Self-test with instant help
Visit: PHSchool.com
Web Code: mya-4083

Comprehension and Critical Thinking

1. **(a) Summarize** What were the goals of the women's rights movement?
   (b) Compare and Contrast How were the goals of the women's rights movement similar to and different from those of the abolitionist movement?

2. **(a) Recall** Why was it considered more important for boys to get a good education than girls in the early 1800s?
   (b) Explain Problems How did the lack of equal educational opportunities hurt women?

Reading Skill

3. **State the Meaning of Evidence** Make a statement about public views regarding women in politics, and then support it with the evidence in this paragraph: "Hers is the domestic altar; there she ministers and commands . . .; let her not seek madly to descend from this eminence to mix with the strife and ambition of the cares of government; the field of politics is not her appropriate arena."

Key Terms

Read each sentence below. If the sentence is true, write YES and explain why. If the sentence is not true, write NO and explain why not.

4. Supporters of women's suffrage opposed the right to vote.

5. The Seneca Falls Convention marked the start of the women's rights movement.

Writing

6. Imagine that you are a reporter in 1848 writing an article about the Seneca Falls Convention. Write a few sentences explaining why the convention met. Then, predict what might be the long-term effects of the convention.

A National Hero

❝Until [James Fenimore] Cooper, most American writers borrowed their subject matter and literary styles from Europe. . . . Cooper proved that such imitation was not necessary. . . . He gave the American public what it desperately wanted—a national hero whose history was theirs.❞

—Frank Magill, editor and literary critic

◄ Natty Bumppo is the hero of Cooper's novel *The Last of the Mohicans.*

American Literature and Arts

Objectives

- Identify the common themes in American literature and art in the mid-1800s.
- Describe the flowering of American literature in the mid-1800s.
- Discuss the development of unique American styles in art and music.

Reading Skill

Draw Logical Conclusions As you review the details and evidence in text, make sure that the conclusions you draw are logical. In other words, they should make sense with all the details and with what you know about the events and about the world. Use your own experience to test, for example, whether particular attitudes make sense in a given situation. Do they fit the historical context?

Key Terms and People

transcendentalism
Ralph Waldo
  Emerson
individualism
Henry David
  Thoreau

civil disobedience
Herman Melville
Nathaniel
  Hawthorne
Louisa May Alcott

Why It Matters While sectionalism and slavery divided the nation, other ideas united the nation. Many Americans shared a belief in optimism and nationalism. They believed that individuals could improve themselves and society. They had pride in the United States of America.

❓ **Section Focus Question: How did American literature and art have an impact on American life?**

An American Culture Develops

Before 1800, American writers and artists modeled their work on European styles. Poets used complex, formal language and filled their poems with references to Greek and Roman myths. Most artists trained in Europe and learned European approaches to painting.

American Themes By the mid-1800s, American writers and artists had begun to develop styles that reflected American optimism and energy. Their work explored subjects that were uniquely American. Two early writers, Washington Irving and James Fenimore Cooper, reflected this interest in American themes.

Irving drew upon the Dutch history of New York in his stories "The Legend of Sleepy Hollow" and "Rip Van Winkle." Rip Van Winkle was a lazy farmer who slept through the American Revolution.

Cooper created the popular character Natty Bumppo, a frontiersman who kept moving westward. Uncomfortable with life in cities and towns, Bumppo criticized the destruction of nature. Cooper's novels about Bumppo, such as *The Deerslayer* and *The Last of the Mohicans,* helped American literature gain popularity in Europe.

Transcendentalism By the early 1800s, a new artistic movement took shape in Europe, called Romanticism. Unlike thinkers of the Enlightenment, who emphasized reason, Romantics placed greater value on nature, emotions, and imagination.

A small but influential group of writers and thinkers in New England developed an American form of Romanticism, called transcendentalism (trahnz ehn DEHNT uhl ihzm). Transcendentalism was a movement that sought to explore the relationship between humans and nature through emotions rather than through reason. It got its name because its goal was to transcend, or go beyond, human reason.

Transcendentalists believed in a close link between humans and nature. They urged people to live simply and to seek beauty, goodness, and truth within their own souls.

Emerson and Thoreau Ralph Waldo Emerson was the leading transcendentalist. In his popular speeches and essays, Emerson asked Americans to question the value of material goods. Civilization might provide wealth, he said, but nature reflected higher values that came from God. Emerson also stressed individualism, the unique importance of each individual. "Trust thyself," he taught. He challenged people to use their "inner light" to guide their lives and improve society.

Henry David Thoreau (thuh ROW) took up Emerson's challenge. He spent two years living in the woods at Walden Pond, meditating on nature. In his 1854 book *Walden*, Thoreau urged people to live

● **INFOGRAPHIC**

≫ MOBY-DICK ≪

Herman Melville's novel *Moby-Dick* tells the story of a sea captain's mad pursuit of a white whale. The novel is still widely read and has been filmed several times.
Critical Thinking: *Apply Information You have read that Melville was interested in extreme, dark emotions. How does the excerpt on the facing page reflect that interest?*

◄ Herman Melville

simply. "Most of the luxuries, and many of the so-called comforts of life, are not only not indispensable, but positive hindrances to the elevation of mankind," he wrote.

Like Emerson, Thoreau believed that individuals must judge right and wrong for themselves. He encouraged civil disobedience, the idea that people should peacefully disobey unjust laws if their consciences demand it. Thoreau spent a night in jail for refusing to pay a tax that he felt supported slavery. Thoreau's ideas about civil disobedience and nonviolent protest influenced later leaders like Martin Luther King, Jr.

Draw Logical Conclusions
Reading Skill
Draw a logical conclusion about Thoreau's values from the information and quotation in this paragraph.

☑**Checkpoint**   **What was the goal of transcendentalism?**

Flowering of American Literature

Irving and Cooper set a high standard for American writers. Two later novelists, Herman Melville and Nathaniel Hawthorne, began to change the tone of American literature.

Melville and Hawthorne Both Hawthorne and Melville were fascinated by psychology and extreme emotions. Melville's novel *Moby-Dick* (1851) told the story of a sea captain who is obsessed with pursuing a white whale. In the end, Captain Ahab's mad pursuit destroys himself, his ship, and his crew. *Moby-Dick* was largely ignored when it was first published. Today, however, it is considered one of the greatest American novels.

“Aye, my hearties all round; it was Moby Dick that dismasted me; Moby Dick that brought me to this dead stump I stand on now. Aye aye,' he shouted with a terrific, loud, animal sob, like that of a heart-stricken moose; 'Aye, aye! it was that accursed white whale that razeed me; made a poor pegging lubber for me for ever and a day!' Then, tossing both arms, with measureless imprecations he shouted out, 'Aye, aye! and I'll chase him round Good Hope, and round the Horn, and round the Norway Maelstrom, and round perdition's flames before I give him up. And this is what ye have shipped for, men! To chase that white whale on both sides of land, and over all sides of the earth. . . .”

◀ Captain Ahab tells his crew that he lost his leg because of the white whale Moby Dick.

Captain Ahab in a movie ▶ version of *Moby-Dick*.

The Hudson River School
This landscape painting by Thomas Cole shows Americans building a home in the middle of the wilderness. Like other paintings of the Hudson River school, it reflects a sense of the beauty and power of nature. **Critical Thinking:** *Evaluate Information* *What is the relationship between people and nature in this painting?*

Hawthorne was descended from the Puritans of Massachusetts. He often used historical themes to explore the dark side of the mind. In his 1850 novel *The Scarlet Letter*, a young minister is destroyed by secret guilt. The novel paints a grim picture of Puritan life.

Alcott Louisa May Alcott presented a gentler view of New England life. In 1868, Alcott published *Little Women*, a novel based on her own experiences growing up with three sisters. The main character, Jo March, was one of the first young American heroines to be presented as a believable, imperfect person rather than as a shining ideal.

Poets of Democracy Poets helped create a new national voice. Henry Wadsworth Longfellow based poems on American history, such as "Paul Revere's Ride." His long poem *The Song of Hiawatha* was one of the first works to honor Native Americans.

Walt Whitman published *Leaves of Grass* in 1855. This book of poems shocked many readers because it rejected formal rules. But today, Whitman is seen as the poet who best expresses the democratic American spirit. His poetry celebrated common people:

> **❝**[T]he policeman travels his beat—the gate-keeper marks who pass; . . .
>
> The clean-hair'd Yankee girl works with her sewing-machine, or in the factory or mill.**❞**
>
> —Walt Whitman, "Song of Myself"

Some poets used their pens to support social reform. John Greenleaf Whittier, a Massachusetts Quaker, and Frances Watkins Harper, an African American woman from Maryland, wrote poems that described and condemned the evils of slavery.

✓**Checkpoint** How did writers explore the American past?

Art and Music

After 1820, artists also began to create a unique American style. Turning away from European themes, they focused on the landscapes around them or on the daily lives of common Americans.

Painting America A group of artists painted scenes of the Hudson River valley. This group became known as the Hudson River school. Thomas Cole and the other painters of this school reflected the values of Romanticism. They sought to stir emotions by reproducing the beauty and power of nature.

Other American painters were inspired by everyday life. George Caleb Bingham created a timeless picture of life on the great rivers. George Catlin captured the ways and dignity of Native Americans.

Popular Songs Most early American songs, such as "Yankee Doodle," had roots in English, Irish, or Scottish tunes. Over time, a wide variety of new American songs emerged. Many were work songs, chanted by men as they sailed on whaling ships, laid railroad tracks, or hauled barges along canals. The spiritual was a special type of song developed by enslaved African Americans.

The most popular American songwriter of the 1800s was Stephen Foster. Many of his tunes, such as "Camptown Races" and "Old Folks at Home," are still familiar today.

☑**Checkpoint** **Identify two themes of American painting.**

☆ **Looking Back and Ahead** American culture of the 1800s had an influence that is still felt today. People still read *Moby-Dick* and *Little Women*. Concepts like individualism and civil disobedience continue to affect people's ideas and actions.

Vocabulary Builder
reproduce (ree prah DYOOS) **v.** to make a copy of

Section 4 | **Check Your Progress**

Progress Monitoring ⬤nline
For: Self-test with instant help
Visit: PHSchool.com
Web Code: mya-4084

Comprehension and Critical Thinking

1. **(a) Recall** Before 1800, what models influenced American writers and painters?
(b) Draw Conclusions How did later works like *The Scarlet Letter* and the paintings of the Hudson River school reflect a change in American art and literature?

2. **(a) Recall** What did Henry David Thoreau mean by "civil disobedience"?
(b) Link Past and Present How did Thoreau's ideas influence Martin Luther King, Jr.?

⦿ Reading Skill

3. **Draw Logical Conclusions** In a novel by James Fenimore Cooper, Natty Bumppo watches as settlers shoot hundreds of pigeons. Based on the following quotation, what conclusion can you draw about Natty's feelings for nature? Explain why your conclusion is logical. **Quotation:** "It's much better to kill only such as you want, without wasting your powder and lead, than to be firing into God's creatures in this wicked manner. . . . Wasn't the woods made for the beasts and birds to harbor in?"

Key Terms

4. Write two definitions for the key term transcendentalism. First, write a formal definition for your teacher. Second, write a definition in everyday English for a classmate.

Writing

5. What is the relationship between artists and society? Using examples from this section, write a paragraph explaining how writers, painters, and musicians reflect the society in which they live and how they help to influence it.

21st Century Learning A summary briefly retells the main ideas of a selection, using different words. It also includes the most important details about the main ideas. Summaries should not include personal opinions about the selection. Read the primary source below, then read summaries A–C.

> In 1852, Frederick Douglass, African American abolitionist, was invited to speak at a July 4th gathering in Rochester, New York.

Primary Source

> Fellow citizens, pardon me, allow me to ask, why am I called upon to speak here today? What have I, or those I represent, to do with your national independence? Are the great principles of political freedom and of natural justice, embodied in that Declaration of Independence, extended to us? . . . This Fourth of July is yours, not mine. You may rejoice. I must mourn. . . . Do you mean, citizens, to mock me by asking me to speak today? . . . My subject then, fellow citizens, is American slavery. I shall see this day and its popular characteristics from the slave's point of view.
>
> —Frederick Douglass,
> Independence Day speech,
> Rochester, 1852

Summary A: Douglass believes that all Americans should celebrate the Fourth of July. The freedoms established in the Declaration of Independence are meant for all.

Summary B: Douglass does not feel he is able to speak. He is a poor man who does not enjoy the wealth and good fortune shared by many members of the audience.

Summary C: Douglass reminds his audience that African Americans did not enjoy the freedoms and independence guaranteed in the Declaration of Independence.

Learn the Skill

Use these steps to determine which summary accurately captures the main idea of the speech.

1. **Identify the subject of the selection.** What is the selection about?

2. **Find the main idea of the selection.** Determine the writer or speaker's most important point about the subject.

3. **Find important details.** What details provide key information about the main idea?

4. **Evaluate the summary.** Does it accurately restate the main idea of the original in different words? Does it include important details? Does it communicate the basic meaning of the original text?

Practice the Skill

Answer the following questions about the summaries on this page.

1. **Identify the subject of the selection.** What is the selection about?

2. **Find the main idea of the selection.** What main point does Frederick Douglass make?

3. **Find important details.** What is one detail that provides information about the main idea?

4. **Evaluate the summary.** Which is the best summary of Douglass's speech? Give three reasons for your answer.

Apply the Skill

See the Review and Assessment at the end of this chapter.

Quick Study Guide

How did reformers and writers inspire change and spark controversy?

Section 1
Improving Society

- Jacksonian democracy encouraged reform by focusing on ideals of liberty and equality.
- In the Second Great Awakening, ministers preached that people had free will and could reform their own lives.
- Reformers tackled a variety of causes, including temperance, prison reform, improved conditions for those with mental illnesses, and public education.

Section 2
The Fight Against Slavery

- Abolitionists such as William Lloyd Garrison and Frederick Douglass called for an end to slavery.
- Conductors on the Underground Railroad helped people escape from slavery to freedom.
- Abolitionists faced strong opposition in both the North and the South.

Section 3
A Call for Women's Rights

- People active in social reform began to demand equal rights for women.
- The Declaration of Sentiments at the Seneca Falls Convention called for women's equality in many areas of public life.
- The women's rights movement focused much of its attention on gaining better education for women.

Section 4
American Literature and Arts

- American writers and artists began to explore American themes in their work.
- Transcendentalists emphasized emotions, nature, and individualism.
- Melville and Hawthorne explored dark areas of psychology, while Whitman wrote poems celebrating democracy.

? Exploring the Essential Question

Use the online study guide to explore the essential question.

Section 1
How did key people bring about reform in education and society?

Section 2
How did abolitionists try to end slavery?

Chapter 12 Essential Question
How did reformers and writers inspire change and spark controversy?

Section 4
How did American literature and art have an impact on American life?

Section 3
How did the women's suffrage movement begin?

Key Terms

Complete each of the following sentences so that the second part further explains the first part and clearly shows your understanding of the key term.

1. The doctrine of free will was almost the exact opposite of predestination, the belief that _____.

2. People in the United States who wanted to end slavery were called abolitionists because they wanted to _____.

3. Women who wanted to _____ supported women's suffrage.

Comprehension and Critical Thinking

4. **(a) Describe** Describe two problems Dorothea Dix uncovered.
   (b) Apply Information What did she do to correct them?
   (c) Link Past and Present How do you think Dix's work benefits people today?

5. **(a) List** Give two reasons why Americans opposed slavery.
   (b) Compare and Contrast Compare how northern abolitionists and southern slaveholders viewed slavery.

6. **(a) Recall** Which rights were denied women in the early 1800s?
   (b) Draw Conclusions What rights did women gain as a result of the victories won in the struggle for equal rights in the 1800s?

History Reading Skill

7. **Draw Conclusions From Sources** Based on the following quotation, what conclusion can you draw about the writer's view regarding education? Explain how you reached this conclusion.

> "Those who have been blessed with a good common-school education rise to a higher and higher point in the kinds of labor performed and also in the rate of wages paid, while the ignorant sink like dregs and are always found at the bottom."
>
> —Annual Reports of the Secretary of the Board of Education of Massachusetts, 1839–1844

Writing

8. **Read the following poem by Frances Watkins Harper. Then, write a paragraph explaining how this poem is related to the spirit of change that swept the United States in the mid-1800s:**

> "I ask no monument, proud and high,
> To arrest the gaze of passers-by;
> All that my yearning spirit craves,
> Is bury me not in a land of slaves."
>
> —Frances Watkins Harper,
> "Bury Me in a Free Land"

9. **Write a Narrative:**
   You are a student in the 1850s. Your parents have taken you to a public meeting about temperance, abolition, or women's rights. Write a letter to a friend describing what you saw and heard at the meeting and how it made you feel. Use information from this chapter to create your description.

Skills for Life

Evaluate Summaries

Review Section 3, "A Call for Women's Rights." Then, look at the three summaries below and answer the questions that follow.

Summary A: The Seneca Falls Convention was a failure. American women failed to make any political or economic gains.

Summary B: The Seneca Falls Convention did not change American society overnight. Still, the convention marked the start of a long struggle for women's rights that eventually succeeded.

Summary C: The Seneca Falls Convention was a great success. Before long, many states gave women property rights and passed laws giving women suffrage.

10. What is the main idea of the section?

11. Which is the best summary of the section? Give three reasons for your answer.

Test Yourself

1. **The idea that God decides the fate of each person is called**

   A prohibition.

   B transcendentalism.

   C romanticism.

   D predestination.

2. **Frederick Douglass and William Lloyd Garrison were**

   A founders of the American Colonization Society.

   B leaders of the antislavery movement.

   C conductors on the Underground Railroad.

   D delegates to the Seneca Falls Convention.

Refer to the quotation below to answer Question 3.

> "Most of the luxuries, and many of the so-called comforts of life, are not only not indispensable, but positive hindrances to the elevation of mankind."

3. **The quotation above describes the core ideas of which American author?**

   A Herman Melville

   B Louisa May Alcott

   C Henry David Thoreau

   D James Fenimore Cooper

Document-Based Questions

Task: Look at Documents 1 and 2, and answer their accompanying questions. Then, use the documents and your knowledge of history to complete this writing assignment:

> Write a short essay about the Second Great Awakening. Include details about the emotional and moral impact of the movement.

Document 1: Charles Grandison Finney, a leading figure of the Second Great Awakening, conducted spellbinding revival meetings in many eastern cities. This excerpt is from Finney's Revival Lectures. *According to Finney, what role do revivals play in religion?*

> "Almost all the religion in the world has been produced by revivals. God has found it necessary to take advantage of the excitability there is in mankind, to produce powerful excitements among them, before he can lead them to obey. Men are so spiritually sluggish, there are so many things to lead their minds off from religion, and to oppose the influence of the Gospel, that it is necessary to raise an excitement among them, till the tide rises so high as to sweep away the opposing obstacles. They must be so excited that they will break over these counteracting influences, before they will obey God."

Document 2: Millions of American flocked to revival meetings, sometimes camping at the sites for several days. *Why were so many Americans attracted to the revival movement?*

Westward Expansion

1820–1860

"*Come through a poor mountainous country... it is difficult to get food for our horses our provisions is getting scarce and have a great trouble to get more here....*"

—Jane Voorhees Lewis,
A Journey by Covered Wagon, 1847

In this painting, settlers travel West by wagon train.

Reading Skill

Frame Research Questions In this chapter, you will learn how to ask questions that can be answered through research.

How did westward expansion change the the determination of its people?

Westward Expansion, 1820–1860

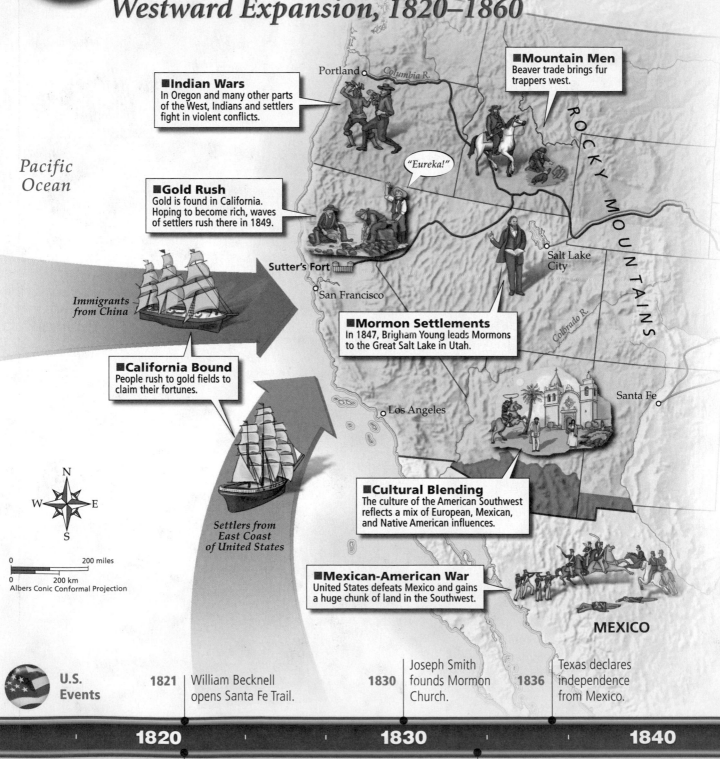

Pacific Ocean

■Indian Wars
In Oregon and many other parts of the West, Indians and settlers fight in violent conflicts.

Portland

Columbia R.

■Mountain Men
Beaver trade brings fur trappers west.

ROCKY MOUNTAINS

"Eureka!"

■Gold Rush
Gold is found in California. Hoping to become rich, waves of settlers rush there in 1849.

Sutter's Fort

San Francisco

Salt Lake City

Immigrants from China

■Mormon Settlements
In 1847, Brigham Young leads Mormons to the Great Salt Lake in Utah.

Colorado R.

■California Bound
People rush to gold fields to claim their fortunes.

Los Angeles

Santa Fe

■Cultural Blending
The culture of the American Southwest reflects a mix of European, Mexican, and Native American influences.

N W E S

Settlers from East Coast of United States

0   200 miles
0   200 km
Albers Conic Conformal Projection

■Mexican-American War
United States defeats Mexico and gains a huge chunk of land in the Southwest.

MEXICO

U.S. Events — **1821** William Becknell opens Santa Fe Trail. — **1830** Joseph Smith founds Mormon Church. — **1836** Texas declares independence from Mexico.

1820   **1830**   **1840**

World Events — **1821** Mexico wins independence from Spain. — **1833** Santa Anna becomes president of Mexico.

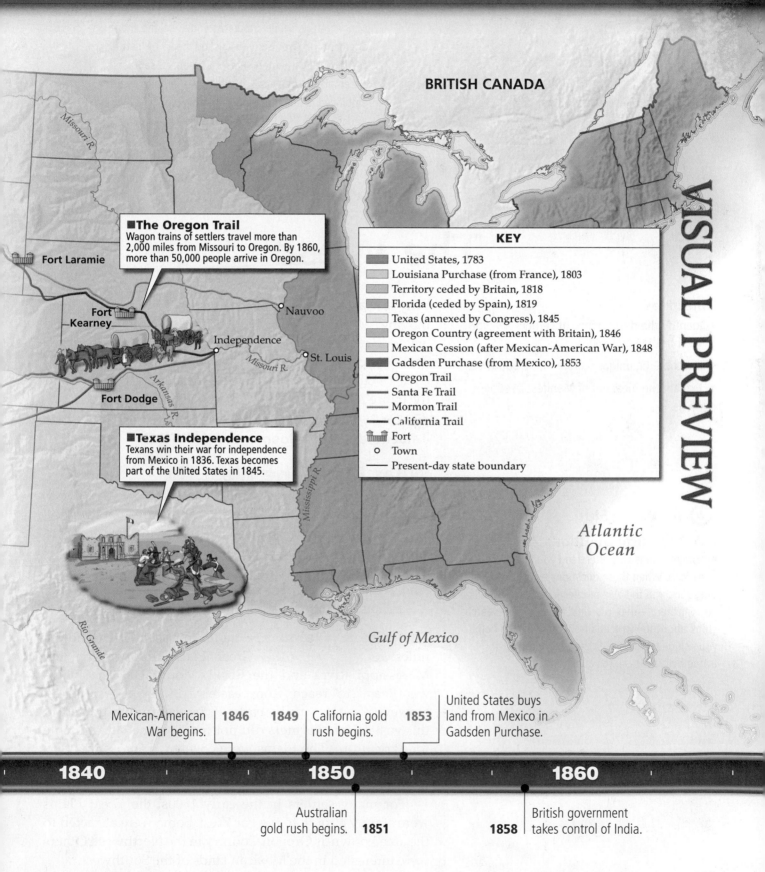

BRITISH CANADA

■**The Oregon Trail**
Wagon trains of settlers travel more than
2,000 miles from Missouri to Oregon. By 1860,
more than 50,000 people arrive in Oregon.

Fort Laramie

Fort
Kearney

Nauvoo

Independence

Missouri R.

St. Louis

Arkansas R.

Fort Dodge

■**Texas Independence**
Texans win their war for independence
from Mexico in 1836. Texas becomes
part of the United States in 1845.

Rio Grande

Mississippi R.

Missouri R.

KEY

	United States, 1783
	Louisiana Purchase (from France), 1803
	Territory ceded by Britain, 1818
	Florida (ceded by Spain), 1819
	Texas (annexed by Congress), 1845
	Oregon Country (agreement with Britain), 1846
	Mexican Cession (after Mexican-American War), 1848
	Gadsden Purchase (from Mexico), 1853
——	Oregon Trail
——	Santa Fe Trail
——	Mormon Trail
——	California Trail
🏰	Fort
○	Town
——	Present-day state boundary

VISUAL PREVIEW

*Atlantic
Ocean*

Gulf of Mexico

Mexican-American
War begins.

1846   **1849** | California gold
rush begins.

1853 | United States buys
land from Mexico in
Gadsden Purchase.

1840   **1850**   **1860**

Australian
gold rush begins. | **1851**

1858 | British government
takes control of India.

443

Mission San Luis Rey

❝At this time (1829) its population was about three thousand Indians. . . . Some were engaged in agriculture, while others attended to the management of over sixty thousand head of cattle. Many were carpenters, masons, coopers, saddlers, shoemakers, weavers . . . while the females were employed in spinning and preparing wool for their looms. . . .❞

—Alfred Robinson, *Life in California*, 1846

▲ Spanish mission in California

The West

Objectives

- Identify the destinations of settlers heading west in the early 1800s.
- Describe the unique culture of the Southwest.
- Explain the meaning of Manifest Destiny.

🔁 Reading Skill

Ask Analytical Questions Reading about historical events will often lead you to ask questions. When these questions are analytical— or require you to solve puzzles in the text to answer them—they can yield interesting research. Think about the *why* and *how* of history to help you ask questions about the text and then to frame possible research questions.

Key Terms

frontier
land grant

ranchero
expansion

Why It Matters Since colonial times, settlers had been moving westward over the Appalachian Mountains and beyond. As these settlers moved further westward, they encountered Native Americans and Mexicans. The mixing of these cultures affected the development of the West and the entire nation.

❷ **Section Focus Question: What cultures and ideas influenced the development of the West?**

What Was "The West"?

As the nation grew, Americans' idea of "the West" changed. Early Americans thought of the area between the Appalachians and the Mississippi River as the western frontier. A **frontier** is the land that forms the farthest extent of a nation's settled regions. By the 1820s, however, much of the land in this area had been settled. As the population soared, Americans began to look beyond the Mississippi River.

The Great Plains Stretching for seemingly endless miles to the west, the Great Plains lie between the Mississippi River and the Rocky Mountains. The Plains were easy to reach from eastern and southern states. However, settlers in the early 1800s were not attracted to this vast region. Farmers did not consider the land suitable for agriculture. The Plains were covered by grass that was anchored to the ground by deep root systems. Breaking up the dense sod would be hard manual labor.

For many settlers in the early 1800s, the Great Plains were simply a route to the Far West. Some were attracted to the area known as Oregon Country in the Northwest. Others were interested in the Mexican lands of the Southwest.

The Northwest In the Northwest, settlers were attracted to the fertile land stretching from beyond the Rocky Mountains to the Pacific Ocean. This region is now occupied by the states of Oregon and Washington as well as by most of British Columbia in Canada. In the early 1800s, the United States, Great Britain, Russia, and Spain all claimed this land as their own.

The Southwest The Mexican settlements in the Southwest were another major destination for settlers heading west. This area, known as the Spanish Borderlands, was part of New Spain. Together with Mexico, these lands had been claimed for Spain in the 1500s.

The lands of the Southwest included present-day California, Utah, Nevada, Arizona, New Mexico, Texas, and about half of Colorado. Ruled first by Spain, then by Mexico, these lands had a culture and history very different from that of the eastern United States.

✓**Checkpoint** What did "the West" mean to Americans in the 1800s?

Ask Analytical Questions
Reading Skill What do you think were the land and climate features that attracted people to the Northwest? Suggest a possible research question to build on this topic.

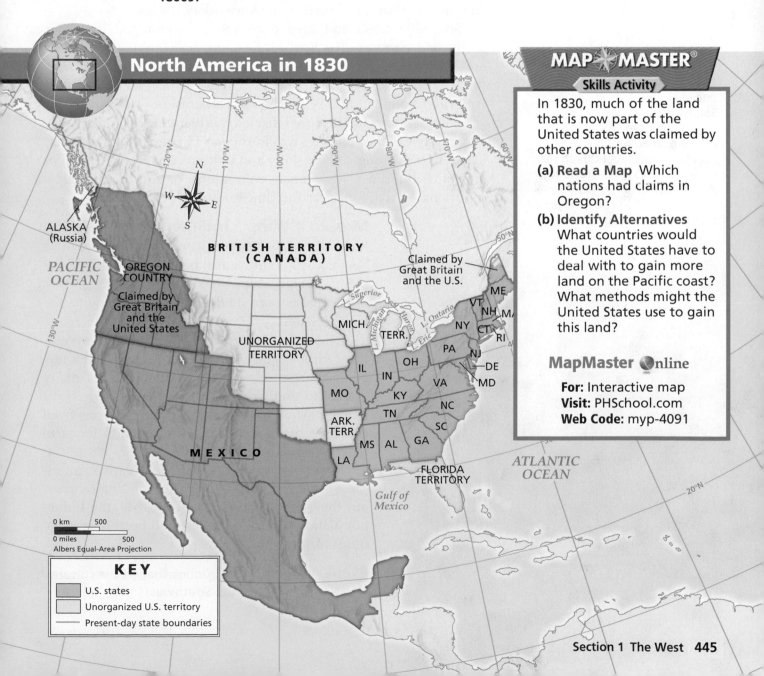

North America in 1830

MAP MASTER®
Skills Activity

In 1830, much of the land that is now part of the United States was claimed by other countries.

(a) Read a Map Which nations had claims in Oregon?

(b) Identify Alternatives What countries would the United States have to deal with to gain more land on the Pacific coast? What methods might the United States use to gain this land?

MapMaster Online

For: Interactive map
Visit: PHSchool.com
Web Code: myp-4091

KEY
- U.S. states
- Unorganized U.S. territory
- Present-day state boundaries

Mexican Settlements

Like England and France, Spain followed a <u>policy</u> of mercantilism toward its colonies. It was illegal for settlers in New Spain to trade with other countries. Raw materials were sent to Spain. Manufactured goods were shipped to the Spanish colonies for sale.

Over the years, many Spanish settlers, or peninsulares, had children. These American-born children were called creoles. Spanish settlers, Native Americans, and Africans also intermarried. The result was another group, the mestizos. By the 1800s, this combination of ethnic groups had created a <u>distinct</u> Southwestern culture.

Native Americans Spanish missionaries, such as Junípero Serro (ho NEE peh roh SEHR rah) in California, were determined to convert Native Americans to Catholicism. Many Indians in the borderlands were forced to live and work at missions. There, they herded sheep and cattle and raised crops. They also learned about the Catholic religion. In the end, the mission system took a terrible toll on Native Americans. Thousands died from overwork or disease.

Spanish settlers and Native Americans exchanged language, foods, and customs. The Spanish brought their language, religion, and laws to the region. The Indians introduced the Spanish to such foods as beans, squash, and potatoes. Spanish settlers adopted Native American clothing, such as ponchos and moccasins.

Southwestern architecture reflected this blending of cultures. The general style of the buildings was European. However, Native American laborers brought their skills and cultural traditions. Churches and other buildings were made from adobe, or sun-dried brick, a traditional Native American building material.

Mexico Wins Independence In 1821, Mexico won its independence from Spain. Unlike Spain, Mexico allowed its people to trade with the many foreign ships that landed on its shores. Mexico also permitted overland trade with the United States.

Under Spanish rule, **land grants,** or government gifts of land, had been given only to a few peninsulares. Mexico, however, made many grants to individual **rancheros,** or owners of ranches. Mexico also removed the missions from church control and distributed mission lands to rancheros and a few American settlers.

Much of this land belonged to Native Americans. Indians often responded by raiding ranches, but they were soon crushed. By 1850, the Indian population in the Southwest had been drastically reduced.

☑ **Checkpoint** What groups shaped the culture of the Southwest?

Mission in the Southwest
Old Spanish missions, like this one in California, still dot the Southwest. Native Americans were forced to live and work on the mission grounds, where Spanish priests taught them about Christianity. **Critical Thinking: Apply Information** *How were missions like these an example of cultural blending?*

Manifest Destiny

From the beginning, Americans had been interested in westward **expansion,** or extending the nation beyond its existing borders. Thomas Jefferson was one of many who believed that the nation must increase in size to make room for its growing population. As you have read, under Jefferson, the Louisiana Purchase doubled the territory of the nation.

By the 1840s, many Americans strongly favored westward expansion. Newspaper editor John L. O'Sullivan wrote in 1845:

> **"**The American claim is by the right of our manifest [obvious] destiny to overspread and possess the whole of the continent which Providence has given us for the development of the great experiment of liberty and . . . self-government entrusted to us.**"**
>
> —John L. O'Sullivan, *United States Magazine and Democratic Review*

The phrase Manifest Destiny quickly became popular. It described the belief that the United States was destined, or meant, to extend from the Atlantic to the Pacific—"from sea to shining sea."

✓**Checkpoint** What did Americans mean by Manifest Destiny?

⭐ **Looking Back and Ahead** The drive to achieve Manifest Destiny would become one of the most powerful forces shaping American history. In the next sections, you will see how Americans pursued the goal of Manifest Destiny.

Section 1 | Check Your Progress

Progress Monitoring Online
For: Self-test with instant help
Visit: PHSchool.com
Web Code: mya-4091

Comprehension and Critical Thinking

1. **(a) Recall** Why did American farmers prefer to settle in the Northwest rather than the Great Plains?
   (b) Evaluate Information How did the geography of the Great Plains affect U.S. settlement of that region in the early 1800s?

2. **(a) Explain** What is Manifest Destiny?
   (b) Detect Points of View How do you think the Mexican government felt about the idea of Manifest Destiny?

Reading Skill

3. **Ask Analytical Questions** Suggest a possible research question related to this topic: The effect of Native American labor on slavery in Mexican settlements.

Key Terms

Fill in the blanks with the correct key terms.

4. Each time Americans settled farther west, the _____ moved.

5. Under Spanish rule, only peninsulares received _____, but under Mexican rule, rancheros received them as well.

Writing

6. Decide which is the best closing sentence for an essay discussing why Americans were drawn to the lands west of the Mississippi River. Explain your choice.
   Sentences:
   (a) So for many Americans, the West was a promise—of wealth, adventure, and freedom.
   (b) The fertile lands of the Northwest drew many people who wanted to own farms.
   (c) Therefore, the southwestern lands ruled by Mexico had developed a culture very different from that of easterners.

◀ A mountain man

Thirty Thousand Beaver Skins

❝The annual quantity of these furs could not be exactly ascertained, but Mr. Smith was informed indirectly that they amounted to about thirty thousand beaver skins, besides otter skins and small furs. The beaver skins alone, at the New York prices, would be worth above two hundred and fifty thousand dollars.❞

—Report of trappers Jedediah Smith, David Jackson, and W.L. Sublette, 1830

Trails to the West

Objectives
- Explain how traders and fur trappers helped open the West.
- List the reasons pioneers traveled along the Oregon Trail and describe the hardships they faced.
- Discuss the issues for women, Native Americans, and new settlers in the West.

⟳ Reading Skill

Ask Inferential Questions You can also ask inferential questions to explore a text and generate research ideas. Inferential questions require you to read between the lines. In other words, you have to use clues in the text and your own knowledge to make reasonable guesses about history. You can then conduct research to confirm or disprove your guesses.

Key Terms and People

William Becknell
John Jacob Astor
mountain man
rendezvous

Marcus and Narcissa Whitman

Why It Matters Like the settlers who traveled across the Atlantic to build the thirteen colonies, settlers who moved westward were drawn by a variety of factors and had to face difficult challenges.

❷ **Section Focus Question: Why did people go west and what challenges did they face?**

Traders Lead the Way

The first Americans to move into the Far West were traders. They were looking for new markets in which to sell their goods. In the process, they blazed important trails for the people who followed.

The Santa Fe Trail As you have read, when Mexico won independence, it began to allow overland trade with the United States. In 1821, Captain William Becknell led a wagon train filled with merchandise from Independence, Missouri, to Santa Fe, New Mexico. The route stretched for about 800 miles.

Becknell crossed treacherous rivers with bottoms of quicksand. He and the traders traveling with him barely survived the desert. Then, he had to find a way through nearly impassable mountains. In spite of these obstacles, Becknell's group reached Santa Fe with their wagons. Other Americans followed Becknell's route. It became known as the Santa Fe Trail. The Santa Fe Trail soon became a busy international trading route.

The Oregon Fur Trade Farther north, fur traders were making huge fortunes. John Jacob Astor, a German immigrant, sent the first American fur-trading expedition to Oregon. Astor established the American Fur Company in 1808 at Fort Astor, now Astoria, Oregon.

Astor's expedition consisted of two groups. The first group sailed around South America and up the Pacific coast. The second group traveled across the continent, using information that had been recorded by Lewis and Clark. On the way, they found the South Pass through the Rocky Mountains. This important route helped to open the Northwest for the missionaries and settlers who followed.

Mountain Men The fur trade made Astor the richest man in the country. The trappers who supplied him with furs were also eager to become rich. These mountain men, or fur trappers of the Northwest, would become legendary.

For most of the year, trappers led isolated lives in a dangerous environment. They endured bitter cold, intense heat, and attacks from wild animals. Jedediah Smith was once scalped by a grizzly bear. He persuaded a companion to sew his scalp back onto his head and to piece together his severed ear. Several weeks later, Smith returned to his work.

Once a year, trappers would bring their furs to a rendezvous (RAHN day voo), a meeting where the trappers would trade furs for supplies. Here, the mountain men would celebrate their time together—singing, laughing, and competing in contests. Then, they got down to serious bargaining. Beaver fur was in great demand in the East, so trappers were able to command high prices for their furs.

By the 1830s, the supply of beavers was nearly exhausted. Most trappers moved back east to become farmers, merchants, or even bankers. Others stayed as guides for the wagon trains that brought thousands of settlers west in the 1840s. One mountain man, an African American named James Beckwourth, discovered a pass through the Sierras that later became a major route to California.

☑ **Checkpoint** **Why did the mountain men travel to Oregon?**

Vocabulary Builder
environment (en VY ruhn mehnt) *n.* surroundings

The Oregon Trail

The first white easterners to build permanent homes in Oregon were missionaries. In the 1830s, they began to travel west for the purpose of bringing their religious beliefs to the Indians.

Missionaries One couple, Marcus and Narcissa Whitman, set up a mission in Oregon to serve the Cayuse Indians. The Whitmans had trouble from the start. The Cayuses mistrusted them, partly because the Whitmans made little effort to understand Cayuse ways.

As more settlers arrived and took over Indian lands, the Cayuses grew increasingly hostile. Then, in 1847, an epidemic of measles killed many Cayuse adults and nearly all their children. Blaming the Whitmans, the Indians killed them along with 12 other settlers.

Still, missionaries like the Whitmans greatly spurred settlement of the West. Their glowing reports of Oregon led more easterners to make the journey west. Farmers sought the free and fertile land, the mild climate, and the plentiful rainfall of the river valleys. Settlers from all over the country were in the grip of "Oregon Fever."

Vocabulary Builder
hostile (HAHS tihl) *adj.* unfriendly; intending to do harm

On the Oregon Trail Most settlers followed the Oregon Trail, a route that stretched more than 2,000 miles from Missouri to Oregon. They set out in spring and had to be in Oregon within five months. Travelers caught by winter in the Rockies risked a slow death. The trip itself was hazardous. Disease and accidents killed about one traveler out of every ten on the Oregon Trail.

Pioneers on the Oregon Trail banded together for protection. Most traveled in long trains of covered wagons. The wagons carried supplies, while the people walked. As the miles went by, the horses and oxen tired more easily. People began to discard personal items to lighten their wagons. The trail was scattered with "leeverites," short for "leave 'er right here."

Dust got into everything. Some people wore masks to keep it out of their faces and lungs. Clean, safe water was hard to find. Francis Parkman, a famous historian, observed the following incident:

> **❝**I saw a tall slouching fellow . . . contemplating the contents of his tin cup, which he had just filled with water. 'Look here, you,' said he; 'it's chock full of animals!' The cup . . . exhibited in fact an extraordinary variety and profusion of animal life.**❞**
>
> —Francis Parkman, *The Oregon Trail*

Despite such hardships, more than 50,000 people reached Oregon between 1840 and 1860.

✔**Checkpoint** **Why did settlers travel by wagon train?**

Ask Inferential Questions

Reading Skill

Why do you think so many Americans were willing to face the hardships of westward settlement? Suggest a possible research topic to answer this question.

● **INFOGRAPHIC**

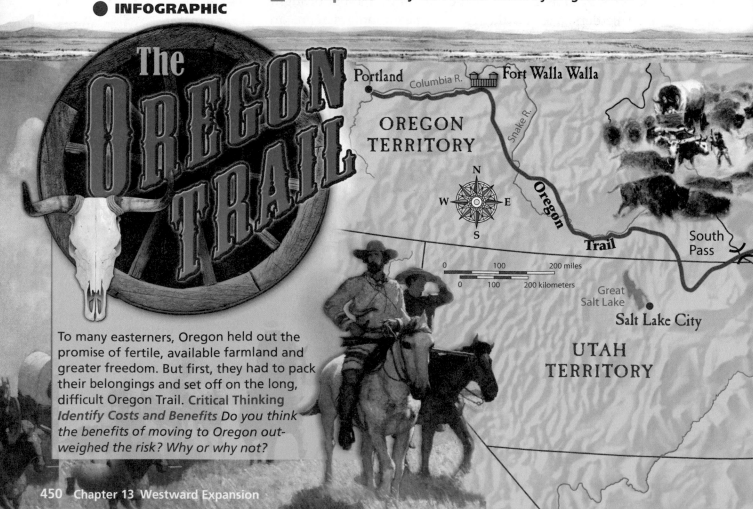

The OREGON TRAIL

Portland · Columbia R. · Fort Walla Walla

OREGON TERRITORY

Snake R.

Oregon Trail

South Pass

Great Salt Lake

Salt Lake City

UTAH TERRITORY

0   100   200 miles
0   100   200 kilometers

To many easterners, Oregon held out the promise of fertile, available farmland and greater freedom. But first, they had to pack their belongings and set off on the long, difficult Oregon Trail. **Critical Thinking** *Identify Costs and Benefits Do you think the benefits of moving to Oregon out-weighed the risk? Why or why not?*

Life in the West

Pioneer life was filled with hardships. Settlers arrived with few possessions. Working only with hand tools, they had to clear the land, plant crops, and build shelters. Disease, accidents, and natural disasters like storms and floods were an ever-present threat.

A. H. Garrison was 15 years old when his family went west in 1846. They traveled along the Oregon Trail with 74 other wagons. Along the way, his father became so ill he was unable to walk. Garrison later recalled the hardships of their first winter in Oregon.

> **"**On Christmas day, it began to snow, and it continued until the ground was covered to a depth of twenty inches. . . . At the beginning of the storm, father had thirteen head of oxen, and twelve head of cows, and one fine American mare. There was no feed to be had, and the grass was so covered that the cattle could get nothing to eat. . . . When spring came, we had four oxen and three cows left.**"**
>
> —*Reminiscences of A. H. Garrison*

Some settlers gave up and returned to the East. Others, like John Bidwell of California, met the challenges and went on to live extraordinary lives. Bidwell and his wife Annie each became civic leaders. John became a United States Congressman and even ran for President, while Annie fought for temperance and the right of women to vote.

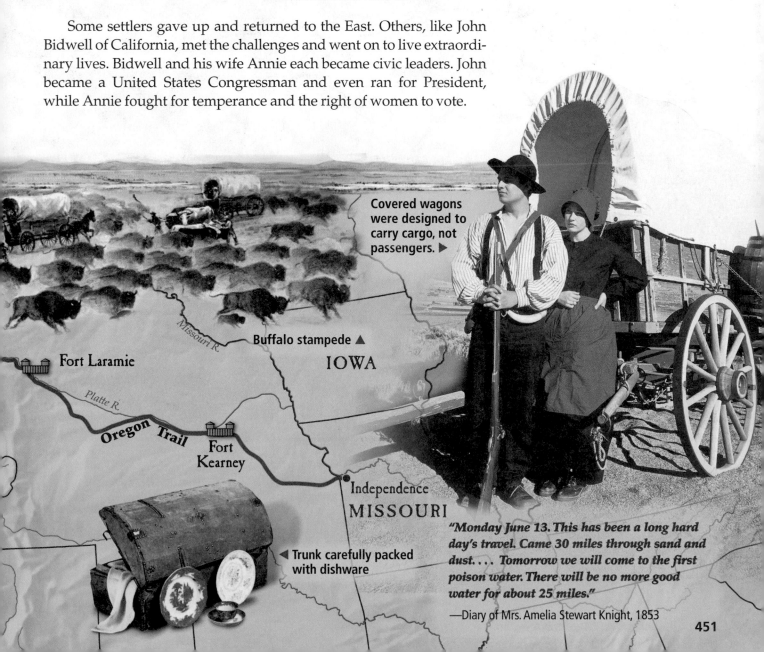

Covered wagons were designed to carry cargo, not passengers. ▶

Buffalo stampede ▲

Fort Laramie

Missouri R.

Platte R.

Oregon Trail

Fort Kearney

IOWA

Independence

MISSOURI

◀ Trunk carefully packed with dishware

"Monday June 13. This has been a long hard day's travel. Came 30 miles through sand and dust. . . . Tomorrow we will come to the first poison water. There will be no more good water for about 25 miles."

—Diary of Mrs. Amelia Stewart Knight, 1853

Trails to the West, 1830–1850

" We proceeded in an easterly direction, and all busied themselves in searching for gold; but my errand was of a different character: I had come to discover what I suspected to be a pass."

— Explorer James Beckwourth, on finding a pass through the Sierra Nevada

BRITISH TERRITORY (CANADA)

PACIFIC OCEAN

Ft. Vancouver
OREGON
Ft. Walla Walla
Portland
Columbia R.
TERRITORY
Willamette R.
Oregon Trail
Snake R.
South Pass
Ft. Laramie
MINNESOTA TERRITORY
Missouri R.
Mississippi R.
WI
MI
L. Michigan
L. Huron
L. Superior
L. Ontario
L. Erie
NY
PA

ROCKY

UNORGANIZED TERRITORY

IA
Chicago
Mormon Trail
Nauvoo
IL
OH
IN

Donner Pass
California Trail
SIERRA
Mormon Trail
Great Salt Lake
Salt Lake City
Oregon Trail
Platte R.
Ft. Kearney
Independence
St. Louis
Ohio R.
VA
KY

Sutter's Fort (Sacramento)
UTAH TERRITORY
Old Spanish Trail
NEVADA
Sonoma
San Francisco
CA
Colorado R.
M O U N T A I N S
Ft. Dodge
Santa Fe Trail
Arkansas R.
MO
TN
NC
SC

Los Angeles
NEW MEXICO TERRITORY
Santa Fe
Albuquerque
Red R.
Ft. Smith
AR
MS
AL
GA

San Diego
El Camino Real
San Antonio
TX
El Camino Real of Texas
Rio Grande
LA
New Orleans
Gulf of Mexico
FL

El Camino Real of the Interior

MEXICO

KEY

← Trails from the eastern United States
← Trails from Mexico
⬆ Forts
● Towns

0 km 300
0 miles 300
Albers Equal-Area Projection

Pioneers packed everything they could carry—from cast-iron stoves to the family Bible—onto covered wagons. ▶

MAP◆MASTER®
Skills Activity

In the mid-1800s, Americans traveled west along many different trails. Mountain passes allowed settlers to cross the Rockies and Sierra Nevada.

(a) Read a Map What pass did travelers on the Oregon Trail use to get across the Rocky Mountains?

(b) Apply Information Describe the route a traveler might take to get from Independence, Missouri, to Los Angeles, California.

MapMaster ●nline

For: Interactive map
Visit: PHSchool.com
Web Code: myp-4097

Women in the West Women in the West worked alongside men to make a success of their family farms. The fact that their labor was necessary for a family's survival raised the status of western women.

Meanwhile, as you have read, women in the East had begun to campaign for greater political and legal rights. Chief among these was the right to vote. On a national level, women's struggle for the vote would take many years. But the West was quicker to reward the hard work of its women. In 1869, the Wyoming Territory became the first area of the United States to grant women the vote.

Native Americans and Settlers Native Americans in Oregon lived in an uneasy peace with the white settlers. Indians in the southern part of Oregon usually got along with whites. In northern Oregon, however, Native Americans were angered by the presence of strangers on their lands.

The discovery of gold in northern Oregon in the 1850s brought large numbers of white and Chinese miners into the area. War broke out there in 1855. The miners killed several dozen Native American men. Three months later, miners massacred an equal number of Indian women, children, and old men.

The Indians fought back, killing white and Chinese alike. The brief war ended when the U.S. government intervened. The Native Americans were forced to accept peace treaties.

Woman harvesting hay on a western farm

✓**Checkpoint** **Why did women enjoy greater equality in the West than in the East?**

☆ **Looking Back and Ahead** The Oregon and Santa Fe trails created close links between east and west. In the next section, you will see how western lands became part of the United States.

Section 2 | **Check Your Progress**

Progress Monitoring Online
For: Self-test with instant help
Visit: PHSchool.com
Web Code: mya-4092

Comprehension and Critical Thinking

1. (a) Recall Why did Americans go to Oregon in the early 1800s?
(b) Analyze Cause and Effect What factors might have discouraged Americans from traveling to Oregon?

2. (a) Explain Why did conflict arise between Native Americans and settlers in Oregon?
(b) Make Predictions Do you think such conflicts would be likely to continue later in the 1800s? Explain.

↺ **Reading Skill**

3. Ask Inferential Questions Reread the text following the heading "The Oregon Fur Trade." What qualities were needed to be successful as a fur trapper in Oregon? Suggest a possible research question to take this topic further.

Key Terms

Read each sentence below. If the sentence is true, write YES and explain why. If the sentence is not true, write NO and explain why not.
4. Mountain men made their living by farming the Great Plains.

5. A trapper would often trade his furs for supplies at a rendezvous.

Writing

6. For each of these transitions (connecting words), write a sentence that expresses a cause-effect relationship about the topic in parentheses. **Transitions:**
(a) *because* (Astor and the Oregon Trail)
(b) *as a result* (the decline in the fur trade)
(c) *therefore* (hardships on the Oregon Trail)

I Wish to See Texas Free

❝I wish to see Texas free from . . . religious intolerance and other anti-republican restrictions, and independent at once; and as an individual have always been ready to risk my all to obtain it: . . . I now think the time has come for Texas to assert her natural rights; and were I in the convention I would urge an immediate declaration of independence.❞

—Stephen Austin, letter to Sam Houston, 1835

◄ Stephen Austin

Conflict With Mexico

Objectives

- Explain how Texas became independent from Mexico.
- Discuss the issues involved in annexing Texas and Oregon.
- Summarize the main events in the Mexican-American War.
- Explain how the United States achieved Manifest Destiny.

🔄 Reading Skill

Ask Questions to Synthesize Information As you read history, recall what you already know about the topic. Consider as well what you know about related topics or experiences—even from modern times. Pull these many pieces of information together to ask and answer questions about the text. Then, use your questions to build research topics.

Key Terms and People

Stephen Austin
dictatorship
siege
Sam Houston

annex
James K. Polk
cede
John C. Frémont

Why It Matters Mexico became independent in 1821. That same year, American traders were traveling to the Southwest along the Santa Fe Trail. Meanwhile, American settlers arrived in the Mexican province of Texas. Growing tensions between Mexicans and Americans led to fighting.

❷ **Section Focus Question: What were the causes and effects of the Texas War for Independence and the Mexican-American War?**

Texas Wins Independence

In 1820, the Spanish governor of Texas gave Moses Austin a land grant to establish a small colony in Texas. After Moses died, his son, Stephen Austin, led a group of some 300 Americans into Texas.

Soon after, Mexico won independence from Spain. The Mexican government agreed to honor Austin's claim to the land. In return, Austin and his colonists agreed to become Mexican citizens and to worship in the Roman Catholic Church.

Growing Conflict Thousands of Americans flooded into Texas. They soon came into conflict with the Mexican government. The new settlers were Protestant, not Catholic. Also, many of the settlers were slaveholders from the American South who wanted to grow cotton in Texas. However, Mexico had abolished slavery.

For a while, Mexico tolerated these violations of its laws. Then, in 1830, Mexico banned further American settlement. Still, Americans kept arriving in Texas. Tensions increased as Mexico tried to enforce its laws banning slavery and requiring settlers to worship in the Catholic Church. Mexico also began to levy heavy taxes on American imports.

Declaring Independence American settlers wanted more representation in the Mexican legislature. Some Tejanos (teh HAH nos), Texans of Mexican descent, also hoped for a democratic government that gave less power to the central government.

These hopes were dashed in 1833 when General Antonio López de Santa Anna became president of Mexico. Santa Anna wanted a strong central government, with himself at the head. Soon after, Santa Anna overturned Mexico's democratic constitution and started a **dictatorship**, or one-person rule.

Austin urged Texans to revolt against the Mexican government. In 1836, Texans declared independence from Mexico and created the Republic of Texas.

Texans at War Santa Anna responded with force. His troops laid siege to the Alamo, a mission in San Antonio where about 185 Anglo-Americans and Tejanos were gathered. A **siege** is an attack in which one force surrounds a city or fort. The defenders of the Alamo held out for 12 days under heavy cannon fire. At last, Mexican forces overran the Alamo. All of the defenders were killed in battle or executed afterward. Inspired by the bravery of the Alamo defenders, many American volunteers joined the Texan army.

The following April, the commander of the Texan forces, **Sam Houston,** led a small army in a surprise attack against Santa Anna's army at San Jacinto. Texans shouted "Remember the Alamo!" Within 18 minutes, the Texans had captured Santa Anna. They forced him to sign a treaty recognizing Texan independence.

Siege at the Alamo
For 12 days, a small group of Texans held off Mexican troops at the Alamo. This print from the 1800s is not an eyewitness portrayal, but it gives an idea of the odds against the defenders of the Alamo. *Critical Thinking: Detect Points of View* Based on this print (right), why do you think many Americans admired the defenders of the Alamo?

The Alamo today

Ask Questions to Synthesize Information
Why was it important whether a new state was a slave state or a free state? Suggest a possible research topic building on this question.

Vocabulary Builder
decade (DEK ayd) *n.* a period of ten years

Republic of Texas Sam Houston became president of the new Republic of Texas. He hoped that the United States would annex, or add on, Texas. But public opinion in the United States was divided. Southerners supported annexation of Texas as a slave state. Northerners opposed this, but still hoped for western expansion.

Presidents Andrew Jackson and Martin Van Buren refused to support annexation. Both feared that adding a slave state might spark a huge political fight that could split the Union.

✓**Checkpoint** Why did Texans want independence from Mexico?

Annexing Texas and Oregon

A decade after Texas won its independence, the annexation of Texas remained an unsettled question. It became a major issue in the presidential election of 1844.

Election of 1844 President John Tyler favored the annexation of Texas. But Tyler was not nominated for a second term. In 1844, the Whigs nominated Henry Clay instead.

Clay hoped to avoid the issue of annexation. But the Democratic candidate, James K. Polk, called for the annexation of both Texas and Oregon. At the time, Oregon was jointly held by Britain and the United States. Polk demanded that the British withdraw from all territory south of latitude 54°40'N. Polk, the candidate of expansion, won the election.

Annexation Shortly before Polk took office, Tyler asked Congress to annex Texas. Congress voted for admission of Texas as a state in 1845, three days before Tyler left office. A convention of Texan delegates quickly met and voted for annexation.

In keeping with his campaign promise, President Polk negotiated a treaty with Britain to divide Oregon. The United States got the lands south of latitude 49°N. Eventually, this territory became the states of Washington, Oregon, and part of Idaho.

Tensions With Mexico The annexation of Texas increased tensions with Mexico. Mexico had never formally recognized Texan independence. The treaty that Santa Anna had been forced to sign at San Jacinto set the southern boundary of Texas at the Rio Grande. The Mexican government claimed that the southern boundary of Texas was the Nueces River, farther to the north.

The Texas War for Independence

KEY
⟵ Texan forces ⟵ Mexican forces
✶ Texan victories ✶ Mexican victories

UNITED STATES

AR

Disputed Area

Red R.

Brazos R.

LA

Colorado R.

Rio Grande

Sabine R.

MEXICO

REPUBLIC OF TEXAS

The Alamo

Houston

San Antonio

San Jacinto

Santa Anna

Gonzales

Goliad

Urrea

Gulf of California

Nueces R.

Gulf of Mexico

0 km 300
0 miles 300
Albers Equal-Area Projection

40°N
110°W
100°W
30°N

N W E S

MAP★MASTER®

Skills Activity

After a brief but bloody war, the Republic of Texas won its independence from Mexico.

(a) Read a Map Key Who won the battle at Goliad?

(b) Make Predictions Based on this map, why might there be future conflict between Texas and Mexico?

MapMaster ●nline
For: Interactive map
Visit: PHSchool.com
Web Code: myp-4094

In fact, Texas had never controlled the area between the two rivers. But setting the Rio Grande as the border between Texas and Mexico would have given Texas much more land. President Polk put pressure on Mexico to accept this claim. Still, Mexico refused.

✓Checkpoint How did the annexation of Texas increase tensions with Mexico?

The Mexican-American War

Polk knew that the Mexican government needed cash. He offered money to settle the claim for the Rio Grande border. He also offered to purchase California and the rest of New Mexico. Outraged Mexicans refused the offer. They did not want to cede, or give up, more land to the United States.

Polk then changed his tactics. Hoping to provoke a Mexican attack on U.S. troops, he sent General Zachary Taylor south to the disputed land south of the Nueces. The Mexicans saw this as an act of war. After Mexican troops ambushed an American patrol on the disputed land, Polk asked Congress for a declaration of war. He claimed that Mexico had forced this war by shedding "American blood upon American soil."

Opposition to War Overall, the war with Mexico was very popular among Americans. Support for the war was strongest among southerners and westerners, who were willing to take up arms to gain more land.

Many northerners, however, argued that Polk had provoked the war. They scornfully referred to it as "Mr. Polk's war" and claimed that he was trying to extend slavery. Abraham Lincoln, a member of the House of Representatives from Illinois, pointed out that the land under dispute was not "American soil." He held that General Taylor's troops had invaded Mexico, not the other way around.

Rebellion in California Polk ordered troops under the command of Stephen Kearny to invade and capture Santa Fe, New Mexico. From there, Kearny was to lead his troops into California.

Even before Kearny's troops reached California, settlers near San Francisco had begun their own revolt against Mexico. Taking up arms, they raised a grizzly bear flag and declared California an independent republic. A bold young explorer, John C. Frémont, soon took command of the Bear Flag Rebellion. He moved to join forces with U.S. troops under the command of Kearny.

Vocabulary Builder
provoke (prah VOHK) **v.** to cause to anger; to excite; to cause an action

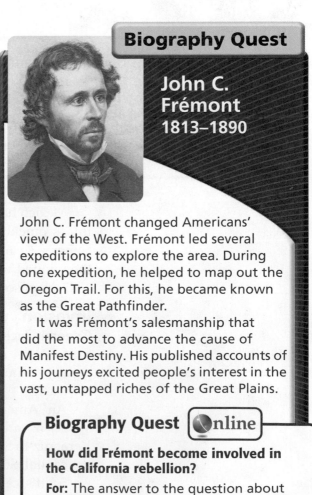

Biography Quest

John C. Frémont
1813–1890

John C. Frémont changed Americans' view of the West. Frémont led several expeditions to explore the area. During one expedition, he helped to map out the Oregon Trail. For this, he became known as the Great Pathfinder.

It was Frémont's salesmanship that did the most to advance the cause of Manifest Destiny. His published accounts of his journeys excited people's interest in the vast, untapped riches of the Great Plains.

Biography Quest ●nline

How did Frémont become involved in the California rebellion?

For: The answer to the question about Frémont

Visit: PHSchool.com

Web Code: myd-4093

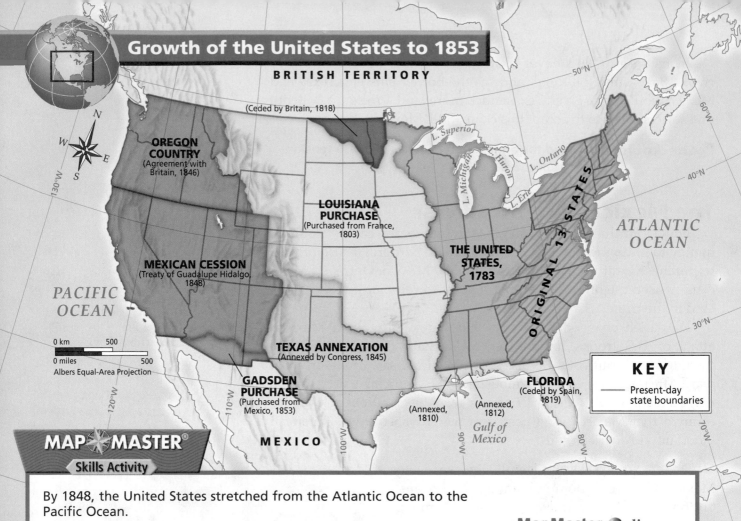

Growth of the United States to 1853

BRITISH TERRITORY

(Ceded by Britain, 1818)

OREGON COUNTRY
(Agreement with Britain, 1846)

LOUISIANA PURCHASE
(Purchased from France, 1803)

THE UNITED STATES, 1783

MEXICAN CESSION
(Treaty of Guadalupe Hidalgo, 1848)

ORIGINAL 13 STATES

ATLANTIC OCEAN

PACIFIC OCEAN

0 km 500
0 miles 500
Albers Equal-Area Projection

TEXAS ANNEXATION
(Annexed by Congress, 1845)

GADSDEN PURCHASE
(Purchased from Mexico, 1853)

FLORIDA
(Ceded by Spain, 1819)

(Annexed, 1810)

(Annexed, 1812)

Gulf of Mexico

MEXICO

L. Superior
L. Michigan
L. Huron
L. Erie
L. Ontario

KEY
Present-day state boundaries

MAP MASTER
Skills Activity

By 1848, the United States stretched from the Atlantic Ocean to the Pacific Ocean.

(a) Read a Map What areas on the map did the United States own in 1853 that it did not own in 1830?

(b) Apply Information Look at a map of the present-day United States. When and how did your state become part of the United States?

MapMaster Online

For: Interactive map
Visit: PHSchool.com
Web Code: myp-4093

Mexico had very little military presence in California. Frémont's forces quickly captured Monterey and San Francisco. Meanwhile, General Kearny's troops captured Santa Fe and San Diego. There they united with naval units to occupy more of California. By early 1847, all of southern California was also under American control.

Invasion of Mexico Moving south from the Rio Grande, General Zachary Taylor captured the Mexican city of Monterrey. Santa Anna attacked Taylor at the Battle of Buena Vista. Though greatly outnumbered, Taylor's forces were better armed. Santa Anna retreated.

An American army under General Winfield Scott captured Veracruz, an important Mexican port. Scott then marched from Veracruz to Mexico City. Scott's army forced the Mexican army into the capital. Still, Santa Anna would not surrender.

Scott's campaign ended at Chapultepec, a stone palace above Mexico City. Like the Texans at the Alamo, the Mexicans fought bravely to defend Chapultepec. Most of them were killed. In Mexico, these young men are still honored for their bravery and patriotism.

After Mexico's defeat at Chapultepec, Santa Anna left Mexico City. The Mexican capital was now in American hands. The United States had won the war. (To learn more about the key battles in the Mexican-American War, see the Geography and History feature.)

✓**Checkpoint** **How did Polk's actions lead to war with Mexico?**

Achieving Manifest Destiny

Polk sent a representative, Nicholas Trist, to help General Scott negotiate a treaty with the Mexican government. Despite many difficulties, Trist negotiated the Treaty of Guadalupe Hidalgo, which was signed in 1848. It formally ended the Mexican-American War.

Under the treaty, Mexico recognized the annexation of Texas and ceded a vast territory to the United States. This territory, known as the Mexican Cession, included present-day California, Nevada, and Utah, as well as parts of Wyoming, Colorado, Arizona, and New Mexico. In return, the United States paid $18 million to Mexico.

In the Gadsden Purchase of 1853, the United States paid Mexico $10 million for a narrow strip of present-day Arizona and New Mexico. Manifest Destiny had been achieved.

✓**Checkpoint** **What was the Mexican Cession?**

☆ **Looking Back and Ahead** By 1853, the United States owned all the territory that would make up the first 48 states. Not until Alaska and Hawaii joined the Union in 1959 would any states outside this area be added.

Section 3 | Check Your Progress

Progress Monitoring ⦿nline
For: Self-test with instant help
Visit: PHSchool.com
Web Code: mya-4093

Comprehension and Critical Thinking

1. (a) Recall Why did the Republic of Texas hope the United States would annex Texas?
(b) Analyze Cause and Effect How would the addition of Texas as a slave state affect the Union? Explain.

2. (a) Recall What did the United States gain as a result of the Mexican-American War?
(b) Draw Conclusions How do you think the Mexican-American War affected the relationship between Mexico and the United States?

🎯 Reading Skill

3. Ask Questions to Synthesize Information Reread the text following the heading "Invasion of Mexico." Why might Santa Anna have been unwilling to surrender? Suggest a possible research topic to explore this question.

Key Terms

Complete each of the following sentences so that the second part clearly shows your understanding of the key term.
4. Many U.S. senators wanted to annex Texas, _____.
5. In Mexico, Santa Anna established a dictatorship, _____.

6. The Mexicans laid siege to the Alamo, _____.

Writing

7. Rewrite the following paragraph to eliminate sentence errors and improve sentence variety. **Paragraph:** Conflict between Mexicans and Anglo-Americans. There was a difference in religion. Mexicans were Catholics. Many Anglo-Americans Protestants. Mexico had outlawed slavery, but many Anglo-Americans owned slaves. This also created problems. Mexico began to tax American imports. Hostilities finally broke out. When Santa Anna attacked the Alamo.

The Mexican-American War

By 1846, the United States and Mexico stood on the brink of war. Mexicans were furious at the American annexation of Texas the year before. Americans felt that Mexico stood in the way of Manifest Destiny. After a border dispute erupted in hostilities, U.S. troops attacked Mexico on two fronts in order to achieve quick victory.

History *Interactive*

Learn More About the Mexican-American War

Visit: PHSchool.com
Web Code: myp-4095

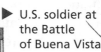

► U.S. soldier at the Battle of Buena Vista

War on Land

American forces invaded Mexico in two directions. John C. Frémont and Stephen Kearny moved west from Fort Leavenworth ❶ to take control of California. They were aided by a revolt of American settlers near San Francisco. Zachary Taylor marched south across the Rio Grande and defeated a large Mexican force at Buena Vista ❷.

► Rebel American settlers declared California a new nation—the Bear Flag Republic.

War at Sea

The U.S. Navy blockaded Mexico's east and west coasts. American sailors helped secure California ❸ while another fleet in the Gulf of Mexico supported the assault at Veracruz ❹. Winfield Scott won a last battle against Mexican soldiers at the Battle of Chapultepec.

The War's Final Days

By the time of General Scott's victory outside Mexico City, U.S. forces had surrounded the Mexican capital. The northern territories of California and New Mexico were under Frémont's and Kearny's control, and Taylor had moved south to press for attack. With the loss of Mexico City, the Mexican government moved to make peace.

WAR AT SEA

KEY
⬅ UNITED STATES FORCES   ⬅ MEXICAN FORCES
✩ UNITED STATES VICTORY

◀ The shako cap—topped with a tall plume of feathers—was part of the American uniform during the war.

▲ U.S. Navy ships guard the American landing at Veracruz.

Analyze GEOGRAPHY AND HISTORY

Select a key battle from the Mexican-American War, and write a journal entry about it from a U.S. soldier's point of view.

Chinese Immigrants

❝Every immigrant group has its own newspaper except for the Chinese. As a result, although the Chinese merchants are many in number, they have no influence. Because they are uninformed, they have no way to exercise their freedom of choice. . . . Since I feel strongly about this situation, I have founded a newspaper called *Golden Hills News* to record in Chinese the commercial news and government affairs happening every day.❞

—William D. M. Howard, announcing a Chinese-language newspaper in San Francisco, 1854

◀ Western miners, including a Chinese immigrant (right)

A Rush to the West

Objectives

- Explain why the Mormons settled in Utah and the issues that divided Mormons and the federal government.

- Discuss the effects of the 1849 California gold rush.

- Describe how California's population had changed by 1850.

🔁 Reading Skill

Ask Questions That Go Beyond the Text Research questions should build on the information you learn in your textbook. Use the many strategies you practiced in Sections 1–3 to build questions that link the text topic to larger issues. For example, you might look at how history fits with modern situations or why the people of history made the decisions they made.

Key Terms and People

Joseph Smith
polygamy
Brigham Young

forty-niner
water rights
vigilante

Why It Matters As a result of the war with Mexico, the United States gained the lands known as the Mexican Cession. Large numbers of Americans began to settle in this vast region.

❓ Section Focus Question: How did Mormon settlement and the gold rush lead to changes in the West?

Mormons Settle Utah

Even before the end of the war, a group of Americans had begun moving into the part of the Mexican Cession that is today Utah. These were the Mormons, members of the Church of Jesus Christ of Latter-day Saints. The church was founded in 1830 by Joseph Smith, a New York farmer. Smith said that heavenly visions had revealed to him the text of a holy book called the *Book of Mormon*.

Seeking Refuge The Mormon Church grew quickly, but some of its teachings often placed its followers in conflict with their neighbors. For example, Mormons at first believed that property should be held in common. Smith also favored **polygamy**, the practice of having more than one wife at a time.

Hostile communities forced the Mormons to move from New York to Ohio and then to Missouri. By 1844, the Mormons had settled in Nauvoo, Illinois. There, Joseph Smith was murdered by an angry mob.

Brigham Young, the new Mormon leader, realized that Nauvoo was no longer safe. He had heard about a great valley in the Utah desert, which at the time was still owned by Mexico. In 1847, he led a party of Mormons on a long, hazardous journey to the valley of the Great Salt Lake. Over the next few years, some 15,000 Mormon men, women, and children made the trek to Utah.

Although Utah was a safe refuge, the land was not hospitable. Farming was difficult in the dry desert. Then, in the summer of 1849, enormous swarms of crickets nearly destroyed the Mormons' first harvest. But a flock of seagulls flew in from the Pacific and devoured the crickets. The Mormons then set out to make the desert bloom. Under strict church supervision, they enclosed and distributed farmland and set up an <u>efficient</u> system of irrigation.

Conflict With the Government In 1848, as a result of the Mexican Cession, Utah became part of the United States. Congress then created the Utah Territory. Mormon leaders immediately came into conflict with officials appointed to govern the territory.

Three issues divided the Mormons and the federal government. First, the Mormon Church controlled the election process in the Utah Territory. Non-Mormons had no say. Second, the church supported businesses that were owned by Mormons. "Outsiders" had difficulty doing business. The third issue was polygamy, which was illegal in the rest of the country.

These issues were not resolved for more than 40 years. In time, Congress passed a law that took control of elections away from the Mormon Church. Church leaders agreed to ban polygamy and to stop favoring Mormon-owned businesses. Finally, in 1896, Utah became a state.

☑**Checkpoint** **Why did the Mormons leave Illinois?**

Mormons Come to Utah

Brigham Young (below) led the first wave of Mormons to migrate to Utah. In later years, settlers continued to arrive. Some, like those shown in the painting, were so poor they had to haul their belongings along the Mormon Trail by hand. **Critical Thinking: Identify Benefits** *Identify two benefits these Mormons might look forward to from settling in Utah.*

The California Gold Rush

When California was ceded to the United States in 1848, about 10,000 Californios, or Mexican Californians, were living in the territory. A handful of wealthy families owned most of the land. They lived an elegant, aristocratic life. Their ranches were worked by poorer Californios or by Native Americans.

After the Mexican Cession, easterners began to migrate to California. The wealthy Californios looked down on the newcomers from the East, and the newcomers felt contempt for the Californios. The two groups rarely mixed or intermarried.

Vocabulary Builder
prospect (PRAHS pehkt) **n.** promise; something looked forward to

Gold Is Discovered An event in January 1848 would bring a flood of other settlers to California. James Marshall was building a sawmill on John Sutter's land near Sacramento. One morning, he found a small gold nugget in a ditch. Sutter tried to keep his discovery a secret. But the news spread like wildfire throughout the country and abroad. By 1849, the California gold rush had begun.

The prospect of finding gold attracted about 80,000 fortune seekers. The nickname "forty-niners" was given to these people who came to California in search of gold. In just two years, the population of California zoomed from 14,000 to 100,000.

Sutter's Mill was just the beginning. Prospectors, or gold seekers, searched throughout the Sacramento Valley for gold. They dug into the land using picks and shovels. They also looked in streams. This process, called placer mining, did not take much labor, money, or skill. Miners washed dirt from a stream in a pan, leaving grains of gold in the bottom. Finding gold was called "hitting pay dirt."

Gold above ground was quickly found. But there was more gold in underground deposits, or lodes. Gold in lodes was difficult and expensive to mine. It required heavy and expensive machinery. As a result, large companies took over the mining of underground lodes.

Water Rights In the gold fields, disputes over water rights were common. Water rights are the legal rights to use the water in a river, stream, or other body. California has an abundance of land, but much of it is desert. Settlers needed water for irrigation and mining.

California had kept older Mexican laws regarding water rights. Landowners had the right to use the water that flowed through their land. At the same time, it was illegal to cut off water to one's neighbors. In most gold rush territories, though, the law was ignored. The first people to reach a stream used as much water as they wanted—sometimes even the whole stream! Disputes over water rights often erupted into violence.

Life in Mining Towns Mining towns were not very permanent places. Most sprang up overnight and emptied just as quickly when miners heard news of a gold strike in another place.

Mining towns attracted both miners and people hoping to make money from miners. Miners were often willing to pay high prices for food and supplies. They also needed entertainment. A typical mining town was made up of a row of businesses with a saloon at its center.

California was not yet a state, so federal law did not apply within the mining towns. To impose some order, miners banded together and created their own rules. Punishment for crimes was often quick and brutal. **Vigilantes,** or self-appointed law enforcers, punished people for crimes, though they had no legal right to do so.

Role of Women Gold rushes were not like other migrations in American history. Most migrations included men and women, young and old. Most forty-niners, however, were young men. By 1850, the ratio of men to women in California was twelve to one!

Still, some women did come to California in search of fortune, work, or adventure. Unlike other areas of the country, California offered women profitable work. Some women mined, but many more stayed in town. They worked in or ran boardinghouses, hotels, restaurants, laundries, and stores.

Drifting and Settling Few forty-niners struck it rich. After the gold rush ended, many people continued to search for gold throughout the West. There were gold or silver strikes in British Columbia, Idaho, Montana, Colorado, Arizona, and Nevada. Other miners gave up the drifting life and settled in the West for good.

✓**Checkpoint** **Why were water rights an important issue?**

Links Across Time

Water Rights in the West

1849 During the gold rush, California law generally gave water rights to the first person to make use of a body of water.

1905 Los Angeles, still a small city, won rights to the Owens River, 200 miles away. Engineers later built aqueducts and dams to carry the water to the city. This water helped Los Angeles grow rapidly. But ranchers and farmers in the Owens Valley protested the loss of their water rights.

Link to Today **Online**

Connection to Today Water rights remain an issue in many areas of the nation today. Farms and communities still compete to win access to clean, available water.

For: Water rights in the news
Visit: PHSchool.com
Web Code: myc-4094

1913 Workers opened the gates of the newly completed Los Angeles aqueduct.

San Francisco During the Gold Rush

This painting shows San Francisco in the 1850s. "Where there was a vacant piece of ground one day," wrote one witness, "the next saw it covered with half a dozen tents or shanties." **Critical Thinking: Distinguish Relevant Information** *What information in this picture supports the conclusion that San Francisco had a diverse population?*

California's Changing Population

San Francisco had only 200 inhabitants in 1848. During the gold rush, immigrants who sailed to California passed through San Francisco's harbor. Its merchants, including a German Jew named Levi Strauss, provided miners with goods and services. Many newcomers remained in the city. Others returned to settle there after working in the mines. By 1870, San Francisco had a population of more than 100,000 people.

An Unusual Mix of People The gold rush brought enormous ethnic diversity to California. People came from Europe, Asia, Australia, and South America. By 1860, the population of California was almost 40 percent foreign-born.

European immigrants often enjoyed more freedom in California than in Europe. They also faced less prejudice than in the East. In some ways, mining societies were more democratic, as men in the gold fields had to rely on one another. One immigrant wrote home:

> **"**We live a free life, and the best thing . . . is that no human being here sets himself up as your lord and master. It is true that we do not have many of the luxuries of life, but I do not miss them.**"**
>
> —quoted in *Land of Their Choice* (Blegen)

Chinese Immigrants China's economy was in trouble in the 1840s. After news reached China of a "mountain of gold," about 45,000 Chinese men went to California. Most hoped to return home to China with enough money to take care of their families.

Chinese laborers faced prejudice. They generally were not given higher-paying jobs in the mines. Instead, they were hired to do menial labor. Some cooked or did laundry. Despite many difficulties, the Chinese worked hard. They helped build railroads and worked on farms. Their labor also helped cities like San Francisco to prosper.

African Americans Several thousand free African Americans lived in California by 1850. They had their own churches and newspapers. Many ran their own businesses. However, they did not have equal rights. They could not vote or serve on juries.

Slavery did not take root in California. Some southerners did bring their slaves with them during the gold rush. However, the other miners objected. They believed that anyone who profited from mining should participate in the hard labor of finding gold.

Native Americans For Native Americans, the gold rush brought even more tragedy. Miners swarmed onto Indian lands to search for gold. Vigilante gangs killed Indians and stole their land. About 100,000 Indians, nearly two thirds of the Native American population of California, died during the gold rush.

Impact on Californios By 1850, only 15 percent of Californians were Mexican. The old ruling families did not have a strong say in the new territorial government. When a constitutional convention was held, only 8 of the 48 delegates were Californios.

Californio politicians could not stop the passage of laws that discriminated against their people. The legislature levied a high tax on ranches and required rancheros to prove that they owned their land. This was often difficult, because most had received their land grants from Spain or Mexico. By the time many Californios could prove ownership, they had had to sell their land to pay legal bills.

☑**Checkpoint** **What effects did the gold rush have on Californios?**

☆ **Looking Back and Ahead** California had enough people by 1850 to apply for admission to the Union as a free state. As you will read in the next chapter, California's request for statehood would cause a national crisis.

Ask Questions That Go Beyond the Text
Ask a question that explores beyond the text and requires research to answer. You might focus on the ways that the lives of Mexicans in California changed after the gold rush.

Section 4 | **Check Your Progress**

Progress Monitoring ⏺nline
For: Self-test with instant help
Visit: PHSchool.com
Web Code: mya-4094

Comprehension and Critical Thinking

1. **(a) Recall** Why did the Mormons decide to move to Utah?
   (b) Identify Alternatives What other options might the Mormons have considered?

2. **(a) List** Which groups migrated to California after 1848?
   (b) Make Inferences Which groups benefited most from the discovery of gold? Which groups suffered most? Explain.

Reading Skill

3. **Ask Questions That Go Beyond the Text** Recall what you just read about California during the gold rush. Ask a question that goes beyond the text and requires research to answer.

Key Terms

4. Write two definitions of the term water rights. First, write a formal definition for your teacher. Second, write a definition in everyday English for a classmate.

Writing

5. Write a short paragraph explaining what happened as a result of the California gold rush in 1849. Then, exchange paragraphs with another student. Check your partner's work for errors. Work together to take the best elements from each paragraph and to create a new version.

21st Century Learning

Historical evidence comes from many sources. Evaluating the validity of written sources is important in putting together a picture of the past.

The following journal entries, written by Elizabeth Wood, describe portions of her two-and-a-half-month journey from Fort Laramie, Wyoming, to eastern Oregon in 1851.

Primary Source

"July 25. Since last date we camped at the ford where emigrants cross from the south to the north side of the Platte. . . . We stopped near the Red Buttes, where the hills are of a red color, nearly square and have the appearance of houses with flat roofs. . . . We also passed Independence Rock and the Devil's Gate, which is high enough to make one's head swim, and the posts reach an altitude of some 4 or 500 feet."

"Monday, September 15th. . . . Mount St. Elias is in the distance, and is covered with snow, so you can imagine somewhat the beauty and grandeur of the scene. We are now among the tribe of Wallawalla Indians."

—Journal of a Trip to Oregon, Elizabeth Wood

Learn the Skill

Use these steps to evaluate written sources.

❶ **Identify the source.** Knowing who the writer is helps you to evaluate that person's account of events.

❷ **Note the context.** When was the account written? In what form did it appear? What was the purpose of the account?

❸ **Analyze the point of view.** What is the writer trying to say? How does the writer feel about the subject?

❹ **Evaluate the validity of the material.** How true is this account? Why do you think so?

Practice the Skill

Answer the following questions to evaluate the source on this page.

❶ **Identify the source.** Who wrote these journal entries?

❷ **Note the context.** (a) When were these entries written? (b) What was their purpose?

❸ **Analyze the point of view.** (a) How does the writer feel about the journey? (b) What words or phrases express the writer's feelings?

❹ **Evaluate the validity of the material.** Do you think this journal entry accurately describes the journey west? Why or why not?

Apply the Skill

See the Review and Assessment at the end of this chapter.

Quick Study Guide

How did westward expansion change the geography of the nation and demonstrate the determination of its people?

Section 1
The West

- By the 1820s, land-hungry Americans often had to look west of the Mississippi River for territory to settle.
- Some Americans moved to the Mexican-controlled lands of the Southwest.
- Manifest Destiny was the idea that the United States had the right to "spread and possess the whole of the continent."

Section 2
Trails to the West

- Traders and trappers helped open the West for settlement.
- Free land and the mild climate attracted settlers from all parts of the United States to Oregon.

Section 3
Conflict With Mexico

- American settlers in Texas rebelled against Mexico and created the independent Republic of Texas.
- American forces defeated Mexican troops in what became known as the Mexican-American War.
- The United States gained vast new territories as a result of the Treaty of Guadalupe-Hidalgo.

Section 4
A Rush to the West

- The Mormons moved west to Utah for religious freedom.
- Gold fever brought thousands of immigrants to California.

? Exploring the Essential Question

Use the online study guide to explore the essential question.

Section 1
What cultures and ideas influenced the development of the West?

Section 2
Why did people go west and what challenges did they face?

Chapter 13 Essential Question
How did westward expansion change the geography of the nation and demonstrate the determination of its people?

Section 4
How did Mormon settlement and the gold rush lead to changes in the West?

Section 3
What were the causes and effects of the Texas War for Independence and the Mexican-American War?

Key Terms

Answer the following questions in complete sentences that show your understanding of the key terms.

1. Why did settlers in California argue over water rights?

2. What did rancheros own?

3. How did wealthy families benefit from land grants?

4. To what did General Santa Anna lay siege in San Antonio during the war for Texas independence?

Comprehension and Critical Thinking

5. **(a) Identify** Who were the peninsulares, the creoles, and the mestizos?
   (b) Draw Inferences Which of these groups were most likely to support Mexican independence from Spain? Why?

6. **(a) Recall** What was Manifest Destiny?
   (b) Identify Economic Benefits What economic benefits could the United States get from following the ideals of Manifest Destiny?

7. **(a) Describe** Describe the life of a mountain man like the one pictured at right.
   (b) Draw Inferences How did these men contribute to the goal of Manifest Destiny?

8. **(a) Explain** What did President James Polk do to bring about Manifest Destiny?
   (b) Draw Conclusions How did Great Britain threaten Manifest Destiny?

Mountain man

9. **(a) Recall** Why did the Mormons immigrate to Utah?
   (b) Compare What other groups in earlier American history came to North America for similar reasons?

10. **(a) Identify** Who were the forty-niners?
    (b) Analyze Cause and Effect How did the forty-niners contribute to California becoming a state?

 History Reading Skill

11. **Frame Research Questions** Frame a research question about any aspect of this chapter. Start by reviewing headings and choosing one that interests you. Remember to frame questions that go beyond the text and require research to answer.

Writing

12. **Write two paragraphs discussing the results of the Mexican-American War.** Then, exchange papers with another student.
    As you look at your partner's paragraphs, you should:
    - correct every error you can find;
    - look for places to add transitions to make the sentences flow better and to connect the two paragraphs;
    - find opportunities to mix short and long sentences.

13. **Write a Narrative:**
    You are an easterner in the 1840s trying to decide whether to go to Oregon, Utah, or California. Write a diary entry in which you weigh the possible costs and benefits of such a trip and reach a final decision.

Skills for Life

Evaluate Written Sources
Use the diary entry below to answer the questions.

> "Tuesday May 20th. Travelled 20 miles and camped . . . saw several antelope, and an animal called prairie dogs, which resemble a puppy. There are acres of them . . . they plough the ground up and form little knolls all over the ground. . . ."
>
> —Journal of Travels to Oregon, Amelia Hadley, 1851

14. Who wrote this journal entry?

15. When was it written?

16. How does the writer feel about the journey?

17. Do you think this journal entry accurately describes prairie wildlife? Why or why not?

Test Yourself

1. **Which of the following most directly led to achieving Manifest Destiny?**

   A Women vote in the West.

   B Mormons move to Nauvoo, Illinois.

   C Santa Anna establishes dictatorship in Mexico.

   D President Polk negotiates a treaty with Great Britain to divide Oregon.

Refer to the quotation below to answer Question 2.

> "I am determined to sustain myself as long as possible and die like a soldier, who never forgets what is due to his honor and that of his country. Victory or Death!"

2. **The person who made this statement was mostly likely**

   A at the Alamo.

   B at a rendezvous.

   C at John Sutter's sawmill.

   D on the Oregon Trail.

Refer to the map below to answer Question 3.

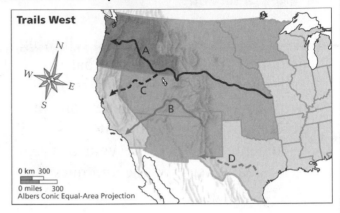

Trails West

0 km 300
0 miles 300
Albers Conic Equal-Area Projection

3. **Which of the trails marked on the map led the forty-niners to their final destination?**

   A trail A

   B trail B

   C trail C

   D trail D

Document-Based Questions

Task: Look at Documents 1 and 2, and answer their accompanying questions. Then, use the documents and your knowledge of history to complete this writing assignment:

List the reasons for and against the Mexican-American War. Then, write a short essay analyzing the arguments of each side. Draw a conclusion about the validity of each argument.

Document 1: In 1846, President Polk asked Congress to declare war against Mexico. *What does Polk accuse Mexico of doing?*

> "The grievous wrongs perpetrated by Mexico upon our citizens throughout a long period of years remain unredressed. . . . We have tried every effort of reconciliation. . . . But now . . . Mexico has passed the boundary of the United States, has invaded our territory and shed American blood upon the American soil. . . .
>
> . . . I involve the prompt action of Congress to recognize the existence of the war, and to place at the disposition of the Executive the means of prosecuting the war with vigor, and thus hastening the restoration of peace."

Document 2: Abraham Lincoln, then a member of Congress, spoke out against the Mexican-American War. *How does Lincoln challenge Polk's reasons for war with Mexico?*

> "I carefully examined the President's messages. . . . The result of this examination was to make the impression that . . . he falls far short of proving his justification [for the war]. . . . The President . . . declares that the soil was ours on which hostilities were commenced by Mexico. . . .
>
> Let [the President] remember he sits where Washington sat, and so remembering, let him answer as Washington would answer. . . . And if, so answering, he can show that the soil was ours, where the first blood of the war was shed, . . . then I am with him. . . . But if he can not do this . . . then I shall be fully convinced . . . that he is deeply conscious of being in the wrong."

ESSENTIAL QUESTION

What forces unite and divide a nation?

DIRECTIONS: Analyze the following documents regarding forces that united and divided the United States in the early 1800s. Answer the questions that accompany each document or set of documents. You will use your answers to build an answer to the unit question.

HISTORIAN'S CHECKLIST

WHO produced the document?

WHERE was it made?

WHEN was it produced?

WHY was it made and for what audience?

WHAT is its viewpoint?

HOW does it connect to what I've learned?

WHY is the document important?

document 1 Industry in the North

What were the effects of industrialization in the North during the early 1800s?

document 2 Cotton in the South

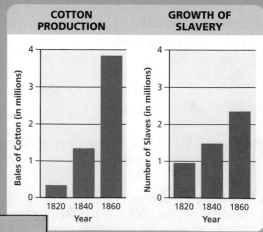

COTTON PRODUCTION — Bales of Cotton (in millions), Year 1820, 1840, 1860

GROWTH OF SLAVERY — Number of Slaves (in millions), Year 1820, 1840, 1860

▲ Cotton Gin invented 1793

How did the South's economy differ from that of the North? Why?

3 Canals, Roads, and Railroads, 1840–1850

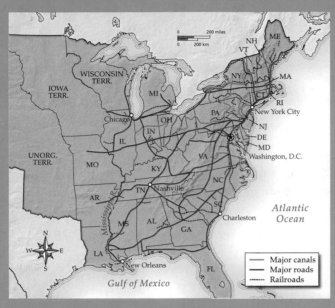

How did the transportation network at left unite or divide the different sections of the United States?

Major canals
Major roads
Railroads

4 Jacksonian Democracy

" It is to be regretted that the rich and powerful too often bend the acts of government to their selfish purposes. . . . There are no necessary evils in government. Its evils exist only in its abuses. If it would confine itself to equal protection, and, as Heaven does its rains, shower its favors alike on the high and the low, the rich and the poor, it would be an unqualified blessing. "

—*President Andrew Jackson, 1832*

THE GROWING ELECTORATE, 1824–1840	
Presidential Election	Total Popular Vote
1824	350,671
1828	1,155,350
1832	1,318,406
1836	1,500,802
1840	2,404,118

Do you think Jacksonian Democracy was a unifying or divisive force in the country? Explain.

 Go On

5 Abolitionism

"What, to the American slave, is your Fourth of July? I answer: a day that reveals to him, more than all other days in the year, the gross injustice and cruelty to which he is the constant victim. To him, your celebration is a sham; your boasted liberty, an unholy license; your national greatness, swelling vanity; your sounds of rejoicing are empty and heartless.... There is not a nation on the earth guilty of practices more shocking and bloody than are the people of the United States at this very hour...."

—*Frederick Douglass, July 4, 1852*

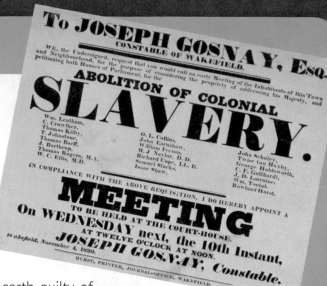

To JOSEPH GOSNAY, Esq.
CONSTABLE OF WAKEFIELD.

ABOLITION OF COLONIAL
SLAVERY.

MEETING
TO BE HELD AT THE COURT-HOUSE,
On WEDNESDAY next, the 10th Instant,
AT TWELVE O'CLOCK AT NOON,
JOSEPH GOSNAY, Constable.

Who do you think agreed with Douglass? Who do you think disagreed with him? Why?

6 Women's Rights

"We hold these truths to be self-evident: that all men and women are created equal; that they are endowed by their Creator with certain inalienable rights; that among these are life, liberty, and the pursuit of happiness....

The history of mankind is a history of repeated injuries and usurpations on the part of man toward woman, having in direct object the establishment of an absolute tyranny over her. To prove this, let facts be submitted to a candid world.

He has never permitted her to exercise her inalienable right to the elective franchise.

He has compelled her to submit to law in the formation of which she had no voice....

He has taken from her all right in property, even to the wage she earns...."

—*Elizabeth Cady Stanton,
Seneca Falls Convention, 1848*

How do you think Stanton and other women's rights leaders felt about Jacksonian Democracy?

7 The Mexican-American War

document

"What is the territory, Mr. President, which you propose to wrest from Mexico? . . . We will not, cannot consent that you shall carry slavery where it does not already exist. . . . Let us abandon all idea of acquiring further territory and by consequence cease at once to prosecute this war. Let us call home our armies. . . ."

—*Senator Thomas Corwin,*
February 11, 1847

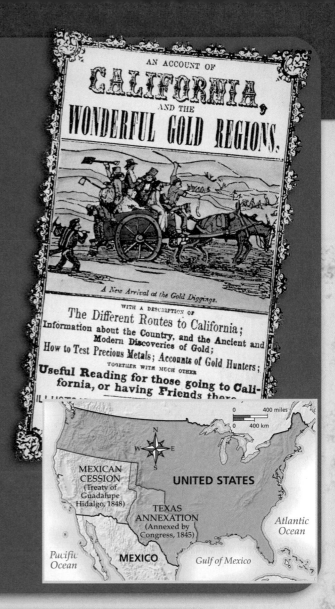

AN ACCOUNT OF

CALIFORNIA,
AND THE

WONDERFUL GOLD REGIONS.

A New Arrival at the Gold Diggings.

WITH A DESCRIPTION OF

The Different Routes to California;
Information about the Country, and the Ancient and Modern Discoveries of Gold;
How to Test Precious Metals; Accounts of Gold Hunters;

TOGETHER WITH MUCH OTHER

Useful Reading for those going to California, or having Friends there.

Why did some Americans oppose the Mexican-American War?
How did the war benefit the United States?

ACTIVITY

Work in pairs or small groups to create a poster that answers the unit question:

? What forces unite and divide a nation?

As a preliminary activity, half of the class should identify and describe forces that united the nation from 1800 to 1860. The other half should identify and describe forces that were dividing the nation during this same period. Then hold a class discussion about these unifying and divisive forces. After the discussion, work in pairs or small groups to create a poster that presents your answer to the unit question.

Unit 5

ESSENTIAL QUESTION

How was the Civil War a political, economic, and social turning point?

History Interactive
Explore Historian's Apprentice Online
Visit: PHSchool.com
Web Code: mvp-5000

Underground Railroad By the middle of the 1830s, opposition to slavery was rising among reformers. Abolitionists aided enslaved people who sought to escape via the Underground Railroad to the North or to Canada.

1830s

Lincoln's Gettysburg Address Lincoln's firm leadership inspired the Union side. In the Gettysburg Address, he vowed that "these dead shall not have died in vain . . . and that government of the people, by the people, for the people, shall not perish from the earth."

1863

Civil War and Reunion

Decision at Gettysburg All attempts at compromise having failed, the United States endured a bloody four-year civil war. After the Battle of Gettysburg, the war turned in favor of the Union army.

1863

A New Voice in Government Before the Civil War, African Americans had no voice in southern government. During Reconstruction, they became a powerful voting force in southern elections. African Americans were elected to public office as sheriffs, mayors, state legislators, and members of Congress.

1868

The Nation Divided

1846–1861

"I then whispered to my wife, 'Come, my dear, let us make a desperate leap for liberty!'"

—*William Craft,*
Running a Thousand Miles for Freedom, *1860*

This painting, *A Ride for Liberty—The Fugitive Slaves*, depicts a black family fleeing toward freedom.

CHAPTER 14

What You Will Learn

Section 1
GROWING TENSIONS OVER SLAVERY

With the addition of new western land, debate over the spread of slavery increased.

Section 2
COMPROMISES FAIL

After all efforts at compromise failed, violent fighting broke out in the Kansas Territory.

Section 3
THE CRISIS DEEPENS

As tensions increased, a new antislavery political party emerged.

Section 4
THE COMING OF THE CIVIL WAR

Abraham Lincoln's election led seven southern states to leave the Union.

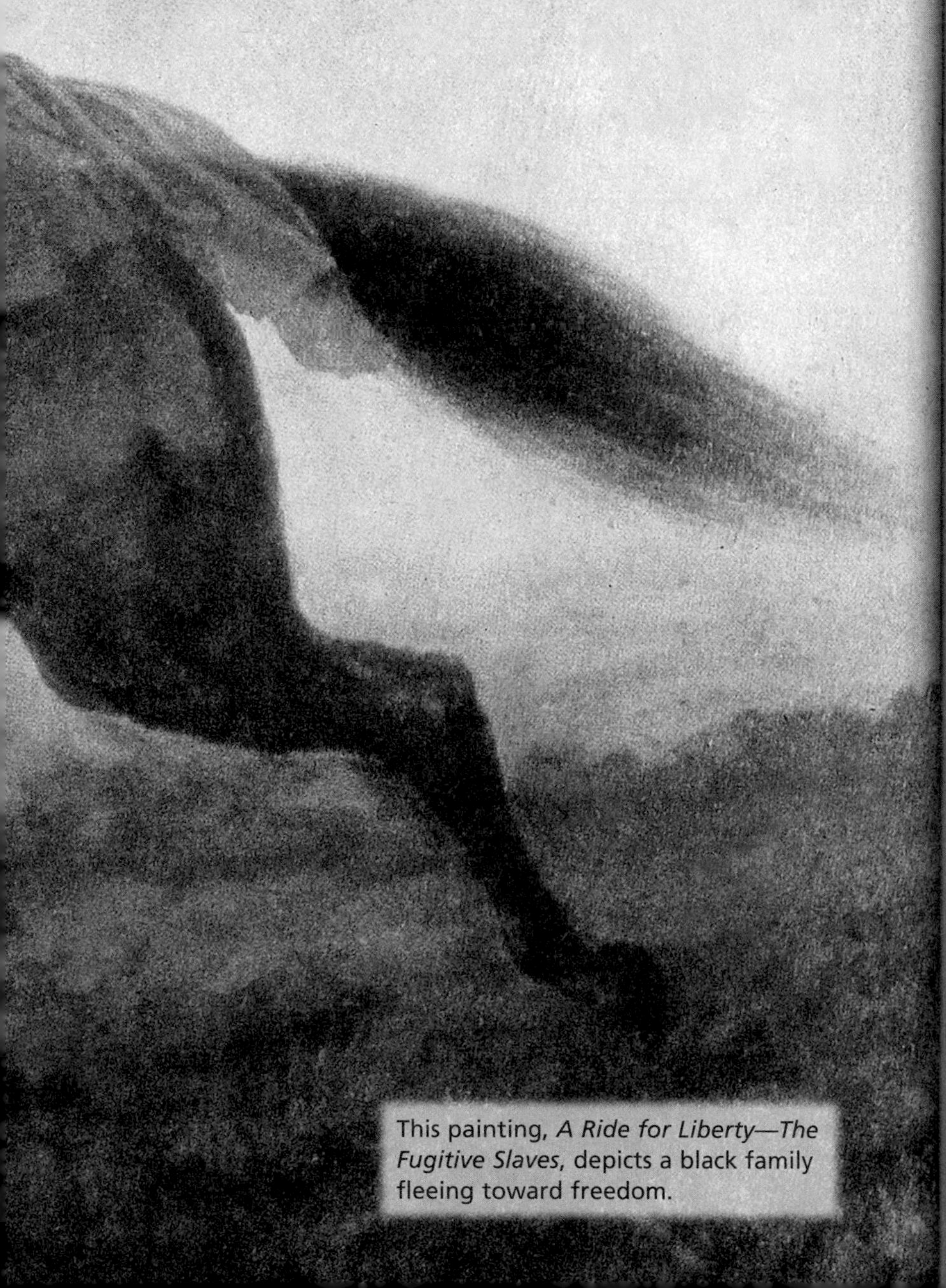

Reading Skill

Analyze Cause and Effect In this chapter, you will learn to identify causes and their effects to help connect and understand historical events and issues.

How did the nation try but fail to deal

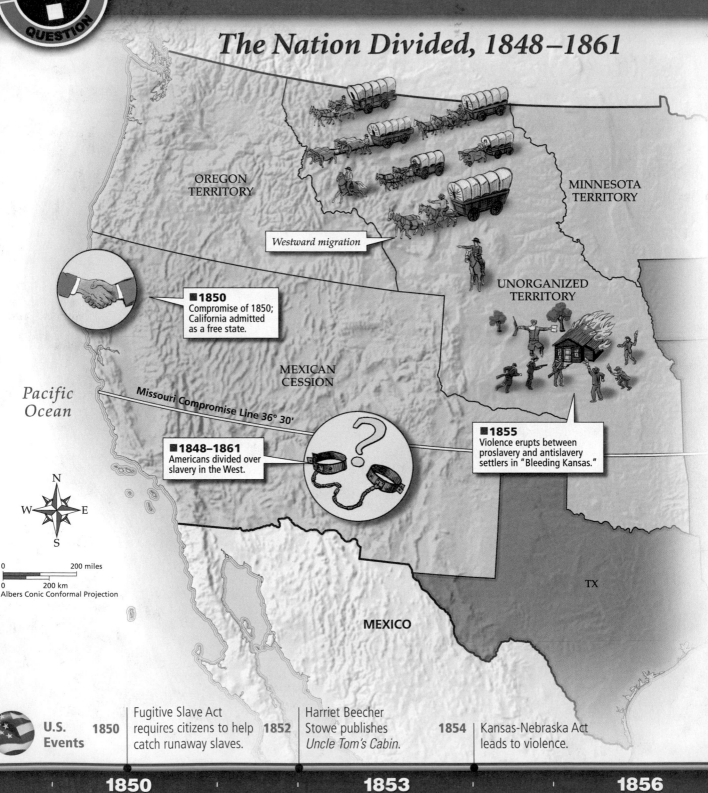

The Nation Divided, 1848–1861

OREGON TERRITORY

MINNESOTA TERRITORY

Westward migration

UNORGANIZED TERRITORY

■ **1850**
Compromise of 1850; California admitted as a free state.

Pacific Ocean

Missouri Compromise Line 36° 30'

MEXICAN CESSION

■ **1848–1861**
Americans divided over slavery in the West.

■ **1855**
Violence erupts between proslavery and antislavery settlers in "Bleeding Kansas."

N W E S

0   200 miles
0   200 km
Albers Conic Conformal Projection

TX

MEXICO

U.S. Events 1850	Fugitive Slave Act requires citizens to help catch runaway slaves.	1852	Harriet Beecher Stowe publishes *Uncle Tom's Cabin.*	1854 Kansas-Nebraska Act leads to violence.

1850   **1853**   **1856**

World Events

1853 Commodore Matthew Perry arrives in Japan to open trade.

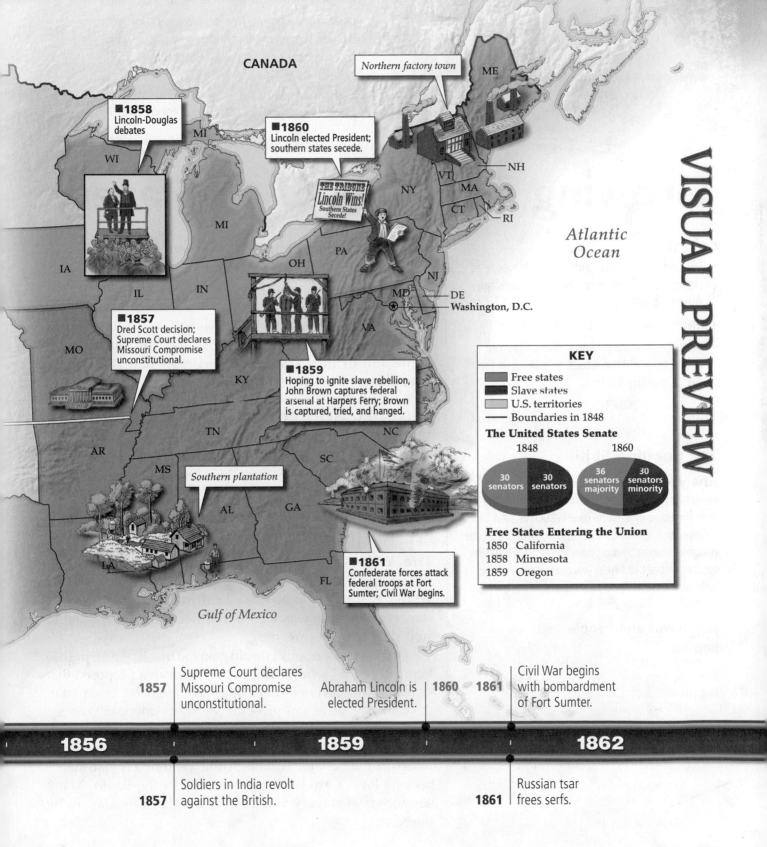

VISUAL PREVIEW

CANADA

Northern factory town

ME

■**1858**
Lincoln-Douglas
debates

MI

■**1860**
Lincoln elected President;
southern states secede.

WI

NH

VT

MA

NY

CT

RI

THE TRIBUNE
Lincoln Wins!
Southern States
Secede!

MI

IA

PA

*Atlantic
Ocean*

IL

IN

OH

NJ

MD — DE
Washington, D.C.

■**1857**
Dred Scott decision;
Supreme Court declares
Missouri Compromise
unconstitutional.

MO

VA

KY

■**1859**
Hoping to ignite slave rebellion,
John Brown captures federal
arsenal at Harpers Ferry; Brown
is captured, tried, and hanged.

TN

NC

KEY

	Free states
	Slave states
	U.S. territories
———	Boundaries in 1848

The United States Senate

1848

1860

30
senators

30
senators

36
senators
majority

30
senators
minority

AR

SC

MS

Southern plantation

AL

GA

Free States Entering the Union
1850 California
1858 Minnesota
1859 Oregon

LA

■**1861**
Confederate forces attack
federal troops at Fort
Sumter; Civil War begins.

FL

Gulf of Mexico

1857	Supreme Court declares Missouri Compromise unconstitutional.	1860	1861	Civil War begins with bombardment of Fort Sumter.
	Abraham Lincoln is elected President.			

1856

1859

1862

1857	Soldiers in India revolt against the British.	1861	Russian tsar frees serfs.

Growing Tensions Over Slavery

Objectives

- Explain why conflict arose over the issue of slavery in the territories after the Mexican-American War.
- Identify the goal of the Free-Soil Party.
- Describe the compromise Henry Clay proposed to settle the issues that divided the North and the South.

⟳ Reading Skill

Analyze Causes Causes are the reasons that events happen. As the United States struggled over the issue of slavery, events such as new laws or important speeches had dramatic effects on the struggle. Understanding how these events made such an impact will help you make sense of this turbulent time in American history.

Key Terms and People

popular
  sovereignty
secede
fugitive

Henry Clay
John C. Calhoun
Daniel Webster

Why It Matters The Missouri Compromise of 1820 seemed to have quieted the differences between North and South. But the American victory in the Mexican-American War added new territory to the United States. As a result, the states renewed their struggle over slavery and states' rights.

❓ Section Focus Question: How did the question of admission of new states to the Union fuel the debate over slavery and states' rights?

Slavery and the Mexican-American War

Between 1820 and 1848, four new slaveholding states and four new free states were admitted to the Union. This maintained the balance between free and slaveholding states, with 15 of each. However, territory gained by the Mexican-American War threatened to destroy the balance.

The Wilmot Proviso The Missouri Compromise did not apply to the huge territory gained from Mexico in 1848. Would this territory be organized as states that allowed slavery? The issue was vital to northerners who wanted to stop slavery from spreading.

Fearing that the South would gain too much power, in 1846 Representative David Wilmot of Pennsylvania proposed that Congress ban slavery in all territory that might become part of the United States as a result of the Mexican-American War.

This proposal was called the Wilmot Proviso. The provision was passed in the House of Representatives, but it failed in the Senate. Although the Wilmot Proviso never became law, it aroused great concern in the South. Many supporters of slavery viewed it as an attack on slavery by the North.

An Antislavery Party The <u>controversy</u> over the Wilmot Proviso also led to the rise of a new political party. Neither the Democrats nor the Whigs took a firm stand on slavery. Each hoped to win support in both North and South in the election of 1848.

The Democratic candidate for President in 1848, Senator Lewis Cass of Michigan, proposed a solution that he hoped would appeal to everyone. Cass suggested letting the people in each new territory or state decide for themselves whether to allow slavery. This process, called **popular sovereignty,** meant that people in the territory or state would vote directly on issues, rather than having their elected representatives decide.

Many Whigs and Democrats wanted to take a stronger stand against the spread of slavery. In August 1848, antislavery Whigs and Democrats joined forces to form a new party, which they called the Free-Soil Party. It called for the territory gained in the Mexican-American War to be "free soil," a place where slavery was banned.

The party chose former Democratic President Martin Van Buren as its candidate. Van Buren did poorly in the election. However, he won enough votes from the Democrats to keep Cass from winning. General Zachary Taylor, a Whig and a hero of the Mexican-American War, was elected instead.

Vocabulary Builder
<u>controversy</u> (KAHN truh vur see)
n. argument or dispute

☑**Checkpoint** **Why was the Free-Soil Party founded?**

The Election of 1848

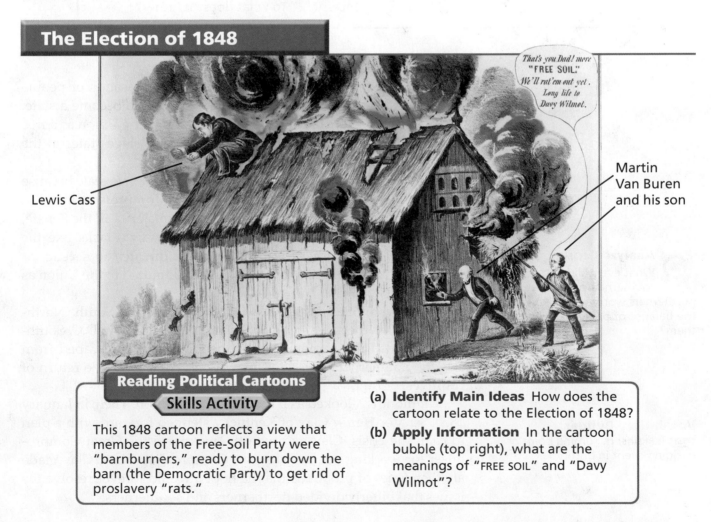

Lewis Cass

That's you Dad! more "FREE SOIL." We'll rat'em out yet. Long life to Davy Wilmot.

Martin Van Buren and his son

Reading Political Cartoons

Skills Activity

This 1848 cartoon reflects a view that members of the Free-Soil Party were "barnburners," ready to burn down the barn (the Democratic Party) to get rid of proslavery "rats."

(a) **Identify Main Ideas** How does the cartoon relate to the Election of 1848?

(b) **Apply Information** In the cartoon bubble (top right), what are the meanings of "FREE SOIL" and "Davy Wilmot"?

Calhoun Versus Webster

"[If] something is not done to arrest it, the South will be forced to choose between abolition and secession. . . . If you are unwilling we should part in peace, tell us so; and we shall know what to do when you reduce the question to submission or resistance."

—John C. Calhoun, March 4, 1850

John C. Calhoun

"I wish to speak today, not as a Massachusetts man, nor as a Northern man, but as an American. . . . I speak today for the preservation of the Union. . . . I speak today . . . for the restoration to the country of that quiet and that harmony which make the blessings of this Union so rich, and so dear to us all."

—Daniel Webster, March 7, 1850

Daniel Webster

Reading Primary Sources
Skills Activity

During the Senate debate on Clay's Compromise of 1850, John C. Calhoun and Daniel Webster wrote dramatic speeches evaluating the compromise.

(a) Detect Points of View For what region does Daniel Webster claim to be speaking?

(b) Apply Information Calhoun says "[If] something is not done to arrest it, the South will be forced to choose between abolition and secession." To what does "it" refer?

A Bitter Debate

After the discovery of gold in California, thousands of people rushed west. California soon had enough people to become a state. Both sides realized that California's admission to the Union as a free state would upset the balance between free and slave states in the Senate.

Northerners argued that California should be a free state because most of the territory lay north of the Missouri Compromise line. But southerners feared that if free states gained a majority in the Senate, the South would not be able to block antislavery attacks like the Wilmot Proviso. Southern leaders began to threaten to secede, or withdraw, from the nation if California was admitted to the Union as a free state.

There were other issues dividing the North and South. Northerners wanted the slave trade abolished in Washington, D.C. Southerners wanted northerners to catch people who had escaped from slavery. Southerners called for a law that would force the return of fugitives, or runaway enslaved people.

For months it looked as if there was no solution. Then, in January 1850, Senator Henry Clay of Kentucky stepped forward with a plan to calm the crisis. Clay had won the nickname the Great Compromiser for working out the Missouri Compromise. Now, Clay made another series of proposals that he hoped would forever resolve the issues that bitterly divided northerners and southerners.

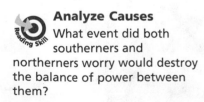

Analyze Causes
What event did both southerners and northerners worry would destroy the balance of power between them?

Vocabulary Builder
crisis (KRĪ sihs) **n.** turning point or deciding event in history

The Senate's discussion of Clay's proposals produced one of the greatest debates in American political history. South Carolina Senator John C. Calhoun was against compromise. Calhoun was gravely ill and just four weeks from death. He was too weak to give his speech, but he struggled to sit upright while his final speech was read to the Senate.

The admission of California as a free state, Calhoun wrote, would expose the South to continued attacks on slavery. There were only two ways to preserve the South's way of life. One was a constitutional amendment to protect states' rights. The other was secession.

Three days later, Massachusetts Senator Daniel Webster rose to support Clay's proposals and called for an end to the bitter sectionalism that was dividing the nation. Webster argued for Clay's compromise in order to preserve the Union.

Which view would prevail? The very existence of the United States depended on the answer.

✓**Checkpoint** **How did California's proposed admission to the Union affect the debate between the North and the South over slavery?**

⭐ **Looking Back and Ahead** With the territories acquired by the Mexican-American War, the nation could no longer overlook the slavery issue. Statehood for each of these territories would upset the balance between free states and slaveholding states. For a short while, it seemed to many that Henry Clay's proposed compromise gave concessions to both sides. But, as you will read in the next section, the compromise soon fell apart. When it did, the nation once again plunged down the road to all-out war between the regions.

Section 1 | **Check Your Progress**

Progress Monitoring Online
For: Self-test with instant help
Visit: PHSchool.com
Web Code: mya-5101

Comprehension and Critical Thinking

1. (a) Recall What was the Wilmot Proviso?
(b) Analyze Cause and Effect Did the Wilmot Proviso successfully address the nation's divisions over slavery? What effect *did* it have on the nation?

2. (a) List What were the main issues that led to Henry Clay's proposed compromise?
(b) Detect Points of View Write a sentence describing how you would feel about the need to compromise if you were a member of Congress from the North.

⊙ Reading Skill

3. Analyze Causes What did southerners want Congress to do about enslaved people who had fled to the North?

Key Terms

Complete these sentences so they clearly show your understanding of the key terms.

4. The status of new western territories would be decided by popular sovereignty, which is
_____.

5. If southern states seceded from the Union, then _____.

6. Many northerners would not report fugitives, who were _____.

Writing

7. Consider the broad topic "Conflicts Between Slave States and Free States Before the Civil War." Divide it into four or five narrower topics. Each of these narrower topics should be covered in a research paper of a few pages.

A Harsh Accusation

" Sir, the Nebraska Bill was in every respect a swindle. It was a swindle by the South of the North. . . . All efforts were now given to the dismal work of forcing slavery on free soil. "

—Senator Charles Sumner of Massachusetts, before being assaulted on the Senate floor, 1856

◀ Newspapers reported Sumner's caning by a southern congressman.

Compromises Fail

Objectives

- Summarize the main points of the Compromise of 1850.

- Describe the impact of the novel *Uncle Tom's Cabin.*

- Explain how the Kansas-Nebraska Act reopened the issue of slavery in the territories.

- Describe the effect of the Kansas-Nebraska Act.

⊙ Reading Skill

Analyze Effects The important events of the 1850s had far-reaching effects around the nation. As you read Section 2, try to identify and understand these effects. Remember that two events do not necessarily have a cause-and-effect link just because they occur in sequence. Use signal words such as *result* to help you identify effects.

Key Terms and People

Harriet Beecher Stowe
propaganda

Stephen Douglas
John Brown

Why It Matters Many Americans hoped that Henry Clay's proposed compromise would quiet the controversy over slavery. However, after 1850, the growing divide only worsened.

❓ **Section Focus Question: What was the Compromise of 1850, and why did it fail?**

The Compromise of 1850

In September 1850, Congress finally passed five bills based on Clay's proposals. This series of laws became known as the Compromise of 1850. President Zachary Taylor had opposed the Compromise. However, Taylor died in 1850. The new President, Millard Fillmore, supported the Compromise and signed it into law.

To Please the North The Compromise of 1850 was designed to end the crisis by giving both supporters and opponents of slavery part of what they wanted. To please the North, California was admitted to the Union as a free state. In addition, the Compromise banned the slave trade in the nation's capital. (However, Congress declared that it had no power to regulate the slave trade between slave states.)

To Please the South Under the terms of the Compromise, popular sovereignty would be used to decide the question of slavery in the rest of the Mexican Cession. People in the states created from that territory would vote whether to be a free state or a slave state when they requested admission to the Union. Also, in return for agreeing to outlaw the slave trade in Washington, D.C., southerners got a tough new fugitive slave law.

The Fugitive Slave Act of 1850 allowed special government officials to arrest any person accused of being a runaway slave. Suspects had no right to a trial to prove that they had been falsely accused. All that was required to <u>deprive</u> them of their freedom was for a slaveholder or any white witness to swear that the suspect was the slaveholder's property. In addition, the law required northern citizens to help capture accused runaways if authorities requested assistance.

Outrage in the North The Fugitive Slave Act became the most controversial part of the Compromise of 1850. Many northerners swore that they would resist the hated new law.

Northerners were outraged to see people accused of being fugitive slaves deprived of their freedom. An Indiana man was torn from his wife and children and given to an owner who claimed the man had escaped 19 years earlier. A wealthy African American tailor was carried back to South Carolina after living in New York for years. His friends quickly raised enough money to buy his freedom. But most who were shipped south remained there. Thousands of northern African Americans fled to the safety of Canada, including many who had never been enslaved.

In city after city, residents banded together to resist the Fugitive Slave Law. When two white Georgians arrived in Boston to seize fugitives, Bostonians threatened the slave catchers with harm if they did not leave the city right away. Another group rescued an accused runaway and sent him to safety in Canada. When the mob leaders were arrested, local juries refused to convict them.

John C. Calhoun had hoped that the Fugitive Slave Law would force northerners to admit that slaveholders had rights to their property. Instead, every time the law was enforced, it convinced more northerners that slavery was evil.

✓**Checkpoint** **How did the Compromise of 1850 deal with the admission of California to the Union?**

Vocabulary Builder
<u>deprive</u> (dee PRĪV) **v.** to keep from happening; to take away by force or intent

Returned to Slavery
Guarded by federal troops, fugitives Anthony Burns and Thomas Sims are captured in Boston and returned to enslavement in South Carolina. Below is a poster distributed by a southern slaveholder. **Critical Thinking:** *Draw Conclusions* What details show the attitude of Bostonians to the return of Burns and Sims?

Uncle Tom's Cabin

One northerner deeply affected by the Fugitive Slave Act was Harriet Beecher Stowe. The daughter of an abolitionist minister, Stowe met many people who had escaped from slavery. She decided to write "something that will make this whole nation feel what an accursed thing slavery is."

In 1852, Stowe published *Uncle Tom's Cabin,* a novel about kindly Uncle Tom, an enslaved man who is abused by the cruel Simon Legree. In this passage, Tom dies after a severe beating:

> **❝**Tom opened his eyes, and looked upon his master. . . . 'There an't no more ye can do! I forgive ye with all my soul!' and he fainted entirely away.
>
> 'I b'lieve, my soul, he's done for, finally,' said Legree, stepping forward, to look at him. 'Yes, he is! Well, his mouth's shut up, at last,—that's one comfort!'**❞**
>
> —Harriet Beecher Stowe, *Uncle Tom's Cabin,* Chapter 38

Reading Skill

Analyze Effects
What was one effect of Harriet Beecher Stowe's horror over slavery? What word in this paragraph highlights the cause-effect link?

Stowe's book was a bestseller in the North. It shocked thousands of people who previously had been unconcerned about slavery. As a result, readers began to view slavery as more than just a political conflict. It was a human, moral problem facing every American.

Many white southerners were outraged by Stowe's book. They criticized it as **propaganda,** false or misleading information that is spread to further a cause. They claimed the novel did not give a fair or accurate picture of the lives of enslaved African Americans.

☑**Checkpoint** What impact did *Uncle Tom's Cabin* have?

Uncle Tom's Cabin
The novel *Uncle Tom's Cabin* had an impact that lasted long after slavery ended. An original illustration from the book and a scene on a decorative plate are shown here. *Critical Thinking: Identify Costs You are a northerner during the 1850s. A fugitive comes to your door seeking help. Will you help her? List the costs and benefits of helping the person.*

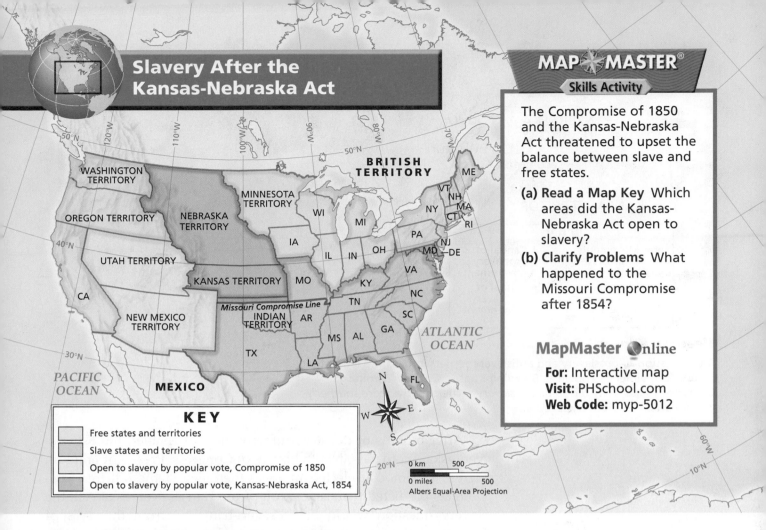

Slavery After the Kansas-Nebraska Act

KEY
- Free states and territories
- Slave states and territories
- Open to slavery by popular vote, Compromise of 1850
- Open to slavery by popular vote, Kansas-Nebraska Act, 1854

MAP MASTER®
Skills Activity

The Compromise of 1850 and the Kansas-Nebraska Act threatened to upset the balance between slave and free states.

(a) Read a Map Key Which areas did the Kansas-Nebraska Act open to slavery?

(b) Clarify Problems What happened to the Missouri Compromise after 1854?

MapMaster Online

For: Interactive map
Visit: PHSchool.com
Web Code: myp-5012

The Kansas-Nebraska Act

The nation moved closer to war after Congress passed the Kansas-Nebraska Act in 1854. The act was pushed through by Senator Stephen Douglas. Douglas was eager to develop the lands west of his home state of Illinois. He wanted to see a railroad built from Illinois through the Nebraska Territory to the Pacific Coast.

In 1853, Douglas suggested forming two new territories—the Kansas Territory and the Nebraska Territory. Southerners at once objected. Both territories lay in an area closed to slavery by the Missouri Compromise. This meant that the states eventually created from these territories would enter the Union as free states.

To win southern support, Douglas proposed that slavery in the new territories be decided by popular sovereignty. Thus, in effect, the Kansas-Nebraska Act undid the Missouri Compromise.

As Douglas hoped, southerners supported the Kansas-Nebraska Act. They were sure that slave owners from Missouri would move across the border into Kansas. In time, they hoped that Kansas would enter the union as a slave state.

Northerners, however, were outraged by the Kansas-Nebraska Act. They believed that Douglas had betrayed them by reopening the issue of slavery in the territories. "The more I look at it the more enraged I become," said one northern senator of Douglas's bill. "It needs but little to make me an out-and-out abolitionist."

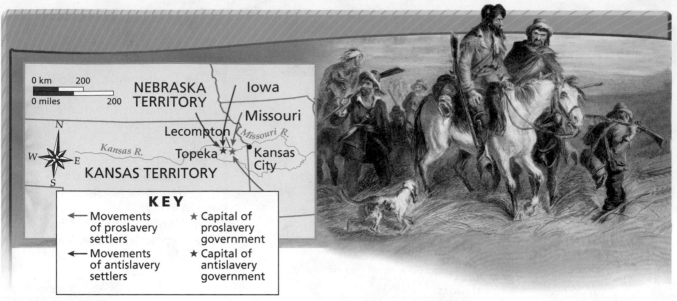

Bleeding Kansas

The migration of proslavery and antislavery settlers into Kansas led to the outbreak of violence known as Bleeding Kansas. **Critical Thinking:** *Interpret Maps* Why did some proslavery settlers take a more southerly route than did antislavery settlers?

After months of debate, southern support enabled the Kansas-Nebraska Act to pass in both houses of Congress. President Franklin Pierce, a Democrat elected in 1852, then signed the bill into law. Douglas predicted that, as a result of the Kansas-Nebraska Act, the slavery question would be "forever banished from the halls of Congress." But events would soon prove how wrong he was.

✓**Checkpoint** **How did Stephen Douglas's plan undo the Missouri Compromise?**

Bleeding Kansas

The Kansas-Nebraska Act left it to the white citizens of the territory to decide whether Kansas would be free or slave territory. Both proslavery and antislavery settlers flooded into Kansas within weeks after Douglas's bill became law. Each side was determined to hold the majority in the territory when it came time for the vote.

Thousands of Missourians entered Kansas in March 1855 to illegally vote in the election to select a territorial legislature. Although Kansas had only 3,000 voters, nearly 8,000 votes were cast on election day! Of 39 legislators elected, all but 3 supported slavery. The antislavery settlers refused to accept these results and held a second election.

Vocabulary Builder
impose (ihm POHZ) **v.** to place a burden on someone or something

Growing Violence Kansas now had two governments, each claiming the right to impose their government on the territory. Not surprisingly, violence soon broke out. In April, a proslavery sheriff was shot when he tried to arrest some antislavery settlers in the town of Lawrence. The next month, he returned with 800 men and attacked the town.

Three days later, John Brown, an antislavery settler from Connecticut, led seven men to a proslavery settlement near Pottawatomie (paht uh wah TOH mee) Creek. There, they murdered five proslavery men and boys.

These incidents set off widespread fighting in Kansas. Bands of proslavery and antislavery fighters roamed the countryside, terrorizing those who did not support their views. The violence was so bad that it earned Kansas the name Bleeding Kansas.

Describe the effect of the Kansas-Nebraska Act on Kansas.

Bloodshed in the Senate Even before Brown's raid at Pottawatomie Creek, the violence in Kansas spilled over into the United States Senate. Charles Sumner of Massachusetts was the leading abolitionist senator. In a fiery speech, Sumner denounced the proslavery legislature in Kansas. He then attacked his southern foes, singling out Andrew Butler, an elderly senator from South Carolina.

Butler was not present the day Sumner made his speech. A few days later, however, Butler's nephew, Congressman Preston Brooks, marched into the Senate chamber. Using a heavy cane, Brooks beat Sumner until he fell to the floor, bloody and unconscious. Sumner never completely recovered from his injuries.

Many southerners felt that Sumner got what he deserved. Hundreds of people sent canes to Brooks to show their support. To northerners, however, Brooks's violent act was just more evidence that slavery was brutal and inhuman.

☑ **Checkpoint** What was the outcome of the election to select a legislature in the Kansas Territory?

⭐ **Looking Back and Ahead** By 1856, all attempts at compromise had failed. The bitterness between the North and the South was about to alter the political landscape of the United States.

Section 2 | **Check Your Progress**

Progress Monitoring Online
For: Self-test with instant help
Visit: PHSchool.com
Web Code: mya-5102

Comprehension and Critical Thinking
1. **(a) Recall** What parts of the Compromise of 1850 were included to please the North?
   (b) Draw Conclusions Why do you think northerners were still not satisfied?
2. **(a) Recall** What was the Kansas-Nebraska Act?
   Evaluate Information How did the Kansas-Nebraska Act contribute to tension between the North and the South?

Reading Skill
3. **Analyze Effects** effect of Harriet Beecher Stowe's book *Uncle Tom's Cabin*

Key Terms
Complete the following sentence so that the second part further explains the first part and clearly shows your understanding of the key term.
4. Many white southerners considered propaganda; _____ an unfair picture of slavery.

Writing
5. Imagine that you are researching the effects of Harriet Beecher Stowe's book *Uncle Tom's Cabin*. Write down five questions that would help you focus your research on this topic. The questions should point you to areas where you need to find more information about the influence of Stowe's book.

Uncle Tom's Cabin

by Harriet Beecher Stowe

Prepare to Read

Introduction

Harriet Beecher Stowe rocked the nation in 1851 when she published *Uncle Tom's Cabin*. The novel won many converts to the antislavery cause. The excerpt below is from the opening chapter. Shelby, a Kentucky slave owner, must sell some of his enslaved servants to Mr. Haley, a slave trader. Haley is especially interested in buying a young woman named Eliza.

Reading Skill

Judging Characters In a work of fiction, characters may say things that the author thinks are wrong. We have to read carefully in order to understand how the author wants us to judge the characters. In the selection below, look for clues as to what Stowe really thinks of Mr. Haley, the slave trader.

Vocabulary *Builder*

As you read this literature selection, look for the following underlined words:

calculation (kal kyoo LAY shuhn) *n.* ability to figure out exactly what something is worth

humane (hyoo MAYN) *adj.* kind; considerate; merciful

candid (KAN dihd) *adj.* frank; honest

virtuous (VIR choo uhs) *adj.* highly moral

Background

Much of *Uncle Tom's Cabin* is written in dialect that reproduces how different types of characters speak. For example, to show the way Haley speaks, Stowe uses "ha'nt" for "haven't," "this yer" for "this here," "uns" for "ones," and "onpleasant" for "unpleasant."

"Come, how will you trade about the gal?—what shall I say for her—what'll you take?"

"Mr. Haley, she is not to be sold," said Shelby. "My wife would not part with her for her weight in gold."

"Ay, ay! women always say such things, cause they ha'nt no sort of calculation. Just show 'em how many watches, feathers, and trinkets, one's weight in gold would buy, and that alters the case, I reckon."

"I tell you, Haley, this must not be spoken of; I say no, and I mean no," said Shelby, decidedly.

"Well, you'll let me have the boy, though," said the trader; "you must own I've come down pretty handsomely for him."

"What on earth can you want with the child?" said Shelby.

"Why, I've got a friend that's going into this yer branch of the business—wants to buy up handsome boys to raise for the market. Fancy articles entirely—sell for waiters, and so on, to rich 'uns, that can pay for handsome 'uns. It sets off one of yer great places—a real handsome boy to open door, wait, and tend. They fetch a good sum; and this little devil is such a comical, musical concern, he's just the article!"

"I would rather not sell him," said Mr. Shelby, thoughtfully; "the fact is, sir, I'm a humane man, and I hate to take the boy from his mother, sir."

"O, you do?—La! yes—something of that ar natur. I understand, perfectly. It is mighty onpleasant getting on with women, sometimes, I al'ays hates these yer screechin', screamin' times. They are *mighty* onpleasant; but, as I manages business, I generally avoids

Slave auction

'em, sir. Now, what if you get the girl off for a day, or a week, or so; then the thing's done quietly,—all over before she comes home. Your wife might get her some ear-rings, or a new gown, or some such truck, to make up with her."

"I'm afraid not."

"Lor bless ye, yes! These critters ain't like white folks, you know; they gets over things, only manage right. Now, they say," said Haley, assuming a <u>candid</u> and confidential air, "that this kind o' trade is hardening to the feelings; but I never found it so. Fact is, I never could do things up the way some fellers manage the business. I've seen 'em as would pull a woman's child out of her arms, and set him up to sell, and she screechin' like mad all the time;—very bad policy—damages the article—makes 'em quite unfit for service sometimes. I knew a real handsome gal once, in Orleans, as was entirely ruined by this sort o' handling. The fellow that was trading for her didn't want her baby; and she was one of your real high sort, when her blood was up. I tell you, she squeezed up her child in her arms, and talked, and went on real awful. It kinder makes my blood run cold to think on 't; and when they carried off the child, and locked her up, she jest went ravin' mad, and died in a week. Clear waste, sir, of a thousand dollars, just for want of management,—there's where 't is. It's always best to do the humane thing, sir; that's been my experience." And the trader leaned back in his chair, and folded his arm, with an air of <u>virtuous</u> decision, apparently considering himself a second Wilberforce.

From *Uncle Tom's Cabin*, by Harriet Beecher Stowe

Judging Characters
Reading Skill
Stowe has Haley refer to enslaved Africans as "critters," showing he does not think of them as human beings. Yet, he also claims that slave-trading has not hardened his feelings. What does this indicate about Stowe's view of Haley?

★ **Background**
William Wilberforce was a famous English politician who campaigned to end slavery.

If you liked this selection, you might want to read more about the antislavery movement in *Escape From Slavery: Five Journeys to Freedom* by Doreen Rappaport, illustrated by Charles Lilly. Harper Collins Publishers. 1991.

Analyze LITERATURE

Imagine that you are a northerner in 1851 reading *Uncle Tom's Cabin* for the first time. Write a letter to a friend explaining how this excerpt made you feel about the slave trade.

▲ Slaves laboring on a southern plantation

Gross Injustice and Cruelty

❝ This rich inheritance of justice, liberty, prosperity, and independence bequeathed by your fathers is shared by you, not by me. . . . What, to the American slave is your Fourth of July? I answer: a day that reveals to him, more than all other days in the year, the gross injustice and cruelty to which he is the constant victim. ❞

—Frederick Douglass, Independence Day speech delivered at Rochester, New York, 1852

The Crisis Deepens

Objectives

- Explain why the Republican Party came into being in the 1850s.
- Summarize the issues involved in the Dred Scott decision.
- Identify Abraham Lincoln's and Stephen Douglas's views on slavery.
- Describe the differing reactions in the North and the South to John Brown's raid.

Reading Skill

Analyze Causes and Effects
Historians often disagree over exactly what caused the Civil War. As you read Section 3, watch carefully for cause-and-effect links. Analyzing these links will help you answer this difficult question for yourself. Remember that sometimes the link is not directly stated. Identify an event, then ask yourself: What caused this event to happen? What were the effects of this event?

Key People

Dred Scott
Roger B. Taney

Abraham Lincoln

Why It Matters Bitterness between northerners and southerners weakened the nation's two major political parties. As a result of the growing struggle over slavery, a new party and new leaders emerged.

❓ **Section Focus Question: Why did the Lincoln-Douglas debates and John Brown's raid increase tensions between the North and South?**

A New Antislavery Party

As the Whig Party split apart in 1854, many northern Whigs joined a new political party. It was called the Republican Party, and its main goal was to stop the spread of slavery into the western territories. The Republicans' antislavery stand also attracted northern Democrats and Free-Soil Party members.

The Republicans quickly became a powerful force in politics. The congressional elections of 1854 were held only months after the party was founded. Of the 245 candidates elected to the U.S. House of Representatives, 105 were Republicans. Republican victories in state races also cost the Democrats control of all but two northern state legislatures.

Two years later, in 1856, the Republican Party ran its first candidate for President. It chose John C. Frémont, the army officer who had helped California win independence during the Mexican-American War. The Republicans waged a strong antislavery campaign. Although the Democrat James Buchanan was elected, Frémont won in 11 of the nation's 16 free states.

✓ **Checkpoint** What was the result of the election of 1856?

The Dred Scott Decision

In March 1857—only three days after Buchanan took office—the U.S. Supreme Court delivered a shattering blow to antislavery forces. It decided the case of *Dred Scott* v. *Sandford*.

Dred Scott was an enslaved person who had once been owned by a U.S. Army doctor. The doctor, and Scott, lived for a time in Illinois and in the Wisconsin Territory. Slavery was illegal in both places. After leaving the army, the doctor settled with Scott in Missouri.

With the help of antislavery lawyers, Scott sued for his freedom. He argued that he was free because he had lived where slavery was illegal. In time, the case reached the Supreme Court. Neither northerners nor southerners were prepared for what the Court decided.

The Court Decides Chief Justice Roger B. Taney wrote the decision for the Court. Scott was not a free man, he said, for two reasons. First, according to Taney, Scott had no right to sue in federal court because African Americans were not citizens. Second, Taney said, merely living in free territory did not make an enslaved person free. Slaves were property, Taney declared, and property rights were protected by the U.S. Constitution.

But the ruling went even further. Taney wrote that Congress did not have the power to prohibit slavery in any territory. Thus, the Missouri Compromise was unconstitutional.

Reaction Supporters of slavery rejoiced at the Dred Scott decision. The decision meant that slavery was legal in all territories—just as white southern leaders had been demanding all along.

Northerners, however, were stunned. African American leaders such as Frederick Douglass condemned the ruling. Still, Douglass declared, "my hopes were never brighter than now." He believed that outrage against the decision would bring more whites to the abolitionist cause.

Indeed, white northerners were also shocked by the ruling. Many had hoped that slavery would eventually die out if it were restricted to the South. Now, however, slavery could spread throughout the West.

One northerner who spoke out against the Dred Scott decision was an Illinois lawyer named Abraham Lincoln. The idea that African Americans could not be citizens, he said, was based on a false view of American history. In a very short time, Lincoln would become a central figure in the fight against the spread of slavery.

☑**Checkpoint** Why did Dred Scott claim he was no longer enslaved?

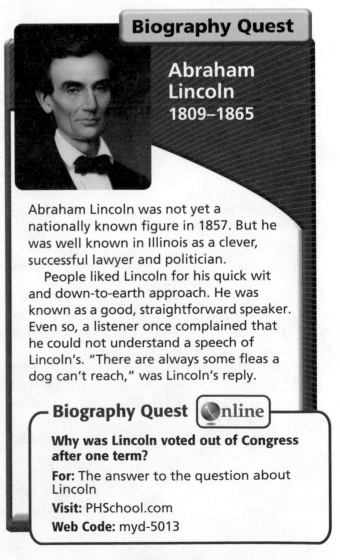

Biography Quest

Abraham Lincoln
1809–1865

Abraham Lincoln was not yet a nationally known figure in 1857. But he was well known in Illinois as a clever, successful lawyer and politician.

People liked Lincoln for his quick wit and down-to-earth approach. He was known as a good, straightforward speaker. Even so, a listener once complained that he could not understand a speech of Lincoln's. "There are always some fleas a dog can't reach," was Lincoln's reply.

Biography Quest **Online**

Why was Lincoln voted out of Congress after one term?

For: The answer to the question about Lincoln

Visit: PHSchool.com

Web Code: myd-5013

Links Across Time

Elections and the Media

1858 Americans followed the Lincoln-Douglas debates as telegraph reports circulated around the country.

1960 Americans were for the first time able to watch presidential candidates debate live on television. Richard Nixon and John F. Kennedy debated before an enormous television audience. Many experts believe that the debates played a major role in Kennedy's victory.

Link to Today Online

Elections and the Media Today The digital revolution is again changing American political campaigns. What media do candidates use today?

For: Voting and the media
Visit: PHSchool.com
Web Code: myc-5103

The Lincoln-Douglas Debates

Lincoln had had only a brief career in politics. After serving in the Illinois state legislature, he was elected to Congress as a Whig. There, he voted for the Wilmot Proviso. After a single term, he returned to Illinois to practice law.

Lincoln's opposition to the Kansas-Nebraska Act brought him back into politics, this time <u>embracing</u> the Republican cause. He had long been a rival of Illinois Senator Stephen Douglas, the author of the Kansas-Nebraska Act. Their rivalry was personal as well as political. Both men had courted Mary Todd, who married Lincoln.

Vocabulary Builder
<u>embrace</u> (ehm BRAYS) **v.** to hold tight; to readily accept

A House Divided In 1858, Illinois Republicans chose Lincoln to run for the Senate against Douglas. Accepting the nomination, Lincoln made a stirring speech in favor of the Union:

> "A house divided against itself cannot stand. I do not believe this government can endure, permanently, half slave and half free. I do not expect the Union to be dissolved—I do not expect the house to fall—but I do expect it will cease to be divided. It will become all one thing or all the other."
>
> —Abraham Lincoln, Springfield, Illinois, June 16, 1858

Lincoln did not state that he wanted to ban slavery. Still, many southerners became convinced that Lincoln was an abolitionist.

Debating Slavery Lincoln then challenged Douglas to a series of public debates. Thousands of people gathered to hear them speak. Newspapers throughout the nation reported what each man said.

Douglas strongly defended popular sovereignty. "Each state of this Union has a right to do as it pleases on the subject of slavery," he said. "In Illinois we have exercised that sovereign right by prohibiting slavery. . . . It is none of our business whether slavery exists in Missouri." Douglas also painted Lincoln as a dangerous abolitionist who wanted equality for African Americans.

Lincoln took a stand against the spread of slavery. He declared, "If slavery is not wrong, nothing is wrong." Lincoln predicted that slavery would die on its own. In the meantime, he said, it was the obligation of Americans to keep it out of the western territories.

In reply to Douglas, Lincoln stated: "I am not, nor ever have been in favor of bringing about in any way the social and political equality of the white and black races." But he did <u>clarify</u> this view. He insisted that "there is no reason in the world why the Negro is not entitled to all the rights enumerated in the Declaration of Independence, the right to life, liberty and the pursuit of happiness."

In the end, Douglas won the Senate election. However, the debates had made Lincoln known throughout the country. Two years later, the men would be rivals again—this time for the presidency.

☑**Checkpoint** What position did Douglas take on slavery?

Vocabulary Builder
clarify (KLAIR ih fī) **v.** to make the meaning of something clear

John Brown's Raid

The nation's attention soon was captured by the actions of John Brown. Driven out of Kansas after the Pottawatomie Massacre, Brown had returned to New England. There he hatched a plot to raise an army and free people in the South who were enslaved.

In 1859, Brown and a small band of supporters attacked the town of Harpers Ferry in Virginia. His goal was to seize guns the U.S. Army had stored there. He thought that enslaved African Americans would support him. He would then give them weapons and lead them in a revolt.

Brown quickly gained control of the arms. But troops commanded by Colonel Robert E. Lee surrounded Brown's force before it could escape. Ten of Brown's followers were killed. Brown was wounded and captured.

Analyze Causes and Effects
How did John Brown's raid affect the national debate over slavery?

John Brown in Kansas
John Steuart Curry began painting this 10-foot-high mural in 1937. It shows John Brown as a fiery abolitionist with a rifle in one hand and a Bible in the other. **Critical Thinking: *Detect Points of View*** *Based on this painting, do you think Curry admired John Brown?*

Death of John Brown

Thomas Hovenden painted this portrait of a saintly John Brown. On his way to his death, Brown stops to kiss a child. Hovenden did not personally witness the events he showed here. **Critical Thinking: *Contrast*** *Compare this painting to the one on the previous page. How do these two paintings try to stir different emotions?*

At his trial, Brown sat quietly as the court found him guilty of murder and treason. Before hearing his sentence, he gave a moving defense of his actions. The Bible, he said, instructed him to care for the poor and enslaved. "If it is deemed necessary that I should forfeit my life for the furtherance of the ends of justice . . . I say, let it be done." He showed no emotion as he was sentenced to death.

When the state of Virginia hanged Brown for treason on December 2, 1859, church bells across the North tolled to mourn the man who many considered a hero. But southerners were shocked. People in the North were praising a man who had tried to lead a slave revolt! More than ever, many southerners were convinced that the North was out to destroy their way of life.

✓Checkpoint **What was John Brown's goal in launching the raid on Harpers Ferry?**

☆ **Looking Back and Ahead** The nation had suffered one dispute after another over the expansion of slavery since the end of the Mexican-American War in 1846. By the election of 1860, talk of the breakup of the United States was everywhere. In the next section, you will read how that breakup came about.

Section 3 | Check Your Progress

Progress Monitoring Online
For: Self-test with instant help
Visit: PHSchool.com
Web Code: mya-5103

Comprehension and Critical Thinking

1. **(a) Summarize** Which groups supported the newly formed Republican Party?
   (b) Draw Conclusions How did the outcomes of the elections of 1854 and 1856 affect the Republican Party?

2. **(a) Identify** On what grounds did Dred Scott sue for his freedom in court?
   (b) Draw Conclusions How did Taney's ruling further divide the North and the South?

3. **(a) Recall** What were the Lincoln-Douglas debates?
   (b) Apply Information Why do you think the Lincoln-Douglas debates received national attention?

Reading Skill

4. **Analyze Causes and Effects** Identify one cause and one effect of John Brown's raid. Why did Brown and his followers attack Harpers Ferry? What happened as a result?

Writing

5. Reread the paragraphs in this section that describe the Lincoln-Douglas debates. When you have finished, paraphrase the excerpt from Lincoln's Springfield speech. Remember, when you paraphrase, you restate something said by someone else, using only your own words.

CHARLESTON MERCURY EXTRA:

Passed unanimously at 1.15 o'clock, P. M. December 20th, 1860.

AN ORDINANCE

To dissolve the Union between the State of South Carolina and other States united with her under the compact entitled "The Constitution of the United States of America."

THE **UNION** is **DISSOLVED!**

◄ Confederate seal

The Confederate States

❝In the exercise of a right so ancient, so well-established, and so necessary for self-preservation, the people of the Confederate states . . . passed [laws] resuming all their rights as sovereign and independent States and dissolved their connection with the other States of the Union.❞

—President Jefferson Davis, message to the Confederate Congress, April 29, 1861

◄ Newspaper announcing secession of southern states

The Coming of the Civil War

Objectives

- Describe the results of the election of 1860.
- Explain why southern states seceded from the Union.
- Summarize the events that led to the outbreak of the Civil War.

🔄 Reading Skill

Analyze Multiple Causes or Effects
Many events in history have more than one cause, as the Civil War certainly did. Other events lead to more than one effect, which is also certainly true of the Civil War. As you read about this turning point in American history, look for causes with multiple effects and effects with multiple causes.

Key Term

civil war

Why It Matters John Brown's raid increased tensions between North and South. So did the growing power of the Republican Party. The nation was on the verge of a civil war.

❓ Section Focus Question: Why did the election of Abraham Lincoln spark the secession of southern states?

The Nation Divides

As the election of 1860 drew near, Americans everywhere felt a sense of crisis. The long and bitter debate over slavery had left the nation seriously divided.

Election of 1860 The Republicans chose Abraham Lincoln as their presidential candidate. His criticisms of slavery during his debates with Douglas had made him popular in the North.

Southern Democrats wanted the party to support slavery in the territories. But northerners refused to do so. In the end, the party split in two. Northern Democrats chose Stephen Douglas as their candidate. Southern Democrats picked Vice President John Breckinridge of Kentucky.

Some southerners still hoped to heal the split between North and South. They formed the Constitutional Union Party and nominated John Bell of Tennessee. Bell promised to protect slavery *and* keep the nation together.

Stephen Douglas was sure that Lincoln would win the election. However, he believed that Democrats "must try to save the Union." He pleaded with southern voters to stay with the Union, no matter who was elected. However, when Douglas campaigned in the South, hostile southerners often pelted him with eggs and rotten fruit.

Election of 1860

KEY

- Lincoln, Republican
- Douglas, Northern Democrat
- Bell, Constitutional Union
- Breckinridge, Southern Democrat

PERCENTAGE ELECTORAL VOTE

4% 13% 24% 59%

PERCENTAGE POPULAR VOTE

12.6% 18.1% 29.5% 39.8%

MAP MASTER
Skills Activity

Due to rising tensions between the North and South, the election of 1860 took place in an atmosphere of distrust and suspicion.

(a) Read a Map Key What do the four colors on the map stand for? Which party won nearly all the northern states? Which party won nearly all the southern states?

(b) Draw Conclusions How does the map show that sectionalism was important in the election?

MapMaster Online

For: Interactive map
Visit: PHSchool.com
Web Code: myp-5104

The election showed just how fragmented the nation had become. Lincoln won in every free state and Breckinridge in all the slave-holding states except four. Bell won Kentucky, Tennessee, and Virginia—all in the upper South. Douglas carried only Missouri. Although Lincoln got only 40 percent of the popular votes, he received enough electoral votes to win the election.

Southern States Secede Lincoln's election sent shock waves through the South. To many southerners, it seemed that the South no longer had a voice in the national government. They believed that the President and Congress were now set against their interests—especially slavery.

One Virginia newspaper expressed the feelings of many southerners. "A party founded on the single sentiment . . . of hatred of African slavery, is now the controlling power," it observed. "The honor, safety, and independence of the Southern people are to be found only in a Southern Confederacy."

South Carolina was the first southern state to secede from the Union. When news of Lincoln's election reached the state, the legislature called for a special convention. On December 20, 1860, the convention passed a declaration that "the union now subsisting between South Carolina and the other states, under the name of the 'United States of America' is hereby dissolved."

The Confederate States of America With the hope of <u>accommodation</u> all but gone, six more states followed South Carolina out of the Union. However, not all southerners favored secession. Tennessee Senator Andrew Johnson and Texas Governor Sam Houston were among those who opposed it. Yet, the voices of the moderates were overwhelmed. "People are wild," said one opponent of secession. "You might as well attempt to control a tornado as attempt to stop them."

In early February, leaders from the seven seceding states met in Montgomery, Alabama, to form a new nation that they called the Confederate States of America. By the time Lincoln took office in March, they had written a constitution and named former Mississippi Senator Jefferson Davis as their president.

☑**Checkpoint** **Why did southern states secede from the Union?**

Vocabulary Builder
<u>accommodation</u> (ak kom moh DAY shuhn) **n.** adjustment; adaptation

The Civil War Begins

On March 4, 1861, Abraham Lincoln became President of a nation facing the greatest crisis in its history. In his inaugural address, he assured the seceded states that he meant them no harm. "I have no purpose, directly or indirectly, to interfere with the institution of slavery where it exists," he promised. But he also warned them about continuing on the course they had chosen:

    "In your hands, my dissatisfied fellow countrymen, and not in mine, is the momentous issue of . . . war. The government will not assail [attack] you. . . . We are not enemies, but friends. We must not be enemies. Though passion may have strained, it must not break our bonds of affection."

    —Abraham Lincoln, Inaugural Address, March 4, 1861

Lincoln's assurance of friendship was rejected. The seceding states took over post offices, forts, and other federal property within their borders. The new President had to decide how to respond.

Fort Sumter Lincoln's most urgent problem was Fort Sumter, located on an island in the harbor of Charleston, South Carolina. The fort's commander would not surrender it. South Carolina authorities decided to starve the fort's 100 troops into surrender. They had been cut off from supplies since late December and could not hold out much longer.

Abraham Lincoln speaks at his first inauguration

501

ATTACK ON FORT SUMTER

America's most tragic conflict began early on the morning of April 12, 1861, at Fort Sumter. The dark night was suddenly lit up by Confederate shells fired from the mainland. Within a few hours, the fort's wooden barracks had caught fire and portions of the fort had crumbled. At midday, a Confederate shell knocked over the fort's flagpole. The firing went on throughout the day and evening. By the next day, the Union garrison was exhausted and every wooden structure in the fort was ablaze. "The men lay . . . on the ground, with wet handkerchiefs over their mouths and eyes, gasping for breath." **Critical Thinking:** *Analyze Cause and Effect What was the cause of the Confederate attack on Fort Sumter? What were the effects?*

History *Interactive*
Inside Fort Sumter
Visit: PHSchool.com
Web Code: myp-5107

American flag from
Fort Sumter ▼

▼ **Confederate Troops Fire on the Fort**
Confederate artillery pounded Fort Sumter for 34 hours. Fires raged out of control and threatened to ignite the fort's magazine, where many barrels of gunpowder were stored. Facing shortages of food and ammunition, the Union commander surrendered. The bloodiest of all American wars had begun.

Major Robert ▶
Anderson, Union
commander of
Fort Sumter

Lincoln did not want to give up the fort. But he feared that sending troops might cause other states to secede. Therefore, he announced that he would send food to the fort, but that the supply ships would carry no troops or guns.

Confederate leaders decided to capture the fort while it was isolated. On April 12, Confederate artillery opened fire on the fort. After 34 hours, with the fort on fire, the U.S. troops surrendered.

Was War Avoidable? The Confederate attack on Fort Sumter marked the beginning of a long civil war. A **civil war** is a war between opposing groups of citizens of the same country.

The Civil War probably attracts more public interest today than any other event in American history. Americans continue to debate why the war took place and whether it could have been avoided.

In 1850, southerners might have been satisfied if they had been left alone. But by 1861, many Americans in both the North and the South had come to accept the idea that war could not be avoided. At stake was the nation's future. Four years later, a weary Lincoln looked back to the beginning of the conflict. He noted:

> **❝** Both parties [condemned] war, but one of them would *make* war rather than let the nation survive, and the other would *accept* war rather than let it perish, and the war came. **❞**
>
> —Abraham Lincoln, Second Inaugural Address, March 4, 1865

Vocabulary Builder
isolate (ī sah layt) *v.* to set apart; to separate

Analyze Multiple Causes or Effects According to this section, what were two causes of the Civil War?

☑Checkpoint Why was Lincoln reluctant to give up Fort Sumter?

☆ Looking Back and Ahead Confederate cannons had nearly destroyed Fort Sumter. To many, it seemed like a huge fireworks display. No one knew that the fireworks marked the beginning of a terrible war that would last four years.

Section 4 | **Check Your Progress**

Progress Monitoring ⏣nline
For: Self-test with instant help
Visit: PHSchool.com
Web Code: mya-5104

Comprehension and Critical Thinking

1. (a) Recall How did divisions among the Democrats help lead to the election of Republican Abraham Lincoln in 1860?
(b) Explain Problems What was the South's reaction to Lincoln's election? How did Lincoln try to reassure the South?

2. (a) Identify What event marked the start of war between the North and the South?

(b) Evaluate Information Explain what Abraham Lincoln meant by the following remark: "Both parties [condemned] war, but one of them would *make* war rather than let the nation survive. . . ."

Reading Skill
3. Analyze Multiple Causes or Effects What were three effects of Lincoln's warning to the South?

Key Terms
4. Write two definitions for the key term civil war. First, write a formal definition for your teacher. Second, write a definition in everyday English for a classmate.

Writing
5. Based on what you have read in this section, write a thesis statement for an essay explaining why the election of Abraham Lincoln caused the South to secede.

Not everything a writer includes in a selection is equally important. Some information is relevant because it is directly related to the subject of the text. Other information is less relevant because it does not directly relate to the subject. When you read, you must focus your attention on the main topic and the most relevant information. Read the fictional letter below to determine relevance.

The letter below is historical fiction. That means that it is based on history, but is not a primary source. In the letter, William, a farmer who had moved to Kansas Territory, writes to his brother Joseph in Vermont.

November 20, 1854
Dear Joseph,

I was pleased to receive your last letter. The success of your store is a great achievement. Our new farm continues to prosper and little Sarah has recovered from the fever that had sickened her for a month. Of course, the issue of the Kansas-Nebraska Act continues to trouble me. I do not agree with your support of Senator Stephen Douglas of Illinois; however, I enjoy reading his speeches. Those who oppose slavery, as I do, do not want that cruel system in place in a territory where it had been banned. Under the terms of the Kansas-Nebraska Act, it is up to the people to decide the issue peacefully by voting their hearts. Yet, settlers who are for and against slavery in the territory seem intent on using force, instead of the ballot box. The elections next year will settle the issue once and for all.

Your loving brother,
William

Learn the Skill

Use these steps to determine which information is relevant and which is irrelevant.

1 **Identify the subject or topic.** What is the main topic of the selection?

2 **Identify your purpose for reading the selection.** Ask yourself: What am I trying to find out?

3 **Identify the information that is relevant to the topic.** What information is directly related to the subject? Why is it relevant?

4 **Identify the information that is irrelevant to the topic.** What information is not directly related to the subject? Why is it irrelevant?

Practice the Skill

Answer the following questions about the letter on the page.

1 **Identify the subject or topic.** What is the main topic of the letter?

2 **Identify the purpose for reading the selection.** Why am I reading this letter?

3 **Identify the information that is relevant to the subject.** (a) What are two statements that are directly related to the topic of the letter? (b) Why is each statement relevant?

4 **Identify the information that is irrelevant to the topic.** (a) What are two statements that are not directly related to the subject? (b) Why is each statement irrelevant?

Apply the Skill

See the Review and Assessment at the end of this chapter.

Quick Study Guide

ESSENTIAL QUESTION

How did the nation try but fail to deal with growing sectional differences?

Section 1
Growing Tensions Over Slavery

- The acquisition of new territories in the West reopened the issue of slavery.
- Lawmakers debated how to keep a balance of power between free and slave-holding states.

Section 2
Compromises Fail

- The Compromise of 1850 attempted to settle the slavery question, but northerners refused to accept the Fugitive Slave Act.
- *Uncle Tom's Cabin* increased northern hatred of slavery and antagonized southern slaveholders.
- Popular sovereignty established by the Kansas-Nebraska Act triggered bloody fighting in Kansas.

Section 3
The Crisis Deepens

- The Republican Party was formed to oppose the spread of slavery.
- In the Dred Scott decision, the Supreme Court ruled that Congress could not ban slavery in any territory.
- Abraham Lincoln became a central political figure when he and Stephen Douglas debated slavery.
- John Brown, an abolitionist, and his followers attacked the federal arsenal at Harpers Ferry, Virginia, to protest slavery.

Section 4
The Coming of the Civil War

- After Lincoln won the presidential election of 1860, some southern states seceded from the Union.
- The Civil War began when Confederate troops fired on Fort Sumter.

? Exploring the Essential Question

Use the online study guide to explore the essential question.

Section 1
How did the question of admission of new states to the Union fuel the debate over slavery and states' rights?

Section 2
What was the Compromise of 1850, and why did it fail?

Chapter 14 Essential Question
How did the nation try but fail to deal with growing sectional differences?

Section 4
Why did the election of Abraham Lincoln spark the secession of southern states?

Section 3
Why did the Lincoln-Douglas debates and John Brown's raid increase tensions between the North and South?

Key Terms
Fill in the blanks with the correct key terms.

1. Many southern states threatened to _____ from the Union if California was admitted as a free state.

2. Southerners claimed that *Uncle Tom's Cabin* was _____ because it did not give a fair picture of the lives of enslaved African Americans.

3. Slavery was the main issue that split the nation apart and led to a violent _____.

Comprehension and Critical Thinking

4. **(a) Recall** Why did Senator Stephen Douglas introduce the Kansas-Nebraska Act?
(b) Understand Sequence How did the events in Kansas demonstrate the unrest that would eventually take shape throughout the nation?

5. **(a) Summarize** What was the Supreme Court's verdict in the Dred Scott case?
(b) Detect Points of View How do you think Harriet Beecher Stowe reacted to the verdict?

6. **(a) Identify** What was the main goal of the Republican Party in the election of 1854?
(b) Distinguish Relevant Information How did Abraham Lincoln represent Republican principles during the Lincoln-Douglas debates?

7. **(a) Identify** What is the subject of the painting below?
(b) Draw Conclusions Do you agree with the artist's view of this person? Why or why not?

8. **(a) Describe** What happened at Fort Sumter?
(b) Draw Conclusions Do you think southerners were justified in seceding despite Lincoln's assurances? Explain.

History Reading Skill
9. **Analyze Cause and Effect** Reread the text in Section 4 under the heading "The Nation Divides." How did the election of 1860 affect the unity of the United States?

Writing
10. **Choose one of the following topics for a research report:**
 • the Kansas-Nebraska Act
 • the Dred Scott decision
 • the early career of Abraham Lincoln

 List five questions you would want to pursue if you were going to research that topic. Write a thesis statement for the topic and find supporting evidence for that thesis from the chapter.

11. **Write a Narrative:**
 Imagine you are from a northern farm family and have just heard of the attack on Fort Sumter. Write a narrative describing your hopes and fears about the future.

Skills for Life
Determine Relevance
Use the fictional letter below to answer the questions that follow.

> October 18, 1856
>
> Dear Margaret,
>
> When the Republican Party was formed two years ago, we had no idea it would grow so quickly. I am so pleased with the party's choice of John Frémont as the Republican candidate for President. I know Mother would have agreed with me. I only hope you and I will be able to cast our votes in a presidential election soon.
>
> Your loving sister, Ellen

12. What is the letter about?

13. What is one statement directly related to the subject of the letter? Why is it relevant?

14. What is one statement that is irrelevant to the subject of the letter? Why is it irrelevant?

Test Yourself

1. **All of the following were causes of the Civil War EXCEPT**

   A John Brown's raid on Harpers Ferry.

   B the Dred Scott decision.

   C the use of child labor in northern factories.

   D the publication of Stowe's *Uncle Tom's Cabin*.

   Refer to the quotation below to answer Question 2.

   > "A house divided against itself cannot stand. . . . I do not expect the Union to be dissolved—I do not expect the house to fall—but I do expect it will cease to be divided. It will become all one thing or all the other."

2. **What division does this quotation describe?**

   A church and state

   B free states and slaveholding states

   C the House of Representatives and the Senate

   D Republicans and Democrats

Refer to the pie chart below to answer Question 3.

Percentage of Popular Vote, 1860

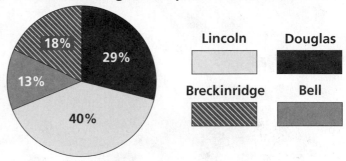

18%   29%   13%   40%

| Lincoln | Douglas |
| Breckinridge | Bell |

3. **What conclusion can you draw from this pie chart?**

   A Southerners voted for Douglas.

   B Lincoln won most of the popular vote.

   C Bell had little support in the North.

   D The two Democrats combined won more votes than Lincoln.

Document-Based Questions

Task: Look at Documents 1 and 2, and answer their accompanying questions. Then, use the documents and your knowledge of history to complete this writing assignment:

> Write a two-paragraph essay comparing the goals of the Fugitive Slave Law with its actual effects.

Document 1: In this speech, Senator John Calhoun of South Carolina explained the need for the Fugitive Slave Law. *According to Calhoun, what would happen if Congress did not pass the law?*

> "How can the Union be saved? . . . There is but one way . . . , and that is by adopting such measures as will satisfy . . . the southern section that they can remain in the Union consistently with their honor and their safety. . . .
>
> But can this be done? Yes, easily. . . . The North has only . . . to conced[e] to the South an equal right in [newly] acquired territory, and to caus[e] the stipulations relative to fugitive slaves to be faithfully fulfilled—to cease the agitation of the slave question. . . ."

Document 2: This poster reveals Bostonians' commitment to protect runaways or kidnapped African Americans. *Why were posters like this illegal?*

A MAN KIDNAPPED!
A PUBLIC MEETING AT
FANEUIL HALL!
WILL BE HELD
THIS FRIDAY EVEN'G,
May 26th, at 7 o'clock,
To secure Justice for A MAN CLAIMED AS A SLAVE by a
VIRGINIA KIDNAPPER!
And NOW IMPRISONED IN BOSTON COURT HOUSE, in defiance of the Laws of Massachusetts. Shall he be plunged into the Hell of Virginia Slavery by a Massachusetts Judge of Probate?
BOSTON, May 26th, 1854.

The Civil War

1861–1865

"The wild cries of charging lines, the rattle of musketry, the booming of artillery and the shrieks of wounded were ...like very hell itself...."

—Lt. Porter Farley,
140th New York Infantry Regiment

In a painting by Don Troiani, a Union soldier and a Confederate soldier fight during the Battle of Gettysburg.

CHAPTER 15

What You Will Learn

Section 1
THE CALL TO ARMS

As the war began and states took sides, the North and the South drew up plans and hoped for an early victory.

Section 2
EARLY YEARS OF THE WAR

The early years of the war were indecisive, as neither side seemed able to defeat the other.

Section 3
THE EMANCIPATION PROCLAMATION

President Lincoln's decision to issue the Emancipation Proclamation opened the way for African Americans to join the Union army.

Section 4
THE CIVIL WAR AND AMERICAN LIFE

The war caused divisions in both North and South while changing the lives of civilians and soldiers alike.

Section 5
DECISIVE BATTLES

Union victories at Gettysburg and Vicksburg in 1863 forced the South's surrender in April 1865.

⤺ Reading Skill

Understand Sequence In this chapter, you will learn to relate the chronological order of events and determine their relationships to one another.

509

How did people, places, and things

The Civil War

KEY

	Union states
	Confederate states
	U.S. Territories
	Union victory
	Union blockade
←	Union advance
	Confederate victory
←	Confederate advance

OR

WASHINGTON TERRITORY

DAKOTA TERRITORY

NEBRASKA TERRITORY

NEVADA TERRITORY

CA

UTAH TERRITORY

COLORADO TERRITORY

Glorieta Pass

NEW MEXICO TERRITORY

Valverde

MEXICO

Union and Confederate Resources, 1861

Population
2.5 to 1

Miles of railroad track
2.4 to 1

Wheat production
4.2 to 1

Iron production
15 to 1

Firearms production
32 to 1

Cotton production
1 to 24

■ Union resources   ■ Confederate resources

U.S. Events

1861 | Eleven states secede from the Union.

1862 | President Lincoln announces plan of emancipation.

Vicksburg surrenders to Union forces. | **1863**

1861   **1862**   **1863**

World Events

1861 | Napoleon III sends French troops to invade Mexico.

1862 | Otto von Bismarck becomes prime minister of Prussia.

VISUAL PREVIEW

MN
ME
WI
VT
MI
NH
NY
IA
MA
CT
RI
OH
PA
Antietam
Gettysburg
IL
IN
Bull Run
NJ
MD DE
VA
Fredericksburg
Chancellorsville
KS
MO
KY
Cold
Harbor
Chattanooga
Seven
Days
NC
Petersburg
TN
Chickamauga
Shiloh
SC
AR
INDIAN
TERRITORY
Atlanta
Fort Sumter
Atlantic
Ocean
AL
MS
GA
Vicksburg
N
TX
LA
W   E
Port
Hudson
FL
S
New Orleans
Sabine Pass
Gulf of Mexico
0   300 miles
Galveston
0   300 km
Albers Conic Equal-Area Projection

| 1863 | Union wins victory at Gettysburg. | Grant invades the South and lays siege to Petersburg. | 1864 | Lee surrenders at Appomattox. | 1865 |

1863   **1864**   **1865**

1864 | French-backed Maximilian of Austria becomes emperor of Mexico.

Miserable Conditions

❝Miserable as our condition was, that of the enlisted men was far worse. . . . There was no shelter for them. There was not enough food. They were thinly clad; many had no shoes, few had overcoats, and hundreds had only ragged trousers and shirt to cover their nakedness. ❞

—Maj. Abner B. Small, Sixteenth Maine Volunteers, *Memoirs of a Prisoner of War*

◄ Union troops

The Call to Arms

Objectives

- Identify the states that supported the Union, the states that seceded, and the states whose loyalties were divided.

- Describe the advantages each side had in the war.

- Compare the different strategies used by the North and the South.

- Summarize the results of the First Battle of Bull Run.

- Describe the conditions soldiers in camp faced.

◉ Reading Skill

Understand Sequence of Events The Civil War began as a result of a complex sequence of events. As that war proceeded in its early days, events continued at a furious pace. To form a full understanding of this phase of the war, pause regularly to summarize the sequence of events. Use your own words to recount the important events in the correct order.

Key Terms

border state   martial law
neutral   blockade

Why It Matters As two American nations prepared for war, many Northerners and Southerners were confident that their side would win a quick victory. They were wrong. The Civil War would be a long, bloody, and costly conflict.

❓ Section Focus Question: Why did each side in the Civil War think the war would be won easily?

Taking Sides in the War

Two days after Fort Sumter's surrender, President Lincoln declared that a rebellion existed in the South. To put it down, he asked the nation's governors to raise 75,000 troops. Across the North, young men eagerly volunteered. Support was so widespread that the governors of Ohio, Indiana, and several other states begged to send more troops than the President had requested.

More States Secede Not all states were so enthusiastic, however. In Tennessee, the governor said that his state "will not furnish a single man" to fight against "our southern brothers." The governors of Kentucky and Missouri made similar replies to Lincoln's request. Maryland and Delaware did not respond at all.

The President's call for troops led more southern states to secede. On April 17, Virginia left the Union. In May, Arkansas, Tennessee, and North Carolina also joined the Confederacy. However, the western counties of Virginia, where there was little support for slavery, refused to secede. In 1863, these 50 counties were admitted to the Union as the state of West Virginia.

The Border States Loyalties remained divided in the border states—slave states that did not secede. Delaware had few enslaved people, and its support of the Union was strong. However, many people in Kentucky, Missouri, and Maryland favored the South. Kentucky and Missouri were important to controlling the Ohio and Mississippi rivers. And unless the Union could hold Maryland, Washington would be surrounded by the Confederacy.

At first, Kentucky declared itself neutral, or not favoring either side. Union generals wanted to occupy Kentucky, but Lincoln refused. He feared that such a move would push the state to secede. His strategy was wise. When Confederate forces invaded it in September 1861, Kentucky decided to support the North.

By contrast, the President acted forcefully to hold Missouri and Maryland. When Missouri's government sided with the South, Union supporters set up their own state government. Fighting broke out within the state. Finally, Lincoln sent troops, and the state stayed in the Union throughout the war.

In Maryland, southern sympathizers destroyed railroad and telegraph lines. So Lincoln placed eastern Maryland under martial law. This is a type of rule in which the military is in charge and citizens' rights are suspended. Maryland officials and others suspected of disloyalty were jailed without trials.

Understand Sequence of Events
Summarize the events as North and South geared up for full-scale conflict. Make sure to recount events in the correct sequence.

✔**Checkpoint** How did the border states line up in the war?

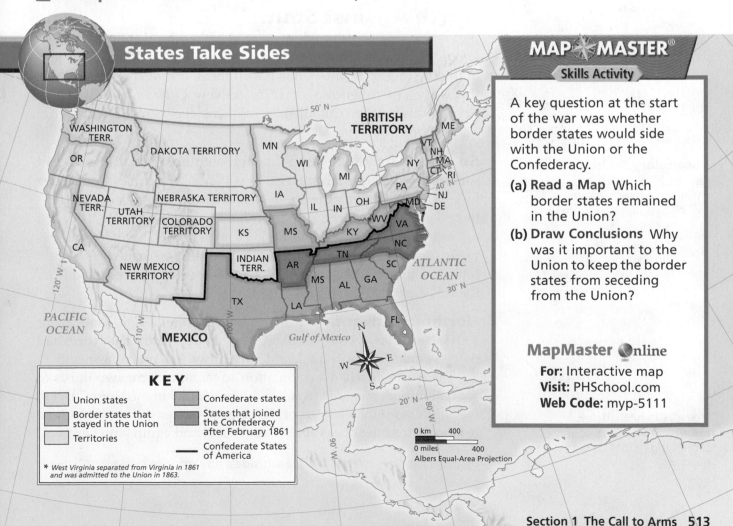

States Take Sides

MAP MASTER®

Skills Activity

A key question at the start of the war was whether border states would side with the Union or the Confederacy.

(a) Read a Map Which border states remained in the Union?

(b) Draw Conclusions Why was it important to the Union to keep the border states from seceding from the Union?

MapMaster Online
For: Interactive map
Visit: PHSchool.com
Web Code: myp-5111

KEY

Union states

Border states that stayed in the Union

Territories

Confederate states

States that joined the Confederacy after February 1861

Confederate States of America

* West Virginia separated from Virginia in 1861 and was admitted to the Union in 1863.

0 km 400
0 miles 400
Albers Equal-Area Projection

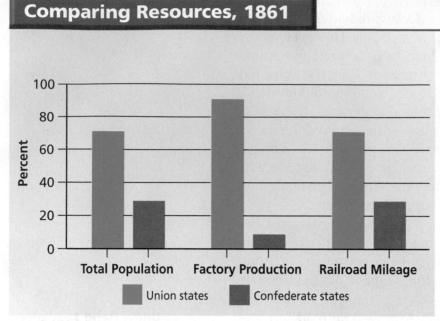

Comparing Resources, 1861

Percent (y-axis): 0, 20, 40, 60, 80, 100

Categories: Total Population, Factory Production, Railroad Mileage

Legend: Union states, Confederate states

Source: *The Times Atlas of World History*

Reading Charts
Skills Activity

The Union had an advantage over the Confederacy in a number of resources.

(a) **Read a Bar Graph** In which of the three comparisons is the Union's advantage the greatest?

(b) **Draw Conclusions** For each of these three resources, how would you expect the Union to benefit from its advantage?

(c) **Make Predictions** Based on the information in these graphs, which side would you expect to win the war? Explain.

North Against South

As the armies prepared, people on both sides were confident. A Union soldier declared that he was "willing . . . to lay down all my joys in this life to help maintain this government." Southerners compared themselves to Americans of 1776. A New Orleans poet wrote of Confederates: "Yes, call them rebels! 'tis the name/Their patriot fathers bore."

Vocabulary Builder
distinct (dihs TIHNKT) **adj.** clear or definite; different in quality

Southern Advantages Although outnumbered, the South had some <u>distinct</u> military advantages. To win, northern armies would have to invade and conquer the South. Confederates would be fighting on their own territory, with help from the local people.

In addition, most of the nation's experienced military officers were southerners. The Confederacy's three top generals—Albert Johnston, Joseph Johnston, and Robert E. Lee—all had resigned from the U.S. Army to fight for the South.

Northern Advantages In 1861, the United States had about 130,000 factories. Of those, 110,000 were in the North. The North had twice as much railroad track and almost twice as much farmland.

The North also had a population advantage. Some two thirds of the nation's people lived in states that remained in the Union, and in the South more than a third of the people were enslaved. With more <u>resources</u>, the North was able to field, feed, and equip larger armies.

Vocabulary Builder
resource (REE sors) **n.** supply of something to meet a particular need

✓**Checkpoint** What were each side's advantages?

The Two Sides Plan Strategies

Union leaders hoped to win a quick victory. To isolate the Confederacy, Lincoln had the navy blockade southern seaports. A **blockade** is a military action to prevent traffic from coming into an area or leaving it. Lincoln hoped to cut off the South's supply of manufactured goods and block overseas sales of cotton.

An important part of northern strategy was to gain control of the Mississippi River, the South's major transportation link. This would split the South in two. The Union also planned to invade Virginia and seize Richmond, the Confederate capital. It was just 100 miles from Washington, D.C.

The South's strategy was simpler. The Confederates did not need to invade the North. They had only to defend their land until northerners got tired of fighting. The Confederates sought aid from Britain and other European nations. They hoped that Britain's need of cotton for its textile mills would force the British to support the South.

☑**Checkpoint** How did strategies on the two sides differ?

Americans Against Americans

On both sides, men rushed to be part of the fight. "I had never dreamed that New England . . . could be fired with so warlike a spirit," wrote Mary Ashton Livermore in Boston. In South Carolina, Mary Chesnut said that men rushed to enlist in the army for "fear the war will be over before they get a sight of the fun."

This war between Americans broke families apart, setting brother against brother, father against son. Kentucky Senator John Crittenden had two sons in the war fighting on different sides. Four brothers of Mary Lincoln, the President's wife, fought for the Confederacy.

Old Enough for War
Soldiers in both the Union and Confederate armies might have been as young as 14. Nearly 4,000 Union troops were 16 or younger. **Critical Thinking: Draw Conclusions** *How do you think the experience of war affected young men?*

Fleeing Bull Run

Before the First Battle of Bull Run, both sides expected an easy victory. But they were wrong. Here, Union soldiers have panicked and are fleeing the Bull Run battlefield. Bull Run was an early sign that the war would be long and costly. **Critical Thinking: *Draw Conclusions*** *What reasons did each side have to think it would win an early victory? Why were both sides' expectations unreasonable?*

History *Interactive*

Explore the Lessons of a Battle
Visit: PHSchool.com
Web Code: myp-5177

The soldiers came from many backgrounds. Nearly half of the North's troops were farmers. One fourth were immigrants.

Three fourths of the South's 1 million white males between ages 18 and 45 served in the army. Two thirds of the 3.5 million northern males of the same age fought for the Union. Some soldiers were as young as 14.

✓Checkpoint Who were the soldiers in this war?

First Battle of Bull Run

Union General Irvin McDowell wanted time to turn his soldiers into an effective fighting force. But by July 1861, northern newspapers were demanding the capture of Richmond and a quick end to the war.

McDowell's 30,000 men left Washington and marched southwest into Virginia. About the same number of Confederates waited at Manassas, a railroad center about 25 miles away. Hundreds of people rode out from Washington to see the battle, expecting an easy Union victory.

The armies clashed along Bull Run, a river just north of Manassas, on July 21. At first, the Union army pushed forward. But a southern commander rallied his men to hold firm. "Look, there is Jackson with his Virginians, standing like a stone wall," he shouted. From then on, the general, Thomas Jackson, was known as "Stonewall" Jackson.

Slowly the battle turned in favor of the Confederates. The poorly trained Union troops began to panic. Soldiers and sightseers fled back to Washington. The Confederates were too exhausted to pursue them.

✓Checkpoint What was the result of the First Battle of Bull Run?

A Soldier's Life

Most soldiers spent three fourths of their time in camp, not fighting. Training took up to 10 hours a day. When not training, soldiers stood guard, wrote home, and gathered firewood. A meal might be simply a dry, cracker-like product called hardtack.

Harsh Conditions Camp conditions were often miserable, especially when wet weather created muddy roads and fields. The lack of clean water was a major health threat. Outbreaks of smallpox, typhoid fever, and other diseases swept through the ranks. It was not unusual for half the men in a regiment to be too sick to fight.

Prisoners of War Both sides built prison camps for captured soldiers. Overcrowded prison camps became deathtraps. Nearly 10 percent of soldiers who died in the war perished in prison camps.

The camps at Elmira, New York, and Andersonville, Georgia, were the worst. Elmira camp, built to hold 5,000 Confederate prisoners, held 10,000. The camp cut rations to bread and water, forcing prisoners to eat rats to survive. Thousands died. At Andersonville, nearly 35,000 Union soldiers lived in a fenced, open field intended to hold 10,000 men. As many as 100 prisoners died each day, usually from starvation or exposure.

Hardtack

✓**Checkpoint** **What conditions did soldiers have to endure?**

☆ **Looking Back and Ahead** The North's hopes for an early victory had been dashed. The war would be long and brutal. In the next section, you will read more about the early years of the war.

Section 1 | **Check Your Progress**

Progress Monitoring Online
For: Self-test with instant help
Visit: PHSchool.com
Web Code: mya-5111

Comprehension and Critical Thinking

1. **(a) Recall** How did President Lincoln respond to the surrender of Fort Sumter?
   (b) Apply Information What caused three border states to remain in the Union?

2. **(a) List** What were three advantages held by the South? What were three advantages held by the North?
   (b) Analyze Cause and Effect How did the First Battle of Bull Run shatter the belief that the Civil War would be a quick Union victory?

Reading Skill

3. **Understand Sequence of Events** Choose a state that wavered about supporting North or the South. Summarize the sequence of events that led this state to a final decision.

Key Terms

Complete each of the following sentences so that the second part explains the first and shows your understanding of the key term.

4. Union leaders planned a blockade; _____.

5. Lincoln placed Maryland under martial law; _____.

Writing

6. Create an outline that covers the information presented in this section, copying the form below. A few entries have been filled in.

   I. Taking sides in the war (first important topic)
   A. More states secede (first issue for that topic)
   1. A number of border states refused to send troops to support the Union (first point)
   2. _____ (second point)
   B.
   1.
   2.

   II.

Battlefield Report

❝Our men were vomiting with excessive fatigue, over-exhaustion, and sunstroke; our tongues were parched and cracked for water, and our faces blackened with powder and smoke, and our dead and wounded were piled indiscriminately in the trenches.❞

—Confederate soldier, describing a battle in Georgia

◀ Confederate troops

Early Years of the War

Objectives

- Explain how new weapons made fighting the war more dangerous.
- Describe the course of the war in the East in 1862.
- Describe the early days of the war in the West and at sea.

Reading Skill

Distinguish Events in Sequence As you read this section, it is important to keep events in sequence. Ask yourself: Which event happened first? Next? Last? You might number events to help you organize their sequence. This will help you to understand the unfolding drama of the Civil War.

Key Terms and People

ironclad
George McClellan

casualty
Ulysses S. Grant

Why It Matters The Union's crushing defeat at Bull Run made northerners realize that a long and difficult struggle lay ahead. Both the North and South tried to find the strategies and the leaders that would ensure victory and preserve their way of life.

❓ **Section Focus Question: How did each side in the war try to gain an advantage over the other?**

New Technology in the War

New weapons made the Civil War more deadly than any previous war. Traditionally, generals had relied on an all-out charge of troops to overwhelm the enemy. But new rifles and cannons were far more accurate and had a greater range than the old muskets and artillery. They could also be loaded much faster. As a result, the attacking army could be bombarded long before it arrived at the defenders' position.

Unfortunately, Civil War generals were slow to recognize the problem and change tactics. Thousands of soldiers on both sides were slaughtered by following orders to cross open fields against these deadly new weapons.

Both sides also made use of **ironclads.** These were warships covered with protective iron plates. Cannon fire bounced harmlessly off this armor. The most famous naval battle of the war occurred when two ironclads, the Union's *Monitor* and the Confederacy's *Merrimack,* fought to a draw in March 1862. The use of ironclads marked the end of thousands of years of wooden warships. The Confederates used ironclads against the Union's naval blockade. Ironclad Union gunboats played an important role in the North's efforts to gain control of the Mississippi River.

✔**Checkpoint** What new technologies were used in the Civil War?

The War in the East

After the Union's defeat at Bull Run, Lincoln removed McDowell and put General George McClellan in command. The general was a good organizer, but he was very cautious. For seven months, he trained his army but did not attack. "If General McClellan does not want to use the army," a frustrated Lincoln complained, "I would like to borrow it for a time."

In March 1862, McClellan was finally ready. He moved some 100,000 soldiers by boat along Chesapeake Bay to a peninsula southeast of Richmond. As McClellan advanced toward the Confederate capital, he discovered that his force was far superior to the 15,000 enemy soldiers blocking the way. However, McClellan still did not have as many soldiers as he wanted because Lincoln had ordered 37,000 soldiers to stay behind to guard Washington, D.C. The general stopped his advance and asked for more troops.

McClellan waited nearly a month before moving again. This delay gave the Confederates time to reinforce their small army of defenders. On May 31, 1862, the Confederates stopped McClellan's advance near Richmond. In late June, McClellan had to retreat.

With Richmond no longer threatened, Lee decided to invade the North. He hoped that a victory on Union soil would help win support for the South in Europe and turn northern public opinion against the war. In early September, he slipped his army into western Maryland.

Now McClellan had a stroke of luck. A Union officer found a paper showing Lee's battle plan. McClellan thus learned that the Confederate army had divided into two parts.

Vocabulary Builder
superior (sah PIR ee ahr) **adj.** of greater importance or value; above average

Vocabulary Builder
reinforce (ree ihn FORS) **v.** to make stronger; to make more effective

● **INFOGRAPHIC**

Battle of Two Ironclads

The Civil War introduced ironclad warships. Here, an artist shows the battle between the Confederacy's *Merrimack* (left) and the Union's *Monitor* (right) off Hampton Roads, Virginia, in 1862.
Critical Thinking: *Draw Conclusions* *How would you expect an ironclad ship to fare in a battle against an older warship that lacked armor? Explain.*

▲ Inset shows the recovery of the *Monitor's* turret, or gun chamber, in 2002.

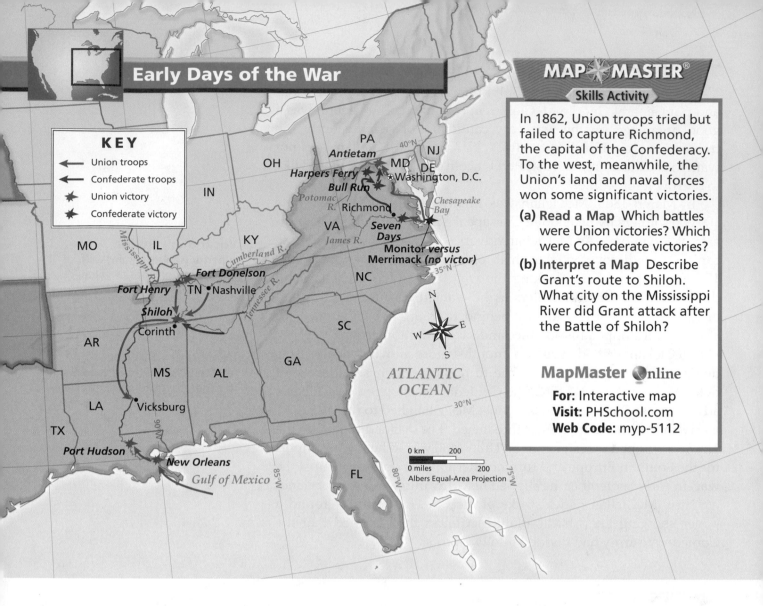

KEY

← Union troops
← Confederate troops
★ Union victory
★ Confederate victory

PA
Antietam
OH
NJ
Harpers Ferry
MD
DE
Bull Run
Washington, D.C.
IN
Potomac R.
Richmond
Chesapeake Bay
VA
Seven Days
Monitor *versus* Merrimack *(no victor)*
MO
IL
Mississippi R.
KY
James R.
35°N
Fort Donelson
NC
Cumberland R.
Fort Henry
TN
Nashville
Shiloh
Tennessee R.
SC
Corinth
AR
GA
MS
AL
ATLANTIC OCEAN
LA
Vicksburg
TX
30°N
Port Hudson
New Orleans
Gulf of Mexico
FL
85°W
80°W
75°W

0 km   200
0 miles   200
Albers Equal-Area Projection

N W E S

MAP★MASTER®
Skills Activity

In 1862, Union troops tried but failed to capture Richmond, the capital of the Confederacy. To the west, meanwhile, the Union's land and naval forces won some significant victories.

(a) Read a Map Which battles were Union victories? Which were Confederate victories?

(b) Interpret a Map Describe Grant's route to Shiloh. What city on the Mississippi River did Grant attack after the Battle of Shiloh?

MapMaster ○nline

For: Interactive map
Visit: PHSchool.com
Web Code: myp-5112

McClellan's troops attacked the larger part of Lee's army at Antietam Creek, near Sharpsburg, Maryland, on September 17, 1862. This was the bloodiest day of the Civil War. The Union army attacked again and again. It suffered about 12,000 casualties—the military term for persons killed, wounded, or missing in action. Lee lost nearly 14,000 men—almost one third of his army. He was forced to pull his battered army back into Virginia. To Lincoln's dismay, McClellan did not press his advantage by pursuing Lee.

Neither side won a clear victory at the Battle of Antietam. But because Lee had ordered a retreat, the North claimed victory.

✓Checkpoint How did McClellan's caution hurt the Union?

The War in the West

As McClellan moved cautiously, Union armies in the West went on the attack. General **Ulysses S. Grant** led the most successful of these armies. McClellan and Grant were very different. McClellan wore carefully fitted uniforms. Grant, once a poor store clerk, wore rumpled clothes. McClellan was cautious. Grant took chances.

Union forces made major advances in western land and naval battles in 1862, seizing control of most of the Mississippi River. In February 1862, Grant moved his army south from Kentucky. First, he captured Fort Henry on the Tennessee River. Then, he captured Fort Donelson on the Cumberland River.

Two water routes into the western Confederacy were now wide open. Grant's army continued south along the Tennessee River toward Corinth, Mississippi, an important railroad center.

Before Grant could advance on Corinth, Confederate General Albert Sidney Johnston attacked. On April 6, 1862, he surprised Grant's troops at the Battle of Shiloh. (For more on this battle, see the Geography and History feature in this chapter.)

The Battle of Shiloh was costly yet important for both sides. The South suffered nearly 11,000 casualties and the North more than 13,000. However, the Union forced the Confederate army to withdraw from the railroad center. Union forces also gained control of western Tennessee and part of the Mississippi River.

Two weeks after the Battle of Shiloh, a Union fleet commanded by David Farragut entered the Mississippi River from the Gulf of Mexico. On April 26, Farragut captured New Orleans, Louisiana. By summer, nearly the entire river was in Union hands.

Distinguish Events in Sequence What was the sequence of battles in the West? When did these occur?

☑**Checkpoint** **What was the result of the Battle of Shiloh?**

☆ **Looking Back and Ahead** Northern and southern generals both tried to carry the war into enemy territory. At first, neither side gained a decisive advantage. In the next section, you will read how the Emancipation Proclamation changed the nature of the war.

Section 2 | Check Your Progress

Progress Monitoring ⬤nline
For: Self-test with instant help
Visit: PHSchool.com
Web Code: mya-5112

Comprehension and Critical Thinking

1. (a) Describe Explain how new weapons made the Civil War more deadly than previous American wars.
(b) Evaluate Information How did harsh conditions and new technology result in a high number of casualties?

2. (a) Summarize Why was General McClellan considered to be an ineffective leader?
(b) Organize Information Make a chart that shows the place, casualties, leaders, outcome, and importance of the battles at Shiloh and Antietam Creek.

🔁 Reading Skill

3. Distinguish Events in Sequence During the Battle of Shiloh, which came first: Grant captured Fort Henry, Johnston attacked, Grant won a stunning victory? Identify the signal clues that you used.

Key Terms
Read each sentence. If the sentence is true, write YES. If the sentence is not true, write NO and explain why.
4. Both the Union and the Confederacy suffered many casualties.
5. Ironclads were of little importance in the war at sea.

Writing

6. Use library or Internet resources to find more information about one of the topics covered in this section. Suggestions for topics include the ironclad warships, the Battle of Shiloh, or the Battle of Antietam. Then, write a short introduction to a research paper that would present information about the topic.

The Battle of Shiloh

In April 1862, the Confederacy seized an opportunity to attack Union forces in the West. Two Union armies were attempting to join each other in south-western Tennessee. Confederate troops were camped close by in Corinth, Mississippi. The Confederates attacked near Pittsburgh Landing, Tennessee, on April 6, hoping to crush one Union force before the other could arrive.

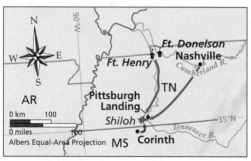

Confederate troops attacked Union forces at the Battle of Shiloh.

KEY

← Union troops

← Confederate troops

1 A Sunken Road

The initial Confederate attack caught Union troops by surprise. They retreated a mile before establishing a defensive position along a sunken road. Troops crouched behind the road bank and fought off a dozen Confederate charges.

2 Exposed to Counterattack

Confederate troops marched toward the Union position without the protection of trees or foxholes. Every charge was met with a flurry of bullets from Union soldiers using vegetation and raised mounds of earth as cover.

Understand Effects:
A Bloody Victory

The Battle of Shiloh was one of the bloodiest engagements of the Civil War. Although the Union emerged the victor, both sides suffered heavy losses. Union General Ulysses S. Grant would continue to guide his army as it gradually seized control of the entire Mississippi Valley.

◀ Rifle bullets

Confederate jacket ▶

3 The "Hornet's Nest"

As the battle wore on, the Confederates nicknamed the Union position the "Hornet's Nest" because of the intense fire the Confederate soldiers encountered. Union bullets caused many Confederate injuries. One officer's jacket shows the devastating results of the battle.

Analyze **GEOGRAPHY AND HISTORY**

Write a paragraph explaining how northern troops used geography to give themselves an advantage over the Confederates.

Justice Has Awakened

❝After two hundred years of bondage and suffering a returning sense of justice has awakened the great body of American people to make amends for the unprovoked wrongs committed against us for over two hundred years. **❞**

—African American Tennesseans,
letter to the Federal Government, 1865

The Emancipation Proclamation

Objectives

- Explain why Lincoln issued the Emancipation Proclamation.
- Identify the effects of the proclamation.
- Describe the contributions of African Americans to the Union.

🔁 Reading Skill

Explain How Events Are Related in Time President Lincoln and others made many choices in fighting the war. They made these choices in the context of the events at the time. When reading about history, it is important to see how events in a period are related in time. Do events influence the attitudes and decisions of people going forward in time? Do they change people's actions and freedoms?

Key Terms and People

emancipate
Horace Greeley

Why It Matters President Lincoln had been reluctant to abolish slavery. But he changed his mind. His Emancipation Proclamation would dramatically alter the nature of the war, the lives of African Americans, and the future of the United States.

❓ Section Focus Question: What were the causes and effects of the Emancipation Proclamation?

Emancipating the Enslaved

Many abolitionists rejoiced when the war began. They urged Lincoln to end slavery and thus punish the South for starting the war.

Lincoln Changes His Mind At first, the President resisted. He knew most northerners did not want to end slavery. "You . . . overestimate the number in the country who hold such views," he told one abolitionist. He feared that any action to emancipate, or free, enslaved African Americans might make the border states secede.

Lincoln said his goal was to restore the Union, even if that meant letting slavery continue. He stated this very clearly in a letter to abolitionist newspaper publisher Horace Greeley.

❝If I could save the Union without freeing *any* slave, I would do it, and if I could save it by freeing *all* the slaves, I would do it. . . . What I do about slavery . . . I do because I believe it helps to save the Union.**❞**

Gradually, Lincoln began to change his mind. He realized how important slavery was to the South's war effort. He told his Cabinet that he intended to issue an Emancipation Proclamation. But Cabinet members advised him to wait until after a success on the battlefield.

A Famous Proclamation On September 22, 1862, a few days after Lee's retreat from Antietam, Lincoln met again with his Cabinet and issued a <u>preliminary</u> proclamation.

On January 1, 1863, Lincoln issued the final Emancipation Proclamation. This document had little immediate effect, however, because it freed enslaved people only in areas that were fighting the Union. Those were places where the Union had no power. The proclamation did not apply to parts of the South already under Union control. Nor did it free anyone in the border states.

The proclamation was both criticized and praised. Some abolitionists said it should be applied throughout the country. White southerners accused Lincoln of trying to cause a slave revolt. But many Union soldiers were enthusiastic. They welcomed anything that weakened the South. "This army will <u>sustain</u> the Emancipation Proclamation and enforce it with the bayonet," an Indiana soldier said.

Effects of the Proclamation Even though the proclamation freed few slaves at first, it had other important effects. Above all, it changed the Civil War into a struggle for freedom. This was no longer just a fight to save the nation. It was now also a fight to end slavery.

Vocabulary Builder
<u>preliminary</u> (pree LIM uh nehr ee) *adj.* leading up to the main action

Vocabulary Builder
<u>sustain</u> (suh STAYN) *v.* to keep going; to endure; to supply with food; to support as just

The Emancipation Proclamation

❝That on the first day of January, in the year of our Lord [1863], all persons held as slaves within any State or designated part of a State, the people whereof shall then be in rebellion against the United States, shall be then, thenceforward, and forever free. . . .❞

—Emancipation Proclamation, January 1, 1863

A Union general posted the announcement at right, declaring the freedom of enslaved African Americans in the part of Virginia occupied by his troops.

FREEDOM TO SLAVES!

Whereas, the President of the United States did, on the first day of the present month, issue his *Proclamation* declaring "that *all persons held as Slaves in certain designated States, and parts of States, are, and henceforward shall be free,"* and that the Executive Government of the United States, including the Military and Naval authorities thereof, would recognize and maintain the freedom of said persons. *And Whereas,* the county of Frederick is included in the territory designated by the Proclamation of the President, in which the *Slaves should become free,* I therefore hereby notify the citizens of the city of Winchester, and of said County, of said Proclamation, and of my intention to maintain and enforce the same.

I expect all citizens to yield a ready compliance with the Proclamation of the Chief Executive, and I admonish all persons disposed to resist its peaceful enforcement, that upon manifesting such disposition by acts, they will be regarded as rebels in arms against the lawful authority of the Federal Government and dealt with accordingly.

All persons liberated by said Proclamation are admonished to abstain from all violence, and immediately betake themselves to useful occupations.

The officers of this command are admonished and ordered to act in accordance with said proclamation and to yield their ready co-operation in its enforcement.

Winchester Va
Jan. 5th, 1863.

R. H. Milroy,
Brig. Gen'l Commanding.

Reading Primary Sources
Skills Activity

President Lincoln's proclamation specified that it applied only to certain parts of the United States.

(a) **Understand Sequence** In what order were these two declarations issued?

(b) **Compare** In what way is the declaration on the right more specific than the one by President Lincoln?

African American Soldiers
These are guards of the 107th Colored Infantry at Fort Corcoran in Washington, D.C. **Critical Thinking: Apply Information** *How did conditions for African American soldiers differ from those for white soldiers?*

Explain How Events Are Related in Time
Explain why these two events are related in time: African American soldiers fought for the Union; President Lincoln issued the Emancipation Proclamation.

Also, the Emancipation Proclamation dashed any hopes that Britain would recognize the South's independence. Britain would not help a government that was fighting to keep people enslaved.

In both the North and the South, Lincoln's proclamation united African Americans in support of the war. "We shout for joy that we live to record this righteous decree," wrote Frederick Douglass.

✓**Checkpoint**   **How did the proclamation affect the war?**

African Americans Help the Union

Slavery existed in small amounts in the North before the Emancipation Proclamation. Enslaved Africans labored in port towns of New England, and inland they worked in homes or as laborers. But even as African Americans were freed in the North, they received unequal treatment. African American volunteers were not permitted to join the Union army until after the Emancipation Proclamation.

Volunteering for Service Ultimately, 189,000 African Americans served in the Union army or navy. More than half were former slaves who had escaped or been freed by the fighting. All faced extra risks. If captured, they were not treated as prisoners of war. Most were returned to slavery and some were killed.

Black and white sailors served together on warships. In the army, however, African American soldiers served in all-black regiments under white officers. They earned less pay than white soldiers.

Despite these disadvantages, African American regiments fought with pride and courage. "They make better soldiers in every respect than any troops I have ever had under my command," a Union general said of an African American regiment from Kansas.

African American troops took part in about 40 major battles and hundreds of minor ones. The most famous was the attack on Fort Wagner in South Carolina by the 54th Massachusetts Infantry on July 18, 1863. The unit volunteered to lead the assault. As the soldiers charged, Confederate cannon fire rained down. Yet the 54th reached the top of the fort's walls before being turned back in fierce hand-to-hand fighting. The regiment suffered terrible losses. Nearly half of its soldiers were casualties.

Thousands of African Americans supported the Union in noncombat roles. Free northern and emancipated southern African Americans often worked for Union armies as cooks, wagon drivers, and hospital aides.

Resisting Slavery In the South, many enslaved African Americans did what they could to hurt the Confederate war effort. Some provided military and other kinds of information to Union armies. Enslaved people had always quietly resisted slavery by deliberately working slowly or damaging equipment. But with many slaveholders off fighting the war, large numbers of slaves refused to work.

✔**Checkpoint** How did African Americans help the Union cause?

⭐ **Looking Back and Ahead** The Emancipation Proclamation made the Civil War a fight to end slavery. After the war, the Thirteenth Amendment banned slavery throughout the nation. The next section tells how the war affected civilians on both sides.

Section 3 | **Check Your Progress**

Progress Monitoring Online
For: Self-test with instant help
Visit: PHSchool.com
Web Code: mya-5113

Comprehension and Critical Thinking

1. (a) **Identify** Why did Lincoln at first resist identifying slavery as an issue of the Civil War?
(b) **Analyze Cause and Effect** What effect did the Emancipation Proclamation have on slavery?

2. (a) **Recall** In what ways did African Americans participate in the Civil War?
(b) **Explain Problems** What were three problems faced by African American soldiers?

🔄 **Reading Skill**

3. **Explain How Events Are Related in Time** Identify events that happened after the Emancipation Proclamation. Explain how these events are connected.

Key Terms

4. Write two definitions for emancipate. First, write a formal definition for your teacher. Second, write a definition in everyday English for a classmate.

Writing

5. Use library or Internet resources to find information about the African American 54th Massachusetts Infantry. Then, list the subtopics to be included in a research paper about the regiment. Write a paragraph about one of those subtopics. Identify some photographs and other nontext items that you would include in a research report on the 54th.

A Nurse's Day

" [Today] I have covered crutches, ripped up arm slings, washed and made them over, gone to commissary with order from doctor for material for pads for wounded or amputated limbs. . . . "

—Elvira Powers,
a nurse at a Northern hospital, 1863

▲ A nurse cares for an injured soldier.

The Civil War and American Life

Objectives

- Explain how opposition to the war caused problems for both sides.
- Identify the reasons that both sides passed draft laws.
- Describe the economic hardships the war caused in the North and the South.
- Describe the contributions of women to the war effort.

🎯 Reading Skill

Explain How Events Are Related in Time As soldiers were fighting the Civil War on the battlefield, Americans in both the North and the South were facing other wartime challenges. You will have a better understanding of the Civil War Era if you can relate events on the battlefield to events in civilian life.

Key Terms

habeas corpus   income tax
draft   inflation

Why It Matters The Civil War was not just about the winning and losing of battles and the freeing of slaves. The conflict affected men and women from all walks of life. In both the North and the South, civilians had to cope with the pains of war.

❷ Section Focus Question: How did the war affect people and politics in the North and the South?

Divisions Over the War

The Civil War not only divided the nation. It also caused divisions *within* the North and the South. Not all northerners supported a war to end slavery or even to restore the Union. Not all white southerners supported a war to defend slavery or secession.

Division in the South In the South, opposition to the war was strongest in Georgia and North Carolina. Barely half of Georgians supported secession. There were nearly 100 peace protests in North Carolina in 1863 alone. Yet only Virginia provided more troops to Confederate armies than did North Carolina. Generally, regions with large slaveholding plantations supported the war more strongly than poor back-country regions, where there were fewer enslaved people.

Strong support for states' rights created other divisions. For example, South Carolina's governor objected to officers from other states leading South Carolina troops. And the governors of Georgia and North Carolina did not want the Confederate government to force men from their states to do military service.

Division in the North Northerners were also divided over the war. Many opposed the Emancipation Proclamation. Others believed that the South had a right to secede. Some northern Democrats blamed Lincoln and the Republicans for forcing the South into a war. Northern Democrats who opposed the war were called Copperheads, after the poisonous snake. Copperheads were strongest in Ohio, Indiana, and Illinois. They criticized the war and called for peace with the Confederacy.

Dealing With Disruptions Some people on both sides tried to disrupt the war effort. A common tactic was to encourage soldiers to desert. Some northerners helped Confederate prisoners of war to escape. In the South, peace groups tried to end the war by working against the Confederacy. They tried to prevent men from volunteering for military service and urged Confederate soldiers to desert.

To deal with such problems, both Lincoln and Confederate President Jefferson Davis suspended the right of habeas corpus in some places during the war. Habeas corpus is a constitutional protection against unlawful imprisonment. It empowers judges to order that imprisoned persons be brought into court to determine if they are being legally held. In the North, more than 13,000 people were arrested and jailed without trials.

Reading Skill

Explain How Events Are Related in Time As the Civil War progressed on the battlefield, what was happening at home? Include information about both North and South in your answer.

✓**Checkpoint** How did the Civil War divide both North and South?

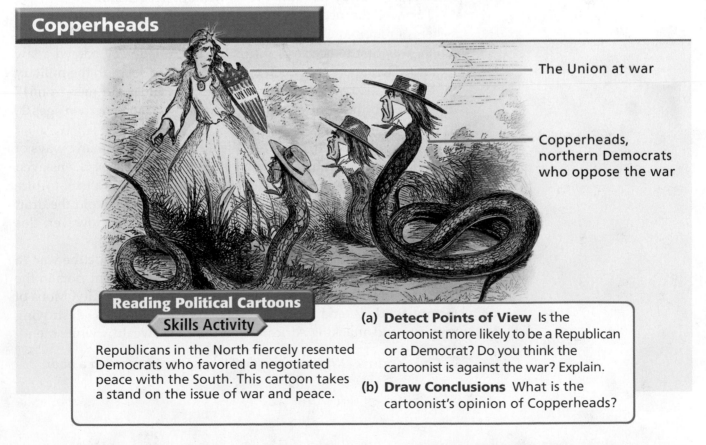

Copperheads

The Union at war

Copperheads, northern Democrats who oppose the war

Reading Political Cartoons

Skills Activity

Republicans in the North fiercely resented Democrats who favored a negotiated peace with the South. This cartoon takes a stand on the issue of war and peace.

(a) Detect Points of View Is the cartoonist more likely to be a Republican or a Democrat? Do you think the cartoonist is against the war? Explain.

(b) Draw Conclusions What is the cartoonist's opinion of Copperheads?

Join or Be Drafted
Volunteers rushed to enlist at first, but antiwar feeling soon grew. During the New York draft riots of 1863, a mob set fire to a home for African American orphans.
Critical Thinking: *Detect Points of View* *What motivated the people who rioted against the draft?*

The Draft Laws

Desertion was a problem for both sides. Between 300,000 and 550,000 Union and Confederate soldiers left their units and went home. About half returned after their crops were planted or harvested. However, at times, from one third to one half of an army's soldiers were away from their units without permission.

To meet the need for troops, each side established a draft, a system of required military service. The South, with its smaller population, was first to act. In April 1862, the Confederacy passed a law requiring white men between ages 18 and 35 to serve in the military for three years. Later, the age range expanded to cover men from 17 to 50. The North adopted a similar draft law in 1863, for men ages 20 to 45.

Exceptions existed, however. Wealthy people had many ways of escaping fighting. In the South, a man who held at least 20 enslaved people did not have to serve. Both sides allowed draftees to hire substitutes to serve in their place. Northerners could avoid the draft by paying the government $300. For many workers, however, this was about a year's pay.

People on both sides complained that the draft made the war "a poor man's fight." Anger against the draft led to violent riots in the North in July 1863. The worst took place in New York City. Mobs of factory workers and laborers rioted for several days, destroying property and attacking African Americans and wealthy white men.

☑**Checkpoint** Why was the Civil War sometimes called a poor man's fight?

The War and Economic Strains

Northern industries boomed as they turned out goods the Union needed in the war. Plenty of jobs were available. But the draft drained away workers so there was a constant shortage.

To pay the costs of fighting the war, Congress <u>levied</u> the first income tax in American history in August 1861. An income tax is a tax on the money people receive. The Union also printed $400 million of paper money to help pay its expenses. This was the first federal paper money, or <u>currency</u>. Putting this additional money into circulation led to inflation, or a general rise in prices. In the North, the prices of goods increased an average of 80 percent during the war.

The South was less able than the North to sustain a war. The Union blockade prevented the South from raising money by selling cotton overseas. Shortages made goods more expensive. This led to much greater inflation than in the North. A pair of shoes that had cost $18 dollars in 1862 cost up to $800 in the South in 1864. The price of a pound of beef soared from 12 cents in 1862 to $8 in 1865.

Southern food production fell as invading Union armies destroyed farmland and crops. Shortages of food led to riots in some southern cities. In Richmond, more than 1,000 women looted shops for food, cloth, and shoes in 1863. A woman in North Carolina complained:

> **❝**A crowd of we poor women went to Greensboro yesterday for something to eat as we do not have a mouthful of bread nor meat. . . . I have 6 little children and my husband in the army and what am I to do?**❞**
>
> —farm woman in North Carolina, April 1863

Enslaved people also suffered from wartime shortages. What little they did have was often seized by Confederate soldiers.

✓Checkpoint   **What strains did the war put on people?**

Women in the Civil War

Women in both the North and the South contributed to the war in many ways. At least 400 women disguised themselves as men and joined the Union or Confederate armies. Others became spies behind enemy lines. Many women took over businesses, farms, and plantations while their fathers, brothers, and husbands served on the battlefields.

In both North and South, women ran farms and plantations. Some southern women worked in the fields to help meet the needs of the Confederacy. They continued to work despite fighting that destroyed their crops and killed their livestock.

Women also ran many northern farms. "I saw more women driving teams [of horses] on the road and saw more at work in the fields than men," a traveler in Iowa reported in 1862.

Vocabulary Builder
<u>levy</u> (LEHV ee) **v.** to impose by law

Vocabulary Builder
<u>currency</u> (KER rehn see) **n.** money used to make purchases

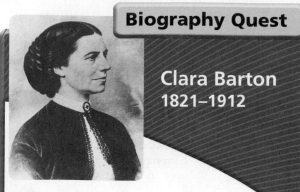

Biography Quest

Clara Barton
1821–1912

Before the Civil War, Clara Barton was a clerk in the U.S. Patent Office. When hostilities began, she became a nurse. Her work under dangerous conditions earned her the nickname Angel of the Battlefield from her Union and Confederate patients.

After the war, Barton worked for a time with the International Red Cross. Returning to the United States, Barton helped set up an American branch of the Red Cross.

Biography Quest Online

How did Barton become involved in a European war?

For: The answer to the question about Barton

Visit: PHSchool.com

Web Code: myd-5114

Women on both sides did factory work. Some performed dangerous jobs, such as making ammunition. Others took government jobs. For example, the Confederate government employed dozens of women to sign and number Confederate currency.

The war created many new opportunities for women. Some women became teachers. About 10,000 northern women became nurses. Men had dominated these professions before the war.

Barriers to women especially fell in the field of nursing. Elizabeth Blackwell, America's first female physician, trained nurses for the Union army. Social reformer Dorothea Dix became the head of Union army nurses. Harriet Tubman, who continued to lead enslaved people to freedom during the war, also served as a Union nurse. Clara Barton cared for wounded soldiers on the battlefield. Although nursing was not considered a "proper" job for respectable southern women, some volunteered anyway.

✓**Checkpoint** How did the war affect women?

☆ **Looking Back and Ahead** Both sides suffered political and economic hardships during the war. Draft laws affected every family, while new jobs opened up for women. In the next section, you will read how the war finally ended in the defeat of the Confederacy.

Section 4 | **Check Your Progress**

Progress Monitoring Online
For: Self-test with instant help
Visit: PHSchool.com
Web Code: mya-5114

Comprehension and Critical Thinking

1. (a) Identify What were two reasons some northerners opposed the war? What were two reasons some southerners opposed the war?
(b) Explain Problems Why did the military draft lead some people to describe the war as a poor man's fight?

2. (a) Describe Explain the changing role for women during the Civil War.
(b) Identify Costs What effects did the Civil War have on the economies of the North and of the South?

⟳ Reading Skill

3. Explain How Events Are Related in Time What was happening to the American economy as the Civil War raged on?

Key Terms

4. Draw a table with four rows and three columns. In the first column, list the key terms from this section: habeas corpus, draft, income tax, inflation. In the next column, write the definition of each term. In the last column, make a small illustration that shows the meaning of the term.

Writing

5. Reread the text under the heading "Women in the Civil War." Then, write a short paragraph about the role that women played in the Civil War. Include material directly quoted from this section. Be sure to copy the quotation exactly, to punctuate it correctly, and to identify the source.

A Valiant Foe

❝I felt . . . sad and depressed at the downfall of a foe who had fought so long and valiantly, and had suffered so much for a cause, though that cause was, I believe, one of the worst for which a people ever fought.❞

—General Grant, expressing his feelings about General Lee

◄ General Grant (left) accepts General Lee's surrender.

Decisive Battles

Objectives
- Describe the significance of the battles at Vicksburg and Gettysburg.
- Explain how Union generals used a new type of war to defeat the Confederacy.
- Explain how the war ended.

🎯 Reading Skill

Relate Events in a Sequence Events in sequence are often connected by a cause-and-effect link. One event causes an event that occurs next. This event in turn can cause another to occur. As you read Section 5, look for sequential events, and then determine if they have a cause-and-effect relationship. Remember, however, that not all events in sequence have this link.

Key Terms and People

siege   total war
William Tecumseh
   Sherman

Why It Matters By 1863, the Civil War had produced hundreds of thousands of dead and wounded. As the fighting raged on, there seemed to be no end in sight. But decisive battles at Gettysburg and Vicksburg would change the war's course and enable the Union to win the Civil War.

❷ Section Focus Question: How did Lincoln and his generals turn the tide of the war?

The Tide Turns

After the Union victory at the 1862 Battle of Antietam, the war again began to go badly for the North. As before, the problem was poor leadership. When McClellan failed to pursue Lee's beaten army, Lincoln replaced him with General Ambrose Burnside.

Confederate Victories Burnside knew McClellan had been fired for being too cautious. So Burnside decided on a bold stroke. In December 1862, he marched his army of 120,000 men directly toward Richmond. Lee massed 75,000 men at Fredericksburg, Virginia, to block their path. Using traditional tactics, Burnside ordered charge after charge. The Union suffered nearly 13,000 casualties in the Battle of Fredericksburg and the Confederates nearly 5,000.

Lincoln next turned to General Joseph Hooker, nicknamed "Fighting Joe." "May God have mercy on General Lee, for I will have none," Hooker boasted as he marched the Union army toward Richmond. In May 1863, Hooker's army was smashed at the Battle of Chancellorsville by a force that was half its size. But the victory was a costly one for the South. During the battle, Stonewall Jackson was shot and wounded. A few days later, Jackson died.

The Battle of Gettysburg

These Confederate victories made Lee bolder. He was convinced that a major victory on Union soil would force northerners to end the war. In June 1863, Lee's troops crossed Maryland and marched into Pennsylvania. The Union army, which was now commanded by General George Meade, pursued them.

On July 1, some Confederate soldiers approached the quiet town of Gettysburg. They were looking for shoes, which were in short supply in the South because of the Union blockade. Instead of shoes, the Confederates <u>encountered</u> part of Meade's army. Shots were exchanged. More troops joined the fight on both sides. By evening, the southerners had pushed the Union forces back through Gettysburg.

The next day, more than 85,000 Union soldiers faced some 75,000 Confederates. The center of the Union army was on a hill called Cemetery Ridge. The center of the Confederate position was nearly a mile away, on Seminary Ridge. The fighting raged into the next day as Confederate troops attacked each end of the Union line.

On the afternoon of July 3, Lee ordered an all-out attack on the center of the Union line. General George E. Pickett led about 15,000 Confederates across nearly a mile of open field toward Cemetery Ridge. As they advanced, Union artillery shells and rifle fire rained down on them. Only a few hundred men reached the Union lines, and they were quickly driven back. About 7,500 Confederates were killed or wounded in what is known as Pickett's Charge.

Vocabulary Builder

<u>encounter</u> (ehn KOWN ter) **v.** to meet in an unexpected way; to experience

Final Battles of the Civil War

MAP MASTER®

Skills Activity

KEY

→ Union troops

← Confederate troops

★ Union victory

★ Confederate victory

‡‡ Union naval blockade

Union victories at Gettysburg and Vicksburg in July 1863 marked a turning point. This map shows the battles in the final years of the Civil War.

(a) Read a Map Which battles were fought in Confederate territory? In Union territory?

(b) Draw Inferences What can this map tell you about the damage suffered by North and South between 1863 and 1865?

MapMaster Online

For: Interactive map
Visit: PHSchool.com
Web Code: myp-5113

In all, the Confederacy suffered more than 28,000 casualties during the three-day Battle of Gettysburg. Union losses <u>exceeded</u> 23,000. For a second time, Lee had lost nearly a third of his troops. "It's all my fault," he said as he rode among his surviving soldiers. "It is I who have lost this fight."

Vocabulary Builder
<u>exceed</u> (ehks SEED) *v.* to go beyond what is expected; to be greater than what was planned

The Fall of Vicksburg On July 4, 1863, as Lee's shattered army began its retreat from Gettysburg, the South suffered another major blow far to the south and west. Vicksburg surrendered to General Grant. It had been one of the last cities on the Mississippi River to remain in Confederate hands. Unable to take Vicksburg by force, Grant had begun a siege of the city in May 1863. A **siege** is an attempt to capture a place by surrounding it with military forces and cutting it off until the people inside surrender.

Day after day, Union guns bombarded Vicksburg. Residents took shelter in cellars and in caves they dug in hillsides. They ate mules and rats to keep from starving. After six weeks, the 30,000 Confederate troops at Vicksburg finally gave up. A few days later, the last Confederate stronghold on the Mississippi River, Port Hudson, Louisiana, also gave up. The entire river was now under Union control.

These events, coupled with Lee's defeat at Gettysburg, make July 1863 the major turning point of the Civil War. Now the Union had the upper hand.

The Gettysburg Address In November 1863, about 15,000 people gathered on the battlefield at Gettysburg to honor the soldiers who had died there. In what is now known as the Gettysburg Address, Lincoln looked ahead to a final Union victory. He said:

Union General Ulysses S. Grant

> **"**We here highly resolve that these dead shall not have died in vain—that this nation, under God, shall have a new birth of freedom—and that government of the people, by the people, for the people, shall not perish from the earth.**"**
>
> —Abraham Lincoln, Gettysburg Address, November 19, 1863

☑**Checkpoint** **Identify two events that marked turning points in the Civil War.**

Closing In on the Confederacy

In Ulysses S. Grant, President Lincoln found the kind of commander he had long sought. In 1864, the President gave him command of all Union forces. Grant decided that he must attack Richmond, no matter how large the Union losses.

Grant Versus Lee Grant's huge army hammered at the Confederates in a series of battles in northern Virginia in the spring of 1864. Grant was unable to break through Lee's troops. But Grant did not retreat. Instead, he continued the attack.

Cause and Effect

CAUSES

- Issue of slavery in the territories divides the North and South.
- Abolitionists want slavery to end.
- Southern states secede after Lincoln's election.

THE CIVIL WAR

EFFECTS

- Lincoln issues the Emancipation Proclamation.
- Total war destroys the South's economy.
- Hundreds of thousands of Americans killed.

Relate Events in a Sequence
What happened first, the Union's victory in Atlanta or President Lincoln's reelection? Explain how these events are related in sequence.

After seven weeks of fighting, Grant had lost about 55,000 men; the Confederates had lost 35,000. Grant realized that his army could count on a steady stream of men and supplies. Lee, on the other hand, was running out of both.

The two armies clashed at Petersburg, an important railroad center south of Richmond. There, in June 1864, Grant began a siege, the tactic he had used at Vicksburg.

While Grant besieged Lee, another Union army under General **William Tecumseh Sherman** advanced toward Atlanta. Like Grant, Sherman was a tough soldier. He believed in **total war**—all-out attacks aimed at destroying an enemy's army, its resources, and its people's will to fight. Sherman later said:

> **❝**We are not only fighting hostile armies, but a hostile people, and must make young and old, rich and poor, feel the hard hand of war.**❞**
>
> —William T. Sherman, *Memoirs*, 1886

March to the Sea The Confederates could not stop Sherman's advance. The Union army marched into Atlanta on September 2, 1864. Atlanta's capture gave President Lincoln's reelection campaign a boost. In the months before the capture of Atlanta, many northerners had grown tired of the war. Support for Lincoln had been lagging. But after Atlanta's fall, Lincoln won a huge election victory over General George McClellan, the Democrats' candidate.

In November, Sherman ordered Atlanta burned. He then marched east toward the Atlantic Ocean. Along the way, Union troops set fire to buildings, seized crops and livestock, and pulled up railroad tracks. They left a path of destruction up to 60 miles wide. In February 1865, the army headed north across the Carolinas.

✓Checkpoint How did Sherman show "the hard hand of war"?

Peace at Last

In March 1865, Grant's army still waited outside Petersburg. For months, Grant had been extending his battle lines east and west of Petersburg. Lee knew it was only a matter of time before Grant would capture the city.

Lincoln, too, saw that the end of the war was near. In his Second Inaugural Address in March 1865, he asked Americans to forgive and forget. "With malice toward none; with charity for all; . . . let us strive together . . . to bind up the nation's wounds," said Lincoln.

Surrender at Appomattox On April 2, Grant's troops finally broke through Confederate lines. By evening, Richmond was in Union hands. Lee's army retreated to the town of Appomattox Court House. There, on April 9, 1865, his escape cut off, Lee surrendered.

Grant offered Lee generous surrender terms. The Confederates had only to give up their weapons and leave in peace. As Lee rode off, some Union troops started to celebrate the surrender. But Grant silenced them. "The war is over," he said. "The rebels are our countrymen again."

The War's Terrible Toll The Civil War was the bloodiest conflict the United States has ever fought. About 260,000 Confederate soldiers gave their lives in the war. The number of Union dead exceeded 360,000, including 37,000 African Americans. Nearly a half million men were wounded. Many returned home disfigured for life.

The war had two key results: It reunited the nation and put an end to slavery. However, a century would pass before African Americans would begin to experience the full meaning of freedom.

✔**Checkpoint** Why did Lee finally decide to surrender?

⭐ **Looking Back and Ahead** With Lee's surrender, the long and bitter war came to an end. In the next chapter, you will read how U.S. leaders tried to patch the Union together again.

Section 5 | Check Your Progress

Progress Monitoring ⬤nline
For: Self-test with instant help
Visit: PHSchool.com
Web Code: mya-5115

Comprehension and Critical Thinking

1. **(a) Identify** Why are the battles at Gettysburg and Vicksburg considered a turning point?
   (b) Understand Sequence How did the advantages of the North at the start of the war continue to be advantages?

2. **(a) Classify** Classify each of the following people as either a Union general or a Confederate general: Ambrose Burnside, Robert E. Lee, Ulysses S. Grant, William Tecumseh Sherman.
   (b) Distinguish Facts From Opinions Write three facts and three opinions Grant might have stated about the Civil War.

Reading Skill

3. **Relate Events in a Sequence** What events led to the turning point of the Civil War in July 1863? How did those events change the war?

Key Terms

Complete each of the following sentences so that the second part further explains the first part and clearly shows your understanding of the key term.

4. Grant placed Vicksburg under a siege; _____.

5. Sherman pursued a total war; _____.

Writing

6. This section says that the Civil War took more than 620,000 American lives. Research and record the number of American deaths in World War I, World War II, Korea, and Vietnam. Compare the total number of American lives lost in these wars to the number lost in the Civil War. Then, write a paragraph to make a point about your findings. Also, credit the sources of published information you used.

21st Century Learning A primary source is information about people or events presented by someone who lived through what is being described. Speeches are primary sources that can give important information about historical figures and events.

> President Lincoln gave this speech at the dedication of the battlefield cemetery at Gettysburg.
>
> **Primary Source**
>
> "Fourscore and seven years ago our fathers brought forth on this continent a new nation, conceived in Liberty, and dedicated to the proposition that all men are created equal.
>
> Now we are engaged in a great civil war, testing whether that nation, or any nation so conceived and so dedicated, can long endure. We are met on a great battlefield of that war. We have come to dedicate a portion of that field as a final resting place for those who here gave their lives that the nation might live. It is altogether fitting and proper that we should do this.
>
> But in a larger sense, we cannot dedicate, we cannot consecrate, we cannot hallow, this ground. The brave men, living and dead, who struggled here have consecrated it, far above our poor power to add or detract. The world will little note, nor long remember, what we say here, but it can never forget what they did here. It is for us the living, rather, to be dedicated here to the unfinished work which they who fought here have thus far so nobly advanced. It is rather for us to be here dedicated to the great task remaining before us—that from these honored dead we take increased devotion to that cause for which they gave the last full measure of devotion—that we here highly resolve that these dead shall not have died in vain—that this nation, under God, shall have a new birth of freedom—and that government of the people, by the people, for the people, shall not perish from the earth."
>
> —Abraham Lincoln, November 19, 1863

Learn the Skill
Use these steps to analyze a speech.

1 Identify the source. Find out who gave the speech, when it was given, and why it was given.

2 Identify the main idea. Read carefully to discover what the main idea of the speech is. What do you think the speaker wanted to tell his or her audience?

3 Identify the point of view. Often a speechmaker wants to persuade listeners to share his or her feelings. Read carefully to determine the point of view of the speechmaker. Look for language that expresses strong feelings.

Practice the Skill
Answer the questions about the speech above.

1 Identify the source. (a) Who wrote the speech? (b) When was the speech given? (c) Why was it given?

2 Identify the main idea. What is the most important idea in the speech?

3 Identify the point of view. (a) What is the speaker's opinion of the Civil War? (b) What words or phrases express his feelings? (c) Why do you think he feels this way?

Apply the Skill
See the Review and Assessment at the end of this chapter.

Quick Study Guide

How did people, places, and things affect the outcome of the Civil War?

Section 1
The Call to Arms

- The Civil War was a war of Americans against Americans.
- Both the North and the South used their advantages in planning military strategy.

Section 2
Early Years of the War

- New weapons made fighting the war more dangerous.
- Despite many battles early in the war, neither side gained a clear advantage.

Section 3
The Emancipation Proclamation

- The Emancipation Proclamation freed enslaved people in areas of rebellion.
- The Emancipation Proclamation changed the Civil War into a fight to end slavery.
- Approximately 189,000 African Americans served in the Union army and navy.

Section 4
The Civil War and American Life

- The Civil War caused divisions in both the North and the South.
- Draft laws that seemed to favor the wealthy led to protests and riots.
- The Civil War caused economic hardships and also led to changes in women's roles.

Section 5
Decisive Battles

- Major Confederate losses at Gettysburg and Vicksburg marked a turning point.
- Lee surrendered to Grant on April 9, 1865, at Appomattox Court House.
- Some 620,000 soldiers died in the Civil War.

? Exploring the Essential Question

Use the online study guide to explore the essential question.

Section 1
Why did each side in the Civil War think the war would be won easily?

Chapter 15 Essential Question
How did people, places, and things affect the outcome of the Civil War?

Section 2
How did each side in the war try to gain an advantage over the other?

Section 5
How did Lincoln and his generals turn the tide of the war?

Section 3
What were the causes and effects of the Emancipation Proclamation?

Section 4
How did the war affect people and politics in the North and the South?

Key Terms

Answer the following questions in complete sentences that show your understanding of the key terms.

1. Which army, the Union or the Confederate, sustained more casualties?

2. Why did Kentucky cease being neutral?

3. What was both Lincoln's and Davis's purpose in suspending habeas corpus?

4. How did Grant's siege of Vicksburg lead to the surrender of Confederate troops?

Comprehension and Critical Thinking

5. **(a) Recall** Why was it critical to keep Maryland in the Union?
   (b) Analyze Cause and Effect What was the effect of Lincoln's declaring martial law in Maryland?

6. **(a) Identify** Why did President Lincoln issue the Emancipation Proclamation?
   (b) Explain Problems What were two limitations of the Emancipation Proclamation?

7. **(a) Describe** What roles did women play in the Civil War?
   (b) Identify Economic Benefits In what way did the hardships of the Civil War provide new opportunities for women?
   (c) Link Past and Present Make a list of three opportunities that are open to women today that once were limited to men.

8. **(a) Classify** Create a chart of the battles fought at these places: Bull Run, Antietam Creek, Shiloh, Fredericksburg, Vicksburg, Gettysburg, Petersburg. Classify each battle as either a Union victory or a Confederate victory.
   (b) Detect Bias Reread the excerpt from Lincoln's Gettysburg Address found in Section 5. Do you think the address gave more comfort to northerners or to southerners? Why?

9. **(a) Summarize** Write three sentences that explain how the Civil War ended.
   (b) Make Predictions Do you think the surrender of the Confederate army at Appomattox Court House brought an end to the conflict between the northern and southern states? Explain.

History Reading Skill

10. **Understand Sequence** In a paragraph, summarize the events in the Civil War on the battlefield and on the home front. Use signal words to clarify the sequence. Where appropriate, show cause-effect links between events in sequence.

Writing

11. **Write on the following topic:**
    Find more information about a Civil War general. Write four paragraphs about him, using the guidelines below.
    - The first paragraph should introduce the general and present a thesis.
    - The second and third paragraphs should support this thesis by giving some background about the general's life, actions, and character.
    - The fourth paragraph should draw a conclusion about the general.

12. **Write a Narrative:**
    Choose one of the following roles: soldier, civilian, or nurse. Write two paragraphs of descriptive narrative telling about your experience in the Civil War.

Skills for Life

Analyze a Speech

Use the quotation below to answer the questions.

> ". . . the people of the Confederate States, in their conventions, determined that the wrongs which they had suffered and the evils with which they were menaced required that they should revoke the delegation of powers to the Federal Government which they had ratified in their several conventions. They consequently passed ordinances [laws] resuming all their rights as sovereign and independent States. . . ."
>
> —Jefferson Davis, April 29, 1861

13. **(a)** Who is the writer?
    (b) When was this written?

14. What is the main idea?

15. **(a)** What words or phrases show the writer's feelings?
    (b) Why do you think he feels this way?

Test Yourself

Refer to the quotation below to answer Question 1.

> "I now hold in contemplation of universal law and of the Constitution [that] the Union of these States is perpetual. . . . It follows from these views that no State upon its own mere motion can lawfully get out of the Union. . . ."
>
> —Abraham Lincoln, March 4, 1861

1. **This quotation shows that Lincoln wanted to**
   A allow southern states to secede.
   B amend the Constitution.
   C abolish slavery.
   D preserve the Union.

2. **Which of the following granted freedom to all African Americans in areas of rebellion against the Union in 1863?**
   A Gettysburg Address
   B Thirteenth Amendment
   C Emancipation Proclamation
   D surrender at Appomattox Court House

3. **Which of the following was the North's most important advantage in the Civil War?**
   A Britain and other European nations sent economic aid.
   B The nation's most experienced military leaders were northerners.
   C The North had a larger population and more resources than the South.
   D Northerners were united in their support for the war.

Document-Based Questions

Task: Look at Documents 1 and 2, and answer their accompanying questions. Then, use the documents and your knowledge of history to complete this writing assignment:

> Write an essay describing the disagreement between the Copperheads and northern supporters of the Civil War. Include specific details about each side's position.

Document 1: Clement L. Vallandigham, an Ohio congressman, gave this speech in New York City in March 1863. *What does Vallandigham propose? How does that represent the Copperhead position?*

> "When I see that the experiment of blood has failed, . . . I am not one of those who proclaim . . . that we shall have separation and disunion. I am for going back to the instrumentality through which this Union was first made, and by which alone it can be restored.
>
> I am for peace, because it is the first step toward conciliation and compromise. You cannot move until you have first taken that indispensable preliminary—a cessation of hostilities. . . .
>
> Let men of intelligence judge: let history attest it hereafter. My theory . . . then, is this—stop this war."

Document 2: Copperheads were probably the most outspoken critics of the war in the North. *What opinion of Copperheads does this cartoon present?*

Reconstruction and the New South

1863–1896

"We knowed freedom was on us....
We thought we was going
to get rich like the white folks....
But it didn't turn out that way."

—Felix Haywood,
former slave, on Reconstruction

Students and teachers pose
outside the Freedmen's Bureau
school in Beaufort, South Carolina.

CHAPTER 16

What You Will Learn

Section 1
REBUILDING THE NATION
As the Civil War ended, Americans faced the problem of how to reunite the nation.

Section 2
THE BATTLE OVER RECONSTRUCTION
Disagreements over Reconstruction led to conflict in the government and in the South.

Section 3
THE END OF RECONSTRUCTION
With the end of Reconstruction, African Americans in the South lost many of the rights they had gained.

Reading Skill
Analyze and Evaluate Proposals
In this chapter, you will learn to identify central issues and frame good research questions in order to analyze and evaluate proposals.

543

What were the short-term and long-

Reconstruction and the New South

Military Districts, 1867

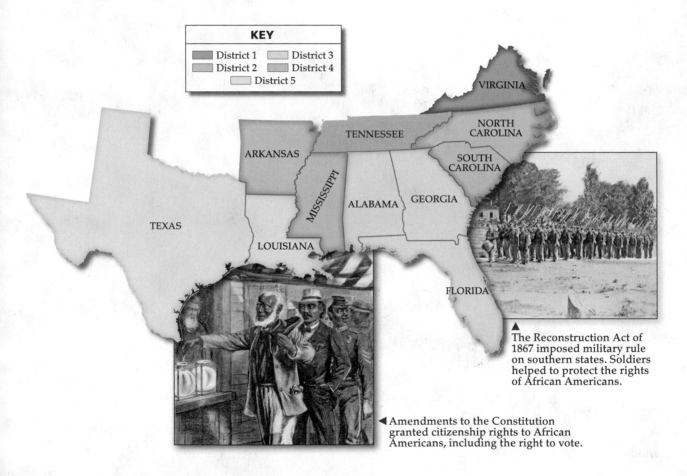

KEY
- District 1
- District 2
- District 3
- District 4
- District 5

VIRGINIA

NORTH CAROLINA

TENNESSEE

ARKANSAS

SOUTH CAROLINA

MISSISSIPPI

ALABAMA

GEORGIA

TEXAS

LOUISIANA

FLORIDA

▲ The Reconstruction Act of 1867 imposed military rule on southern states. Soldiers helped to protect the rights of African Americans.

◄ Amendments to the Constitution granted citizenship rights to African Americans, including the right to vote.

U.S. Events

President Lincoln proposes mild Reconstruction plan. **1863**

1865 Lincoln is assassinated five days after war ends.

1867 Radical Reconstruction begins.

1860   **1865**   **1870**

World Events

1867 Dominion of Canada is formed.

Self-Rule Returns to the South

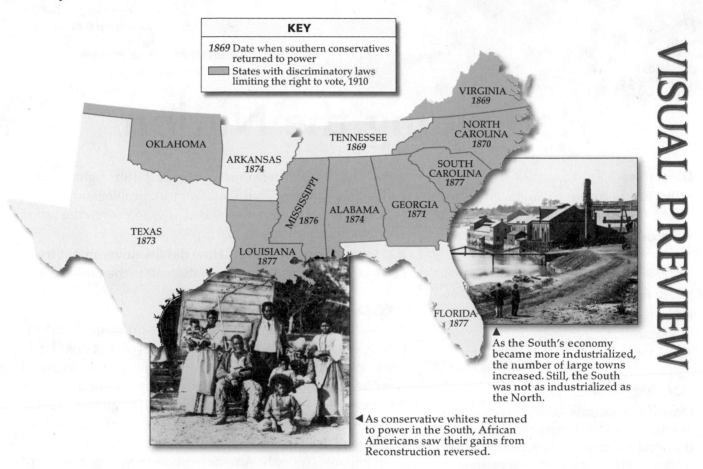

KEY

1869 Date when southern conservatives returned to power

☐ States with discriminatory laws limiting the right to vote, 1910

VIRGINIA
1869

NORTH CAROLINA
1870

TENNESSEE
1869

SOUTH CAROLINA
1877

OKLAHOMA

ARKANSAS
1874

MISSISSIPPI
1876

ALABAMA
1874

GEORGIA
1871

TEXAS
1873

LOUISIANA
1877

FLORIDA
1877

VISUAL PREVIEW

▲ As the South's economy became more industrialized, the number of large towns increased. Still, the South was not as industrialized as the North.

◄ As conservative whites returned to power in the South, African Americans saw their gains from Reconstruction reversed.

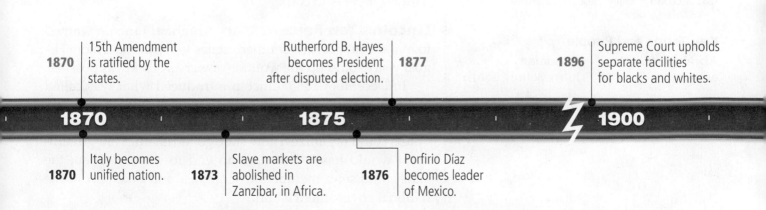

1870 15th Amendment is ratified by the states.

1877 Rutherford B. Hayes becomes President after disputed election.

1896 Supreme Court upholds separate facilities for blacks and whites.

1870   **1875**   **1900**

1870 Italy becomes unified nation.

1873 Slave markets are abolished in Zanzibar, in Africa.

1876 Porfirio Díaz becomes leader of Mexico.

Bind Up the Nation's Wounds

❝With malice toward none, with charity for all, with firmness in the right as God gives us to see the right, let us strive on to finish the work we are in, to bind up the nation's wounds, to care for him who shall have borne the battle and for his widow and his orphan—to do all which may achieve and cherish a just and lasting peace . . . .❞

—Abraham Lincoln,
Second Inaugural Address, 1865

◄ As Civil War soldiers returned home, President Lincoln hoped to swiftly heal the nation.

Rebuilding the Nation

Objectives

- Describe the postwar challenges that faced the nation.
- Compare and contrast President Lincoln's plan for Reconstruction with the plan proposed by Congress.
- Identify the goals of the Freedmen's Bureau.
- Describe the immediate impact of Lincoln's assassination.

🎯 Reading Skill

Identify Proposals In turbulent times, such as after the Civil War, people may have many different ideas about how to move forward. They identify goals to achieve and propose solutions to problems. For example, each proposal made by a government leader was intended to achieve a specific goal. As you read Section 1, identify these proposals and goals.

Key Terms and People

Abraham Lincoln   freedman
amnesty   John Wilkes Booth

Why It Matters After four years of bitter fighting, the Union had won the Civil War. Even so, problems remained as Americans tried to find the best way to restore the union and rebuild the nation.

❓ Section Focus Question: How did the government try to solve key problems facing the nation after the Civil War?

Preparing for Reunion

As the Civil War ended, enormous problems faced the nation, especially the South. Vast stretches of the South lay in ruins. What provisions would be made for people who had been freed from slavery? Homeless refugees—both African American and white—needed food, shelter, and work. (For more on conditions in the South after the Civil War, see the Life at the Time feature at the end of this section.)

Somehow, though, Americans had to master their hard feelings and bring the North and the South together again. This process, known as Reconstruction, would occupy the nation for years to come.

Lincoln's Ten Percent Plan Abraham Lincoln wanted to make it easy for the southern states to rejoin the Union. His goal was to bind up the wounds of war as quickly as possible.

In December 1863, Lincoln introduced what was called the Ten Percent Plan. As soon as ten percent of a state's voters swore an oath of loyalty to the United States, the voters could organize a new state government. That government would have to declare an end to slavery. Then, the state could send members to Congress and take part in the national government again.

Lincoln's plan included amnesty for former Confederates who took the loyalty oath. An amnesty is a group pardon. The offer of amnesty did not apply to Confederate government leaders and top military officers.

The Wade-Davis Bill Six months later, Congress passed a much stricter plan for Reconstruction called the Wade-Davis Bill. Under that bill, 50 percent of voters would have to sign a loyalty oath before a state could return to the Union. Moreover, anyone who had <u>voluntarily</u> fought for the Confederacy would be barred from voting for delegates to a convention to write a new state constitution. The bill did not give them a right to vote. Lincoln would not sign the Wade-Davis Bill, so it never became law.

Lincoln and his fellow Republicans hoped to see a strong Republican Party in the new South. Lincoln thought that his "soft," or lenient, Reconstruction policy would win support from influential southerners. Supporters of a strict policy toward the South, known as Radical Republicans, disagreed. They argued that only a strict plan would keep the people who had led the South into secession from regaining power and weakening the control of the Radical Republicans.

☑️**Checkpoint** How did Lincoln's plan for Reconstruction differ from that of the Radical Republicans in Congress?

Identify Proposals
What did Lincoln propose in his Ten Percent Plan?

Vocabulary Builder
<u>voluntary</u> (VAHL ahn tair ee) *adj.* not forced; done of one's own free will

Destruction in the South
Parts of Richmond, capital of the Confederacy, lay in ruins at war's end. **Critical Thinking: *Interpret Photographs*** *What do you think would be the most urgent need of the people of Richmond?*

The Freedmen's Bureau

It was urgent to deal with the needs of freedmen, enslaved people who had been freed by the war, as well as other war refugees. Congress created the Freedmen's Bureau in March 1865. The bureau's first duty was to provide emergency relief to people displaced by the war.

Education The Freedmen's Bureau set up schools to teach freedmen to read and write. So great was the hunger for education that many African American communities started schools on their own. To pay a teacher, people pooled their pennies and dollars.

Many teachers were northern white women, but a large number were northern African American women. Edmonia Highgate, the daughter of freed slaves, taught at a Freedmen's Bureau school in Louisiana. "The majority of my pupils come from plantations, three, four and even eight miles distant," she wrote. "So anxious are they to learn that they walk these distances so early in the morning."

Most southern states had lacked systems of public education before the war. Now, public schools began to educate both blacks and whites. The Freedmen's Bureau helped to start schools at which African Americans could extend their education. These schools gave rise to such present-day institutions as Fisk University in Tennessee and Hampton University in Virginia.

Defending Freedmen The Freedmen's Bureau helped freedmen find jobs and <u>resolved</u> disputes between whites and blacks. Some people tried to cheat the freedmen. The Freedmen's Bureau set up its own courts to deal with such disputes.

☑**Checkpoint** What was the Freedmen's Bureau?

Vocabulary Builder
<u>resolve</u> (ree SAHLV) **v.** to decide; to solve

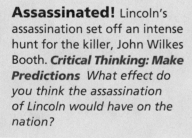

Assassinated! Lincoln's assassination set off an intense hunt for the killer, John Wilkes Booth. *Critical Thinking: Make Predictions* *What effect do you think the assassination of Lincoln would have on the nation?*

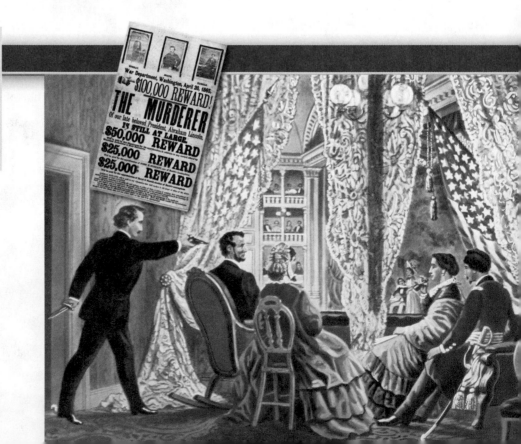

Lincoln Is Murdered

As the war drew to a close, President Lincoln hoped for a peaceful Reconstruction. But Lincoln had no chance to put his plans into practice. He was shot dead on April 14, 1865, five days after Lee's surrender.

A Confederate sympathizer, John Wilkes Booth, slipped up behind Lincoln while he and his wife were attending a play at the Ford's Theatre in Washington. Booth fired a single pistol shot into the President's head. Lincoln died a few hours later.

Booth was shot dead two weeks later after pursuers trapped him in a barn and set it on fire. Eight people were convicted and four were hanged for their parts in the plot to kill Lincoln.

News of Lincoln's death shocked the nation. A special funeral train carried Lincoln's body back to Illinois for burial. In town after town, vast crowds paid their last respects.

Lincoln's successor was Vice President Andrew Johnson of Tennessee. Johnson was a southern Democrat who had remained loyal to the Union. Because Johnson had expressed bitterness toward the Confederates, many expected him to take a strict approach to Reconstruction.

✔**Checkpoint** **Why did many people expect Johnson to take a hard line on Reconstruction?**

☆ **Looking Back and Ahead** Many people feared the effect of Lincoln's assassination on the process of Reconstruction. In the next section, you will learn how Reconstruction was affected by tensions between Lincoln's successor and members of Congress.

Section 1 | **Check Your Progress**

Progress Monitoring Online
For: Self-test with instant help
Visit: PHSchool.com
Web Code: mya-5121

Comprehension and Critical Thinking

1. **(a) Recall** What problems faced the South at the end of the Civil War?
   (b) Contrast Why did the South have greater difficulty than the North in recovering from the Civil War?

2. **(a) Recall** How did Lincoln's plan for Reconstruction differ from the Wade-Davis Bill?
   (b) Explain Problems What problems do you see for reuniting the nation in each plan?

Reading Skill

3. **Identify Proposals** Reread the paragraphs under the heading "The Freedmen's Bureau." What did the bureau propose to do to help the freedmen?

Key Terms

Answer the following questions in complete sentences that show your understanding of the key terms.

4. What did former Confederates have to do to get amnesty under Lincoln's plan to rebuild the Union?

5. Who were the freedmen?

Writing

6. Choose the best sentence to end a research paper about Abraham Lincoln. Explain your choice.
   Sentences:
   (a) Abraham Lincoln was humbly born on February 12, 1809, but he went on to be one of our greatest Presidents.
   (b) Because Abraham Lincoln did not win a majority of the votes cast, his presidency turned out to be the nation's most turbulent period.
   (c) His trials as President changed Lincoln into the steady leader who saved the Union in its darkest hour.

The South After the Civil War

The Civil War had a devastating impact on the South. All southerners—rich and poor, black and white—faced a long struggle to rebuild their lives and their land.

Confederate battle flag

Destroyed plantation

▲ Physical Destruction

Most of the fighting during the Civil War took place in the South. After Confederate bombardment at the beginning of the War, the interior of Fort Sumter was destroyed. Cities and plantations lay in charred ruins. Two thirds of the railroads were destroyed.

► Wounded Soldiers

A quarter of a million Confederate soldiers died in the war. Thousands more were disabled by their wounds.

Returning Confederate veteran

Freedmen's school

Teaching people to read

▲ Freedmen

For nearly 4 million freedmen, the end of the Civil War was a time of both hope and fear. They were no longer enslaved. But most had no land, no jobs, and no education. The first task was to teach them to read.

Confederate money

◄ Financial Ruin

The economy of the South was ruined. Confederate money was suddenly worthless. Many banks closed, and people lost their life's savings.

Analyze LIFE AT THE TIME

Take one of the following roles: a wounded veteran; a planter whose plantation has been destroyed; a freedman. Write a paragraph explaining how you feel about the end of the war and the possibilities for the future.

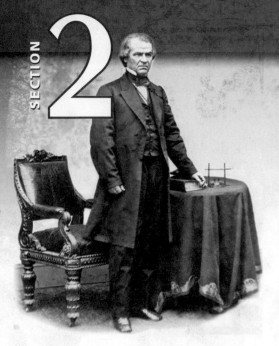

Who Shall Rule the South?

❝ Rebels found themselves in places of trust, while the truehearted Unionists, who had watched for the coming of our flag and ought to have to have enjoyed its protecting power, were driven into hiding places. ❞

—Senator Charles Sumner, criticizing President Johnson's Reconstruction actions in the South, 1868

◀ President Andrew Johnson

The Battle Over Reconstruction

Objectives
- Explain why conflicts developed over plans for Reconstruction.
- Describe the changes in the South brought about by Radical Reconstruction.
- Explain how Congress tried to remove President Johnson from office.
- Describe how the Ku Klux Klan and other secret societies tried to prevent African Americans from exercising their rights.

🎯 Reading Skill

Analyze Proposals Proposals must be carried out in order to be effective. The proposal must include details on how to put the proposal into action. As you read Section 2, look at the suggested ideas for carrying out proposals.

Key Terms and People

Andrew Johnson	scalawag
black codes	carpetbagger
Hiram Revels	impeachment
Blanche Bruce	

Why It Matters The Radical Republicans in Congress wanted a strict form of Reconstruction. However, President Johnson had a more lenient plan. The stage was set for a battle between Congress and the Presidency.

❓ **Section Focus Question: How did disagreements over Reconstruction lead to conflict in government and in the South?**

A Growing Conflict

Like President Lincoln, Andrew Johnson proposed a relatively lenient plan of Reconstruction. He followed Lincoln's example in putting his plan into effect himself, without consulting legislators.

The Thirteenth Amendment In January 1865, Congress approved a constitutional amendment to abolish slavery throughout the nation. When ratified later that year, the Thirteenth Amendment banned both slavery and forced labor. It gave Congress the power to make laws to enforce its terms.

Johnson's Plan Like Lincoln, Johnson issued a broad amnesty to most former Confederates. Johnson allowed southern states to organize new governments and elect representatives to Congress. Each state, though, was required to abolish slavery and ratify the Thirteenth Amendment. By late fall, most of the states had met Johnson's requirements. When Congress met in December 1865, the representatives and senators elected by white southerners included many former Confederate leaders.

Congress quickly rejected Johnson's approach. First, it refused to seat the southern senators and representatives. Next, the two houses appointed a committee to form a new plan for the South.

In a series of public hearings, the committee heard testimony about black codes—new laws used by southern states to control African Americans. Critics claimed that the codes replaced the system of slavery with near-slavery. In Mississippi, for example, African Americans could not vote or serve on juries. If unable to pay a fine as ordered by a court, they might be hired out by the sheriff to any white person who paid the fine.

Anger at these developments led Congress to adopt an increasingly hard line. The hardest line was taken by the Radical Republicans. The Radicals had two key goals. One was to prevent former Confederates from regaining control over southern politics. The other was to protect the freedmen and guarantee them a right to vote.

Vocabulary Builder

critic (KRIHT ihk) *n.* someone who makes judgments on the value of objects or actions

☑ Checkpoint **How did Congress respond to Johnson's plan for Reconstruction?**

The Fourteenth Amendment

The struggle over Reconstruction led to direct clashes between the President and Congress during 1866. At issue were two laws and a constitutional amendment.

Voicing alarm at the treatment of African Americans in the South, Congress passed the Civil Rights Act of 1866. It granted citizenship rights to African Americans and guaranteed the civil rights of all people except Native Americans.

President Johnson vetoed the bill and another one extending the life of the Freedmen's Bureau. Congress voted to overturn both vetoes. Under the Constitution, a vetoed bill becomes law if it wins the votes of two thirds of each house. Both bills received enough votes to become law.

Opposing Plans for Reconstruction

I want a quick reunion.

President Andrew Johnson (1865)	Radical Republicans (1867)
• Majority of white men must swear oath of loyalty • Must ratify 13th Amendment • Former Confederate officials may vote and hold office	• Must disband state government • Must write new constitution • Must ratify 13th and 14th Amendments • Must allow African American men to vote

President Andrew Johnson

We want real change.

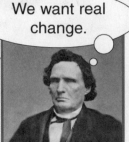

Congressman Thaddeus Stevens

Reading Charts
Skills Activity

President Andrew Johnson and Republican members of Congress, led by Thaddeus Stevens, disagreed about the process of Reconstruction.

(a) **Read a Chart** Which plan required states to write new constitutions?

(b) **Detect Points of View** Why did Radical Republicans think Johnson's plan was not strict enough?

Congress also drew up the Fourteenth Amendment to the Constitution, seeking to make sure that the Supreme Court did not strike down the Civil Rights Act. Republicans remembered the Court's Dred Scott decision. In that ruling, the Court declared that no one descended from an enslaved person could be a United States citizen.

The amendment failed at first to win the approval of three fourths of the states. It finally was approved in 1868, after Radicals took control of Reconstruction.

The Fourteenth Amendment says that all people born or naturalized in the United States are citizens. The amendment also declares that states may not pass laws that take away a citizen's rights. Nor can a state "deprive any person of life, liberty, or property, without due process of law; nor deny to any person . . . the equal protection of the laws."

Another provision declares that any state that denies the vote to any male citizen over the age of 21 will have its representation in Congress reduced. That provision was not enforced until the 1970s.

The Fourteenth Amendment became a powerful tool for enforcing civil rights. However, almost a century passed before it was used for that purpose.

Analyze Proposals

Congress proposed the Fourteenth Amendment to give freedmen a way to defend their rights. How would the amendment put that goal into action?

✔**Checkpoint** How did the Fourteenth Amendment seek to protect the freedmen?

Radical Reconstruction

Tempers rose as the elections of 1866 approached. White rioters and police attacked and killed many African Americans in two southern cities, Memphis and New Orleans. Outrage at this violence led Congress to push a stricter form of Reconstruction.

Radicals in Charge By early 1867, the Radical Republicans had won enough support from moderates to begin a "hard" Reconstruction. This period is known as Radical Reconstruction.

The Reconstruction Act of 1867 removed the governments of all southern states that had refused to ratify the Fourteenth Amendment. It then imposed military rule on these states, dividing them into five military districts. Before returning to the Union, each state had to write a new constitution and ratify the Fourteenth Amendment. Each state also had to let African Americans vote.

Under military rule, the South took on a new look. Soldiers helped <u>register</u> southern blacks to vote. In five states, African American voters outnumbered white voters. In the election of 1868, Republicans won all southern states. The states wrote new constitutions and, in June 1868, Congress seated representatives from seven "reconstructed" states.

Time of Hope and Advancement For the first time, African Americans in the South played an active role in politics. Prominent among them were free-born African Americans—carpenters, barbers, preachers—and former Union soldiers.

African Americans were elected as sheriffs, mayors, judges, and legislators. Sixteen African Americans served in the U.S. House of Representatives between 1872 and 1901. Two others, Hiram Revels and Blanche Bruce, served in the Senate.

Historians once took a critical view of Radical Reconstruction, focusing on the widespread corruption and excessive spending during this period. More recently, however, historians have written about important accomplishments of Reconstruction. They noted that during Reconstruction, southern states opened public schools for the first time. Legislators spread taxes more evenly and made fairer voting rules. They gave property rights to women. In addition, states rebuilt bridges, roads, and buildings destroyed by the war.

Radical Reconstruction brought other sweeping changes to the South. Old leaders lost much of their power. The Republican Party built a strong following based on three key groups. One group, called **scalawags** by their opponents, were southern whites who had opposed secession. Freedmen voters made up a second group.

The third group were **carpetbaggers**, a name given by southerners to northern whites who went south to start businesses or pursue political office. Critics claimed that these northerners were in such a rush to head south that they just tossed their clothes into cheap satchels called carpetbags.

Vocabulary Builder
<u>register</u> (REJ is tur) *v.* enroll or record officially

Biography Quest

Hiram Revels
1822–1901

In his early years, Hiram Revels was a minister and preached to African American congregations across the Midwest. Throughout the Civil War, he was a staunch supporter of the Union.

In 1870, Revels was elected to the U.S. Senate and thus became the nation's first African American senator. He was elected to complete the unfinished term of former Confederate President Jefferson Davis.

Biography Quest

How did some senators try to keep Revels out of the Senate?

For: The answer to the question about Revels

Visit: PHSchool.com

Web Code: myd-5122

The terror– "WORSE THAN SLAVERY"

Burning school-house

Reading Political Cartoons

Skills Activity

The Ku Klux Klan used terror and violence to keep African Americans from voting. Northern cartoonist Thomas Nast shows his point of view about the Klan and other secret societies in this cartoon.

(a) Distinguish Relevant Information Point out two negative images in the cartoon. Give one word to describe the family.

(b) Detect Points of View What do you think is Nast's opinion of the Ku Klux Klan?

Targeting President Johnson Meanwhile, the Radicals mounted a major challenge against President Johnson. The Radicals tried to remove Johnson from office by impeachment. **Impeachment** is the bringing of formal charges against a public official. The Constitution says the House may impeach a President for "treason, bribery, or other high crimes and misdemeanors." After impeachment, there is a trial in the Senate. If convicted, the President is removed from office.

Johnson escaped removal—but barely. The House voted to impeach him in February 1868. The Senate trial took place from March to May. In the end, the votes went 35 for and 19 against Johnson. This was one vote short of the required two-thirds majority.

The Election of 1868 General Ulysses S. Grant, a war hero, won the presidential election for the Republicans in the fall of 1868. With southern states back in the Union under military rule, some 500,000 African Americans voted, mainly for Republicans. Grant won the electoral votes of 26 of the 34 states.

Grant was a moderate who had support from many northern business leaders. With his election, the Radicals began losing their grip on the Republican Party.

Fifteenth Amendment Over opposition from Democrats, Congress approved the Fifteenth Amendment in 1869. It barred all states from denying African American males the right to vote "on account of race, color, or previous condition of servitude."

Some African Americans said the amendment was too weak. It did not prevent states from requiring voters to own property or pay a voting tax. The amendment took effect in 1870, after three fourths of the states gave their approval.

The Ku Klux Klan Angry at being shut out of power, some whites resorted to violence. They created secret societies to terrorize African Americans and their white allies.

The best-known secret society was the Ku Klux Klan. Its members donned white robes with hoods that hid their faces. Klansmen rode by night to the homes of African American voters, shouting threats and burning wooden crosses. If threats failed, the Klan would whip, torture, shoot, or hang African Americans and white Republicans. Klan violence took hundreds of lives during the election of 1868.

The terror went on even after Congress responded with new laws. The Ku Klux Klan Acts of 1870 and 1871 barred the use of force against voters. Although the original Klan dissolved, new groups took its place. In the face of the terrorism, voting by African Americans declined. The stage was set for the end of Reconstruction.

☑ Checkpoint **What were the key elements of Radical Reconstruction?**

⭐ **Looking Back and Ahead** Although Reconstruction guaranteed rights to more Americans, huge challenges remained. In the next section, you will learn more about the process of rebuilding the South. You will also learn that as time went on, Americans became less interested in Reconstruction. This set the scene for a return of power to former Confederates.

Terror and Violence
To spread terror, Ku Klux Klan members wore hoods like the one above when they attacked their victims. They also left miniature coffins as warnings. **Critical Thinking: *Draw Conclusions*** *Why do you think the hoods helped spread terror?*

Progress Monitoring ⬤nline
For: Self-test with instant help
Visit: PHSchool.com
Web Code: mya-5122

Section 2 | **Check Your Progress**

Comprehension and Critical Thinking

1. (a) Recall Which amendment guaranteed African Americans the right to vote: the Thirteenth, Fourteenth, or Fifteenth?
(b) Apply Information How did each of these three amendments help to expand democracy?

2. (a) Recall What was the Ku Klux Klan?
(b) Evaluate Information Why do you think the Klan was not formed before the Civil War?

Reading Skill

3. Analyze Proposals In 1867, the Radical Republicans in Congress proposed the Reconstruction Act. What actions did this proposal involve?

Key Terms

Complete each of the following sentences so that the second part clearly shows your understanding of the key term.
4. Radical Republicans in the House of Representatives tried to remove the President by impeachment, which is _____.

5. Former Confederates wanted to control the lives of freedmen through black codes, which were _____.

Writing

6. Rewrite the following passage to correct the grammar, spelling, and punctuation errors that you find. **Passage:** President Johnson wanting to show mercy to the defeated confederacy. Many of the republicans in Congress, however, opposed him. Because they wanted to protect the freedman. This conflict led congress to held impeechment hearings.

A Southern Viewpoint

❝It would be best for the peace, harmony, and prosperity of the whole country that there should be an immediate restoration, an immediate bringing back of the states into their original practical relations.❞

— Alexander H. Stephens, urging an end to federal control of southern states, 1866

◄ Cartoon criticizing northern carpetbaggers in the South

The End of Reconstruction

Objectives

- Explain why support for Reconstruction declined.
- Describe how African Americans in the South lost many newly gained rights.
- Describe the sharecropping system and how it trapped many in a cycle of poverty.
- Identify the signs that the South began to develop a stronger economy by the 1880s.

◎ Reading Skill

Evaluate Proposals When you read a proposal, ask yourself: Is the proposal likely to work as a way of advancing its goal?

Key Terms and People

poll tax
literacy test
grandfather clause

segregation
Homer Plessy
sharecropper

Why It Matters The South experienced reforms during the Reconstruction era. However, many of the changes were quite temporary. When Reconstruction ended, African Americans were subjected to new hardships and injustices. It would take more than a century to overcome these injustices.

❷ Section Focus Question: What were the effects of Reconstruction?

Reconstruction's Conclusion

Support for Radical Republicans declined as Americans began to forget the Civil War and focus on bettering their own lives. Scandals within President Grant's administration played an important role. Grant made poor appointments to public offices, often appointing personal friends. Many of the appointees proved to be corrupt. Although Grant himself had no part in the corruption that took place, his reputation suffered. Grant won reelection in 1872, but many northerners lost faith in the Republicans and their policies.

Self-rule for the South Meanwhile, many people in both North and South were calling for the withdrawal of federal troops and full amnesty for former Confederates. Starting with Virginia in 1869, opponents of Republicans began to take back the South, state by state. Slowly, they chipped away at the rights of African Americans.

In some states, campaigns of terror by secret societies were a major factor in restoring their power. By 1874, Republicans had lost control of all but three southern states. By 1877, Democrats controlled those, too.

The Election of 1876 The end of Reconstruction was a direct result of the presidential election of 1876. Because of disputes over election returns, the choice of the President was decided by Congress. There, a deal between the Republicans and Democrats settled the election—and sealed the fate of Reconstruction.

The candidates in 1876 were Rutherford B. Hayes of Ohio for the Republicans and Samuel J. Tilden of New York for the Democrats. The Republicans said they would continue Reconstruction, and the Democrats said they would end it.

Tilden won the popular vote by 250,000 votes. However, 20 electoral votes were in dispute. Without them, Tilden fell one vote short of the 185 needed to win in the electoral college.

To resolve the issue, Congress appointed a special commission of 15 members. Most of them were Republicans. The commission gave all 20 electoral votes to Hayes. Rather than fight the decision in Congress, Democrats agreed to accept it. Hayes had privately told them that he would end Reconstruction. Once in office, Hayes removed all federal troops from the South.

Evaluate Proposals
What proposal did Hayes make to the Democrats in order to end their opposition? How did this proposal meet the goals of both the Democrats and Republicans?

☑ **Checkpoint** **What factors contributed to the end of Reconstruction?**

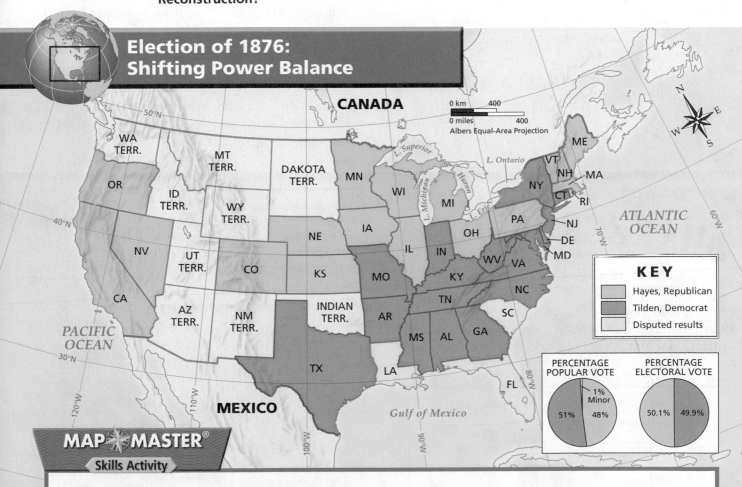

Election of 1876: Shifting Power Balance

KEY

- Hayes, Republican
- Tilden, Democrat
- Disputed results

PERCENTAGE POPULAR VOTE
51% | 48% | 1% Minor

PERCENTAGE ELECTORAL VOTE
50.1% | 49.9%

MAP☀MASTER®
Skills Activity

Although Samuel Tilden won the popular vote, Rutherford B. Hayes was declared the winner in the election.

(a) Read a Map Key In which region did Tilden have the most support?
(b) Draw Conclusions Based on this map, do you think the Civil War ended sectionalism? Explain.

MapMaster ●nline

For: Interactive map
Visit: PHSchool.com
Web Code: myp-5123

African Americans Lose Rights

With the end of Reconstruction, African Americans began to lose their remaining political and civil rights in the South. Southern whites used a variety of techniques to stop African Americans from voting. They passed laws that applied to whites and African Americans but were enforced mainly against African Americans.

One such law imposed a **poll tax**—a personal tax to be paid before voting. This kept a few poor whites and many poor freedmen from voting. Another law required voters to pass a **literacy test,** or a test to see if a person can read and write. In this case, voters were <u>required</u> to read a section of the Constitution and explain it.

However, a grandfather clause allowed illiterate white males to vote. The **grandfather clause** was a provision that allowed a voter to avoid a literacy test if his father or grandfather had been eligible to vote on January 1, 1867. Because no African American in the South could vote before 1868, nearly all were denied the right to vote.

Southern states created a network of laws requiring **segregation,** or enforced separation of races. These so-called Jim Crow laws barred the mixing of races in almost every aspect of life. Blacks and whites were born in separate hospitals and buried in separate cemeteries. The laws decreed separate playgrounds, restaurants, and schools. They required African Americans to take back seats or separate cars on railroads and streetcars. When African Americans challenged the restrictions in court, they lost. State and local courts consistently ruled that Jim Crow laws were legal.

Vocabulary Builder
<u>require</u> (rih KWYR) **v.** to order or command

● **INFOGRAPHIC**

SHARECROPPING
CYCLE OF POVERTY

Farming land they did not own, sharecroppers were locked into a cycle of debt, as shown by the illustration.
Critical Thinking: *Draw Conclusions Why was it hard for sharecroppers to escape the debt cycle?*

1. Planting the Crop
Landowners give the sharecropper land, seed, and tools in exchange for a share in the crop. Sharecroppers buy goods and supplies from the landowner on credit.

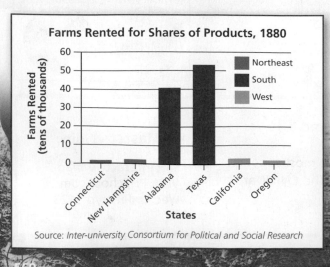

Farms Rented for Shares of Products, 1880

Farms Rented (tens of thousands)

- Northeast
- South
- West

States: Connecticut, New Hampshire, Alabama, Texas, California, Oregon

Source: *Inter-university Consortium for Political and Social Research*

In 1896, the U.S. Supreme Court upheld segregation laws. Homer Plessy had been arrested for sitting in a coach marked "for whites only." In the case of *Plessy* v. *Ferguson*, the Court ruled in favor of a Louisiana law requiring segregated railroad cars. The Court said a law could require "separate" facilities, so long as they were "equal."

This "separate but equal" rule was in effect until the 1950s. In fact, facilities for African Americans were rarely equal. For example, public schools for African Americans were almost always <u>inferior</u> to schools for whites.

Vocabulary Builder
<u>inferior</u> (ihn FIR ee uhr) *adj.* of lower rank or status, or of poorer quality

☑️**Checkpoint** **What methods did southern states use to deprive African Americans of their rights?**

A Cycle of Poverty

At emancipation, many freedmen owned little more than the clothes they wore. Poverty forced many African Americans, as well as poor whites, to become sharecroppers. A **sharecropper** is a laborer who works the land for the farmer who owns it, in exchange for a share of the value of the crop.

The landlord supplied living quarters, tools, seed, and food on credit. At harvest time, the landlord sold the crop and tallied up how much went to the sharecroppers. Often, especially in years of low crop prices or bad harvests, the sharecroppers' share was not enough to cover what they owed the landlord for rent and supplies. As a result, most sharecroppers became locked into a cycle of debt.

2. Harvesting the Crop and Settling Accounts
The sharecropper gives the landowner his crop. Landowner sells it and gives the tenant his share, minus the amount owed at the company store.

History *Interactive,*
Explore the Sharecropping Cycle
Visit: PHSchool.com
Web Code: myp-5127

3. Cycle of Debt
After a year of hard work, the sharecroppers often owed more than they had earned and had no choice but to offer the landlord a greater percentage of next year's crop.

Links Across Time

1963 Dr. Martin Luther King, Jr., speaks to Americans in Washington, D.C.

Fighting for Civil Rights

1896 In *Plessy* v. *Ferguson*, the Supreme Court upheld segregation laws in the South. These restrictions continued for more than 50 years.

1950s–1960s Some Americans launched a campaign to bring equal rights to African Americans. This civil rights movement used marches, petitions, and other public actions to end discrimination in education, use of public facilities, and voting.

Link to Today Online

Civil Rights Today Did the civil rights movement win equal rights for all Americans? Not everyone agrees. Go online to find out more about recent developments in civil rights.

For: Civil rights in the news
Visit: PHSchool.com
Web Code: myc-5123

Opportunities dwindled for African Americans in southern towns and cities, too. African American artisans who had been able to find skilled jobs during Reconstruction increasingly found such jobs closed to them. Those with some education could become schoolteachers, lawyers, or preachers in the African American community. But most urban African Americans had to take whatever menial job they could find.

✓Checkpoint How did many freedmen and whites become locked in a cycle of poverty?

Industrial Growth

It would be a long process, but during Reconstruction the South's economy began to recover. By the 1880s, new industries appeared. Southerners hailed a "New South," based on industrial growth.

The first element of the South's economy to begin recovery was agriculture. Cotton production, which had lagged during the war, quickly revived. By 1875, it was setting new records. Planters put more land into tobacco production, and output grew.

Southern investors started or expanded industries to turn raw materials into finished products. The textile industry came to play an important role in the southern economy.

The South had natural resources in abundance, but it had done little to develop them in the past. Atlanta newspaper editor Henry Grady described the funeral of a man from Georgia as follows:

> **"**They buried him in the heart of a pine forest, and yet the pine coffin was imported from Cincinnati. They buried him within touch of an iron mine, and yet the nails in his coffin and the iron in the shovel that dug his grave were imported from Pittsburgh.**"**
>
> —Henry Grady to the Bay State Club of Boston, 1889

The South began to develop its own resources. New mills and factories grew up to use the South's iron, timber, and oil. Lumber mills and furniture factories processed yellow pine and hardwoods from southern forests.

Southern leaders took great pride in the region's progress. They spoke of a "New South" that was no longer dependent on "King Cotton." An industrial age was underway, although the North was still far more industrialized.

✓**Checkpoint** What was the "New South" that was emerging by 1900?

⭐ **Looking Back and Ahead** When Reconstruction ended in 1877, its record showed many successes and some failures. Most importantly, all African Americans were finally citizens. Laws passed during Reconstruction, such as the Fourteenth Amendment, became the basis of the civil rights movement that took place almost 100 years later.

Factory in the "New South"

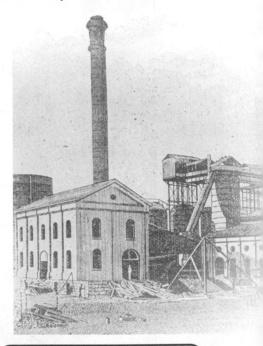

Section 3 | Check Your Progress

Comprehension and Critical Thinking

1. **(a) Identify** Who were sharecroppers? How did they differ from landowners?
   (b) Draw Conclusions Why did so many sharecroppers live in poverty?

2. **(a) Recall** What is segregation?
   (b) Analyze Cause and Effect How did *Plessy* v. *Ferguson* make the fight against segregation more difficult?

🔄 Reading Skill

3. **Evaluate Proposals** In *Plessy* v. *Ferguson*, the Supreme Court proposed the idea of "separate but equal" facilities. Do you think this idea meets the goal of ensuring equal rights?

Key Terms

Complete each of the following sentences so that the second part clearly shows your understanding of the key term.

4. African Americans and whites had to pay a poll tax before _____.

5. Because of laws in the South requiring segregation, African Americans and whites _____.

Writing

6. Rewrite the following passage to correct the errors. **Passage:** The 1876 presidential election decided by a special commission. Samuel J. Tilden a democrat won the Popular vote over republican Rutherford B. Hayes. However, their were 20 disputed electorial votes. A special commission made an agreement with the democrats.

21st Century Learning Thematic maps focus on special topics, such as food products, physical features, or political boundaries. Information presented in a visual way is easier to understand and absorb. One type of thematic map shows the migration or movement of people within a particular area.

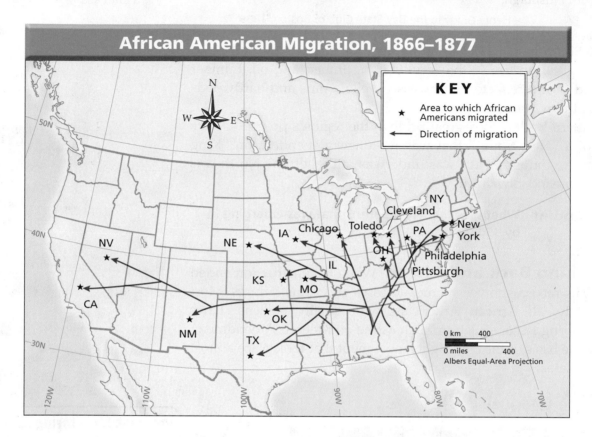

African American Migration, 1866–1877

KEY

★ Area to which African Americans migrated

← Direction of migration

0 km 400
0 miles 400
Albers Equal-Area Projection

Learn the Skill

Use these steps to learn how to trace migrations on maps.

1 **Identify the subject of the map.** Read the title of the map. Look for dates that identify the time period.

2 **Look at the map key.** The map key explains special symbols and colors used on the map.

3 **Determine direction.** To trace the route of a migration, use the direction arrows on the compass rose to identify north, south, east, and west. Then, identify the direction or directions of the route.

4 **Make a generalization.** Use the information on the map to make a general statement about the historic migration.

Practice the Skill

Answer the following questions about the map on this page.

1 **Identify the subject of the map.** What is the title of the map?

2 **Look at the map key.** What does the star symbol show?

3 **Determine direction.** In which direction did African Americans travel to migrate to New York?

4 **Make a generalization.** In general, to which areas of the country did African Americans migrate during Reconstruction?

Apply the Skill

See the Review and Assessment at the end of this chapter.

Quick Study Guide

What were the short-term and long-term effects of the Civil War?

Section 1
Rebuilding the Nation

- The South faced major economic and social challenges at the end of the Civil War.
- Reconstruction plans and programs like the Freedmen's Bureau were designed to rebuild the South.
- The death of Abraham Lincoln threatened lenient plans for Reconstruction.

Section 2
The Battle Over Reconstruction

- President Andrew Johnson and the Radical Republicans clashed over Reconstruction plans.
- Conflict over Reconstruction led to Andrew Johnson's impeachment.
- During Reconstruction, African American males gained the right to vote. Republicans came to power in each southern state.

Section 3
The End of Reconstruction

- With the end of Reconstruction, African Americans in the South lost many rights they had gained after the Civil War.
- Many African Americans and poor whites were forced to become sharecroppers.
- The South's agriculture revived, and its industries expanded.

? Exploring the Essential Question

Use the online study guide to explore the essential question.

Section 1
How did the government try to solve key problems facing the nation after the Civil War?

Chapter 16 Essential Question
What were the short-term and long-term effects of the Civil War?

Section 2
How did disagreements over Reconstruction lead to conflict in government and in the South?

Section 3
What were the effects of Reconstruction?

Key Terms

Fill in the blanks with the correct key terms.

1. _____ were people who had been enslaved before emancipation.

2. Northerners who moved south after the Civil War were sometimes called _____.

3. Southern states gave _____, which required voters to read and explain part of the Constitution.

4. A _____ farmed land in return for a portion of the value of the crop.

Comprehension and Critical Thinking

5. **(a) Recall** How did the Wade-Davis Bill differ from Lincoln's plan for reuniting the country?
(b) Make Predictions How do you think southerners would have reacted to Reconstruction if Lincoln's plan had been followed?

6. **(a) Recall** How did Johnson and the Radicals come into conflict?
(b) Analyze Cause and Effect How effective do you think Johnson was after the failure of the impeachment process?

7. **(a) Recall** What right is guaranteed by the Fifteenth Amendment?
(b) Interpret Art How does the painting *His First Vote* (below) reflect how the Fifteenth Amendment affected African Americans?

8. **(a) Recall** How did the Freedman's Bureau help African Americans after the Civil War?
(b) Make Predictions Which of the actions of the Freedmen's Bureau has probably had the longest lasting impact on African Americans? How?

9. **(a) Recall** What were the terms of the compromise that gave Rutherford B. Hayes the presidency in 1876?
(b) Draw Conclusions How were African Americans in the South affected by this compromise?

History Reading Skill

10. **Analyze and Evaluate Proposals** Review what you have read about the conflict between Johnson and Radical Republicans. What did each side propose? Which proposal makes the most sense to you? Explain.

Writing

11. **Write an essay on the following topic:**
Explain how events and developments during Reconstruction highlighted differences between North and South, even as the two tried to reunite.

Your essay should:
- state a thesis or purpose for writing;
- explain the subject you are writing about;
- offer evidence, examples, or details to support your explanation;
- conclude with a short summary of your main points.

12. **Write a Narrative:**
Imagine you are Hiram Revels. Write a narrative describing your first days in the Senate.

Skills for Life

Analyze a Migration Map

Use the map in the Skills for Life feature to answer the questions that follow.

13. What time period is covered in this map?

14. What does the arrow symbol show?

15. In which direction did African Americans travel to migrate to Oklahoma and New Mexico?

16. Based on the information in the map, what decision did many African Americans make during Reconstruction?

Test Yourself

Refer to the quotation below to answer Question 1.

> "A system of oppression so rank that nothing could make it seem small except the fact that [African Americans] had already been ground under it for a century and a half."

1. **Which system does this quotation refer to?**
   A amnesty
   B Reconstruction
   C sharecropping
   D segregation

2. **How did African Americans benefit from the passage of the Fourteenth Amendment?**
   A Their right to vote was protected.
   B They became citizens.
   C They were given land.
   D They no longer had to pass literacy tests.

3. **A chief goal of the Freedmen's Bureau was to promote**
   A abolition.
   B industrial growth.
   C education.
   D segregation.

Document-Based Questions

Task: Look at Documents 1 and 2, and answer their accompanying questions. Then, use the documents and your knowledge of history to complete the following writing assignment:

> Write a two-paragraph essay about the goals and methods of the Ku Klux Klan. Using specific details, draw a conclusion about whether Document 1 or Document 2 gives a more accurate description of the Klan.

Document 1: The "Organization and Principles" of the Ku Klux Klan, stated below, was written in 1868. It describes the goals of the Klan. *What does the Klan say is its attitude toward violence?*

> "This is an institution of chivalry, humanity, mercy, and patriotism; embodying in its genius and its principles all that is chivalric in conduct, noble in sentiment, generous in manhood, and patriotic in purpose; its peculiar objects being:
>
> First, to protect the weak, the innocent, and the defenseless from the [insults], wrongs, and outrages of the lawless, the violent, and the brutal; to relieve the injured and oppressed. . . .
>
> *Questions to be asked each [Klan] candidate:*
> • Are you in favor of a white man's government in this country? . . ."

Document 2: This political cartoon was published in a northern magazine in 1874. *Describe what has happened to the African American family.*

Historian's Apprentice

Workshop

How was the Civil War a political, economic, and social turning point?

DIRECTIONS: Analyze the following documents from the years before, during, and after the Civil War. Answer the questions that accompany each document or set of documents. You will use your answers to build an answer to the unit question.

HISTORIAN'S CHECKLIST

WHO produced the document?

WHERE was it made?

WHEN was it produced?

WHY was it made and for what audience?

WHAT is its viewpoint?

HOW does it connect to what I've learned?

WHY is the document important?

document 1

Handbill, Boston, 1851

CAUTION!!
COLORED PEOPLE
OF BOSTON, ONE & ALL,
You are hereby respectfully CAUTIONED and advised, to avoid conversing with the
Watchmen and Police Officers of Boston,
For since the recent ORDER OF THE MAYOR & ALDERMEN, they are empowered to act as
KIDNAPPERS
AND
Slave Catchers,
And they have already been actually employed in KIDNAPPING, CATCHING, AND KEEPING SLAVES. Therefore, if you value your LIBERTY, and the *Welfare of the Fugitives* among you, *Shun* them in every possible manner, as so many *HOUNDS* on the track of the most unfortunate of your race.
Keep a Sharp Look Out for KIDNAPPERS, and have TOP EYE open.
APRIL 24, 1851.

Was this poster antislavery or proslavery? Explain.

document 2

Battle of Antietam, 1862

Why did hostility between the North and the South continue even after the Civil War was over?

document 3 · The Emancipation Proclamation

" Coming generations will celebrate the first of January as the day which brought liberty and manhood to American slaves.... That paper Proclamation must now be made iron, lead and fire, by the prompt employment of the negro's arm in this contest. "

—*Frederick Douglass, 1863*

What were the effects of the Emancipation Proclamation?

document 4 · Northern Newspaper's Viewpoint

" There is one, and only one, sure and safe policy for the immediate future: namely: the North must remain the absolute Dictator of the Republic until the spirit of the North shall become the spirit of the whole country....

The South is still unpurged of her treason. Prostrate in the dust she is no less a traitor at this hour than when her head was erect.... They cannot be trusted with authority over their former slaves.... The only hope for the South is to give the ballot to the Negro and in denying it to the rebels. "

—The Independent, *May 5, 1865*

Do you think this editorial helped the nation heal after the Civil War? Why or why not?

document 5 · The South's Postwar Economy

" Our losses have been frightful, and we have, now, scarcely a support. My Father had five plantations on the coast, and all the buildings were burnt, and the negroes ... are roaming in a starved condition. Our farm near Charleston was abandoned.... All is now lost, and the negroes, left to themselves ... seek a little food, about the city. Our residence in the city, was sacked ... and the house well riddled by shell & shot. Our handsome Residence in the country was burnt. The Enemy passed over all our property on the coast in their march from Savannah to Charleston, the whole country, down there, is now a howling wilderness.... [I]t will be many years, before this once productive country will be able to support itself. "

—*Edward Barnwell Heyward, South Carolina planter, 1866*

How did the Civil War affect the South's economy?

 Go On

continued

6 An African American Senator

"[M]y downtrodden people . . . bear toward their former masters no revengeful thoughts, no hatreds, no animosities. They aim not to elevate themselves by sacrificing one single interest of their white fellow-citizens. They ask but the rights which are theirs by God's universal law . . . [to] enjoy the liberties of citizenship on the same footing with their white neighbors and friends."

—Hiram Revels, speech in the U.S. Senate, March 16, 1870

Do you think Senator Revels' goals could be achieved in the late 1800s? Why or why not?

7 Worse Than Slavery

How did radical white southerners oppose rights for African Americans?

8 Sharecropping

Percentage of sharecropped farms (by county)

- 0%–20%
- 21%–34%
- 35%–80%

Conic Projection
0   100   200 mi
0   100 200 km

VIRGINIA

TENNESSEE

NORTH CAROLINA

ARKANSAS

SOUTH CAROLINA

MISS.   ALABAMA   GEORGIA

Atlantic Ocean

TEXAS

LOUISIANA

FLORIDA

Gulf of Mexico

95°W   85°W

Why did many African American farmers remain trapped in poverty?

ACTIVITY

Divide into three groups to prepare a documentary news program on the unit question:

How was the Civil War a political, economic, and social turning point?

One group should use the Historian's Apprentice Workshop documents to describe the Civil War's political effects. Another group should use the documents to describe the economic effects of the war. The last group should cover the war's social effects. After each group has had time to prepare a presentation, it should report its findings to the rest of the class in the format of a documentary news program.

Epilogue

1865–Present

> *"There are all kinds of exciting new technologies that can create millions of new good jobs, put the U.S. back in a position of leadership in the world economy, and solve lots of problems at the same time."*
>
> —Al Gore,
> economic policy speech, 2002

Since 1865, the United States has become an industrial giant and a global superpower. But in the 21st century, America faces new challenges to its prosperity.

Makkos

EPILOGUE

What You Will Learn

Section 1
THE NATION GROWS
An expanding economy and a surge of immigration led to an explosive growth in American cities.

Section 2
A NEW ROLE FOR THE NATION
Around 1900, the United States reversed a century of isolation and began taking an active role in world events.

Section 3
TOWARD THE MODERN AGE
After World War II, the United States entered a long period of heightened tensions with the Soviet Union, known as the Cold War.

Section 4
INTO THE FUTURE
Challenges to Americans today include the threat of terrorism, technological change, and preservation of the environment.

Reading Skill
Frame Research Questions In this chapter, you will learn how to ask questions that can be answered through research.

573

How has the American nation met

The Growing Nation, 1865–Present

1 **Settling the West**
Attracted by open land, farmers settled across the West.

4 **Dealing With Other Nations**
Today, the United States continues to play a leading role in international affairs around the world.

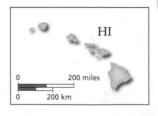

 U.S. Events

1869 | First transcontinental railroad completed.

United States Steel Corporation founded. | **1901**

Wall Street panic marks beginning of Great Depression. | **1929**

1860 **1885** **1910** **1935**

 World Events

United States defeats Spain in Spanish-American War. | **1898**

Adolf Hitler becomes chancellor of Germany. | **1933**

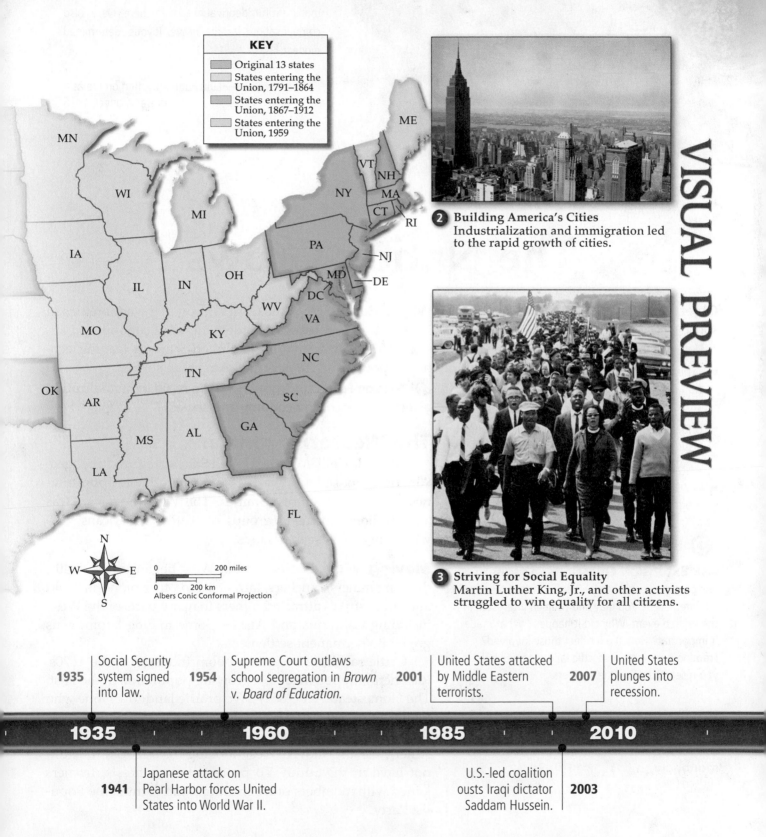

KEY

- Original 13 states
- States entering the Union, 1791–1864
- States entering the Union, 1867–1912
- States entering the Union, 1959

ME
VT
NH
NY
MA
CT
RI
PA
NJ
MD
DE
DC
WV
VA
NC
SC
GA
FL
MN
WI
MI
IA
IL
IN
OH
KY
TN
AL
MS
LA
AR
OK
MO

N
W E
S

0   200 miles
0   200 km
Albers Conic Conformal Projection

VISUAL PREVIEW

2 **Building America's Cities**
Industrialization and immigration led to the rapid growth of cities.

3 **Striving for Social Equality**
Martin Luther King, Jr., and other activists struggled to win equality for all citizens.

1935 Social Security system signed into law.	**1954** Supreme Court outlaws school segregation in *Brown v. Board of Education*.	**2001** United States attacked by Middle Eastern terrorists.	**2007** United States plunges into recession.

1935   **1960**   **1985**   **2010**

1941 Japanese attack on Pearl Harbor forces United States into World War II.

U.S.-led coalition ousts Iraqi dictator Saddam Hussein. **2003**

The Pioneer Spirit

❝ There were many tearful occasions for the tearful type. There were days and months without human fellowship, there were frightful blizzards... and many pitiful deprivations, but there were also compensations for the brave, joyous, determined pioneer. ❞

—Lulu Fuhr, reflecting on life as a Kansas pioneer, 1916

▲ A farm family on the Great Plains

The Nation Grows

Objectives

- Describe the impact of western settlement on Native Americans.

- Explain the connection between the expansion of industry and the growing labor union movement.

- Understand how an expanding economy and a surge of immigration led to an explosive growth of American cities.

- Identify the leading reforms of the Progressive Era.

🔄 Reading Skill

Ask Extension Questions In discussing one central event, history books will often mention a related event. You may find yourself interested in the related event. Why did it happen? What made it important? How did it affect those involved? Framing questions in specific language will help you research to find the answers.

Key Terms and People

reservation
corporation
monopoly

Theodore
Roosevelt
suffrage

Why It Matters With the Civil War over, the nation turned its attention to westward settlement and economic expansion. This growth made the United States a leading economic power and transformed American society.

❓ Section Focus Question: How did rapid industrialization affect the American economy and society?

The Western Frontier

After the Civil War, the United States grew and changed. Americans looked westward, hoping to find new opportunities in the wide, empty prairies. The West, however, was already home to many groups of Native Americans who would, in time, lose their lands.

Moving West A rush to the West began in the 1840s, drawing miners, ranchers, farmers, and other pioneers. Gold and silver strikes attracted miners to many parts of the West, including California and Alaska. Some mining boomtowns grew into permanent settlements.

Cattle ranching became a boom industry in the 1870s. Ranchers shipped meat to a growing population in the East. The Homestead Act (1862) gave prairie land to anyone who would farm it for five years. Eager for land, families from the East endured hardships and harsh weather. African Americans also moved West, looking for freedom they did not have in the South. To protect their interests, farmers joined with members of labor unions and formed the Populist Party.

Technology helped sustain western settlement. With the new steel plow, farmers could cut the tough prairie soil. To encourage railroad building, the government granted the railroad 10 square miles of land for every mile of track. In 1869, the Union Pacific Railroad, building west, met the Central Pacific, building east, at Promontory, Utah. This first transcontinental railroad helped unite the country.

Plains Indians Lose Their Lands Settlement of the West meant the near destruction of Native American cultures. Plains Indians were buffalo hunters. The buffalo supplied meat for food and skins for clothing, warm rugs, and tepees.

In spite of treaties protecting Indian lands, miners and settlers claimed ownership. Soldiers and hunters wiped out the huge buffalo herds. Leaders such as Sitting Bull, Crazy Horse, Chief Joseph, and Geronimo led their people in wars with government troops. The contest was hopeless. Gradually, the federal government forced Native Americans onto reservations, land set aside for Native Americans to live on.

☑**Checkpoint** **What impact did the destruction of the buffalo herds have on Native Americans of the Great Plains?**

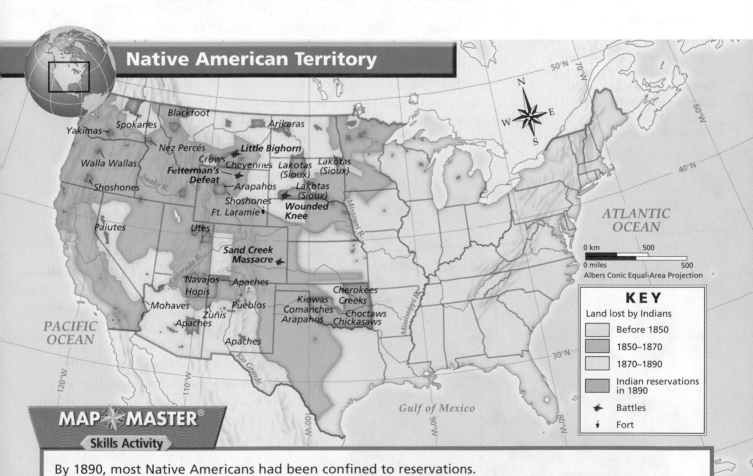

Native American Territory

KEY

Land lost by Indians

- Before 1850
- 1850–1870
- 1870–1890
- Indian reservations in 1890
- ✶ Battles
- ⚑ Fort

MAP✶MASTER®

Skills Activity

By 1890, most Native Americans had been confined to reservations.

(a) Read a Map During what period did Native Americans lose most of their land in California?

(b) Draw Conclusions How did being restricted to reservations change the way of life of Native Americans on the Great Plains?

MapMaster ⦿nline
For: Interactive map
Visit: PHSchool.com
Web Code: myp-6132

Business and Labor

American business and industry boomed after the Civil War. A network of rail lines crossed the country. Railroads carried materials to factories and cattle to meatpacking plants. Inventions such as refrigeration, the telephone, and the electric street car changed both business and daily life. Thomas Edison and his workers invented products that shaped today's world—not only the first practical light bulb but also the electric power plant, the phonograph, and motion pictures. Late in the 1800s, inventors in America and Europe built the first automobiles.

Growth of Big Business The railroad industry <u>dominated</u> the American economy. "Railroad barons" bought up smaller lines and built great railroad empires. The most powerful was Cornelius Vanderbilt, owner of the New York Central Railroad. Railroad owners sometimes abused their power by fixing prices and bribing public officials. At the same time, though, the railroads created jobs and spurred the growth of industry.

To expand, businesses organized as corporations. A **corporation** sells shares of stock to investors in exchange for money, or capital. If the business prospers, investors get dividends, and the value of their stock grows. The corporate structure protects individual owners if a company fails because they could not lose more than they invested.

Business tycoons became successful in other areas, particularly steel, banking, and oil. The steel industry expanded quickly, creating great fortunes. Steelmaker Andrew Carnegie gained control of all aspects of the business, from iron mines to steel mills to shipping lines. Believing the wealthy had a duty to society, Carnegie gave millions to charity.

Big banks grew along with industry. They invested in corporations, allowing bankers to control company policies. With his fortune, banker J. P. Morgan bought railroads and steel companies. He merged several companies to form U.S. Steel, the first billion-dollar American business. Other fortunes were based on a new resource—oil. John D. Rockefeller built his family fortune with an oil refinery that grew into the Standard Oil Company. Rockefeller organized a trust to control the stock of rival companies. That made Standard Oil a **monopoly**—a company that dominates an industry.

Critics charged that these business practices reduced competition, hurting smaller companies and consumers. Others defended giant corporations, saying they brought lower prices and improved people's lives.

Inventive Genius

Thomas Edison once said, "Genius is one percent inspiration and ninety-nine percent perspiration."
Critical Thinking: *Draw Conclusions What did Edison mean? Do you think his opinion is true in other areas of life?*

Rise of Organized Labor The growth of American industry created thousands of new jobs. Working conditions, however, were often harsh and dangerous. Many workers were immigrants, women, and children, who labored for long hours and low pay in crowded sweatshops.

Workers began to organize for better conditions. The Knights of Labor wanted shorter hours and an end to child labor. In 1886, the American Federation of Labor (AFL) brought together trade unions, which represented workers who were skilled in particular crafts. Some unions used strikes to gain better pay. In the 1886 Haymarket Riot in Chicago, police clashed violently with protesting workers. Public officials and the courts generally sided with factory owners.

✓ **Checkpoint** How did economic conditions affect the labor union movement?

Immigration and the Growth of Cities

In the late 1800s, millions of immigrants streamed into the United States. Fleeing poverty, they hoped for factory jobs or to acquire farmland. The immigrants swelled city populations. Housing was scarce, and city services were lacking. At the same time, city life offered a rich mix of cultures and amusements.

The New Immigrants Before the Civil War, most immigrants were from northern and western Europe. In the late 1800s, this pattern changed. More people came from southern or eastern Europe, including Catholics from Italy and Jews from Russia. A growing number of Asians, mainly Chinese, arrived on the West Coast.

Language, religion, and culture set newcomers apart from their neighbors. Usually the older immigrants kept traditional ways, and their children hurried to learn English and become citizens.

Many Americans opposed the flood of immigrants, saying that newcomers would never fit into American culture. On the West Coast, anti-Chinese feelings were especially strong. An 1882 federal law barred most Chinese immigrants. Other laws set limits on immigration.

American Cities Grow and Change The United States was once mainly a rural, farming nation. That changed as people flocked to cities. One large group of migrants was African Americans from the South. They formed thriving new communities in northern cities such as Chicago and Detroit.

City life was very different for the rich and the poor. The poor often lived in small, dark, crowded tenement apartments. In these unhealthy conditions, diseases like tuberculosis spread easily. Fires were frequent and crime common. Middle-class families, on the other hand, lived in comfortable houses. The very wealthy built mansions far from the crowds.

✓ **Checkpoint** How did industrialization and immigration change life in American cities?

Child coal miners

Suffragettes march for the right to vote in the early 1900s

The Progressive Era

Though prosperity created the Gilded Age in the late 1800s, American society had many problems. In the Progressive Era, reformers worked to reduce the power of big business, improve social conditions, and clean up political corruption.

Progressive Reformers Though they had different targets, Progressives were united in wanting to improve society. Some reformers were journalists, known as muckrakers. They reported on slum conditions and unsafe meatpacking plants. Other Progressives backed political reforms such as primary elections.

Progressives also attacked corruption in government. Powerful "bosses," such as Boss Tweed in New York City, controlled business and politics. One early reform set up the Civil Service Commission. It awarded federal jobs on the basis of exam scores rather than political influence. Reformers also tried to <u>minimize</u> the power of big business. In 1887, Congress passed the Interstate Commerce Act to regulate railroads. The Sherman Antitrust Act (1890) limited business tactics that hurt competition.

Progressive Presidents By 1900, reform ideas reached presidential politics. Theodore Roosevelt became President in 1901, after William McKinley's assassination. Roosevelt believed the presidency could influence the quality of American life. He attacked unfair business practices and supported labor. His conservation policy set aside land for national parks and forests. New laws made food products and medicines safer. Roosevelt's successor, William Howard Taft, continued reforms.

In 1912, Woodrow Wilson, also a Progressive, was elected President. He backed laws to encourage business competition. Congress also began to regulate the banking system.

The Women's Suffrage Movement Even though many leading reformers were women, American women had few political rights. Reformers such as Elizabeth Cady Stanton had long fought

Vocabulary Builder
<u>minimize</u> (MIHN ah mīz) **v.** to reduce; to make smaller; to make of less importance

Ask Extension Questions

Reading Skill

The conflict between Theodore Roosevelt and William Howard Taft is an interesting aspect of American history. Suggest a possible research question building on the election of 1912.

for **suffrage**—the right to vote. American women first gained the vote in some western states. In 1920, the Nineteenth Amendment to the Constitution protected women's right to vote.

Women sought equality in other areas, too, such as the chance to study law and medicine. They tried to end social problems such as child labor. Women also led the fight to ban alcoholic beverages. In 1919, the Eighteenth Amendment established Prohibition, a ban on the sale of alcohol in the United States.

Seeking Equality The reforms of the early 1900s did not achieve much for nonwhites. Since Reconstruction's end, African Americans had lost many rights. They faced prejudice and segregation in schools, housing, and jobs. Two leaders offered different answers. Booker T. Washington advised people to concentrate on education and gradual progress. W.E.B. Du Bois believed that African Americans should work actively against discrimination. Du Bois joined with white reformers to found the National Association for the Advancement of Colored People (NAACP).

Other minority groups also faced discrimination. The Mexican American population in the Southwest grew quickly after 1910. Immigration to the United States from China was barred, but Asians from Japan and the Philippines immigrated to the West Coast. Discrimination against the Asians was widespread. An agreement with Japan kept out more workers.

Booker T. Washington

W.E.B. Du Bois

☑**Checkpoint** **List some accomplishments of the Progressive Presidents Roosevelt, Taft, and Wilson.**

⭐ **Looking Back and Ahead** By the beginning of the twentieth century, Americans were settled across the continent. American industry was thriving, and immigration had swelled the nation's cities. In the next section, you will see how this new status thrust the United States into a leading role on the world scene.

HISTORIAN'S APPRENTICE ACTIVITY PACK

To further explore the topics in this chapter, complete the activity in the Historian's Apprentice Activity Pack to answer this essential question:

How did industrialization affect the United States?

Section 1 | Check Your Progress

Comprehension and Critical Thinking

1. **(a) Identify** Who was Chief Joseph?
   (b) Detect Points of View In 1879, Chief Joseph appeared before Congress. He said, "Treat all men alike. Give them all the same law. Give them all an even chance to live and grow. All men were made by the same Great Spirit Chief." What was Chief Joseph trying to tell Congress? How do you think members of Congress responded to his words?

2. **(a) Describe** Why did cities grow rapidly after the Civil War?
   (b) Apply Information How did the growth of cities lead to problems for many residents?

Reading Skill

3. **Ask Extension Questions** The displacement of Native Americans of the Great Plains and Southwest is a controversial part of American history. Suggest a possible research question building on this topic.

Key Terms

4. Draw a table with four rows and two columns. In the first column, list the key terms from this section: reservation, corporation, monopoly, suffrage. In the next column, write the definition of each term.

Writing

5. "Life in a city is more rewarding than life outside a city." List two or three arguments in favor of that opinion, and list two or three arguments opposing that opinion.

An Immigrant's Journey

From all over the world, immigrants poured into the United States. Wherever they came from, these newcomers shared many of the same hopes, fears, and challenges.

 Passage

Immigrants faced a long, difficult ocean crossing crowded into ship holds that were designed to carry cargo or cattle.

"Day after day the weather was bad and the sea stormy. The hatch was tightly closed and there was no circulation of air, so we were all tortured by the bad odor."

—Japanese immigrant
describes the voyage

European immigrants arrive in New York

 Arrival

New York's Ellis Island was the point of entry for many European immigrants. Asians were detained on Angel Island outside San Francisco.

"Immigration officials slammed a tag on you with your name, address, country of origin, etc. . . . Then they pushed you and they'd point, because they didn't know whether you spoke English or not."

—Irish immigrant
describes arrival at Ellis Island

3 ▸ Ethnic Neighborhoods

Crowded into ethnic neighborhoods, immigrants preserved familiar ways as they adjusted to their new culture.

"When we first arrived we still wore our wooden shoes. . . . We conquered the English language beautifully. My father spoke well. But in the home we spoke Frisian."

–Dutch immigrant describes life in America

A street in a Jewish neighborhood in New York

4 ▸ Citizenship

For many immigrants, becoming a citizen was the proudest moment of their lives.

"I am the youngest of America's children, and into my hands is given all her priceless heritage. . . . Mine is the whole majestic past, and mine is the shining future."

–Russian immigrant expresses pride in becoming U.S. citizen

A new citizen is sworn in

Analyze LIFE AT THE TIME

Suppose that you are an immigrant in 1900. For each stage of the journey from passage to citizenship, write a sentence describing your hopes or your fears.

The Fifteen Millionth Ford

Americans Mean Business

❝The chief business of the American people is business. They are profoundly concerned with producing, buying, selling, investing, and prospering in the world. . . . We want peace and honor, and that charity which is so strong an element of all civilization. The chief ideal of the American people is idealism.❞

—President Calvin Coolidge, 1925

◄ Automobile production strengthened U.S. trade around the world.

A New Role for the Nation

Objectives

- Describe how the United States gained an empire after the Spanish-American War.
- Identify the causes of World War I.
- Explain the social changes that occurred in the United States during the 1920s.
- Describe how hard times affected American families during the 1930s.

🔁 Reading Skill

Ask Analytical Questions Reading about history may sometimes leave you puzzled. Ask questions that focus on these puzzles, and then research to find answers. Start by looking at what does not make sense to you, such as why people acted in a particular way. Use the question starters *who, what, when, why,* and *how.* Then, think about how events changed over time and what caused the changes.

Key Terms and People

Woodrow Wilson
isolationism
on margin

Franklin Delano
Roosevelt

Why It Matters Following George Washington's early advice to avoid the political affairs of other nations, later Presidents pursued policies that limited U.S. involvement in world affairs. Yet, as American trade expanded, the United States abandoned isolationism and emerged as a new power on the global stage.

❷ Section Focus Question: How did a more powerful United States expand its role in the world?

Becoming a World Power

Once Americans reached the Pacific Coast, they looked toward winning even more trade and territory. In the 1850s, visits by the U.S. Navy opened ports in Japan to trade with the West. In 1867, the United States purchased the resource-rich Alaska Territory from Russia.

U.S. expansion in the Pacific rested on naval power. The country acquired the islands of Midway and Samoa, where ships bound for Asia could refuel. The next large acquisition was the island chain of Hawaii, ruled by its royal family. Starting in the mid-1800s, Americans had set up large sugar plantations in Hawaii. In 1893, with the help of the U.S. Marines, American sugar planters overthrew the last Hawaiian queen, Liliuokalani. The United States soon annexed the islands. In mainland Asia, the United States competed with European nations for influence in China. The Open Door Policy guaranteed access to Chinese ports and trade.

The United States and Latin America Backers of expansion next looked closer to home. In nearby Cuba, people were rebelling against rule by Spain. Sensational newspaper stories made many Americans want to help the rebels. In 1898, the American battleship *Maine* blew up in Havana harbor. Newspaper headlines blamed Spain. Soon the country was at war with Spain, not only in Cuba but also in the Philippine Islands. A quick victory gave the United States control of Cuba, Puerto Rico, Guam, and the Philippines. Cubans were given self-rule, though under American control.

Theodore Roosevelt believed in using power to promote American expansion. He actively followed a "big stick" policy in challenging European expansion in Latin America. One of his goals was a canal across the narrow Isthmus of Panama. It would let ships sail between the Atlantic and the Pacific oceans rather than going around South America. Taking advantage of a local rebellion, Roosevelt obtained land for the canal. Despite tropical diseases and engineering challenges, the Panama Canal was completed by 1914. Roosevelt took another step in establishing an American role in Latin America. The Roosevelt Corollary stated the right of the United States to intervene in Latin American affairs in order to prevent European nations from trying to establish control. U.S. troops protected American investments in Haiti and the Dominican Republic. From 1914 through 1916, U.S. troops intervened in the Mexican Revolution.

✓**Checkpoint** **What lands did the United States gain control of as a result of the Spanish-American War?**

The Big Stick in the Caribbean Sea

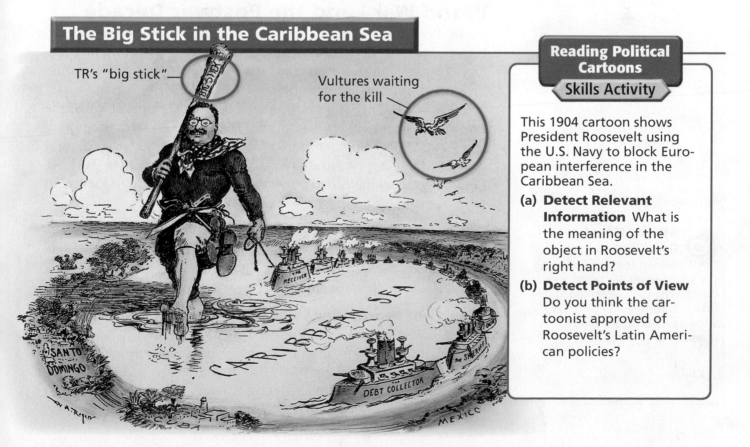

TR's "big stick"

Vultures waiting for the kill

SANTO DOMINGO

CARIBBEAN SEA

THE RECEIVER

DEBT COLLECTOR

MEXICO

Reading Political Cartoons

Skills Activity

This 1904 cartoon shows President Roosevelt using the U.S. Navy to block European interference in the Caribbean Sea.

(a) **Detect Relevant Information** What is the meaning of the object in Roosevelt's right hand?

(b) **Detect Points of View** Do you think the cartoonist approved of Roosevelt's Latin American policies?

Links Across Time

Today an honor guard keeps 24-hour watch at the Tomb of the Unknowns.

Honoring Veterans

1921 The day World War I ended has been remembered ever since. On November 11, 1921, the body of an unidentified American soldier was laid to rest in the Tomb of the Unknowns at Arlington National Cemetery.

1938 November 11 was made a national holiday, Armistice Day. The name of Armistice Day was later changed to Veterans Day.

Link to Today

Veterans Day Today Each year, on November 11, we continue to honor those who have served in our nation's armed forces.

For: Veterans Day in the news
Visit: PHSchool.com
Web Code: mvc-7213

Ask Analytical Questions

Reread the text following the subheading "Entering the War." Why did the United States finally enter the war in 1917? Suggest a possible research question on this topic.

World War I and the Postwar Decade

In 1914, long-standing tensions in Europe erupted into war. Imperialism was one cause—major nations were competing for territory. To maintain power, nations made alliances with one another, promising support if their allies were attacked.

In June 1914, in Sarajevo, Bosnia, a Serbian nationalist killed the heir to the Austro-Hungarian throne. The alliance system soon drew one nation after another into war. The war pitted the Central powers—Germany, Austria-Hungary, and the Ottoman, or Turkish, Empire—against the Allied powers of France, Britain, and Russia. In time, more than 20 countries were involved.

Entering the War President Woodrow Wilson tried to keep the United States neutral. However, American opinion soon became anti-German because of German submarine attacks on American ships. The United States entered the war in April 1917.

Results of World War I When the United States joined the war, things looked bad for the Allies—Britain, France, and Russia. Then, Russia withdrew from the war after a revolution overthrew the tsar's government. However, by June 1918, the Germans were in retreat. The war ended in November. Its costs were staggering. More than 8 million people were dead. Much of Europe was in ruins.

President Wilson tried to shape the peace settlement. His Fourteen Points plan outlined a League of Nations, an organization that would settle international disputes. However, the final peace treaty left out many of Wilson's ideas. Instead, the Treaty of Versailles imposed extremely harsh terms on Germany. Congress sought a return to **isolationism,** avoiding becoming involved in world affairs. It rejected U.S. membership in the League of Nations.

The Prosperous Twenties The 1920s began as a hopeful, prosperous time. The postwar economy grew quickly.

The auto industry was important in the booming economy. Factories turned out new consumer goods such as radios, vacuum cleaners, and refrigerators. Many people also <u>invested</u> in the stock market for the first time. Stock prices rose steadily.

American society changed during the 1920s. Women could now vote. More women joined the workforce. Some young women, known as flappers, shocked older Americans with their short skirts and unconventional behavior. Having more leisure time, people enjoyed sports, radio programs, and movies, along with a new kind of music—jazz. African American culture flourished during the Harlem Renaissance.

Reformers had tried to change society by banning alcoholic beverages. Prohibition had disastrous side effects, however. Many people broke the law. Organized crime thrived by supplying liquor to illegal speakeasies. Prohibition was repealed in 1933.

The Crash Some of the prosperity of the 1920s was not real. People bought things they could not afford, paying in installments. They bought stocks **on margin,** paying only a fraction of the cost.

Then, the economy began to slow. Though factories still made goods, people could not afford them. Factories laid off workers or closed. Some investors began to sell their stocks. Stock prices fell. Brokers demanded full payment for stocks bought on margin. Many investors had to sell. In October 1929, panic struck the stock market.

☑️ **Checkpoint** · **What were the results of World War I?**

The Great Depression

The economy now plunged into the worst economic slump in American history. The Great Depression deepened throughout the 1930s. Banks closed, wiping out people's savings. Unemployment soared. Hungry people lined up at soup kitchens. A severe drought in the Great Plains made things worse. High winds and dust storms blew away the topsoil, turning farmland into a region named the Dust Bowl.

President Herbert Hoover tried to fight the Great Depression with some public works programs. Still, people blamed him for the hard times. They wanted a leader who would act more forcefully. In 1932, they elected **Franklin Delano Roosevelt,** also known as FDR. The new President made people feel more confident.

Vocabulary Builder
invest (ihn VEHST) *v.* to purchase something with money with the hope that its value will grow; to give power or authority

Flappers balance on the ledge of a building.

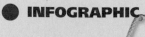

THE GREAT DEPRESSION:
Misery in the Cities

The misery of the Great Depression touched all Americans. Much of the most visible suffering took place in the nation's cities. **Critical Thinking:** *Link Past and Present How do you think you would react if another depression like this one struck the United States?*

Desperate for food, the jobless lined up at soup kitchens operated by churches and private charities. ▼

FREE SOUP COFFEE & DOUGHNUTS FOR THE UNEMPLOYED

◄ Apple sellers were a common sight on street corners.

BUY APPLES 5

Unemployment, 1927–1933

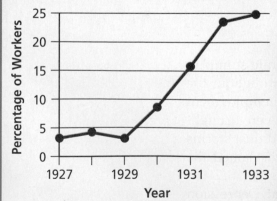

Source: *Historical Statistics of the United States*

Unemployment reached its highest levels in American history during the 1930s.

The homeless gathered in miserable shantytowns, nicknamed Hoovervilles.

FDR's Program FDR promised the American people a New Deal. His programs had three main goals: relief for the unemployed, plans for recovery, and reforms to prevent another severe depression. The Works Progress Administration (WPA), for example, built schools and public buildings and gave work to artists and writers. The Tennessee Valley Authority (TVA) built dams to supply electric power and control floods in parts of the South. The Federal Deposit Insurance Corporation (FDIC) protected bank accounts. The Social Security system provided benefits for retired or disabled people.

Impact of the New Deal Some critics thought the New Deal went too far. They wanted less government interference in business.

Other critics said that it did not go far enough to assist the poor. The New Deal did not <u>restore</u> the prosperity of the 1920s. However, it changed people's relationship with the federal government. Government grew bigger, with more influence on everyday life. Government spending increased greatly, building up a deficit. On the other hand, New Deal programs helped millions of people. Many thought that social programs helped people keep their faith in democracy during the crisis.

Vocabulary Builder
<u>restore</u> (ree STOR) **v.** to bring back to a normal state; to put back; to reestablish

☑**Checkpoint** **What were the three goals of the New Deal?**

☆ **Looking Back and Ahead** By the late 1930s, the New Deal had restored hope, though it had not ended the Depression. While Americans fought the Depression, ominous events were occurring in other parts of the world. Dictatorships in Germany, Italy, the Soviet Union, and Japan took aggressive actions that once again threatened the security of the United States.

Section 2 | Check Your Progress

Comprehension and Critical Thinking

1. (a) **Identify** What role did the press play in rallying American support for a war in Cuba?
(b) **Analyze Cause and Effect** By the end of the war, how had the United States replaced Spain as a colonial power?

2. (a) **Recall** Why did the United States enter World War I?
(b) **Draw Conclusions** Do you think the United States should have stayed out of World War I?

3. (a) **List** Name three ways American society changed during the 1920s.

(b) **Detect Points of View** In 1925, President Calvin Coolidge commented, "The business of America is business." What did Coolidge mean by this? How did his words reflect the confidence of Americans in the strength of their economy?

⟳ **Reading Skill**
4. **Ask Analytical Questions** Reread the text following the subheading "The United States and Latin America." What were the reasons why Theodore Roosevelt wanted a canal built across the Isthmus of Panama? Suggest a possible research question on this topic.

Key Terms
Read each sentence below. If the sentence is true, write YES. If the sentence is not true, write NO and explain why.

5. Isolationism was based on the desire of Americans to take a leading role in world affairs.

6. Investors who bought on margin always paid in full for the stocks they were purchasing.

Writing
7. What evidence in this section suggests the reasons why poor Americans were so drawn to the wealthy FDR? Write a paragraph explaining your opinion.

Our National Policy

" Our national policy in foreign affairs has been based on a decent respect for the rights and dignity of all nations, large and small. And the justice of morality must and will win in the end. . . . In fulfillment of this purpose we will not be intimidated by the threats of dictators. "

—President Franklin D. Roosevelt,
Four Freedoms Speech, 1941

◄ A soldier returns home after World War II.

Toward the Modern Age

Objectives

- Describe the causes and results of World War II.
- Explain the major events of the Cold War.
- Tell how the civil rights movement changed American society.
- Examine U.S. involvement in the Vietnam War.

Reading Skill

Focus Research Topics Research topics must be specific. Formulate questions for which information to answer them is likely to be available. Frame questions to a particular time and place. Avoid questions that would require *yes* or *no* answers. Connect questions to the context of your history reading. Work toward asking questions that can be answered with evidence from available and reliable research sources.

Key Terms and People

totalitarian state
appeasement
Harry S Truman

Cold War
Martin Luther
  King, Jr.

Why It Matters After World War I, Americans were threatened by yet another war as dictators in Europe and Asia threatened democracy. The United States would defeat this threat by winning World War II. After defending democracy abroad, Americans looked inward to expand civil liberties and freedoms at home.

? Section Focus Question: How has the United States tried to increase democracy at home and abroad?

World War II

World War I was supposed to make the world "safe for democracy." In the 1930s, however, democracy disappeared in many places. Fascist dictators took power in Germany, Italy, and Spain. In the Soviet Union, Joseph Stalin established a totalitarian Communist state. In a totalitarian state, a single party controls the government and every aspect of people's lives. In East Asia, Japan built an empire.

Fascism was fostered by the troubles many countries had with their economies. In Italy, Benito Mussolini and the Fascist Party played on extreme nationalist feelings. In Germany, there was much resentment of the harsh peace treaties that ended World War I. Adolf Hitler blamed Germany's losses in the war on Jews and others. His National Socialist—or Nazi—Party was brutal and militaristic. During the war years, Hitler and his officers carried out his systematic plan to destroy European Jews. In what is now called the Holocaust, Nazi troops rounded up Jews in every occupied country. More than 6 million died or were killed in concentration camps. Millions of other "enemies" of the Nazis were also brutally murdered.

Hitler secretly began to rebuild the German army and break peace treaty terms. Then, his armies invaded neighboring countries. At first, Britain and France followed a policy of **appeasement,** a policy of giving in to aggression in order to avoid war. However, when Hitler invaded Poland in 1939, they declared war. Soon, Italy, Japan, and other nations joined Germany to form the Axis powers. The Allies included Britain, France, China, the Soviet Union, and many others.

At first, the United States tried to remain neutral, though it sent aid to the Allies. On December 7, 1941, Japan launched a surprise attack on American military bases in Hawaii. The United States went to war alongside the Allies.

The Home Front America mobilized for war quickly. Factories <u>converted</u> to war production. To conserve supplies for the military, the government rationed the amounts of meat, gasoline, sugar, clothing, and other goods that civilians could buy. Millions of women went to work in defense jobs.

During the war, prejudice against Americans of Japanese ancestry caused a great injustice. Fearing that they might be disloyal, the U.S. government moved about 110,000 Japanese Americans into "relocation camps." They lost homes and businesses.

The Allied Victory In 1942, the Allies faced losses on most fronts. Then, several Allied victories marked turning points in the war: The U.S. Navy defeated the Japanese at Midway Island. Russians held back the German siege of Stalingrad, and the British drove back the Germans in North Africa. In 1943, the Allies invaded Italy. The major invasion of western Europe came on D-Day, June 6, 1944. Allied troops landed on the coast of Normandy, France, and pressed eastward toward Germany.

Vocabulary Builder
<u>convert</u> (kuhn VERT) **v.** to change from one purpose or function to another; to change from one political party or religion to another

Fighting Front and Home Front
Winning World War II depended on the bravery of soldiers and the strength of the economy. At left, GIs storm onto the Normandy beachhead. At right, women respond to the urgent need to produce the goods of war.
Critical Thinking: *Make Inferences* *How did the growth of the American economy make the United States a more formidable fighting force?*

The Cold War in Europe

KEY

- NATO nations, 1955
- Warsaw Pact, 1955
- Neutral nations
- Areas added to the Soviet Union after World War II

By 1955, the Cold War divided Europe into two camps: those nations belonging to NATO and those nations belonging to the Warsaw Pact.

(a) Read a Map Which NATO nations bordered Warsaw Pact nations?

(b) Apply Information Do you think it would be difficult for Yugoslavia to remain neutral? Explain.

MapMaster Online
For: Interactive map
Visit: PHSchool.com
Web Code: mvp-8251

President Roosevelt died in April 1945 and was succeeded by Harry S Truman. However, the Allies' march to victory continued. In May, Germany surrendered. Use of a new weapon—the atomic bomb—brought Japan's surrender. People everywhere hoped that a new world body, the United Nations (UN), would prevent future wars.

☑ **Checkpoint** What victories for the Allies marked turning points in World War II?

The Cold War Begins

At the end of the war, the Allies divided Germany into occupation zones. Although the other Allies objected, Soviet troops set up Communist satellites in Eastern Europe.

President Truman resolved to contain Soviet expansion. Hostility developed into a Cold War, a state of tension. An arms race began, and both superpowers spent billions on defense and weapons.

Vocabulary Builder
<u>satellite</u> (SAT uh lyt) **n.** a small state that is economically or politically dependent on a larger, more powerful state

Postwar Crises The war had left Europe in ruins. Secretary of State George C. Marshall proposed to rebuild the continent. With $12 billion of Marshall Plan help, Western Europe began to recover.

The East-West split led to serious clashes. In 1948, the Soviets blockaded supplies coming into West Berlin. Truman's answer was the Berlin Airlift. For nearly a year, American planes dropped tons of food and supplies to West Berliners. In May 1949, Stalin lifted the blockade. Berlin remained a trouble spot. In 1961, the East German government built a wall dividing East and West Berlin.

The Korean War After World War II, communism gained a foothold in Asia. On the Korean Peninsula, a Communist government ruled the north and a non-Communist government ruled the south.

In June 1950, North Korean troops invaded the South. UN troops organized to stop them. As the UN troops fought their way northward, Chinese soldiers joined the North Koreans. Douglas MacArthur, the American commander, wanted to invade China. Truman, however, wanted to limit the war. He fired MacArthur. In 1953, a truce was negotiated, but Korea remained divided.

Cold War Fears Communist advances in Asia and Europe frightened many Americans. They worried that Communists were working inside the United States. In 1950, Wisconsin Senator Joseph McCarthy made dramatic charges about Communists in government, in schools, and even in the army. McCarthy attracted attention but had little real evidence.

Global Conflicts In 1959, communism came closer to home. Fidel Castro led a Communist revolution in Cuba. Thousands of Cubans fled to the United States.

In October 1962, the Soviets attempted to ship weapons to Castro. President John F. Kennedy then announced that American ships would stop any Soviet ships taking missiles to Cuba. After a few tense days, the Soviet ships turned back.

☑️ **Checkpoint** How did the Korean War end?

The Civil Rights Movement

All Americans had worked together to win the war. Many people, though, still faced discrimination in jobs, education, and housing.

The Movement Begins In many southern states, laws supported "separate but equal" facilities in schools and other public places. In *Brown* v. *Board of Education of Topeka* (1954), the Supreme Court ruled that segregated schools could not provide children with an equal education. It ordered schools everywhere to integrate black students and white students.

In 1955, African Americans in Montgomery, Alabama, organized a boycott of the city's segregated bus system. It followed the arrest of Rosa Parks, who had refused to give up her seat to a white man, as the law required.

There were many black activists, but Dr. Martin Luther King, Jr., soon emerged as a fearless and compelling national leader. King urged the use of nonviolent protests against unjust laws.

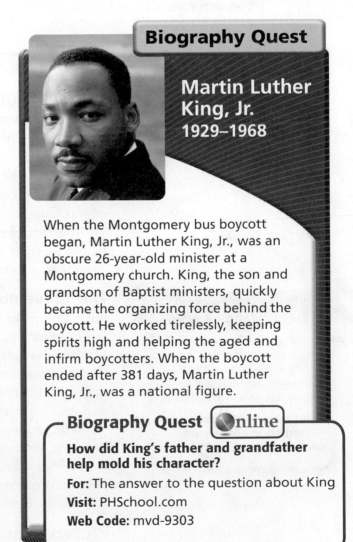

Biography Quest

Martin Luther King, Jr.
1929–1968

When the Montgomery bus boycott began, Martin Luther King, Jr., was an obscure 26-year-old minister at a Montgomery church. King, the son and grandson of Baptist ministers, quickly became the organizing force behind the boycott. He worked tirelessly, keeping spirits high and helping the aged and infirm boycotters. When the boycott ended after 381 days, Martin Luther King, Jr., was a national figure.

Biography Quest 🌐**Online**

How did King's father and grandfather help mold his character?

For: The answer to the question about King
Visit: PHSchool.com
Web Code: mvd-9303

A Nurse Reflects

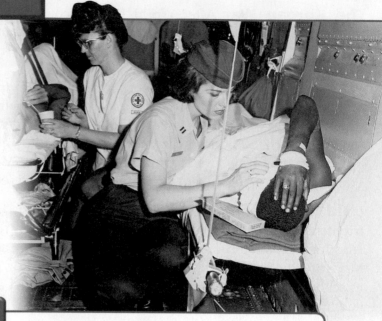

"Those of us who went to Vietnam practiced a lifetime of nursing in one year—our tour of duty there. We were the young, caring for the young. The average age of the wounded soldier in Vietnam was 19.4 years. The average age of the nurse was 23. We quickly learned that the primary reason we were in Vietnam was to get each other home."

—Diane Carlson Evans, speech in Washington, D.C., 1998

Nurses care for wounded soldiers about to be shipped home.

Reading Primary Sources
Skills Activity

As many as 10,000 women served in uniform with U.S. military forces in the Vietnam War, most as nurses.

(a) **Rank** What three characteristics do you think were most important for a nurse serving in Vietnam?

(b) **Draw Conclusions** What does the speaker mean when she says the main goal was "to get each other home"?

The 1960s The 1960s brought great social change. Civil rights became a national issue. In August 1963, more than 200,000 people gathered on the Mall in Washington, D.C., where King made his famous "I have a dream" speech.

In 1963, John F. Kennedy was assassinated. His successor, Lyndon Johnson, was skilled in getting laws passed. Under his leadership, Congress passed strong Civil Rights and Voting Rights acts.

The 1960s brought other protests. Despite new civil rights laws, many thought that change was coming too slowly. In the hot summers, riots broke out in several cities.

The Movement Widens The struggle for civil rights inspired other groups to demand greater equality. Latinos had several goals. For example, many Mexican Americans were migrant farm workers, working for low pay in dangerous conditions. In the 1960s, César Chávez organized the United Farm Workers. With a national boycott of grapes, the union won better working conditions. Native American and Asian American groups also gained political influence.

Women were not a minority, but they faced many barriers. Working women earned less than men—about 63 cents for every dollar—for doing the same kind of work. It was hard for women to enter professions. The National Organization for Women (NOW) worked for equality in those areas.

☑ **Checkpoint** What did the Supreme Court rule in *Brown* v. *Board of Education of Topeka*?

HISTORIAN'S APPRENTICE ACTIVITY PACK

To further explore the topics in this chapter, complete the activity in the Historian's Apprentice Activity Pack to answer this essential question:

What major influences have helped shape American society and culture?

The Vietnam War

After World War II, a civil war broke out in Vietnam. That war divided Vietnam into a Communist North and a non-Communist South. Over several years, the United States built up its forces in Vietnam. Fighting in Vietnam was jungle warfare against guerrilla fighters. There were few clear-cut victories.

Americans were bitterly divided over the war. Some, often referred to as "hawks," wanted to escalate the war for a victory over the Communist North. Others, referred to as "doves," however, believed that the United States should not be in Vietnam at all. Antiwar protests were widespread.

President Johnson did not run again in 1968. The new President, Richard Nixon, promised to end the war. Peace talks led to a cease-fire agreement in 1973. In 1975, the last American soldiers left, and all of Vietnam fell under Communist rule.

☑ **Checkpoint** What was the outcome of the Vietnam War?

☆ **Looking Back and Ahead** The Vietnam War was a painful episode in American history. Besides its huge cost, the war deeply divided the nation. But, as the war wound down, the Cold War showed signs of a thaw. In the next section, you will see how the nation turned its attention to new issues in the 1980s.

Focus Research Topics

Reread the text under the heading "The Vietnam War." Suggest a more focused research topic that is based on the divisions between "hawks" and "doves" during the Vietnam era.

Section 3 | **Check Your Progress**

Comprehension and Critical Thinking

1. (a) Recall How did Americans feel about world involvement during the 1930s?
(b) Link Past and Present Do you think it is possible for the United States to be isolationist today? Explain your answer.

2. (a) Recall Describe two results of the Vietnam War.
(b) Contrast Contrast the Korean War and the Vietnam War in terms of causes and results.

3. (a) Recall Who was Senator Joseph McCarthy?
(b) Link Past and Present Television played a key role in the downfall of Senator McCarthy.

Give at least three examples of how television influences public opinion today.

Reading Skill

4. Focus Research Topics Reread the text under the heading "World War II." Suggest a more-focused research question that is based on the following: Why do democracies sometimes try to appease dictators?

Key Terms

5. Write two definitions for the following key terms: totalitarian state, appeasement, Cold War. First, write a formal definition for your teacher. Second, write a definition in everyday English for a classmate.

Writing

6. Choose two details from within this section that support the topic sentence that follows. Then, write a paragraph developing the topic based on these details. **Topic sentence:** The 1960s were a time of conflict for Americans both home and abroad.

REAGAN

FOR PRESIDENT
Let's make America great again.

A Renewal of Spirit

❝ I want my candidacy to unify our country, to renew the American spirit and sense of purpose. I want to carry our message to every American, regardless of party affiliation. ❞

—Ronald Reagan, addressing the Republican National Convention, 1980

◄ Ronald Reagan ushered in a new conservative era in 1980.

Into the Future

Objectives

- List the goals of the conservative Presidents such as Ronald Reagan and George H.W. Bush.
- Tell how different foreign policy challenges arose after the end of the Cold War.
- Examine U.S. foreign policy in the Middle East after the September 11 attacks.
- Discuss environmental, technological, and economic challenges that face Americans today.

🎯 Reading Skill

Ask Questions That Connect to the Present Does history repeat itself? Investigate by asking questions that connect history to the present. Compare or contrast a historical situation with a current situation. Or look at ways that historical situations have led to current situations. Ask questions that require research to answer.

Key Terms and People

Ronald Reagan
deregulation
George H.W. Bush
George W. Bush

détente
terrorism
al Qaeda

Why It Matters Just like generations before them, Americans of today face challenges at home and abroad. American leaders continue to search for the best way to secure democracy and prosperity at home. At the same time, they must confront how best to deal with foreign threats.

❷ Section Focus Question: What changes and challenges are shaping the United States today?

Rise of the Conservative Movement

The unpopular Vietnam War helped bring Richard Nixon, a Republican, to office. In response to an economic crisis—rising prices, slow growth, and high unemployment—Nixon cut back spending. Then, political scandal rocked his administration.

The Watergate affair began during Nixon's 1972 reelection campaign, with a break-in at the Democratic headquarters. A Senate investigation showed that Nixon and his advisers had lied in trying to cover up the incident. By midsummer 1974, the House of Representatives seemed ready to impeach Nixon and the Senate ready to convict him. Instead, he resigned—the first President to do so.

Vice President Gerald Ford succeeded Nixon. Wanting to end the scandal, he pardoned the former President, though many people objected. Ford was also beset by economic problems, and in 1976, he lost the election to Jimmy Carter, a Democrat. Carter had trouble working with Congress. Inflation remained a problem, made worse by an energy crisis. In 1980, voters preferred the upbeat message of the Republican candidate, Ronald Reagan.

The New Conservative Movement Conservative voters backed Reagan for different reasons. Some wanted a smaller federal government and deregulation, or reduction of restrictions on business. Others focused on morality and a return to traditional family values. Many belonged to evangelical Christian churches, which emphasized a personal experience with God.

As President, Reagan put conservative ideas into action. His economic plan cut taxes and dropped many regulations. Spending for social programs fell, and military spending soared. After Reagan's two terms, his Vice President, George H.W. Bush, was elected in 1988. He continued many of Reagan's policies.

Presidents Clinton and Bush Conservatives remained strong in Congress in the 1990s. Now, however, there was a Democrat in the White House—Bill Clinton, a former Arkansas governor. President Clinton was often at odds with Congress. However, Congress and the President managed to agree on major changes in the welfare system and on balancing the federal budget.

Clinton's personal popularity was high. The economy was growing so fast that there was a budget surplus. However, an investigation turned up evidence of his improper relationship with a White House intern, which he at first denied under oath. In late 1998, the House of Representatives voted to impeach Clinton. In a historic trial in February 1999, the Senate acquitted him.

The impeachment trial was only the second in history, but the 2000 election was unique. Clinton's Vice President, Al Gore, ran against Texas Governor George W. Bush, a son of the former President. Gore won the popular vote by a narrow margin. The electoral college tally, however, was in doubt while votes were recounted in Florida. In December 2000, the Supreme Court ruled the Florida recount illegal, making Bush the President. In his first term, Bush won major victories by fulfilling campaign pledges to lower taxes and to raise standards for public schools. Reelected by a comfortable margin in 2004, Bush experienced frustration in his next term. Controversy over American policy in the Middle East and an economic collapse brought his approval rating to 29 percent, among the lowest in history.

✔**Checkpoint** List two main goals of Presidents Reagan and George W. Bush.

Clinton Signs a Bill
Children of minimum-wage earners cluster around President Clinton as he signs a bill to raise the minimum wage. **Critical Thinking: *Contrast*** *Contrast the records of Ronald Reagan and Bill Clinton.*

Strengthening America's Families
A New Minimum Wage

New Conflicts in the World

From the late 1940s on, the Cold War dominated foreign policy. Then, Communist rule began to crumble all over Europe. By the mid-1990s, communism was no longer a major threat. New kinds of conflicts erupted in trouble spots all over the world.

The Cold War Ends The Cold War began to thaw during the Nixon administration. Although a strong anti-Communist, Nixon established ties with Communist China. He visited China and the Soviet Union in 1972. The policy of détente—a relaxing of tensions—continued during the Ford and Carter administrations.

All this time, however, the arms race was putting great pressure on the failing Soviet economy. A new Soviet leader, Mikhail Gorbachev, attempted to save communism by relaxing controls on speech and political opposition. However, the Soviet system was too corrupt to survive. Beginning in 1989, every Communist government in Eastern Europe eventually collapsed. The Berlin Wall was torn down. East and West Germany were soon reunited under a democratic government.

Change overtook the Soviet Union itself. In August 1991, hardline Communists tried to reverse the reforms, but thousands of Russian people opposed them. One by one, the Soviet republics declared their independence. By the end of 1991, the Soviet Union was gone. The United States began to help Russia and the other republics build democracy and a free-market economy.

An Age of Regional Conflicts The end of the Cold War did not mean world peace. Civil wars tore apart countries in Africa and Central America. When the Communist government of Yugoslavia fell, old ethnic and religious hatreds flared up in the Balkans. In 1991, the republics of Croatia and Bosnia split off from Yugoslavia. Millions of people were displaced as Serbs, Croats, and Bosnians fought one another. A second Balkan war erupted in 1998 between Serbs and Albanians in Kosovo. NATO forces intervened, and American soldiers joined European troops as peacekeepers.

The Middle East was another hot spot. A major source of trouble was a series of wars between Israel and the Arab countries that surround it. Another was ongoing violence between Palestinians and Israelis. Ever since the founding of Israel in 1948, each U.S. President tried to bring peace, but terrorism and reprisals continued.

American support for Israel angered some Arab countries. In 1973, oil-producing Arab countries cut off oil shipments, causing shortages and high prices. The supply of Mideastern oil also caused the brief Persian Gulf War in 1991. Saddam Hussein, the dictator of Iraq, invaded neighboring oil-rich Kuwait. A UN coalition of the United States and its allies launched an air attack. After six weeks, Iraq left Kuwait, although Hussein remained in power.

✓**Checkpoint** What was the immediate result of the collapse of the Soviet Union?

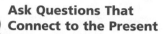

Ask Questions That Connect to the Present
The end of the Cold War changed the relationship of the United States with Russia and the former Soviet republics. Ask a question that connects the collapse of communism in the Soviet Union with events in the region today. Your question should require research to answer.

Breaking down the Berlin Wall

New Directions in Foreign Policy

After the 1960s, terrorist bombings, kidnappings, and hijackings became more common in Europe, the Middle East, and elsewhere. Terrorism is the deliberate use of random acts of violence, often against civilians, in order to achieve a political goal.

The Challenge of Terrorism In the Middle East, a number of radical Muslim groups sponsored terrorism. These extremists were outraged by U.S. support for Israel, as well as by the Persian Gulf War. As a result, Americans overseas sometimes became targets of terrorism.

Terrorism also became a threat within the United States itself. In 1993, a bomb rocked the World Trade Center in New York City. Six Arab men were later convicted of the crime. In 1995, two Americans who resented the government exploded a bomb that destroyed a federal office building in Oklahoma City, killing 168 people.

The United States Is Attacked On September 11, 2001, terrorists seized control of four American passenger airplanes. The hijackers crashed two of the planes into the Twin Towers of the World Trade Center in New York City. As onlookers watched in horror, the two skyscrapers collapsed. A third hijacked airliner crashed into the Pentagon near Washington, D.C. The fourth airplane crashed in Pennsylvania after courageous passengers attacked the hijackers. More than 3,000 people were killed in the terrorist attacks of September 11.

Vocabulary Builder
radical (rad ih kul) *adj.* favoring fundamental or extreme change

HISTORIAN'S APPRENTICE ACTIVITY PACK

To further explore the topics in this chapter, complete the activity in the Historian's Apprentice Activity Pack to answer this essential question:

How has the United States tried to remain safe and to defend democracy?

Attack on America
After the September 11 attack on the World Trade Center, President George W. Bush went to New York City to give encouragement to rescue workers. The events of September 11 produced dramatic changes in American foreign policy. *Critical Thinking: Analyze Cause and Effect Do you think the attacks had the impact on the American people that the attackers expected?*

EXTRA EXTRA EXTRA
St. Petersburg Times

AMERICA UNDER ATTACK

PLANES CRASH INTO WORLD TRADE CENTER AND PENTAGON
OFFICE TOWERS COLLAPSE; HUNDREDS ARE MISSING
ALL FLIGHTS GROUNDED; TWO UNITED PLANES CRASH
MARKETS CLOSE; DISNEY SHUTS PARKS; U.S. ON ALERT

Gulf Oil Spill

On April 20, 2010, the largest accidental, deep sea oil spill occurred. An estimated 62,000 barrels of oil, per day, seeped into the Gulf of Mexico. Although attempts were made to capture the leaking oil, much of the oil made it to shore. In the image above workers attempt to clean the oil, from this spill, that made it onto Pensacola Beach. **Critical Thinking: *Analyze Effects*** *How does the environment affect people? How do people affect the environment?*

Vocabulary Builder
consume (kahn SYOOM) ***v.*** to use up; to eat or drink

Americans Respond American citizens were quick to respond to the tragedy. Millions lined up to give blood, aided in rescue efforts, or donated money and supplies to help the victims and rescuers.

It soon became clear that the attack was the work of al Qaeda (ahl KY duh) (also spelled *al-Qaida*). Al Qaeda is a terrorist network led by a wealthy Saudi, Osama bin Laden. Bin Laden was living in Afghanistan, protected by a brutal dictatorship, the Taliban. In November 2001, an American-led force attacked military sites and terrorist training camps in Afghanistan. The Taliban were soon toppled. However, Osama bin Laden escaped, and the search for him continued.

War in Iraq President Bush next targeted Iraq as a threat. Bush accused Iraqi dictator Saddam Hussein of having ties with Bin Laden. He also claimed that Hussein was developing weapons of mass destruction (WMD), such as nuclear and chemical weapons.

In March 2003, the United States and Britain led a coalition of about 30 nations in an attack on Iraq. Using advanced weapons, coalition forces smashed Iraq's defenses in six weeks. As the fighting subsided, coalition advisers set up the Coalition Provisional Authority to supervise the establishment of a new democratic government for Iraq. In 2005, Iraqis voted in the nation's first free election in 50 years.

Despite these efforts at reconstruction, militants began a terror campaign to kill American troops and Iraqis. Attacks continued even after Hussein was brought to justice. Captured in 2003, the dictator was tried and executed in 2006. Meanwhile, Shiite and Sunni Muslims took up arms against each other across Iraq.

Americans Divided Many Americans supported the Iraq War. Bush's strong actions, they said, toppled a brutal dictator and promoted democracy. Others criticized Bush's actions. They felt Iraq had not posed an immediate threat. Other critics charged that the war consumed valuable money, supplies, and troops.

☑ Checkpoint What reasons did President Bush give for toppling the government of Saddam Hussein?

Changes and Challenges

The United States faced crucial new challenges in the twenty-first century. A new President confronted economic uncertainty and promised great change.

The Historic Election of 2008 After only two years in the U.S. Senate, Barack Obama won the nomination of Democrats for the presidency. Republicans nominated Arizona senator John McCain.

Many were attracted to the 47-year-old Obama's youth and fresh political face. Obama won the election. Nearly 150 years after the end of slavery, the first African American President headed to the White House.

Financial Meltdown Late in 2007, the economy of the United States plunged into recession. Unemployment rose and consumer spending fell. The stock market dropped by nearly 40 percent.

The problem began with mortgages—loans from banks to pay for homes. Many banks made risky loans. As the economy slowed, many borrowers found they could not repay what they owed.

In 2008, Congress advanced up to $750 billion to cash-strapped lenders by creating the Troubled Assets Relief Program, or TARP. In 2009, Congress enacted a massive aid package to stimulate the economy.

Barack Obama won the 2008 presidential election.

Other Challenges The U.S. will face these and other hurdles:

- **Technology.** Technology has improved our lives, but depending on technology can make Americans vulnerable to crime and attacks.

- **The environment.** The natural world can be destructive. For example, in 2005 Hurricane Katrina caused tremendous damage along the Gulf of Mexico. Global warming and other problems persist.

- **Immigration.** America's population is changing as new immigrants continue to arrive.

☑ **Checkpoint** What are two challenges facing Americans today?

⭐ **Looking Back and Ahead** Today, the U.S. faces complex issues. Yet, Americans have met such challenges before.

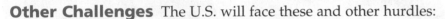

Section 4 | Check Your Progress

Comprehension and Critical Thinking

1. (a) Summarize Why did the Soviet Union collapse in the late 1980s?
(b) Explain Problems Describe two ways in which the United States could help former Communist nations make the shift to democracy.

2. (a) Recall Describe two environmental problems the United States faces.
(b) Explain Problems Why are these problems also global in impact?

Reading Skill

3. Ask Questions That Connect to the Present Ask a question that connects the Cold War to the present and requires research to answer. You might focus on the relationships of the nations of Eastern Europe to the United States.

Key Terms

4. Draw a table with three rows and two columns. In the first column, list these key terms: deregulation, détente, terrorism. In the next column, write the definition of each word.

Writing

5. Imagine that you will be writing an editorial meant to influence readers of your school newspaper about environmental issues in your community. Create an outline for the editorial that organizes your thoughts. Create two main topic headings for the editorial: I. Environmental problems in our community; II. What can be done about them.

21st Century Learning To predict consequences, or results, you must analyze what has happened in the past and compare it to the present situation. The data below show demographic, or population, trends. Demographic data help social scientists, as well as town and city planners, form a more complete picture of a certain population and establish trends over a period of time.

Percent of Total U.S. Population by Age Group, 1960–2050

1960

- 29.2%
- 35.7%
- 35%

2000

- 25.7%
- 39.8%
- 34.4%

2050

- 23.8%
- 42.4%
- 33.9%

■ 0–17 years   ■ 18–44 years   ■ 45 years & Over

Source: U.S. Bureau of the Census, *Projections of the Population of the U.S., by Age, Sex, and Race: 1995 to 2050* (2002)

Learn the Skill

Use these steps to make predictions.

1 Identify the subject of the data. Read the graph or chart title to understand what is being measured. Always look for the source of the data.

2 Analyze the data. Study the data to see trends or patterns. Remember, information can be presented in different ways: tables, graphs, charts, or as text. Data may appear as percentages or in thousands or millions.

3 Predict possible future developments. Draw conclusions or make generalizations based on the data on the chart.

Practice the Skill

Answer the following questions about the data on this page.

1 Identify the subject of the data. (a) What is the title of the pie graphs? (b) What years are shown on the graphs? (c) What is the source of the data?

2 Analyze the data. (a) What percentage of the population was between 0 and 17 years of age in 1960? (b) Which age group shows the most growth between 1960 and 2050? (c) Which group decreases the most?

3 Predict possible future developments. (a) How do you think changes in the population will affect the construction of schools and houses built between 2000 and 2050? (b) What advice would you offer to hospitals and health care facilities based on this data?

Apply the Skill

See the Review and Assessment at the end of this chapter.

Quick Study Guide

How has the American nation met challenges at home and abroad?

Section 1
The Nation Grows

- Settlement of the western frontier led to the near destruction of the Plains Native American way of life.
- A booming economy led to the rise of wealthy business tycoons and a growing labor union movement.
- A surge in immigration swelled city populations and helped change the United States from a rural to an urban nation.

Section 2
A New Role for the Nation

- After the Civil War, the United States extended its control over parts of the Pacific region and Latin America.
- After its victory in World War I, the United States enjoyed a period of prosperity.
- The 1929 stock market crash marked the beginning of the Great Depression.

Section 3
Toward the Modern Age

- After early defeats on all fronts, the Allies rallied to win victory in World War II.
- Cold War tensions led to a number of dangerous confrontations.
- After World War II, African Americans began to demand their full civil rights.
- The Vietnam War was a costly conflict that deeply divided Americans.

Section 4
Into the Future

- The conservative movement sought to reduce the role of the federal government.
- U.S. foreign policy focused on the Middle East and the Balkans.
- After the 9/11 attacks, the U.S. invaded Afghanistan and Iraq.
- Economic problems began in 2007.

? Exploring the Essential Question

Use the online study guide to explore the essential question.

Section 1
How did rapid industrialization affect the American economy and society?

Section 2
How did a more powerful United States expand its role in the world?

Epilogue Essential Question
How has the American nation met challenges at home and abroad?

Section 4
What changes and challenges are shaping the United States today?

Section 3
How has the United States tried to increase democracy at home and abroad?

Key Terms

Answer the following questions in complete sentences that show your understanding of the key terms.

1. Why did many Native Americans of the Plains move onto reservations?

2. Which amendment of the Constitution guaranteed American women the right of suffrage?

3. How did isolationism in the United States affect the peace settlement after World War I?

4. Why did the European democracies resort to appeasement of Adolf Hitler?

5. What action by President Richard Nixon established the policy of détente during the Cold War?

Comprehension and Critical Thinking

6. (a) **Describe** How did the westward migration of Americans change the lives of Plains Indians?
   (b) **Analyze Cause and Effect** How did wars with government troops affect Native American life?

7. (a) **Recall** How did changes in the economy affect workers in the late 1800s?
   (b) **Draw Conclusions** Why was there an effort to organize workers into labor unions?

8. (a) **Identify** Identify two devices invented by Thomas Edison.
   (b) **Draw Conclusions** How did Edison's inventions improve daily life in American cities?

9. (a) **Summarize** The newspaper editor Horace Greeley said, "We cannot all live in cities, yet nearly all seem determined to do so." What did he mean?
   (b) **Evaluate Information** How did the growth of industry affect the way people lived in the cities?

10. (a) **Describe** What were the results of the Japanese attack on Pearl Harbor?
    (b) **Link Past and Present** How was the reaction of Americans to the attack on Pearl Harbor similar to the reaction of Americans to the terrorist attacks of September 11, 2001?

History Reading Skill

11. **Frame Research Questions** Review Sections 1 through 4 of the Epilogue, and frame one research question for each section. For every research question, choose a general topic. Then, narrow your question to make it more specific. Remember to frame questions that go beyond the text and require research to answer.

Writing

12. **Write a Persuasive Paragraph:**
    Choose one headline from the list below, and write a persuasive paragraph that gives your opinion on the issue. Remember to support your opinion with facts, examples, and reasons.
    • Settlement of the West: Triumph or Tragedy?
    • Rockefeller and Carnegie: Heroes or Tyrants?
    • The Vietnam War: Justified or Unjustified?

13. **Write a Narrative:**
    Imagine that you are an immigrant arriving in New York City around 1900. Write a narrative describing your experiences at Ellis Island.

Skills for Life

Make Predictions
Use the graph below to answer the questions.

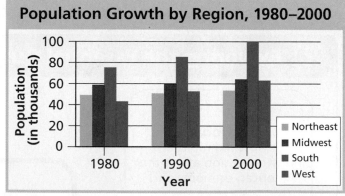

Population Growth by Region, 1980–2000

Source: U.S. Bureau of the Census, *The Statistical History of the U.S.* (1976) and 2000 Census of the U.S. www.census.gov

14. What is being measured by the data?

15. (a) In 1980, how many people lived in the Northeast? (b) What happened to the population of the South from 1980 to 2000?

16. Make a prediction about how this graph might look in 2020.

Test Yourself

1. Which of the following most benefited big business?

A rise of the American Federation of Labor

B strikes called by unions

C dangerous working conditions in sweatshops

D development of the corporation

Refer to the quotation below to answer questions 2 and 3.

> "My fellow Americans, our long national nightmare is over. Our Constitution works; ours is a Government of laws and not of men. . . . [L]et us restore the golden rule to our political process, and let brotherly love purge our hearts of suspicion and hate."
>
> —President Gerald Ford, August 9, 1974, hours after the resignation of Richard Nixon

2. Of what is President Ford speaking when he refers to a "long national nightmare"?

A Vietnam

B Watergate

C the rule of law

D inflation

3. Which phrase suggests that President Ford is thinking of pardoning Nixon?

A "Our Constitution works"

B "ours is a government of laws"

C "restore the golden rule"

D "purge our hearts of . . . hate"

Document-Based Questions

Task: Look at Documents 1 and 2, and answer their accompanying questions. Then, use the documents and your knowledge of history to complete the following writing assignment:

Write a three-paragraph essay about the role of government in American life today. Using specific details, indicate whether you think that President Roosevelt's views or President Reagan's views are more appropriate to the role of government in our society today.

Document 1: FDR's first inaugural address was given at a time when the economy was in shambles and Americans were desperate for action. *How does Roosevelt propose to attack the Depression?*

> "This Nation asks for action, and action now. Our greatest primary task is to put people to work. This is no unsolvable problem if we face it wisely and courageously. It can be accomplished in part by direct recruiting by the Government itself, treating the task as we would treat the emergency of a war, but at the same time, through this employment, accomplishing greatly needed projects to stimulate and reorganize the use of our natural resources."
>
> —Franklin Delano Roosevelt, First Inaugural Address, 1933

Document 2: Forty-eight years later, Ronald Reagan's first inaugural address was given at a time when many Americans were concerned by the growing size of federal government programs. *What does Reagan suggest is the core of the problem?*

> "In this present crisis, government is not the solution to our problem; government is the problem. From time to time we've been tempted to believe that society has become too complex to be managed by self-rule, that government by an elite group is superior to government for, by, and of the people. But if no one among us is capable of governing himself, then who among us has the capacity to govern someone else?"
>
> —Ronald Reagan, First Inaugural Address, 1981

Reference Section

Table of Contents

Primary Source Readings in American History

Primary Sources

The Creation of Cherokee Country

Background

The Cherokees were one of the dominant Native American groups of the Southeast culture region. They originally lived in the area that is now North Carolina, South Carolina, and Georgia. Other major groups in the Southeast included the Natchez and Creeks.

Like other Native Americans, the Cherokees had a strong tradition of oral literature.

History, folk tales, and religious beliefs were memorized and recited, passing from one generation to the next. Creation stories were an important part of this oral tradition. The following story tells how the Cherokee lands in Georgia and the surrounding area were created. The mountains described are the Appalachians.

Vocabulary Builder

suspend (suh SPEND) *v.* to hang from

cardinal (KAHRD uh nuhl) *adj.* main; most important

vault (vawlt) *n.* arched roof or ceiling

dart (dahrt) *v.* to move suddenly or rapidly

alight (uh LĪT) *v.* to come to rest from the air

buzzard (BUHZ uhrd) *n.* any of various breeds of vultures

The earth is a great island floating in a sea of water, and <u>suspended</u> at each of the four <u>cardinal</u> points by a cord hanging down from the sky <u>vault</u>, which is of solid rock. When the world grows old and worn out, the people will die and the cords will break and let the earth sink down into the ocean, and all will be water again. The Indians are afraid of this.

When all was water, the animals were above . . . beyond the arch, but it was very much crowded, and they were wanting more room. They wondered what was below the water and at last . . . the little Water-beetle, offered to go and see if it could learn. It <u>darted</u> in every direction over the surface of the water, but could find no firm place to rest. Then it dived to the bottom and came up with some soft mud, which began to grow and spread on every side until it became the island which we call the earth. It was afterward fastened to the sky with four cords, but no one remembers who did this.

At first the earth was flat and very soft and wet. The animals were anxious to get down, and sent out different birds to see if it was yet dry, but they found no place to <u>alight</u> and came back

again to [the world above]. At last it seemed to be time, and they sent out the Great <u>Buzzard</u>, the father of all the buzzards we see now. He flew all over the earth, low down near the ground, and it was still soft. When he reached the Cherokee country, he was very tired, and his wings began to flap and strike the ground, and wherever they struck the earth there was a valley, and where they turned up again there was a mountain. When the animals above saw this, they were afraid that the whole world would be mountains, so they called him back, but the Cherokee country remains full of mountains to this day.

Nineteenth Annual Report of the Bureau of American Ethnology, 1897–1898

Comprehension and Critical Thinking

1. Why did the animals want dry land?
2. According to this creation story, how were the Appalachian Mountains formed?
3. Critical Thinking: *Apply Information* Why do you think animal figures play an important role in this and other creation stories?

Chapter 1

Pericles, *Funeral Oration*

Background

Ancient Greece was divided into many small city-states, among them Athens and Sparta. Today, we consider Athens the birthplace of democracy.

In the fifth century B.C., a great conflict called the Peloponnesian War broke out between Athens and an alliance of city-states under the leadership of Sparta. At the time, the most respected leader in Athens was Pericles.

While the war was going on, Pericles was asked to deliver a speech honoring the city's war dead. He chose the occasion to also praise Athens, its government, its military, and its way of life. In the following selection from the speech, Pericles explains why he thinks the government of Athens is superior to those of other city-states.

Vocabulary *Builder*

capacity (kuh PAS ih tee) *n.* ability; skill

obscurity (ahb SKYOOR uh tee) *n.* state of being unclear or unknown

surveillance (suhr VAIL uhns) *n.* careful watching

injurious (ihn JYOOR ee uhs) *adj.* harmful

magistrate (MAJ uh strayt) *n.* official who enforces the law

statute (STACH oot) *n.* formal written law

Our constitution does not copy the laws of neighboring states; we are rather a pattern to others than imitators ourselves. Its administration favors the many instead of the few; this is why it is called a democracy. If we look to the laws, they afford equal justice to all in their private differences; if to social standing, advancement in public life falls to reputation for capacity, class considerations not being allowed to interfere with merit; nor again does poverty bar the way, if a man is able to serve the state, he is not hindered by the obscurity of his condition.

The freedom which we enjoy in our government extends also to our ordinary life. There, far from exercising a jealous surveillance over each other, we do not feel called upon to be angry with our neighbor for doing what he likes, or even to indulge in those injurious looks which cannot fail to be offensive, although they inflict no positive penalty. But all this ease in our private relations does not make us lawless as citizens. Against this fear is our chief safeguard, teaching us to obey the magistrates and the laws, particularly such as regard the protection of the injured, whether they are actually on the statute book, or belong to that code which, although unwritten yet cannot be broken without acknowledged disgrace.

Thucydides, *History of the Peloponnesian War*

Bust of Pericles

Comprehension and Critical Thinking

1. According to Pericles, what makes Athens a democracy?

2. What freedoms do Athenians enjoy in their private lives?

3. **Critical Thinking: *Compare*** Based on this description, in what ways was the government of Athens similar to the government of the United States today?

Primary Sources

Bartolomé de Las Casas, *The Destruction of the Indies*

Background

Bartolomé de Las Casas was a Roman Catholic priest born in Seville, Spain, in 1484. In his youth, he met Christopher Columbus and traveled to the West Indies. There, he observed the conquest of the Americas and was horrified by the treatment of Native Americans by the conquistadors.

Las Casas dedicated his long life to protecting Native Americans from Spanish abuse.

On several occasions, he returned to Spain to plead their case before the Spanish throne. His writings and discussions shocked Spanish leaders who attempted to pass laws to protect the Indians. The conquistadors' friends at court, however, often had the policies reversed. Below is an excerpt from a 1542 work detailing the abusive policies of the Spanish.

Vocabulary *Builder*

tyrannical (tih RAN ih kuhl) *adj.* harsh; using power unjustly

instrumental (ihn struh MEHN tuhl) *adj.* serving as an important tool; very helpful

annihilation (uh nī uh LAY shuhn) *n.* complete destruction

Sacrament (SAK ruh mehnt) *n.* sacred rite of the Christian church

indigenous (ihn DIHJ uh nehs) *adj.* native to a region or counry

tribulation (trihb yoo LAY shuhn) *n.* great sorrow or trouble

---

There are two main ways in which those who have traveled to this part of the world pretending to be Christians have uprooted these pitiful peoples and wiped them from the face of the earth. First, they have waged war on them: unjust, cruel, bloody and <u>tyrannical</u> war. Second, they have murdered anyone and everyone who has shown the slightest sign of resistance. . . . This latter policy has been <u>instrumental</u> in suppressing the native leaders, and, indeed, given that the Spaniards normally spare only women and children, it has led to the <u>annihilation</u> of all adult males. . . .

The reason the [Spanish] have murdered on such a vast scale and killed anyone and everyone in their way is purely and simply greed. They have set out to line their pockets with gold. . . . The Spaniards have shown not the slightest consideration for these people, treating them (and I speak from first-hand experience, having been there from the outset) not as brute animals—indeed, I would to God they had done and had shown them the consideration they afford their animals—so much as piles of dung in the middle of the road. They have had as little concern for their souls as for their bodies, all the millions that have perished having gone to their deaths with no knowledge of God and without the benefit of the <u>Sacraments</u>. . . .

The <u>indigenous</u> peoples never did the Europeans any harm whatever; on the contrary, they believed them to have descended from the heavens, at least until they or their fellow-citizens had tasted, at the hands of these oppressors, a diet of robbery, murder, violence, and all other manner of trials and <u>tribulations</u>.

Bartolomé de Las Casas, *The Destruction of the Indies*

Comprehension and Critical Thinking

1. According to Las Casas, why did the Spanish treat Native Americans the way they did?

2. Who did the Native people think the Europeans were at first?

3. Critical Thinking: *Detect Points of View* Why does Las Casas accuse the conquistadors of "pretending to be Christians"? What evidence does he offer for this accusation?

Chapter 2

Jacques Marquette, *Reaching the Mississippi*

Background

Jacques Marquette was born in northern France in 1637. He joined the Jesuits at the age of 17 and worked as a priest in France for more than a decade.

In his late twenties, Marquette was sent to Quebec, in the heart of France's North American empire. Marquette served as a missionary to the native people of the continent. There, he heard rumors of a great river southwest of Quebec, which the French hoped would be a "Northwest Passage" to the Pacific Ocean. In 1673, Marquette joined Canadian-born explorer Louis Joliet and five other adventurers to find the river. Here, he describes reaching the Mississippi River.

Vocabulary *Builder*

dissuade (dihs WAYD) *v.* to advise against; discourage

salvation (sal VAY shuhn) *n.* saving of a person's soul, especially referring to life after death

depute (dee PYOOT) *v.* to select someone for a task or mission

---

On the 17th day of May, 1673, we started from the mission of St. Ignatius. . . . [T]he first nation that we came to was that of the Folle Avoine [Menominee]. . . . I told these people . . . of my design to go and discover those remote nations, in order to teach them the mysteries of our holy religion. They . . . did their best to <u>dissuade</u> me. They represented to me that I would meet nations who never show mercy to strangers. . . .

I thanked them for their advice . . . but told them that I could not follow it, because the <u>salvation</u> of souls was at stake. . . .

We left the waters flowing to Quebec . . . to float on those that would thenceforward take us through strange lands.

. . . [W]e arrived at . . . the Mississippi on the 17th of June, with a joy that I cannot express.

Finally on the 25th of June we perceived on the water's edge some tracks of men, and a narrow . . . beaten path. . . . [A]fter walking about two leagues, we discovered a village. . . . We . . . decided to reveal ourselves. . . . by shouting with all our energy, and stopped without advancing any farther. On hearing the shout, the savages [the Illinois] . . . having probably recognized us as Frenchmen, especially when they saw a black gown—or, at least, having not cause for distrust, as we were only two men, and had given them notice of our arrival—they <u>deputed</u> four old men to come and speak to us. . . . They afterward invited us to enter their village.

Jacques Marquette, *The Jesuit Relations,* Vol. LIX

Comprehension and Critical Thinking

1. What warning did the Menominee give Marquette and Joliet?

2. How long was the journey from St. Ignatius to the Mississippi?

3. **Critical Thinking:** *Predict* What dangers do you think Marquette and Joliet will face as they continue on their journey?

Marquette and Joliet on the Mississippi

William Bradford, *History of Plimoth Plantation*

Background

On September 6, 1620, the Pilgrims departed from Plymouth, England, on board the *Mayflower.* The journey across the Atlantic Ocean took 66 days. Their intended destination was the mouth of the Hudson River, site of present-day New York City. During the second half of the trip, they encountered rough weather. The threat of shipwreck if they continued on to the Hudson led them to halt, explore Cape Cod, and settle in Massachusetts.

Among the passengers was William Bradford. He later served as governor of the Plymouth Colony for more than 25 years. Bradford also wrote *History of Plimoth Plantation,* a valuable source of information about the colony. In this excerpt, Bradford describes the arrival of the Pilgrims at Cape Cod.

Vocabulary *Builder*

succor (SUHK uhr) *n.* help or aid

barbarian (bahr BEHR ee uhn) *n.* uncivilized person

desolate (DEHS uh liht) *adj.* empty; lacking in life or comfort

sustain (SUH stayn) *v.* support; keep alive

Being thus arrived in a good harbor and brought safe to land, they fell upon their knees and blessed the God of Heaven who had brought them over the vast and furious ocean and delivered them from all the perils and miseries thereof, again to set their feet on the firm and stable, their proper element.

But here I cannot but stay and make a pause and stand half amazed at this poor people's present condition; and so I think will the reader too, when he well considers the same. Being thus past the vast ocean and a sea of troubles before in their preparation . . . they had now no friends to welcome them, nor inns to entertain or refresh their weather-beaten bodies, no houses or much less towns to repair to, to seek for succor. . . . These savage barbarians, when they met with them (as after will appear) were readier to fill their sides of arrows than otherwise. And for the season, it was winter, and they that know the winters of that country know them to be sharp and violent and subject to cruel and fierce storms, dangerous to travel to known places, much more to search an unknown coast. Besides, what could they see but a hideous and desolate wilderness full of wild beasts and wild men? And what multitudes there might be of them they knew not. . . . What could now sustain them but the spirit of God and his grace?

William Bradford, *History of Plimoth Plantation*

Pilgrims of Plymouth Colony

Comprehension and Critical Thinking

1. What does Bradford mean when he speaks of the Pilgrims' "proper element"?

2. What fears do the Pilgrims face? According to Bradford, what is their one source of hope?

3. **Critical Thinking: *Detect Bias*** What is Bradford's view of Native Americans? How do you think Native Americans viewed the Pilgrims?

Chapter 3

Maryland Act of Toleration

Background

Lord Baltimore was the founder of the Maryland Colony and served as Lord Proprietary, or head of the government. He had hoped to make Maryland a Catholic colony. However, the majority of colonists turned out to be Protestants. Nevertheless, Catholic settlers got the large grants and held the positions of power in the colony. Protestant settlers were unhappy with those conditions.

In 1649, Lord Baltimore encouraged the Maryland legislature to pass an act of toleration. The law gave the colony a measure of religious freedom. The act was designed to protect Protestants but, in fact, protected the Catholic minority as well. The following excerpt from the Act of Toleration identifies some of the people and actions that would and would not be tolerated in the colony.

Vocabulary *Builder*

blaspheme (blas FEEM) *v.* to speak against God or holy matters

confiscation (kahn fihs KAY shuhn) *n.* seizure of property by a government

forfeiture (FOR fuh chuhr) *n.* act of giving up something as a penalty

amity (AM ih tee) *n.* peaceful relations

discountenance (dihs KOWNT uhn ehns) *v.* make to feel shame

Forasmuch as, in a well-governed and Christian commonwealth, matters concerning religion and the honor of God ought in the first place to be taken into serious consideration, . . . be it therefore ordered and enacted by the Right Honorable Cecilius Lord Baron of Baltimore, absolute Lord and Proprietary of this Province with the advise and consent of this General Assembly:

That whatsoever person or persons within the Province thereunto belonging shall from henceforth blaspheme God, that is, curse Him; or deny our Savior Jesus Christ to be the son of God, or shall deny the Holy Trinity, the Father, Son, and Holy Ghost . . . shall be punished with death and confiscation or forfeiture of all his or her lands and goods to the Lord Proprietary and his heirs.

And be it also enacted . . . that whatsoever person or persons shall from henceforth use or utter any reproachful words or speeches concerning the Blessed Virgin Mary, the Mother of our Savior, or the Holy Apostles . . . shall in such case for the first offense forfeit to the said Lord Proprietary and his heirs . . . the sum of five pounds sterling. . . . And that every person or persons before mentioned offending herein the third time, shall for such third Offence forfeit all his lands and Goods and be for ever banished and expelled out of this Province. . . .

And for the more quiet and peaceable government of this Province, and the better to preserve mutual love and amity amongst the Inhabitants thereof, be it therefore [enacted] that no person or persons whatsoever within this Province . . . professing to believe in Jesus Christ, shall from henceforth be any ways troubled, molested or discountenanced for or in respect of his or her religion nor in the free exercise thereof within this Province or the Islands thereunto belonging nor any way compelled to the belief or exercise of any other Religion against his or her consent.

An Act Concerning Religion, April 24, 1649

Comprehension and Critical Thinking

1. What actions were punishable by death under the Maryland Act of Toleration?

2. What people were given religious freedom in Maryland? Why?

3. Critical Thinking: *Contrast* Based on your reading, how did colonial Maryland differ from Puritan New England in terms of religious toleration?

Primary Sources

The Magna Carta

Background

King John ruled England from 1199 to 1216. During his troubled reign, he found himself in conflict with England's feudal barons. The nobles especially resented John's attempts to tax them heavily.

In 1215, the barons forced John to sign the Magna Carta, or Great Charter. Most of this document was intended to protect the rights of the barons.

However, over time, the document came to guarantee some basic rights of English citizens. When English colonists came to North America, they brought these ideas with them. Eight of the 63 clauses of the Magna Carta are printed here.

Vocabulary *Builder*

counsel (KOWN suhl) *n.* advice; consent

bailiff (BAY lihf) *n.* tax collector in medieval England

credible (KREHD uh buhl) *adj.* believable

peer (peer) *n.* person of equal rank

realm (rehlm) *n.* kingdom

enjoin (ehn JOIN) *v.* to order; to enforce

12. No [tax] nor aid shall be imposed on our kingdom, unless by common <u>counsel</u> of our kingdom, except for ransoming our person, for making our eldest son a knight, and for once marrying our eldest daughter; and for these there shall not be levied more than a reasonable aid. . . .

30. No sheriff or <u>bailiff</u> of ours, or other person, shall take the horses or carts of any freeman for transport duty, against the will of the said freeman.

31. Neither we nor our bailiffs shall take, for our castles or for any other work of ours, wood which is not ours, against the will of the owner of that wood. . . .

38. No bailiff for the future shall, upon his own unsupported complaint, put any one to his "law," without <u>credible</u> witnesses brought for this purpose.

39. No freeman shall be taken or imprisoned . . . or exiled or in any way destroyed, nor will we go upon him nor send upon him, except by the lawful judgment of his <u>peers</u> or by the law of the land.

40. To no one will we sell, to no one will we refuse or delay, right or justice. . . .

45. We will appoint as justices, constables, sheriffs, or bailiffs only such as know the law of the <u>realm</u> and mean to observe it well. . . .

63. Wherefore it is our will, and we firmly <u>enjoin</u>, that the English Church be free, and that the men in our kingdom have and hold all the aforesaid liberties, rights, and concessions, well and peaceably, freely and quietly, fully and wholly, for themselves and their heirs, of us and our heirs, in all respects and in all places for ever, as is aforesaid.

The Magna Carta, in Source Problems in English History,
ed. White and Notestein

Comprehension and Critical Thinking

1. Which clauses of the Magna Carta listed here protect the right of people to their own private property?

2. What promise is made in clause 12?

3. **Critical Thinking: *Link Past and Present***
   How do the principles expressed in clauses 38–40 apply to the United States today?

Chapter 4

Jonathan Mayhew, *On Unlimited Submission to Rulers*

Background

During the Great Awakening, American preachers spoke out on both political and religious issues. One of these preachers was Jonathan Mayhew, the Congregationalist minister at Boston's West Church. In a 1750 sermon, Mayhew argued against the idea that people owed complete submission, or obedience, to their rulers. Mayhew based his argument on the teachings of an early Christian leader, the apostle Paul.

Mayhew's lengthy sermon was printed and widely read in the colonies. In this excerpt, he explains his view of the purpose of government.

Vocabulary *Builder*

welfare (WEHL fair) *n.* well-being

parity (PAR ih tee) *n.* similarity

allegiance (uh LEE jehntz) *n.* loyalty

implicit (ihm PLIH siht) *adj.* by suggestion; not stated directly

---

The [goal of government] is the good of civil society. . . .

If it be our duty, for example, to obey our king merely for this reason, that he rules for the public <u>welfare</u> (which is the only argument the apostle makes use of), it follows, by a <u>parity</u> of reason, that when he turns tyrant and makes his subjects his prey to devour and to destroy instead of his charge to defend and cherish, we are bound to throw off our <u>allegiance</u> to him and to resist. . . . Not to discontinue our allegiance, in this case, would be to join with the sovereign in promoting the slavery and misery of that society, the welfare of which we ourselves, as well as our sovereign, are indispensably obliged to secure and promote as far as in us lies.

It is true the apostle puts no such case of such a tyrannical prince; but, by his grounding his argument for submission wholly upon the good of civil society, it is plain he <u>implicitly</u> authorizes and even requires us to make resistance whenever this shall be necessary to the public safety and us to make happiness.

Jonathan Mayhew, *A Discourse Concerning Unlimited Submission and Non-Resistance to the Higher Powers*

Jonathan Mayhew

JONATHAN MAYHEW, D.D. PASTOR OF THE WEST CHVRCH IN BOSTON, IN NEW ENGLAND, AN ASSERTOR OF THE CIVIL AND RELIGIOVS LIBERTIES OF HIS COVNTRY AND MANKIND, WHO OVERPLIED BY PVBLIC ENERGIES DIED OF A NERVOVS FEVER

Comprehension and Critical Thinking

1. According to Mayhew, what is the chief goal of a government?

2. What does Mayhew think people should do if a ruler becomes tyrannical?

3. Critical Thinking: *Make Predictions* How do you think ideas like Mayhew's might contribute to a spirit of resistance and revolution in the colonies?

Primary Sources

Patrick Henry, *Speech in the House of Burgesses*

Background

Patrick Henry was born in Virginia in 1735. Trained as an attorney while a young man, he became known for his speaking skills. Henry was elected to the Virginia House of Burgesses in 1765 and strongly opposed the Stamp Act. In a speech related to the crisis, he spoke against Parliament and the king, declaring, "If this be treason, make the most of it." Bitter criticism from delegates forced him to apologize for the statement and affirm his loyalty to the king.

In March 1775, Henry made the following speech, which became his best known. Some credit this speech with being the deciding act in gaining Virginia's troops for the Revolutionary cause. At the end of the speech, members of the assembly jumped from their seats and shouted, "To Arm! To Arms!"

Vocabulary *Builder*

adversary (AD vehr sayr ee) *n.* enemy; opponent

irresolution (ih rehz oh LOO shuhn) *n.* uncertainty on how to act

supine (soo PĪN) *adj.* lying on one's back

delusive (dih LOOS ihv) *adj.* unreal; misleading

vigilant (VIHJ uh lehnt) *adj.* on the alert for danger

extenuate (ihk STEHN yuh wayt) *v.* to excuse; to make light of

They tell us, sir, that we are weak; unable to cope with so formidable an <u>adversary</u>. But when shall we be stronger? Will it be the next week, or the next year? Will it be when we are totally disarmed, and when a British guard shall be stationed in every house? Shall we gather strength by <u>irresolution</u> and inaction? Shall we acquire the means of effectual resistance by lying <u>supinely</u> on our backs and hugging the <u>delusive</u> phantom of hope, until our enemies shall have bound us hand and foot?

Sir, we are not weak if we make a proper use of those means which the God of nature hath placed in our power. Three millions of people armed in the holy cause of liberty, and in such a country as that which we possess, are invincible by any force which our enemy can send against us. . . . The battle, sir, is not to the strong alone; it is to the <u>vigilant</u>, the active, the brave.

Besides, sir, we have no election. If we were base enough to desire it, it is now too late to retire from the contest. There is no retreat but in submission and slavery! Our chains are forged! Their clanking may be heard on the plains of Boston! The war is inevitable—and let it come! I repeat, sir, let it come!

It is vain, sir, to <u>extenuate</u> the matter. The gentlemen may cry, Peace, peace! But there is no peace. The war has actually begun! The next gale that sweeps from the north will bring to our ears the clash of resounding arms! Our brethren are already in the field! Why stand we here idle? What is it that gentlemen wish? What would they have? Is life so dear or peace so sweet as to be purchased at the price of chains and slavery? Forbid it, almighty God. I know not what course others may take, but as for me, give me liberty or give me death!

Patrick Henry, speech to the Virginia Assembly, March 23, 1775

Comprehension and Critical Thinking

1. According to Henry, why would the Americans be difficult to defeat?

2. Why does Henry think the Americans have no "election," or choice, but to fight?

3. **Critical Thinking: *Detect Points of View*** How do you think a colonist who did not want to break away from Britain might respond to Henry's argument?

Chapter 5

William Sutherland, *The Battle of Lexington*

Background

After the Boston Tea Party, the British government passed the Intolerable Acts. The acts were designed to punish Massachusetts for the crime of its colonists. Massachusetts became an armed camp, with British control limited to Boston. Parliament declared the colony in rebellion.

On April 18, 1775, some 700 British troops left Boston to march on Concord and seize arms stored there by the colonists. One of these British soldiers was William Sutherland. Along the way, the troops passed through the town of Lexington. In this letter, Sutherland describes what happened next.

Vocabulary *Builder*

instantaneous (ihn sten TAY nee uhs) *adj.* immediate; at once
grenadier (grehn uh DIR) *n.* member of a European military force formerly armed with grenades
consequence (KAHN suh kwehns) *n.* result of an action

On coming within gunshot of the village of Lexington, a fellow from the corner of the road, on the right hand, [aimed his weapon] at me. . . . I immediately called to Mr. Adair and the party to observe this circumstance, which they did, and I acquainted Major Pitcairn of it immediately.

We still went on farther when three shots more were fired at us, which we did not return, this is sacred truth as I hope for mercy. These three shots were fired from a corner of a large house to the right of the church. When we came up to the main body, which appeared to me to exceed four hundred in and about the village, who were drawn up in a plain opposite to the church, several officers called out, "Throw down your arms and you shall come to no harm," or words to that effect. Which, they refusing to do, instantaneously the gentlemen who were on horseback rode in amongst them, of which I was one, at which instant I heard Major Pitcairn's voice call out, "Soldiers, don't fire; keep your ranks; form and surround them." Instantly some of the villains, who got over the hedge, fired at us, which our men for the first time returned, which set my horse a-going, who galloped with me down a road above six hundred yards among the middle of them before I turned him. And in returning, a vast number who were in a wood at the right of the grenadiers fired at me, but the distance was so great that I only heard the whistling of the [musket balls], but saw a great number of people in the wood. In consequence of their discovering themselves by firing, our grenadiers gave them a smart fire.

William Sutherland, letter, April 27, 1775

Comprehension and Critical Thinking

1. What do the British want the colonists gathered in Lexington to do? What do the British promise in return?

2. According to Sutherland, who started the shooting?

3. Critical Thinking: *Evaluate Information* Do you think Sutherland's version of the events is believable? Why or why not?

Statue of a minuteman

Thomas Paine, *Common Sense*

Background

Born in England in 1737, Thomas Paine left school at the age of 12. Later, he unsuccessfully tried a variety of careers, from sailor to tax collector. Then, he met Benjamin Franklin in London. Franklin helped Paine come to the American colonies and find work as a journalist.

Two years later, in 1776, Paine published *Common Sense* in order to stir up support for American independence. In different parts of the pamphlet, Paine gives political, military, and moral arguments for breaking away from Britain. In the excerpt below, Paine discusses economic reasons.

Vocabulary *Builder*

advocate (AD vuh kiht) *n.* person who speaks in favor of something

reconciliation (rehk uhn sihl ee AY shuhn) *n.* making peace after a disagreement

renounce (ree NOWNS) *v.* to promise to give up

variance (VAIR ee uhns) *n.* quarrel; dispute

contention (kuhn TEHN shun) *n.* disagreement; conflict

I challenge the warmest <u>advocate</u> for <u>reconciliation</u>, to show a single advantage that this continent can reap, by being connected with Great Britain. I repeat the challenge, not a single advantage is derived. Our corn will fetch its price in any market in Europe, and our imported goods must be paid for, buy them where we will.

But the injuries and disadvantages we sustain by that connection, are without number; and our duty to mankind at large, as well as to ourselves, instruct us to <u>renounce</u> the alliance: Because, any submission to, or dependence on Great Britain, tends directly to involve this continent in European wars and quarrels; and sets us at <u>variance</u> with nations, who would otherwise seek our friendship, and against whom, we have neither anger nor complaint. As Europe is our market for trade, we ought to form no partial connection with any part of it. It is the true interest of America to steer clear of European <u>contentions</u>. . . .

Europe is too thickly planted with kingdoms to be long at peace, and whenever a war breaks out between England and any foreign power, the trade of America goes to ruin, because of her connection with Britain.

Thomas Paine, *Common Sense*

Thomas Paine

Comprehension and Critical Thinking

1. According to Paine, what advantages can the colonies gain by remaining connected with Britain?

2. What effect does Paine say Britain has on American trade?

3. Critical Thinking: *Evaluate Information* Paine's purpose was to persuade colonists to support independence. Which colonists do you think would be most persuaded by the arguments given above?

Chapter 6

Joseph J. Ellis, *His Excellency George Washington*

Background

George Washington gained his first real military experience during the French and Indian War in the 1750s. He was credited with saving the remains of a large American and British army that had been cut to pieces by the French and their Indian allies early in the war.

When the American Revolution started in 1775, Washington was the obvious choice to command American forces. Compared to the best British generals, Washington was inexperienced. But John Adams felt that choosing a Virginian would secure the loyalty of that important colony. It turned out to be a wise decision.

In the following excerpt, a modern historian discusses Washington as a military leader.

Vocabulary *Builder*

<u>protracted</u> (proh TRAKT ehd) *adj.* drawn out; lasting a long time

<u>indefatigable</u> (ihn dih FAT ih guh buhl) *adj.* impossible to tire out; energetic

<u>arrogant</u> (AR uh gehnt) *adj.* full of pride

<u>align</u> (uh LĪN) *v.* to bring into close agreement; to fit

<u>decisive</u> (dee SĪ sihv) *adj.* leading to a final outcome or decision

---

Washington spent the entire war in the field with the Continental army. He was not, by any standard, a military genius. He lost more battles than he won; indeed, he lost more battles than any victorious general in modern history. Moreover, his defeats were frequently a function of his own overconfident and aggressive personality, especially during the early stages of the war, when he escaped to fight another day only because the British generals opposing him seemed choked with the kind of caution that, given his resources, Washington should have adopted as his own strategy. But in addition to being fortunate in his adversaries, he was blessed with personal qualities that counted most in a <u>protracted</u> war. He was composed, <u>indefatigable</u>, and able to learn from his mistakes. He was convinced that he was on the side of destiny—or, in more <u>arrogant</u> moments, sure that destiny was on his side. Even his critics acknowledged that he could not be bribed, corrupted, or compromised. Based on his bravery during several battles, he apparently believed he could not be killed. Despite all his mistakes, events seemed to <u>align</u> themselves with his own instincts. He began the war at the siege of Boston determined to deliver a <u>decisive</u> blow against more disciplined and battle-tested British regulars. He ended it at the siege of Yorktown doing precisely that.

Joseph J. Ellis, *His Excellency George Washington*

Comprehension and Critical Thinking

1. According to the author, why was Washington able to survive early defeats in battle?

2. How did Washington's army at Boston differ from his army at Yorktown?

3. **Critical Thinking:** *Support Opinions* (a) Make a table with two columns, one listing Washington's strengths and the other listing his weaknesses as a general. (b) Based on the information in your table, discuss why Washington was or was not the right man to lead the American army in the Revolutionary War.

Thomas Jefferson, *Virginia Statute for Religious Freedom*

Background

In 1786, the Virginia legislature adopted the Statute for Religious Freedom, written by Thomas Jefferson. The law is still part of the Virginia state constitution.

Other states followed Virginia's lead. The Statute for Religious Freedom later became the basis for the First Amendment to the United States Constitution, which guarantees freedom of religion.

Jefferson himself recognized the importance of this document. Later in life, he directed that his tombstone list what he considered his three greatest accomplishments: writing the Declaration of Independence, founding the University of Virginia, and writing the Virginia Statute for Religious Freedom.

Vocabulary *Builder*

<u>propagation</u> (prahp uh GAY shuhn) *n.* spread

<u>abhor</u> (ab HOR) *v.* to hate

<u>civil</u> (SIHV uhl) *adj.* relating to citizenship

<u>diminish</u> (dih MIHN ihsh) *v.* to lessen

<u>irrevocable</u> (ih REHV uh kuh buhl) *adj.* unchangeable

<u>infringement</u> (ihn FRIHNJ mehnt) *n.* violation

I. *Whereas* Almighty God hath created the mind free . . . that to compel a man to furnish contributions of money for the <u>propagation</u> of opinions which he disbelieves and <u>abhors</u>, is sinful and tyrannical . . . that our <u>civil</u> rights have no dependence on our religious opinions, any more than our opinions in physics or geometry . . .

II. *Be it . . . enacted by the General Assembly*, that no man shall be compelled to frequent or support any religious worship, place, or ministry whatsoever, nor shall be enforced, restrained, molested, or burdened in his body or goods, nor shall otherwise suffer, on account of his religious opinions or belief; but that all men shall be free to profess, and by argument to maintain, their opinions in matters of religion, and that the same shall in no wise <u>diminish</u>, enlarge, or affect their civil capacities.

III. And although we well know that this Assembly, elected by the people for the ordinary purpose of legislation only, have no power to restrain the acts of succeeding assemblies, constituted with powers equal to our own, and that therefore to declare this act to be <u>irrevocable</u> would be of no effect in law; yet we are free to declare, and do declare, that the rights hereby asserted are of the natural rights of mankind, and that if any act shall hereafter be passed to repeal the present, or to narrow its operation, such an act will be <u>infringement</u> of natural right.

Thomas Jefferson, Virginia Statute for Religious Freedom

Comprehension and Critical Thinking

1. According to Jefferson, what is the relationship between civil rights and religious belief?

2. What does Jefferson mean when he calls freedom of religion a "natural right"?

3. **Critical Thinking:** *Compare* Read the First Amendment to the Constitution. How does the First Amendment reflect ideas similar to those in the Virginia Statute for Religious Freedom?

Chapter 7

James Madison, *The Federalist, No. 39*

Background

The *Federalist Papers* is a name given to a series of 85 essays written in 1787 by Alexander Hamilton, James Madison, and John Jay. Their goal was to win support for the Constitution.

Originally, the three authors did not sign the essays with their own names. Instead, they used the Roman name *Publius*, from the Latin word for "public." Using such pen names was a common practice in political writing of the time. It indicated the great respect the early leaders of the United States had for the ancient Roman Republic.

The following excerpt is from *The Federalist* No. 39. Here, James Madison shows that the government formed by the Constitution is a republic.

Vocabulary *Builder*

bestow (bee STOH) *v.* to give

inconsiderable (ihn kuhn SIHD uhr uh buhl) *adj.* small; unimportant

standard (STAN duhrd) *n.* something against which other things are judged

conformable (kuhn FORM uh buhl) *adj.* in harmony or agreement

magistrate (MAJ ihs trayt) *n.* official who enforces the law

We may define a republic to be, or at least may <u>bestow</u> that name on, a government which derives all its powers directly or indirectly from the great body of the people, and is administered by persons holding their offices during pleasure, for a limited period, or during good behavior. It is ESSENTIAL to such a government that it be derived from the great body of the society, not from an <u>inconsiderable</u> proportion, or a favored class of it. . . .

On comparing the Constitution planned by the convention with the <u>standard</u> here fixed, we perceive at once that it is, in the most rigid sense, <u>conformable</u> to it. The House of Representatives, like that of one branch at least of all the State legislatures, is elected immediately by the great body of the people. The Senate, like the present Congress, and the Senate of Maryland, derives its appointment indirectly from the people. The President is indirectly derived from the choice of the people, according to the example in most of the States. . . . The Senate is elective, for the period of six years; which is but one year more than the period of the Senate of Maryland, and but two more than that of the Senates of New York and Virginia. The President is to continue in office for the period of four years; as in New York and Delaware, the chief <u>magistrate</u> is elected for three years, and in South Carolina for two years.

James Madison, *The Federalist* No. 39

James Madison

Comprehension and Critical Thinking

1. What does Madison consider to be the most important quality of a republic?

2. Describe two examples Madison uses to show that the government under the Constitution fits the definition of a republic.

3. **Critical Thinking:** *Draw Inferences* Why do you think Madison tries to show that the proposed new government has many similarities to the state governments?

Thomas Jefferson, *On Majority Rule*

Background

The early leaders of the United States thought long and hard about the meaning of republican government.

One of the key issues was the question of the majority versus the minority. In a republic, the people who make laws have to be elected. They therefore represent the views of the largest number of people. How can the rights of the minority—especially those who hold unpopular views—be protected in a nation where the majority rules? This issue is still debated today.

In these two excerpts, Thomas Jefferson talks about what he calls *lex majoris partis*—Latin for "the law of the majority." The first reading is from a letter written by Jefferson to a friend. The second is from his First Inaugural Address.

Vocabulary *Builder*

fundamental (fuhn duh MEHNT uhl) *adj.* basic

enounce (ee NOWNS) *v.* to express

unanimous (yoo NAN uh muhs) *adj.* agreed upon by everyone

despotism (DEHS puh tihz uhm) *n.* rule by a tyrant

prevail (pree VAIL) *v.* to win out; to gain the advantage

countenance (KOWN tuh nehns) *v.* to approve or accept

The first principle of republicanism is that the *lex majoris partis* is the <u>fundamental</u> law of every society of individuals of equal rights; to consider the will of the society <u>enounced</u> by the majority of a single vote as sacred as if <u>unanimous</u> is the first of all lessons in importance, yet the last which is thoroughly learnt. This law once disregarded, no other remains but that of force, which ends necessarily in military <u>despotism</u>.

Thomas Jefferson, letter to Alexander von Humboldt, 1817

All, too, will bear in mind this sacred principle, that though the will of the majority is in all cases to <u>prevail</u>, that will to be rightful must be reasonable; that the minority possess their equal rights, which equal law must protect, and to violate would be oppression. . . . Having banished from our land that religious intolerance under which mankind so long bled and suffered, we have yet gained little if we <u>countenance</u> a political intolerance as despotic, as wicked, and capable of as bitter and bloody persecutions.

Thomas Jefferson, First Inaugural Address, 1801

Comprehension and Critical Thinking

1. In his letter to Humboldt, what does Jefferson say about the importance of majority rule in a republic?

2. Restate in your own words what Jefferson says in his First Inaugural Address about people who hold minority or unpopular opinions.

3. **Critical Thinking:** *Apply Information* Based on the above, do you think Jefferson would agree with the following statements? Explain.
   (a) "The President is still the President, even though he won by only a few votes."
   (b) "She lost the election, so we can ignore the opinions of the people who voted for her."

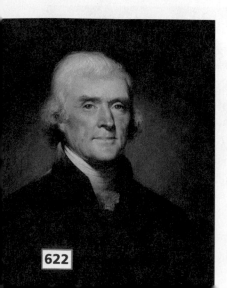

Thomas Jefferson

Hillary Rodham Clinton, *The Importance of Voting*

Background

The right to vote is one of the most basic rights guaranteed by the Constitution. Over the years, different groups of Americans—such as women and African Americans—have struggled long and hard to secure their right to vote. Yet, many Americans have failed to exercise this right. This drop in voter turnout has worried leaders of all political parties, including Hillary Rodham Clinton.

Clinton served as First Lady of the United States and, later, as a senator from New York. In this column, written before the presidential election of 2000, Clinton urges young people to go out and vote.

Vocabulary *Builder*

<u>cite</u> (sīt) *v.* to mention or refer to

<u>survey</u> (SER vay) *n.* process for gathering public opinion

<u>factor</u> (FAK tor) *n.* condition or quality that causes something else to happen

<u>aspect</u> (AS pehkt) *n.* single part or element among many

<u>incumbent</u> (ihn KUHM behnt) *adj.* required as a duty

<u>privilege</u> (PRIHV uh lihj) *n.* special right not shared by everybody

In 1998, fewer than one in five 18- to 24-year-olds voted. When asked why . . . they <u>cite</u> a number of reasons: They feel ignored by politicians; they feel their vote doesn't really count; and they say that they don't get the kind of information they need to make an informed decision.

The <u>survey</u> concludes that the single <u>factor</u> that most influences whether a young person will vote is whether his or her parents vote. But almost half of this group reported that they never—or almost never—talked about politics, government, or current events with their parents.

There is at least one hopeful sign that might help us bring this generation into the process: More than half of them volunteer on a regular basis, and 94 percent define the most important <u>aspect</u> of citizenship as "helping others." I hope that the trend toward service learning in the schools will provide the opportunity for young people to see that the work they do in their communities, and the issues they care about as a result, can be and are affected by what happens in the voting booth.

There are 70.2 million people in this country under 20. The thought that this huge segment of the population might never bother to vote for President or governor, state legislator or town clerk, is extraordinarily alarming. It is <u>incumbent</u> on those of us who do vote, who do believe in the power of one vote to change history, and who do believe in our system of government, to consider very carefully how best to bring them into the political process. . . .

It doesn't matter if you're black or white, old or young, rich or poor, male or female, Republican or Democrat. Don't throw this precious <u>privilege</u> away. When you wake up next Tuesday, please go vote.

Hillary Rodham Clinton, *Talking It Over*, November 1, 2000

Comprehension and Critical Thinking

1. What major concern or worry does Clinton express?

2. According to Clinton, in what way are the majority of young Americans good citizens?

3. **Critical Thinking: *Draw Conclusions*** Why do you think Clinton calls voting a precious privilege? Do you agree with this view? Explain.

Primary Sources

Washington Irving, *Rip Van Winkle*

Background

Washington Irving was born in New York City in 1783. He was the first American to make a living as a popular writer, as well as the first American writer to win a wide readership in Europe. Irving is best known for *The Sketch Book* (1819), a collection of essays that also contains two famous short stories, "The Legend of Sleepy Hollow" and "Rip Van Winkle."

"Rip Van Winkle" is a humorous fantasy about a lazy New York farmer who goes to sleep in the mountains before the American Revolution—and does not wake up for 20 years! In this selection, Rip returns to his village for the first time since his long nap.

Vocabulary *Builder*

incomprehensible (ihn kahm pree HEHN suh buhl) *adj.* impossible to understand

disputatious (dihs pyoo TAY shuhs) *adj.* fond of arguing

bilious (BIHL yuhs) *adj.* bad-tempered

harangue (huh RANG) *v.* to speak in a noisy, scolding manner

vehement (VEE uh mehnt) *adj.* strong; violent

jargon (JAR guhn) *n.* incomprehensible language

He now hurried forth, and hastened to his old resort, the little village inn—but it too was gone. A large rickety wooden building stood in its place, with great gaping windows, some of them broken, and mended with old hats and petticoats, and over the door was painted, "The Union Hotel, by Jonathan Doolittle." Instead of the great tree that used to shelter the quiet little Dutch inn of yore, there now was reared a tall naked pole, with something on the top that looked like a red night-cap, and from it was fluttering a flag, on which was a singular assemblage of stars and stripes—all this was strange and <u>incomprehensible</u>. He recognized on the sign, however, the ruby face of King George . . . but even this was singularly [changed]. The red coat was changed for one of blue and buff, a sword was held in the hand instead of a sceptre, the head was decorated with a cocked hat, and underneath was painted in large characters, GENERAL WASHINGTON.

There was, as usual, a crowd of folk about the door, but none that Rip recollected. The very character of the people seemed changed. There was a busy, bustling, <u>disputatious</u> tone about it, instead of the accustomed . . . drowsy tranquility. He looked in vain for the sage Nicholas Vedder, with his broad face, double chin, and fair long pipe, uttering clouds of tobacco smoke instead of idle speeches; or Van Bummel, the schoolmaster, doling forth the contents of an ancient newspaper. A lean, <u>bilious</u>-looking fellow, with his pockets full of handbills, was <u>haranguing</u> <u>vehemently</u> about rights of citizens—elections—members of congress—liberty—Bunker's Hill—heroes of seventy-six—and other words, which were a perfect Babylonish <u>jargon</u> to the bewildered Van Winkle.

Washington Irving, *The Sketch Book*

Comprehension and Critical Thinking

1. Identify two objects Rip sees at the hotel that he does not understand.

2. What are the men talking about when Rip arrives? Why doesn't Rip understand them?

3. **Critical Thinking:** *Draw Inferences* Rip thinks that "the very character of the people seemed changed." How did the people change? What do you think caused this change?

Chapter 8

George Washington, *Farewell Address*

Background

As he prepared to leave office, President George Washington made a speech describing his vision of the nation's future. The speech became known as Washington's Farewell Address.

The speech deals with a wide range of topics, from the need to keep down the nation's debt to the importance of education. Washington also warns against the dangers of forming political parties, which began during his presidency.

The following excerpt from Washington's Farewell Address deals with relations between the United States and other countries. Washington's ideas about foreign relations influenced American foreign policy for generations.

Vocabulary *Builder*

commercial (KUH MER shuhl) *adj.*
relating to trade

caprice (kuh PREES) *n.*
sudden change

patronize (PAY truh nīz) *v.*
to support

infidelity (ihn fuh DEHL uh tee) *n.*
disloyalty; unfaithfulness

maxim (MAK sihm) *n.*
wise saying

The great rule of conduct for us in regard to foreign nations is, in extending our <u>commercial</u> relations, to have with them as little political connection as possible. So far as we have already formed engagements, let them be fulfilled with perfect good faith. Here let us stop. Europe has a set of primary interests which to us have none; or a very remote relation. Hence she must be engaged in frequent controversies, the causes of which are essentially foreign to our concerns. . . . Why, by interweaving our destiny with that of any part of Europe, entangle our peace and prosperity in the toils of European ambition, rivalship, interest, humor or <u>caprice</u>?

It is our true policy to steer clear of permanent alliances with any portion of the foreign world; so far, I mean, as we are now at liberty to do it; for let me not be understood as capable of <u>patronizing</u> <u>infidelity</u> to existing engagements. I hold the <u>maxim</u> no less applicable to public than to private affairs, that honesty is always the best policy. I repeat, therefore, let those engagements be observed in their genuine sense. But, in my opinion, it is unnecessary and would be unwise to extend them.

George Washington, Farewell Address

George Washington

Comprehension and Critical Thinking

1. Restate the main point of the first sentence of the excerpt in your own words.

2. How does Washington think the United States should deal with agreements that it has already made with other nations?

3. **Critical Thinking:** *Identify Costs* Based on the above, what is one way the United States might suffer from forming permanent alliances with a European country?

Primary Sources

Tecumseh, *Speech at Vincennes*

Background

The great Shawnee leader Tecumseh was born in 1768 in what is now the state of Ohio. In the early 1800s, Tecumseh became the chief spokesman for Native Americans who opposed white settlement of western lands. Along with his brother, known as the Prophet, Tecumseh sought to organize Native Americans into a united league.

In 1810, Tecumseh was outraged that some Indians near the Wabash River had sold land to the United States government. In 1810, he met at Vincennes, Indiana, with the territorial governor, William Henry Harrison, to protest the sale. The following excerpt is from the speech Tecumseh gave that day.

Vocabulary *Builder*

<u>traverse</u> (truh VERS) *v.*
to travel over or across

<u>encroach</u> (ehn KROHCH) *v.*
to intrude upon the rights or property of another

<u>stationary</u> (STAY shuh nair ee) *adj.* fixed; unmoving

Until lately, there was no white man on this continent; that it then all belonged to red men, children of the same parents, placed on it by the Great Spirit that made them, to keep it, to <u>traverse</u> it, to enjoy its productions, and to fill it with the same race, once a happy race, since made miserable by the white people who are never contented but always <u>encroaching</u>. The way, and the only way, to check and to stop this evil, is for all the red men to unite in claiming a common and equal right in the land, as it was at first, and should be yet; for it never was divided, but belongs to all for the use of each. For no part has a right to sell, even to each other, much less to strangers—those who want all, and will not do with less.

The white people have no right to take the land from the Indians, because they had it first; it is theirs. They may sell, but all must join. Any sale not made by all is not valid. The late sale is bad. It was made by a part only. Part do not know how to sell. It requires all to make a bargain for all. All red men have equal rights to the unoccupied land. The right of occupancy is as good in one place as in another. There can not be two occupations in the same place. The first excludes all others. It is not so in hunting or traveling; for there the same ground will serve many, as they may follow each other all day; but the camp is <u>stationary</u>, and that is occupancy. It belongs to the first who sits down on his blanket or skins which he has thrown upon the ground; and till he leaves it no other has a right.

Tecumseh, speech at Vincennes, in *The World's Famous Orations*, ed. William Jennings Bryan

Comprehension and Critical Thinking

1. Why does Tecumseh object to the recent sale of land by Native Americans?

2. What solution does Tecumseh suggest for the increase in white settlement?

3. Critical Thinking: *Detect Points of View* Based on this speech, how does Tecumseh's view of property differ from that of the Americans who settled in the West?

Chapter 9

Francis Scott Key, *The Star-Spangled Banner*

Background

The War of 1812 gave birth to an enduring American tradition. On September 13, 1814, British ships bombarded Fort McHenry near Baltimore. A young lawyer, Francis Scott Key, waited anxiously to find out if the fort would fall. The next morning, Key was relieved to see the American flag still flying over the fort.

Key described his feelings in the poem "The Star-Spangled Banner." The poem was then set to a traditional English tune and quickly became popular. In 1889, it was officially chosen to be played at all military flag raisings. The tradition of performing the song at Major League baseball games began in 1918. Finally, in 1931, Congress adopted "The Star-Spangled Banner" as the national anthem of the United States.

Vocabulary Builder

twilight (TWĪ līt) *n.* dim light between sunset and dark

perilous (PEHR uh luhs) *adj.* dangerous

rampart (RAM pahrt) *n.* defensive wall

haughty (HAWT ee) *adj.* overly proud

repose (ree POHZ) *v.* to rest

fitful (FIHT ful) *adj.* at irregular intervals

Oh, say, can you see by the dawn's early light
   What so proudly we hailed at the <u>twilight</u>'s
last gleaming,
Whose broad stripes and bright stars through
the <u>perilous</u> fight,
   O'er the <u>ramparts</u> we watched were so
gallantly streaming?
And the rockets' red glare, the bombs bursting
in air,
Gave proof through the night that our flag
was still there.
Oh, say, does that star-spangled banner yet wave
O'er the land of the free and the home of
   the brave?

On the shore, dimly seen through the mists
of the deep,
   Where the foe's <u>haughty</u> host in dread silence
<u>reposes</u>,
What is that which the breeze, o'er the
towering steep,
   As it <u>fitfully</u> blows, half conceals,
half discloses?
Now it catches the gleam of the morning's
first beam,
In full glory reflected, now shines on
the stream.
'Tis the star-spangled banner; oh long
may it wave
O'er the land of the free and the home of
the brave!

Francis Scott Key, "The Star-Spangled Banner"

**The flag as it
was in 1812**

Comprehension and Critical Thinking

1. How did Key know that Fort McHenry had not fallen to the British?

2. What words does Key use to describe the people of the United States?

3. Critical Thinking: *Apply Information* Based on what you have read, why would Key have been concerned about the safety of Fort McHenry?

John Marshall, *Gibbons v. Ogden*

Background

In 1824, the Supreme Court decided the case of *Gibbons* v. *Ogden*.

The case involved steamboat traffic between different states. The state of New York had granted Aaron Ogden a license giving him the sole right to operate steamboats on state waterways between New York and New Jersey. When Thomas Gibbons began operating steamboats on the same waterways, Ogden sued him. Gibbons had a license granted by the federal government.

In his decision, Chief Justice John Marshall upheld the constitutional right of Congress to regulate interstate commerce. In this excerpt, Marshall discusses the meaning of the "commerce clause" of the Constitution, which is also reprinted below.

Vocabulary *Builder*

comprehend (kahm pree HEHND) *v.* to include

inconvenient (ihn kuhn VEEN yehnt) *adj.* causing difficulty or trouble

commence (kuh MEHNS) *v.* to begin

terminate (TER muh nayt) *v.* to end

jurisdiction (joor ihs DIHK shuhn) *n.* area in which a government has legal and political authority

From the Constitution of the United States ("commerce clause")

Article 1, Section 8.
The Congress shall have the power . . .
3. To regulate commerce with foreign nations, and among the several states, and with the Indian tribes.

From *Gibbons* v. *Ogden*

Commerce among the states cannot stop at the external boundary line of each state, but may be introduced into the interior. It is not intended to say that these words <u>comprehend</u> that commerce which is completely internal, which is carried on between man and man in a state, or between different parts of the same state, and which does not extend to or affect other states. Such a power would be <u>inconvenient</u> and is certainly unnecessary. Comprehensive as the word "among" is, it may very properly be restricted to that commerce which concerns more states than one. . . .

[States] either join each other, in which case they are separated by a mathematical line, or they are remote from each other, in which case other states lie between them. What is commerce "among" them, and how is it to be conducted? Can a trading expedition between two adjoining states <u>commence</u> and <u>terminate</u> outside of each? And if the trading intercourse be between two states remote from each other, must it not commence in one, terminate in the other, and probably pass through a third? Commerce among the states must, of necessity, be commerce with the states. . . . The power of Congress, then, whatever it may be, must be exercised within the territorial <u>jurisdiction</u> of the several states.

Gibbons v. *Ogden*, in *The Annals of America*, Volume 5

Comprehension and Critical Thinking

1. According to Marshall, what kind of trade does Congress not have the power to regulate?

2. Does Marshall believe that Congress can control certain kinds of trade within a state? Explain.

3. Critical Thinking: *Identify Benefits*
   How might the constitutional power of Congress to regulate interstate commerce benefit the nation's economy?

Chapter 10

Alexis de Tocqueville, *Democracy in America*

Background

Alexis de Tocqueville, a young French writer, visited the United States in 1831. During his travels, he observed firsthand the impact of Jacksonian democracy. After returning to France, Tocqueville began writing *Democracy in America,* a detailed look at American politics, society, economics, religion, and law. The first volume was published in 1835. The book is still studied and quoted by historians and politicians today.

Following are two excerpts from *Democracy in America*. In the first, Tocqueville discusses the role of the American people in their government. In the second, he gives his view of the American character.

Vocabulary *Builder*

infraction (ihn FRAK shuhn) *n.* violation

random (RAN duhm) *adj.* chosen without plan or control

ardent (AHRD uhnt) *adj.* intense; enthusiastic

enterprising (EHNT uhr prī zihng) *adj.* full of energy; willing to undertake new projects

innovator (IHN uh vayt uhr) *n.* person who creates a new way of doing something

From Part Two, Chapter 1

In America the people name those who make the law and those who execute it; they themselves form the jury that punishes <u>infractions</u> of the law. Not only are the institutions democratic in their principle, but also in all their developments; thus the people name their representatives directly and generally choose them every year in order to keep them more completely under their dependence. It is therefore really the people who direct. . . . This majority is composed principally of peaceful citizens who, either by taste or by interest, sincerely desire the good of the country. Around them parties constantly agitate. . . .

From Part Two, Chapter 10

The American taken <u>randomly</u> will therefore be a man <u>ardent</u> in his desires, <u>enterprising</u>, adventurous—above all, an <u>innovator</u>. This spirit is in fact found in all his works; he introduces it into his political laws, his religious doctrines, his theories of social economy, his private industry; he brings it with him everywhere, into the depths of the woods as into the heart of towns.

Alexis de Tocqueville, *Democracy in America*, trans. by Harvey C. Mansfield and Delba Winthrop

Alexis de Tocqueville

Comprehension and Critical Thinking

1. According to Tocqueville, who controls the American government?

2. How does Tocqueville's view of American government fit what you have learned about the Jackson era?

3. Critical Thinking: *Link Past and Present* How does Tocqueville describe what he sees as the typical American? What people today might fit Tocqueville's description?

Primary Sources

Fredrika Bremer, *A Day Among the Swedes at Pine Lake*

Background

Like Ireland and Germany, Sweden became a great source of immigrants to the United States in the mid-1800s. Many Swedish immigrants left home because Sweden did not have enough good farmland to support its growing population. The majority of Swedish immigrants settled in the Midwest, especially in Minnesota, where the land and climate were similar to those in their homeland.

Fredrika Bremer was a Swedish writer who traveled extensively in the United States. In 1853, she described her travels in the book *Homes of the New World: Impressions of America.* In this excerpt, she describes her visit to a community of Swedish immigrants in Minnesota.

Mrs. Petterson, a large woman, who in her youth must have been handsome, came out to receive me, bent double and supported on a crutch-stick, but her open <u>countenance</u> beaming with kindness. She is not yet fifty, but is aged and broken down before her time by severe labor and trouble. . . .

Her husband began here as a farmer, but neither he nor his wife were accustomed to hard work; their land was poor (with the exception of Bergvall's farm, all the land around Pine Lake appears to be of a poor quality), they could not get help, and they were without the conveniences of life; they had a large family, which kept increasing; they endured incredible hardships. Mrs. Petterson, while [nursing] her children, was compelled to do the most <u>laborious</u> work; bent double with <u>rheumatism</u>, she was often obliged to wash for the whole family on her knees. Her husband was at last obliged to give up farming; he then took to shoemaking, and at this trade succeeded in making a livelihood for himself and his family.

He had now been dead a few years, and his widow was preparing to leave the little house and garden, which she could no longer look after, and remove to her son-in-law, Bergvall's. She felt herself worn out, old, and finished before her time, as she said; but still did not regret having come to America, because, as regarded her children and their future, she saw a new world opened to them, richer and happier than that which the mother country could have offered them, and she would have been glad to have purchased this future for them at the sacrifice of her own life; she would be well contented to go down to the grave, even before her time, and there to have done with her crutch.

Fredrika Bremer, *Homes of the New World: Impressions of America*

Comprehension and Critical Thinking

1. What hardships did Mrs. Petterson and her husband face when they first came to the United States?

2. Why is Mrs. Petterson glad that they decided to immigrate?

3. **Critical Thinking:** *Identify Costs and Benefits* Based on this selection and your reading, make a chart showing some of the costs and benefits of coming to the United States in the 1840s.

Chapter 11

Solomon Northrup, *Twelve Years a Slave*

Background

Solomon Northrup was a free African American in New York State. But in 1841, he was kidnapped by slave traders. Separated from his wife and three children, he ended up on a plantation in Louisiana. After 12 years, he finally regained his freedom, thanks to the efforts of a group of white and black New Yorkers.

In 1853, Northrup published *Twelve Years a Slave*, a book about his experiences under slavery. In this excerpt, Northrup describes a slave auction. Eliza, an enslaved woman, watches as her son Randall is sold by the slave dealer, Freeman.

Vocabulary *Builder*

besought (bee SAWT) *v.*
begged (past tense of *beseech*)

paroxysm (PAR uhks ihz uhm) *n.*
sudden, violent outburst

plaintive (PLAYN tihv) *adv.*
sad; sorrowful

afflict (uh FLIHKT) *adj.*
to cause pain

avail (uh VAYL) *n.*
help; usefulness

All the time the trade was going on, Eliza was crying aloud, and wringing her hands. She <u>besought</u> the man not to buy him, unless he also bought her self and Emily. She promised, in that case, to be the most faithful slave that ever lived. The man answered that he could not afford it, and then Eliza burst into a <u>paroxysm</u> of grief, weeping <u>plaintively</u>. Freeman turned round to her, savagely, with his whip in his uplifted hand, ordering her to stop her noise, or he would flog her. . . .

All the frowns and threats of Freeman, could not wholly silence the <u>afflicted</u> mother. She kept on begging and beseeching them, most piteously not to separate the three. Over and over again she told them how she loved her boy. A great many times she repeated her former promises—how very faithful and obedient she would be; how hard she would labor day and night, to the last moment of her life, if he would only buy them all together. But it was of no <u>avail</u>; the man could not afford it. The bargain was agreed upon, and Randall must go alone. Then Eliza ran to him; embraced him passionately; kissed him again and again; told him to remember her— all the while her tears falling in the boy's face like rain.

Solomon Northrup, *Twelve Years a Slave: Narrative of Solomon, a Citizen of New-York, Kidnapped in Washington City in 1841*

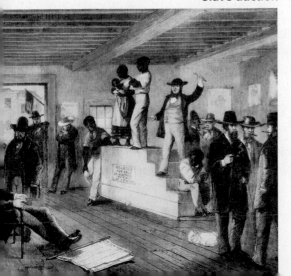

Slave auction

Comprehension and Critical Thinking

1. What does Eliza want? How does she try to get it?

2. How does the slave dealer respond to Eliza?

3. Critical Thinking: *Draw Conclusions* Northrup's book was widely read in the North. What effect do you think descriptions like this one had on readers?

Primary Sources

Elizabeth Cady Stanton, *Letter From Seneca Falls*

Background

Elizabeth Cady Stanton was the leading figure of the early women's rights movement. In 1848, she and Lucretia Mott organized the first American women's rights convention at Seneca Falls, New York. She also authored the Declaration of Sentiments, issued by the Seneca Falls convention. Echoing the Declaration of Independence, the Declaration of Sentiments stated that "all men and women are created equal." Until her death in 1902, Stanton worked to win the right for women to vote.

Stanton also spoke out in support of education for women. She believed that education was needed to prepare women for full citizenship. In the following passage, she describes a new approach to educating women.

Vocabulary *Builder*

<u>untrammeled</u> (uhn TRAM uhld) *adj.* without limitations; free

<u>romp</u> (rahmp) *v.* to play actively and noisily

<u>metropolis</u> (muh TRAHP uh lihs) *n.* large city

<u>melancholy</u> (MEHL ehn kahl ee) *adj.* sad; depressing

<u>drone</u> (drohn) *n.* male bee that does no work

<u>lucrative</u> (LOO kruh tihv) *adj.* well-paying; profitable

---

The great work before us is the proper education of those just coming on the stage. Begin with girls of this day, and in twenty years we can revolutionize this nation. The childhood of women must be free and <u>untrammeled</u>; the girl must be allowed to <u>romp</u> and play, climb, skate, and swim. Her clothing must be more like those of the boy—strong, loose-fitting garments, thick boots, etc.—that she may be out in all seasons and enter freely into all kinds of sports. Teach the girls to go alone, by night and day—if need be, on the lonely highway or through the busy streets of the <u>metropolis</u>.

The manner in which all courage and self-reliance is early educated out of the girl—her path portrayed with danger and difficulties that never exist, is <u>melancholy</u> indeed. Better, far, suffer occasional insults, or die outright, than live the life of a coward, or never more without a protector. The best protection that any woman can have, one that will serve her at all times and in all places, is courage, and this she must get by experience. . . .

The girl must early be impressed with the idea that she is to be "a hand and not a mouth"—a worker, and not a <u>drone</u>—in the great hive of human action. She must be taught to look forward to a life of self-dependence, and like the boy, prepare herself for some <u>lucrative</u> trade or profession.

Elizabeth Cady Stanton, *History of Suffrage*

Comprehension and Critical Thinking

1. In what ways does Stanton think the education of girls should be like that of boys?

2. What does Stanton mean when she says that a woman should be "a hand and not a mouth"?

3. Critical Thinking: *Make Generalizations* Summarize in one sentence Stanton's goal for women.

Chapter 12

Ralph Waldo Emerson, *Self-Reliance*

Background

Ralph Waldo Emerson was not only the most influential thinker of the transcendentalist movement, he was also one of the most admired Americans of his day. His essays and poems won a wide readership. In his lifetime, Emerson was best known for his popular lectures. He traveled across the country, especially the Northeast, addressing large crowds on a wide variety of topics. His early training as a minister helped make him a powerful speaker—especially when he was speaking out against slavery.

In one of his most important essays, *Self-Reliance,* Emerson warned against conformity, or blind following of standards set by others. Instead, he argued in favor of individualism.

Vocabulary *Builder*

envy (EHN vee) *n.* desire for or resentment of what others have

bestow (bee STOH) *v.* to give as a gift

integrity (ihn TEHG ruh tee) *n.* state of being true and sincere

arduous (AHR joo uhs) *adj.* very difficult

solitude (SOL uh tood) *n.* state of being alone

There is a time in every man's education when he arrives at the conviction that <u>envy</u> is ignorance; that imitation is suicide; that he must take himself for better for worse as his portion; that though the wide universe is full of good, no kernel of nourishing corn can come to him but through his toil <u>bestowed</u> on that plot of ground which is given to him to till. . . .

Trust thyself: every heart vibrates to that iron string. . . . Nothing is at last sacred but the <u>integrity</u> of your own mind. . . .

What I must do is all that concerns me, not what the people think. This rule, equally <u>arduous</u> in actual and in intellectual life, may serve for the whole distinction between greatness and meanness. It is the harder because you will always find those who think they know what is your duty better than you know it. It is easy in the world to live after the world's opinion; it is easy in <u>solitude</u> to live after our own; but the great man is he who in the midst of the crowd keeps with perfect sweetness the independence of solitude.

Ralph Waldo Emerson, *Self-Reliance*

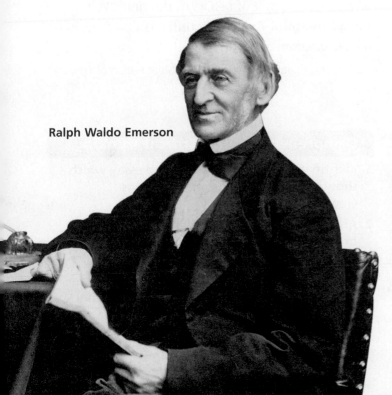

Ralph Waldo Emerson

Comprehension and Critical Thinking

1. According to Emerson, who has the right to judge a person's actions?

2. How does Emerson define greatness?

3. Critical Thinking: *Apply Information* If you were designing a T-shirt devoted to the idea of individualism, what words from *Self-Reliance* would you put on it? Why?

Primary Sources

John O'Sullivan, *Manifest Destiny*

Background

John O'Sullivan was a very influential journalist. In 1837, he founded the *United States Magazine and Democratic Review*. This monthly publication became highly popular among Jacksonian Democrats. In fact, the first person to subscribe to the magazine was Andrew Jackson himself!

In 1839, O'Sullivan published a series of newspaper editorials in which he outlined his view of the United States and its destiny or mission. He called the United States the "Great Nation of Futurity" because he believed the rise of America marked the beginning of a great new era in human history. O'Sullivan's editorials gave rise to the phrase "manifest destiny," the idea that the United States was meant to extend its borders to the Pacific Ocean.

Vocabulary *Builder*

domain (doh MAYN) *n.*
area under someone's rule

inevitable (ihn EHV ih tuh buhl) *adj.* certain; unable to be stopped

smite (smīt) *v.* to strike dead

hierarch (HĪ uhr ahrk) *n.* chief priest in ancient times

oligarch (AHL uh gahrk) *n.* one of a small group of rulers

myriad (MEER ee uhd) *n.* extremely large number

Our national birth was the beginning of a new history, the formation and progress of an untried political system, which separates us from the past and connects us with the future only; and so far as regards the entire development of the natural rights of man, in moral, political, and national life, we may confidently assume that our country is destined to be the great nation of futurity. . . .

The far-reaching, the boundless future will be the era of American greatness. In its magnificent <u>domain</u> of space and time, the nation of many nations is destined to manifest to mankind the excellence of divine principles; to establish on earth the noblest temple ever dedicated to the worship of the Most High—the Sacred and the True. . . .

Yes, we are the nation of progress, of individual freedom, of universal enfranchisement. . . . We must onward to the fulfillment of our mission—to the entire development of the principle of our organization—freedom of conscience, freedom of person, freedom of trade and business pursuits, universality of freedom and equality. This is our high destiny, and in nature's eternal, <u>inevitable</u> decree of cause and effect we must accomplish it. . . .

For this blessed mission to the nations of the world, which are shut out from the life-giving light of truth, has America been chosen; and her high example shall <u>smite</u> unto death the tyranny of kings, <u>hierarchs</u>, and <u>oligarchs</u>, and carry the glad tidings of peace and good will where <u>myriads</u> now endure an existence scarcely more enviable than that of beasts of the field. Who, then, can doubt that our country is destined to be *the great nation* of futurity?

John O'Sullivan, "The Great Nation of Futurity"

Comprehension and Critical Thinking

1. Identify three words in the above essay which show that O'Sullivan takes a religious viewpoint.

2. According to O'Sullivan, what is the mission of the United States?

3. Critical Thinking: *Apply Information* How could O'Sullivan's ideas be used to support the idea that the United States should expand to the Pacific Ocean?

Chapter 13

David Rohrer Leeper, *Gold Rush Journal*

Background

In 1848, gold was discovered in California. The gold rush that followed attracted fortune-seekers from all over the nation and all over the world. Many of these forty-niners recorded their experiences in letters, diaries, and memoirs. One of the forty-niners was David Rohrer Leeper.

Leeper was barely 17 years old when he left Indiana to try his luck in the California gold fields. He spent five years in California.

In 1894, when he was 62, he retold his experiences in the book *The Argonauts of '49, some recollections of the plains and the diggings.* In this excerpt, Leeper describes how it felt to be a teenager leaving home in search of gold and adventure.

Vocabulary *Builder*

yoke (yohk) *n.* pair of pack animals bound together by a wooden collar

pang (pang) *n.* sudden physical or emotional pain

wrought (rawt) *adj.* made; fashioned

intensify (ihn TEHN suh fī) *v.* to make stronger or sharper

On February 22, 1849, our little party of six set out from South Bend, Indiana, for the newly discovered gold-fields of California. . . . All were young—the oldest twenty-five, the youngest seventeen. Our equipment consisted of two wagons, seven <u>yoke</u> of oxen, and two years' supplies. The long journey before us, the comparatively unknown region through which it lay, and the glamour of the object for which it was undertaken, lent our adventure considerable local interest, so that many friends and spectators were present to witness our departure, our two covered wagons being objects of much curious concern as they rolled out of Washington street, with their three thousand miles chiefly of wilderness before them.

But for us the occasion had few <u>pangs</u>. The diggings had been discovered but a twelvemonth before, and the glowing tales of their marvelous richness were on every tongue. Our enthusiasm was <u>wrought</u> up to the highest pitch, while the hardships and perils likely to be incident to such a journey were given scarcely a passing thought. Several parties of our acquaintance had already gone, and others were preparing to go, which still further <u>intensified</u> our eagerness.

David Rohrer Leeper, "The Argonauts of '49" from *California as I Saw It*, Library of Congress

California forty-niner

Comprehension and Critical Thinking

1. According to Leeper, what was the mood of him and his friends as they left for California?

2. What were their reasons for going?

3. Critical Thinking: *Make Predictions* Based on your reading, do you think Leeper and his friends would have faced any unexpected challenges? Explain.

Defiance of the Fugitive Slave Law

Background

In the North, the most hated part of the Compromise of 1850 was the Fugitive Slave Law. The law required all citizens to help catch runaway slaves. Anyone who let a fugitive slave escape could be fined $1,000 and jailed.

Some northern abolitionists banded together to form "vigilance committees." Their purpose was to resist efforts to return African Americans to slavery. The *Liberator*, the abolitionist newspaper founded by William Lloyd Garrison, published this list of instructions for vigilance committees. Garrison strongly opposed the use of violence but suggested other ways to interfere with slave catchers.

Vocabulary *Builder*

induce (ihn DOOS) *v.* to persuade

infamous (IHN fuh muhs) *adj.* having a bad reputation; disgraced

resolute (REZ uh loot) *adj.* determined; firm

loathe (lohth) *v.* to hate

detest (dee TEHST) *v.* to hate

As soon as the kidnappers arrive in any town, large handbills should be posted in all public places, containing their names, with a description of their persons and the business on which they come.

An attempt should be made to <u>induce</u> the landlord of any hotel or boardinghouse to which they may go, to refuse them entertainment, on the ground of their being persons <u>infamous</u> by profession, like pick-pockets, gamblers, or horse-stealers. . . .

Two <u>resolute</u>, unarmed men should follow each of them wherever he goes, pointing him out from time to time with the word SLAVE-HUNTER. . . . He should not have a moment's relief from the feeling that his object is understood, that he cannot act in secret, that he is surrounded by those who <u>loathe</u> his person and <u>detest</u> his purpose, and who have means always at hand to prevent the possibility of success.

"Reception and Treatment of Kidnappers," *Liberator*, January 31, 1851

Poster defying the Fugitive Slave Law

Comprehension and Critical Thinking

1. In one sentence, describe this writer's approach to opposing the Fugitive Slave Law.

2. How can you tell that the writer of this article does not favor the use of violence?

3. Critical Thinking: *Detect Points of View* How does the writer of this article use emotionally charged words to express strong feelings about the Fugitive Slave Law? Give three examples.

Chapter 14

Abraham Lincoln and Stephen Douglas, *Debate at Alton, Illinois*

Background

The 1858 Illinois Senate race pitted Democratic candidate Stephen Douglas against Republican candidate Abraham Lincoln. During the campaign, Lincoln challenged Douglas to a series of debates. Over the course of two months, the candidates held seven fiery debates in different towns. Thousands of people came from miles around to listen.

The main issue of the debates was the extension of slavery into the western territories. The Lincoln-Douglas debates set out in clear terms the difficult issue of slavery in the territories. These excerpts are from their final debate.

Vocabulary *Builder*

controversy (KAHN truh ver see) *n.* debate; argument

sentiment (SEHN tuh mehnt) *n.* feeling

proposition (prahp uh ZIHSH uhn) *n.* basic principle or argument

radiate (RAY dee ayt) *v.* to spread outward

LINCOLN: The real issue in this <u>controversy</u>—the one pressing upon every mind—is the <u>sentiment</u> on the part of one class that looks upon the institution of slavery as a wrong, and of another class that does not look upon it as a wrong. The sentiment that contemplates the institution of slavery in this country as a wrong is the sentiment of the Republican Party. It is the sentiment around which all their actions, all their arguments, circle, from which all their <u>propositions</u> <u>radiate</u>. They look upon it as being a moral, social, and political wrong; and while they contemplate it as such, they nevertheless have due regard for its actual existence among us, and the difficulties of getting rid of it in any satisfactory way and to all the constitutional obligations thrown about it. Yet, having a due regard for these, they desire a policy in regard to it that looks to its not creating any more danger. They insist that it should, as far as may be, be treated as a wrong; and one of the methods of treating it as a wrong is to make provision that it shall grow no larger. They also desire a policy that looks to a peaceful end of slavery at some time, as being wrong.

DOUGLAS: He says that he looks forward to a time when slavery shall be abolished everywhere. I look forward to a time when each state shall be allowed to do as it pleases. If it chooses to keep slavery forever, it is not my business, but its own; if it chooses to abolish slavery, it is its own business, not mine. I care more for the great principle of self-government, the right of the people to rule, than I do for all the Negroes in Christendom. . . . Hence, I say, let us maintain this government on the principles that our fathers made it, recognizing the right of each state to keep slavery as long as its people determine, or to abolish it when they please.

The Lincoln-Douglas Debates, in *Annals of America*, Volume 9

Comprehension and Critical Thinking

1. According to Lincoln, what is the basic idea behind the Republican Party?

2. Summarize Douglas's attitude toward the abolition of slavery.

3. Critical Thinking: *Detect Points of View* Did Lincoln favor the immediate abolition of slavery? Why or why not?

Primary Sources

Robert E. Lee, *Letter to His Sister*

Background

The Lees were one of the most respected families in Virginia as well as in the United States. In 1776, Richard Henry Lee had introduced the resolution in the Continental Congress calling for independence. His cousin, Harry Lee, was a cavalry commander in the Revolutionary War.

Harry's son, Robert E. Lee, also had a distinguished career in the U.S. military. He served in the Mexican War and acted as superintendent of the Military Academy at West Point. But when Virginia seceded from the Union in April 1861, Lee faced a difficult choice. He had to decide whether to keep his position or remain loyal to Virginia. In this letter, he tells his sister of his decision. He later agreed to accept command of the Confederate army.

Vocabulary *Builder*

<u>forborne</u> (for BORN) *v.* to stop or avoid (*past tense of* forbear)

<u>redress</u> (ree DREHS) *n.* fair settlement

<u>commission</u> (kuh MIHSH uhn) *n.* official document making someone a military officer

<u>endeavor</u> (ehn DEHV uhr) *v.* to try

The whole South is in a state of revolution, into which Virginia, after a long struggle, has been drawn; and though I recognize no necessity for the state of things, and would have <u>forborne</u> and pleaded to the end for <u>redress</u> of grievances, real or supposed, yet in my own person I had to meet the question whether I should take part against my native State.

With all my devotion to the Union, and the feeling of loyalty and duty of an American citizen, I have not been able to make up my mind to raise my hand against my relative, my children, my home. I have, therefore, resigned my <u>commission</u> in the Army, and save in defense of my native State (with the sincere hope that my poor services may never be needed) I hope I may never be called upon to draw my sword.

I know you will blame me, but you must think as kindly as you can, and believe that I have <u>endeavored</u> to do what I thought right.

The Wartime Papers of Robert E. Lee

Robert E. Lee

Comprehension and Critical Thinking

1. Based on this reading, was Lee in favor of secession?

2. What reason does he give for resigning his commission with the Union army?

3. Critical Thinking: *Draw Conclusions* How would you describe Lee's feelings about his decision? Would you consider him a traitor? Why or why not?

Chapter 15

James Henry Gooding, *Letters From an African American Soldier*

Background

James Henry Gooding was a free African American born in New York. At the age of 19, he went to Massachusetts to find work on a whaling ship. He made a good living, married, and settled down in Massachusetts. Then, in February 1863, he became one of the first people to volunteer for the 54th Massachusetts, the famous African American regiment of the Union army. He soon rose to the rank of corporal.

From March 1863 until he was killed in battle in February 1854, Gooding wrote a series of letters that were published in a Massachusetts newspaper. The first excerpt here was written while the 54th was still in training camp. The second was written after the assault on Fort Wagner.

Vocabulary *Builder*

vie (vī) *v.* to compete

ignoble (ihg NOH buhl) *adj.* shameful

parapet (PAR uh peht) *n.* barrier used to shield troops from enemy fire

bayonet (bay uh NEHT) *n.* short blade attached to the end of a rifle

battery (BAT uhr ree) *n.* set of heavy guns, such as cannons

May 24, 1863

We have received marching orders; the order was read at dress parade last Thursday, so next Sunday I think we shall be on our way to Dixie. . . .

It seems that most every man in the regiment <u>vies</u> with each other in excellence in whatever they undertake. It is, I think, one of the best guarantees that the 54th will be a credit to old Massachusetts wherever it goes. The citizens of this Commonwealth need not be ashamed of the 54th now; and if the regiment will be allowed a chance, I feel confident the Colored Volunteers will add glory to her already bright name. There is not a man in the regiment who does not appreciate the difficulties, the dangers, and maybe <u>ignoble</u> death that awaits him, if captured by the foe, and they will die upon the field rather than be hanged like a dog; and when a thousand men are fighting for their very existence, who dare say them men won't fight determinedly? The greatest difficulty will be to stop them.

July 20, 1863

The 54th, the past week, has proved itself twice in battle. . . .

Gen. Strong asked us if we would follow him into Fort Wagner. Every man said, yes—we were ready to follow wherever we were led. . . . We went at it, over the ditch and on to the <u>parapet</u> through a deadly fire; but we could not get into the fort. We met the foe on the parapet of Wagner with the <u>bayonet</u>—we were exposed to a murderous fire from the <u>batteries</u> of the fort, from our Monitors and our land batteries, as they did not cease firing soon enough. Mortal men could not stand such a fire, and the assault on Wagner was a failure.

On the Altar of Freedom: A Black Soldier's Civil War Letters From the Front, ed. Virginia M. Adams

Comprehension and Critical Thinking

1. What is Gooding's attitude about going into battle? What prediction does he make?

2. Does Gooding's prediction come true?

3. **Critical Thinking:** *Draw Inferences* Why do you think the men of the 54th Massachusetts were unwilling to be captured alive?

Primary Sources

Walt Whitman, *O Captain! My Captain!*

Background

Walt Whitman was born in 1819 on Long Island and grew up in Brooklyn. In 1855, he published his greatest collection of poems, *Leaves of Grass*. He kept adding to the collection for the rest of his life. During the Civil War, Whitman volunteered to care for men in military hospitals.

After the assassination of Abraham Lincoln, Whitman wrote two poems honoring the fallen President that became very famous. "When Lilacs Last in the Dooryard Bloom'd" is considered one of his best works. "O Captain! My Captain!" is a shorter poem and one of the few Whitman wrote using rhyme. The poem was greatly loved by the American people. Whitman was so often asked to recite it, he said he almost regretted writing it.

O Captain! my Captain! our fearful trip is done,
The ship has weather'd every <u>rack</u>, the prize we
  sought is won,
The port is near, the bells I hear, the people all
  <u>exulting</u>,
While follow eyes the steady <u>keel</u>, the vessel
  grim and daring;
     But O heart! heart! heart!
      O the bleeding drops of red,
       Where on the deck my Captain lies,
        Fallen cold and dead.

O Captain! my Captain! rise up and hear the bells;
Rise up—for you the flag is flung—for you the
  bugle <u>trills</u>,
For you bouquets and ribbon'd wreaths—for you
  the shores a-crowding,
For you they call, the swaying mass, their eager
  faces turning;
     Here Captain! dear father!

This arm beneath your head!
   It is some dream that on the deck,
    You've fallen cold and dead.

My Captain does not answer, his lips are pale
  and still,
My father does not feel my arm, he has no pulse
  nor will,
The ship is anchor'd safe and sound, its voyage
  closed and done,
From fearful trip the victor ship comes in with
  object won;
   Exult O shores, and ring O bells!
    But I with mournful tread,
     Walk the deck my Captain lies,
      Fallen cold and dead.

Walt Whitman, *Leaves of Grass*

Comprehension and Critical Thinking

1. Who is the Captain in the poem? What is the ship?

2. Why does Whitman write "our fearful trip is done" and "the prize we sought is won"?

3. Critical Thinking: *Detect Points of View* What is Whitman's attitude toward the Captain and the events discussed in the poem?

Walt Whitman

Chapter 16

Frederick Douglass, *What the Black Man Wants*

Background

Frederick Douglass was born into slavery in Maryland in 1817. Escaping to the North, he became a leading abolitionist. He spoke at antislavery conventions, published the antislavery newspaper the *North Star,* and wrote a best-selling autobiography that awakened many people to the injustices of slavery. In addition, Douglass was a delegate to the 1848 women's rights convention at Seneca Falls.

Only a few days after the end of the Civil War, Douglass addressed the annual meeting of the Massachusetts Anti-Slavery Society. He discussed one of the key issues of Reconstruction: the enfranchisement of, or giving the vote to, African Americans. This is an excerpt from that speech.

Vocabulary *Builder*

unconditional (uhn kuhn DIHSH uhn uhl) *adj.* without limits or reservations

mockery (MAHK uhr ee) *n.* false imitation

sufficient (suh FIHSH uhnt) *adj.* enough

deprivation (deh prih VAY shuhn) *n.* act of taking something away

incapacity (ihn kuh PAS ih tee) *n.* lack of ability

I am for the "immediate, <u>unconditional</u>, and universal" enfranchisement of the black man, in every State in the Union. Without this, his liberty is a <u>mockery</u>; without this, you might as well almost retain the old name of slavery for his condition; for in fact, if he is not the slave of the individual master, he is the slave of society, and holds his liberty as a privilege, not as a right. He is at the mercy of the mob, and has no means of protecting himself. . . .

It may be asked, "Why do you want it? Some men have got along very well without it. Women have not this right." Shall we justify one wrong by another? This is the <u>sufficient</u> answer. Shall we at this moment justify the <u>deprivation</u> of the Negro of the right to vote, because some one else is deprived of that privilege? I hold that women, as well as men, have the right to vote, and my heart and voice go with the movement to extend suffrage to woman; but that question rests upon another basis than which our right rests.

We may be asked, I say, why we want it. I will tell you why we want it. We want it because it is our right, first of all. No class of men can, without insulting their own nature, be content with any deprivation of their rights. We want it again, as a means for educating our race. Men are so constituted that they derive their conviction of their own possibilities largely by the estimate formed of them by others. If nothing is expected of a people, that people will find it difficult to contradict that expectation. By depriving us of suffrage, you affirm our <u>incapacity</u> to form an intelligent judgment respecting public men and public measures; you declare before the world that we are unfit to exercise the elective franchise, and by this means lead us to undervalue ourselves.

Frederick Douglass, *What the Black Man Wants*

Comprehension and Critical Thinking

1. According to Douglass, when should the government grant African Americans the right to vote? Under what conditions?

2. What is Douglass's view of women's suffrage?

3. Critical Thinking: *Evaluate Information* Summarize one argument Douglass uses in favor of granting the vote to African Americans. Explain whether you find that argument persuasive and why.

Primary Sources

Robert G. Kaiser, *America and the Aftermath of September 11*

Background

September 11, 2001, was a day of incredible horror and incredible bravery. Terrorists flew planes into both towers of New York's World Trade Center. Within a short time, both buildings crumbled to the ground, killing thousands of people. In Washington, D.C., a third plane, under the command of another terrorist, crashed into the Pentagon, destroying a large part of the building and killing hundreds more.

A fourth hijacked airplane might have brought more destruction on the nation's capital. However, heroic passengers took action. Following is the story of the passengers of United Airlines Flight 93, as reported in an essay for the 2001 *Encyclopaedia Britannica Year in Review.*

The horror planned for September 11 was supposed to be worse, and very nearly was. The fourth hijacked airplane was evidently aimed at the Capitol or the White House in Washington—we may never know its target for certain. A direct hit on either would have been <u>symbolically devastating</u>, adding enormously to the impact of the attacks. But a group of brave and <u>resourceful</u> passengers on United Airlines Flight 93 prevented its hijackers from fulfilling their mission. . . .

Passengers on board the flight, who thought they were flying . . . to San Francisco, made calls to relatives on the ground with cellular telephones and learned that a hijacked plane already had been flown into the World Trade Center. . . . One of them was Jeremy Glick, 31, sales manager for a technology firm, who told his wife to "have a good life" and promised to go down fighting against the terrorists. Glick and several other passengers . . . were plotting to rush the cockpit . . . to disrupt whatever plan their hijackers had in mind. One of the other plotters, Todd Beamer, told a telephone operator whom he had reached via an onboard "airfone" about this plan. The operator heard him shout to his comrades, "Are you guys ready? Let's roll!" The operator then heard screams and sounds of a <u>scuffle</u> before the line went dead. In the next few moments, the plane took a series of sharp turns and then plunged into the Pennsylvania countryside. . . . Somehow, the passengers had disrupted the hijackers and forced the plane to Earth.

In that case, the technological wizardry of the age contributed to heroism and self-sacrifice that may have saved many lives in Washington.

Encyclopaedia Britannica Year in Review: The Events of 2001 and How They Shaped the World

Comprehension and Critical Thinking

1. What did the terrorists plan to do with United Airlines Flight 93?

2. What role did technology play in the passengers' plan?

3. **Critical Thinking: *Identify Alternatives*** What other course of action might the passengers on Flight 93 have followed? Why do you think people like Glick and Beamer chose to act as they did?

Presentes of the United States
Presidents of the United States

1 George Washington (1732–1799)

Years in office:
1789–1797
Party:
none
Elected from:
Virginia
Vice President:
John Adams

2 John Adams (1735–1826)

Years in office:
1797–1801
Party:
Federalist
Elected from:
Massachusetts
Vice President:
Thomas
   Jefferson

3 Thomas Jefferson (1743–1826)

Years in office:
1801–1809
Party:
Democratic
   Republican
Elected from:
Virginia
Vice President:
1) Aaron Burr,
2) George Clinton

4 James Madison (1751–1836)

Years in office:
1809–1817
Party:
Democratic
   Republican
Elected from:
Virginia
Vice President:
1) George Clinton,
2) Elbridge Gerry

5 James Monroe (1758–1831)

Years in office:
1817–1825
Party:
Democratic
   Republican
Elected from:
Virginia
Vice President:
Daniel Tompkins

6 John Quincy Adams (1767–1848)

Years in office:
1825–1829
Party:
National
   Republican
Elected from:
Massachusetts
Vice President:
John Calhoun

7 Andrew Jackson (1767–1845)

Years in office:
1829–1837
Party:
Democratic
Elected from:
Tennessee
Vice President:
1) John Calhoun,
2) Martin Van
   Buren

8 Martin Van Buren (1782–1862)

Years in office:
1837–1841
Party:
Democratic
Elected from:
New York
Vice President:
Richard Johnson

9 William Henry Harrison* (1773–1841)

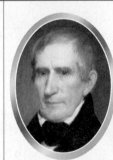

Years in office:
1841
Party:
Whig
Elected from:
Ohio
Vice President:
John Tyler

10 John Tyler (1790–1862)

Years in office:
1841–1845
Party:
Whig
Elected from:
Virginia
Vice President:
none

11 James K. Polk (1795–1849)

Years in office:
1845–1849
Party:
Democratic
Elected from:
Tennessee
Vice President:
George Dallas

12 Zachary Taylor* (1784–1850)

Years in office:
1849–1850
Party:
Whig
Elected from:
Louisiana
Vice President:
Millard Fillmore

*Died in office

13 Millard Fillmore (1800–1874)

Years in office:
1850–1853
Party:
Whig
Elected from:
New York
Vice President:
none

14 Franklin Pierce (1804–1869)

Years in office:
1853–1857
Party:
Democratic
Elected from:
New Hampshire
Vice President:
William King

15 James Buchanan (1791–1868)

Years in office:
1857–1861
Party:
Democratic
Elected from:
Pennsylvania
Vice President:
John Breckinridge

16 Abraham Lincoln** (1809–1865)

Years in office:
1861–1865
Party:
Republican
Elected from:
Illinois
Vice President:
1) Hannibal Hamlin,
2) Andrew Johnson

17 Andrew Johnson (1808–1875)

Years in office:
1865–1869
Party:
Republican
Elected from:
Tennessee
Vice President:
none

18 Ulysses S. Grant (1822–1885)

Years in office:
1869–1877
Party:
Republican
Elected from:
Illinois
Vice President:
1) Schuyler Colfax,
2) Henry Wilson

19 Rutherford B. Hayes (1822–1893)

Years in office:
1877–1881
Party:
Republican
Elected from:
Ohio
Vice President:
William Wheeler

20 James A. Garfield** (1831–1881)

Years in office:
1881
Party:
Republican
Elected from:
Ohio
Vice President:
Chester A. Arthur

21 Chester A. Arthur (1829–1886)

Years in office:
1881–1885
Party:
Republican
Elected from:
New York
Vice President:
none

22 Grover Cleveland (1837–1908)

Years in office:
1885–1889
Party:
Democratic
Elected from:
New York
Vice President:
Thomas Hendricks

23 Benjamin Harrison (1833–1901)

Years in office:
1889–1893
Party:
Republican
Elected from:
Indiana
Vice President:
Levi Morton

24 Grover Cleveland (1837–1908)

Years in office:
1893–1897
Party:
Democratic
Elected from:
New York
Vice President:
Adlai Stevenson

**Assassinated

25 William McKinley** (1843–1901)

Years in office:
1897–1901
Party:
Republican
Elected from:
Ohio
Vice President:
1) Garret Hobart,
2) Theodore Roosevelt

26 Theodore Roosevelt (1858–1919)

Years in office:
1901–1909
Party:
Republican
Elected from:
New York
Vice President:
Charles Fairbanks

27 William Howard Taft (1857–1930)

Years in office:
1909–1913
Party:
Republican
Elected from:
Ohio
Vice President:
James Sherman

28 Woodrow Wilson (1856–1924)

Years in office:
1913–1921
Party:
Democratic
Elected from:
New Jersey
Vice President:
Thomas Marshall

29 Warren G. Harding* (1865–1923)

Years in office:
1921–1923
Party:
Republican
Elected from:
Ohio
Vice President:
Calvin Coolidge

30 Calvin Coolidge (1872–1933)

Years in office:
1923–1929
Party:
Republican
Elected from:
Massachusetts
Vice President:
Charles Dawes

31 Herbert C. Hoover (1874–1964)

Years in office:
1929–1933
Party:
Republican
Elected from:
California
Vice President:
Charles Curtis

32 Franklin D. Roosevelt* (1882–1945)

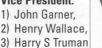

Years in office:
1933–1945
Party:
Democratic
Elected from:
New York
Vice President:
1) John Garner,
2) Henry Wallace,
3) Harry S Truman

33 Harry S Truman (1884–1972)

Years in office:
1945–1953
Party:
Democratic
Elected from:
Missouri
Vice President:
Alben Barkley

34 Dwight D. Eisenhower (1890–1969)

Years in office:
1953–1961
Party:
Republican
Elected from:
New York
Vice President:
Richard M. Nixon

35 John F. Kennedy** (1917–1963)

Years in office:
1961–1963
Party:
Democratic
Elected from:
Massachusetts
Vice President:
Lyndon B. Johnson

36 Lyndon B. Johnson (1908–1973)

Years in office:
1963–1969
Party:
Democratic
Elected from:
Texas
Vice President:
Hubert Humphrey

*Died in office
**Assassinated

37 Richard M. Nixon*** (1913–1994)

Years in office:
1969–1974
Party:
Republican
Elected from:
New York
Vice President:
1) Spiro Agnew,
2) Gerald R. Ford

38 Gerald R. Ford (1913–2006)

Years in office:
1974–1977
Party:
Republican
Appointed from:
Michigan
Vice President:
Nelson
   Rockefeller

39 Jimmy Carter (b. 1924)

Years in office:
1977–1981
Party:
Democratic
Elected from:
Georgia
Vice President:
Walter Mondale

40 Ronald W. Reagan (1911–2004)

Years in office:
1981–1989
Party:
Republican
Elected from:
California
Vice President:
George H.W.
   Bush

41 George H.W. Bush (b. 1924)

Years in office:
1989–1993
Party:
Republican
Elected from:
Texas
Vice President:
J. Danforth
   Quayle

42 William J. Clinton (b. 1946)

Years in office:
1993–2001
Party:
Democratic
Elected from:
Arkansas
Vice President:
Albert Gore, Jr.

43 George W. Bush (b. 1946)

Years in office:
2001–2009
Party:
Republican
Elected from:
Texas
Vice President:
Richard Cheney

44 Barack H. Obama (b. 1961)

Years in office:
2009–
Party:
Democratic
Elected from:
Illinois
Vice President:
Joseph R. Biden

***Resigned

The Fifty States

State	Date of Entry to Union (Order of Entry)	Land Area in Square Miles	Population (In Thousands)	Number of Representatives in House*	Capital	Largest City
Alabama	1819 (22)	50,750	4,447	7	Montgomery	Birmingham
Alaska	1959 (49)	570,374	627	1	Juneau	Anchorage
Arizona	1912 (48)	113,642	5,131	8	Phoenix	Phoenix
Arkansas	1836 (25)	52,075	2,673	4	Little Rock	Little Rock
California	1850 (31)	155,973	33,872	53	Sacramento	Los Angeles
Colorado	1876 (38)	103,730	4,301	7	Denver	Denver
Connecticut	1788 (5)	4,845	3,406	5	Hartford	Bridgeport
Delaware	1787 (1)	1,955	784	1	Dover	Wilmington
Florida	1845 (27)	53,997	15,982	25	Tallahassee	Jacksonville
Georgia	1788 (4)	57,919	8,186	13	Atlanta	Atlanta
Hawaii	1959 (50)	6,423	1,212	2	Honolulu	Honolulu
Idaho	1890 (43)	82,751	1,294	2	Boise	Boise
Illinois	1818 (21)	55,593	12,419	19	Springfield	Chicago
Indiana	1816 (19)	35,870	6,080	9	Indianapolis	Indianapolis
Iowa	1846 (29)	55,875	2,926	5	Des Moines	Des Moines
Kansas	1861 (34)	81,823	2,688	4	Topeka	Wichita
Kentucky	1792 (15)	39,732	4,042	6	Frankfort	Louisville
Louisiana	1812 (18)	43,566	4,469	7	Baton Rouge	New Orleans
Maine	1820 (23)	30,865	1,275	2	Augusta	Portland
Maryland	1788 (7)	9,775	5,296	8	Annapolis	Baltimore
Massachusetts	1788 (6)	7,838	6,349	10	Boston	Boston
Michigan	1837 (26)	56,809	9,938	15	Lansing	Detroit
Minnesota	1858 (32)	79,617	4,919	8	St. Paul	Minneapolis
Mississippi	1817 (20)	46,914	2,845	4	Jackson	Jackson
Missouri	1821 (24)	68,898	5,595	9	Jefferson City	Kansas City
Montana	1889 (41)	145,556	902	1	Helena	Billings
Nebraska	1867 (37)	76,878	1,711	3	Lincoln	Omaha
Nevada	1864 (36)	109,806	1,998	3	Carson City	Las Vegas
New Hampshire	1788 (9)	8,969	1,236	2	Concord	Manchester
New Jersey	1787 (3)	7,419	8,414	13	Trenton	Newark
New Mexico	1912 (47)	121,365	1,819	3	Santa Fe	Albuquerque
New York	1788 (11)	47,224	18,976	29	Albany	New York
North Carolina	1789 (12)	48,718	8,049	13	Raleigh	Charlotte
North Dakota	1889 (39)	68,994	642	1	Bismarck	Fargo
Ohio	1803 (17)	40,953	11,353	18	Columbus	Columbus
Oklahoma	1907 (46)	68,679	3,451	5	Oklahoma City	Oklahoma City
Oregon	1859 (33)	96,003	3,421	5	Salem	Portland
Pennsylvania	1787 (2)	44,820	12,281	19	Harrisburg	Philadelphia
Rhode Island	1790 (13)	1,045	1,048	2	Providence	Providence
South Carolina	1788 (8)	30,111	4,012	6	Columbia	Columbia
South Dakota	1889 (40)	75,898	755	1	Pierre	Sioux Falls
Tennessee	1796 (16)	41,220	5,689	9	Nashville	Memphis
Texas	1845 (28)	261,914	20,852	32	Austin	Houston
Utah	1896 (45)	82,168	2,233	3	Salt Lake City	Salt Lake City
Vermont	1791 (14)	9,249	609	1	Montpelier	Burlington
Virginia	1788 (10)	39,598	7,079	11	Richmond	Virginia Beach
Washington	1889 (42)	66,582	5,894	9	Olympia	Seattle
West Virginia	1863 (35)	24,087	1,808	3	Charleston	Charleston
Wisconsin	1848 (30)	54,314	5,364	8	Madison	Milwaukee
Wyoming	1890 (44)	97,105	494	1	Cheyenne	Cheyenne
District of Columbia		61	572	1 (nonvoting)		

Self-Governing Areas, Possessions, and Dependencies	Land Area in Square Miles	Population (In Thousands)	Capital
Puerto Rico	3,515	809	San Juan
Guam	209	155	Agana
U.S. Virgin Islands	132	121	Charlotte Amalie
American Samoa	77	65	Pago Pago

Sources: Department of Commerce, Bureau of the Census　　　　*As of 108th Congress.

Alabama

Alaska

Arizona

Arkansas

California

Colorado

Connecticut

Delaware

Florida

Georgia

Hawaii

Idaho

Illinois

Indiana

Iowa

Kansas

Kentucky

Louisiana

Maine

Maryland

Massachusetts

Michigan

Minnesota

Mississippi

Missouri

Montana

Nebraska

Nevada

New Hampshire

New Jersey

New Mexico

New York

North Carolina

North Dakota

Ohio

Oklahoma

Oregon

Pennsylvania

Rhode Island

South Carolina

South Dakota

Tennessee

Texas

Utah

Vermont

Virginia

Washington

West Virginia

Wisconsin

Wyoming

ILLUSTRATED ATLAS
OF AMERICAN HISTORY

Table of Contents

Introduction

This illustrated atlas contains dramatic maps and vibrant pictures and graphs to bring your study of American history to life. You can use these pages to compare regions or to make connections between past and present. The atlas has been placed at the front of your textbook, so you will have it as a ready reference throughout the year.

Get up-to-date information about any country in the world. Use the World Desk Reference Online to learn about the world today, practice critical thinking skills, and get updated statistics and data.

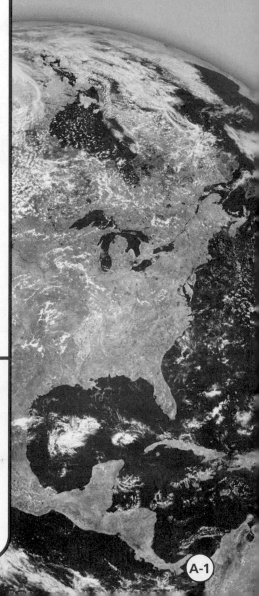

UNITED STATES
POLITICAL

Golden Gate Bridge, San Francisco, California

115°W   110°W   105°W   100°W

Seattle
Spokane
Olympia **Washington**

Great Falls
Helena **Montana**

Minot   Grand Forks
North Dakota
Bismarck

Portland
Salem
Eugene

Oregon

Billings

Boise
Idaho

Pocatello

Wyoming

Casper

Ogden

South Dakota
Rapid City   Pierre
Sioux Falls

Reno
San Francisco Carson City
Sacramento
Oakland
San Jose

Nevada

Great
Salt Lake   Salt Lake
City

Utah

Cheyenne

Nebraska

Lincoln

Denver
Colorado
Colorado
Springs

Kansas
Wichita

California

Las
Vegas

Los Angeles
Long Beach

**PACIFIC
OCEAN**

125°W

Salton
Sea
San Diego

Arizona

Phoenix

Tucson

Santa Fe
Albuquerque

New Mexico

Las
Cruces
El Paso

Oklahoma
Oklahoma
City

Fort Worth

Texas

Austin

San
Antonio

30°N

115°W

120°W

110°W

105°W

160°W   155°W

Honolulu **Hawaii**

PACIFIC OCEAN

0 km   100
0 miles   100
Mercator Projection

20°N

160°E   170°E

**PACIFIC
OCEAN**

50°N

180° 70°N 170°W 160°W 150°W

RUSSIA

140°W

Arctic Circle

130°W

Alaska
Fairbanks

60°N

CANADA

Anchorage

Bering
Sea

Gulf of
Alaska

Juneau

MEXICO

0 km   400
0 miles   400
Albers Conic Equal-Area Projection

100°W

A-2

95°W　90°W　85°W　50°N　80°W　75°W　70°W　65°W

45°N

CANADA

L. Superior

Duluth

Minnesota

Michigan

L. Huron

Vermont

Maine

• Bangor

Augusta

Burlington ★

Montpelier

Lewiston

Portland

Wisconsin

St. Paul ★

Minneapolis ★

Green Bay

Madison ★

Milwaukee

Grand Rapids

Lansing

L. Michigan

New York

Concord ★

Manchester

New Hampshire

Albany ★

Boston

Massachusetts

Providence

Hartford

Rhode Island

Connecticut

L. Ontario

Rochester

Buffalo

L. Erie

Sioux City

Iowa

Omaha

Des Moines ★

Chicago

Peoria

Gary

Fort Wayne

Detroit

Toledo

Cleveland

Akron

Ohio

Columbus ★

Pennsylvania

Harrisburg ★

Pittsburgh

Newark

Jersey City

Philadelphia

Trenton

Wilmington

New York

New Jersey

Illinois

Springfield ★

Indiana

Indianapolis ★

Cincinnati

West Virginia

Baltimore

Washington, D.C. ⊛

Annapolis

Dover

Delaware

Maryland

Missouri

Topeka ★

Kansas City

St. Louis

Jefferson City ★

Louisville

Frankfort ★

Lexington

Huntington

Charleston

Virginia

Richmond ★

Norfolk

Capitol, Washington, D.C.

35°N

ATLANTIC OCEAN

Springfield

Kentucky

Knoxville

Winston-Salem

Greensboro

Raleigh ★

Tulsa

Nashville ★

Tennessee

North Carolina

Charlotte

Arkansas

Fort Smith

Memphis

Little Rock ★

Columbia ★

South Carolina

N

W — E

S

Dallas

Mississippi

Atlanta ★

Macon

Birmingham

Alabama

Columbus

Charleston

KEY

⊛ National capital

★ State capital

• Other city

Savannah

Shreveport

Jackson ★

Montgomery ★

Georgia

Jacksonville

30°N

70°W

Louisiana

Mobile

Pensacola

Tallahassee ★

0 km　　　300

0 miles　　　300

Albers Conic Equal-Area Projection

Baton Rouge ★

L. Pontchartrain

Florida

35°N

New Orleans

Houston

Gulf of Mexico

Tampa

L. Okeechobee

Miami

B A H A M A S

25°N

Tropic of Cancer

CUBA

20°N

Gateway Arch, St. Louis, Missouri

80°W　　75°W

A-3

UNITED STATES
PHYSICAL

Grand Canyon

CANADA

ROCKY MOUNTAINS

CASCADE RANGE

SIERRA NEVADA

GREAT PLAINS

Missouri R.

Great Salt Lake

Colorado R.

Pikes Peak (14,110 ft.)

NORTH

Mt. Whitney (14,491 ft.)

GRAND CANYON

PACIFIC OCEAN

30°N
125°W

120°W

115°W

110°W

Rio Grande

MEXICO

160°W   155°W

PACIFIC OCEAN

Hawaii

20°N

0 km 100
0 miles 100
Mercator Projection

ARCTIC OCEAN

70°N

Arctic Circle

Yukon R.

Mt. McKinley (20,320 ft.)

ALASKA RANGE

0 km 500
0 miles 500
Albers Conic Equal-Area Projection

Bering Sea

Gulf of Alaska

60°N

25°N

105°W

100°W

170°E
PACIFIC OCEAN

180°

170°W

160°W

150°W

140°W

Mississippi River

L. Superior

L. Huron

L. Michigan

L. Ontario

L. Erie

St. Lawrence R.

Mississippi R.

Ohio R.

A M E R I C A

APPALACHIAN MOUNTAINS

ATLANTIC COASTAL PLAIN

GULF COASTAL PLAIN

Mississippi R.

KEY

Land Elevation

Feet		Meters
14,000		4,000
7,000		2,000
1,500		500
700		200
0		0
Below sea level		Below sea level

N E W S

0 km   300

0 miles   300

Albers Conic Equal-Area Projection

ATLANTIC OCEAN

Gulf of Mexico

The Everglades, southern Florida

Tropic of Cancer

C U B A

Hispaniola

Caribbean Sea

65°W   60°W   45°N   40°N   35°N

95°W   90°W   85°N   80°W   75°W   70°W   20°N

UNITED STATES
RESOURCES & THE ECONOMY

Grain harvest, an example of commercial farming

Washington

Montana

North Dakota

Oregon

Idaho

South Dakota

Wyoming

Nevada

Utah

Nebraska

California

Colorado

Kansas

Arizona

New Mexico

Oklahoma

Texas

PACIFIC OCEAN

45°N

40°N

115°W

110°W

105°W

100°W

115°W

110°W

160°W

155°W

180°

170°W

160°W

150°W

140°W

130°W

RUSSIA

Hawaii

PACIFIC OCEAN

0 km   100
0 miles   100
Mercator Projection

70°N

Arctic Circle

Alaska

CANADA

MEXICO

Bering Sea

Gulf of Alaska

60°N

50°N

170°E

0 km   400
0 miles   400
Albers Conic Equal-Area Projection

PACIFIC OCEAN

105°W

100°W

CANADA

90°W 85°W 50°N 80°W 75°W 70°W 65°W

L. Superior

Michigan

L. Huron

L. Ontario

L. Michigan

L. Erie

esota

Wisconsin

Iowa

Illinois

Indiana

Ohio

Pennsylvania

West Virginia

Virginia

Missouri

Kentucky

North Carolina

Tennessee

Arkansas

South Carolina

Mississippi

Alabama

Georgia

Louisiana

Florida

Gulf of Mexico

Maine

Vermont

New Hampshire

Massachusetts

Rhode Island
Connecticut

New York

New Jersey

Delaware

Maryland

ATLANTIC
OCEAN

Medical research, a key service industry in the U.S. economy

0 km   300
0 miles   300
Albers Conic Equal-Area Projection

N
W   E
S

20°N

75°W

KEY

▮ Hunting and gathering		⚒ Iron
▮ Forestry		▱ Copper
▮ Livestock raising		🛒 Bauxite
▮ Commercial farming		▭ Gold
▮ Manufacturing and trade		▱ Silver
🐟 Commercial fishing		● Phosphates
▮ Little or no activity		⚛ Uranium
🛒 Coal		⚒ Lead
⛏ Petroleum		△ Nickel
⚡ Hydroelectric power		▢ Tungsten

Oil wells pump petroleum, an important natural resource

THE WORLD: POLITICAL

Greenland
(Den.)

Alaska
(U.S.)

CANADA

**NORTH
AMERICA**

Ottawa ⊛

UNITED STATES

⊛ Washington, DC

Bermuda (U.K.)

ATLANTIC OCEAN

See inset
map

Tropic of Cancer

Hawaii
(U.S.)

MEXICO

*Gulf of
Mexico*

60°N

40°N

20°N

100°W   80°W   60°W

Mexico City ⊛

Caribbean Sea

Caracas ⊛

GUYANA

Paramaribo ⊛

VENEZUELA

Bogotá ⊛   Georgetown ⊛   ⊛ Cayenne

COLOMBIA   *French Guiana
(Fr.)*

SURINAME

*Galápagos Is.
(Ecuador)*

⊛ Quito

ECUADOR

**SOUTH
AMERICA**

Equator   0°

PACIFIC OCEAN

PERU

⊛ Lima

BRAZIL

SAMOA

*American
Samoa (U.S.)*

TONGA

*French Polynesia
(Fr.)*

*Cook Is.
(N.Z.)*

*Pitcairn I.
(U.K.)*

Tropic of Capricorn

*Easter Is.
(Chile)*

BOLIVIA

⊛ La Paz   Brasília ⊛

⊛ Sucre

PARAGUAY

CHILE

Asunción ⊛

20°S

International Date Line

40°S

Santiago ⊛

Buenos
Aires ⊛

URUGUAY

⊛ Montevideo

ARGENTINA

*Falkland Is.
(U.K.)*

60°S

SOUTHERN OCEAN

Antarctic Circle

ANTARCTICA

Central America
and the Caribbean

30°N

0 km   300

0 miles   300

Azimuthal Projection

**UNITED
STATES**

*Gulf of
Mexico*

N

Tropic of Cancer   W ⊕ E

S

Nassau ⊛

B A H A M A S

Havana ⊛

CUBA

20°N

MEXICO

Br. Virgin Is.
(U.K.)

**DOMINICAN
REPUBLIC**   *Puerto
Rico
(U.S.)*

HAITI

Kingston ⊛   Port-au-Prince ⊛   Santo
Domingo ⊛

JAMAICA   *Virgin Islands (U.S.)*

**ANTIGUA
AND BARBUDA**

Guadeloupe (Fr.)

ST. KITTS AND NEVIS

DOMINICA

BELIZE

⊛ Belmopan

GUATEMALA

Guatemala ⊛
San Salvador ⊛

HONDURAS

⊛ Tegucigalpa

NICARAGUA

⊛ Managua

EL SALVADOR

Caribbean Sea

Martinique (Fr.)

ST. LUCIA

Neth. Antilles (Neth.)

*Aruba
(Neth.)*

**ST. VINCENT AND
THE GRENADINES**

GRENADA

BARBADOS

10°N

**COSTA
RICA**   ⊛ San José

PANAMA   ⊛ Panamá

*PACIFIC
OCEAN*

80°W

COLOMBIA

Caracas ⊛

20°W

VENEZUELA

**TRINIDAD
AND
TOBAGO**

⊛ Port of Spain

60°W

*ATLANTIC
OCEAN*

GUYANA

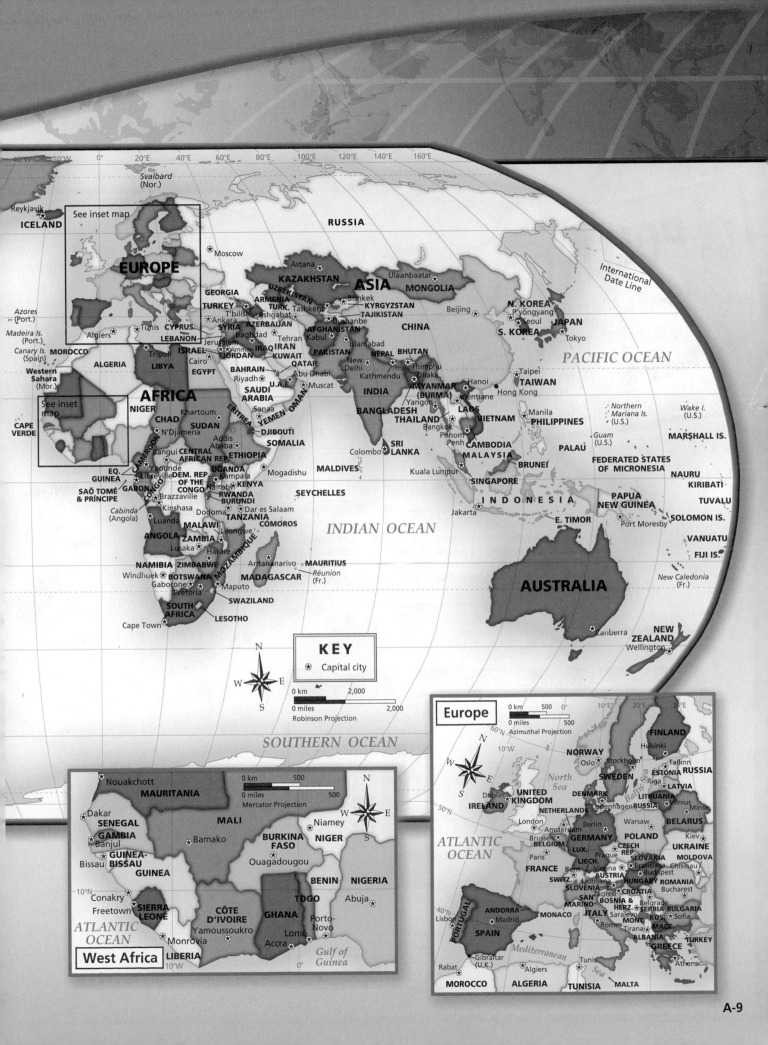

THE UNITED STATES
A DIVERSE NATION

POLLING PLACE
投票站 CASILLA ELECTORAL
投票所 LUGAR NG BOTOHAN
투표소 PHÒNG PHIẾU

Sign at a California polling place

ASIA

CANADA

UNITED

Asian Migration

According to the 2000 census, 10.2 million Asian Americans make up 3.6 percent of the total U.S. population. Asian immigrants include people from China, Japan, Korea, the Philippines, as well as those from countries in Southeast Asia and South Asia.

0 km   3,000
0 miles   3,000
Mercator Projection

PACIFIC OCEAN

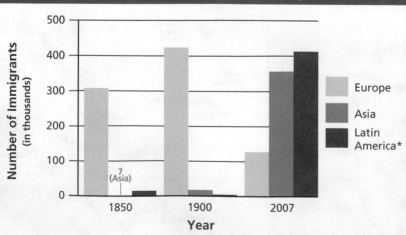

Immigration: Countries of Origin

- Europe
- Asia
- Latin America*

Number of Immigrants (in thousands)

500
400
300
200
100
0

7 (Asia)

1850   1900   2007
Year

*Latin America includes the Caribbean, Mexico, and the countries of Central America and South America.

Sources: *Historical Statistics of the United States* and *Statistical Yearbook of the Immigration and Naturalization Service*

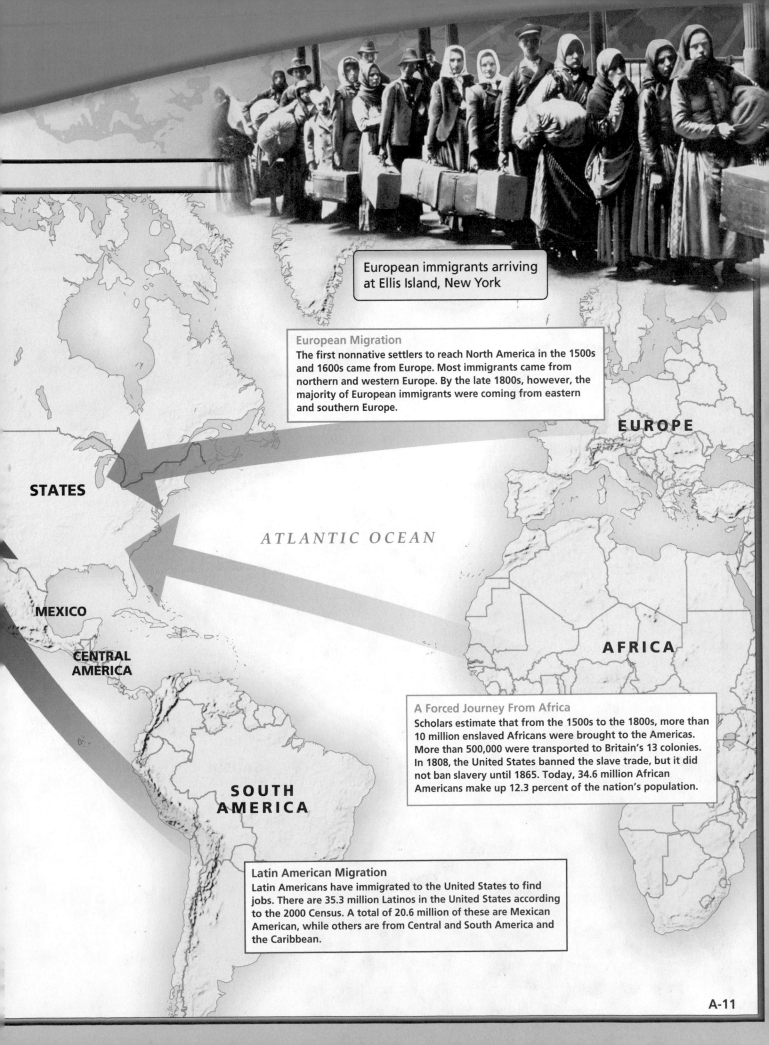

European immigrants arriving
at Ellis Island, New York

European Migration

The first nonnative settlers to reach North America in the 1500s and 1600s came from Europe. Most immigrants came from northern and western Europe. By the late 1800s, however, the majority of European immigrants were coming from eastern and southern Europe.

EUROPE

STATES

ATLANTIC OCEAN

MEXICO

CENTRAL
AMERICA

AFRICA

A Forced Journey From Africa

Scholars estimate that from the 1500s to the 1800s, more than 10 million enslaved Africans were brought to the Americas. More than 500,000 were transported to Britain's 13 colonies. In 1808, the United States banned the slave trade, but it did not ban slavery until 1865. Today, 34.6 million African Americans make up 12.3 percent of the nation's population.

SOUTH
AMERICA

Latin American Migration

Latin Americans have immigrated to the United States to find jobs. There are 35.3 million Latinos in the United States according to the 2000 Census. A total of 20.6 million of these are Mexican American, while others are from Central and South America and the Caribbean.

UNITED STATES
TERRITORIAL EXPANSION TO 1853

Mandan Village, like the one visited by Lewis and Clark during their exploration of the Louisiana Territory

A covered wagon, the mode of transportation for people moving west in the 1800s

PACIFIC OCEAN

OREGON COUNTRY
(Agreement with Britain, 1846)

(Ceded by Britain, 1818)

LOUISIANA PURCHASE
(Purchased from France, 1803)

MEXICAN CESSION
(Treaty of Guadalupe-Hidalgo, 1848)

The Alamo, site of a key battle in the war for Texas independence; Texas became part of the Mexican Cession

TEXAS ANNEXATION
(Annexed by Congress, 1845)

GADSDEN PURCHASE
(Purchased from Mexico, 1853)

MEXICO

CANADA
(BRITISH TERRITORY)

L. Superior

L. Michigan

L. Huron

L. Ontario

L. Erie

THE UNITED
STATES,
1783

A. M. Willard's *The Spirit of '76*, symbol
of courage during the American Revolution,
fought by the 13 colonies against Great Britain

ATLANTIC
OCEAN

KEY

Present-day
state boundaries

Original thirteen states

0 km   500
0 miles   500
Albers Conic Equal-Area Projection

50°W

N
W   E
S

30°N

St. Augustine, oldest permanent
settlement in the United States

(Annexed,
1810)

(Annexed,
1812)

FLORIDA
(Ceded by Spain,
1819)

*Gulf of
Mexico*

60°W

UNITED STATES
POPULATION DENSITY

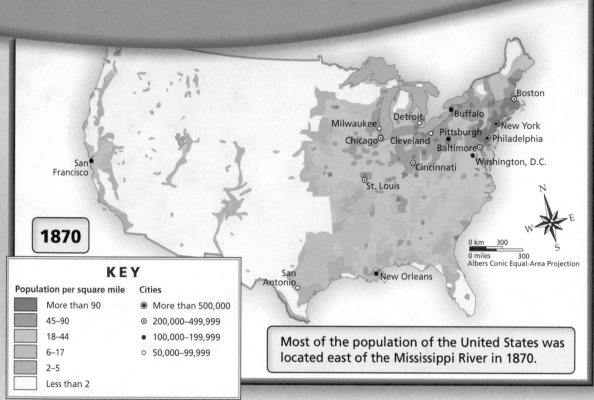

1870

KEY

Population per square mile
- More than 90
- 45–90
- 18–44
- 6–17
- 2–5
- Less than 2

Cities
- More than 500,000
- 200,000–499,999
- 100,000–199,999
- 50,000–99,999

Most of the population of the United States was located east of the Mississippi River in 1870.

By 1960, the Midwest and the West had become more populated. A number of large cities had grown in these regions.

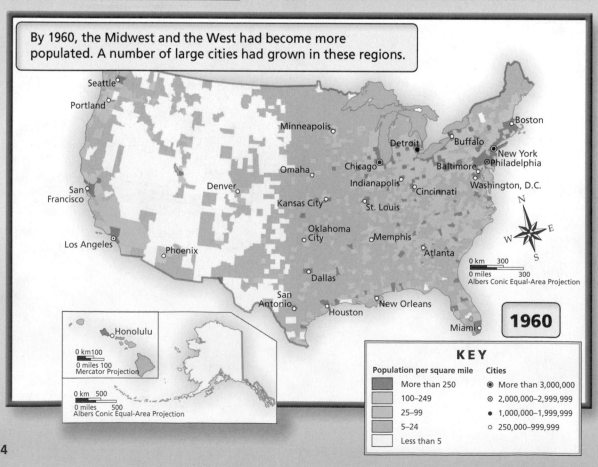

1960

KEY

Population per square mile
- More than 250
- 100–249
- 25–99
- 5–24
- Less than 5

Cities
- More than 3,000,000
- 2,000,000–2,999,999
- 1,000,000–1,999,999
- 250,000–999,999

In the 1880s, Anaheim, California, outside of Los Angeles was rural. By the twenty-first century Los Angeles, as well as surrounding cities like Anaheim, were modern bustling cities connected by freeways.

Large cities and their suburbs formed huge metropolitan areas by the year 2000. The largest city is New York, followed by Los Angeles and Chicago.

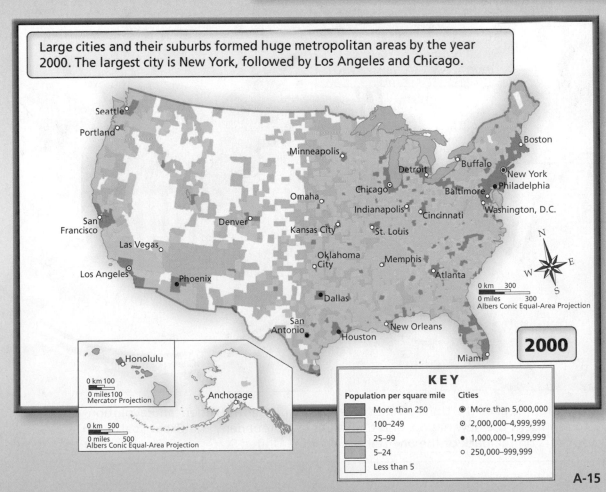

2000

KEY

Population per square mile	Cities
More than 250	◉ More than 5,000,000
100–249	⊙ 2,000,000–4,999,999
25–99	● 1,000,000–1,999,999
5–24	○ 250,000–999,999
Less than 5	

SYMBOLS OF OUR NATION

Today's American flag has thirteen red and white stripes representing the original thirteen states. Fifty white stars stand for the current number of states. The first official flag had thirteen stars and was approved in 1777.

Thirteen white stars

American bald eagle

Scroll reading *E Pluribus Unum* ("Out of Many, One")

Olive branch (symbol of peace)

Thirteen arrows (symbol of war)

The Great Seal of the United States was designed after the American Revolution to represent the new nation, and the values of its founders. The Great Seal appears on the back of the one-dollar bill of the United States.

Economics and Civics Handbooks

Contents

The Economics Handbook will provide you with key economic concepts and terms, so you may understand economic issues and decision making throughout history.

As you study history, you will learn certain rights and responsibilities of being an American citizen. The Civics Handbook will show you how to conduct important civics activities.

What is Economics?

Making Choices About Resources

Which sweater to buy? How many hours to study? Which restaurant to go to? If you are like most people, you constantly face decisions because you don't have enough time and money to do everything. Economics is the study of how people make choices when they face a limited supply of resources.

The study of economics begins with the idea that people cannot have everything they need and want. A **need** is something like air, food, or shelter. A **want** is an item that we would like to have but that is not necessary for survival. Because people cannot have everything they need or want, they must consider their choices and decide how best to fill their needs.

As an individual, you have to decide what to do with your time and money. Businesses have to decide how many people to employ and how much to produce. A city government may have to decide whether to spend its budget to build a park or a library.

Trade-offs and Opportunity Costs

When people make decisions, they face **trade-offs** because they choose one course of action over another. A person who chooses one item gives up other opportunities. The thing a person gives up is called the **opportunity cost.** Suppose you have to choose between sleeping late or getting up early to study for a test. The opportunity cost of extra study time is less sleep.

Review Questions

1. What is economics?
2. Define trade-off and opportunity cost.

Scarcity

Why Must People Make Choices?

People have to make choices because of scarcity. Scarcity is the term used to explain that there are not enough resources to meet everyone's wants or needs. One person may be able to buy hundreds of bicycles or guitars, but no one can have an unlimited supply of everything. At some point, a limit is reached. Scarcity always exists because our needs and wants are always greater than our resource supply.

Meeting Basic Needs
Agriculture allowed early Native Americans to grow and store food for survival.

Meeting Needs and Wants

Until modern times, people mostly focused on resources related to agriculture to meet their needs and wants. They farmed the land to produce food, mainly for their own use. This traditional way of meeting basic needs still exists in some countries today. However, modern societies have also developed other economic systems to deal with increased trade and industry. An economic system is the method used by a society to produce and distribute goods and services.

Review Questions

1. What is scarcity?

2. How does scarcity cause people to make choices?

Economics Handbook

Basic Economic Questions

Through its economic system, society answers **three key questions.** **1)** What goods and services should be produced? **2)** How should goods and services be produced? **3)** Who consumes the goods and services? **Goods** are objects, such as cars and clothes. **Services** are actions that people do for others, such as teaching. **Producers** make and sell goods and services. **Consumers** buy and use goods and services.

How a society answers these three questions shows what economic goals it values and shapes its economic system.

Three Key Economic Questions

What goods and services should be produced?	How should goods and services be produced?	Who consumes the goods and services?
How much of our resources should we devote to national defense, education, public health, or consumer goods? Which consumer goods should we produce?	Should we produce food on large corporate farms or on small family farms? Should we produce electricity with oil, nuclear power, coal, or solar power?	How do goods and services get distributed? The question of who gets to consume which goods and services lies at the very heart of the differences between economic systems. Each society answers the question of distribution based on its combination of social values and goals.

Economic Goals

Economic efficiency	Making the most of resources
Economic freedom	Freedom from government intervention in the production and distribution of goods and services
Economic security and predictability	Assurance that goods and services will be available, payments will be made on time, and a safety net will protect individuals in times of economic disaster
Economic equity	Fair distribution of wealth
Economic growth and innovation	Innovation leads to economic growth, and economic growth leads to a higher standard of living.
Other goals	Societies pursue additional goals, such as environmental protection.

Review Questions

1. List examples of both goods and services.

2. Which economic goals are most valued in the U.S.?

Modern Economic Systems

As you read on page 651, an economic system is the method a society uses to produce and distribute goods and services. Four different economic systems have developed as societies attempt to answer the three economic questions according to their goals. This table provides information about the main economic systems in the world today.

Modern Economic Systems

	Description	Origin	Location Today
Traditional	People make economic decisions based on custom or habit. They produce what they have always produced and just as much as they need, using long-established methods.	Accompanied the rise of agriculture and home crafts	Mainly in rural areas within developing nations
Market (Capitalist, Free-Enterprise)	Economic decisions are made in the marketplace through interactions between buyers and sellers according to the laws of supply and demand. Individuals own the means of production. Government regulates some economic activities and provides such "public goods" as education.	Capitalism has existed since the earliest buying and selling of goods in a market. The market economic system developed in response to Adam Smith's ideas and the shift from agriculture to industry in the 1800s.	Australia, Canada, Japan, United States, and a handful of other nations
Centrally Planned (Command, Socialist, Communist)	Central government planners make most economic decisions for the people. In theory, the workers own the means of production. In practice, the government does. Some private businesses, but government is in control.	In the 1800s, criticism of capitalism by Karl Marx and others led to calls for distributing wealth according to need. After the 1917 Russian Revolution, the Soviet Union developed the first command economy.	Communist countries, including Cuba, North Korea, Venezuela and Vietnam
Mixed (Social Democratic, Liberal Socialist)	A system with markets in which the government plays an important role in making economic decisions.	The Great Depression of the 1930s ended laissez-faire capitalism in most countries. People insisted that government take a stronger role in fixing economic problems. The fall of communism in Eastern Europe in the 1990s ended central planning in most countries. People insisted on freer markets.	Most nations, including Brazil, France, India, Italy, Poland, Russia, and Sweden

The Market Economy

Individuals Buy and Sell

What do a crafts fair, a music store, and the New York Stock Exchange all have in common? All are examples of markets. A **market** is an arrangement that allows buyers and sellers to exchange things.

Markets exist because none of us can make, or produce, all we require to satisfy our needs and wants. You probably didn't grow the wheat used to make the cereal you had for breakfast. Instead, you purchased your cereal at a store, which is an example of a market. Markets allow us to exchange the things we have for the things we want.

In a market system, people and businesses have the freedom to make, to sell, and to buy what they want. Producers choose what to make and sell. Consumers decide what goods and services to buy. In other words, individuals answer the three key economic questions that you learned about on page 652. It is an efficient system because producers make only what buyers want, when they want it, and generally at prices they are willing to pay.

New York Stock Exchange

Review Questions

1. Why do markets exist?

2. In a free market, who decides what to make, to sell, and to buy?

Centrally Planned Economies

The Government Decides

In a **centrally planned economy**, the central government alone answers the key economic questions. Centrally planned economies are sometimes called **command economies** because a central authority is in command of the economy. It owns all resources and decides what is produced and at what price things will be sold.

The government in centrally planned economies tries to encourage faster economic growth and more equal distribution of goods and services. **Economic growth** means there is an increase in production and people are spending more money.

Often, the government has a hard time making a plan that will meet these goals. There is no competition among sellers and producers do not keep the profit if they make better products. As a result, producers do not try to improve their products, and consumers must accept poorly made merchandise.

Centrally planned economies mostly exist in countries with a communist form of government, such as North Korea and the former Soviet Union. In communist countries, the government controls both economic and political decisions. Individual freedoms are limited.

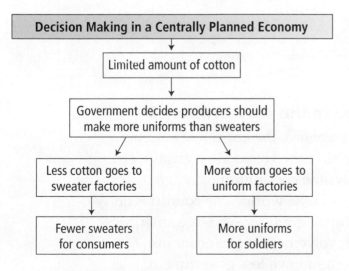

Decision Making in a Centrally Planned Economy

↓

Limited amount of cotton

↓

Government decides producers should make more uniforms than sweaters

↓ ↓

Less cotton goes to sweater factories | More cotton goes to uniform factories

↓ ↓

Fewer sweaters for consumers | More uniforms for soldiers

Review Questions

1. In a centrally planned economy who makes the important economic decisions?

2. **Diagram Skills** How does the government's decision affect consumers and soldiers?

Mixed Economies

Government Helps the Economy

No country has an economy that is strictly a free market or a command economy. Most economies are actually market economies, with some level of government involvement. This is called a **mixed economy**. While most areas of the economy may be free, the government may step in to provide certain goods and services. In a mixed economy, the government generally provides defense, education, and public roads.

Review Questions

1. Describe a mixed economy.

2. In a mixed economy, the government enforces safety standards. If a product is found to be unsafe, the government requires that the product be recalled, or removed from stores. Do research on the Internet to identify two products that have been recalled in the last year. Explain the reasons for the recalls.

A Continuum of Economic Systems

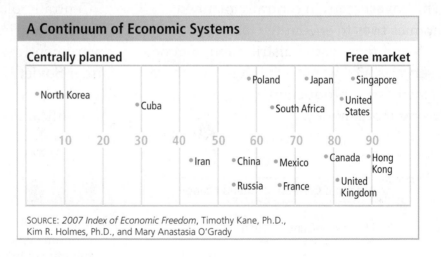

SOURCE: *2007 Index of Economic Freedom*, Timothy Kane, Ph.D., Kim R. Holmes, Ph.D., and Mary Anastasia O'Grady

How Involved Is the Government?

As you read on page 653, the economic systems of the nations around the world vary greatly. The chart above shows the continuum or range of economic systems in the world. The countries on the left side of the diagram have a large amount of government involvement in the economy. The countries on the right have less government involvement in the economy. Compared to most other countries, the United States has an economy with little government involvement and a great deal of economic freedom. Its system is called a **free enterprise** system.

Economics at Work

Factors of Production

Now that you are familiar with the different economic systems that exist, it is important to understand how producers make decisions about resources and how the marketplace works.

All the resources that are used to make all goods and services are called factors of production. As the diagram below shows, there are three types: land, labor, and capital. Because resources are scarce, societies try to make the most of the resources they have to work with. When societies use resources efficiently, the economy grows. Efficiency means an economy is using resources in such a way as to maximize the production of goods and services.

The Marketplace

In a local market, goods and services are exchanged among people who live within a smaller community such as a town or city. Over the years, however, technology and improved transportation systems have allowed producers to exchange goods with people who live across the world. As you will read on the next page, the relationship between sellers and buyers help decide how much to produce and at what price.

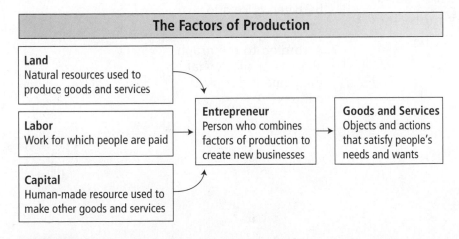

The Factors of Production

Land
Natural resources used to produce goods and services

Labor
Work for which people are paid

Capital
Human-made resource used to make other goods and services

Entrepreneur
Person who combines factors of production to create new businesses

Goods and Services
Objects and actions that satisfy people's needs and wants

Entrepreneurs are individuals who take risks to develop new ideas and start businesses. Their efforts help the economy grow.

Review Questions

1. **Diagram Skills** What are the three types of resources used to make goods and services?

2. Why is it important to use resources efficiently?

3. How has technology and transportation changed the marketplace?

Consumer Demands

Producers make decisions about how to use resources, but consumers decide which goods to buy and use. Economists use the term demand to describe the ability and desire of consumers to buy a good.

In a market system, buyers demand goods and sellers supply those goods. Both buyers and sellers help to set prices through their interactions. For example, more people will buy a slice of pizza if it costs $1 than if it costs $10. As the price of an item increases, people will buy less of it. As the price goes down, people will buy more of the same item. Buying more when prices are low, and buying less when prices are high is called the law of demand.

When fewer people buy pizza because the price is too high, economists say that the quantity demanded of pizza has dropped. When prices drop and people buy more, they say the quantity demanded of pizza has increased.

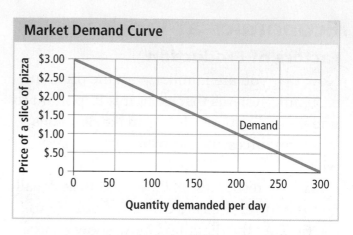

Market Demand Curve

Economists use a line graph to show how price and the demand for a good relate to each other. Because quantity demanded increases as prices decrease, the line on the graph above slopes down to the right.

Review Questions

1. What is the relationship between price and consumer demand?

2. According to the graph, at $.50 per slice, what is the demand for pizza per day?

The Supply of Goods and Services

When demand for a good increases, the price rises. In order to make more money, companies will supply more of the good or service as prices increase. Supply is the amount of goods available in the marketplace. When prices rise, other companies might begin producing the good because they also want to make money. As a result, there is a greater supply of the good available to consumers. If the price of a good decreases, companies will produce less and some companies may stop selling the good completely. The law of supply states that producers will offer more of a good if prices rise, and less of a good if prices fall.

Market Supply Curve

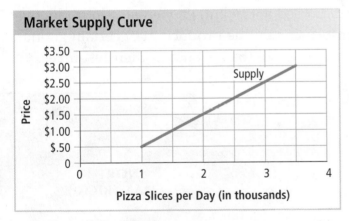

The line on a supply graph will always rise from left to right. The line shows that higher prices lead to higher production. If the price of a slice of pizza is $2.00, all the pizzerias in a city will produce 2,500 slices.

Review Questions

1. According to the law of supply, what happens to the quantity of goods produced if prices fall?

2. **Graph Skills** According to the graph, how many slices of pizza will be produced if the cost per slice is $1.00?

Why Nations Trade

Making the Best Use of Resources

As you have read, markets exist because people cannot produce all we require to satisfy our needs and wants. This is true of nations, as well.

Countries produce different goods and services because they have different resources. They focus on certain products that they can make easily and cheaply. For example, coffee can be grown easily in warm areas like Central America, so it is inexpensive to produce there. If Canadians wanted to produce coffee, however, they would have to grow it in greenhouses, which would be more difficult and costly. Because countries cannot efficiently produce everything their citizens need and want, they engage in trade. By specializing or focusing on the production of certain goods and services, nations make the best use of their resources.

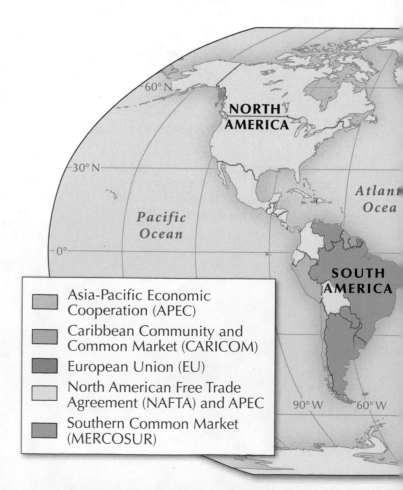

Asia-Pacific Economic Cooperation (APEC)

Caribbean Community and Common Market (CARICOM)

European Union (EU)

North American Free Trade Agreement (NAFTA) and APEC

Southern Common Market (MERCOSUR)

Nations Work Together

Trading among nations is an exchange of goods and services in an international market. It has played an important role in the U.S. economy. Free-trade zones help encourage trade among nations. A free-trade zone is a region where a group of countries agree to reduce or eliminate tariffs, or taxes on imported goods. These agreements make trading less expensive.

The North American Free Trade Agreement (NAFTA) was developed to eliminate all fees and other trade barriers between Canada, Mexico, and the United States. Supporters of NAFTA say the agreement increases trade between the countries. Approximately 100 trading organizations like NAFTA operate throughout the world today.

Major Trade Organization Members

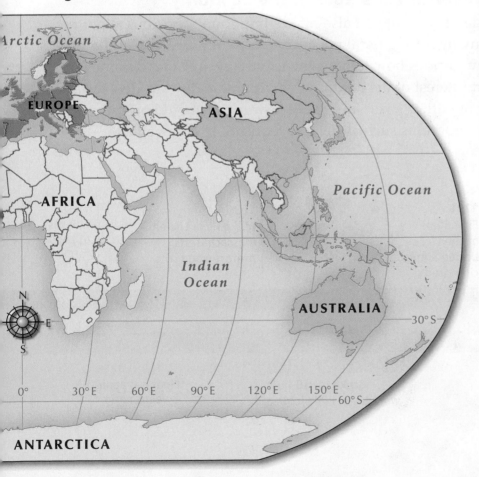

Review Questions

1. How does trade help societies meet their needs and wants?

2. How do countries join together to encourage economic growth for all?

The American Economy

A Tradition of Free Enterprise

The United States economy encourages free enterprise, which means people are allowed to try out their business ideas and compete in the free market. Its vast land, resources, and many people who are willing to work have all contributed to economic growth in the United States.

The free market has helped the economy in the United States, but the government set up the foundation for economic success. Government laws, such as those protecting the right to private property and enforcing contracts, help Americans profit from free enterprise. The Constitution also specifies limits on how government can tax, and it prohibits government from interfering in business contracts. Federal and state agencies regulate industries whose goods and services affect the well-being of the public.

The Government's Role in the Economy

The federal government also makes important decisions about the economy by setting fiscal policy. Fiscal policy means that the government decides how to both collect money and spend money in the best interest of the economy. Government officials debate about raising or cutting taxes and about how much should be spent on specific programs such as defense, education, and welfare.

Key Events in American Economic History

1791
First Bank of the United States chartered

1834
Mill girls in Lowell, Massachusetts, protest wage cuts

1867
Knights of Labor formed

1750   1800   1850

1835
Strike for 10-hour workday in Philadelphia

1869
Financial panic sweeps nation

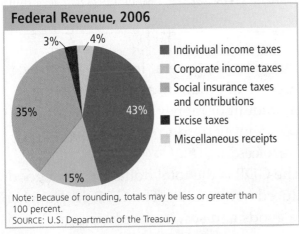

Americans often argue about the proper balance of government involvement in the economy. Some people want more government services, while others say that the government already intervenes too much in the economy.

Sometimes government fiscal policy decisions bring gradual shifts or changes to an established system. For example, in the United States during the Great Depression many new federal programs changed the role of the government in the American economy. With the New Deal, the federal government moved away from laissez faire, or leaving the economy alone. Instead, the federal government took specific actions to improve the economy.

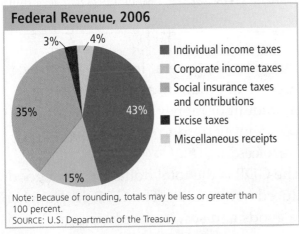

Federal Revenue, 2006

- 3%
- 4%
- Individual income taxes
- Corporate income taxes
- Social insurance taxes and contributions
- Excise taxes
- Miscellaneous receipts

35%
43%
15%

Note: Because of rounding, totals may be less or greater than 100 percent.
SOURCE: U.S. Department of the Treasury

This graph shows the revenue sources or sources of money in the government's budget.

Review Questions

1. Describe the economic system of the United States.

2. **Graph Skills** What are the largest sources of the U.S. Government's income?

3. What are two ways the government encourages economic growth in the U.S. economy?

1886
American Federation of Labor formed

1913
Federal Reserve System created

1929
Stock market crash

1947
Taft-Hartley Act

1955
AFL and CIO merge

1980
Savings and Loan crisis begins

2007
United States plunges into recession

1900

1950

2000

1892
Homestead Strike in Pennsylvania

1930
Great Depression begins

1933
Federal Deposit Insurance Corporation (FDIC) created

1963
Equal Pay Act

1997
More than 160,000 ATMs operate in United States

Measuring the Economy

The Federal Reserve or Fed is the central banking system of the United States. It functions as a bank for other banks and for the federal government. The Fed is responsible for monetary policy, which means it makes decisions that help to manage the growth of the economy. The Fed attempts to encourage economic growth by controlling the money supply, availability of credit, and interest rates.

Monetary policy is based on careful study of economic indicators including the rate of inflation and the Gross Domestic Product (GDP). These factors help economists predict changes in the economy.

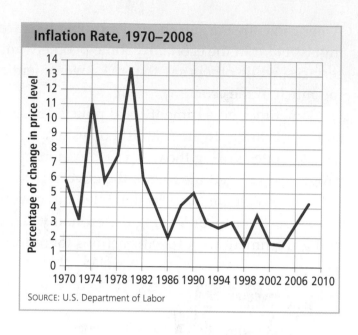

Inflation Rate, 1970–2008

SOURCE: U.S. Department of Labor

Inflation is a general increase in prices. In a period of inflation, as prices rise, the same amount of money buys less. As a result, people cannot afford to buy as many goods and services.

The GDP is the total dollar value of goods produced in a country. The GDP grows when more goods and services are being produced. If consumers spend less, fewer goods and services will be produced and the GDP decreases.

The strength of the economy can also be measured by how much people are saving and investing. When you save money, it doesn't just stay in the bank. Banks use your saved money to make loans to businesses. This investment helps the economy grow.

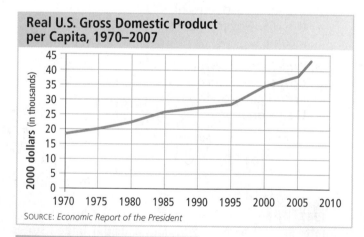

Real U.S. Gross Domestic Product per Capita, 1970–2007

SOURCE: *Economic Report of the President*

Review Questions

1. What is monetary policy?

2. What factors do economists study to measure the economy?

How to Volunteer

Americans are known for their strong tradition of community involvement. You too can become involved by contributing your time and talents to make a difference in your school and community.

Below, Carlos Lopez describes his experience looking for a volunteer job. As you read, think about the steps he took to become a volunteer for a program that teaches inline skating to inner city children.

Carlos Lopez comes from a family of volunteers. His mother, a teacher, volunteers her time after school to help recent immigrants learn English. His father helps out once a month in a local soup kitchen.

Carlos too wanted to help his community, so he looked into possibilities for community service. He talked to friends in the Service Learning Club at school. He also looked online to learn more about national organizations such as Habitat for Humanity and Meals on Wheels. He looked at volunteer opportunities listed in his local newspaper. Soon Carlos had a list of ten possibilities to consider.

Carlos then had to decide how much time he could spend volunteering. Between homework, chores, and sports, Carlos figured he could volunteer about three hours a week, as long as his volunteer job was close by.

Carlos also considered his strengths and interests in choosing where to volunteer. He liked teaching younger children, and he wanted to be outdoors.

Carlos saw a notice at school asking for volunteers to teach inline skating to inner city children, using donated skates and gear. He talked to classmates who volunteered for the program and visited it the next week.

Today the children are learning a new skill and getting fresh air and exercise. Carlos has the satisfaction of helping others who would not otherwise have this opportunity.

Learn the Skill

To find a volunteer job, follow these steps:

1 **Research your options.** Find out about possible volunteer jobs in your community.

2 **Determine your strengths, interests, and availability.**

Practice the Skill

1 Make a list of at least five volunteer opportunities you have heard or read about.

2 List your own strengths, interests, and availability.

3 Decide which volunteer opportunities on your list would be best for you.

Apply the Skill

Find out about volunteer opportunities in your community. Research one and report your findings to the class.

How to Cast Your Vote

One of the most important ways to voice your opinion is through your vote. By voting for those representatives who reflect your own opinions, you can exercise some influence over the choices the government makes. The process of casting a vote is quite simple. See the box below for some of the most frequently asked questions and answers about voting.

Who can vote?

- American citizens
- at least 18 years of age
- who live in the state in which they wish to vote

How do you register to vote?

- Go to city hall or the county courthouse, or register when you apply for or renew your driver's license.
- Take proof of your age along, such as a birth certificate.
- Check to see if you can register on the Internet.

Who should you vote for?

- Read newspaper and magazine articles that tell you the candidates' views on important issues.

- Check online to see if the candidates have Web sites that tell you more about them.
- Listen to candidates' speeches.

Learn the Skill

To cast your vote, follow these steps:

❶ Find the location of your polling place. Your voter registration card should identify your polling place.

❷ Go to your polling place on Election Day. Your name will be checked against a list of registered voters.

❸ Cast your vote. You will mark your ballot or make your choices on a touch screen or another type of voting device.

Practice the Skill

Call your local courthouse or city hall to find out where you should register to vote. Then find out where people in your area go to cast their votes.

Apply the Skill

Choose a recent presidential election. Decide for whom you would have voted in that election.

How to Evaluate Leadership

What sort of person should you choose to represent you? Part of the answer depends on the position being filled. You may find certain qualities important for town supervisor and others important for U.S. Senator.

No matter what the position, you must evaluate the candidate before you cast your ballot. Consider the scenario below, which describes one citizen's evaluation of a candidate for state representative.

Hannah is planning to vote in an upcoming election for state representative. Three people are running for the office—a Democrat, a Republican, and a third-party candidate.

Hannah decides that a few qualities top her list as the most important for a public servant to possess. They are honesty, experience, and creative approaches to solving problems. Hannah also knows that her state is suffering from high unemployment and a substandard educational system.

Hannah watches the candidates on television, reads newspaper articles, and visits their Web sites. She learns that the third-party candidate is mainly concerned with a narrow list of issues and decides to eliminate him.

Hannah learns that the Republican candidate has served in public office before, while the Democratic candidate is new to politics.

Since she believes that an experienced candidate can accomplish more, she is considering eliminating the Democrat. She continues her research and finds that the Republican was a high school teacher for 15 years before entering politics and that during his time as mayor of a small city, he boosted the local economy. Based on these factors, Hannah decides to vote for the Republican candidate.

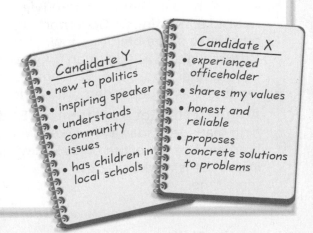

Candidate Y
- new to politics
- inspiring speaker
- understands community issues
- has children in local schools

Candidate X
- experienced officeholder
- shares my values
- honest and reliable
- proposes concrete solutions to problems

Learn the Skill

To learn how to evaluate leadership, follow these steps.

1 Choose the qualities that make a good leader. Make a list of your criteria.

2 Rate your subject. Using your criteria, rate the person you are evaluating on the basis of their actions, speeches, and other's experiences with them.

Practice the Skill

1 What resources does Hannah use to find out about the candidates?

2 What state issues does Hannah believe her representative will have to address?

Apply the Skill

Choose someone in a leadership position, such as a member of Congress or the President. Evaluate that person based on your leadership criteria.

How to Work on a Political Campaign

If you are interested in politics, consider volunteering to work on a political campaign. It takes the support of hundreds of volunteers to run for national office. State and local campaigns also depend on volunteer help. The diary entries below describe how one volunteer found work on a political campaign.

July 20th Talked to Tyler today about the upcoming election. We both support the Independent Party. I like their position on the environment, and Tyler supports their government reform efforts.

August 12th Tyler and I have both decided to volunteer to work on Adam Santini's campaign for governor! I was on Adam's Web site and noticed that they had a form to fill out for people who want to help in the campaign. Tyler noticed a "Santini for Governor" sign outside an office building downtown. He went in and filled out an application to volunteer. Looks like we'll both be trying to get an Independent into office!

August 27th Got a call from the Santini field manager today, who asked whether I can work in the office on Saturday mornings. Tyler is working at the same time.

September 3rd I sure had my eyes opened at the Santini headquarters today! It takes a lot of work, and a lot of workers, to get someone elected! There are field workers, communications workers, a policy team, a fundraising department, and a scheduling department.

October 15th Things are really heating up now that the election is so close. We've been handing out fliers and making phone calls. Other people are making posters and entering data into the computer. We need all the help we can get!

November 10th Well, the election is officially over and—WE WON!! It was a lot of hard work, but we did it together and now we can watch things change with Santini in office!

Learn the Skill

To work on a political campaign, follow these steps:

1 Choose a candidate. Why did the volunteers above decide to work for Santini?

2 Find out how to contact the candidate's organization. How did the volunteers get in touch with the Santini campaign?

3 Find out about volunteer opportunities. What tasks did the volunteers do?

Practice the Skill

1 Choose a candidate you wish to support in the next national, state, or local election.

2 Think about your availability and what kind of transportation you will need.

Apply the Skill

Contact the candidate's campaign headquarters to learn about volunteer opportunities.

How to Write a Letter to the Editor

The Constitution of the United States guarantees all citizens the right to express their views on political issues. One way to do this is to write a letter to the editor of your local newspaper. If your letter is printed, other citizens will be able to read your opinion.

Below is a letter to the editor from a concerned citizen. Read the letter, and think about the citizen's opinion. Has he expressed it clearly? Has he given good reasons for feeling the way he does? Does the letter influence you?

Editor:

Thank you for the articles in your paper identifying the importance of recycling. It is the responsibility of every citizen to care for our environment, and recycling is a simple and effective way of caring. Before our family began recycling, we were not aware of how much newspaper, glass, aluminum, paper, and plastic we used. We have been amazed at the amounts we accumulate each week.

The new city program offering curbside pickup service makes recycling easy and convenient. We urge everyone to participate in the new program. To learn more, contact the city manager's office.

Sincerely,
Matt Reilly

Learn the Skill

To write an effective letter to the editor, follow these steps:

1. **Find out about volunteer opportunities.** What tasks did the volunteers do?

2. **State your opinion.** Give two reasons why you feel the way you do. Support your reasons with evidence or examples.

3. **Reaffirm your point of view.** You may also share your suggestions for overcoming the problem or working out the issue.

Practice the Skill

1. Brainstorm a list of three issues. For each one, write one statement that expresses your opinion. Write at least two reasons or examples to support your opinion.

2. Take turns sharing your ideas with a classmate. You should be able to understand each other's views on the issues each of you has chosen.

Apply the Skill

1. Select one of your three issues and write a letter to the editor.

2. Send your letter to the editor of your local newspaper.

How to Conduct a Poll

The United States is a representative democracy. This means that public officials act on behalf of the citizens who elected them. To do this effectively, they must know how citizens feel about different issues.

Polls are a good way of determining public opinion. A poll is a list of questions like those below. Many people answer these questions. The results of a poll give a good idea of how people may feel about different issues.

Forced-Choice Questions

A forced-choice question makes the person give a definite answer. For example, the person may have to choose either "yes" or "no."

Example: The minimum voting age should be raised to 21.

____ yes ____ no

Scaled Questions

Scaled questions ask a person to gauge how strongly they feel about an issue.

Example: Circle your reaction to the following statement: The Constitution continues to meet the needs of Americans today.

Disagree   Uncertain   Agree

Ranked Questions

A ranked question gives a list of items. The person must put them in order of importance to him or her.

Example: Rank the following in order of importance. Use a 1 for the freedom you think is most important and a 3 for the freedom you think is least important.

____ freedom of the press

____ freedom of speech

____ freedom of assembly

Learn the Skill

To conduct a poll, follow these steps:

❶ Choose an issue and write poll questions that ask about people's opinions of it. Think of an issue that is of importance to many people. Include each type of question in your poll.

❷ Ask people to take the poll. Ask at least ten people.

❸ Compile the results. How many people answered each question the same way?

Practice the Skill

❶ Write two examples of each type of question.

❷ Have a partner read your questions to make sure they are clear and worded fairly.

Apply the Skill

❶ Choose an issue and write six poll questions about it.

❷ Ask 20 people to complete your poll.

❸ Compile the results and report them to the class.

How to Use the Internet as a News Source

If you have a particular news topic you'd like to research, you can use a combination of magazines, newspapers, and Internet sources. The major television networks, newspapers, and magazines all have Web sites.

Reggie wanted to learn about the President's recent visit to Latin America. Read the material below to find out how he went about his search for information.

8:30 a.m.

"Let's see. The President went to Latin America on Monday. The press should have been covering his visit all week. First, I'll look in the local newspaper for information, starting on Tuesday. . . .

9:00 a.m.

"Our paper had one story about the visit. I think I'll stop at the library and see what some of the bigger newspapers and news magazines reported. . . .

11:00 a.m.

"That was interesting. Those sources included some photographs, and the main newspapers discussed the President's visit each day. I wonder what I can find on the Internet? . . .

1:00 p.m.

"Wow! A search online turned up lots of news articles on the subject. Each article had links to related articles on the same subject. The search also turned up some editorials on the President's trip and official news releases from the White House. It will be easy to compare their different points of view."

Learn the Skill

To learn how to use the Internet as a news source, follow these steps.

1 Use a search engine to find Internet news sources.

2 Be sure that your sources have a reputation for accurate news coverage. If you are unsure of a source's reliability, compare it to sources you know to be trustworthy.

Practice the Skill

1 What information was Reggie able to locate online?

2 How did the online information differ from the print information?

Apply the Skill

1 Choose a topic in the news. Type a keyword or phrase about the topic into a search engine.

2 Follow those results that appear to be good news sources.

3 Explain how each site helped broaden your understanding of the topic.

How to Write a Letter to a Public Official

Public officials are elected in order to carry out the political goals of citizens. One way to participate in government is to let your elected representatives know how you feel about certain issues.

You can write a letter to convey your opinion about an issue. Your letter should state your views clearly and give reasons why you feel the way you do. Below, a concerned citizen asks her representative to take action on an issue.

2213 Essex Road
Castle City, CA 94320
August 28, 1994

The Honorable Carmen Mendoza
House of Representatives
Washington, D.C. 20515

Dear Representative Mendoza:

Last evening, I saw your interview on the news. You said you were concerned about the lack of recreational facilities for teenagers in many areas. I share your concern. Unlike me, you can do much to solve this problem. You could propose a bill that provides federal funds to build such facilities.

Opponents of this bill might say that building such facilities would be very expensive. But what would be more expensive in the long run—abandoning many teens to a life of crime or providing an alternative to life on the streets? Many older people have testified that they were saved from the evils of street life by an opportunity to channel their energies into sports and other programs provided at recreational centers.

I have seen you express your concern on television. Now I would like to know what you plan to do about this problem.

Respectfully yours,
Cleotis Larkin

Learn the Skill

To write a letter to a public official, follow these steps:

❶ **Find out to whom you should write.** Do some research or call a few offices to find the best person to hear your comments.

❷ **Address the letter.** Follow the correct format for a letter.

❸ **Clearly state your purpose.** Provide reasons to back it up.

Practice the Skill

❶ Read the letter above. Find the writer's address, the receiver's address, the greeting, and the signature.

❷ Analyze the body of the letter. Did the writer convey her purpose clearly?

Apply the Skill

❶ Choose an issue that concerns you. Find out which public official handles that issue.

❷ Write a letter. Have a teacher or classmate read it over. Send it to the public official.

How to Analyze Television News Programs

Most Americans get information about local, national, and world events by watching the news on television. This means that television has a great influence on public opinion. When you watch the news, you should think critically about how information is presented to you.

A news program can make people think a certain way about issues. It could leave out important information without which you might think differently. Also, television news networks choose which stories to report and how much time to spend on them.

For a school project, Darius Heely is tracking the news. Every evening for the past two weeks, he has watched the same news program. He sits by the television with his notebook in hand.

When the program starts, he gets his pencil and his stopwatch ready. For each story, Darius jots down the subject and records the time. He makes notes, such as whether a story was national or international, if it covered violent content, or if it seemed more like entertainment than news.

At the end of the program, Darius reads over the notes that he has taken. Sometimes he disagrees with how the news was presented by this program.

For the last part of his project, Darius will compare his notes about all of the news content aired during the two weeks. He will see which stories were reported several days in a row and which got the most attention. By doing this, Darius will get a good idea of how the news networks shape public issues.

Learn the Skill

To analyze the news, follow these steps:

1. **Make a chart.** The columns should show the subject, length of time, location, and other notes.

2. **Watch the news.** Fill in the chart.

3. **Think about it.** What did you think was the most important story? Which was given the most emphasis? Were some less important than others? How long were most stories?

Practice the Skill

1. Watch the news with a friend or family member. Each of you should fill out a chart.

2. Decide which story you thought was the most important. Choose one thing you liked and one thing you didn't like about the program.

3. Compare your reactions with others.

Apply the Skill

1. With a group of classmates, read through a newspaper.

2. Plan a television news program with the stories from the newspaper.

3. Explain your group's decisions to the class.

How to Serve on a Jury

The Constitution of the United States guarantees all persons the right to trial by jury. Ordinary citizens serve on a jury. They are the ones to hear and judge the facts in a case.

As major participants, jurors are vitally important in the American system of justice. If you are called to serve on a jury, keep in mind that you will help to ensure that the defendant will be treated fairly by the courts.

A Juror's Responsibilities

When the Court . . .	the Juror must . . .
sends the potential juror a summons to appear in court on a specific date and time, . . .	. . . appear in court as requested.
requests the juror to swear that he or she will tell the truth, . . .	. . . swear an oath.
questions the juror to determine whether he or she is qualified and suitable to serve on the jury, . . .	. . . answer truthfully.
presents the case against the defendant . . .	. . . give careful attention to the testimony and evidence.
excuses the jury to deliberate and decide the case, . . .	. . . weigh the evidence and decide the case, being careful to follow the steps below.

Learn the Skill

To learn how to serve on a jury, follow these steps.

1. **Avoid bias.** Do not allow likes or dislikes for either side to influence you.

2. **Remember that the defendant is presumed innocent.** The government must prove guilt "beyond a reasonable doubt."

Practice the Skill

1. As a juror, how might you avoid bias?

2. Consider the phrase "beyond a reasonable doubt." What does this phrase mean?

Apply the Skill

1. Consider the following: A woman named Linda Wright has been accused of stealing from the cash drawer at the store where she works. She claims to be innocent.

2. Conduct a mock jury trial as a class based on the scenario above.

How to Identify Your Political Roots and Attitudes

A person's political roots can be traced back to early childhood and the influence of family, friends, and teachers.

The excerpt below is from the Web site of a fictional presidential candidate. As you read, look for hints about his political roots and attitudes.

"My name is Joshua Heckman, and I am running for President. Since I wouldn't vote for someone whom I know nothing about, I wouldn't expect you to, either. I've set up this Web site to help you get to know me.

"I was born into a working class neighborhood in Detroit, Michigan. I went to public school and played baseball and basketball. When I was 12 years old, my dad got sick. He couldn't work anymore, and we didn't have any health insurance, so things got pretty tight financially. My mom went to work, but we still had to sell our house. A few years later, my dad recovered and things improved enough that I was able to attend college by taking out several student loans.

"I studied public administration in college, and got a job as business manager of a large Michigan hospital. My years there taught me a lot about people and the challenges they face. Later I ran for the state legislature and have served there for 10 years. I believe these experiences will motivate and enable me to make a real difference for the people of the United States."

Learn the Skill

To learn how to identify your political roots and attitudes, follow these steps.

① **Identify any early political experiences you have had.** Recall, for example, family conversations about politics.

② **Identify the influences of the place where you live, your ethnic and religious ties, and your personal interests.**

③ **Consider the effects of personal experiences.** Describe an experience with a specific person or event that influenced your political attitudes.

Practice the Skill

In what ways would you expect Heckman's background to influence his later political attitudes?

Apply the Skill

Interview a friend or family member. Use the steps above to help this person identify the influences on his or her political attitudes.

How to Participate in Public Debate

Government institutions and policies affect citizens' lives every day. You may sometimes disagree with the way the government has handled an issue, or you may have a suggestion for solving a public problem. There are many ways you can share your views with government officials.

Mia Renatti was upset by her city's plan to tear down her school and build a new one. As you read about Mia, think about what issues you might want to speak out about.

Mia Renatti lives in one of the oldest neighborhoods in her city. She attends the same school that her older sisters, her father, and her grandmother attended. She lives just down the street from the school and grew up playing on its playground.

Mia was very upset when the city announced that it was considering tearing down the school and completely rebuilding it. Mia didn't think a whole new building was necessary. She thought about the different ways she could convince her neighborhood to fight the new school.

Mia decided she could reach out to other concerned citizens by speaking at a public school board meeting. She thought about all the reasons why her school was important to her and about how expensive the long-term construction project would be.

The day of the meeting came, and Mia was very nervous. But she knew that many people in the audience felt the way she did. She delivered her speech, and everyone applauded. At the end of the meeting, the school board decided that it would be best to preserve the old school.

Learn the Skill

To express your views publicly, follow these steps:

1 Identify a local issue.

2 **Find out which government bodies are involved.** Do some research on the issue to find out which offices handle it and what impact they have on the issue.

3 **Decide the best way to express your opinion.** Write a letter to one of the government offices, attend a city council meeting, or speak with your neighbors.

Practice the Skill

1 With a partner, research a community issue.

2 Contact relevant local organizations to receive information.

3 Send a letter to one organization expressing your views on the issue.

Apply the Skill

1 Prepare a short speech about the issue you have researched.

2 Hold a "city council meeting" in class and deliver your speech.

English and Spanish Glossary

The glossary defines all high-use words and many key historical words and terms. The high-use words appear underlined the first time that they are used in the text. The key words and terms appear in blue type the first time that they are used. Each word in the glossary is defined in both English and Spanish. The page number(s) after the English definition refers to the page(s) on which the word or phrase is defined in the text. For other references, see the index.

Pronunciation Key

When difficult names or terms first appear in the text, they are respelled to help you with pronunciation. A syllable printed in small capital letters receives the greatest stress. The pronunciation key below lists the letters and symbols that will help you pronounce the word. It also includes examples of words using each of the sounds and shows how each word would be pronounced.

Symbol	Example	Respelling
a	hat	(hat)
ay	pay, late	(pay), (layt)
ah	star, hot	(stahr), (haht)
ai	air, dare	(air), (dair)
aw	law, all	(law), (awl)
eh	met	(meht)
ee	bee, eat	(bee), (eet)
er	learn, sir, fur	(lern), (ser), (fer)
ih	fit	(fiht)
ī	mile	(mīl)
ir	ear	(ir)
oh	no	(noh)
oi	soil, boy	(soil), (boi)
oo	root, rule	(root), (rool)
or	born, door	(born), (dor)
ow	plow, out	(plow), (owt)

Symbol	Example	Respelling
u	put, book	(put), (buk)
uh	fun	(fuhn)
yoo	few, use	(fyoo), (yooz)
ch	chill, reach	(chihl), (reech)
g	go, dig	(goh), (dihg)
j	jet, gently bridge	(jeht), (JEHNT lee), (brihj)
k	kite, cup	(kīt), (kuhp)
ks	mix	(mihks)
kw	quick	(kwihk)
ng	bring	(brihng)
s	say, cent	(say), (sehnt)
sh	she, crash	(shee), (krash)
th	three	(three)
y	yet, onion	(yeht), (UHN yuhn)
z	zip, always	(zihp), (AWL wayz)
zh	treasure	(TREH zher)

A

abolitionist (a boh LIH shuhn ihst) person who wanted to end slavery (p. 423)
abolicionista persona que quería abolir la esclavitud

accommodation (ak kom moh DAY shuhn) adjustment; adaptation (p. 501)
acomodo ajuste; adaptación

accumulate (uh KYOOM yoo layt) to collect slowly; to increase in amount over time (p. 81)
acumular reunir lentamente; aumentar una cantidad con el tiempo

adobe (uh DOH bee) sun-dried, unburned brick made of clay and straw (p. 12)
adobe seco al sol, ladrillo no quemado hecho de arcilla y paja

alien (AY lee ihn) outsider; someone from another country (p. 300)
extranjero persona que no pertenence a un grupo; persona de otro país

alliance (ah LĪ ans) agreement between nations or groups to aid and support one another (pp. 57, 141, 183)
alianza convenio entre países por el que se comprometen a ayudarse y apoyarse mutuamente

ally (AL eye) a person joined with another for a common purpose (p. 429)
aliado una persona ensambló con otra para un propósito común

alter (AWL ter) to change; to make different (p. 315)
alterar cambiar; hacer algo diferente

alternative (awl TUR nuh tiv) providing a choice between two or among more than two things (p. 19)
alternativa opción de escoger entre dos o más cosas

amend (ah MEHND) to change or revise (p. 264)
enmendar cambiar o revisar

amendment (ah MEHND mehnt) revision or addition to a bill, law, or constitution (p. 221)
enmienda revisión o adición a un proyecto de ley, ley o constitución

amnesty (AM nehs tee) government pardon (p. 547)
amnistía indulto que otorga el gobierno

annex (an NEHKS) to add on or take over (p. 456)
anexar agregar o apoderarse de algo

appeal (ah PEEL) to ask that a court decision be reviewed by a higher court (p. 262)
apelar pedir que una decisión de un tribunal sea revisada por un tribunal superior

appeasement (uh PEEZ mehnt) policy of giving into aggression in order to avoid war (p. 591)
apaciguamiento política de consentir la agresión para evitar la guerra

apprentice (uh PREHN tihs) person who learns a trade or craft from a master (p. 110)
aprendiz persona que aprende un oficio o destreza de un maestro

aristocratic (uh ris tuh KRAT ik) of an aristocracy or upper class (p. 311)
aristocrático de la aristocracia o clase alta

B

backcountry (bak KUHN tree) frontier region located along the eastern slope of the Appalachian Mountains (p. 81)
backcountry región fronteriza ubicada a lo largo de la ladera oriental de los montes Apalaches

bill (bihl) proposed law (p. 259)
proyecto de ley ley propuesta

bill of rights (bihl uhv rīts) written list of freedoms that a government promises to protect (p. 103)

declaración de derechos lista escrita de las libertades que un gobierno se compromete a proteger

black codes (blak kohds) southern laws that severely limited the rights of African Americans after the Civil War (p. 553)
códigos negros leyes sureñas que limitaron severamente los derechos de los afroamericanos después de la Guerra Civil

blockade (BLAHK ayd) shutting a port or roadway to prevent people or supplies from coming into or leaving an area (pp. 161, 328, 515)
bloqueo cierre de un puerto o camino para impedir que entren o salgan personas o provisiones en cierta zona

bond (bahnd) certificate issued by a government for a certain amount of money that the government promises to pay back with interest (p. 284)
bono certificado emitido por un gobierno por cierta cantidad de dinero que el gobierno promete devolver con intereses

border state (BOR der stayt) slave state that remained in the Union during the Civil War (p. 513)
estado fronterizo estado esclavista que permaneció en la Unión durante la Guerra Civil

borderland (BOR der land) land along a frontier (p. 91)
tierra limítrofe tierra a lo largo de una frontera

boycott (BOI kaht) organized campaign to refuse to buy or use certain goods and services (p. 147)
boicot campaña organizada para rehusar comprar o usar ciertos bienes y servicios

C

canal (kah NAHL) artificial waterway dug across land to improve transportation (p. 403)
canal vía navegable artificial excavada a lo largo de un terreno para mejorar el transporte

capitalism (KA piht ahl ihz uhm) economic system in which people put money, or capital, into a business or project in order to make a profit later on; economic system in which privately owned businesses compete in a free market (p. 344)

capitalismo sistema económico en el que las personas invierten dinero (capital) en un negocio o proyecto para obtener ganancias más adelante; sistema económico en el que los negocios de propiedad privada compiten en un mercado libre

capitalist (KA piht ahl ihst) person who invests capital, or money, in a business to earn a profit (p. 383)
capitalista persona que invierte capital (dinero) en un negocio para obtener ganancias

carpetbagger (KAHR peht BAG er) uncomplimentary nickname for a northern white who went to the South after the Civil War to start a business or pursue a political career (p. 555)
carpetbagger sobrenombre despreciativo dado a los norteños blancos que se mudaron al Sur después de la Guerra Civil para emprender un negocio o seguir una carrera política

casualty (KA su ahl tee) military term for a person killed, wounded, or missing in action (p. 520)
baja término militar que describe a una persona muerta, herida o desaparecida en combate

caucus (KAW kuhs) private meeting of members of a political party (p. 352)
reunión de comité encuentro privado de los integrantes de un partido político

cavalry (KAV uhl ree) units of troops on horseback (p. 183)
caballería unidades de tropas a caballo

cease (sees) to stop; to come to an end (p. 296)
cesar detenerse; llegar a su fin

cede (seed) to give up (pp. 144, 345, 457)
ceder entregar

censorship (SEHN sor shihp) the power to review, change, or prevent the publication of news (p. 267)
censura poder de revisar, cambiar o evitar la publicación de noticias

charter (CHAHR ter) official document that gives certain rights to an individual or a group (pp. 67, 342)
carta de privilegio documento oficial que confiere ciertos derechos a un individuo o grupo

checks and balances (chehks and BAL an sez) a principle of the U.S. Constitution that gives each branch of government the power to check, or limit, the actions of the other branches (p. 257)
control y equilibrio principio de la Constitución de Estados Unidos que otorga a cada rama del gobierno el poder de controlar o limitar las acciones de las otras ramas

circumnavigate (ser kuhm NAV ih gayt) to travel all the way around Earth (p. 40)
circunnavegar hacer un recorrido completo alrededor de la Tierra

citizen (SIHT ih zehn) person who owes loyalty to a particular nation and is entitled to all its rights and protections (p. 270)
ciudadano persona que debe lealtad a una determinada nación y que tiene derecho a recibir todos sus derechos y protecciones

civil disobedience (SIHV ihl dih soh BEE dee ehns) idea based on nonviolence that people have a right to disobey a law they consider unjust, if their consciences demand it (p. 433)
desobediencia civil idea de que las personas tienen derecho, sin usar la violencia, a desobedecer una ley que consideren injusta, si su conciencia así lo exige

civil war (SIHV ihl wor) war between people of the same country (p. 503)
guerra civil guerra entre habitantes de un mismo país

civilian (suh VIHL yuhn) person not in the military (p. 187)
civil persona que no pertenece a las fuerzas armadas

civilization (sihv uh luh ZAY shuhn) advanced culture in which people have developed cities, science, and industries (p. 8)
civilización cultura avanzada en la cual la gente ha desarrollado ciudades, la ciencia y la industria

clan (klan) group of families that are related to one another (p. 15)
clan grupo de familias que están relacionadas entre sí

clarify (KLAIR ih fī) to make the meaning of something clear (p. 497)
aclarar explicar el significado de algo

Cold War (kohld wor) after World War II, long period of intense rivalry between the Soviet Union and the United States (p. 592)
guerra fría después de la Segunda Guerra Mundial, largo período de intensa rivalidad entre la Union Soviética y Estados Unidos

compromise (KAHM proh mīz) agreement in which each side gives up part of what it wants to end a disagreement (p. 214)
acuerdo compromiso por el que cada una de las partes renuncia a una parte de lo que desea con el fin de acabar con una desavenencia

confine (kuhn FĪN) to keep within certain limits; to shut or imprison (p. 188)
confinar mantener dentro de ciertos límites; encerrar o encarcelar

conquistador (kahn KWIHS tuh dor) conqueror, especially one of the sixteenth-century Spanish soldiers who defeated the Indian civilizations of Mexico, Central America, or Peru (p. 44)
conquistador persona que conquista, especialmente uno de los soldados españoles del siglo XVI que derrotaron a las civilizaciones indígenas de México y América Central o Perú

constitution (kahn stih TYOO shuhn) document in which the laws, principles, organization, and processes of a government are established (p. 204)
constitución documento que establece las leyes, principios, organización y procedimientos de un gobierno

consume (kuhn SYOOM) to use up (p. 600)
consumir usar

continental (kahn tihn EHN tuhl) paper money printed during the American Revolution (p. 188)
continental forma de papel moneda impreso durante la Guerra de la Independencia

continental divide (kahn tihn EHN tuhl dih VĪD) mountain ridge that separates river systems flowing toward opposite sides of a continent (p. 318)
divisoria continental cadena montañosa que separa sistemas fluviales que corren hacia lados opuestos de un continente

contract (KAHN trakt) agreement between two or more parties that can be enforced by law (p. 344)

contrato convenio entre dos o más partes que se puede hacer valer por ley

contrast (KAHN trast) difference shown between things when compared (pp. 89, 214)
contraste diferencia que se manifiesta entre dos cosas cuando son comparadas

controversy (KAHN truh vur see) argument or dispute (p. 483)
controversia discusión o disputa

convert (kuhn VERT) to change from one purpose or function to another; to change from one political party or religion to another (pp. 91, 415, 591)
convertir cambiar de un propósito o función a otro; cambiar de un partido político o de una religión a otra

corduroy road (KOR der oi rohd) road made of sawed-off logs, laid side by side (p. 403)
camino de troncos camino hecho de troncos aserrados y colocados uno al lado de otro

corporation (kor por AY shuhn) business owned by many investors (p. 578)
compañía empresa que es propiedad de muchos inversionistas

cotton gin (KAHT tuhn jihn) machine that removed seeds from cotton fibers (p. 396)
despepitadora de algodón máquina que servía para quitar las semillas a las fibras de algodón por medio de un cilindro de madera con púas

coureur de bois (koo REHR duh BWAH) French term for "runner of the wood" (p. 54)
coureur de bois término francés para "corredor del bosque" o contrabandista de pieles

crisis (KRĪ sihs) turning point or deciding event; situation involving great risk (p. 484)
crisis momento crucial o acontecimiento decisivo; una situación que implica un gran riesgo

critic (KRIHT ihk) someone who makes judgments about objects or actions (pp. 331, 553)
crítico persona que hace juicios sobre objetos o acciones

culture (KUHL cher) way of life (p. 10)
cultura forma de vida

culture area (KUHL cher AIR ee uh) region in which groups of people have a similar way of life (p. 11)
área cultural región en la cual grupos de personas tienen una forma de vida similar

currency (KER rehn see) money used to make purchases (pp. 11, 531)
moneda dinero que se usa para realizar compras

D

dame school (daym skool) school run by a woman, usually in her own home (p. 119)
escuela de señoritas escuela administrada por una mujer, generalmente en su propia casa

debtor (DEH tor) person who cannot pay his or her debts (p. 87)
deudor persona que no puede pagar sus deudas

decade (DEK ayd) a period of ten years (p. 456)
década un período de diez años

decline (dee KLĪN) to lose strength or power over a period of time (pp. 54, 324)
decaer perder fuerza o poder a lo largo de cierto tiempo

deprive (dee PRĪV) to keep from happening; to take away something needed by force or intent (pp. 7, 487)
privar impedir que suceda; tomar por la fuerza o con intención algo que se necesita

deregulation (dee rehg yuh LAY shuhn) reduction of federal or state restrictions on businesses (p. 597)
desregulación reducción de las restricciones federales o estatales sobre los negocios

détente (day TAHNT) policy to reduce tension between two countries (p. 598)
détente política de reducir las tensiones entre las superpotencias

devise (dee VĪZ) to carefully think out; to invent (p. 206)
idear hacer planes cuidadosamente; inventar

devote (dee VOHT) to commit; to apply time and energy (p. 397)
dedicar comprometer; destinar tiempo y energía

dictatorship (dihk TAY tor shihp) government in which one person or a small group holds complete authority (pp. 252, 455)
dictadura gobierno en el que una persona o un grupo pequeño ejerce una autoridad total

direct democracy (dir EHKT deh MAH kra see) system of government in which ordinary citizens have the power to govern (p. 24)
democracia directa sistema de gobierno en el que los ciudadanos comunes tienen poder para gobernar

discrimination (dihs krihm ihn AY shuhn) denial of equal rights or equal treatment to certain groups of people (p. 395)
discriminación negación de igualdad de derechos o de un tratamiento igualitario a ciertos grupos de personas

dissent (dihs SEHNT) disagreement (p. 267)
disensión desacuerdo

dissolve (dih ZAHLV) to break up into smaller parts (p. 365)
disolver separar en partes más pequeñas

distinct (dihs TIHNKT) clear or definite; clearly different in its quality (pp. 12, 446, 514)
distinto claro o definido; que difiere claramente en cuanto a su calidad

divine right (dih VĪN rīt) belief that a ruler's authority comes directly from God (p. 122)
derecho divino creencia en que la autoridad de un gobernante proviene directamente de Dios

domestic (doh MEHS tihk) having to do with the home or household; pertaining to a country's internal affairs (pp. 108, 348)
doméstico relacionado con la casa o el hogar; relativo a los asuntos internos de un país

dominant (DAHM uh nunt) dominating; ruling; prevailing (p. 315)
dominante que domina, rige, o prevalence

dominate (DAHM uh nayt) to rule or control (p. 578)
dominar regir o controlar

draft (draft) system of required military service (p. 530)
leva sistema del servicio militar obligatorio

dumping (DUHMP ing) selling goods in another country at very low prices (p. 342) *inundación de mercado* venta de productos en otro país a precios muy bajos

duration (doo RAY shun) length of time (p. 300)
duración un tiempo determinado

duty (DOOT ee) import tax (p. 146)
aranceles impuestos a las importaciones

E

economic depression (eh koh NAH mihk dee PREH shuhn) period when business activity slows, prices and wages drop, and unemployment rises (p. 208)
depresión económica período en el que la actividad comercial disminuye, los precios y los salarios bajan y el desempleo aumenta

efficient (ee FISH ehnt) acting effectively, without wasted cost or effort (pp. 386, 463)
eficiente que actúa con eficacia, sin desperdiciar costos ni esfuerzos

emancipate (ee MAN sih payt) to set free (p. 524)
emancipar liberar

embargo (ehm BAHR goh) government order that forbids foreign trade (p. 324)
embargo orden gubernamental que prohíbe el comercio exterior

embrace (ehm BRAYS) to accept; to hold tight to; to readily accept (p. 496)
abrazar aceptar; aferrarse a; aceptar sin dificultad

emotion (ee MOH shuhn) strong feeling such as sadness, anger, or love (pp. 214, 432)
emoción sentimiento intenso; por ejemplo, tristeza, ira o amor

emotional (ee MOH shuh nuhl) appealing to the emotions, or feelings, of people (p. 147)
emocional relativo a las emociones o sentimientos de la gente

emphasis (EM fuh sis) special importance or significance (p. 341)
énfasis importancia o significado importante

emphasize (EM fuh syz) to stress; to make more important (p. 297)
recalcar destacar; dar más importancia

encomienda (ehn koh mih EHN dah) land granted to Spanish settlers that included the right to demand labor or taxes from Native Americans (p. 147)
encomienda terreno otorgado a los colonos españoles, que incluía el derecho a exigir trabajo o impuestos de los indígenas americanos

encounter (ehn KOWN ter) to meet in an unexpected way; to experience (p. 534)
tropezar con encontrar de modo inesperado; experimentar

enlist (ehn LIHST) to sign up for military duty (p. 187)
enlistarse inscribirse para el servicio militar

environment (en VY run munt) surroundings (p. 449)
entorno lo que rodea

establish (uh STAB lish) to set up, found (p. 67)
establecer instituir, fundar

exceed (ehks SEED) to go beyond what is expected or planned (p. 535)
exceder ir más allá de lo esperado; superar lo proyectado

exclude (ehks KLOOD) to keep out or expel; to reject or not be considered (p. 428)
excluir mantener fuera o expulsar; rechazar o no considerar

executive (ehks ZEHK yoo tihv) in government, person who runs the government and sees that the laws are carried out (p. 205)
ejecutivo en un gobierno, persona que dirige el gobierno y hace cumplir las leyes

expansion (ehks PAN shuhn) extending of a nation beyond its existing borders (p. 447)
expansión acto de extender un país más allá de sus fronteras existentes

expedition (ehks peh DIH shuhn) journey undertaken by a group of people with an objective (p. 317)

expedición viaje que emprende un grupo de personas con un objetivo concreto

extended family (ehks TEHN dehd FAM ih lee) close-knit family group that includes parents, children, grandparents, aunts, uncles, and cousins (p. 107)
familia extensa grupo familiar unido que incluye a los padres, hijos, abuelos, tías, tíos y primos

F

faction (FAK shuhn) organized political group (p. 290)
facción grupo político organizado

factor (FAK tor) condition or quality that causes something else to happen (p. 45)
factor condición o cualidad que provoca que ocurra algo distinto

factory system (FAK tor ee SIHS tehm) methods of production that bring workers and machinery together in one place (p. 383)
sistema de fábricas métodos de producción que reúnen trabajadores y maquinaria en un mismo lugar

famine (FAM ihn) widespread starvation (p. 394)
hambruna escasez generalizada de alimentos

fateful (FAYT ful) having important consequences; decisive (p. 192)
fatídico de graves consecuencias; decisivo

federalism (FEHD er uhl ihz uhm) principle of the U.S. Constitution that establishes the division of power between the federal government and the states (p. 257)
federalismo principio de la Constitución de Estados Unidos que establece la división de poderes entre el gobierno federal y los estados

feudalism (FYOOD uhl ihz uhm) system in which a ruler grants parts of his land to lords in exchange for military service and financial assistance (p. 25)
feudalismo sistema en el cual el gobernante otorga parte de su tierra a los señores a cambio de servicio militar y ayuda financiera

finance (FĪ nans) to pay for; to supply with money (p. 120)
financiar pagar por algo; proveer dinero

flexible (FLEHKS ah bahl) capable of change (p. 221)
flexible capaz de cambiar

forty-niner (FOR tee NĪ ner) person who came to California in search of gold (p. 464)
los del cuarenta y nueve personas que vinieron a California en busca de oro

fragment (FRAG mehnt) broken part or piece; small section of something (p. 501)
fragmento parte rota o pieza de algo; sección pequeña de algo

freedmen (FREED mehn) men and women who were legally freed from slavery after the Civil War (p. 548)
libertos hombres y mujeres liberados jurídicamente de la esclavitud después de la Guerra Civil

freedom of the press (FREE duhm uhv thuh prehs) right of newspapers and other public media to publish articles believed to be accurate (p. 105)
libertad de prensa derecho de los diarios y otros medios públicos de comunicación a publicar artículos cuyo contenido consideran como cierto

frontier (fruhn TIR) land that forms the furthest extent of a nation's settled regions (p. 444)
frontera territorio que constituye la extensión más lejana de las regiones establecidas de un país

fugitive (FYOO jih tihv) runaway (p. 484)
fugitivo persona que huye

function (FUHNK shuhn) purpose; proper use; official duty (p. 91)
función propósito; uso adecuado; responsabilidades que conlleva un cargo

fundamental (fuhn duh MEHN tahl) most important part; foundation of an idea or action; the essential quality (pp. 78, 293)
fundamental lo más importante; la base de una idea o acción; la cualidad esencial

G

gentry (JEHN tree) upper class of colonial society (p. 110)
alta burguesía clase alta de la sociedad colonial

glacier (GLAY sher) thick sheet of ice (p. 6)
glaciar gruesa capa de hielo

grandfather clause (GRAND fah ther klawz) law that excused a voter from a literacy test if his father or grandfather had been eligible to vote on January 1, 1867 (p. 560)
cláusula del abuelo ley que eximía a un votante de la prueba de alfabetización si su padre o abuelo había tenido derecho a votar el 1 de enero de 1867

grievance (GREE vans) formal complaint (p. 172)
querella queja formal

guerrilla (guh RIHL uh) fighter who works as part of a small band to make hit-and-run attacks (p. 191)
guerrillero combatiente dentro de un pequeño grupo que realiza ataques relámpago

H

habeas corpus (HAY bee ihs KOR puhs) the right not to be held in prison without first being charged with a specific crime; constitutional protection against unlawful imprisonment (pp. 104, 252, 529)
habeas corpus derecho a no ser encarcelado sin antes haber sido acusado de un delito específico; protección constitucional contra el encarcelamiento ilegal

hostile (HAHS tihl) unfriendly; intending to do harm (pp. 291, 449)
hostil poco amistoso; que se propone hacer daño

I

impeachment (ihm PEECH mehnt) process of bringing formal charges against a public official (p. 556)
juicio político proceso que consiste en presentar una acusación formal contra un funcionario público

impose (ihm POHZ) to place a burden on something or someone (pp. 285, 490)
imponer colocar una carga sobre algo o alguien

impressment (ihm PREHS mehnt) practice of seizing sailors on American ships and forcing them to serve in the British navy (pp. 296, 388)
leva práctica de obligar a una persona a prestar servicio militar; captura de marineros de navíos estadounidenses para obligarlos a servir en la armada británica

impulse (IHM puhls) sudden push or driving force; sudden action; driving force behind an action (p. 415)
impulso empujón repentino o fuerza motriz; acción repentina; la fuerza motriz detrás de una acción

inauguration (ihn awg er AY shuhn) ceremony in which the President officially takes the oath of office (p. 283)
toma de mando ceremonia en la que el presidente hace el juramento propio de su cargo

incident (IN suh dunt) happening; occurrence (p. 151)
incidente acontecimiento; suceso

income tax (IHN kuhm taks) tax on the money people earn or receive (p. 531)
impuesto a los ingresos impuesto sobre el dinero que la gente gana

indentured servant (ihn DEHN cherd SER vehnt) person who signs a contract to work for a set number of years in exchange for ocean passage to the colonies (p. 111)
sirviente contratado persona que firma un contrato para trabajar durante un número determinado de años a cambio de un pasaje oceánico a las colonias

individual (in duh VIJ oo ul) of, for, or by a single person or thing (p. 205)
individual de, para o por una sola persona o cosa

individualism (ihn dih VIHD yoo uhl ihz uhm) concept that stresses the importance of each individual (p. 432)
individualismo concepto que hace hincapié en la importancia de cada individuo

Industrial Revolution (ihn DUHS tree uhl rehv oh LYOO shuhn) gradual replacement of many hand tools by machines (p. 382)
Revolución Industrial sustitución gradual de muchas herramientas manuales por máquinas

inferior (ihn FIR ee uhr) less worthy; less valuable; of lower rank; of poorer quality (pp. 395, 561)
inferior menos digno; menos valioso; de categoría más baja; de menor calidado

inflation (ihn FLAY shuhn) general rise in prices (p. 531)
inflación aumento generalizado de los precios

infrastructure (IHN frah struhk cher) basic public works needed for a society to function, including the systems of roads, bridges, and tunnels (p. 343)
infraestructura obras públicas básicas necesarias para el funcionamiento de una sociedad, como los sistemas de carreteras, puentes y túneles

interchangeable parts (ihn ter CHAYNJ ah buhl pahrts) identical pieces that can be assembled quickly by unskilled workers (p. 386)
partes intercambiables piezas idénticas que pueden ser ensambladas con rapidez por trabajadores no calificados

interest group (IHN trehst groop) organization that represents the concerns of a particular group (p. 271)
grupo de intereses organización que representa los asuntos que conciernen a un grupo en particular

interstate commerce (IHN ter stayt KAHM mers) trade between two or more states (p. 344)
comercio interestatal intercambio comercial entre dos o más estados

invest (ihn VEHST) to purchase something with money with the hope that its value will grow; to supply money for a project in order to make a profit (pp. 284, 383, 587)
invertir adquirir algo a cambio de dinero con la esperanza de que su valor aumente; facilitar dinero para un proyecto para que dé ganacias

ironclad (Ī ern klad) warship covered with protective iron plates (p. 518)
acorazado barco de guerra cubierto con placas protectoras de hierro

irrigate (IR uh gayt) to water crops by channeling water from rivers or streams (p. 7)
irrigar regar los cultivos canalizando el agua de los ríos o arroyos

isolate (Ī soh layt) to set apart; to separate (p. 503)
aislar apartar; separar

isolated (Ī soh lay tehd) set apart; separated (p. 403)
aislado apartado; separado

isolationism (Ī soh LAY shuhn ihz uhm) avoiding involvement in other countries' affairs (p. 587)
aislacionismo práctica de evitar la participación en los asuntos de otros países

J

judicial branch (jyoo DIH shuhl branch) system of courts to settle disputes involving national issues (p. 213)
poder judicial sistema de tribunales para dirimir pleitos referentes a cuestiones nacionales

judicial review (jyoo DIH shuhl ree VYOO) principle that the Supreme Court has the right to decide whether acts of Congress are constitutional or not (p. 313)
revisión judicial principio según el cual la Corte Suprema tiene derecho a decidir si los actos del Congreso son constitucionales

jurisdiction (jer ihs DIHK shuhn) power of a court to hear and decide cases (p. 262)
jurisdicción potestad de un tribunal para conocer y resolver sobre casos

K

kayak (KĪ ak) boat consisting of a light wooden frame covered with watertight skins and propelled by a double-bladed paddle (p. 12)

kayac bote que consta de una ligera estructura de madera cubierta de pieles impermeables a excepción de una única o doble abertura en el centro, y que se impulsa por medio de un remo de dos paletas

L

laissez faire (LAY seh fair) idea that government should not interfere in the economy (p. 311)
laissez faire idea de que el gobierno no debe entrometerse en la economía

land grant (land grant) government gift of land (p. 446)
concesión de tierras donación de tierras por parte del gobierno

legislature (LEHJ ihs lay cher) part of a government that makes laws (p. 103)
legislatura parte de un gobierno que se encarga de elaborar leyes

levy (LEHV ee) to impose a tax by law; to force to be paid (pp. 104, 531)
gravar imponer una contribución por ley; obligar a que se pague

libel (LĪ behl) publishing of false statements that unjustly damage a person's reputation (pp. 105, 267)
libelo publicación de afirmaciones falsas que dañan injustamente la reputación de una persona

limited government (LIHM ih tehd GUHV ern mehnt) the principle that the government has only the powers that the Constitution gives it (p. 256)
gobierno limitado el principio de que el gobierno tiene únicamente los poderes que la Constitución le otorga

literacy test (LIH ter ah see tehst) examination to see if a person can read and write; used in the past to restrict voting rights (p. 560)
prueba de alfabetización examen para establecer si una persona sabe leer y escribir, se usaba en el pasado para restringir el derecho al voto

logic (LAH jihk) reason; good sense; careful thought (p. 171)
lógica razón; buen juicio; reflexión cuidadosa

M

martial law (MAHR shuhl law) type of rule in which the military is in charge and citizens' rights are suspended (p. 513)
ley marcial tipo de gobierno en el que los militares están al mando y se suspenden los derechos de los ciudadanos

mass production (mas proh DUHK shuhn) manufacturing of large numbers of identical products quickly and cheaply (p. 386)
producción en masa manufactura rápida y a bajo costo de un gran número de productos idénticos

mercantilism (MER kan tihl ihz uhm) economic policy that held that a nation prospered by exporting more goods to foreign nations than it imported from them (p. 50)
mercantilismo principio económico según el cual una nación prospera exportando más bienes a países extranjeros que los que importa de ellos

mercenary (MER sehn air ee) soldier who fights merely for pay, often for a foreign country (pp. 161, 181)
mercenario soldado que combate tan sólo por una paga, casi siempre en favor de un país extranjero

middle class (MIHD uhl klas) a portion of the colonial population that included small planters, independent farmers, and skilled craftsworkers (p. 111)
clase media en las 13 colonias, parte de la población colonial que incluía a los pequeños cultivadores, a los granjeros independientes y a los artesanos

militia (mih LIH shah) organized body of armed volunteers (p. 140)
milicia cuerpo organizado de voluntarios armados

minimize (MIHN ah mīz) to reduce to the lowest possible amount (p. 580)
reducir al mínimo disminuir a la cantidad más pequeña posible

minimum (MIHN ah muhm) smallest amount possible or allowed (p. 146)
mínimo cantidad más pequeña posible o permitida

minuteman (MIHN uht man) colonial militia volunteer who was prepared to fight at a minute's notice (p. 152)
miliciano de la Guerra de Independencia voluntario de la milicia colonial que estaba siempre preparado para luchar

mission (MIHSH uhn) religious settlement run by Catholic priests and friars; settlement that aims to spread a religion into a new area (p. 47)
misión colonía religiosa administrada por sacerdotes católicos y frailes; asentamiento cuya finalidad es diseminar la religión en una nueva zona

monopoly (muhn AH poh lee) company that controls all or nearly all business in a particular industry (pp. 151, 578)
monopolio compañía que controla toda o casi toda la actividad de una industria en particular

monotheism (MAHN oh thee ihz uhm) belief that there is only one God (p. 22)
monoteísmo creencia de que solamente hay un Dios

motive (MOH tihv) thought or feeling behind an action (p. 55)
motivo pensamiento o sentimiento detrás de una acción

mountain man (MOWN tehn man) fur trapper of the Northwest (p. 449)
hombre de montraña cazador de pieles del Noroeste

myth (mihth) story or legend; imaginary object; invented story (p. 37)
mito cuento o leyenda; objeto imaginario; relato inventado

N

nationalism (NA shuhn uhl ihz uhm) devotion to the interests of one's own country; pride in one's own nation or ethnic group (p. 327)
nacionalismo lealtad a los intereses del propio país; orgullo respecto a la propia nación o grupo étnico

nativist (NAY tihv ihst) person who was opposed to immigration (p. 394)
nativista persona que buscaba reservar Estados Unidos para los protestantes blancos nacidos en el país, y que se oponía a la inmigración

natural rights (NA cher uhl rīts) rights that belong to every human being from birth (p. 122)
derechos naturales derechos de los que goza todo ser humano desde el momento de su nacimiento

naturalization (na cher uhl ih ZAY shuhn) legal process guaranteeing citizenship (p. 270)
naturalización procedimiento jurídico que garantiza la ciudadanía

navigation (nav uh GAY shuhn) science of locating the position and plotting the course of ships (p. 19)
navegación ciencia de ubicar la posición y de trazar el trayecto de los barcos

negative (NEHG ah tihv) in opposition to an idea; not positive (p. 41)
negativo opuesto a una idea; no positivo

neutral (NEW truhl) not favoring either side in a dispute (pp. 295, 513)
neutral que no favorece a ninguna de las partes en un pleito

nominating convention (NAHM ih nay ting kuhn VEHN shuhn) large meeting of party delegates to choose candidates for office (p. 352)
convención de postulación gran encuentro de delegados de un partido para elegir candidatos a un cargo

northwest passage (NORTH wehst PAS saj) water route through or around North America (p. 51)
paso del noroeste ruta navegable a través o alrededor de América del Norte

nullification (nuhl ih fih KAY shuhn) idea that a state has the right to nullify, or cancel, a federal law that the state leaders consider to be unconstitutional (p. 364)
anulación idea de que un estado tiene derecho a anular o cancelar una ley federal que los dirigentes del estado consideran inconstitucional

nullify (NUHL ih fī) to cancel a federal law; to deprive of legal force (p. 301)
anular cancelar una ley federal; privar de fuerza jurídica

O

occupy (AHK yoo py) take possession of (p. 158)
ocupar tomar posesión o apoderarse de algo

on margin (ohn MAHR jehn) practice that allows people to buy stock with a down payment of a portion of the full value (p. 587)
con margen práctica que permite a las personas comprar acciones abonando una entrada del diez por ciento del valor total

option (AHP shuhn) choice; possible course of action (p. 192)
opción elección; posible manera de actuación

override (OH ver rīd) set aside; disregard; overrule; replace (p. 259)
invalidar dejar de lado; no tener en cuenta; no admitir; sustituir

P

participate (pahr TIHS ah payt) to take part in; to share in an activity (pp. 24, 351)
participar tomar parte en algo; compartir una actividad

peninsular (peh nihn suh LAR) Spanish colonist who was born in Spain (p. 48)
peninsular colono español nacido en España

petition (peh TIH shuhn) formal written request to someone in authority that is signed by a group of people (p. 147)
petición solicitud formal por escrito, firmada por un grupo de personas y dirigida a una autoridad

phase (fayz) stage of development (p. 143)
fase etapa de desarrollo

pilgrim (PIHL gruhm) person who takes a religious journey (p. 69)
peregrino persona que emprende un viaje religioso

plantation (plan TAY shuhn) large estate farmed by many workers (pp. 47, 87)
plantación finca grande cultivada por muchos trabajadores

policy (PAHL uh see) plan or course of action, as pursued by a government (p. 446)
política plan o normas a seguir por un gobierno

poll tax (pohl taks) personal tax to be paid before voting (p. 560)
impuesto al voto impuesto personal que debía pagarse para poder votar

polygamy (poh LIHG ah mee) practice of having more than one wife at a time (p. 462)
poligamia práctica de tener más de una esposa al mismo tiempo

popular sovereignty (PAH pyoo lahr SAH ver ehn tee) principle that asserts that people are the primary source of the government's authority; right of people to vote directly on issues (pp. 256, 483)
soberanía popular derecho de los habitantes de un territorio o estado a votar directamente sobre ciertas cuestiones en vez de que sus representantes electos decidan

potlatch (PAHT lach) ceremony held by some Native American groups at which the hosts showered their guests with gifts such as woven cloth, baskets, canoes, and furs (p. 12)
potlach ceremonia realizada por algunos grupos de indígenas americanos en la cual los anfitriones agasajaban a sus huéspedes con regalos como tejidos, cestas, canoas y pieles

preamble (PREE am buhl) introduction to a declaration, constitution, or other official document (p. 172)
preámbulo introducción a una declaración, constitución u otro documento oficial

precedent (PREH seh dehnt) example to be followed by others in the future (p. 283)
precedente ejemplo a seguir por otros en el futuro

precise (pree SĪS) exact; accurate (p. 27)
preciso exacto; acertado, certero

predestination (pree dehs tihn AY shuhn) idea that God decides the fate of a person's soul even before birth (p. 415)
predestinación idea de que Dios decide el destino del alma de una persona incluso antes de su nacimiento

preliminary (pree LIM uh nehr ee) leading up to the main action (p. 525)
preliminar preámbulo a la acción principal

presidio (prih SIHD ee oh) military post where soldiers lived in the Spanish colonies (p. 92)
presidio puesto militar donde vivían los soldados en las colonias españolas

private property (PRĪ veht PRAH per tee) property owned by an individual (p. 252)
propiedad privada propiedad que pertenece a una persona

privateer (prī vuh TEER) armed civilian ship that had the government's permission to attack enemy ships and keep goods seized (p. 190)
corsario barco civil armado con el permiso del gobierno para atacar a los barcos enemigos y quedarse con los bienes capturados

prohibition (proh ih BIH shuhn) total ban on the sale and consumption of alcohol (p. 416)
ley seca prohibición total de la venta y consumo de alcohol

propaganda (prah peh GAN dah) false or misleading information that is spread to further a cause; information used to sway public opinion (p. 488)
propaganda información falsa o engañosa que se difunde para apoyar una causa; información usada para influir en la opinión pública

proprietary colony (proh PRĪ eh tair ee KAHL uhn ee) English colony in which the king gave land to one or more proprietors, or owners, in exchange for a yearly payment (p. 78)
colonia de propietarios colonia inglesa donde el rey concedía tierras a uno o más propietarios o dueños a cambio de un pago anual

proprietor (proh PRĪ ah tor) owner of a business or colony (p. 86)
propietario dueño de una empresa o colonia

prospect (PRAHS pehkt) expectation; something to look forward to happening (pp. 110, 464)

prospecto expectativa; algo que se desea que ocurra

province (PRAHV ahns) governmental division of a country, similar to a state (pp. 51, 346)
provincia división gubernamental de un país, semejante a un estado

provoke (prah VOHK) to cause to anger; to excite; to cause an action (pp. 301, 457)
provocar incitar al enojo; excitar; dar lugar a una acción

public school (PUHB lihk skool) school supported by taxes (pp. 118, 417)
escuela pública escuela financiada con impuestos

pueblo (PWEHB loh) town in the Spanish colonies; Anasazi village (p. 93)
pueblo asentamiento en las colonias españolas; aldea anasazi

pursue (per SYOO) to chase after; to try to capture (p. 402)
perseguir ir tras de algo; tratar de capturar

Q

quote (kwoht) to repeat the exact words spoken or written (p. 357)
citar repetir las palabras exactas habladas o escritas

R

racism (RAY sihz uhm) belief that one race is superior or inferior to another (p. 116)
racismo creencia de que una raza es superior o inferior a otra

radical (RAD ih kul) favoring fundamental or extreme change (pp. 423, 599)
radical que favora cambio fundamental o extreme

ranchero (ran CHAIR oh) owner of a ranch (p. 446)
ranchero dueño de un rancho

ratify (RAT ih fī) to approve (pp. 218, 264)
ratificar aprobar

react (ree AKT) to act in response to an action; to respond (pp. 152, 350)

reaccionar actuar en respuesta a una acción; responder

register (REJ is tur) enroll or record officially (p. 555)
registrar inscribir o anotar oficialmente

reign (rayn) period of dominance or rule (p. 393)
reinado período de dominación o gobierno

reinforce (ree ihn FORS) to strengthen; to make more effective (pp. 122, 328, 519)
reforzar fortalecer; hacer más eficaz

rendezvous (RAHN day voo) yearly meeting where trappers would trade furs for supplies (p. 449)
rendezvous encuentro anual en el que los tramperos intercambiaban pieles por provisiones

repeal (ree PEEL) to cancel (pp. 152, 255)
revocar cancelar

representative government (reh pree SEHN tah tihv GUHV ern mehnt) political system in which voters elect others to make laws (p. 69)
gobierno representativo sistema político en el que los votantes eligen a otras personas para que elaboren las leyes

reproduce (ree prah DOOS) to make a copy (p. 435)
reproducir hacer una copia

republic (ree PUHB lihk) system of government in which the people choose representatives to govern them (pp. 25, 252)
república sistema de gobierno en el que la gente elige representantes que los gobernarán

require (rih KWYR) to order or command (p. 560)
requerir ordenar o mandar

reservation (reh zer VAY shuhn) area set aside by the government for Native Americans to live on (p. 577)
reservación territorio que el gobierno destina a ser habitado por indígenas americanos

reside (ree ZĪD) to live in; to dwell for a while; to exist in (p. 8)
residir vivir en algún lugar; habitar por un tiempo; existir

resolution (rehz uh LOO shuhn) formal statement of opinion or policy (p. 171)
resolución declaración formal de una opinión o política

resolve (ree SAHLV) strong determination; *also* to decide; to solve (pp. 143, 364, 548)

resolver decidir; dar solución

resource (REE sors) supply of something to meet a particular need (pp. 188, 514)
recurso abasto de algo que satisface una necesidad en particular

restore (ree STOR) to bring back to a normal state; to put back; to reestablish (pp. 50, 158, 326, 589)
restaurar devolver a una condición normal; reponer; restablecer

restrict (ree STRIHKT) to confine; to keep within a certain boundary or limit; to place limitations on something or somebody (p. 75)
restringir confinar; mantener dentro de ciertas fronteras o límites; poner limitaciones a algo o alguien

retain (rih TAYN) to keep (p. 103)
retener mantener

revenue (REV uh noo) the income from taxes, licenses, etc., as of a city, state, or nation (p. 312)
ingreso utilidad de impuestos, licencias, etc., de la ciudad, estado o la nación

revival (ree VĪ vuhl) huge outdoor religious meeting (p. 415)
reunión evangelista encuentro religioso de grandes proporciones al aire libre

revolt (ree VOHLT) uprising; rebellion; to rebel (pp. 116, 400)
revuelta sublevación; rebelión

rigid (RIH jihd) strict; not easily bent or changed (p. 48)
rígido estricto; que no se dobla o cambia con facilidad

royal colony (ROI uhl KAHL uh nee) colony under direct control of the English crown (p. 78)
colonia real colonia bajo control directo de la corona inglesa

S

sachem (SAY chuhm) member of the tribal chief council in the League of the Iroquois (p. 15)
sachem (representante en tiempo de paz) miembro del consejo del jefe tribal de la Liga de los iroqueses

salvation (sal VAY shuhn) in Christianity, the means for saving one from evil; everlasting afterlife (p. 23)
salvación en la cristiandad, la manera para librarse del mal; la vida eterna

satellite (SAT uh lyt) a small state that is economically or politically dependent on a larger, more powerful state (p. 592)
satélite un estado pequeño dependiente económicamente y políticamente de un estado más grande y poderoso

scalawag (SKAL eh wag) southern white who had opposed secession (p. 555)
scalawag blanco sureño que se oponía a la secesión

secede (seh SEED) to withdraw from membership in a group (pp. 331, 484)
separarse retirarse como miembro de un grupo

sedition (seh DIH shuhn) stirring up of rebellion against a government (p. 300)
sedición acto de fomentar la rebelión contra un gobierno

segregation (sehg reh GAY shuhn) enforced separation of races (p. 560)
segregación separación obligada de dos razas

self-government (sehlf GUHV ern mehnt) right of people to rule themselves independently (p. 348)
autogobierno derecho de las personas a gobernarse a sí mismas de forma independiente

separation of powers (seh pahr AY shuhn uhv POW ers) principle by which the powers of government are divided among separate branches (pp. 123, 253)
separación de poderes principio por el cual los poderes del gobierno se dividen entre sus distintas ramas

sharecropper (SHAIR krah per) person who rents a plot of land and farms it in exchange for a share of the crop (p. 561)
aparcero persona que alquila un terreno y lo cultiva a cambio de una parte de la cosecha

siege (seej) military blockade or bombardment of an enemy town or position in order to force it to surrender (pp. 455, 535)

sitio cerco militar o bombardeo de una población o posición enemiga a fin de obligarla a rendirse

slave code (slayv kohd) laws that controlled enslaved African Americans' lives and denied them basic rights (pp. 116, 399)
código de la esclavitud una de un grupo de leyes que regulaban la vida de los esclavos afroamericanos y les negaban los derechos fundamentales

smuggling (SMUH glihng) act of illegally importing or exporting goods (p. 324)
contrabando importación o exportación ilegal de mercancías

social reform (SOH shuhl ree FORM) organized attempts to improve conditions of life (p. 414)
reforma social intentos organizados de mejorar las condiciones de vida

specify (SPEHS uh fī) to describe or to point out in detail (p. 73)
especificar describir o señalar en detalle

speculator (SPEHK yoo lay tor) person who invests in a risky venture in the hope of making a large profit (p. 284)
especulador persona que invierte en una empresa arriesgada con la esperanza de tener grandes ganancias

sphere (sfeer) rounded shape; area of interest or influence (p. 17)
esfera figura redondeada; zona de interés o influencia

spirituals (SPIR ih chyoolz) religious folk songs that blended biblical themes with the realities of slavery (p. 400)
canto espiritual canto religioso tradicional que combinaba temas bíblicos con las realidades de la esclavitud

spoils system (spoilz SIHS tehm) act of replacing government officials with supporters of a newly elected President (p. 354)
sistema de sinecuras sustitución de funcionarios gubernamentales por partidarios del presidente recién electo

states' rights (stayts rīts) the right of states to limit the power of the federal government (p. 301)

derechos de los estados derecho de los estados a limitar el poder del gobierno federal

strait (strayt) narrow passage that connects two large bodies of water (p. 40)
estrecho travesía estrecha que conecta dos grandes masas de agua

suffrage (SUH frihj) right to vote (pp. 351, 581)
sufragio derecho al voto

superior (suh PIR ee er) of greater importance or value; above average in quality; higher in position or rank (p. 519)
superior de mayor importancia o valor; por encima del promedio en cuanto a calidad; que ocupa una posición o categoría más alta

surplus (SER pluhs) excess; quantity that is left over (p. 7)
superávit excedente; cantidad sobrante

sustain (suh STAYN) to keep going; to support as just (pp. 68, 525)
sostener mantener en marcha; apoyar como justo

T

tariff (TAIR ihf) tax placed on goods entering a country from another country (p. 286)
arancel impuesto con que se gravan las mercancías que entran en un país provenientes de otro

telegraph (TEHL eh graf) invention that allows messages to be sent quickly by sending electrical signals along a wire (p. 391)
telégrafo invento que permite enviar mensajes rápidamente a grandes distancias por medio de señales eléctricas que viajan por un cable

temperance movement (TEHM per ehns MOOV mehnt) organized effort to end alcohol consumption (p. 416)
movimiento por la temperancia esfuerzo organizado en contra del consumo de alcohol

temporary (TEM puh rehr ee) not permanent (p. 115)
temporal que no es permanente

terrorism (TEHR er ihz uhm) deliberate use of violence, often against civilian targets, to achieve political or social goals (p. 599)

terrorismo uso deliberado de la violencia, a menudo en contra de objetivos civiles, con el fin de alcanzar objetivos políticos o sociales

toleration (tahl er AY shuhn) recognition that other people have the right to different opinions (p. 73)
tolerancia reconocimiento de que otras personas tienen el derecho de mantener opiniones distintas

total war (TOH tuhl wor) all-out attacks aimed at destroying not only an enemy's army but also its resources and its people's will to fight (p. 536)
guerra total ataques masivos encaminados a destruir no sólo al ejército enemigo, sino también sus recursos y la voluntad de luchar de la población

totalitarian state (toh tal uh TER ee uhn stayt) nation in which a single party controls the government and every aspect of people's lives (p. 590)
estado totalitario país en el que un sólo partido político controla el gobierno y todos los aspectos de la vida de las personas

town meeting (town MEET ing) meeting in colonial New England during which settlers discussed and voted on issues; form of direct democracy in which residents meet to make decisions for the community (p. 75)
cabildo abierto reunión en la Nueva Inglaterra colonial donde los colonos discutían y votaban sobre sus asuntos; forma de democracia directa en la que los residentes se reúnen para tomar decisiones que conciernen a la comunidad

traitor (TRAY ter) person who betrays his or her country or cause and helps the other side (p. 192)
traidor persona que traiciona a su país

transcendentalism (trans sehn DEHN tuhl ihz uhm) movement that sought to explore the relationship between humans and nature through emotions rather than through reason (p. 432)
trascendentalismo movimiento que se proponía explorar la relación entre los seres humanos y la naturaleza mediante las emociones en vez de la razón

transform (trans FORM) to change in appearance or form; to change the condition of something (p. 183)
transformar cambiar la apariencia o la forma; cambiar la condición de algo

triangular trade (trī ANG yuh ler trayd) three-way colonial trade route between the colonies, the islands of the Caribbean, and Africa (p. 115)
comercio triangular ruta de comercio colonial a tres bandas entre las colonias, las islas del Caribe y África

tribute (TRIH byoot) money paid by one country to another in return for protection (p. 322)
tributo dinero que un país paga a otro a cambio de protección

turnpike (TERN pīk) road built by a private company that charges a toll to use it (p. 402)
camino de peaje camino construido por una compañía privada que cobra una cuota por su uso

U

unconstitutional (uhn kahn stih TOO shuhn uhl) contrary to what is permitted by the U.S. Constitution (pp. 263, 285)
inconstitucional contrario a lo que permite la Constitución de Estados Unidos

urbanization (er ban ihz AY shuhn) movement of large numbers of people from rural areas to cities; rapid growth of city populations (p. 390)
urbanización desplazamiento de un gran número de personas de las zonas rurales a las ciudades; crecimiento rápido de la población de las ciudades

V

veto (VEE toh) to reject, as when the President rejects a law passed by Congress (p. 259)
vetar rechazar, como cuando el Presidente rechaza una ley aprobada por el Congreso

via (VEE ah) by way of (p. 424)
vía paso por algún lugar

vigilante (vihj ihl AN tee) self-appointed law enforcer (p. 465)
vigilante persona que se designa a sí misma para hacer cumplir la ley

violate (VY uh layt) fail to keep or observe; infringe on (p. 172)
violar que no logra adherirse o observar; que infringe

vital (VĪ tuhl) necessary for life; of great importance; spirited; lively (p. 183)
vital necesario para la vida; de gran importancia; lleno de vida; animado

voluntary (VAHL ahn tair ee) not forced; done of one's free will (pp. 357, 547)
voluntario no forzado; hecho por voluntad propia

W

war hawk (wor hawk) one of the members of Congress who called for war with Britain prior to the War of 1812 (p. 327)
halcón de guerra uno de los miembros del Congreso de representantes del Sur y del Oeste que instaban a la guerra con Gran Bretaña antes de la guerra de 1812

water rights (WAW ter rīts) legal right to use water from a body of water (p. 464)
derecho de aguas derecho jurídico a utilizar el agua de un río, arroyo u otra masa de agua con un fin determinado

women's rights movement (WOO mehns rīts MOOV mehnt) organized campaign to win property, education, and other rights for women (p. 429)
movimiento por los derechos femeninos campaña organizada para obtener el derecho a la propiedad, a la educación y otros derechos para la mujer

women's suffrage (WOO mehns SUH frihj) right of women to vote (p. 428)
sufragio femenino derecho de las mujeres a votar

writ of assistance (riht uhv uh SIHS tehns) court order that allowed officials to make undefined searches (p. 148)
auto de asistencia orden judicial que permitía a determinados funcionarios a realizar registros sin tener que revelar lo que andaban buscando

Acknowledgments

Staff Credits

The people who made up the *America: History of Our Nation* team—representing design services, editorial, editorial services, education technology, manufacturing and inventory planning, market research, marketing services, planning and budgeting, product planning, production services, publishing processes, and rights and permissions—are listed below. Boldface type denotes the core team members.

Scott Andrews, Rosalyn Arcilla, **Jane Breen, Laura Chadwick, Eugennie Chang,** Bob Craton, **Brett Creane,** Harold DelMonte, **Glenn Diedrich, Jim Doris, Kerry Dunn,** Patricia Fromkin, **Elizabeth Good, Shelby Gragg,** Michael Hornbostel, Judie Jozokos, **Patrick Keithahn,** John Kingston, **Doreen Kruk, Ann-Michelle Levangie, Marian Manners, Grace Massey, Anne McLaughlin,** Michael McLaughlin, **Xavier Niz, Jennifer Paley, Paul Ramos, Ryan Richards, Melissa Shustyk,** Kristen VanEtten, **Al Velasquez, Roberta Warshaw**

Map and Art Credits

Maps: Mapping Specialist Limited, except where noted with additional type set by Justin Contursi **Visual Preview Maps** XNR Productions 4–5, 34–35, 64–65, 100–101, 138–139, 168–169, 202–203, 280–281, 308–309, 338–339, 380–381, 412–413, 442–443, 450–451, 510–511, 544–545, 574–575 and TLAH Maps 131, 373, 472, 475, 571 Anthony Morse 20, 82, 210, 320–321, 425, 460–461 with additional type set by Artur Mkrtchyan **Illustrated Maps** Anthony Morse 20, 82, 210, 320–321, 425 Kevin Jones Associates 13

Art: Keithley and Associates, all charts/graphs/instructional art and photo composites except where noted **Illustrations** XNR Productions 4–5, 13, 34–35, 64–65, 100–101, 138–139, 168–169, 202–203, 280–281, 308–309, 338–339, 380–381, 412–413, 442–443, 450–451, 480–481, 510–511, 544–545, 574–575 **Timelines** Humberto Ugarte **Instructional Art/Photo Composites** One Visual Mind 13, 38–39, 72–73, 109, 160, 194, 216, 286, 328, 350–351 Kerry Cashman 398–399, 425, 432–433, 450–451, 502, 560–561 Humberto Ugarte 74, 80, 450–451, 452, 588 Justin Contursi **Atlas design and Skills Activity photo treatments** GDPS **All Skills for Life art** Brainworx 210–211, 288–289, 320–321, 341, 420–421, 460–461, 522–523, 550–551

Every effort has been made to credit all vendors. Any omissions brought to our attention will be corrected in subsequent printings.

Photo Credits

Cover and Title page Getty Images **A-1** Getty Images, Inc.; **A-2 T** Esbin/Anderson/Omni-Photo Communications, Inc.; **A-3 B** Dallas and John Heaton/CORBIS; **A-3 T** AP/Wide World Photos; **A-4 T** Tom & Susan Bean; **A-5 T** Julie Habel/CORBIS; **A-5 B** Marvin Newman; **A-6 T** © DK Images; **A-7 T** Giancarlo de Bellis/Omni-Photo Communications, Inc.; **A-7 B** Bill Ross/CORBIS; **A-10** Larry Downing/Reuters/CORBIS; **A-11** © CORBIS; **A-12 TL** Connie Ricca/CORBIS; **A-12 TR** Smithsonian American Art Museum, Washington, DC/Art Resource, NY; **A-12 B** Bettmann/CORBIS; **A-13 T** Bettmann/CORBIS; **A-13 B** Jay Dorin/Omni-Photo Communications, Inc.; **A-15 T** Anaheim Public Library; **A-15 B** D. Boone/CORBIS; **A-16 TL** © Royalty-Free/Corbis; **A-16 B** © CORBIS; **ii** Jamestown-Yorktown Educational Trust, VA, USA/The Bridgeman Art Library, London/New York; **v** John Guthrie, Guthrie Studios; **vii** The Granger Collection, New York; **viii** Courtesy National Archives; **ix** © The Granger Collection, NY; **x** Collection of The New-York Historical Society, negative no. 26280ON; **xi** AP/Wide World Photos; **xii** © Royalty-Free/Corbis; **HT 01** Omni-Photo Communications, Inc.; **HT 02 L** Courtesy National Archives; **Ht 02 R** Omni-Photo Communications, Inc.; **HT 03** Lawrence Migdale/Pix; **HT 04** © CORBIS/Bettmann; **HT 05** © David Young-Wolff/PhotoEdit inc.; **HT 08 L** David Stoecklein/CORBIS; **HT 08 R** Sime s.a.s./eStock/PictureQuest; **HT 10** Silver Burdett Ginn; **HT 14** Copyright © North Wind/North Wind Picture Archives—All rights reserved; **HT 15** CC Lockwood/Animals Animals; **HT 16** Mary Evans Picture Library; **HT 17** The Granger Collection, New York; **HT 21** KAL/The Baltimore Sun/CartoonArts International/CWS; **HT 23** Brand X Pictures/PictureQuest; **HT 24** © Jeff Greenberg/PhotoEdit Inc.; **0 B** Copyright © North Wind/North Wind Picture Archives—All rights reserved.; **0 T** The Art Archive/Museo de la Torre del Oro Seville/Dagli Orti/The Picture Desk; **01 TR** Jamestown-Yorktown Educational Trust, VA, USA/The Bridgeman Art Library, London/New York; **01 TL** The Trustees of the British Museum/Art Resource, NY; **01 B** © CORBIS/Bettmann; **02–03** Tom Bean/CORBIS; **04 B** Jorge Ianiszewski/Art Resource, NY; **04 M** Stock Montage, Inc.; **05 T** The Granger Collection, New York; **05 R** Figure of Shou Lao (jade), Chinese School, (17th century)/Fitzwilliam Museum, University of Cambridge, UK/Bridgeman Art Library; **06** Erich Lessing/Art Resource, NY; **08** Charles & Josette Lenars/CORBIS; **08 Inset** The Granger Collection, New York; **09** Jorge Ianiszewski/Art Resource, NY; **10** Richard Nowitz Photography; **11 R** The Granger Collection, New York; **11 L** Michel Zabe/© Dorling Kindersley; **11 M** Michel Zabe/© Dorling Kindersley; **14** The Trustees of the British Museum/Art Resource, NY; **15** The Art Archive/Cherokee Indian Museum North Carolina/Mireille Vautier; **16** Courtesy, Dept. of Library Services, American Museum of Natural History; **17 L** Courtesy of the Freer Gallery of Art, Smithsonian Institution, Washington, D.C.: Purchase, F1946.12, f. 38b; **17 TR** Peter Chadwick/© Dorling Kindersley; **17 BR** Roger Phillips/© Dorling Kindersley; **17 MR** Philip Dowell © Dorling Kindersley; **18** Giraudon/Art Resource, NY; **19** Figure of Shou Lao (jade), Chinese School, (17th century)†/Fitzwilliam Museum, University of Cambridge, UK/Bridgeman Art Library; **20 L** photolibrary.com; **20 R** © Tom Stoddart/Woodfin Camp & Associates; **21 M** The Granger Collection, New York; **21 T** © Markus Matzel/Peter Arnold, Inc.; **21 B** Philip Dowell © Dorling Kindersley; **22** The Granger Collection, New York; **23** Tissot, James Jacques Joseph (1836–1902) Moses and the 10 Commandments c. 1896–1902. Gouache on board. 10 11/16 × 5 5/8". Gift of the Heirs of Jacob Schiff, x1952-190. Photo by John Parnell. The Jewish Museum, New York, NY, U.S.A./Art Resource, NY; **24** Bildarchiv Preussischer Kulturbesitz/Art Resource, NY; **25** AP/Wide World Photos; **26** The Granger Collection, New York; **29** Bildarchiv Preussischer Kulturbesitz/Art Resource, NY; **30** Figure of Shou Lao (jade), Chinese School, (17th century)†/Fitzwilliam Museum, University of Cambridge, UK/Bridgeman Art Library; **31** © Royalty-Free/CORBIS; **32–33** Amos Zemer/Omni-Photo Communications, Inc.; **36** © Bettmann/CORBIS; **37** Ridolfo Ghirlandaio (1483–1561) "Christopher Columbus". Museo Navale di Pegli, Genoa, Italy. Scala/Art Resource, NY.; **38 B** Astrolabe, copper, by Ahmad Ibn Khalaf an Iraqi Arab, 9th century, O_DATA†/†Bibliotheque Nationale de Cartes et Plans, Paris, France/Bridgeman Art Library; **39 R** The Art Archive/Museo de la Torre del Oro Seville/Dagli Orti/The Picture Desk; **39 L** The Art Archive/Marine Museum Lisbon/Dagli Orti; **40 (5)** Corel Professional Photos CD-ROM™; **40 MR** Roger Phillips/© Dorling Kindersley; **42 M** National Gallery Collection; by kind permission of the Trustess of the National Gallery, London/CORBIS; **42 TL** Copyright © North Wind/North Wind Picture Archives—All rights reserved; **43 BL** Photo Researchers, Inc.; **43 M** Mary Evans Picture Library; **43 TR** The Granger Collection, New York; **44** © Bettmann/CORBIS; **45** The Granger Collection, New York; **47** The Granger Collection, New York; **49** © HIP/Art Resource; **50 R** Peter M. Fisher/Corbis; **50 TL** © Dorling Kindersley; **50 B** Bettmann/CORBIS; **51** Queen Elizabeth I playing the lute (miniature) (see also 3912), Hilliard, Nicholas (1547–1619), Berkeley Castle, Gloucestershire, UK/Bridgeman Art Library; **52** Tate Gallery, London/Art Resource, NY; **53** The Granger Collection, New York; **55** The Granger Collection, New York; **56** © Monica Graff/The Image Works; **57** The Granger Collection, New York; **60** Copyright © North Wind/North Wind Picture Archives—All rights reserved; **62–63** © CORBIS/Bettmann; **66** © Alamy Images; **68** State Capitol, Commonwealth of Virginia. Courtesy The Library of Virginia; **69** Courtesy of the Library of Congress. Art © Romare Bearden Foundation/Licensed by VAGA, New York, NY; **70** Head of Squanto (d.1622), an American Indian of the Pawtuxet tribe who became a good friend to the Pilgrims (wood), American School, (17th century)/Private Collection/Bridgeman Art Library; **71** North Wind Picture Archives; **72 B** Courtesy of The Salem Witch Museum, Salem, Massachusetts; **72 TL** Getty Images; **72 TR** Getty Images Inc.–Hulton Archive Photos; **72–73 Bkgrnd** Getty Images/Richard Dobson; **73 L** © CORBIS; **74 TR** North Wind Picture Archives; **74 B** Portrait of Anne Hutchinson (1591–1643), American School, (20th century)/Schlesinger Library, Radcliffe Institute, Harvard University,/The Bridgeman Art Library; **74 TL** © H. Stanley Johnson/SuperStock; **74 MR** SuperStock, Inc.; **76** Mary Evans Picture Library; **77** The Picture Collection of the New York Public Library; **78** © Private Collection/© Philip Mould Ltd, London/The Bridgeman Art Library; **79** The Granger Collection, New York; **80 MR** The Granger Collection, New York; **80 TL** Library of Congress; **80 B** The New York Public Library/Art Resource, NY; **83 T** Roy Rainford/Robert Harding World Imagery;

83 M © Charles E. Rotkin/CORBIS; **83 B** © Philip Gould/CORBIS; **84 Bkgrnd** SuperStock Inc.; **84** The Granger Collection, New York; **85** The Granger Collection, New York; **87** Portrait of General James Edward Oglethorpe (1696–1785) founder of the State of Georgia, copy of original portrait in Atlanta, c.1932 (oil on canvas), Ravenet, Simon Francois (1706/21-74) (after)/Corpus Christi College, Oxford, UK/Bridgeman Art Library; **89** Hulton Archive/Getty Images Inc.; **90** © Jon Arnold/SuperStock; **92 L** Tumacacori Mission, 1855 (oil on canvas), Pratt, Henry Cheever (1803-80)/© Phoenix Art Museum, Arizona, Francis Hover Stanley and Carolanne Smurthwaite/ Bridgeman Art Library; **92 R** Jack Dykinga/Getty Images; **96** The Granger Collection, New York; **98–99** © Granger Collection, Ltd.; **100 M** The Granger Collection, New York; **100 TR** Copyright © North Wind/North Wind Picture Archives—All rights reserved; **100 BL** Slaves preparing tobacco, Virginia, America, c.1790, from 'Le Costume Ancien et Moderne', Volume II, plate 50, by Jules Ferrario, engraved by Angelo Biasioli (1790–1830), published c.1820s-30s (colour litho), Bramati, G. (19th century) (after)/Private Collection, The Stapleton Collection/Bridgeman Art Library; **101 B** North Wind Picture Archives; **102** Private Collection, © John Noott Galleries, Broadway, Worcestershire, UK/The Bridgeman Art Library; **103** The Granger Collection, New York; **105 R** The New York Public Library, Rare Book Division/Art Resource; **105 L** Copyright © North Wind/North Wind Picture Archives—All rights reserved; **106** Courtesy of the Library of Congress; **107** The Granger Collection, New York; **109 BR** © CORBIS/Bettmann; **109 BL** © Richard T. Nowitz/CORBIS; **109 TL** The Granger Collection, New York; **109 R** Wilberforce House, Hull Museums, Hull City Council, UK. DK; **110 R** Victoria & Albert Museum, London/Art Resource, NY; **111** The Granger Collection, New York; **112** The Granger Collection, New York; **113** SuperStock, Inc.; **115** The Granger Collection, New York; **116** Slaves preparing tobacco, Virginia, America, c.1790, from 'Le Costume Ancien et Moderne', Volume II, plate 50, by Jules Ferrario, engraved by Angelo Biasioli (1790–1830), published c.1820s-30s (colour litho), Bramati, G. (19th century) (after)†/ Private Collection, The Stapleton Collection/Bridgeman Art Library; **118** The Granger Collection, New York; **119 B** © CORBIS; **119 M** The Granger Collection, New York; **119 R** The Granger Collection, New York; **120** Schomburg Center/Art Resource, NY; **121** Copyright © North Wind/North Wind Picture Archives—All rights reserved; **123** Archivo Icongrafico, S.A/ CORBIS; **125 T** Collection of The New-York Historical Society; **125 B** Pearson Education/PH School Division; **128** The Granger Collection, New York; **129** The Granger Collection, New York; **130** Maryland Province of the Society of Jesus. Photo by Don Doll, SJ; **131** The Granger Collection, New York; **132 T** Library of Congress; **132 B** North Wind Picture Archives; **133** The Granger Collection, New York; **134–135 BL** Courtesy National Archives; **134 T** Tony Freeman/PhotoEdit; **135 BR** Copyright © North Wind/North Wind Picture Archives—All rights reserved; **135 TL** The Granger Collection, New York; **136–137** © Bettmann/CORBIS; **140** The Granger Collection, New York; **141** The Granger Collection, New York; **143** Robert Griffing/Paramount Press, Inc.; **144** Mary Evans Picture Library; **145 L** Colonial Williamsburg Foundation; **145 R** Corbis/Bettmann; **147** Copyright © North Wind/North Wind Picture Archives—All rights reserved; **148** The Granger Collection, New York; **149** The Granger Collection, New York; **150** © North Wind Picture Archive; **151 T** The Granger Collection, New York; **151 BL** Courtesy, American Antiquarian Society; **153** Jim Conaty/Omni-Photo Communications, Inc.; **154 T** Courtesy of the Library of Congress; **154 B** The Granger Collection, NY; **154 BR** Jim Barber/StockRep, Inc.; **154 M** The Granger Collection, New York; **155** The Granger Collection, New York; **156** © Art Resource, NY; **157** The Granger Collection, New York; **158** Fort Ticonderoga Museum; **159** Fort Ticonderoga Museum; **160 M** Copyright © North Wind/North Wind Picture Archives—All rights reserved; **160 BL** American 18th Century, Attack on Bunker's Hill, with the Burning of Charles Town, oil on canvas, .533 × .708 (21 × 27 7/8); framed: .603 × .774 × .038 (23 3/4 × 30 1/2 × 1 1/2). Gift of Edgar Williams and Bernice Chrysler Garbisch, Photograph (c) 2000 Board of Trustees, National Gallery of Art, Washington, 1783 or after, oil on canvas.; **160 TR** The Granger Collection; **160 BR** The Granger Collection; **160 T** © CORBIS; **166–167** Paintings by Don Troiani, historicalartprints.com; **170** The Granger Collection, New York; **171** Bettmann/ CORBIS; **172** The Granger Collection, New York; **173** Maryland Historical Society, Baltimore; **174** Courtesy National Archives and Records Administration, College Park, Maryland, photo no. (USH001TF 011 004); **175** Index Stock Imagery, Inc.; **179** The Granger Collection, New York; **181** The Granger Collection, New York; **182 BL** Uniforms of the American Revolution: 1777 Private Field Dress from the 1st Georgia Continental Infantry (gouache & w/c on paper), Lefferts, Charles MacKubin (1873–1923)/© New-York Historical Society, New York, USA/Bridgeman Art Library; **182 TR** Colonial Williamsburg Foundation; **182 BR** Courtesy National Park Service, Museum Management Program and Valley Forge National Historical Park. Rifle, 1760–1770, Pennsylvania "Mountain" flintlock rifle. Steel, iron, wood. L 137.8 Barrel L 99.7 cm. The George C. Neumann Collection, Valley Forge Historical Park, VAFO 172. http://www.cr.nps.gov/museum/exhibits/revwar/image_gal/vafoimg/ vafo172.html; **182 BM** The Connecticut Historical Society Museum, Hartford, Connecticut; **183** The Granger Collection, New York; **184** PhotoDisc, Inc./ Getty Images; **185** Pearson Education/PH School Division; **186** The Granger Collection, New York; **187** © CORBIS/Bettman; **188** The Granger Collection, New York; **190** The Granger Collection, New York; **191** SuperStock, Inc.; **192** Copyright © North Wind/North Wind Picture Archives—All rights reserved.; **194 TL** The Granger Collection, New York; **194 M** The Granger Collection, New York; **194 TR** The Granger Collection, New York; **194 BL** The Granger Collection, New York; **194 BR** Fort Ticonderoga Museum; **194 Bkgrnd** The Granger Collection, New York; **197** PhotoDisc, Inc./Getty Images; **198** Corel Professional Photos CD-ROM; **200–201** Independence National Historical Park; **204 (4)** The Granger Collection, New York; **205** Virginia Tourism Corp; **208** The Granger Collection, New York; **211 B** Richard Hamilton Smith/ CORBIS; **211 T** Raymond Bial; **212** The Granger Collection, New York; **213 R** Gary Randall/Getty Images, Inc.-Taxi; **213 L** Bob Krist/CORBIS; **214** James Wilson (1742–1798) American Revolutionary Statesman, 1792 by Jean Pierre Henri Louis. (1755–1799) Watercolor on ivory, 6.7 × 5.2 cm., detail, Smithsonian American Art Museum, Washington, D.C./Art Resource, NY; **216 BR** © CORBIS/Bettmann; **216 TL** Art Resource, NY; **216 BL** © CORBIS/ Bettmann; **216 BR** (BR, Bkgrd) Shutterstock; **216 TR** © CORBIS/Bettmann; **218** © CORBIS; **219** © CORBIS; **220** Courtesy of the Library of Congress; **225** Courtesy of the Library of Congress; **227 & 228** Donovan Reese/Getty Images-Photodisc-; **244** © Corbis Royalty Free; **250** Photograph by Robin Miller, 2001. Independence National Historical Park; **251** © Bettmann/ CORBIS; **252** © CORBIS/Bettmann; **253 T** © CORBIS/Bettmann; **253 B** © CORBIS; **254** Steve Bronstein/Getty Images; **255 R** Courtesy of the Library of Congress; **255 MR** Drug Enforcement Administration; **255 ML** Tony Freeman/PhotoEdit; **255 L** California Historical Society, San Francisco; **258** © Joseph Sohm; ChromoSohm, Inc./CORBIS; **263** Steve Petteway/The Collection of the Supreme Court of the United States; **265** Jeff Cadge/Getty Images; **267 L** Jeff Greenberg/Omni-Photo Communications, Inc.; **267 R** Nick Ut/AP/Wide World Photos; **269** © Michael S. Yamashita/CORBIS; **270** Paul Sakuma/AP/Wide World Photos; **271** © Paul Conklin/PhotoEdit; **272 B** © Corbis/Bettmann; **273 R** Portrait of George Washington (1732-99), 1853 (oil on canvas), Peale, Rembrandt (1778–1860)/© Collection of the New-York Historical Society, USA,/The Bridgeman Art Library; **273 B** Jim Conaty/Omni-Photo Communications, Inc.; **274** The Granger Collection, New York; **275 T** The Granger Collection, New York; **275 M** National Geographic Society; **276 T** Gift of James Speyer/Museum of the City of New York/The Art Archive; **276 BL** Thomas Sully, Andrew Jackson, detail, Andrew W. Mellon Collection. Photograph © Board of Trustees, National Gallery of Art, Washington; **276 T** The Art Collection of the Union League of Philadelphia; **277 TL** The Granger Collection, New York; **277 TR** Copyright © North Wind/North Wind Picture Archives—All rights reserved.; **277 B** John Guthrie, Guthrie Studios; **278–279** Washington's Inauguration at Philadelphia in 1793 (ca. 1900), Jean Leon Jerome Ferris. Watercolor on paper. Private Collection/The Bridgeman Art Library; **282** The Granger Collection, New York; **283** The Granger Collection, New York; **285** Art Resource, NY (detail); **286 B** The Metropolitan Museum of Art, Gift of Edgar William and Bernice Chrysler Garbisch, 1963. (63.201.2) Photograph © 1983 The Metropolitan Museum of Art; **286 L** The Granger Collection, New York; **286 TL** © CORBIS; **286 TR** © Bettmann/CORBIS; **288** Library of Congress, Prints & Photographs Division, LC-USZC4-1495; **289 T** Abby Aldrich Rockefeller Folk Art Museum, Colonial Williamsburg Foundation, Williamsburg, VA; **289 B** Dave King/© Dorling Kindersley; **290** The Granger Collection, New York; **291 L** White House Historical Association (White House Collection) (55); **291 R** The Granger Collection, New York; **292 B** Joe Raedle/Newsmakers/ Getty Images; **292 T** Shutterstock; **294 L** The Granger Collection, New York; **294 R** Kevin Fleming/CORBIS; **296** Mary Evans Picture Library/Alamy Images; **298** The Granger Collection, New York; **299** The Granger Collection, New York; **301** © National Portrait Gallery, Smithsonian Institution/Art Resource, NY; **304** The Metropolitan Museum of Art, Gift of Edgar William and Bernice

Acknowledgments

Chrysler Garbisch, 1963. (63.201.2) Photograph © 1983 The Metropolitan Museum of Art; **305** Courtesy of the Library of Congress; **306–307** The Granger Collection, New York; **308 TL** White House Collection, copyright White House Historical Association; **308 TR** © National Portrait Gallery, Smithsonian Institution/Art Resource, NY; **309 L** Field Museum of Natural History; **309 R** North Wind Picture Archives/Alamy Images; **310** SuperStock, Inc.; **311** Nathan Beck/Omni-Photo Communications, Inc.; **314** The Granger Collection, New York; **315** The Granger Collection, New York; **317** NASA/Johnson Space Center; **318** © The Granger Collection, NY; **320 B** Dick Durrance/National Geographic Society; **320 T** The Granger Collection, New York; **321 M** Independence National Historical Park; **321 TR** Smithsonian Institution, Photo no. 95-3550; **321 B** Missouri Historical Society, St. Louis; **321 TL** Independence National Historical Park; **321 M** Independence National Historical Park; **322** The Granger Collection, New York; **323** Copyright © North Wind/North Wind Picture Archives—All rights reserved.; **324** The Fotomas Index; **327** North Wind Picture Archives/Alamy Images; **328 L** The Granger Collection; **330** Field Museum of Natural History; **336–337** Art Resource, NY; **340** The Bridgeman Art Library; **341 TR** Daniel Webster, c.1828., detail, National Portrait Gallery, Smithsonian Institution/Art Resource, NY; **341 TL** The Granger Collection, New York; **341 B** John Caldwell Calhoun, ca. 1818-25, detail, National Portrait Gallery, Smithsonian Institution/Art Resource, NY; **343** Copyright © V&A Images/—All rights reserved.; **344** Courtesy of the Metropolitan Museum of Art, Rogers Fund, 1942 (42.95.7). Photograph © 1995 By the Metropolitan Museum of Art, NY; **345** The Granger Collection, New York; **349 R** © CORBIS; **349 L** Thomas Sully, Andrew Jackson, detail, Andrew W. Mellon Collection. Photograph Board of Trustees/National Gallery of Art, Washington, DC; **351 L** THE COUNTY ELECTION, 1852 (detail), George Caleb Bingham, American, 1811–1879, oil on canvas, 38 × 52", The Saint Louis Art Museum. Gift of Bank of America.; **351 R** Courtesy of the Library of Congress; **352** Thomas Sully, Andrew Jackson, detail, Andrew W. Mellon Collection. Photograph © Board of Trustees, National Gallery of Art, Washington; **353** Robert Cruikshank. "The President's Levee, or all Creation going to the White House. Courtesy of the Library of Congress; **355** Mary Evans Picture Library; **358 Inset** Trail of Tears Commission, Inc.; **358 L** John Guthrie, Guthrie Studios; **361 L** Courtesy of the Library of Congress; **361 R** Pearson Education/PH School Division; **362** SuperStock, Inc.; **363** Courtesy of the Library of Congress; **365** Courtesy of the Library of Congress; **366 BR** The Granger Collection, New York; **366 BL** Corning Museum of Glass; **366 TR** Getty Images Inc.–Hulton Archive Photos; **366 TL** © New-York Historical Society, New York, USA/Bridgeman Art Library, London/New York; **371** The Granger Collection, New York; **372** The Metropolitan Museum of Art, Gift of Edgar William and Bernice Chrysler Garbisch, 1963. (63.201.2) Photograph © 1983 The Metropolitan Museum of Art; **373** © CORBIS; **374 T** © Bettmann/CORBIS; **374 BR** Courtesy of the Library of Congress; **374 BL** Courtesy of the Library of Congress; **375** © Bettmann/CORBIS; **376 T** © CORBIS; **376 B** © CORBIS; **377 TR** © CORBIS; **377 TL** Alamy Images; **377 B** Collection of The New-York Historical Society, negative no. 26280ON; **378–379** Clyde DeLand/SuperStock; **382** © Bettmann/CORBIS; **383** Dave King/© Dorling Kindersley; **384** The Granger Collection, New York; **385** Michael Newman/PhotoEdit Inc.; **386 L** The Granger Collection, New York; **386 Inset** American Textile History Museum, Lowell, Mass.; **389 T** Copyright © North Wind/North Wind Picture Archives—All rights reserved.; **390** © Roger-Viollet/The Image Works; **391** The Granger Collection, New York; **392** Matthew Brady/Library of Congress, Washington, D.C. USA/The Bridgeman Art Library, London/New York; **393** The Granger Collection, New York; **394** © CORBIS; **396** SuperStock, Inc.; **398 B** Hunter Museum of Art; **398 Inset** Liz McAulay (c) Dorling Kindersley; **399 L** Collection of The New-York Historical Society, New York, USA/The Bridgeman Art Library, London/New York; **400** The Granger Collection, New York; **401** © North Wind Picture Archives; **403** Courtesy of the Library of Congress; **410–411** Library of Congress; **414** © CORBIS; **415** Courtesy of the Library of Congress; **416** © New Bedford Whaling Museum. †detail; **417 R** The Granger Collection, New York; **418** Brooke/Topical Press Agency/Getty Images; **420 T** © Kevin Fleming/CORBIS; **420 B** Fine Art Photographic Library/CORBIS; **421 TL** Culver Pictures, Inc., **421 TR** The Granger Collection, New York; **421 TM** © CORBIS; **421 BR** © CORBIS; **421 BL** The Metropolitan Museum of Art, The Elisha Whittelsey Collection, The Elisha Whittelsey Fund, 1951. MM 55138 Photograph, all rights reserved, The Metropolitan Museum of Art.; **422** The Granger Collection, New York; **423** Getty Images Inc.–Hulton Archive Photos; **424** Alamy Images;

425 BR © CORBIS; **425 B** Smithsonian American Art Museum, Washington, DC/Art Resource; **427** Adelaide Johnson, Portrait monument to Lucretia Mott, Elizabeth Cady Stanton and Susan B. Anthony. Marble, c. 1920. Architect of the Capitol.; **428** © CORBIS; **430** Maria Mitchell Association; **431 R** The Granger Collection, New York; **431 L** 20th Century Fox/Everett Collection; **432 L** Courtesy of the Library of Congress; **432 R** Else Bostelmann/NGS Image Collection/The Art Archive; **433** © Corbis/Bettmann; **434** Thomas Cole. Oil on Canvas 23 3/4 × 31 1/2. The Minneapolis Institute of Arts; **439** © New Bedford Whaling Museum; **440–441** SuperStock; **444** North Wind/North Wind Picture Archives; **446** CLAVER CARROLL/photolibrary.com; **448** The Granger Collection, New York; **450 BR** The Granger Collection, New York; **450 T** © Michael T. Sedam/CORBIS; **450–451 T** William Henry Jackson/Scotts Bluff National Monument; **450 TL** Shutterstock; **450 M** Geoff Brightling/© Dorling Kindersley; **451 BL** Courtesy of the Lane County Historical Museum. photo by John Zimmerman; **451 TR** Bruce Forster/© Dorling Kindersley; **452 B** The Art Archive/Gift of Ruth Koerner Oliver/Buffalo Bill Historical Center, Cody, Wyoming/6922.1; **452 T** The Granger Collection, New York; **453** PhotoDisc, Inc./Getty Images; **454** Center for American History/University of Texas at Austin; **455 R** The Granger Collection, New York; **455 B** John M. Roberts/CORBIS; **457** Bettmann/CORBIS; **460 B** Corel Professional Photos CD-ROM™; **460 T** © Bettmann/CORBIS; **461 M** Chicago Historical Society; **461 B** Color lithograph by unknown artist, Landing of the Troops at Vera Cruz, 1847. Anne S.K. Brown Military Collection, John Hay Library, Brown University; **462** California State Library; **463 T** Used by permission, Utah State Historical Society, all rights reserved; **463 L** "Handcart Pioneers" by CCA Christensen (c) by Intellectual Reserve, Inc. Courtesy of Museum of Church History and Art Used by Permission.; **464 B** Andrew McKinney/© Dorling Kindersley; **465** USC Regional History Center; **466** San Francisco, general view, ca. 1850-52; detail, engraving by S. Frank Marryat, Collection of The New-York Historical Society, negative no. 26280; **470** The Granger Collection, New York; **472 L** © North Wind/North Wind Picture Archives—All rights reserved.; **472 R** Library of Congress; **473** Robertstock; **474 TR** Abolition of Colonial Slavery Meeting, 1830 (letterpress), English School, (19th century)/Private Collection,/The Bridgeman Art Library; **474 M** The Granger Collection, New York; **474 TL** © Bettmann/CORBIS; **475** The Granger Collection, New York; **476 B** © CORBIS; **476 T** The Granger Collection, NY; **477 T** Mary Evans Picture Library; **477 B** His First Vote, 1868 (oil on canvas), Wood, Thomas Waterman (1823–1903)/Private Collection, Christie's Images/www.bridgeman.co.uk/The Bridgeman Art Library, London/New York; **478–479** The Granger Collection, New York; **482** © David J. & Janice L. Frent Collection/CORBIS; **483** Courtesy of the Library of Congress; **484 L** Matthew Brady/Library of Congress; **484 R** The Granger Collection, New York; **486 L** The Granger Collection; **486 L** Picture History; **487 L** Copyright © North Wind/North Wind Picture Archives—All rights reserved.; **487 R** Illinois State University; **488** © Bettmann/CORBIS; **488 Inset** RÈunion des MusÈes Nationaux/Art Resource, NY; **490** The Granger Collection, NY; **493 T** The Granger Collection, New York; **493 B** Pearson Education/PH School Division; **494** Courtesy of the Library of Congress; **495** John Henry Brown, "Abraham Lincoln" (1809–1865), Sixteenth US President. Watercolor on ivory, c. 1860. National Portrait Gallery, Smithsonian Institution/Art Resource, NY. (detail); **496** © CORBIS/Bettmann; **497** Kansas State Historical Society; **498** The Granger Collection, New York; **499** National Portrait Gallery, Smithsonian Institution/Art Resource, NY (NPG.71.29); **499** © Bettmann/CORBIS; **499** © CORBIS; **501** Hulton-Deutsch Collection/CORBIS; **502 B** The Granger Collection, New York; **502 T** United States Department of the Interior; **502 M** Adoc-photos/Art Resource, NY; **506** Kansas State Historical Society; **507** The Granger Collection, New York; **508–509** Painting by Don Troiani/historicalartprints.com; **512** © Medford Historical Society Collection/CORBIS; **515 L** Omni-Photo Communications, Inc.; **515 R** Omni-Photo Communications, Inc.; **516** Courtesy Beverley R. Robinson Collection, US Naval Academy Museum; **517** Dave King/Dorling Kindersley (c) Confederate Memorial Hall, New Orleans; **518** The Granger Collection, New York; **519 L** © Bettmann/CORBIS; **519 R** Steve Helber/AP/Wide World Photos; **522–523** from Great Battles of the Civil War by kind permission of Marshall Editions Ltd; **523 BL** Publisher's Press, Inc.; **523 BR** Collection of Picture Research Consultants, Inc. Photo © Collection of David and Kevin Kyle; **524** © Bettmann/CORBIS; **525** Collection of the personal papers of General Robert H. Milroy, Courtesy of the Jasper County Public Library, Rensselaer, Indiana (detail); **526** AP/Wide World Photos; **528** The Granger Collection, New York;

529 The Granger Collection, New York; **530 R** The Granger Collection, New York; **530 L** Getty Images Inc.–Hulton Archive Photos; **532** AP/Wide World Photos; **533** SuperStock, Inc.; **535** Courtesy of the Library of Congress; **541** The Granger Collection, New York; **542–543** © CORBIS; **544 R** Medford Historical Society Collection; **544 L** The Granger Collection, New York; **545 L** © Corbis/Bettmann; **545 R** The Granger Collection, New York; **546** Smithsonian American Art Museum, Washington, DC/Art Resource, NY; **547** © CORBIS/Bettmann; **548 R** © CORBIS/BETTMANN; **548 L** Getty Images-Hulton Archive Photos; **550 M** Alamy Images; **550 B** The Granger Collection, New York; **550 T** Dave King/Dorling Kindersley © Confederate Memorial Hall, New Orleans; **551 TL** Copyright © North Wind/North Wind Picture Archives—All rights reserved.; **551 M** Douglas Mudd, National Numismatic Collection, The Smithsonian Institution; **551 TR** neg. #86-113-74, Rudolf Eickmeyer, National Museum of American History, Smithsonian Institution; **551 B** The Museum of the Confederacy, Richmond, Virginia, Photography by KATHERINE WETZEL; **552** Courtesy of the Library of Congress; **553 L** The Granger Collection, New York; **553 R** Courtesy of the Library of Congress; **554 R** Courtesy of the Library of Congress; **554 L** Courtesy of the Library of Congress; **555** The Granger Collection, New York; **556** The Granger Collection, New York; **557 T** Old Court House Museum, Vicksburg, Photo by Bob Pickett; **557 B** Collection of Mississippi State Historical Museum/Mississippi Department of Archives and History; **558** © Bettmann/CORBIS; **560 Inset** Courtesy of the Library of Congress; **560–561** © CORBIS; **562** © CORBIS/Bettmann; **563** © CORBIS; **565** © CORBIS; **566** His First Vote, 1868 (oil on canvas), Wood, Thomas Waterman (1823–1903)/Private Collection, Christie's Images/www.bridgeman.co.uk/The Bridgeman Art Library, London/New York; **567** The Granger Collection, New York; **568 L** © North Wind/North Wind Picture Archives—All rights reserved.; **568 B** CORBIS; **BM** United States Department of the Interior; **BR** Dave King/Dorling Kindersley © Confederate Memorial Hall, New Orleans; **568 T** Library of Congress; **569 T** Library of Congress; **B** Bettmann/CORBIS; **570 (2)** The Granger Collection, New York; **571** © CORBIS; **571** The Granger Collection, New York; **572–573** © Royalty-Free/Corbis; **574 T** Solomon D. Butcher Collection, Nebraska State Historical Society; Bettmann/CORBIS AP Photo/Hiroko Ami, Japan Pool; **575 T** Getty Images; **B** Bettmann/CORBIS; **576** Solomon D. Butcher Collection, Nebraska State Historical Society; **578** The Granger Collection, New York; **579** Snark/Art Resource, NY; **580** © CORBIS; **581 T** Getty Images Inc.–Hulton Archive Photos; **581 B** Schomburg Center for Research in Black Culture/Art Resource; **582 B** © Bettmann/CORBIS; **582 M** © Bettmann/CORBIS; **582 T** © Bettmann/CORBIS; **583 T** Hulton Archive/Getty Images; **583 B** © Bettmann/Corbis; **584** © Bettmann/CORBIS; **585** The Granger Collection, New York; **586** © royalty-free/CORBIS; **587** © Underwood & Underwood/CORBIS; **588 B** © CORBIS/Bettmann; **588 TR** Popperfoto/Retrofile; **588 TL** AP/Wide World Photos; **590** © Swim Ink 2, LLC/CORBIS; **591 R** Courtesy of the Library of Congress; **591 L** © CORBIS; **593** Getty Images; **594** © Bettmann/CORBIS; **596** Image by © David J. & Janice L. Frent Collection/CORBIS; **597** AP/Wide World Photos; **598** David Brauchli/Reuters/CORBIS; **599 R** © Reuters/CORBIS; **599 L** "USA TODAY (9/12/2001) Reprinted with Permission"; **600** AP/Wide World Photos; **606–607** Corel Professional Photos CD-ROM; **609** Heritage Image Partnership; **611** Copyright © North Wind/North Wind Picture Archives—All rights reserved.; **612** Jamestown-Yorktown Educational Trust/Bridgeman Art Library; **615** © Bettmann/CORBIS; **617** Jim Conaty/Omni-Photo Communications, Inc.; **618** © Bettmann/CORBIS; **621** © CORBIS/Bettmann; **625** The Granger Collection, New York;

627 Copyright © North Wind/North Wind Picture Archives—All rights reserved.; **629** The Granger Collection, New York; **631** The Granger Collection, New York; **633** The Granger Collection, New York; **635** Seaver Center for Western History Research, Natural History Museum of Los Angeles County; **636** The Granger Collection, New York; **638** Valentine Museum, Richmond, Virginia; **640** Courtesy of the Library of Congress; **643 01** © National Portrait Gallery, Smithsonian Institution/Art Resource, NY; **643 01** © National Portrait Gallery, Smithsonian Institution/Art Resource, NY; **643 02** © National Portrait Gallery, Smithsonian Institution/Art Resource, NY; **643 03** White House Collection, copyright White House Historical Association; **643 04** © National Portrait Gallery, Smithsonian Institution/Art Resource, NY, **643 05** © National Portrait Gallery, Smithsonian Institution/Art Resource, NY; **643 06** National Portrait Gallery, Smithsonian Institution/Art Resource, NY; **643 07** White House Collection, copyright White House Historical Association; **643 08** White House Collection, copyright White House Historical Association; **643 09** © National Portrait Gallery, Smithsonian Institution/Art Resource, NY; **643 10** © National Portrait Gallery, Smithsonian Institution/Art Resource, NY; **643 11** White House Collection, copyright White House Historical Association; **643 12** © National Portrait Gallery, Smithsonian Institution/Art Resource, NY; **644 13** White House Collection, copyright White House Historical Association; **644 14** © National Portrait Gallery, Smithsonian Institution/Art Resource, NY; **644 15** © National Portrait Gallery, Smithsonian Institution/Art Resource, NY; **644 16** White House Collection, copyright White House Historical Association; **644 17** White House Collection, copyright White House Historical Association; **644 18** © National Portrait Gallery, Smithsonian Institution/Art Resource, NY; **644 19** White House Collection, copyright White House Historical Association; **644 20** © National Portrait Gallery, Smithsonian Institution/Art Resource, NY; **644 21** © National Portrait Gallery, Smithsonian Institution/Art Resource, NY; **644 22** White House Collection, copyright White House Historical Association; **644 23** White House Collection, copyright White House Historical Association; **644 24** White House Collection, copyright White House Historical Association; **645 25** © National Portrait Gallery, Smithsonian Institution/Art Resource, NY; **645 26** © National Portrait Gallery, Smithsonian Institution/Art Resource, NY; **645 27** © National Portrait Gallery, Smithsonian Institution/Art Resource, NY; **645 28** White House Collection, copyright White House Historical Association; **645 29** White House Collection, copyright White House Historical Association; **645 30** White House Collection, copyright White House Historical Association; **645 31** White House Collection, copyright White House Historical Association; **645 32** White House Collection, copyright White House Historical Association; **645 33** White House Collection, copyright White House Historical Association; **645 34** White House Collection, copyright White House Historical Association; **645 35** © National Portrait Gallery, Smithsonian Institution/Art Resource, NY; **645 36** White House Collection, copyright White House Historical Association; **646 37** White House Collection, copyright White House Historical Association; **646 38** White House Collection, copyright White House Historical Association; **646 39** White House Collection, copyright White House Historical Association; **646 40** White House Collection, copyright White House Historical Association; **646 42** White House Historical Association (White House Collection) (6196) (detail); **646 43** George W. Bush Presidential Library; **646 41** White House Historical Association (White House Collection) (6196) (detail); **646 B** White House Photo Office; **650** Lawrence Migdale/Pix; **651** The Granger Collection, New York; **654** © Monica Graff/The Image Works; **662** © North Wind Picture Archives; **663** Getty Images; **666** Shutterstock; **671** Shutterstock

Acknowledgments

Text Credits

Grateful acknowledgment is made to the following for copyrighted material:

Alfred A. Knopf, Inc.
"I, Too" by Langston Hughes from *American Negro Poetry, Revised Edition*, copyright © 1974 by the Estate of Arna Bontemps. First edition copyright © by Arna Bontemps.

American Heritage
Excerpt from *Christopher Columbus, Hero and Villain* by Christine Gibson, from AmericanHeritage.com.

Bantam Books
Excerpt from *Dauntless: A Novel of Midway and Guadalcanal* by Barrett Tillman, copyright © 1992 by Barrett Tillman. Used by permission of Bantam Books, a division of Random House, Inc.

Bedford/St. Martin's
Excerpt from *Reading the American Past* by Michael P. Johnson, copyright © 2005 by Bedford/St Martin's.

Close Up Publishing
from "I Never Cared Much for Machinery" by Lucy Larcom, from *Ordinary Americans: U.S. History Through The Eyes Of Everyday People, Second Edition*, copyright © 2003 Close Up Foundation.

Creators Syndicate, Inc.
Excerpt from "The Importance of Voting" from *Talking it Over* by Hillary Rodham Clinton, copyright © 2000 by Creators Syndicate, Inc.

Da Capo Press
Excerpt from *Life in California During a Residence of Several Years in That Territory* by Alfred Robinson, copyright © 1969 by Da Capo Press, a Division of Plenum Publishing Corporation.

Doubleday
Excerpt from *Lone Star Nation* by H. W. Brands, copyright © 2004 by Doubleday, a division of Random House, Inc. Excerpt from "Valley Forge" by Maxwell Anderson, from *America On Stage*, copyright © 1934 by Maxwell Anderson. Copyright renewed © 1962 by Gilda Oakleaf Anderson, Alan Anderson, Terence Anderson, Quentin Anderson, and Hesper A. Levenstein.

Encyclopedia Britannica, Inc.
Excerpt from *The Annals of America, Volume 3: 1784-1796: Organizing the New Nation*, copyright © 1976 by Encyclopedia Britannica, Inc. "Criticizing Presidential Power" by Edward Livingston, from *The Annals of America, Volume 4: 1797-1820: Domestic Expansion and Foreign Entanglements*, copyright © 1976 by Encyclopedia Britannica, Inc. "We're Almost Froze" from *The Annals of America, Volume 10: 1866-1883: Reconstruction and Industrialization*, copyright © 1976, 1977, 1987, 2003 by Encyclopedia Britannica, Inc. "You Will Be Astounded by Davy Crockett, from *The Annals of America, Volume 6: 1833-1840: The Challenge of a Continent*, copyright 1976 by Encyclopedia Britannica, Inc." Drawing the Country Together by Henry Clay, from *The Annals of America, Volume 4: 1797-1820: Domestic Expansion and Foreign Entanglements*, copyright © 1976 by Encyclopedia Britannica, Inc. "Advancing Wealth and Power" by Andrew Jackson, from *The Annals of America, Volume 5: 1821-1832: Steps Toward Equalitarianism*, copyright © 1976 by Encyclopedia Britannica, Inc. "An Interfering Government" by John C. Calhoun, from *The Annals of America, Volume 5: 1821-1832: Steps Toward Equalitarianism*, copyright © 1976 by Encyclopedia Britannica, Inc. "A Burdensome Tax" by John Adams, from *The Annals of America, Vol. 2, 1755-1783*, copyright © 1976 by Encyclopedia Britannica, Inc. "A Bill of Rights" by Thomas Jefferson, from *The Annals of America, Volume 3: 1784-1796: Organizing the New Nation*, copyright © 1976 by Encyclopaedia Britannica, Inc. "Bind Him No Longer" by John Greenleaf Whittier, from *The Annals of America, Vol. 6: 1833-1840: The Challenge of A Continent*, copyright © 1976, 1977, 1987, 2003 by Encyclopedia Britannica, Inc. "Sacred Fire of Liberty" by George Washington, from *The Annals of America, Volume 3: 1784-1796: Organizing the New Nation*, copyright © 1976 by Encyclopedia Britannica, Inc. "Good Government" by Thomas Jefferson from *The Annals of America, Volume 4: 1797-1820: Domestic Expansion and Foreign Entanglements*, copyright © 1976 by Encyclopaedia Britannica, Inc. A Well-Regulated Militia from *The Annals of America, Vol. 2, 1755-1783* by Maryland Delegates, from *The Annals of America, Vol. 2, 1755-1783*, copyright © 1976 by Encyclopedia Britannica, Inc. "Four Bullets Through My Coat" from *The Annals of America, Vol. 2, 1755-1783*, copyright © 1976 by Encyclopedia Britannica, Inc.

Facts On File, Inc.
"Their Hearts Will Be Changed" by Rev. Charles Grandison Finney, from *Encyclopedia of American Historical Documents, Volume II*, copyright © 2004, Susan Rosenfeld, Ed. "The Public Good" from *Encyclopedia of American Historical Documents* by Susan Rosenfeld (Ed.), copyright © 2001 by Susan Rosenfeld.

Paul Halsall
Excerpt from *Medieval Sourcebook: Christopher Columbus: Extracts from Journal*, from Fordham.edu, copyright © Paul Halsall March 1996.

HarperCollinsCustomBooks
Excerpt from *Leo Africanus: Description of Timbuktu*, translated by Paul Brians et al.

Heidelberg College
"Vital to Its Survival" by G. Michael Pratt, from Fallen Timbers Battlefield: Archaeological Project at Heidelberg College from *The Battle of Fallen Timbers: An historical perspective*.

Holt, Rinehart and Winston, Inc.
Excerpt from *Eyewitnesses and Others: Readings in American History, Volume 1: Beginnings to 1865* by Patrick Henry, copyright © 1991 by Holt, Rinehart and Winston, Inc.

Hon. Heather Wilson
Excerpt from "H.R. 4766, Esther Martinez Native American Languages Preservation Act of 2006" from *Library of Congress* by Hon. Heather Wilson.

Hutchinson of London
Excerpt from *Passage to America: A history of emigrants from Great Britain and Ireland to America in the mid-nineteenth century*, copyright © 1972 Terry Coleman.

Coretta Scott King
Excerpt from the Statement by Mrs. Coretta Scott King against Apartheid given at the United Nations on March 21, 1988, copyright © 1988 by Coretta Scott King.

Estate of Martin Luther King
Excerpt from *I Have a Dream* by Martin Luther King, Jr., copyright © 1963 Martin Luther King Jr., copyright renewed © 1991 Coretta Scott King.

The Library of America
Excerpt from *The American Revolution: Writings from the War of Independence* by Philip Vickers Fithian, copyright © 2001 by Literary Classics of the United States, Inc., New York, NY. Excerpt from *The American Revolution: Writings from the War of Independence* by George Rogers Clark, copyright © 2001 by Literary Classics of the United States, Inc., New York, NY.

Longman
Excerpt from "Master of his own labour" from *America Past and Present* by Robert A. Divine, copyright © 2002 by Addison-Wesley Educational Publishers Inc.

Marshall Cavendish Corporation
Excerpt from "A National Hero" from *Magill's Survey of American Literature, Volume 1*, Frank N. Magill, Ed., copyright © 1991 by Salem Press, Inc.

National Geographic
Excerpt from "Ancient Pyramid Found at Mexico City Christian Site" from *National Geographic News, April 6, 2006*, copyright © 2006 National Geographic Society. All rights reserved.

Oxford University Press
Excerpt from *Early American Writings*, copyright © 2002 by Oxford University Press, Inc. Carla Mulford, General Editor.

Pearson Education, Inc.
Excerpt from *Sequoyah and the Cherokee Alphabet* by Robert Cwiklik, copyright © 1989 by Robert Cwiklik. Reprinted by permission of Pearson Education, Inc.

Pearson Prentice Hall, Inc.
Excerpt from "Election Fever" from *Jacksonian America: 1815-1840—New Society, Changing Politics* by Frank Otto Gatell and John M. McFaul., copyright 1970 by Prentice-Hall Inc.

Scott, Foresman and Company
Excerpt from "Dog-tax Dispute" from *Sources of the American Republic: A Documentary History of Politics, Society, and Thought* by Marvin Meyers, Alexander Kern & John G. Cawelti, copyright © 1960 by Scott, Foresman and Company.

St. Martin's Press
Excerpt from *America Firsthand: Volume I: From Settlement to Reconstruction* by Robert D. Marcus and David Burner, copyright © 1989 by St. Martin's Press, Inc.

Stonesong Press Book/Penguin
Excerpt from *Witnessing America: The Library of Congress Book of Firsthand Accounts of Life in America 1600-1900*, copyright © Noel Rae (Ed.) and The Stonesong Press, Inc., 1996.

University of California
Excerpt from *Chinese American Voices; From the Gold Rush to the Present* by Judy Yung, Gordon H. Chang, and Him Mark Lai (Ed.), copyright © by the Regents of the University of California

The University of Massachusetts Press
from *On the Altar of Freedom: A Black Soldier's Civil War Letters from the Front* by James Henry Gooding, copyright © 1991 by The University of Massachusetts Press

University of Nebraska Press
Excerpt from *The War for America: 1775-1783* by Piers Mackesy, copyright © 1993 by the University of Nebraska Press, renewal copyright © 1992 by Piers Mackesy. Excerpt from *Jedediah Smith* by Dale L. Morgan, copyright © 1953 by Dale L. Morgan, University of Nebraska Press

Viking Penguin
Excerpt from *American Colonies* by Alan Taylor, Copyright Alan Taylor, copyright © 2001, Viking Penguin

Note: Every effort has been made to locate the copyright owner of material reprinted in this book. Omissions brought to our attention will be corrected in subsequent editions.